THE MUMMY!
A Tale of the Twenty-Second Century

By Jane Webb Loudon

Edited by
Nickianne Moody and Andy Sawyer

EER
Edward Everett Root Publishers, Brighton, 2021

EER
Edward Everett Root, Publishers, Co. Ltd.,
Atlas Chambers, 33 West Street, Brighton, Sussex, BN1 2RE, England.
www.eerpublishing.com

edwardeverettroot@yahoo.co.uk

Full details of our overseas agents in America, Australia, Canada, China,
Europe, and Japan and how to order our books are given on our website.

Jane Webb Loudon
The Mummy! A Tale of the Twenty-Second Century
Edited by Nickianne Moody and Andy Sawyer

The Mummy first published in three-volumes by Henry Colburn in London, 1827.

This edition © Edward Everett Root Publishers Co. Ltd., 2021.

ISBN: 9781911204930 Paperback
ISBN: 9781911204954 Hardback

Andrew Sawyer and the estate of the late Nickianne Moody
have asserted their rights to be identified as the authors
of this Work in accordance with the Copyright, Designs and
Patents Act 1988 as the owner of this Work.

All rights reserved. No part of this publication may be reproduced,
stored in a retrieval system or transmitted in any form or by any
means, electronic, mechanical, photocopying, recording or otherwise,
without the prior permission of the copyright owner.

Production by Pageset Limited, High Wycombe, Buckinghamshire.

To
Nickianne Moody
(1963–2019)

Contents

Acknowledgements v

Note on the text vii

Preface: "A Strange, Wild Novel": Jane Webb Loudon and
  The Mummy! viii

The Mummy! A Tale of the Twenty-Second Century 1

Volume 2 111

Volume 3 227

The Mummy! A Tale of the Twenty-Second Century: Part Two 351

Acknowledgements

To have a work dedicated to one of its co-creators is perhaps unusual. This edition of *The Mummy! A Tale of the Twenty-Second Century* stems from the fascination both of its editors had with the life and work of Jane Webb Loudon, a pioneer of the literature that came to be known as science fiction and the idea of horticulture as a practical activity for women. This fascination began to take its form as a series of "Loudon Lunches" in which we discussed JWL's position as a strangely hybrid figure, recognised as important by two widely-different and rarely-speaking interest-groups but rarely seen in a fuller context of literature and the championing of women's scientific interests in the first half of the nineteenth century. While my recognition that JWL's "Introduction" to *The Mummy!* was a manifesto for a new kind of subject-matter at least as important as Mary Shelley's arguments for *Frankenstein* and Hugo Gernsback's editorials for *Amazing Stories* led to a couple of short essays and conference papers, it was Nickianne who made the initial moves towards proposing and planning this book. However, as we were about to prepare work on the text and editorial matter, Nickianne became seriously ill.

It is something of a cliché to note, at the beginning of a work of scholarship, that, once the debts to other colleagues and teachers have been thanked, errors remain the responsibility of the editors/compilers. This book would probably not exist without the work of Alan Rauch (whose abridged 1994 edition of the novel first sparked our interest) , Paul Alkon, Bea Howe, and Ann B. Shtier and many others, and I owe much (for answering tangential questions, furthering my knowledge, or simply putting up with my constant arguments that histories of science fiction were *all wrong*) to colleagues in Liverpool University, the Science Fiction Foundation, the British Science Fiction Association, the Science Fiction Research Association, and the Fictionmags discussion group. I am grateful for the support of my former co-workers in Special Collections and Archives, Liverpool University Library. I am particularly grateful to the late Professor I. F. Clarke, the pioneer of the history of the "tale of the future", whose research papers (now held in Liverpool University Library) included a photocopy of the rare First Edition of *The Mummy!* Thanks also to go Lisa Tuttle and Sara Porter for their aid with further research after the completion of this book.

However, it is more important than ever to note that in this particular case, the buck stops here. Nickianne's untimely death prevented her from having significant input into the shape and content of this book, but it began as a collaboration and is offered as such in memory of a good friend and inspiring colleague. Any omissions and errors, however, are the responsibility of one and one only member of the partnership.

* * *

I would also, however, like to thank John Spiers of EER for his support of this project, and above all my wife Mary Sawyer for encouraging me to complete this task and, unlike, those mentioned above, for *living* with someone with this strange obsession with the work of a young woman who needed to find a *new* idea for a novel.

Andy Sawyer (February 2021)

Note on the text

The Mummy! A Tale of The twenty-Second Century was published anonymously, although the author was soon revealed to be "Miss Webb": a second novel, *Stories of a Bride*, was published as by "The Author of The Mummy". For most of her writing life, which was largely in collaboration with her husband John Claudius Loudon, the author was "Mrs Loudon" or "JWL". The initials presumably stand for "Jane Wells [her second forename] Loudon" rather than "Jane Webb Loudon", but we have chosen to use the latter nomenclature rather the former, referring to "Jane Webb" only when her life before her marriage is explicitly referenced and to celebrate the slight ambiguity of her preferred signature "JWL", which is used herewith as an abbreviation.

The key text for this book is the revised second edition, although the changes from the first (1827) edition are indicated. In Volume One, Chapters 2, 4, 5, 6, and 7 are extensively rewritten, with characters lost and their dialogue reassigned to others, but there were also a large number of major or minor changes throughout. These changes are presented in the final section of this *EER* edition.

Spelling and punctuation is as printed (e.g. "stedfastly" rather than the more modern "steadfastly", except for occasional silent corrections of obvious errors ("is" instead of "it") and insertions of full stops at the end of sentences, where omitted (JWL's usual practice, where sentences end with a dash, is to omit full stops and this has been followed.

JWL's use of words that are now single words ("mean time"/"every thing" /"every one" instead of "meantime"/"everything"/"everyone") is retained.

Obvious typographical errors such as "xecute" for "execute" and missing or duplicated words have been silently corrected.

Preface: "A Strange, Wild Novel": Jane Webb Loudon and The Mummy![1]

In 1827 a young woman named Jane Webb published "a strange, wild novel" called *The Mummy! A Tale of the Twenty-Second Century*. In 2126, a despotic Queen rules Catholic England. The complicated plot involves the strange electoral politics through which the next queen is to be chosen, an invasion from Ireland, two brothers with very different ambitions in life, entangled romantic rivalries, hidden identities, Machiavellian plotting, and the revived mummy of the Egyptian Pharoah Cheops, who acts as a kind of moral chorus to events. As Alan Rauch argues (Rauch, 2001: 74), the novel's future-setting was almost certainly influenced by Mary Shelley's *The Last Man*, published the previous year. There, in a fictional future, we also saw the extrapolative use of contemporary technology such as ballooning, a feature of invasion fears and social satire (Holmes, 2013: 34; 50–51, but also public spectacle (Holmes, 2008: 55).

The Last Man may be closer to the world of the symbolically Fantastic than it is to modern science fiction, but it recognises nothing essentially odd or wonderful (in the diegetic world) about "this very hour I will engage a sailing balloon" (Shelley, *The Last Man*, 1998: 70). A new vision of the world is taking shape. In *The Mummy!* we have the beginnings of a new way of *writing* this vision.

This is still a world of traditional romance and rivalry. Sir Ambrose Montagu and his friend the Duke of Cornwall want to marry Cornwall's daughter, Elvira and his niece Rosabella to Sir Ambrose's sons, the stalwart soldier Edmund and Edric, the scientist with a "romantic disposition". Rosabella, though, is in love with Edmund, and storms at her uncle about his unceremonious disposal of her. Edric refuses outright to marry her, estranging himself from his father and escaping to explore the possibilities of reanimating the dead. Further complications ensue on the death of Queen Claudia: Rosabella and Elvira are next in succession, and whoever gains the throne must rule with no consort. Romantic entanglements become a net as Cornwall's confessor Father Morris and a group of aristocrats set conspiracies in motion.

Claudia's death happens after her horse is panicked by an entanglement of *balloons* just before the resurrected Cheops lands in London to begin looming over the guilty with his staring eyes and diabolical laugh. This exotic emblem of difference and futurity exists in a world of weather-control, mobile homes travelling by rail, "steam-valets", and trials argued by automaton lawyers. The revival of Cheops is not by supernatural means, but through more "new technology"; electric current from Dr Entwerfen's "galvanic battery", making more explicit the hints about the use of electricity as a kind of vital fluid in Shelley's first great novel *Frankenstein* (1818).[2]

It is not insignificant that the novel to which one reviewer, struggling to compare *The Mummy!* to something, turned was *Frankenstein*. If, as Brian Aldiss argued in *Billion Year Spree*, *Frankenstein* was the first novel which we can unambiguously call science fiction (Aldiss,1973: 22–34), we need to point to *The Mummy!* to understand how this as-yet-unnamed mode developed.

Like *Frankenstein*, it is more than a contribution to genre-history. It is part of the conversation of understanding science in the early Nineteenth Century. Although another contemporary reviewer (for the *Monthly Review*) has no sympathy for the novel's "farrago of nonsense", their flagging of the "effects of the progress of science and the 'march of intellect' in the lapse of three hundred years" (*Monthly Review:* November 1927, 411) implicitly recognises the way the author set out, as she writes in her introduction, to imagine "strange discoveries" and "stranger modes of life".

Among readers the novel attracted was the horticulturalist John Claudius Loudon (1783–1843), who in the March 1828 issue of his *Gardener's Magazine* drew attention to its "new and useful combinations" of ideas. Impressed by these speculative technologies, Loudon wanted to meet the author. As Jane Webb Loudon told it in "A Short Account of the Life and Writings of John Claudius Loudon" introducing the second edition of his *Self-Instruction for Young Gardeners* (1847: 478–9):

"Mr. Loudon chanced to see the review of this book in the *Literary Gazette*, and, as among other things I had mentioned a steam-plough[3], it attracted his attention, and he procured the work from a circulating library. He read it, and was so much pleased with it, that he published, in *The Gardener's Magazine* for 1828, a notice of it under the head of "Hints for Improvements;" and he had from that time a great desire to become acquainted with the author, whom he supposed to be a man. In February 1830, Mr. Loudon chanced to mention this wish to a lady, a friend of his, who happened to be acquainted with me, and who immediately invited him to a party, where she promised him he should have the wished-for introduction. It may be easily supposed that he was surprised to find the author of the book a woman; but I believe that from that evening he formed an attachment to me, and, in fact, we were married on the 14th of the following September."

This charmingly romantic element— interestingly reminiscent of the story told of how in 1936 the American science fiction writer Henry

Kuttner wrote a fan letter to "Mr." C. L. Moore not knowing she was a woman[4]—may be rosily recalled, if not absolutely reworked. John Loudon may well have assumed initially that the anonymous author of *The Mummy!* was male, although a review of *The Literary Souvenir for 1829* in the *Literary Gazette* of October 1828 notes among the contributors "Miss Webb, author of the Mummy". Would the mutual friend, possibly Susan Martin, wife of the artist John, not revealed Jane Webb's gender, on the request to be introduced to "him"? It seems likely that Webb's friends (trying to encourage her career in other ways)[5] were introducing a couple for their mutual benefit. Leopold Martin recalls that the marriage came about "by the advice of my mother", whom he recalls as having a "special motherly friendship" with Jane Webb and the poets Emma Roberts and L. E. L. (Letitia Elizabeth Landon) (Martin: 1889 [12 Jan]). Another acquaintance of the Martins was William Jerdan, editor of the *Literary Gazette*, who lists JWL in his autobiography as among a number of women whose literary careers he aided and encouraged,[6] remarking that he "saved her from sinking" at a crisis in her life. He was also a friend of John Loudon (Jerdan 1853, [Vol 4: 321–323).

Webb was a young woman on her own struggling to make a mark in the literary world. Loudon, already a respected authority with his *Encyclopedia of Gardening* (1822) had employed an amanuensis since the amputation of his right arm. The pair may well have needed each other for intellectual and emotional reasons, but there were very practical motives for their partnership.

A partnership, however, it was. On her marriage, Jane Webb began a gradual and then increasingly involved collaboration with her husband on his major publication *Gardener's Magazine and Register of Rural and Domestic Improvement*, the first illustrated horticultural journal published for a general readership, aiming to provide a forum for gardeners outside scientific and learned societies. She had an accessible written style which could negotiate scientific knowledge for an amateur audience. There were certainly limits to her territory: her first task was to attend lectures by John Lindley, newly-appointed professor of Botany at London University. And she participated in professional journalism because of the cultural capital accrued by her husband and which he was willing to share with her. However, despite the constraints within which she worked, she is not "the wife of John Claudius Loudon" but, as many of her contemporaries realised, a ground-breaking figure in her own right.

Conversations upon Comparative Chronology (1830) showed her interest in educational texts. *Gardening for Ladies* (1840) established her as an author of informative and accessible handbooks for the non-specialist: as significant a name, "in gardening circles as Mrs Beeton's in the home) (Howe, 9). Compendia of useful knowledge such as *The Ladies' Flower-*

Garden of Ornamental Annuals (1840) and *Botany for Ladies* 1842) followed. Following her husband's death in 1843, she continued to publish, and for a brief period (1849–51) edited the *Ladies' Companion* magazine. Although she abandoned novels after *Stories of a Bride* (1829), she assisted her daughter Agnes to publish fiction. Towards the end of her life, (she died in 1858) she was a peripheral part of a loose circle of literary figures which included Charles Dickens, Wilkie Collins, Elizabeth Gaskell, the artists John Millais and Edwin Landseer, and the novelist and ghost story writer Catherine Crowe, who lodged with the Loudons in the 1850s.

The Mummy! was reprinted in 1872 by Frederick Warne, in the context of their reissues of several of her and her husband's books between 1860 and 1880, and the late-Victorian fascination with supernatural fiction, but has not since seen print until Alan Rauch's abridged 1994 edition. Her gardening books still attract interest – *Gardening for Ladies* was reprinted as recently as 2013 – but not as central, liberating texts.

Rauch sees *The Mummy!* as a remarkable novel of technological and moral speculation. "The 1820s were troubled by social, political and intellectual instability, and Loudon's work is one of a few novels that attempts to make sense of the time," (Loudon, 1994: x). However, it is seen by others as a kind of interlude or side-step. Paul Alkon says that "Webb's disappearance from literary history was *unfortunately* [my emphasis] hastened by marriage to the landscape gardener John Claudius Loudon, who sought her out and proposed after reading *The Mummy*. Life with this ardent fan deflected Webb from science fiction to writing a series of botanical books with such unappealing titles as *The Ladies' Flower Garden of Ornamental Annuals.*" (Alkon, 2002: 38). Lisa Hopkins sees *The Mummy!* as a deliberate engagement with the issues raised by *Frankenstein*, a "sensational but ultimately pious corrective to the pessimism and atheism of Mary Shelley" (Hopkins, 2003: 14), but leaves it as a fascinating but isolated "sport" rather than as an attempt to engage knowingly with literary difference, the idea of science, or the writing of futurity.[7] In contrast, to Geoffrey Taylor in *Some Nineteenth Century Gardeners The Mummy!* is "not really readable today, but it is hardly less so than any other fantasy of the future" (Taylor, 1951: 26). Loudon's biographer Bea Howe is full of sentimental suppositions of what "Jane" might have said or thought, and concentrates upon her status as a gardening-writer, though Howe is clearly entertained by Jane's "Wellsian fantasy":

> ... unlike any other book written by a woman in the 19th century, that age for great women writers.... a diverting and striking novel for its time. (33)

Leonore Davidoff and Catherine Hall, in Family Fortunes: Men and

Women of the English Middle Class 1780–1850 (1987) focus upon John Loudon as one of their examples of the practical ideologues who promoted social virtue through domestic suburban life but wave Jane aside as "the daughter of Thomas Webb, a manufacturer of Birmingham." (188) Although they note that she wrote nineteen books including The Lady's Companion to the Flower Garden (1841) which sold 20,000 copies in nine editions, they pay no attention to her career as an independent writer.

Melanie Louise Simo, in her Loudon and the Landscape (1988), while concentrating on JWL's husband and his horticultural work, shows how the Loudons' reformist passions complimented each other (268–278), and Ann B. Shteir's discussion of her botanical works in *Cultivating Women, Cultivating Science* (1996) places her firmly in the tradition of those eighteenth and nineteenth female science writers who found botanical studies a rewarding area with which to encourage the participation of women in a more formal and "serious" education. Sara Dewis (2014) devotes a sympathetic, informative chapter to her, but in the context of the Loudons' horticultural work. She offers detailed insight to the *Ladies' Companion* but only a few paragraphs on the early literary work. Rauch's positioning of *The Mummy!* in the context of 19th century debates about "useful knowledge" (Rauch, *Useful Knowledge*, 2001) is the best groundwork for appreciation of JWL's achievement as both satirist and speculator.

We argue (see the introductory essay to Part Two) that *The Mummy!* is as important a text in science fiction and the establishment of the "future" as a speculative space as anything by Mary Shelley or H. G. Wells. But her work as a propagandist for women's ownership of the technological and scientific "spaces" of the suburban garden and her editorship of the *Ladies' Companion*, in which she encouraged her readers to examine the scientific elements of the female "social sphere" are not separate from the playfulness of *The Mummy!*, but closely-woven strands in a life that deserves to be looked at as a whole.

"… a stirring fight with literary exertion."[8]

JWL's early background is hazy. The most authoritative source is Howe's 1961 biography, written with access to Agnes Loudon's diaries but prone to speculation. Christened Jane Wells Webb, she was the daughter of Thomas Webb, an attorney, owner of Kitwell House in Bartley Green seven miles south-west of Birmingham, and his wife, as yet unidentified. It is tempting to follow Rauch in ascribing her interest in science and scientific education to the influence (albeit indirect) of the Lunar Society, the Birmingham-based group of savants including James Watt, Erasmus Darwin, Josiah Wedgewood, and Joseph Priestley (Rauch, 2001: 59). Not enough, however, is known about her parents to firmly establish involvement with individuals known to be associated with the Society.[9]

Her mother died in 1819 (Howe, 28). Father and daughter toured Europe, but on their return in 1820 Thomas Webb found himself in financial difficulties and retired to Kitwell House. He died in 1824. JWL's life and literary struggles after her father's death are sometimes a matter of guesswork. How she made acquaintance with William Jerdan is unknown. She was clearly in London at some point between 1824 and 1827, as her "Martin" connection suggests, but Rauch believes that she was in Edinburgh at the time of a letter to Sir Walter Scott dated 12th December 1829 (Rauch, 2001: 221–2, n.15). Friendship with the Martins links her to William Godwin, who attended their *"petit soupers"* (Martin, 5 Jan 1889). Godwin, however, may not have met Martin socially until 1830, according to his diary.[10] Through Godwin, JWL could have known his daughter Mary, or at least known of her in more detail than through reading her novels. There is, however, no evidence that they ever met. No work by or about Mary Shelley suggests acquaintanceship with the woman whose work owes so much to her.

Details of her life and works are sometimes confused. She is occasionally confused with the "Mrs Loudon" (Margracia Loudon) who published several novels beginning with *First Love* (1830) and a treatise called *Philanthropic Economy or The Philosophy of Happiness* (1835). She has been credited as a botanical artist (McCouat, 2017) although this may be confusion with the work of her husband's sister (also Jane Loudon) who supplied art for both John Claudius and JWL (Dewis, 2014: 132–7; 189–92).

Most significantly in the light of many references to her as a teenager when she wrote *The Mummy!*; accounts of JWL's life give her birthdate as 19 August 1807 (Howe: 26). This cannot be so. She died 13 July 1858 aged, according to her death burial register, 57; suggesting a birthdate of 1800. Her obituary in *Lloyd's Weekly Newspaper* 1 Aug 1858 (and elsewhere) notes of Thomas Webb that following his death "his daughter, at the age of twenty-five, found herself an orphan dependent on her own exertions for support." She also states in the Introduction to *Gardening for Ladies* that for three-fourths of her life she was ignorant of horticultural matters (specifically citing ten years of instruction from her husband as, presumably the other "fourth"); also suggesting an 1800 rather than 1807 birth.[11] This weakens the romance of seventeen-year-old "Jane" thrown upon her own resources (Howe: 32, and many subsequent references), but it possibly allows her more agency in the circumstances of her marriage.

She was probably working on her first book (*Prose and Verse*, by Jane Webb), before her father's death. It was issued by a Birmingham publisher in 1824, and includes stories translated/adapted from French and Spanish sources and original and translated poems, including one written by her father (on his purchase of Kitwell House) and another written on visiting Kenilworth Castle after reading Walter Scott's *Kenilworth* (1821).

The Mummy! was successful enough to achieve a second edition, which was heavily revised, not always to its benefit. Her next novel, *Stories of a Bride*, linked three tales set in Central Europe intertwining gothic, romantic and philosophical themes, with a spirited and often cynically amusing framing narration by a young woman determined to control her own life. A review in the *Dublin Evening Packet* (21 November 1829) compared it favourably with her "insufferably tedious" first novel and praised "really effective and powerfully descriptive scenes". However, her career as novelist did not progress.

Illness and lack of confidence played a part in this. Jerdan recalls her telling him "I cannot put myself forward, and I cannot make bargains [i.e. with publishers]" (Jerdan, *Autobiography* vol 4: 322). The attempt to establish *Tabby's Magazine* with her as editor failed. At the beginning of 1829, backed by Jerdan, she applied to the Royal Literary Fund for relief and was awarded £25. The December 1829 letter to Sir Walter Scott perhaps shows this tension between self-interest and diffidence. JWL apologises for her "presumption" in previously contacting him for what might have been support in her application to the Fund (Rauch, 2001 221–2, n.15), or possibly a request that he review *Stories of a Bride*.

Science Writing: Knowledge Within Boundaries

Jane Webb's introduction to her future husband in February 1830 provided a niche for her talents to expand. "A Walk in a Flower-Garden" (1833) published in the *Juvenile Forget-Me-Not*, presents the mother and daughters of *Conversations Upon Comparative Chronology* again holding pedagogical conversations reminiscent of the dialogues in Jane Marcet's influential *Conversations on Natural Philosophy* (1819). This time Mrs. Seymour is instructing her children in botanical science. By showing them the structures of plants and explaining botanical classification, she passes on the information the author has gained from Lindley's lectures and her husband. *The Ladies Country Companion, or How to Enjoy Country Life Rationally* published in 1845 when she was a widow, is seen by Schenker as possessing "an empowering subtext for middle class women", offering the garden as a space for creative outlet and rational occupation (Schenker, 2002:349). *Gardening for Ladies*, her major work, begins, as Schenker notes, practically; with a chapter entitled "Stirring the soil – digging."

In the short-lived *Lady's Magazine of Gardening* (1841–2) she constructed a safe environment for amateur gardeners to express appreciation of flowers, share innovations, and make particular enquiries about the hundreds of new species being offered by nurseries during this period. After John Loudon's death, Bradbury and Evans were prepared to use her name and reputation to launch *The Ladies' Companion: At Home and Abroad* in 1849. While this did not succeed under Loudon's editorship, in Margaret

Beetham's assessment (Beetham, 2009) it was ahead of its time with early contributions from Mary Howitt, Mary Mitford, Geraldine Jewsbury and Eliza Acton's column on household hints and recipes. The commercial style that Loudon attempted to innovate would culminate in Samuel Beeton's *Englishwoman's Domestic Magazine* in 1852.

Amongst typical periodical offerings of fiction, fairy tales, puzzles, notes on fashion and the "Letters-Bag", *The Ladies' Companion* included Loudon's visits to the British Museum and Tom Taylor's series on "the governess". It is distinguished by its interest in science, presented as a series of letters on the chemistry of everyday life, physical geography and diet. The three main scientist-contributors were Edward Solly, Professor of Chemistry at Addiscombe College, the East India Company Military Seminary; David T Ansted, formerly Professor of Geology at King's College; and Edwin Lankester, a naturalist and surgeon who would become president of the The Microscopial Society of London. All three were fellows of the Royal Society.

In the first issue and for each introduction of a new correspondent, science is positioned carefully as healthy enjoyment. At different points Solly and JWL express concern about men who are "bores" and clever women who are "blues" (i.e. "bluestockings").[12] This perception is dismissed as old fashioned. JWL takes up the theme of mental cultivation in her second editorial, reiterating that "the old fancy, that learning must make women pedantic and disagreeable is rapidly passing away" (no. 2 p. 29). However, by issue five her contributions were focused elsewhere. She commented that although she was glad that readers appreciated the scientific papers, "I do not think, however, that all my readers would like the articles on dress and work omitted to make more room for science" (no. 5. p. 71).

This tension perhaps contributed to Bradbury and Evans' loss of confidence in Loudon's ability to attract an audience for the paper. By then, the "wildness" of her early fiction had been overtaken by the practicalities of a very different social milieu. *The Mummy!*, however, remains a significant step in understanding how the territory of "the future" is developed in English fiction, as speculation about possibilities and as satire of the present. It establishes Jane Webb Loudon as a pioneering writer who is much more than the sum of her largely separate lives as would-be best seller and propagandist for middle-class gardening.

(Nickianne Moody & Andy Sawyer)

Bibliography

Aldiss, Brian, *Billion Year Spree* [1973] (London, Corgi; 1975).
Alkon, Paul K. *Origins of Futuristic Fiction* (Athens, Georgia, University of Georgia Press; 1987.

Alkon, Paul K. *Science Fiction before 1900* (London, Routledge; 2002).
[Anon.] '[Review of] *The Mummy*' *Literary Gazette*, 360 (October 1827), 660–1.
[Anon.] '[Review of] *The Mummy*' *John Bull*, (October 22), 1827, 330.
[Anon.] '[Review of] *The Mummy*' *Monthly Review*, 6:27 (November 1827), 411–2.
[Anon.] 'Obituary Notes' *Lloyd's Weekly Newspaper* (August 1 1858) 9.
Beetham, M. *A Magazine of Her Own* (London, Routledge; 1996).
Beetham, M. 'Ladies Companion 1849–1870' (eds) Laurel Brake and Marysa Demoor, *Dictionary of Nineteenth-Century Journalism* (Ghent and London, Academia Press and the British Library, 2009), 340.
Belzoni, Gionvanni, *Narrative of the Operations and recent Discoveries in Egypt and Nubia* (London: John Murray, 1820).
Clarke, I. F, *The Tale of the Future* (London, The Library Association;1961).
David, Rosalie, *Discovering Ancient Egypt* (London, 1993; Michael O'Mara).
Davidoff, Lenore and Catherine Hall, *Family Fortunes: Men and Women of the English Middle Class 1780–1850* (London, Hutchinson; 1987).
Dewis, Sara, *The Loudons and the Gardening Press: A Victorian Cultural Industry* (Farnham, Ashgate; 2014).
Goldstein, Laurence, *The Flying Machine & Modern Literature* (Basingstoke, Macmillan; 1986).
Herodotus *The Histories* (trans. Aubrey de Selincourt) (Harmondsworth; Penguin, 1955).
Holmes, Richard, *The Age of Wonder* (London, HarperPress; 2008).
Holmes, Richard, *Falling Upwards: How We Took To the Air* (London, Collins; 2013).
Hopkins, Lisa., 'Jane C. Loudon's The Mummy!: Mary Shelley Meets George Orwell, and They Go in a Balloon to Egypt', Cardiff Corvey: *Reading the Romantic Text* 10 (June 2003). Online: Internet (5. 12. 2019): <www.cf.ac.uk/encap/corvey/articles/cc10_n01.pdf>.
Howe, Bea, *Lady With Green Fingers: The Life of Jane Loudon* (London, Country Life Ltd; 1961).
Jerdan, William, *The Autobiography of William Jerdan* (4 vols.) (London, Arthur Hall, Virtue And Co.; 1853.
Knellwolf, Christa and Jane Goodall (eds.), *Frankenstein's Science: Experimentation and Discovery in Romantic Culture, 1780–1830* (Aldershot, Ashgate; 2008).
Kuttner, Henry, *A Gnome There Was* (New York, Simon & Schuster; 1950).
Lawford, Cynthia, 'Diary' *London Review of Books* 21 September 2000: 36–37.
Loudon, Agnes, *Tales For Young People* (London, Bowdery and Kerby; 1846).
Loudon, Agnes, *Tales Of School Life* (London, Grant and Griffith; 1850).
Loudon, Jane Webb, *Prose and Verse* (Birmingham, R. Wrightson; 1824)
Loudon, Jane Webb, *The Mummy! A Tale of the Twenty-Second Century* [1st ed], (London, Henry Colburn; 1827).

Loudon, Jane Webb, *The Mummy! A Tale of the Twenty-Second Century* [2nd ed.] (London, Henry Colburn; 1828).
Loudon, Jane Webb, *Stories of a Bride* (London, Henry Colburn and Richard Bentley; 1829).
Loudon, Jane Webb, 'Letter to Sir Walter Scott, December 12, 1929) (National Library of Scotland, MS 3911:149).
Loudon, Jane Webb, *Conversations Upon Comparative Chronology and the Outlines of General History* (London, Longman Rees, Orme, Brown and Green; 1830).
Loudon, Jane Webb, 'A Walk in a Flower-Garden' in S. C. Hall, (ed.) *Juvenile Forget-Me-Not* (London, Ackermann; 1833),103–120.
Loudon, Jane Webb, *Agnes, or, The Little Girl Who Could Keep Her Promise* (London, Harvey and Darton; 1846).
Loudon, Jane Webb, *The Ladies' Country Companion, or, How to Enjoy a Country Life Rationally* (London, Longman, 1845).
Loudon, Jane (ed.), *The Ladies' Companion, At Home and Abroad* (London, Bradbury and Evans; 1849–50).
Loudon, Jane Webb, *The Mummy! A Tale of the Twenty-Second Century* [1827] (Introduction and abridgement by Alan Rauch) (Ann Arbor, University of Michigan Press; 1994).
Loudon, Jane Webb, *Gardening for Ladies* 2nd ed. (London, John Murray; 1841).
Loudon Jane Webb, *Gardening for Ladies* (London, Constable; 2013).
Loudon, John Claudius, 'Hints for Improvements', *The Gardener's Magazine* (March 1829), 478–9).
Loudon, John Claudius, *Self-Instruction for Young Gardeners*, 2nd ed., (London, Longman, Brown, Green and Longmans, 1847).
Luckhurst, Roger, *The Mummy's Curse: The True History of a Dark Fantasy* (Oxford, Oxford University Press; 2012).
McCouat, Philip, "Forgotten Women Artists #2: Jane Loudon: Artist, Futurist, Horticulturalist and Author" *Journal of Art in Society* (November 2017) http://www.artinsociety.com/forgotten-women-artists-2-jane-loudon.html.
Martin, Leopold 'Reminiscences of John Martin, K. L. by His Son' *Newcastle Weekly Chronicle* (5. Jan 1889 – 20 April) 1889.
Matoff, Susan, *Conflicted Life: William Jerdan, 1782–1869*, (Eastbourne, Sussex, Academic Press; 2011).
Rauch, Alan, *Useful Knowledge: The Victorians, Morality, and the March of Intellect* (Durham, North Carolina, Duke University Press; 2001).
Schenker, Heath, 'Women, Gardens, and the English Middle Class in the Early Nineteenth Century', in Michel Conan, *Bourgeois and Aristocratic Cultural Encounters in Garden Art, 1550–1850* (Washington DC, Dumbarton Oaks Research Library and Collection; 2002), 337–360.
Schofield, Robert S., 'The Lunar Society of Birmingham; A Bicentenary Appraisal' *Notes and Records of the Royal Society of London*, Vol. 21, No. 2 (December, 1966), 144–161.

Seymour, Miranda. *Mary Shelley* (New York, Grove Press; 2001).
Shelley, Mary *Frankenstein* (London, Penguin,1992).
Shelley, Mary, *Frankenstein: The 1818 Text* (New York, Penguin; 2018).
Shelley, Mary, *The Last Man* [1826] (Oxford; Oxford University Press; [Oxford World's Classics],1998.
Shteir, Ann B. *Cultivating Women, Cultivating Science: Flora's Daughters and Botany in England 1760–1860* (Baltimore, Johns Hopkins University Press; 1996).
Shteir, Ann B., 'Green-Stocking or Blue? Science in Three Women's Magazines, 1800–50', *Culture and Science in the Nineteenth-Century Media* ed. Louise Henson *et. al.* (London, Ashgate; 2004) 3–13.
Simo, Melanie Louise, *Loudon and the Landscape: From Country seat to Metropolis 1783–1843* (New Haven, Yale University Press; 1988).
Sutherland, John and Veronica Melnyk, *Rogue Publisher: The 'Prince of Puffers'. The Life and Works of the Publisher Henry Colburn* (Brighton, Edward Everett Root; 2018.
Taylor, Geoffrey, *Some Nineteenth Century Gardeners* (London, Skeffington; 1951).
Uglow, Jenny, *The Lunar Men: The Friends Who Made the Future* (London, Faber and Faber; 2003).
'Wilkinson, Toby, *A World Beneath The Sands: Adventurers and Archaeologists in the Golden Age of Egyptology* (London: Picador, 2020).

Endnotes

1 Parts of this preface were delivered in substantially different form at the British Society for Literature and Science conference, University of Liverpool 16–18 April 2015.
2 See Jane Goodall's account of "Electrical Romanticism" in Knellwolf and Goodall, (117–132).
3 In fact, a "steam-mowing apparatus" (Vol. 1 Ch. 2).
4 "About the Author", interior back dust-jacket to Henry Kuttner, *A Gnome There Was* (New York, Simon & Schuster, 1950). They married in 1940 and worked together under their own names and various pseudonyms until Kuttner's death in 1958.
5 See also Nickianne Moody's "Gardening in Print: Profession, Instruction and Reform" (footnote 38): "Between her father's death and her marriage in 1830 Jane Loudon supported herself through her writing, publishing a book of poetry, *The Mummy*, and a second novel *Stories of a Bride* as well as being a salaried contributor to the *Literary Gazette* edited by William Jerdan. It is in this circle that the Loudons could have had mutual friends and have been introduced. Jerdan was the same age as John Loudon, a Scot who had also moved to London to start his professional career. After working on a range of different professional and news orientated publications Jerdan assumed editorship of the *Literary Gazette* in 1817 and remained there until 1850. As a weekly publication the *Literary Gazette* was aimed at a general readership and Jerdan assembled a number of well known contributors including William Blackwood, Edward Bulwer-Lytton, Thomas Hood, Walter Scott and the poet Laetitia Landon. Jerdan and Landon were going to act as advisors to Jane Loudon's editorship of *Tabby's Magazine* which they were planning to set up just prior to Jane's marriage and assumption of a different kind of writing career." The plans for the magazine fell through, possibly because of failure to convince the publisher Henry Colburn to back it. Jerdan hired JWL to provide *The History of Africa* (1830), the third volume in his "Juvenile Library" series for Colburn and Bentley. It proved to be the final volume in the badly-reviewed series, and by then Jane Webb had become Jane Loudon.

6 In the case of Landon, to the extent that he fathered three children with her between 1823 and 1829 (Lawford 2000; Matoff 2011 577–580).
7 JWL specifically references *Frankenstein* in the first volume of *Stories of a Bride* where the narrator comments that "The Germans have all a comfortable, contented look. The women are reckoned handsome; but they are beauties on a large scale, and if a manufactory á la Frankenstein were carried on, I verily believe one Austrian belle would make three Parisiennes." (*Stories of A Bride*, vol 1 p. 37)
8 Jerdan, 320.
9 For the Lunar Society see Jenny Uglow, (2003) and Schofield (1966). Thomas Webb was a generation younger than the men who made up the "Society", an informal group of which no formal records such as membership lists survive. They were (relatively) local men who published widely and whose influence was great. A letter in the *Birmingham Chronicle* 13 July 1824 suggests an acquaintanceship (if indirect) with Richard Lovell Edgeworth (1844–1817) who was a member of the Lunar Society. I am grateful to Lisa Tuttle for drawing my attention to this (AS).
10 http://godwindiary.bodleian.ox.ac.uk/people/MAR03.html#MAR03-notes. Godwin records meeting "Miss Webb" on two occasions in July 1830 (once with Martin) and meets the "Loudons" on 11 October (after their marriage).
11 Loudon 1841: v-vi. George Glenny's characterisation of her as a "lying old woman" in the *Horticultural Journal and Florists Register* of July 1833 (qtd. Dewis, 197) seems simple abuse, but makes better sense if she was not, in fact, in her twenties.
12 This debate is examined by Shtier (2004:10).

THE MUMMY!
A TALE OF THE TWENTY-SECOND CENTURY

"Why has thou disquieted me, to bring me up?"[1]

(1 Sam. xxviii.15)

Volume 1: Introduction

I have long wished to write a novel, but could not determine what it was to be about. I could not bear any thing common-place, and I did not know what to do for a hero. Heroes are generally so much alike, so monotonous, so dreadfully insipid—so completely brothers of one race, with the family likeness so amazingly strong—" This will not do for me," thought I as I sauntered listlessly down a shady lane, one fine evening in June; "I must have something new, something quite out of the beaten path:— but what?—ay, that was the question. In vain did I rack my brains—in vain did I search the storehouse of my memory: I could think of nothing that had not been thought of before.

"It is very strange!" said I, as I walked faster, as though I hoped the rapidity of my motion would shake off the sluggishness of my imagination. It was all in vain! I struck my forehead and called Wit to my assistance, but the malignant deity was deaf to my entreaty. "Surely," thought I," the deep mine of invention cannot be worked out; there must be some new ideas left, if I could but find them." To find them, however, was the difficulty.

Thus lost in meditation, I walked onwards till I reached the brow of a hill, and a superb prospect burst upon me. A fertile valley richly wooded, studded with sumptuous villas and romantic cottages, and watered by a noble river, that wound slowly its lazy course along, spread beneath my feet; and lofty hills swelling to the skies, their summit lost in clouds, bounded the horizon. The sun was setting in all its splendour, and its lingering rays gave those glowing tints and deep masses of shadow to the landscape that sometimes produce so magical an effect. It was quite a Claude Lorraine[2] scene; and more fully to enjoy it, I entered a hay-field, and seated myself upon a grassy bank. The day had been sultry; and the evening breeze, as it murmured through the foliage, felt cool and refreshing. "It is a lovely world," thought I, "notwithstanding all that cynics can say against it. Our own passions bring misery upon our heads, and then we rail at the world, though we only are in fault. Why should I seek to wander in the regions of fiction? Why not enjoy tranquilly the blessings Heaven has bestowed upon me?"

I felt too indolent to answer my own question; a delicious stillness crept over my senses, and the heaving chaos of my ideas was lulled to repose. A majestic oak stretched its gnarled arms in sullen dignity above my head; myriads of busy insects buzzed around me; and woodbines and wild roses, hanging from every hedge, mingled their perfume with that of the new-mown hay. I reclined languidly on my grassy couch, listening to the indistinct hum of the distant village, and feeling that delightful sense of exemption from care, which a faint murmur of bustle afar off gives to the weary spirit, when suddenly the bells struck up a joyous peal—the cheerful notes now swelling loudly upon the ear, then sinking gently away with the retiring breeze, and then again returning with added sweetness. I listened with delight to their melody, till their softness seemed to increase; the sounds became gradually fainter and fainter; the landscape faded from my sight: a soft languor crept over me: in short, I slept.

It would be of no use to go to sleep without dreaming; and, accordingly, I had scarcely closed my eyes when, methought, a spirit stood before me. His head was crowned with flowers; his azure wings fluttered in the breeze, and a light drapery, like the fleecy vapour that hangs upon the summit of a mountain, floated round him. In his hand he held a scroll, and his voice sounded soft and sweet as the liquid melody of the nightingale.

"Take this," said he, smiling benignantly; "it is the Chronicle of a future age. Weave it into a story. It will so far gratify your wishes, as to give you a hero totally different from any hero that ever appeared before. You hesitate," continued he, again smiling, and regarding me earnestly: "I read your thoughts, and see you fear to sketch the scenes of which you are to write, because you imagine they must be different from those with which you are acquainted. This is a natural distrust: the scenes will indeed be different from those you now behold; the whole face of society will be changed: new governments will have arisen; strange discoveries will be made, and stranger modes of life adopted. The restless curiosity and research of man will then have enabled him to lift the veil from much which is (to him at least) at present a mystery; and his powers (both as regards mechanical agency and intellectual knowledge) will be greatly enlarged. But even then, in the plenitude of his acquirements, he will be made conscious of the infirmity of his nature, and will be guilty of many absurdities which, in his less *enlightened* state, he would feel ashamed to commit.

"To no one but yourself has this vision been revealed: do not fear to behold it. Though strange, it may be fully understood, for much will still remain to connect that future age with the present. The impulses and feelings of human creatures must, for the most part, be alike in all ages: habits vary, but nature endures; and the same passions were delineated, the same weaknesses ridiculed, by Aristophanes, Plautus, and Terence, as in after-times were described by Shakspeare[3] and Moliere; and as will be in the times of which you are to write,— by authors yet unknown.

"But you still hesitate; you object that the novelty of the illusions perplexes you. This is quite a new kind of delicacy; as authors seldom trouble themselves to become acquainted with a subject before they begin to write upon it. However, since you are so very scrupulous, I will endeavour, if possible, to assist you. Look around."

I did so; and saw, as in a magic glass, the scenes and characters, which I shall now endeavour to pass before the eyes of the reader.

Volume 1: Chapter 1

In the year 2126, England enjoyed peace and tranquillity under the absolute dominion of a female sovereign. Numerous changes had taken place for some centuries in the political state of the country, and several forms of government had been successively adopted and destroyed, till, as is generally the case after violent revolutions, they all settled down into an absolute monarchy. The religion of the country was mutable as its government; and in the end, by adopting Catholicism,[4] it seemed to have arrived at nearly the same result: despotism in the state, indeed, naturally produces despotism in religion; the implicit faith and passive obedience required in the one case, being the best of all possible preparatives for the absolute submission of both mind and body necessary in the other.

In former times, England had been blessed with a mixed government and a tolerant religion, under which the people had enjoyed as much freedom, as they perhaps ever can do, consistently with their prosperity and happiness. But it is not in the nature of the human mind, to be contented: we must always either hope or fear; and things at a distance appear so much more beautiful than they do when we approach them, that we always fancy what we have not, infinitely superior to any thing we have; and neglect enjoyments within our reach, to pursue others, which, like *ignes fatui*,[5] elude our grasp at the very moment when we hope we have attained them.

Thus it was with the people of England:— Not satisfied with being rich and prosperous, they longed for something more. Abundance of wealth caused wild schemes and gigantic speculations; and though many failed, yet, as some succeeded, the enormity of the sums gained by the projectors, incited others to pursue the same career. New countries were discovered and civilized; the whole earth was brought to the highest pitch of cultivation; every corner of it was explored; mountains were levelled, mines were excavated, and the globe racked to its centre. Nay, the air and sea did not escape, and all nature was compelled to submit to the overwhelming supremacy of Man.

Still, the English people were not satisfied: —enabled to gratify every wish till satiety succeeded indulgence, they were still unhappy; perhaps, precisely because they had no longer any difficulties to encounter. Education became universal, and the technical terms of abstruse sciences familiar to the lowest mechanics; whilst questions of religion, politics, and metaphysics, agitated by them daily, supplied that stimulus, for which their minds, enervated by over cultivation, constantly craved. The consequences may be readily conceived. It was impossible for those to study deeply who had to labour for their daily bread; and not having time to make themselves masters of any given subject, they only learned enough of all to render them disputatious and discontented. Their heads were filled with words to which they affixed no definite ideas, and the little sense Heaven had blessed them with was lost beneath a mass of undigested and misapplied knowledge.

Conceit inevitably leads to rebellion. The natural consequence of the mob thinking themselves as wise as their rulers, was, that they took the first convenient opportunity that offered, to jostle these aforesaid rulers from their seats. An aristocracy was established, and afterwards a democracy; but both shared the same fate; for the leaders of each, in turn, found the instruments they had made use of to rise, soon become unmanageable. The people had tasted the sweets of power, they had learned their own strength, they were enlightened; and, fancying they understood the art of ruling as well as their quondam directors, they saw no reason why, after shaking off the control of one master, they should afterwards submit to the domination of many. "We are free," said they; "we acknowledge no laws but those of nature, and of those we are as competent to judge as our would-be masters. In what are they superior to ourselves? Nature has been as bountiful to us as to them, and we have had the same advantages of education. Why then should we toil to give them ease? We are each capable of governing ourselves. Why should we pay them to rule us? Why should we be debarred from mental enjoyments and condemned to manual labour? Are not our tastes as refined as theirs, and, our minds as highly cultivated? We will assert our independence, and throw off the yoke. If any man wish for luxuries, let him labour to procure them for himself. We will be slaves no longer; we will all be masters."

Thus they reasoned, and thus they acted, till government after government having been overturned, complete anarchy prevailed; and the people began to discover, though, alas! too late, that there was little pleasure in being masters when there were no subjects; and that it was impossible to enjoy intellectual pleasures, whilst each man was compelled to labour for his daily bread. This was, however, inevitable, for, as perfect equality had been declared, of course no one would condescend to work for his neighbour; and every thing was done badly; as, however skilful any man may be in any particular art or profession, it is quite impossible he can excel in all.

In the meantime, the people, who had, though they scarcely knew why, attached to the idea of equality that of exemption from toil, found to their infinite surprise, that their burthens had increased tenfold, whilst their comforts had unaccountably diminished in the same proportion. The blessings of civilization were indeed fast slipping away from them. Every man became afraid lest the hard-earned means of existence should be torn from his grasp; for, as all laws had been abolished, the strong tyrannized over the weak, and the most enlightened nation in the world was in imminent danger of degenerating into a horde of rapacious barbarians.

This state of things could not continue; and the people, finding from experience that perfect equality was not quite the most enviable mode of government, began to suspect that a division of labour and a distinction of ranks were absolutely necessary to civilization; and sought out their ancient nobility, to endeavour to restore something like order to society. These illustrious personages were soon found: those who had not emigrated, had retired to their seats in the country, where, surrounded by their dependants, and the few friends who had remained faithful to them, they enjoyed the *otium cum dignitate*,[6] and consoled themselves for the loss of their former greatness, by railing most manfully at those who had deprived them of it.

Amongst this number, was the lineal descendant of the late royal family, and to him the people now resolved humbly and unconditionally to offer the crown; imagining, with the usual vehemence and inconsistency of popular commotions, that an arbitrary government must be best for them, as being the very reverse of that, the evils of which they had just so forcibly experienced.

The prince however, to whom a deputation from the people made this offer, happened not to be ambitious. Like another Cincinnatus,[7] he placed all his happiness in the cultivation of a small farm, and had sufficient prudence to reject a grandeur which he felt must be purchased by the sacrifice of his peace. The deputies were in despair at his refusal; and they re-urged their suit with every argument the distress of their situation could inspire. They painted in glowing colours the horrors of the anarchy that prevailed, the misery of the kingdom, the despair of the people, and at last wound up their arguments by a solemn appeal to Heaven, that if he persisted in his refusal, the future wretchedness of the people might fall upon his head. The prince continued inexorable; and the deputies were preparing to withdraw, when the prince's daughter, who had been present during the whole interview, rushed forward and prevented their retreat:—"Stay! I will be your Queen," cried she energetically; "I will save my country, or perish in the attempt!"

The princess was a beautiful woman, about six-and-twenty; and at this moment, her fine eyes sparkling with enthusiasm, her cheeks glowing, and her whole face and figure breathing dignity from the exalted purpose of her soul, she appeared to the deputies almost as a supernatural being; and, regarding her offer as a direct inspiration from Heaven, they bore her in triumph to the assembled multitude who awaited their return: whilst the people, ever caught by novelty, and desirous of any change to free them from the misery they were enduring, hailed her appearance with delight, and unanimously proclaimed her Queen.

The new sovereign soon found the task she had undertaken a difficult one; but happening luckily to possess common sense and prudence, united with a firm and active disposition, contrived in time to restore order, and to confirm her own power, whilst she contributed to the happiness of her people. The face of the kingdom rapidly changed—security produced improvement—and the self-banished nobles of the former dynasty crowding round the new Queen, she chose from amongst them the wisest and most experienced for her counsellors, and by their help compounded an excellent code of laws. This book was open to the whole kingdom; and cases being decided by principle instead of precedent, litigation was almost unknown: for as the laws were fully and clearly explained, so as to be understood by every body, few dared to act in open violation of them, punishment being certain to follow detection; and all the agonizing delights of a lawsuit were entirely destroyed, as every body knew, the moment the facts were stated, how it would inevitably terminate. This renewal of the golden age continued several years without interruption, the people being too much delighted with the personal comforts they enjoyed, to complain of the errors inseparable from all human institutions; whilst the remembrance of what they had suffered during the reign of anarchy, made them tremble at a change, and patiently submit to trifling inconveniences to avoid the risk of positive evils.

This generation passed away, and with it died, not only the recollection of the past misfortunes of the kingdom, but also the spirit of content they had engendered. A new race arose, who, with the ignorance and presumption of inexperience, found fault with every thing they did not understand, and accused the Queen and her ministers of dotage, merely because they did not accomplish impossibilities. The government, however, was too firmly established to be easily shaken. The judicious economy of the Queen had filled her treasury with riches; her prudent regulations had extended the commerce of her subjects to an almost incredible extent; whilst her firm and decided disposition made her universally respected both at home and abroad. The malcontents were therefore awed into submission, and obliged, in spite of themselves, to rest satisfied with growling at the government they were not strong enough to overturn. At this time the Queen died, and the state of affairs experienced an important change.

It has been before mentioned, that the religion of the country had altered with its government. Atheism, rational liberty, and fanaticism, had followed each other in regular succession; and the people found, by fatal experience, that persecution and bigotry assimilated as naturally with infidelity as with superstition. A fixed government seemed to require an established religion; and the multitude, ever in extremes, rushed from excess of liberty to intolerance. The Catholic faith was restored, new saints were canonized, and confessors appointed in the families of every person of distinction. These priests, however, were far from having the power they had possessed in former times. The eyes of men had been too long opened to be easily closed again. Education still continued amongst the lower classes; and though, at the time this history commences, it was going out of fashion with persons of rank, its influence was felt even by those most prejudiced against it. During the reign of the late Queen, the minds of the public not having any state affairs to occupy them, had been directed to the improvement of the arts and sciences; and so many new inventions had been struck out, so many wonderful discoveries made, and so many ingenious contrivances put into execution, that poor Nature seemed to be degraded from her throne, and usurping man to have stepped up to supply her place.

Before the Queen died, she chose her niece Claudia to succeed her; and as she enacted that none of her successors should marry, she ordered that all future queens should be chosen, by the people, from such female members of her family as might be between twenty and twenty-five years of age, at the time of the throne's becoming vacant. Every male throughout the kingdom who had attained the age of twenty-one, was to have a voice in this election; but as it was presumed it might be inconvenient to convoke these numerous electors into one place, it was agreed that every ten thousand should choose a deputy to proceed to London to represent them, and that a majority of these deputies should elect the Queen. It seemed probable to thinking minds, however, that this scheme, like most feasible in theory, would present some difficulties when it was to be put in practice; but of these, the old Queen never troubled herself to think. She had provided against any immediate disturbance by choosing her own successor, and she left posterity to take care of itself.

Queen Claudia was one of those *fainéant*[8] sovereigns of whom it is extremely difficult to write the history, for the simple but unanswerable reason, that they never perform any action worthy of being recorded. But as she seldom did any harm, though she did not do much good, she contrived to escape either violent censure or applause; and in short, to get through life very decently, without making much bustle about it. She continued the same counsellors that had been employed by her predecessor, appointing the sons, when the fathers died, to save trouble. She left the laws as she found them for the same reason; and, in short, she let the affairs of government go on so quietly, and so exactly in the same routine as before, that for two or three years after her accession, the people were scarcely aware that any change had taken place.

Volume 1: Chapter 2

The indolent Claudia had already reigned three years in the most profound tranquility; and the year 2127 was beginning also to roll placidly away, when early in its spring the peace of the kingdom was interrupted, and the Council of the Queen thrown into most distressing consternation by the intelligence that Roderick, King of Ireland, had landed in Wales, at the head of an invading army, and that the malcontents from every part of the kingdom were flocking to his standard.

The crisis was alarming. The pacific reign of the late Queen, and inertness of the present one, had occasioned the standing army of England to be a splendid toy kept rather for show than use; and universal education had made its component parts reasoning pedants, rather than active agents. It was, indeed, no uncommon occurrence to see a regiment thrown into confusion on a review day, in consequence of the orders of the general not exactly coinciding with the notions entertained of military tactics by the privates, who, whilst arguing the point, quite forgot what they had been ordered to perform. Little could reasonably be expected from an army thus constituted, but the native spirit of Englishmen, and their hatred of foreigners, rose triumphant over every obstacle; and the soldiers unanimously professed themselves ready to obey the orders of the council, and to die in defence of their Queen and government if necessary.

Unfortunately, however, the Council were in no condition to give orders. This worthy and sapient body had hitherto contrived to manage their affairs very comfortably, by referring in all cases of doubt and difficulty to decisions made in the reign of the late Queen; but this case was quite unprecedented, and the illustrious lawgivers were consequently completely at a loss as to what was best to be done. Meanwhile the enemy, who had no such scruples to contend with, entered the suburbs of London, and attacking the Queen's palace in Hammersmith Street, upon the banks of the Thames, would inevitably have taken her Majesty prisoner, had not this fatal outrage been prevented by the courage and activity of Edmund Montagu, a captain in the Queen's body guard, who had obtained his commission through the interest of the Queen's great uncle, the old Duke of Cornwall, only a short time previously.

This youthful hero luckily had command of the guard at the time of the enemy's attack and by his decision and presence of mind, he succeeded in animating his soldiers to defend the post committed to their charge, till a body of regular troops under the Duke of Exeter, a veteran officer of the late Queen, came to their relief, and compelled the invaders to retreat.

The Duke of Exeter was a good soldier, and a sensible man. He saw the danger of his country, and like another Washington,[9] left his beloved retirement to save it from destruction. The counsellors of the Queen gladly submitted to his dictation. They felt their own weakness, and cheerfully gave up the reins of government to hands better qualified to guide them. The Queen was equally glad to escape all responsibility; and the Duke of Exeter, appointing young Montagu, with whose conduct he had been much pleased, second in command, soon, by a succession of vigorous and consistent measures, drove the enemy from the kingdom: their retreat indeed being hastened by the news Roderick received of an insurrection having broken out in Dublin during his absence.

Whilst these intestine commotions were agitating England, the Emperors of Greece and Germany, who had long envied the prosperity of "the little sea-girt isle,"[10] took the opportunity of declaring war against it; and Claudia only found herself freed from domestic foes, to contend with foreign ones. Her army, however, encouraged by success, professed themselves ready to encounter any enemy, and they set off for Germany, in high spirits under the command of General Montagu; the Duke of Exeter's age and infirmities making him decline leaving England.

The youthful general was the son of a baronet in the West of England, and rapid as his promotion had been at court, it was by no means greater than he deserved. His face and figure were such as the imagination delights to picture as a hero of antiquity; and his character accorded well with the majestic graces of his person. Haughty and commanding in his temper— ambition was his God, and the love of glory his strongest passion; yet his very pride had a nobleness in it, and his soldiers loved though they feared him.

Very different was the character of his younger brother Edric, whose romantic disposition and contemplative turn of mind often excited the ridicule of his friends. As usual, in similar cases, the persecution he endured only wedded him more firmly to his peculiar opinions, and determined him to sustain them with the constancy of a martyr, whilst he secluded himself from society, and despised the opinion of the world, because he found it was against him; supposing himself capable of resisting every species of temptation, simply because, as yet, he had met with nothing adequate to tempt him. Older and more experienced persons have made the same mistake.

Perhaps the striking difference perceptible in the character of these young men, might be occasioned more by education than nature. Until the period of Edmund's obtaining his commission, they had both resided entirely at the country seat of their father, Sir Ambrose, where the care of their instruction was confided to Dr. Entwerfen,[11] a German enthusiast, whom an unlucky propensity for trying experiments had banished from his native land. This philosopher, however, was unfortunately better skilled in the knowledge of the sciences, than in that of the human heart; and the lofty spirit of Edmund, despising his control, soon sought a more congenial companion in Father Morris, confessor to the Duke of Cornwall, who resided in the neighbourhood; and who, having been a warrior in his youth,[12] was well calculated to sympathise with the feelings of a young aspirant for military glory.

The confessor was an intelligent, well informed man, and feeling flattered by the fondness Edmund showed for his society, he devoted all his leisure hours to the instruction of his young friend, leaving Dr. Entwerfen to occupy himself entirely with Edric, whose disposition accorded better with his own. Sir Ambrose was well satisfied with the change. Edmund was always his favourite son, and possessing the happy privilege of favourites, found no difficulty in persuading his father that whatever he preferred, was the best and most prudent plan that could possibly have been adopted. He thus easily contrived in due time to get permission to enter the army, and being naturally ardent and enterprising, success had hitherto attended all his efforts.

Country gentlemen have always been allowed to form a genus perfectly distinct from every other class of the community; there being something in the mere circumstance of a man's living entirely upon his own estate, which never fails to produce a peculiar effect upon the mind. An English 'Squire is indeed almost a petty monarch: surrounded by his tenants and dependants, he rarely, except upon occasions of ceremony, meets with any superior, or even equal to himself; and he becomes the sun of his own system, around whom the doctor, the parson, and the lawyer of his village, roll as attendant planets.

Notwithstanding all the changes that had taken place in the political, moral, and religious state of England, this caste remained the same; and Sir Ambrose was as warm in his feelings; as hasty in his temper, and as violent in his prejudices as any of his predecessors. He was nevertheless far superior to the generality of his class, and amongst innumerable other good qualities was an indulgent master and an affectionate father. His foible,—for alas! where shall we find a character without one,—was a desire to show occasionally how implicitly he could be obeyed: though, in general. he was easy to a fault, and it was only when roused by opposition, that the natural obstinacy of his disposition displayed itself. Edmund's military glory was flattering to his parental pride, and his eyes would glisten with delight at the bare mention of his darling's name.

In common with most persons of his class, Sir Ambrose Montagu considered regularity as a cardinal virtue; and in his own habits, he was as undeviating and exact as the machinery which performed the principal domestic operations in his mansion. Every day after dinner at the same hour, he proceeded regularly to his library, where Abelard, an old butler, who had grown grey in his service, as regularly presented him with a splendid hookah, which he smoked with infinite satisfaction; whilst Davis, his steward, reported all that had occurred relative to the affairs of the farm during the day, and received orders for all that was to take place during the morrow.

One fine evening in June, 2127, Davis was not listened to with the accustomed interest; and the smoke of the hookah, instead of being gently puffed out with its usual air of calm enjoyment, rose rapidly in volumes, or sank entirely away, as Sir Ambrose appeared alternately excited by strong feeling, or lost in meditation. Parental affection occasioned this unwonted agitation; letters had been received from Edmund, announcing him to be upon the eve of battle with an army far superior to his own, and impatience with which the doating[13] father expected intelligence of the event, may be easier imagined than described. Still the force of habit prevailed, and the accustomed hour found him with his faithful attendants, Davis and Abelard, at their usual posts in the library.

The worthy baronet was above seventy; and his long white hair hung in waving curls upon his shoulders, as he sat in his comfortable elastic arm-chair, leaning one elbow upon the table before him. His features had been very handsome, and his complexion still retained that look of health and clearness, which, in a green old age, is the sure indication of a well-spent life. His countenance, though intelligent, was unmarked by the traces of any stormy passions; the cares and troubles of life seemed to have passed gently over him, and content had smoothed the wrinkles age might have made upon his brow; whilst the tall thin figure of Mr. Davis, as he stood reverentially bending forward, his hat in his hand, and his whole demeanour expressing a singular mixture of preciseness and habitual respect, contrasted strongly with the dignified appearance of his master.

The windows of the library opened to the ground, and looked out upon a fine terrace, shaded by a verandah, supported by trellis-work, round which, twined roses mingled with vines. Below, stretched a smiling valley, beautifully wooded, and watered by a majestic river winding slowly along; now lost amidst the spreading foliage of the trees that hung over its banks, and then shining forth again in the light as a lake of liquid silver. Beyond, rose hills majestically towering to the skies, their clear outline now distinctly marked by the setting sun, as it slowly sank behind them, shedding its glowing tints of purple and gold upon their healthy sides; whilst some of its brilliant rays even penetrated through the leafy shade of the verandah, and danced like summer lightning upon the surface of a mirror of polished steel which hung directly in the face of Sir Ambrose.

"What a lovely evening!" exclaimed the worthy baronet, gazing with a delightful eye upon the rich landscape before him; "often as I have looked upon this scene, methinks every time I see it I discover some new beauty. How finely the golden tint the sun throws upon the tops of those trees, is relieved by the deep masses of shadow below! That was Edmund's favourite grove, poor fellow!" and the anxious father sighed, as he puffed his hookah.

"It is a fine evening," said Davis, bowing low, "and if your honour pleases, I think we had better get the steam-mowing apparatus[14] in motion tomorrow. If the sun should be as hot tomorrow as it has been to-day I am sure the hay will make without using the burning glass at all."

"Do as you like, Davis," returned his master, puffing the smoke violently from bis pipe. "I leave it entirely to you."

"And does not your honour think I had better give the barley a little rain? It will be all burnt up, if this weather should continue; and if your honour approve, it may be done immediately, for I saw a nice black heavy-looking cloud sailing by just now, and I can get the electrical machine out in five minutes to draw it down, if your honour thinks fit."

"I have already told you I give you permission to do as you like, Davis," returned the baronet, puffing out volumes of smoke from his hookah. "Inundate the fields if you will, so that you don't trouble me any more about the matter."

"But I would not wish to act without your honour's full conviction," resumed the persevering steward. "Your honour must be aware of the aridity of the soil, and of the impossibility that exists of a proper developement[15] of the incipient heads, unless they be supplied with an adequate quantity of moisture."

"You are very unreasonable, Davis," said Sir Ambrose; "most of your fraternity would be satisfied with being permitted to have their own way; but you—"

"Excuse my interrupting your honour," cried Davis, bowing profoundly; "but I can not bear it to be thought that I was capable of persuading your honour to take any steps your honour might not thoroughly approve. Now as to the germinization and ripening—"

"My good fellow!" exclaimed Sir Ambrose, smiling at the energy with which Davis spoke— his thin figure waving backwards and forwards in the sunshine, and his earnest wish to convince his master, almost depriving his voice of its usual solemn and sententious tone: "My mind is too much occupied to think of these things now, so I give you full and free liberty to burn, dry, or drown my fields, as you may think fit; empowering you to take all necessary steps, either to germinate or ripen corn upon any part of my estate, only premising, that you do not trouble me upon the subject any longer; and so good night."

This being spoken in a tone of voice Davis did not dare to disobey, he slowly retired, apparently as much annoyed at having his own way, as some people are at being contradicted; when suddenly a brilliant dash of light gleamed on the baronet's polished mirror. "Ah! what was that?" exclaimed Sir Ambrose, starting up, and dashing his pipe upon the ground.

He gazed eagerly upon the mirror for a few seconds in breathless anxiety, bending forwards in a listening attitude, and not daring to stir, as though he feared the slightest movement might destroy the pleasing illusion. The flash was repeated again and again in rapid succession, whilst a peal of silver bells began to ring their rounds in liquid melody. "Thank God! thank God!" exclaimed the aged baronet, sinking upon his knees, and clasping his hands together, whilst the big tears rolled rapidly down his face, "My Edmund has conquered! my Edmund is safe!"

The faithful servants of Sir Ambrose followed the example of their master, and for some minutes the whole party appeared lost in silent thanksgivings; the silver bells still continuing their harmonious sweetness, though in softer and softer strains, till at last they gradually died away upon the ear. Sir Ambrose started from his knees as the melody ceased, and desiring Abelard to summon Edric and Father Morris, who was then with the youthful philosopher in his study, he rushed upon the terrace, followed by Davis, to examine a telegraph[16] placed upon a mount at a little distance, so as to be seen from one end of it: the light and music just mentioned, being a signal always given when some important information was about to be transmitted.

The sun had now sunk behind the hills, and the shades of evening were rapidly closing in as the baronet, with straining eyes, watched the various movements of the machine. "One, two, and six!" said he; "yes, that signifies he has won the battle, and is safe. My heart told me so, when I saw the signal flash. My darling Edmund!—two, four, and eight—he has subdued the Germans, and taken the whole of the fine province of France. Six, six, and four—alas! my failing eyes are too weak to see distinctly. Davies, look I implore you! The signal is changing before we have discovered its meaning! For mercy's sake look before it be too late! Alas! alas! I had forgotten your eyes are as feeble as mine own. Oh, Davis! where is Edric? Why is not he here to assist his poor old father at such a moment as this?"

But Edric was otherwise engaged. After the departure of Edmund for the continent, the attention of Father Morris had been directed to his brother, and the mind of Edric, which had long craved for stronger food than it could obtain from the good-natured Dr. Entwerfen, expanded rapidly beneath the culture bestowed upon it. He had long been fond of abstract studies and visionary speculations, but they now formed the only pleasure of his existence; and he pursued them with an eagerness which made all the ordinary affairs of life appear tasteless and insipid. An idea, suggested by Father Morris in one of their conferences, as to the possibility of reanimating a dead body, took forcible possession of his mind. His imagination became heated by long dwelling upon the same theme; and a strange, wild, undefinable craving to hold converse with a disembodied spirit haunted him incessantly. For some time he buried this feverish anxiety in his own breast, and tried in vain to subdue it; but it seemed to hang upon his steps, to present itself before him wherever he went, and, in short, to pursue him with the malignancy of a demon.

"What is the matter with you, Edric?" said Father Morris to his proselyte, the day we have already mentioned. "You are so changed, I scarcely know you, and your eyes have a wild expression, absolutely terrific."

"I am, indeed, half mad," returned Edric, with a melancholy smile; "and yet, perhaps, you will. laugh when I tell you the reason of my uneasiness: to say truth, the conversation we had together the other day has occasioned it. You convinced me so clearly of the possibility of resuscitating a dead body,[17] that since that moment have been tormented by an earnest desire to communicate with one who has been an inhabitant of the tomb. I would fain know the secrets of the grave, and ascertain whether the spirit be chained after death to its earthly covering of clay, condemned till the day of final resurrection to hover over the rotting mass of corruption that once contained it; or whether the last agonies or death free it from its mortal ties, and leave it floating, free as air, in the bright regions of ethereal space?"

"You know my opinion," said the priest.

"I do," replied the pupil: "but forgive me if I add—I do not feel satisfied with it: in fact, mine is not a character to be satisfied with building my faith upon that of any other man. I would see and judge for myself."

"I do not blame you," resumed Father Morris; "a reasonable being should believe nothing he cannot prove; and to remove your doubts, I would advise you to step into the adjoining church-yard, where you can try Dr. Entwerfen's galvanic[18] battery of fifty surgeon power, (which you must allow is surely enough to re-animate the dead,) upon a body which then—"

"Hold! hold!" cried Edric, shuddering. "My blood freezes in my veins, at the thought of a church-yard:—your words recall a horrible dream that I had last night, which even now, dwells upon my mind, and resists all the efforts I can make to shake it off."

"Tell it, then," said the Confessor sternly, "for when the imagination is possessed by horrible fantasies it is relieved by speaking of them to another person."

"I thought," said Edric, "that I was wandering in a thick gloomy wood, through which I had the utmost difficulty to make my way. The black trees, frowning in awful majesty above my bead, twined together in masses so as almost to obstruct my path. Suddenly, a fearful light flashed upon me, and I saw at my feet a horrid charnel house, where the dying mingled terrifically with the dead. The miserable living wretches turned and writhed with pain, striving in vain to escape from the mass of putrescence heaped upon them. I saw their eye-balls roll in agony—I watched the distortion of their features, and, making a violent effort to relieve one who bad almost crawled to my feet, I shrank back with horror as I found the arm I grasped soften to my touch, and a disgusting mass of corruption gave way beneath my fingers!—Shuddering I awoke—a cold sweat hanging upon my brows, and every nerve thrilling with convulsive agony."

"Mere visionary terrors," said the father. "You have suffered your imagination to dwell upon one subject, till it is become morbid."

"Is it not strange" continued Edric, apparently pursuing the current of his own thoughts, "that the mind should crave so earnestly what the body shudders at; and yet, how can a mass of mere matter, which we see sink into corruption the moment the spirit is withdrawn from it, shudder? How can it even feel? I can scarcely analyse my own sensations; but it appears to me that two separate and distinct spirits animate the mass of clay which composes the human frame. The one, the merely vital spark which gives it life and motion, and which we share in common with brutes, and even vegetables; and the other, the divine ethereal spirit, which we may properly term the soul, and which is a direct emanation from God himself, only bestowed upon man."

"In my opinion," said Father Morris, "the organs of thought, reflection, imagination and reason, are material; and as long as the body remains uncorrupted all may be restored, provided circulation can be renewed: for that I think the principle essentially necessary to set the animal machine in motion."

"I confess," resumed Edric, "we all know that circulation and the action of the lungs are inseparably connected, and that if the latter be arrested, death must ensue. How frequently are apparently dead bodies recovered by friction, which produces circulation; and inflation of the lungs with air, which restores their action. If the idea be correct, that the soul leaves the body the instant what we call death takes place, how can these instances of resuscitation be accounted for? Think you that the soul can be recalled to the body after it has once quitted it? Or that it hovers over it in air, attached to it by invisible ligatures, ready to be drawn back to its former situation, when the body shall resume its vital functions? It cannot surely remain in a dormant state and be re-awakened with the body; for this would be inconsistent with the very idea of an incorporeal spirit."

"If you could overcome your childish reluctance to trying an experiment upon a corpse," said Father Morris, "your doubts would be set at rest. For if you could succeed in reanimating a dead body that had been long entombed, so that it might enjoy its reasoning faculties in full perfection, my opinion would be completely established."

"But where shall I find a body, which has been dead a sufficient time to prevent the possibility of its being only in a trance, and which yet has not begun to decompose? —For even if I could conquer the repugnance I feel at the thought of touching such a mass of cold mortality, as that presented in my dream, according to your own theory, the organs must be perfect, or the experiment will not be complete."

"What think you of trying to operate upon a mummy? You know a chamber has been lately discovered in the great pyramid,[19] which is supposed to be the real tomb of Cheops; and where, it is said, the mummies of that great king and the principal personages of his household, have been found in a state of wonderful preservation."

"But mummies are so swathed up."

"Not those of kings and princes. You know all travellers, both ancient and modern, who have them, agree, that they are wrapped merely in folds of red and white linen, every finger and even every toe distinct; thus, if you could succeed in resuscitating Cheops you need not even touch the body; as the clothing in which it is wrapped, would not at all encumber its movements."

"The idea is feasible, and, as you rightly say, if it can be put into execution, will set the matter at rest for ever. I should also like to visit the pyramids, those celebrated monuments or antiquity, whose origin is lost in the obscurity of the darker ages, and which seem to have been spared by the devastating hand of Time, purposely to perplex the learned."

Dr. Entwerfen had been present during the whole of this conversation, though he had been so busied with some philosophical experiments, that he had not joined in it; roused, however. by the word "pyramid," he now started forward.

"You are right," cried he, with enthusiasm, "they are, indeed a mystery—which it has puzzled ages to develope[20]—go to Egypt, and I will accompany you. I feel an inward voice call me to the spot. Yes, we will explore these monuments, and who can tell but that we may be the favoured mortals destined to raise the mystic veil which so long has covered them? We may be decreed to revive their mummies, and force them to reveal the secrets of their prison house. It was Cheops raised the pyramids from the dust by science, and Cheops, by the force of science, shall be compelled to disclose their origin.[21]

"I am glad," resumed Father Morris, "to find the opinions of Dr. Entwerfen coincide so exactly with my own, and that he will have the kindness to accompany your expedition. You will want a companion who can enter into your feelings. and participate in your hopes. My monastic vows chain me to this spot, or I would gladly lend my humble aid to accomplish so valuable a discovery."

"Well, well, we can easily fancy that," cried Dr. Entwerfen, impatiently; "but though you can't go, we can: and—and—when shall we set off, Edric, dear?"

"Stay, stay!" replied Edric, smiling at the doctor's impetuosity; "though I own I should like to visit Egypt, yet there are many things to be considered before such an expedition can be undertaken. I must obtain my father's consent. I must—"

Here a gentle tap at the door interrupted Edric's argument; and made the doctor, whose nerves were rather susceptible, leap two or three yards in a fright:—whilst Father Morris, with his usual air of calm composure, opened the door to the unwelcome intruder.

It was old Abelard the butler. Half ashamed of the unphilosophic terror he had evinced, the doctor felt glad to be able to hide his emotion under the appearance of anger, and demanded peevishly, what was the matter. "Have I not told you a hundred times," continued he, "that I do not like to be interrupted at my studies! and that nothing is more disagreeable than to have one's attention distracted, when it has been fixed upon an affair of importance!"

"I do not attempt to controvert the axiom you have just propounded," returned Abelard, speaking in a slow precise manner, as though he weighed every syllable before he drawled it forth: "for undeniable facts do not admit of contradiction. However, the message with which I stand charged at the present moment relates to Master Edric and the reverend Father Morris, instead of yourself, I humbly opine, no blame can attach itself to me, on account of the unpremeditated interruption of which you allege me culpable."

"And what have you to say to me?" demanded Edric.

"That the worthy gentleman, your respectable progenitor, requests you instantly to put in exercise your locomotive powers to join him on the terrace, to the end, that there your superior visual faculties may afford *soulagement*[22] to the mental anxiety under which he at present labours, by aiding him to develope the intelligence conveyed to him by the telegraphic machine."

"What!" exclaimed Edric, eagerly, and then, without waiting a reply, he darted forward, and in a few seconds was by the side of his father: whilst Father Morris followed with nearly equal expedition.

Abelard gazed after them with amazement: "There is something very astonishing," said he, addressing Dr. Entwerfen, "in the effervescence of the animal spirits during youth. I labour under a complete acatalepsy[23] upon the subject; I should think it must arise from the excessive elasticity of the nerves. Ideas strike—" but here, happening unfortunately to look up, he too was struck to find Dr. Entwerfen had also vanished: and being unwilling to waste his eloquence upon the empty air, he departed, slowly and solemnly, however, according to his custom, to join the party assembled on the terrace.

Volume 1: Chapter 3

"My dear Edric," exclaimed Sir Ambrose, throwing himself into the arms of his son, "my dear, dear Edric! your brother has gained the battle! The Germans are completely overthrown. He has taken their king, and several of their princes prisoners; and the fine province of France is ceded to us entirely!"

"I am rejoiced to hear it," cried Edric, returning his father's embrace with emotion, "and he, I hope, is safe?"

"I hope so too," replied Sir Ambrose; "though he says nothing of himself: but you know Edmund: 'Our troops won this,' 'our army gained that!' 'the soldiers fought bravely!'—he never speaks of himself.[24] To hear him relate a battle, nobody would imagine he had ever had any thing to do with it."

"It is too dark to see any more," said Father Morris, who, during this conversation, had been watching the telegraph, and now turned from it in despair; "the machine is still in motion, but it is too dark for me to decipher what it means."

The attention of all present was directed to the sky as he spoke. It was indeed become of pitchy blackness, a general gloom seemed to hang over the face of nature; the boards flew twittering for shelter, a low wind moaned through the trees, and, in short, every thing seemed to portend a storm.

"Had we not better return to the house?" said Dr. Entwerfen, looking round with something like fear at these alarming indications for his heated imagination had not yet quite recovered the effect of the awful speculations in which he had been so lately indulging. "What is that black spot there? I declare it moves! Good heavens! what can it be?"

"Really, doctor!" returned Abelard, "you provoke the action of my risible faculties. That opaque body which you perceive at a little distance, and which seems to have occasioned such a fearful excitement of your nervous system, is only a living specimen of the corvus genus, who has probably descended upon earth to search for his vermicular repast."[25]

"I beg your pardon, Mr. Abelard," rejoined Mr. Davis, speaking with his usual precision, "but, according to my humble apprehension, you labour under a slight mistake as to that particular. The feathered biped that has so forcibly attracted your attention, appears to me, not one of the corvi, but rather one of the graculi;[26] a variety of extremely rare occurrence in this vicinity, and which are sometimes called incendriae aves,[27] from their unfortunate propensity to put habitations in combustion, by picking up small pieces of phlogisticated carbon,[28] and carrying them in their beaks to the combination of straw and other materials, sometimes piled upon the apex of a house, to defend it from the inroads of pluviosity."[29]

"It is of no use," sighed Sir Ambrose, still straining his eyes to endeavour to decipher the movements of the telegraph, the outlines of which now only appeared, stamped as if in jet, and strongly relieved by the dark grey sky beyond.

"It is of no use," reiterated Father Morris, and the whole party were preparing to retire, when suddenly a vivid light flashed upon them from the hill, and instantly a long line of torches seemed to stream along the horizon. "He is coming home, but will write more tomorrow," exclaimed the whole party simultaneously; for all knew well by experience, the meaning of that signal. "He is coming home, thank God!" repeated Sir Ambrose, his pallid lips quivering, and every limb trembling with agitation.

"Look to my father," cried Edric, "he will faint."

"Oh no, no!" repeated Sir Ambrose: "thank God! thank God!"

"Lean upon me, at least," said Edric, affectionately.

Sir Ambrose complied; and, supported by his son, gazed anxiously on the torches, the red glare of which, by shedding an unnatural light around them, made the surrounding darkness only appear more intense. Thunder now growled in the distance, and rain began to fall in large drops; yet still Sir Ambrose stood, with his eyes fixed upon the torches, and no persuasions could induce him to leave the terrace. These wild, fearful-looking lights, gleaming through the tempest, seemed a connecting link between him and his darling son; and it was not till they were obscured by the thick heavy rain, and even the outline of the telegraph vanished in the gathering clouds around, that he could be induced to seek for shelter.

Sir Ambrose slept little that night: the sleep of age is easily broken, and perhaps the joyful agitation of his spirits had produced a slight access of fever. He rose with the dawn; and, long before the rest of his family had descended, summoned Abelard, that he might dispatch him to inform the Duke of Cornwall of the news: as Father Morris, on account of the storm, had passed the night at the house of Sir Ambrose.

"Go," said he, as soon as the drowsy butler made his appearance. "I am sure the duke feels nearly as great an interest in the success of Edmund as myself, and will not be displeased if he be disturbed a little earlier than usual upon such an occasion."

"I obey," replied Abelard. "I will shake off my somnolent propensities, and speed with the velocity of the electric fluid[30] to the castle of the noble chieftain."

"Take heed you do not forget your message by the way," repeated Sir Ambrose, smiling.

"Not all the waters of Lethe could wash such somnifugous[31] tidings from my memory," replied the butler. "Your honour's words are imprinted upon the mnemonic organ of my brain; and my sensorium must be divided from my cerebellum ere they can be effaced."

The Duke of Cornwall had been the intimate friend of Sir Ambrose almost from infancy. They had been companions at school and at college; besides which, peculiar circumstances which had happened in their youth, had linked them together in indissoluble ties. What these circumstances were, however, no one exactly knew, except the parties concerned, and they always avoided alluding to them. All that was generally understood upon the subject being, that Sir Ambrose had, in some manner, been instrumental in saving the duke's life; but how, when, or where, was never clearly explained.

The Duke of Cornwall was of the royal family of England, and closely allied to the throne. His father had been brother to that prince who had so stedfastly refused the crown when it was offered to him by the ambassadors from the people; and as that prince had left no male descendants, the duke might be considered as legitimately entitled to reign. The thought of disturbing by his claims the female dynasty now established, had, however, never entered into his mind, for having taken it into his head that he would marry his daughter Elvira to Edmund Montagu, and his niece Rosabella to Edric, he turned all his thoughts, plans, and wishes to the accomplishment of this object, and suffered no other idea to interfere with it.

Like most persons living in complete retirement, the duke was exceedingly fond of petty mysteries and needless manoeuvres, and he wasted as much ingenuity and as many contrivances over this scheme, as might, if differently applied, have sufficed to overturn a kingdom. It was true, the interest of the plot was somewhat spoiled, by the fear that the instant he made known his intentions, every one would be delighted to comply with them: yet still, as long as it was kept secret, it was a plot, and as it was the best the duke could muster, he resolved to make the most of it

For this purpose he made Father Morris his confidant, and held long private conferences every day with him upon the subject. The duke was now completely happy: he had not only something to plan, and something to think about, but he had also some one to oppose, for Father Morris's opinion as to the dispositions of the young people, was diametrically opposite to his own; he thinking the strong mind and haughty spirit of Rosabella better suited to the ambitious Edmund, whilst the soft yielding disposition and feminine graces of Elvira seemed to harmonize exactly with the taste of the philosophic Edric. No persuasions, however, could induce the duke to deviate in the slightest degree from his design. Like many of the higher classes of society in those days of universal education, he affected an excessive plainness: and simplicity in his language; so much so, indeed, as sometimes almost to degenerate into rudeness, in order that it might be clearly distinguished from the elaborate and scientific expressions of the vulgar; and when urged by his confessor upon the subject of these intended marriages, he would roughly say, "Don't talk to me; there is nothing like a little contradiction in the married life. If two people were to agree to live together, who were always of the same opinion, they would die of ennui in six months. No, no, I'm right, and so they'll find it in the end."

He would then shake his head, and put on such a look of positive determination, that Father Morris would generally retire in silence, feeling it perfectly in vain to attempt to alter his resolution. As to consulting the inclinations of the young people themselves, the idea never entered his imagination. "Children don't know what is good for them," he would reply sharply, if such a thought were suggested to him, "and it is the duty of parents and guardians to decide in such matters."

The duke had already risen, and was in his garden, when the messenger of Sir Ambrose arrived panting for breath, and quite exhausted by the velocity, as he expressed it, which he had employed in endeavouring to execute with the utmost expedition, the wishes of his master. The duke was surprised to see him.—"What brings you out so early, Abelard?" demanded he.

"Oh, your grace," replied the butler, gasping for utterance, "the haste I have made has impeded my respiration; and the blood, finding the pulmonary artery free, rushes with such force along the arterial canal to the aorta, that—that—I am in imminent danger of being suffocated."

"Pshaw!" said the duke.

"Besides," continued Abelard, "a saline secretion distils from every pore of my skin[32], in a serous transudation, from the excessive exertions I have made use of."

"And what has occasioned these violent exertions?"

"The earnest desire experienced by Sir Ambrose to transmit with all the expedition possible, to your grace, the intelligence he has just received of the acquisition of a victory by Master Edmund, in the hostile territory of Germany."

"Victory!" shouted the duke, "Victory!—Rosabella! Elvira! where are you, girls? Here's tidings to rouse you from your slumbers.—And how is he, Abelard? Is the brave boy safe himself? God bless him! victory will be nothing to us, if we are to lose him."

"It occasions me excessive chagrin," replied Abelard, "that I am totally unable to resolve that interrogatory to your grace's complete satisfaction. Taciturnity, however, upon some subjects, is, I believe, generally considered synonymous with prosperity; and, as Master Edmund, to the best of my credence, conveyed no information relative to his sanity in the communication made by him to his paternal ancestor, I humbly opine that there are no reasonable grounds for supposing it has suffered any material deterioration in consequence of the late sanguinary encounter in which he has been engaged."

The duke had not patience to wait the conclusion of this speech; but hobbled away as fast as his infirmities would permit, vociferating for Elvira and Rosabella, in a voice that might have silenced Stentor;[33] and Abelard, finding himself alone, was fain to follow his example, marvelling as he went along, at the excessive impatience of the fiery spirits of the age, which would not permit people to remain stationary, even to hear, what he called, a compendious replication to the very questions which they themselves had propounded.

Whatever faults might fall to the share of the Duke of Cornwall, that of a cold heart was certainly not amongst the number, and the delight he felt on hearing of Edmund's triumph could not have been greater if the youthful hero had been his own son. His eyes, indeed, absolutely sparkled with transport, when he communicated the intelligence to his niece and daughter; and his tidings were not bestowed upon insensible ears, for the breasts of both his youthful auditors throbbed with pleasure at the news. Elvira had been the idol of Edmund's homage from her childhood; and she fancied she returned his passion with equal fervour; but she deceived herself, and love was as yet a stranger to her heart. Endowed with great beauty and superior talents; accustomed from her earliest infancy to be worshipped by all around her; surrounded by flatterers, till even flattery had lost its charm, Elvira had yet never loved; why she had not, we leave to philosophers to explain; we merely state facts and leave others to draw conclusions.

Rosabella's character was much more easy to decipher than that of her cousin. Passion was the essence of her existence; and her dark eyes flashed a fire that bespoke the intensity of her feelings. She loved Edmund, but though she loved him with all that overwhelming violence, which only a soul like hers could feel, yet she would not have scrupled to sacrifice even him to her revenge, if she had thought he treated her with negligence or contempt. She scorned the opinion of the world, and regarded mankind in general but as slaves, whom she should honour by trampling beneath her feet. Ambition was her leading passion, and even her love for Edmund struggled in vain for mastery against it. This feeling was now highly gratified by the tidings of Edmund's victory. She triumphed in his glory; and a deeper glow burnt upon her cheek, from the proud consciousness she felt that she had not placed her affections upon an unworthy object.

"We have no time to lose, girls," said the duke. "I would not miss being with Sir Ambrose when he receives his letter, for kingdoms. Here, Hyppolite! Augustus! get a balloon ready, and let us be off directly.[34] How tedious these fellows are! They might have removed a church steeple in the time they have wasted about that balloon."

"If your grace would have a moment's patience," said Hyppolite, holding the cords of the balloon. But his Grace had no patience; it was an ingredient Nature had quite forgotten to put into his composition; and, without waiting for the ascending ladder to be put down, he sprang into the car in such haste the moment the balloon was brought to the door, that he was in imminent danger of oversetting it. "So! so," said he, "very well! that will do,—and now girls, that you are safely embarked, we will be off. Hyppolite! you will steer us:— and, Abelard, go you into the buttery, and let my fellows give you something to eat; you will want something after your fatigues. There! there, that will do; don't let us hinder a moment—;" and the rest of his speech was lost in air, as the balloon floated majestically away.

"It has often appeared very astonishing to me," said Abelard, after watching the balloon till it was out of sight, "to observe how partial great people are generally to an aerial mode of travelling; for my part, I think the pedestrian manner infinitely more agreeable."

"*De gustibus non est disputandum*"[35] replied Augustus, the duke's footman, to whom this observation was addressed:—" But I think I observe symptoms of lassitude about you, Mr. Abelard. Will you not adjourn to the apartment of Mrs. Russel, our housekeeper, to repair by some alimentary refreshment, the excessive exhaustion you have sustained in the course of your morning's exertions?"

"Willingly, Mr. Augustus.—I own candidly, I feel the want of a little wholesome nutrition. I shall, besides, be extremely happy to avail myself of the opportunity fortune so benignantly presents, of paying my respects to Mrs. Russel, whom I have not seen these three days."

The worthy, housekeeper was equally rejoiced with Abelard at this instance of Fortune's benignity; a sort of sentimental flirtation having been going on between them for the last thirty years. She accordingly stroked down her snow-white apron, re-adjusted her mob cap,[36] and smoothed her grey hairs, which were divided upon her forehead, with the most scrupulous exactness, before she advanced to welcome her visitors. "What will you take, my dear Mr. Abelard?" said she, as soon as he was within hearing; "what can you fancy? I have a delicious corner of a cold venison pasty in my pantry."

"Words are altogether too feeble to express the transports of my gratitude at receiving so gracious an accolade, beauteous Eloisa," replied the romantic butler; for thus, in allusion to his own name,[37] was he wont to call her. "But though you had only the rigours of the Paraclete[38] to invite me to, instead of the comforts of your well-stored pantry, still would words be wanting to express the feelings of my bosom on thus again beholding you."

"Spare my blushes!" said Mrs. Russel, casting her eyes upon the ground, and playing with a corner of her apron. "I feel a roseate suffusion glow upon my cheeks, as your flattering accents strike upon the tympanum of my auricular organs."

"Oh, Mrs. Russell" sighed Abelard, gazing upon her tenderly;—then, after a short pause, he continued: "As to the aliments with which your provident kindness would soulage my appetite—though venison be a wholesome viand, and was reckoned by the ancients efficacious in preventing fevers, and though the very mention of the savoury pasty makes the eryptae,[39] usually employed in secreting the mucus of my tongue, erect themselves, thereby occasioning an overflow of the saliva, yet will I deny myself the indulgence, and content myself simply with a boiled egg, as being more likely to agree with the present enfeebled state of the digestive organs of my stomach."

"You shall have it instantly," cried Mrs. Russel.

"And will you have the kindness to superintend the culinary arrangement of it yourself?" rejoined Abelard. "I do not like the albumen too much coagulated; and I prefer it without any butyraceous[40] oil, simply flavoured by the addition of a small quantity of common muriate of soda."[41]

The egg was soon prepared and devoured. "Thank you, thank you! dear Mrs. Russell," said Abelard; "this refection was most acceptable. I had felt for some time the gastric juice corroding the coats of my stomach; and still, though I have now given it some solid substance to act upon, I think it would not be amiss to dilute its virulence by the addition of a little fluid. Have you any thing cool and refreshing?"

"I have some bottled beer" replied Mrs. Russel; "but I am afraid the carbonic acid gas has not been sufficiently disengaged during the process of the vinous fermentation to render it wholesome; and there is scarcely any alcohol in the whole composition—"

"That is exactly what I want," said Abelard, "for my physicians have expressly forbidden stimulants. Provided the gluten that forms the germ was properly separated in the preparation of the malt, and the seed sufficiently germinated to convert the fecula[42] into sugar, I shall be perfectly satisfied."

"I can guarantee the accuracy of its preparation both with regard to the malt and the beer," repeated Mrs. Russel; and the frothing fluid soon sparkled in a goblet, to the infinite satisfaction of the thirsty butler, who, after a hearty draught, vowed nectar itself was never half so delicious; and that all the gods on Olympus would envy him, if they could but taste his fare, and see the blooming Hebe[43] that was his cup-bearer.

Volume 1: Chapter 4

WHEN the balloon of the duke approached the habitation of Sir Ambrose, its occupiers perceived the worthy baronet walking with hasty strides towards the mount of the telegraph, which commanded an extensive view of the surrounding country, followed by Edric, Father Morris, and Dr. Entwerfen, who appeared vainly endeavouring to persuade him to relax a speed so little suited to his advanced years.

"Talk not to me of going slowly, when I expect news of my darling Edmund!" exclaimed Sir Ambrose, continuing his rapid pace —his heart beating with paternal pride, and his countenance beaming with exultation.

"I am also anxious to hear of my brother," said Edric, "but after the information we have already received by the telegraphic dispatch, it appears to me that we have little more to learn of importance."

"Edric, you are not a father, and you can have no idea of a father's anxiety," replied Sir Ambrose, hurrying on to the mount, as though he hoped the rapidity of his motion would afford some relief to the impatience of his mind; whilst the party of the duke, seeing the point to which he was hastening, opened the valves of their balloon, and made preparations to descend upon the same spot.

The duke and Sir Ambrose were always glad to meet, but as the present occasion was one of more than ordinary interest, so they now greeted each other with more than ordinary pleasure. The duke had always been warmly attached to Edmund, and his voice actually trembled with agitation as he exclaimed:—

"Well, my old friend, you see your brave boy is determined to keep us alive still. Our blood would stagnate in our veins, if he did not give us a fillip now and then to rouse us. But what does the young rogue say of himself? I hope he's not wounded?"

"He never mentions himself," replied Sir Ambrose, tears glistening in his eyes, as he pressed the hand of his friend warmly in his own; "Edmund loves his country too devotedly to think of himself when he is engaged in her service."

"Well, well, it is all right," cried the duke, "he is a brave boy, that is certain."

Sir Ambrose did not reply, for he had now reached the summit of the mount, and was too eagerly looking round in every direction to attend to his friend's remark.

In those days, the ancient method of conveying the post having been found much too slow for so enlightened a people, an ingenious scheme had been devised,[44] by which the letters were put into balls and discharged by steam-cannon, from place to place; every town and district having a piece of *toile metallique*, or woven wire, suspended in the air, so as to form a kind of net to arrest the progress of the ball, and being provided with a cannon to send it off again, when the letters belonging to that neighbourhood should have been extracted: whilst, to prevent accident, the mail-post letter-balls were always preceded by one of a similar description, made of thin wood, with a hole in its side, which, collecting the wind as it passed along, made a kind of whizzing noise, to admonish people to keep out of the way.

The mount on which Sir Ambrose now stood, commanded an extensive view, and the scene it presented was beautiful in the extreme. On one side, innumerable grass fields, richly wooded, and only divided from each other by invisible iron fences, appeared like one vast park; whilst, on the other, the waving corn, its full heads beginning to darken in the sun, gave a rich glowing tint to the landscape. But Sir Ambrose thought not of the prospect, he did not even see the murmuring brooks and shady groves, the smiling vales and swelling hills, that constituted its beauty; no, his attention was wholly occupied by a small black spot he had just discovered on the edge of the horizon. In breathless anxiety, his eyes almost starting from their sockets, he bent eagerly forwards, gazing on this small and at first almost imperceptible speck. It gradually grew larger and larger—it rapidly approached! and in a few seconds a slight noise buzzed through the air as the long-expected balls whizzed past him.

Sir Ambrose's agitation was excessive; with trembling limbs and livid lips, he hurried to the nearest station, which luckily was close at hand, and round which several of his household were assembled, in their impatience to hear the news. Sir Ambrose could not speak, but the person whose province it was to sort the letters guessed his errand, and opening the bag held forth the ardently expected treasure. Gasping for breath, Sir Ambrose eagerly attempted to take it, but his hands were unequal to the task, the violence of his emotion overpowered him, and after a short, but fruitless struggle, he fell senseless on the ground.

The confusion produced by this unexpected incident was indescribable. The old duke walked up and down, wringing his hands, and exclaiming, "What shall we do? What will become of us?" whilst the rest of the party endeavoured to give assistance to Sir Ambrose.

"Parental affection," said Davis, who had an unfortunate propensity for making long speeches precisely at the moment when nobody was likely to attend to him; "parental affection has been universally allowed by all writers, both ancient and modern, to be one of the strongest passions of the soul, and the most exalted instances might be produced of the surprising energy of this universal sentiment."

"For Heaven's sake help me to raise my father," cried Edric: "Give him air, or he will die!"

"Patience," continued Davis, "is necessary in all things, and is perhaps one of the most useful and estimable qualities of life. It enables us to bear, without shrinking, the bitterest evils that can assail us. Without patience, philosophy would never have made those wonderful discoveries that subjugate nature to our yoke."

"Fetch me some water," exclaimed Edric, "or he will expire before your eyes."

"It appears to me," said a labourer, who had been mending a steam digging-machine in a neighbouring field, and who now stood leaning upon his work, and looking on gravely at all that passed, without attempting to offer the least assistance;—" It appears to me that it would be highly improper to administer the aqueous fluid in its natural state of frigidity, under the existing circumstances. The present suspension of animation under which Sir Ambrose labours, is evidently occasioned by want of circulation. Now, as it is the property of hot liquors, rather than cold ones, to supply the stimulant necessary for the reproduction of circulation, I opine that hot water would answer the purpose better than cold."

In the mean time Father Morris had brought some water from a neighbouring fountain, and throwing it on the patient's face, Sir Ambrose opened his eyes: for some moments he stared wildly around him, but, as soon as he began to recollect what had passed, he implored Father Morris to give him his ardently desired letter.

"You are not yet equal to reading it," said Father Morris compassionately; "I fear the exertion will be too much for you."

"Oh give it me! give it me," exclaimed the poor old man; "if a spark of mercy remain in your soul, do not keep me in this agony!"

It was impossible to resist the tone of real anguish that accompanied these words, and Father Morris put the letter into his hands.— Sir Ambrose took it eagerly; though he trembled so, that he could scarcely break the seal. At last, he tore it open and gazed at its contents, but he could not read a word; he dashed away his tears, and rubbed his eyes impatiently —all was in vain—the writing was still illegible —"Read! read!" cried he, in a voice trembling with agitation, "For Heaven's sake read! —will no one have pity on me?"

Father Morris took the letter, and read it aloud, whilst Sir Ambrose sate—his eyes raised to Heaven, his hands clasped together, and the tears rolling down his aged cheeks, listening to his words, and drinking in every syllable. After giving a circumstantial account of the battle, and assuring his father that he had not been wounded, Edmund proceeded thus. "The Queen has written me a letter of approbation in her own hand, and has been graciously pleased to signify her intention of honouring me with a triumphal entry into London; she has likewise conferred upon me letters of nobility. The goodness of my sovereign makes a deep impression upon my breast; but for the rest, I assure you that neither the applauses of the multitude, nor the privilege of writing Lord before my name, can afford a moment's satisfaction to a heart that pants only for the pleasure of seeing again those most dear to it; nor shall I enjoy my triumph unless those I love be present to give it zest."

"I congratulate you, my dear sir!" exclaimed Father Morris, as soon as he had finished;" I congratulate you from my inmost soul!"

"Go to his triumph!" exclaimed the duke, rubbing his hands in ecstacy; "Yes, yes, that we will: won't we, my old friend? God bless him! I'm glad he is not hurt, though. And so you see, in spite of all his glory, he can't be happy without us. How prettily he says that!—'Not all the approbation of my sovereign, the praises of the people'—nor—nor—what is it? I don't remember the exact words, but I know the sense was, that he couldn't be happy without us, and, God bless him! I'm sure I'm as happy as he can be, at the thought of seeing him."

Sir Ambrose could not reply, but the tears ran down his aged cheeks like rain, as his heart breathed a silent offering of thanksgiving to the Almighty Being who had thus bestowed victory upon his son; and his lips murmured some inarticulate sounds of transport; whilst Elvira and Rosabella mingled their tears with his, for joy often becomes painful, and seeks for a relief like grief.

The party now slowly returned to the mansion of Sir Ambrose, so completely occupied in discussing Edmund's letter, as to be totally unaware that Edric had not accompanied them; yet such was the case. The youthful philosopher's heart had swelled almost to bursting, as he had listened to the reading of his brother's letter, and he now rushed into a thick wood, shelving down to a romantic stream, which formed part of the pleasure-grounds of Sir Ambrose.

Almost without knowing where he was going, Edric plunged amongst the trees, and threw himself upon a grassy bank under their shade, upon the border of the rivulet. The gentle murmuring of the water, gave a delightful sense of refreshing coolness, particularly agreeable from the burning heat of the day; and Edric lay, his eyes fixed upon the sparkling waves as they danced in the sunbeams, with both his hands pressed firmly upon his throbbing temples, endeavouring in vain to analyze the new and strange emotions that struggled for mastery in his bosom. By degrees he became more calm; and though his heart still beat with feelings he could not quite explain, he felt soothed by the softly gliding streamlet; and the stormy passions of his breast seemed lulled to tranquillity as one hand fell carelessly down by his side, and the other merely supported the head it no longer strained.

It was not envy that occasioned Edric's emotions; but shame and indignation burnt in his bosom when he recollected that he was wasting his days in comparative obscurity, whilst his brother, only a few years older than himself, was ennobling the name bequeathed to him by his ancestors.

"And cannot I also become famous?" thought he, his heart swelling with emulation. "Though I abhor the profession of a soldier are not other ways open to me of attaining eminence? Why should I not exert myself? I will remain in indolence no longer. I, too, will prove myself worthy of my forefathers, and show the world that the exalted blood of the Montagues has not degenerated in my veins!" His eyes sparkled with the thought, and he half raised himself, as though eager to put it into immediate execution. A moment's reflection, however, restored him to himself, and he could not help smiling at his own folly. "And yet I call myself a philosopher," thought he: "Alas! alas! how little do we know ourselves, for after all, the pursuit of knowledge for its own sake is the only employment worthy of a man of sense: and the transitory applause of the multitude, it is beneath him to accept. Nature is the goddess I adore; and if it should be granted to me to explore her secrets, I shall be the happiest of mankind. But why should I pass my life in anxious cravings never destined to be realized? The events of to-day have only proved clearly the little value my society is of to my father: he is too much occupied with my brother to even think of me, and were I absent, I should soon be forgotten. Why then should I not travel and satisfy these restless wishes that gnaw at my heart and poison every pleasure? I was not born to rest contented with the dull routine of domestic life, and I detest hypocrisy: I will seek my father; and, explaining my real sentiments, set off for Egypt immediately."

Satisfied with this resolution, Edric rose and walked hastily towards his father's mansion, with all that inward vigour which the consciousness of having made up one's mind is certain to bestow; and which, perhaps, is one of the most agreeable sensations that can be experienced by the human mind, as that of suspense or indecision is undoubtedly one of the most unpleasant.

Edric found his father and the duke busily engaged in consulting upon their intended journey, which was an event in both their lives; for as, since the universal adoption of balloons, journeys were performed without either trouble or expense, the rich had lost all inducement to undertake them, and it was rare for a man of rank to quit his family mansion unless he had some post at court.

"I have a palace in London," said the duke, "which I hope you will make your home; though it has been so long unused that I doubt whether it will be fit for your reception."

"Do not distress yourself about making arrangements for my family," replied Sir Ambrose; "there will be only Edric and myself, and we can make shift with any thing."

"Indeed I shall not consent to any such arrangement," said Elvira, who now entered the room with Rosabella and Clara Montagu, the orphan niece of the baronet, who had been brought up in his family; "What has Clara done that she is to be excluded from the party?"

"Oh, Clara is too young to think of such things," returned Sir Ambrose, smiling.

"Not she," cried the duke; "I'll engage for it; are you my pretty rosebud?" continued he, drawing the smiling, blushing girl to his knee. Shouldn't you like to go to London, eh?"

"Oh, yes," cried Clara, with all the eagerness and innocence of fifteen, for that was her age; "very much indeed, if my uncle has no objection."

"My dear Sir Ambrose," said Elvira, coaxingly, "do pray indulge us."

"Well, well, we shall see," replied the good-humoured baronet, smiling.

"Thank you, thank you, my dear, dear uncle!" cried Clara, flying to him, and almost smothering him with kisses.

"But I have not consented yet, you know." No, but I'm sure you will, you look so good-natured."

"Go, go, you are a little coaxing puss: but why did you not come home last night, Clara?"

"My nurse was so ill, and it rained so: besides, you know, uncle, you gave me leave to stop, if I liked."

"Well, well, I believe I did. It was of no great consequence; you are always safe under the care of Mrs. Robson: she is a very respectable woman—I hope she's better?"

"Oh, she'll soon be well now. I'm going to tell her of Edmund's victory; and she said yesterday, if she could but hear that he had conquered, it would cure her, if she were dying."

"Off with you, then," said Sir Ambrose, laughing, "you are always on the wing; and harkye, you may tell your nurse also, that you are going to London."

Clara's delight and gratitude were unbounded, and she sprang away like a young fawn to tell her nurse the joyful news, while Elvira's eyes sparkled with pleasure, as she thanked Sir Ambrose warmly for his kindness. The duke was also highly gratified. "You must bring Abelard and Davis also," said he, "for I'm sure you won't be happy without them."

Sir Ambrose owned he should not; and the duke, being like most people who lead dull, monotonous lives, quite delighted with an event that promised a little change, bustled off, followed by his fair companions, fully determined to make the most of it.

Edric's heart throbbed violently when he found himself alone with his father; the moment was arrived he had been so ardently wishing for, and yet he was silent. He had scarcely had patience to wait the end of his father's conference with the duke; and whilst it had lasted, he had been arranging and rearranging a thousand times in his mind, the phrases he meant to make use of; yet now they seemed to have all vanished from his memory, and he stood gazing through the open window, his mind feeling a perfect chaos, and without being able to recollect one single word of what he had determined to say. After continuing for some time in this state of irresolution, he was suddenly startled by his father's exclaiming, "Well, Edric, my dear boy, I am very glad I have an opportunity of speaking to you alone, as I have something of importance to communicate."

The voice of Sir Ambrose sounded harsh and abrupt in the ears of his son, and Edric felt incapable of uttering a single word in reply.

"What is the matter?" cried Sir Ambrose, after a short pause; "surely you are not ill? Edric, my dear boy, do speak; shall I send for Dr. Coleman?"

"Oh, no, no!" cried Edric, faintly; "I am not ill, I assure you."

"What is the matter, then?" resumed Sir Ambrose, impatiently; "Perhaps, you want some new philosophical instrument, and you don't like to ask for it, because you know the low state of my finances. But don't distress yourself on that account, for you are going to marry a rich wife, and then you can indulge yourself with any thing you like."

"Marry!" cried Edric, in alarm. "Yes," returned his father, "the duke has just most generously proposed that you shall marry Rosabella; and that he will give her a fortune equal to what he gives Elvira."

"But I do not love Rosabella, and nothing shall induce me to marry her: I should be utterly miserable even to think of it."

"Not marry Rosabella!" exclaimed Sir Ambrose, in the utmost astonishment.

"Indeed, I cannot. I am convinced she would make me wretched, for our tempers don't assimilate, and we should both be miserable. I should be very sorry to cause either you or the duke a moment's uneasiness. But in an affair like this, which concerns the happiness of my whole life.—"

"Don't talk to me, Sir," cried Sir Ambrose, in a violent passion, "I won't hear a word, Sir—not a syllable: *my* son shall obey *my* orders. Go to your room, Sir, and prepare to marry Rosabella immediately, or never expect to see my face again."

"My dear father!" said Edric, attempting to take Sir Ambrose's hand.

"Away, Sir!" cried the baronet, shaking him off; "obedience far outweighs words. If I *am* your *dear* father, you will act in compliance with my wishes; and if you do not, it is a mockery to call me 'dear.'"

"I cannot marry Rosabella!"

"Was ever such obstinacy!—such folly! The world will think you distracted."

"I care not for the world!" cried Edric, impatiently.

"But you must care for the world—the world must not be slighted! and as long as you live in it, you must conform to its opinions. I don't like to hear people say they don't care for the world; when people pretend to scorn it, it is generally because they have done something to make it scorn them."

"But, my dear father! you would not wish me to sacrifice my conscience to its dictates."

"And pray, Sir, what has your conscience to do with the matter in question?"

"Should I not sacrifice it by marrying a woman I feel I could never love? In my opinion, nothing can be more sacred than the marriage vow; and with what feelings could I enter into this solemn engagement in the presence of Almighty God, calling upon him to witness it, when I knew my heart was at variance with my words? My soul would recoil with horror at such blasphemy."

"You talk about your conscience, Edric,—but should you not rather say your inclinations? The person of Rosabella does not please your fancy, I suppose; and to gratify a capricious whim, you would destroy the happiness of your father, and ruin your own prospects for ever."

"It is not of the person of Rosabella that I complain; I allow her to be beautiful as a Venus, and that her talents even exceed her personal charms: but when I see her dark eyes flashing fury, and her lips curved into an expression of pride, hatred, or scorn, I forget her beauty, and think only of the fearful passions of her soul."

"Your objections are futile, Edric; at any rate, they are of no avail. You must marry her—I am sorry it is against your inclination, but I will not have my authority disputed:—however, as I have always been an indulgent father, I do not wish you to decide hastily, and I give you four-and-twenty hours to make up your mind: at the expiration of which time you shall marry Rosabella or quit my house for ever. No reply, young man; I won't hear a word."

It was in vain to attempt a reply; and Edric left his father's presence oppressed by that strange, mysterious presentiment of evil, which, like a fearful cloud, dark, gloomy, and impenetrable, sometimes hangs upon our thoughts, foreboding horrors; though so dimly and indistinctly, that, like the gigantic phantoms we sometimes fancy through the mist of twilight, their terrors seemed increased tenfold by the very uncertainty that half shrouds them from our sight. Mingled with these feelings, was one of wild, unearthly joy. Driven from his father's house, he would be free to travel— his doubts might be satisfied—he might, at last, penetrate into the secrets of the grave; and partake, without restraint, of the so ardently desired fruit of the tree of knowledge. Nothing would then be hidden from him. Nature would be forced to yield up her treasures to his view— her mysteries would be revealed, and he would become great, omniscient, and god-like. His mind filled with a chaos of thoughts like these, which he strove in vain to arrange, and which seemed to swell his brain almost to bursting, Edric sought the study of Dr. Entwerfen to inform his worthy tutor of the change a few short hours had wrought in his destiny.

Volume 1: Chapter 5

"Why did not you join with your cousin in inviting Clara Montagu to go with us to London?" said the Duke to Rosabella, as their balloon proceeded homewards.

"I thought the humility of my situation rendered it improper," returned Rosabella, with an affected air of modesty. "It surely would be wrong for a poor dependant like myself, to take the liberty of inviting guests to the house of her patron."

"Rosabella! you know I can't bear to hear you talk so ridiculously—I hate to hear of your dependant situation, and humility, and nonsense; we all know that you are not humble, you are as proud as Lucifer; and as to dependance, I never make any distinction between you and Elvira. You are my daughters whilst I live, and shall be my heiresses when I die—aye, and perhaps before I die, but you'll see."

"I am sure my cousin did not mean to offend you, Sir," said Elvira; "She loves you tenderly, and—"

"*Apropos de bottes!*"[45] exclaimed the Duke, "what letter was that which I saw you receive this morning?"

"It was from Edmund," replied Elvira trembling and blushing, as she drew it from her bosom, and gave it to her father.

In case of Claudia's death, Elvira and Rosabella were the next heiresses to the throne; and as neither had attained the age which would prevent their being eligible candidates, they had not the least idea the duke would wish them to marry until after that period. Thus both earnestly regarded the duke as he perused the epistle, which Elvira knew, and Rosabella suspected, breathed only love; and both expected a torrent of rage when he had concluded it. To their infinite surprise however, he folded it up, and putting it into his pocket, merely told Elvira, that he wished a private conference with her in his library, as soon as they reached home. Poor Elvira turned pale at the mention of the library: for when aught went wrong in the duke's household, it was there he was accustomed to lecture the unfortunate offender, and there Elvira herself had often trembled in her childhood; in short, the place was associated in her mind with only disagreeable recollections, and anticipating nothing pleasant connected with it, she sat completely absorbed in a gloomy silence.

Rosabella seemed equally disinclined for conversation. Though the conduct of her uncle was quite different from what she had expected, her active mind had already suggested a thousand explanations for it, each less consonant to her judgment than her wishes. "His letter must have been one of mere friendship—and it is possible that he does not love her," thought she; whilst, as the idea flashed across her mind she turned eagerly to Elvira, to read its confirmation in her countenance: —but, alas! those timid, downcast looks—and those glowing cheeks, told but too plainly a tale that drove Rosabella to distraction. Scarcely had the balloon stopped when she sprang from the car, and rushed to her own room in a state little short of madness, whilst Elvira, with a beating heart followed her father to the library.

Rosabella was met at the entrance to her apartments by her favourite attendant, Marianne, who had lived with her from her childhood, and who governed her with despotic sway. It is strange, but the most haughty people are generally the most submissive slaves to those who have acquired power over them, and the proud-spirited female who would spurn indignantly all control from her titled relatives, will obey implicitly—nay, almost servilely, the wishes of a favourite servant. Thus it was with Rosabella. Marianne was perfectly aware of her power, and she occasionally used it tyrannically, but on the present occasion she was really alarmed at the glowing cheeks, flashing eyes, and agitated frame of Rosabella, and asked with an appearance or deep interest, if she were ill.

Rosabella did not speak, but throwing herself upon a sofa, hid her face in both her hands.

What *is* the matter?" asked Marianne, gazing at her with astonishment.

"He loves her! he adores her!" cried Rosabella, starting from her couch and traversing the room rapidly. "Curse on her beauty! Oh that a look of mine could wither it! or that she could feel the burning fire that rages here!" Then stopping suddenly, she gazed upon her attendant with the wildness of a maniac, and, pressing her hand firmly against her side, threw herself again upon her couch, exclaiming, "Oh, Marianne! why am I not beloved like Elvira?"

"And are you certain that she is beloved?"

"Certain!" reiterated Rosabella, wringing her hand; Alas! alas! would I were not so certain; but can I doubt the evidence of my senses? This day—this very day! she has received. a letter from him. I saw a blush of conscious pleasure glow upon her cheeks, and I could have stabbed her to the heart,—yes, and exulted in her dying agonies,—triumphed in her groans. Oh, Marianne! is it not extraordinary that one so great, so noble, and so exalted as Edmund, can love such a poor, weak, feeble being as Elvira? But she loves him not; at least not as he should be loved. She is incapable of it."

"I think she is,—and that though he now admires her beauty, yet, when he discovers the feebleness of her soul, he must despise her."

"But he is so blinded that be fancies her very faults perfections."

"That blindness cannot continue. When Edmund knew Elvira, he had seen nothing of the world; and people thus situated, who have warm imaginations, generally amuse themselves by conjuring up an idol of perfection to which they attach all kinds of merit, probable or improbable. They invest the first face or figure that takes their fancy, with these imagined charms, no matter whether they accord or not, and then fall in love with the image they have created-whilst the delusion under which they labour, makes them see every action of the beloved object under a false light; just as people wearing green spectacles fancy the whole creation tinged with emerald. Intercourse with the world dispels these visions, and when Edmund returns he will be as one awakening from a dream: he will look in vain for the charms which once bewitched him."

"Oh, that you may be right! but yet I fear—"

"Fear nothing—Edmund will return quite changed. Though in reality he has been absent only a few months, he will have acquired more knowledge of the world, than in all his previous life. He will now know himself, and will feel that he wants a companion in a wife: one that can enter into his views, participate in his wishes, and if necessary, aid him in his plans. Then will he be able to properly estimate your character, and despising the feeble

Elvira, he will lay his heart and hand humbly at your feet."

"Alas! alas! were even this flattering vision realised, it would be then too late."

"Too late! what mean you?"

"That even now Elvira is confessing his attachment to her father, and, perhaps—oh, there is madness in the thought!—even at this moment she may be receiving his approval."

"Then we are lost," said Marianne, and a pause ensued, interrupted only by the convulsive sobs of Rosabella, who wrung her hands and wept aloud in the bitterest agony.

"But are you sure you have not deceived yourself?" resumed the confidant; "your jealousy may have given weight to trifles not worthy of serious attention."

"The Duke asked her if she had heard from him, and she gave him Edmund's letter. My uncle read it calmly, and when he had finished desired her to attend him to his library."

"I confess this does not look well," said Marianne, and another long pause ensued, which was broken by the sound of rapid footsteps, and in an instant Elvira rushed into the apartment with a face radiant with joy.

"Oh, my dear cousin," cried she, "my father is so kind I so good! I have told him every thing, and he is not in the least angry. He has given his consent, and all is settled. I am to marry Edmund, and you Edric, and—"

"I marry Edric!" exclaimed Rosabella, the crimson flush of anger darkening over her fine features, and proud scorn curling her beautiful lips; "I marry that feeble inanimate wretch! When we meet, and he offers his hand to greet me, his very touch seems to freeze my veins. Cold, prudent, and calculating, he has all the vices of age without its excuses. And shall I marry such a being? No, if all other resources fail, death shall free me before the hated moment arrives!" and starting from her couch, she paced the room in violent agitation.

"My dear Rosabella," said Elvira following, and trying to soothe her, "do pray compose yourself. Consider my father—how angry he would be if he were to hear you! He is so positive he might—" Here Elvira stopped, her delicacy making her averse to remind her cousin how completely she was in the duke's power.

"Go on," cried Rosabella, tauntingly; "I know what you would say. Upbraid me with my meanness—trample upon me—spurn me—do not even spare the memory of my poor dear father;—I am prepared for every thing; I know the worst; I know that my uncle is positive, and that I am a poor dependant, subsisting upon his bounty, and that it is in his power to turn me this instant from his door, without a shilling to procure me food or shelter. But not even this shall control my will. Poor and dependant as I am, I am free; and I would sooner labour in the meanest servitude, beg my bread, or even perish for want, than reside in a palace surrounded by crowds of adoring slaves, if the price were that I must call Edric husband."

"My dear mistress," exclaimed Marianne, soothingly, "you are too violent."

"I am very much hurt, Rosabella," said Elvira, "to find you think me capable of saying any thing intentionally to wound your feelings. As to your unhappy father, you must be aware I know his history only vaguely, as it is a subject to which the duke never suffers any one to allude; and I assure you he was not even in my thoughts when I spoke—"

"Oh!" cried Rosabella, clasping her hands together energetically as she spoke; "Oh! that it were but permitted to me to clear my father's name from the shade that hangs over it. I know, I feel, that he cannot have been guilty! He must have been the victim of slander; of vile contrivance or malice of plots raised against him by those who envied his fair fame. Oh, that I knew the facts, and could clear him from all blame! By heaven! neither the gratification of my love, nor any revenge, could afford me half the pleasure!"

"You use strange language, Rosabella," said Elvira, blushing at her cousin's warmth; "I own I cannot comprehend such violent feelings. Thank God! nature formed mine in a more temperate mould."

"Your feelings!" cried Rosabella, scornfully; "you have none—you cannot even fancy them—you are incapable of love!"

"There you do me injustice, "replied Elvira; "such passions as yours I am indeed incapable of feeling—but love; real, pure, undefiled love; that absorbing affection which prefers another's happiness to its own; that devotion which would sink unknown to the grave, to procure another's happiness; that seeks not its own gratification, but would sacrifice all the world can give, to promote the welfare of another; that can taste of no pleasure and partake of no delight, unless it be participated by the beloved object, and even then, joys in his satisfaction more than in its own; this I *can* feel; my heart tells me that I can, and this, I hope, I shall in time feel for Edmund."

"Then you own you do not love him yet?" asked Rosabella, with a bitter smile.

"I fear I do not," returned Elvira, sighing, "at least not as he should be loved. But," continued she, after a short pause, "perhaps my ideas of love are foolish and romantic, and I shall in time become more reasonable."

A smile of contempt was Rosabella's only answer, when their conference was interrupted by a summons for them both to attend the duke. They obeyed in silence, and found him sitting in his library, with Father Morris standing beside his chair.

"Of course, Elvira has told you what I mean to do for you" said the duke, addressing Rosabella.

"Yes! My lord, she has," returned Rosabella with dignity.

"Well, and what do you say to it?"

"I thought your Grace did not intend either my cousin, or myself to marry, till we were past the age fixed by the late Queen?"

"Pooh! nonsense; you neither of you have the least chance of ascending the throne. Claudia is not thirty: and she is likely to live these fifty years."

Rosabella did not speak, but the colour fled from her cheeks, and her eyes were cast upon the ground, whilst her strongly compressed lips showed that it was with infinite difficulty that she controlled her feelings sufficiently to hear her uncle with patience.

"In short," continued the duke, "I have made up my mind that you shall both marry and as Edmund it seems has fixed upon Elvira, I think I cannot do better than to give you to his younger brother."

"And do you know of whom you are disposing so unceremoniously?" asked Rosabella, raising her brilliant eyes from the ground, and fixing them upon him with a look of proud scorn. The duke shrunk involuntarily from the withering glare, which seemed to fall upon him with the fabled power of that of the basilisk.

"Of whom I am disposing?" stammered he, unconsciously repeating her words, "Of whom I am disposing? Why, of my niece, to be sure," he continued, arranging with difficulty his scattered ideas. "You are my niece, are you not?"

"Yes," returned Rosabella, "unfortunately I am your niece; and I blush for an uncle who does not scruple to abuse so barbarously the last legacy bequeathed to him by an unfortunate brother. Yes, my lord duke, I am your niece—your protégée—your dependant. I am not ashamed to own that I owe my daily bread to your bounty; but notwithstanding all this, I am not aware that I am your slave, nor do I think the pecuniary obligations I am under to you sufficient to give you the right of disposing of me as an article of furniture, or a beast of burthen."

"You mistake the matter entirely, Rosabella," said the duke; "I do not wish to hurt your feelings."

"Do you think, then, that I am formed of stone or iron, that I am to be told to marry when and where you list, without having my inclinations consulted or my affections gained? I am not so quiescent. Were my poor father alive you would not treat me thus."

"Beware, Rosabella, you tread on dangerous ground!" said the duke, violently agitated.

"Alas! alas!" cried Rosabella, wringing her hands, "why am I treated thus? Have I no friend to take my part? Will no one interpose to save me from destruction? Oh that my poor father were alive!—he, at least, would pity his unhappy daughter. Father Morris, *you* have always professed to love me. I have been told you were my father's friend. Can you stand and see me thus cruelly oppressed, and not proffer one single word in my behalf? I appeal to you as a friend, as a Christian, as a man.'"

Father Morris made no answer to this appeal, but his lips turned of a livid paleness, and uttering a low groan, he sank into a chair, hiding his face in his hands, whilst every nerve quivering with agitation.

"Go to your chamber, Rosabella," said the duke, in a trembling voice, "and when you have learnt to express yourself more temperately towards one who has been your only friend and benefactor, perhaps I may send for you again."

Rosabella attempted to speak, but the duke sternly forbade her. "Go," said he, "your ignorance of your real situation may now plead in excuse for your conduct. But the time will shortly come when you will shudder at your folly, and wonder at my present forbearance."

Awed by his manner, and the mysterious emotion of Father Morris, Rosabella withdrew in silence, followed by Elvira, and each retired to her separate chamber, to muse in solitude upon the strange events which had occurred during the day.

Volume 1: Chapter 6

When Edric left his father to seek Dr. Entwerfen, he encountered Father Morris in the way and so absorbed was he in his own meditations that he had almost passed the reverend father without seeing him.

"This is quite *en philosophe*,"[46] said the priest with a smile, as he intercepted his pupil's path. "What is the matter, Edric? I did not think King Cheops[47] himself could have made you so soon forget your old friends."

"Indeed I had not forgotten you, for I was thinking of you that very moment. Do you really think it possible, that if I went to Egypt, I might succeed in resuscitating a mummy?"

"I do not doubt it. The ancient Egyptians you know believed that the souls of their mummies were chained to them in a torpid state till the final day of judgment, and supposing this hypothesis to be correct, there is every reason to imagine that by employing so powerful an agent as galvanism, re-animation may be produced."[48]

"If I recollect rightly, the ancient Egyptians did not imagine the souls of their dead remained in their bodies, but. that they would return to them at the expiration of three thousand years."

"And it is now about three thousand years since Cheops was entombed."

"It is strange," continued Edric, musing, "what influence your words have upon my mind: whilst I listen to you, the racking desire I feel to explore these mysteries becomes almost torture; and I muse upon it till I fancy it an impulse from a superior power, and that I am really selected to be the mortal agent of their revelation to man."

"And why may not this impulse, which seems to operate with such irresistible force upon your mind, and which you say *you fancy*,[49] be a real feeling implanted in you by the Divine Author of your being, to guide you to a country where you are destined to attain immortality? Egypt is rich in monuments of antiquity; and all historians unite in declaring her ancient inhabitants to have possessed knowledge and science far beyond even the boasted improvements of modern times. For instance, could we attempt to erect stupendous buildings like the pyramids, where enormous masses are arranged with geometrical accuracy, and the labours of man have emulated the ever lasting durability of nature? Are we even capable of conceiving works so majestic as those they put in execution? We assuredly are not; and in every point, excepting in their religion, they surpass us."

"And though," returned Edric, "every scheme of religion falls infinitely below the divine perfection of Christianity; yet as Christianity was not revealed in the times we are speaking of, it cannot be denied that the Egyptians made some approach to wisdom even in their devotions. They worshipped Nature, though they disguised her under the symbols of her attributes, and gratified the vulgar taste by giving them tangible objects to represent ideas too sublime for their unenlightened comprehension. That they entertained the divine idea of a resurrection, and of rewards and punishment in a future life, is evident, not only from their favourite fable of the Phoenix, and the use they made of the now hackneyed image of the Butterfly; but by the care they bestowed upon the preservation of the body; their mournings for the loss of Osiris, and rejoicings when he was found; and the kind of trial to which they subjected the human corpse after death, when, if serious crimes were alleged and proved against it, it was denied the rites of sepulture,[50] and left to decay unlamented. Then, can any modern institutions excel the wisdom of the laws enacted by the Pharaohs? or can any modem magnificence equal that displayed in the cities of Memphis and Thebes? And since this will hardly be disputed, what country can be more fitting than that once so highly favoured, to be the scene of the most important discovery ever made by Man."

"I perfectly agree with you;" replied Father Morris "and only wonder, with these impressions upon your mind, that you can hesitate an instant about undertaking your voyage to Egypt."

"Alas! I have no longer any occasion to hesitate!"

"What do you mean?"

"My father has just ordered me to quit his house immediately, unless I marry Rosabella; and *that* no tortures shall ever induce me to do;—for I hate her!"

"Then the duke has spoken," said Father Morris, gloomily; "I thought this success of Edmund's would open his lips; but," continued he, addressing Edric, "I think you ought to rejoice at such a circumstance, as your principal objection to visiting the pyramids, was the difficulty of getting your father to consent to such an expedition; that objection, at least, is now removed."

"But how removed, Father Morris? Think you, that I could bear to leave England, perhaps for ever, and upon an expedition so awful in its tendency and consequences, whilst labouring under a father's curse? I cannot do it. I must again see my father, and obtain his forgiveness before I go."

"You are then prepared to comply with his wishes?"

"Never! I have before told you, no force shall compel me to marry Rosabella!"

"And do you imagine Sir Ambrose will relinquish his project so easily? Is it not more probable that your opposition will only increase his determination; and that another interview, if you still refuse to obey his commands, may provoke the curse you now seem to dread?"

"What shall I do then? For in my present state of mind, life is a burthen to me;—my brain feels bewildered."

"Go to Dr. Entwerfen's study, and remain there concealed for the present, till the effervescence of your father's rage shall have evaporated. My duty now calls me to my patron but I shall soon return; I will then see your father, and perhaps a conversation with me may bring him to reason."

"I trust my cause in your hands, father," said Edric "and may your eloquence bring it to a happy issue."

"You may depend upon me," rejoined the reverend father; "I feel deeply interested in the business:" and they parted, Edric proceeding to seek his tutor, and Father Morris returning to the house of the Duke of Cornwall,

When Edric entered the study of Dr. Entwerfen, he found him engaged in what, considering his age and station, seemed a very extraordinary amusement., He was apparently dancing a hornpipe, drawing his heels together, and alternately rising and sinking like a clown in a pantomime, twisting his face, in the mean time, into the most hideous grimaces.

"What is the matter?" cried Edric, gazing at him with surprise.

"I—I—I am galvanized," cried the doctor, in a piteous tone; nodding his head with a sudden jerk; that seemed to threaten every instant to throw it out of its socket; and then, suddenly starting, he kicked out one leg horizontally, and twirled round upon the other with an air of an opera dancer.

"How did it happen?" cried Edric, excessively shocked at the unnatural contrast exhibited between the doctor's serious countenance, and involuntary antics.

"I can't—exactly—tell," replied the doctor, bolting forth his words with difficulty, and still swimming, grinning, and capering, to the inexpressible horror of his companion, till.by degrees his grimaces subsided, and he was enabled at last to stand tolerably steady. He now informed his pupil, that trying some experiments with his galvanic battery, he had unfortunately operated upon himself; and in his turn listened to the account of what had passed between Edric and Sir Ambrose. Instead of expressing sorrow, however, when he found his pupil had quarrelled with his father, the doctor's eyes sparkled with joy— "Then you must inevitably travel," exclaimed he. "We shall visit the pyramids, we shall animate the mummies; and we shall attain immortality."

"No! I cannot leave England without being reconciled to my father: he is old, and I may never see him again; I could not bear to part from him in anger."

"But consider the object you have in view and the countries you will visit: all the English travel. I never knew a young Englishman in my life who was not fond of it. The inhabitants of other countries journey for what they can get, or what they hope to learn; but an Englishman travels because he does not know what to do with himself. He spares neither time, trouble, nor money; he goes every where, sees every thing; after which, he returns-just as wise as when he set out. Not that I blame curiosity—no—I admire it above all things!— it is that which has led to all the great discoveries that have been made since the creation of the world, and it is that which now impels us to explore the pyramids."

Edric looked annoyed at the conclusion of this speech, and, to change the subject; asked the doctor, if he thought his galvanic battery powerful enough for the experiment they meant to try with it.

"Powerful!" exclaimed the doctor; "why I feel it even now tingling to my fingers' ends. I should think, Sir, the effect it has had upon me is a sufficient proof of the force of the machine."

"If we *do* go," said Edric, apparently pursuing the thread of his own reflections, "I should feel inclined to visit other countries besides Egypt."

"And so should I—I should like particularly to see India, for some black-letter pamphlets in my possession, allude to its being once governed by an old woman,[51] and as the regular historians make no mention of the fact, I should like to see what traditions I could gather respecting it on the spot. The religion of the ancient Hindoos, before they were converted to Christianity[52], has been said to have resembled that of the ancient Egyptians; by comparing the monuments of both, one might be made to illustrate the other. I should also like, before we quit Africa, to see the celebrated court of Timbuctoo.[53] I have long been in correspondence with a learned pundit there, who has communicated to me some of the most sublime discoveries.

"The whole of the interior of Africa must be interesting, particularly the rising states on the banks of the Niger.[54] It is generally instructing as well as amusing to watch the birth and struggles of infant republics; and to remark first how fast the people encroach, and then the governors. Whilst the rulers are weak, they are always liberal; but their exalted sentiments in general decrease in exact proportion as they become powerful.

"In short," resumed the doctor, "I would willingly traverse the whole world; I know but one country that I should dislike to visit."

"And which is that?" asked Edric.

"America.[55] I have no wish to have my throat cut, or my breath stopped by a bowstring. I have a perfect horror of despotic governments."

"Then how do you endure the one we live under?"

"The case is quite different. With us, the spur of despotism is scarcely felt; and the people, being permitted occasionally to think and act for themselves, are not debased and brutalized as the slaves of absolute power are in general. Despotism, with us, is like a rod which the schoolmaster keeps hung up in sight of his boys, but which he has very seldom any occasion to make use of. From such despotism as that of the Americans, however, Heaven defend us!

"Amen! For, as we are happy now, we should be idiots to desire a change."

"What an unphilosophical sentiment!" exclaimed the doctor: "I am really quite shocked that you, Edric, should utter such a speech. What an abominable doctrine! Remember, that if you once allow innovation to be dangerous, you instantly put a stop to all improvement—you absolutely shut and bolt your doors against it. Oh! it is horrible, that such a doctrine should be ever broached in a civilized country. You surely could not be aware of what you were saying?"

"Perhaps I was not: for I own candidly I scarcely do know what I am doing!"

"To amuse you then, I will give you a treat. I will show you a curious collection of ballads, all of which are at least three hundred years old, which a friend of mine picked up in London for me the other day, and sent me down this morning by the stage-balloon.[56] They are all of the genuine rag paper, a certain proof of their antiquity; for, you know, the asbestos paper we now use has not been invented more than two hundred years. But you shall see them: follow me."

So saying, the doctor trotted off to his library, that paradise of half-forgotten volumes, most of which had been accidentally saved from their well-merited destination of covering over butter, and wrapping up. cheese, to be drawn from the dust and obscurity of which they had lain for centuries, to ornament the shelves of Doctor. Entwerfen; and whose authors, if they could have taken a peep upon earth, and beheld them, would have been quite astonished to find themselves immortal. Entering this emporium of neglected learning, the doctor hastily advanced to a table, on which lay his newly acquired treasures, and holding them up, exclaimed, "Look, Edric, bow beautifully dirty the paper is; no art could counterfeit this dingy hue. This sooty tinge is the genuine tint of antiquity. You know, Edric, in ancient times, the caloric employed in culinary purposes, and indeed for all the common usages of life, was produced by the combustion of wood, and of a black bituminous substance, or amphilites, drawn from the bowels of the earth, called coal, of which you may yet see specimens in the cabinets of the curious. As these substances decomposed, or rather expanded, by the force of heat, the attraction of cohesion was dissolved, and the component parts flew off in the shape of smoke or soot. This smoke, rising into the air, was dispersed by it, and the minute particles, or atoms, of which it was composed, falling and resting upon every thing that chanced to be in their way, produced that incomparable dusky hue, which the moderns have so often tried, though in vain, to imitate. I beg your pardon, Edric, for using such vulgar language to express what I wished to say, but really, treating upon such a subject, I did not know how to explain myself elegantly."

"Oh! I understood you very well, Sir. After all, the only true use of language is to convey the ideas of one person to the understanding of another; and, provided that end be attained, I really do not see that it is of any consequence what words we make use of."

"True, Edric dear! you make very just observations sometimes. Well, but the ballads; I was going to show you my treasures, —my jewels! as the Roman lady said of her children. Look what beautiful specimens these are! A little torn here and there, and with a few of the lines illegible-but genuine antiques. I'll warrant every one of them above three hundred years old.[57] Look, it is real linen paper; you may tell it by the texture; and then the spelling, see what a number of letters they put into their words that were or no use. Look at the titles of them. Here is the 'Tragical end of poor Miss Bailey'[58]—and here 'Cherry Ripe'[59]—and 'I've been roaming[60].' Here is 'The loves of Captain Wattle and Miss Roe'[61]—and here are 'Jessy the flower of Dumblane,'[62] and 'Dunois the brave.'[63] But this is my Phoenix—here is what will be the envy of collectors! here is my invaluable treasure. This, I believe, is absolutely unique, and that I am so blest as to possess the only copy extant. The date is wanting, but the manners it describes are so unpolished, that I should almost think it might be traced back to the times of the aboriginal Britons.—Thus it begins:—

> 'At Wednesbury there was a cocking,[64]
>   A match between Newton and Scroggins;
> The nailors and colliers left work,
>   And to Spittle's they all went jogging.
>   Tol de rol lol.'

I used to be very much puzzled at this burthen, which is one of frequent recurrence in ancient songs. At first, I thought it a relic of some language now irrevocably lost. Then it struck me, it might be an invocation to the deities of the aborigines. In short, I was quite perplexed, and knew not what to think, when a learned friend of mine hit upon an idea the other day, which seems completely to solve the difficulty. He suggests that it was an ancient manner of running up and down the scale; and that 'Tol de rol lol' had the same signification as 'Do re mi fa;'—which solution is at once so simple and ingenious, that I am sure you, as well as myself, must be struck by it. I here omit a few stanzas, in which the author enumerates his heroes exactly in the Homeric manner. The names are so barbarous, that I am afraid of loosening my teeth in pronouncing them:—

> 'There was plenty of beef at the dinner,
>   Of a bull that was baited to death;
> Bunny Hyde got a lump in his throat,
>   Which had like to have stopt[65] his breath.'

What a beautiful simplicity there is in that last line,

> 'Which had like to have stopt his breath.'

Oh, we moderns have nothing equal to it!—

> 'The company fell in confusion,
>   To see this poor Bunny Hyde choke,
> So they hurried him down to the kitchen,
>   And held his head over the smoke.'

This developes[66] a curious practice of antiquity. You know, Edric, I explained to you just now the manner in which combustion was formerly effected, and the causes of the production of what was called smoke. I own, however, it seems a strange way of reviving a half-suffocated man, to hold his head over smoke, which, being loaded, as I said before, with innumerable atoms of all sorts and sizes, would, one might think, be more likely to impede respiration than restore it. The fact, however, is undoubted; and it not only affords a curious illustration of the manner of the ancients, but is of itself a strong proof of the authenticity of the ballad; for such an idea never could have entered the head of a modern. To return to poor Hyde—

> 'One gave him a kick o' th' stomach,
>   And another a thump o' th' brow,
> His wife cried throw him i' th' stable,
>   And he will be better just now.'

This unfeeling conduct of his wife does not say much in commendation of the ladies of those times. Here follows an hiatus of several stanzas: I find, however, by a word or two here and there, that they celebrated the exploits of two gallic heroes:—

> 'The best i' th' country bred;
> The one was a brassy-wing black,
>   And the other a dusky-wing'd red.'

These unfortunate victims of the cruelty of man seem both to have perished. There is a stanza, however, before this catastrophe, which seems to relate to the combat.

> 'The conflict was hard upon each,
>   Till glossy-wing'd blacky was choked,
> The colliers were nationally vex'd,
>   And the nailers were all provoked.'

This passage seems very obscure: 'Nationally' is evidently a sign of comparison, but I cannot say I ever saw it employed before. It is, however, another proof of the amazing antiquity of the ballad. After this, it appears that the people broke in upon the ring, and both cocks were crushed to atoms. I don't know whether you are acquainted with the manner in which these gallic combats were conducted, Edric. A kind of Amphitheatre was formed, upon which the birds were pitted one against the other, whence the name cock-pit. The combatants were armed with large iron spurs, and the victor generally left his rival dead upon the field. The ballad proceeds:—

> 'The cock-pit was near to the church,
>   As an ornament to the town;
> One side was an old coal-pit,
>   And the other was well gorsed round.'

Gorse was a kind of heath or furze.

> 'Peter Hadley peep'd through the gorse,
>   In order to see the cocks fight;
> Spittle jobb'd his eye out with a fork,
>   And said, "Blast you, it sarves you right!"'

This is very spirited and expressive, though the false quantities render it difficult to read.

'Some folks may think this is strange,
   Who Wednesbury never knew,
But those who have ever been there,
   Won't have the least doubt but it's true.

For they are all savage by nature,
   And guilty of deeds that are shocking,
Jack Baker he whack'd his own feyther,
   And so ended the Wednesbury cocking.'"

"It is very fine certainly," said Edric, who was half asleep.

"Upon my word," returned the doctor, "I don't think you have heard a single word I have been saying."

"Oh! yes, I have," replied Edric, "every syllable. It was about a man killing his own father, and putting his eyes out with a fork."

"Eh!" cried the doctor, somewhat annoyed at this unequivocal proof that though his words might have struck upon the auricular organs of his pupil, they had not reached his brains. The exclamation of the doctor restored Edric to his senses, and he began to apologize.

"I am really very sorry," said he, "but you must excuse my inattention. Sometimes, you know, the mind is not in tune for literary discussions, even when proceeding from the most eloquent lips. This is my case at the present moment. My mind is so occupied by the important change that has just taken place in my affairs, that, I own, even your learning and eloquence were thrown away upon me."

"If that be the state of your mind," replied the doctor, with chagrin, "'it is of no use to show you any more of my literary treasures; else I have some of matchless excellence. Here is a letter addressed to Sheridan,[67] a witty writer of comedies, in the eighteenth century, which has never been opened,—and here is a tailor's bill of the immortal Byron,[68] which may possibly never have been looked at. But here is the most inestimable of my relics. Look, at least, at this. This piece of paper, covered carelessly with irregular strokes and lines, was once in the possession of that enchanting, that inimitable novelist of the nineteenth century, generally distinguished in the works of contemporary writers by the mysterious title of "The Great Unknown!"[69] See, here is half the word 'Waverley,' written upon it, and doubtless all these other irregular marks and scratches proceeded directly from his pen. I confess, Edric, I never contemplate this relic of genius without a feeling of reverence, and almost of awe. 'Perhaps,' say I to myself, when I look at it, 'when these letters were formed, the first idea had but just arisen in the mind of the author of those immortal works, which were afterwards destined to improve and delight mankind. Perhaps, at that very moment gigantic thoughts were rushing through his brain, and a variety of new ideas opening their treasures to his imagination.' Oh, there is something in the mere random stroke of the pen of a celebrated character, inexpressibly affecting to the mind;—it carries one back to the very time when he lived —it seems to make one acquainted with him, and to let us into the secrets of his inmost thoughts. But I see you are not attending to me, Edric!"

"I am very sorry—another time I should be happy—but now—I cannot. However, when we return, perhaps—"

"It may be then too late," said the doctor, with solemnity; and locking up his cabinet, he led the way back to his common sitting-room, in high dudgeon.

Volume 1: Chapter 7

When Father Morris had left Edric, he proceeded to the house of the Duke of Cornwall, intending to return to that of Sir Ambrose almost immediately; but the scene which took place between the duke and his niece, altered his determination. It is not in the power of language to describe the agony of Father Morris at the appeal of Rosabella. She had accidentally touched upon a chord that thrilled through every nerve, and almost drove him to madness. The duke, after attempting in vain to console him, retired, leaving him a prey to the bitterest torments; for, like the votaries of Eblis, he felt unquenchable fire burning in his bosom, and like them, he sought in vain to escape. He was roused from this state of unutterable anguish, by a summons from Sir Ambrose to attend him instantly, and with a heavy heart he obeyed.

Repenting the sins he had committed, yet meditating more, Father Morris endeavoured, as he slowly retraced his steps to Sir Ambrose's mansion, to soothe his feelings, by dwelling upon the good he meant to do when he should attain power, rather than on the means by which that power was to be obtained: for it is a remarkable fact, that no man likes to appear a villain to himself; and even when his crimes escape the eyes of the world, be is not satisfied, unless he can frame plausible excuses for them in his own mind: though it is true that these excuses would not bear strict examination; as self-love is an able sophist, and slight reasons look brilliant when set off by such colouring.

Nearly reconciled to himself by arguments, the fallacy of which he would have been the first to detect, if they had been offered by another, Father Morris entered the house of Sir Ambrose with his usual calm smile; but his equanimity was almost again upset, when he found Dr. Coleman, a highly respectable physician in the neighbourhood, already closeted with the worthy baronet. Father Morris hated Dr. Coleman, it would perhaps be difficult to say why; unless it was that the priest, feeling conscious his designs would not bear exposure, shrank from the penetrating eye of the physician, whose natural shrewdness was considerably heightened by his professional acumen. There are, indeed, no classes of society better acquainted with the vices of mankind, than the professors of law and physic: a great writer has called law the chimney through which the fiery passions of the world expend themselves in smoke[70]—and the experience of the medical man. sometimes even surpasses that of his legal brethren. Admitted into the very bosom of families—often the unavoidable confidant of the most delicate secrets—an experienced physician becomes naturally cautious, penetrating, and suspicious.

This was the case with Dr. Coleman; and Father Morris now felt particularly annoyed by his presence: as, however, there was no remedy, the father was too good a politician to suffer his annoyance to be seen, and smoothing his brow, he expressed in his usual soft, low voice, the pleasure he said he felt at meeting so unexpectedly with his old friend.

"I am glad to hear that you are pleased to see me," said Dr. Coleman, with marked emphasis.

"How can it be otherwise? It is so kind of you, who have so many professional engagements to occupy your time, to bestow any of it upon your friends."

Dr. Coleman did not speak, but he. fixed his eyes upon Father Morris, with an expression which the latter could not bear. Hastily drawing the cowl, in which his features were generally shrouded, still closer over his face, he turned to Sir Ambrose, and asked what had occasioned the hasty summons he had received.

"The conduct of Edric," replied the baronet abruptly; "he refuses to see me, and as I understand he had a long conference with you this morning, I have sent for you to know what he means."

"That, my dear Sir," returned Father Morris, with gentle smile, and half-closed eyes, "you must allow, it would be impossible for me even to guess. The minds of young men are wayward and capricious; they scarcely know their own wishes; how then can one so ignorant of the world as I, be expected to divine them? Our good friend Dr. Coleman is much more competent to advise you upon the subject than I am."

"Oh, you are too humble, father!" said Dr. Coleman ironically; "pray have a juster sense of your own merit.

"All this has nothing to do with the business," exclaimed Sir Ambrose, getting into a passion. "I want to know what you said to Edric this morning, and what he said to you."

"He told me that he would sooner die than marry Rosabella."

"The young villain! then let him die, if he likes it. But it's all nonsense—a mere figure of speech. It is very easy to talk about dying; but few people like it when they are put to the test. Not that he's the least intention of any thing of the kind. He thinks I'm an old fool, and only says it to frighten me: but I see through his schemes! I'm not to be duped, and I won't give up the point. I shall be deaf to all his prayers and supplications."

"I do not think that he intends to offer any."

"Not offer any! What do you mean?"

"That I think he has a project in his head, which makes him rather glad of the quarrel that has taken place, than otherwise."

"Impossible! this must be false," cried Dr. Coleman, starting from his seat.

"See him, and judge for yourself," returned Father Morris, scowling at his opponent.

"And what is this project?" asked Sir Ambrose, as soon as he had recovered a little from his astonishment.

"He intends to go to Egypt, and visiting the Pyramids, to try to resuscitate a mummy!"

Dr. Coleman groaned in the spirit: Sir Ambrose shook his head.

"I fear it is but too true," said he, "it is just like one of his plans. The boy is mad; evidently distracted: that silly tutor of his has quite turned his brain.

"I really am afraid he is deranged," sighed Dr. Coleman "If he seriously entertains so mad a scheme: but you will excuse me, Father Morris, if I still entertain some doubts upon the subject. He may only have mentioned such a thing in joke."

"Talk to him yourself; he is in the chamber of Dr. Entwerfen: I do not wish you to confide in my representations. It is always painful to me to interfere in family disputes. Indeed, when Edric this morning wished me to explain his intentions to his father, I declined doing so; and you were witness, that it was only in compliance with the earnest entreaty of my worthy friend, that I spoke at all on the subject."

"Notwithstanding," said Dr. Coleman, after musing a short time, "I shall be better satisfied when I have seen Edric myself."

"I beg you will do no such thing," interrupted Sir Ambrose, "he will fancy you an ambassador from me, and I could not bear that. It is his place to submit, not mine. He shall not triumph over me in that manner."

"I am sure he would feel no triumph."

"But I tell you he would, Sir! He would rejoice, exult, and glory in such a thing. I will be master in my own house, and over my own sons: you shall not see him, nobody shall see him; and he shall remain shut up in the asylum he' has chosen, till he comes to his senses."

"It is useless to enrage Sir Ambrose by farther opposition now," whispered Father Morris to Dr. Coleman; "Edric cannot go to Egypt without money, and you know he never has any in hand. It can do no harm to adjourn the subject till to-morrow: they will both then be calmer, and more likely to listen to reason."

Dr. Coleman could not deny the policy of this advice, though he felt reluctant to follow it, as it was suggested by Father Morris: discarding the presentiment of evil, however, as a prejudice which it was his duty to overcome, aa it was contrary to his reason, the worthy physician took his leave, fully determining to reconcile the father and son on the morrow.

But the morrow—(alas! who shall dare speculate upon the morrow!) was destined to see Edric and his tutor on their way to Egypt. When Father Morris returned to the adytum[71] of Dr. Entwerfen, he informed Edric, that his father, so far from expressing anger at his intended expedition to Egypt, seemed glad of the opportunity to get rid of him, as he said his presence would only spoil Edmund's triumph. "He says you always look so gloomily," continued the wily priest, "that even when he is disposed to enjoy himself, you throw a damp upon his spirits the instant you appear. He, therefore, gave his free consent to your journey, and commissioned me to supply you with the funds necessary for the expedition."

It had ever been the prevailing weakness of Edric to believe his brother more beloved by Sir Ambrose than himself; and Father Morris knowing this, had framed his tale accordingly. We easily believe what we fear; and Edric, though not generally credulous, placed implicit faith in the father's story, though it gave him acute anguish.

"I knew he did not love me," said he, "but to bid me go thus, on so perilous an enterprise, without seeing me, I did not expect," and involuntary tears rolled down his cheeks as he spoke, whilst the good-natured Dr. Entwerfen sobbed for sympathy.

"Never mind it, Edric dear!" said he, throwing his arms round his pupil's neck; "you have one friend, at any rate, who loves you dearly, and will never desert you."

"I know it," exclaimed Edric, warmly returning his tutor's embrace; "Yes, doctor, you are my friend, of that I am fully satisfied; and we will succeed, or perish together."

"You will want many things to enable you to proceed in your enterprise," said Father Morris, "with which you must furnish yourselves in London. Besides, as Edric has never been ten miles from home in his life, he should stay a short time to see the wonders of that vast metropolis, before he leaves his native country. Foreseeing this, and thinking, as strangers in London, you would feel awkward in having no place to go to on your arrival, I have dispatched a carrier pigeon to a friend of mine in town, Lord Gustavus de Montfort, who will, am sure, give you a hearty welcome, and will afford you both the shelter of his house, and the aid of his advice."

"I know not how to express my gratitude," returned Edric.

"Then say nothing about it—if you really feel obliged, profit by my directions. A stage balloon will pass through the village in an hour, shall you. be ready to avail yourselves of the opportunity?"

"I would go this instant," exclaimed Edric.

The doctor, with some difficulty, consented to this arrangement, and, at the appointed moment; Edric and his tutor were on their way to London: though the doctor could scarcely be persuaded to set off; for, again and again, he would return to survey the treasures he was leaving behind, and the moment Edric thought he had him safe, he would recollect some indispensable requisite for their journey, and hurry back again to find it. At last they were fairly started, and a favourable wind blew them rapidly towards London. Edric had never seen this vast metropolis, and his astonishment and delight, when its magnificent palaces, its superb streets, its public buildings, its theatres, and its churches, broke upon him, was quite beyond description. His transports and exclamations, indeed, at length became so violent, as quite to annoy the learned doctor.

"If you feel such rapture at the sight of London," said he, peevishly, "I suppose you will be reluctant to quit it; and I dare say you already repent having proposed to travel."

"Oh! what is that?" cried Edric, without attending to him, as, lost in amazement, he saw a house in the suburbs gently slide out of its place,[72] and glide majestically along the road, a lady at one of the windows kissing her hand to tome one in another house as she passed. "Do my eyes deceive me, or does that house move?"

"Certainly it does," replied the doctor. "Did you never see a moving house before? You must have heard of them at any rate, for nothing can be more common. It certainly is convenient, when one wants to go into the country for a few weeks, to be able to take one's house with one: it saves a great deal of trouble in packing, and permits one to have all one's little conveniences about one. You see there are grooves in the bottom of the houses that just fit on the iron railways: and as they are propelled by steam, they slide on without much trouble. It does not answer, however, with any but small houses, for large ones can't well be made compact enough. However, you must postpone your admiration of that, as well as of the other wonders of London, for here we are at Lord Gustavus's door. What a noble mansion! is it not? This street, Edric, is called the Strand, and is the most fashionable in London; because it adjoins the Queen's favourite palace at Somerset House."[73]

"Is that the palace?" said Edric. "It seems a noble pile of building."

"The gardens are fine," replied the doctor; "but as they are thrown open to the public, and nothing is paid for admission, it is reckoned vulgar to walk in them. You English do not like any thing you do not pay for; but more of this hereafter. We must now prepare to pay our respects to our noble host."

Lord Gustavus de Montfort received them very kindly, but Edric found something in his voice and manners excessively forbidding. He had a pompous disagreeable manner of speaking, with a nasal accent so strong, that it was absolutely torture to Edric, whose sense of hearing was uncommonly fine, to listen to him; he had also a conceited dictatorial way of delivering his opinion, which Edric thought extremely unpleasant. He generally commenced his speeches with "Thinking as I think, and as I am positive every one who hears me must think, or at least ought to think;" and this exordium[74] formed an epitome of his character; as he was firmly persuaded that every one who differed in the slightest degree from his opinion, was decidedly wrong, whilst the possibility of his ever being mistaken himself never entered his imagination. His father had been one of the counsellors of the late Queen, and his eldest brother having declined to take the father's place upon his death, Lord Gustavus had been appointed to it. Thus he was really a person of some consequence in the state; and though his being so was quite a matter of chance, arising from the circumstances above-mentioned and the indolence of the Queen, he affected to regard it as a matter of personal favour to himself, and endeavored to persuade his hearers that the affairs of government could not possibly go on without him. Knowing his foible of wishing to be thought of importance in the realm, and feeling the want of a leader of rank, some of the discontented spirits of the kingdom had endeavoured to gain him over to their party; and though Lord Gustavus was strictly loyal, and even particularly fond of talking of her gracious Majesty the Queen, and boasting of the confidence she placed in him, yet his vanity could not altogether resist the able attacks made upon it by the rebels. He wavered, he began to talk of reform, and to mingle boasts of his popularity amongst the people, with those he had before indulged in, of enjoying the favour of his sovereign. Thus he hung upon the balance, ready to incline to either side, according to the circumstances that time or chance might produce.

"I am extremely happy," said he, as he advanced to meet his guests, "that my worthy and respected friend Father Morris, has procured me the honour of such illustrious visitors. The holy father has informed me of the sublime purpose that animates your bosoms, and leads you to traverse realms of air, to explore the hitherto undiscovered secrets of the grave. His partiality for me has also led him to imagine that my humble means may perchance prove conducive to so great an. end, and he has requested me to give you all the assistance in my power to promote the gigantic objects you have in view. Thus, you may rest assured, no efforts shall be wanting on my part to fulfil his wishes, and as, though insignificant in myself, I am so happy as to be honoured by the protection and favour of her Majesty the Queen, my most gracious sovereign; and also as my feeble attempts to promote the public good have been rewarded by the gratitude of the people; it may perchance be in my power to serve you; and in the meantime I hope you will do me the honour to partake of such hospitality as my humble mansion can afford."

So saying, Lord Gustavus led the way through a sumptuous suite of rooms, to one where an elegant cold collation was laid out, of which he invited his guests to partake. Nothing could be more splendid than the furniture and embellishments of this apartment. The rooms were hung with crimson silk, trimmed with gold; valuable paintings decorated the walls; statues of inestimable price filled each corner, and magnificent mirrors increased tenfold the magic of the scene. Lord Gustavus secretly enjoyed the astonishment and admiration painted upon the countenances of his guests; and whilst he openly affected to talk of his "poor house," and his "humble attempts to entertain them," &c. his heart covertly exalted in the grandeur around him, and his eyes sparkled with pleasure at the effect he saw it produced upon the strangers. Nothing makes one so much disposed to be in a good humour with the world, as being in a good humour with oneself and nothing is so certain to produce that delightful sensation, as to see what we possess excite the admiration of others. Thus, as the flattery conveyed by looks far outweighs that expressed by words, and as the looks of Edric and the doctor unequivocally declared their sentiments, Lord Gustavus was quite enchanted with his visitors, and spared no pains to render them equally happy as himself. He ordered a large apartment to be prepared for the doctor, that he might make his arrangements for the intended Egyptian expedition quite at his ease; he commanded his servants to obey his directions implicitly, and he directed tradesmen to supply every thing that might be wanted at his own expense.

Having thus given the doctor *carte blanche*,[75] he next turned his attention to Edric, and, finding it was his first visit to London, volunteered to show him all the wonders of that immense metropolis, which then, spreading enormously in every direction, seemed like the fabled monster of the Indians, to stretch its enormous arms on every side and swallow up all the hapless villages which were so unfortunate as to fall within its reach.

Sir Ambrose being too proud to make any enquiries respecting his rebellious son, Edric's departure was not suspected by his father. till the arrival of Dr. Coleman on the following day. As Father Morris had predicted, the worthy baronet was become much more cool, and by the persuasions of Dr. Coleman, at length consented to see his son, and not to insist upon his marrying Rosabella, until he had given the subject more mature consideration. After this concession, his astonishment and indignation, when he learnt the truth, may he easier conceived than described. Nothing is so mortifying to a passionate man, as to find his intended kindness of no avail; and Sir Ambrose, in the transport of his rage, vowed never to see his offending son again.

"Let me implore you to consider what you are doing!" said Dr. Coleman, when he heard this oath.

"Oh, my dear uncle!" cried Clara, clinging to his knees, "don't say that you will never forgive him."

"I never will!" exclaimed the. enraged baronet, "I swear by all my hopes of happiness, here and hereafter, that I never will see his face again."

"You will repent this rashness," said Dr. Coleman, "when it is too late. I feel confident there must be some deception in the business."

"Deception!" cried Sir Ambrose, eagerly, "by whom can it have been practised, and for what purpose? Pray explain yourself,"

"You will perhaps feel offended at what I am about to say, and probably will not believe me—but in my opinion—

Here the worthy doctor was interrupted by the appearance of a round, fat, rosy-looking face, which just popt[76] in for a moment at the door of the apartment, and was then instantly withdrawn.

"Good Heavens! I should surely know those features," exclaimed Dr. Coleman, "and yet I hope—I trust—it cannot be."

"Who is there?" cried Sir Ambrose, pettishly, "what do you want? and why are you ashamed of showing your face?"

That jolly face again made its appearance, but it was now accompanied by a portly body, which certainly did it no discredit, though it was clad in the garments of a priest.

"Sure and it is not my face that I'd be ashamed of showing, any how," said the apparition, with a strong south country brogue;[77] "but it was that myself[78] didn't like to inthrude, and I was just looking for the docthor there."

"And what is your will with me, Father Murphy?" asked Dr. Coleman, with an air of melancholy.

"Sure and I'd be afther telling ye directly barring that I've a bit o' a note here, that'll spak' fasther than I can."

So saying he presented a letter to Dr. Coleman, who opened and read it with considerable agitation.

"You'll excuse me, Sir Ambrose, this is a matter of the greatest importance. So my young friend is waiting without? I must see him instantly. I must bid you adieu for the present, Sir Ambrose, but you shall see me again in a day or two. have a friend, the son of an old friend, Mr. Henry Seymour[79], come to spend some time with me. I hope you will permit me to have the honour of introducing him to you; I am sure you will like him. He is a young Irishman; a very nice young man."

After running through this speech with astonishing volubility, he hurried away, leaving Sir Ambrose excessively annoyed at his departure; and totally at a loss how to account for it, or how to class his strange visitor, till he recollected that Dr. Coleman had passed many years in Ireland; and that it was the illiberal policy of the king of that country to have his priests lowly descended and ill-educated men, lest they should acquire too much influence over his subjects, and become dangerous to his government. The Irish priests, thus divested of all the dignity of the sacerdotal character, gradually degenerated into a kind of privileged jesters, tolerated in every great house for the amusement they afforded, and obliged if they had any wit, to conceal under the appearance of folly. Father Murphy was evidently one of this humiliated class, and his connexion with Dr. Coleman was easily accounted for, by supposing him to belong to some family Dr. Coleman had formed an acquaintance with, when in Ireland; but the mysterious allusion which the Doctor had made respecting Edric, was not so comprehensible, and Sir Ambrose waited eagerly for several days, in the hope that he would call to explain what he had meant. No doctor, however, arrived, and as the Duke's mind was completely occupied by another subject, Sir Ambrose was left entirely to his own reflections, without having a single creature to whom he could impart them, or from whom he could hope for sympathy. The Duke, in fact, was a specimen of a class common enough in the world, of men whose minds will not hold more than one idea at a time, and his head was now so full of the splendid images connected with Edmund, that Edric's rejection of Rosabella and subsequent departure were almost forgotten.

It was far otherwise with Sir Ambrose, who now began to repent, though secretly, of the unwarrantable severity with which he had treated his son. It is a trite though undeniable observation, that we never know the real value of any possession till we have lost it; and thus Sir Ambrose, though he had thought nothing of the respectful and dutiful attentions of his son, whilst he was in the habit of constantly receiving them, now felt their want, and regretted bitterly the ill-timed harshness that had deprived him of them for ever. Still, however, he was too obstinate to own he had been wrong; and though he knew that by recalling his son he should restore his lost happiness, he, like many other persons in. similar situations, most magnanimously determined to persist in being miserable.

Four days had elapsed since that on which Dr. Coleman had so abruptly left Sir Ambrose, ere he called again, and when he made his reappearance, he was accompanied by a tall, handsome young man, whom he introduced as Henry Seymour, and the good-humoured, though eccentric Father Murphy. Sir Ambrose received his guests very coldly for he felt hurt by the doctor's neglect; but the Duke, who, attended by Father Morris, happened to be with Sir Ambrose when they arrived, was quite enchanted with them, and when they rose to depart, gave them a general invitation to his castle. This courtesy, which seemed to displease alike Father Morris and Dr. Coleman, was accepted with transports by the strangers, especially by the younger, whose enthusiastic expressions of gratitude quite delighted the old duke.

From this moment the fancy the duke had suddenly conceived for the strangers, rapidly became intimacy, and they were soon quite domesticated at the castle. Henry Seymour listened to the duke's stories-laughed at his jokes-admired his dogs and horses, and above all, approved of his improvements; whilst he talked and walked with Elvira, or read to her as she worked, or accompanied her when she sang or played, with his voice or flute. In short, he became quite *l'ami de la maison*,[80] and was beloved by every one in it, excepting Father Morris, Marianne, and Rosabella. Marianne he seemed to consider as quite beneath his notice, and Rosabella he was uniformly polite to; but Father Morris he evidently hated, and took very little pains to conceal his feelings. When these broke forth a little too strongly, Doctor Coleman would often look grave and shake his head, but in vain; prudence was not Henry Seymour's forte: wit and good-humour danced gaily in his bright blue eyes; but the expression of violent passions often flitted in quick transition over his animated features, and he frequently appeared to have the greatest difficulty in restraining himself within due bounds.

His manners, too, were much too familiar for his station, and when disappointed in trifles, he often treated the duke and princesses with unwarrantable haughtiness. Like a petted child, he was always either offending, or suing to be forgiven, and though on these occasions Doctor Coleman always whispered "Beware!" the admonition was generally forgotten at the very moment when it might have been of service. Notwithstanding this perverseness, it was impossible to know Henry Seymour without loving him, and his own affections seemed as warm as those he inspired. He loved the duke and Elvira, respected Doctor Coleman, and was evidently tenderly attached to Father Murphy, though no two beings could be imagined more different than he and that reverend personage. Father Murphy, indeed, was a general favourite, and the whole household of the duke concurred in thinking him quite a nonpareil of a priest; for, as he was not very fond of doing penance himself, so he was not very rigid in imposing it upon others, and consequently he and his penitents were always upon the best terms imaginable. In short, he seemed especially designed by Nature to be good friends with all the world; and on his side he certainly did the utmost not to thwart the beneficent old lady's kind intentions.

The time now rapidly approached for Edmund's return; letters had been received from him, announcing that he should be in England in a couple of days and the duke having made all the preparations possible, and twice as many as were necessary, for removing his whole household to town, became- in an agony of impatience to set off. He had not permitted either Sir Ambrose or Elvira to inform Edmund of his approbation of his attachment; and he anticipated, with almost childish delight, the effect that would be produced on Edmund's mind by the joyful intelligence. Elvira, however, did not appear to participate in her father's pleasure, and as the hour approached for their departure for town, her spirits became evidently more and more depressed; whilst Henry Seymour's gaiety seemed also to have quite deserted him, till the good-natured duke compassionating his dejection, and really feeling sorry to part with so agreeable a companion, invited him to accompany them to London. Henry Seymour's bright eyes sparkled with joy at this proposition, and seizing the duke's hand, he exclaimed,—

"I'll go with all my heart—and you are a dear good creature for thinking of asking me!"

"There's nobody shall be more welcome," returned the duke, not at all offended with the familiarity of his young friend's address, though it was quite out of all rule according to the *bienseances*[81] of the age; "for I don't know any body I love better, excepting my old friend here, Sir Ambrose, and Edmund."

"And Elvira and Rosabella, and me?" said Clara Montagu coaxingly.

"What should I love such a little hussey[82] as you for, I wonder?"

"Oh, that I don't know; but I'm sure you do love me, let you say what you will!" returned Clara, whom delight at the idea of her expected journey had made half wild.

"Good Heaven! Henry Seymour!" said Doctor Coleman, in an impressive tone; "you cannot surely be so mad as to intend going to London?"

"Why not? There is no danger, and if there were, would it not be worth braving in such a cause? By Heaven! I would leap over the crater of Mount Etna with such an object in view."

"Well, you must do as you like. I know it is in vain to attempt to reason with you when you have made up your mind."

"Quite, my dear doctor, so don't waste your eloquence."

"We shall set off to-morrow," said the duke: "I wish we were there."

"What a pity," remarked Henry, "that nature did not mingle a little patience with your Grace's other good qualities."

"It is, indeed;—'for patience,' as Father Murphy says, 'robs care of its bitterest sting.'"

"Och! and is it me ye're quoting from, yere Grace? And where's the use of that, pray? when ye know I'm just here and ready to quote for myself."

"If all your observations are as good as that the duke has just repeated said Sir Ambrose, "I don't know any body that might be quoted from with more advantage."

"Sure! and is it of myself ye're saying that?" asked Father Murphy, "for if ye are, ye never made a betther spach in all your life; only there's a little misthake if ye think the observation ye're talking of came out of my own head, for it didn't do any such thing."

"Do not be alarmed," said Father Morris, who now approached, and who spoke with his usual satirical sneer: "No one who knows you will ever suspect you of any thing so atrocious."

"Good-nature and integrity are sometimes more than equivalent to brilliant talents," said Sir Ambrose bitterly.

"True," rejoined Father Morris, in one of his softest, most insinuating tones; "but they become inestimable when united, as in the example before us:" bowing to Father Murphy as he spoke. Sir Ambrose turned, and looked earnestly at the tall thin figure of the monk as he stood before him, his arms crossed upon his breast, and his head, as usual, bent towards the ground, but he did not speak.

"By the way," said the duke, "is it not strange that we have never heard any thing of Edric since he left? I begin to think that it was all a planned thing, and they would have gone just the same if nothing had been said of Rosabella."

"Impossible!" exclaimed Sir Ambrose.

"I see no impossibility in the business," resumed the duke. "I think the case is clear. They did not know how to get off decently; and so Edric pretended to quarrel with you and me, to give the thing a face."

"I cannot fancy Edric guilty of such meanness," cried Sir Ambrose passionately.

"I don't think the matter admits of a single doubt: I only wish I had not offered him my niece. What is your opinion of the subject, Father Morris?"

"Men devoted to austere professions like myself," replied the priest, without raising his eyes from the ground, "know but little of what is passing in the world. Thus, though my body be no longer shrouded in the gloom of a cloister, my mind still remains too much abstracted from the busy scenes around me, for me to be a competent judge of the effect of human passions."

"Och! then, ye are very right to say nothin' about them," cried Father Murphy; "for though I'm in a passion every day of my life, I nevher know what to say when I begin to talk of it. And so I jist think it's the wisest way to holdth my tongue."

Neither Sir Ambrose nor the duke made any reply; and after settling that they should commence their journey on the following morning, they separated.

Volume 1: Chapter 8

The journey of the duke and his party to London had nothing in it to distinguish it from hundreds of other journeys, they did not meet with a single adventure worthy of being recorded; and they arrived in perfect safety at the palace of the duke, which was situated in the Strand, (that being, as we have before stated, in those days the most fashionable part of London,) and had beautiful gardens shelving down to the Thames.

The duke had brought all his establishment to town; and it would be difficult to conceive any one in a greater bustle than the worthy Mrs. Russel for several days after their arrival. The tender Abelard could. not find her at liberty for a single moment, to listen to his poetical effusions. One day, however, having been, as he conceived, particularly happy, be determined to make himself heard. He accordingly waited upon the fair Eloisa, whom he found busily employed in giving directions to the servants.

"Mrs. Russel!" sighed he, in love's softest cadence; but Mrs. Russel heard him not; she was talking to the cook. "You must quite alter your style, Angelina," said she, "remember, nothing can be too plain for great people.[83] Fricasees and ragouts are only devoured by the *canaille*.[84]

"I am instructed of that, Ma'am," replied Angelina, a great, fat, bonny-looking cook,—"but I flatter myself I know how to concoct dishes—"

"That is the very thing you must avoid," interrupted Mrs. Russel, "any thing did for the country, but here the case is different: the duke's rank requires a certain degree of style, and it is the fashion now for great people to have only one dish, and that as plainly cooked as possible. I have been told by a friend of mine, who got a peep at the great dinner the Queen gave the other day to the foreign ambassadors, that there was nothing in the world upon the table, but a huge round of boiled beef, and a great dish of smoking potatoes, with their jackets on."

"Well, Ma'am," returned Angelina, "I will rally both my physical and mental energies to afford you all the satisfaction in my power; notwithstanding which, I am free to confess, that, in my opinion, the gastronomic science is now cruelly neglected, and that I do not think the digestive powers of the stomach can be properly excited from their dormant state by such unstimulating food as that you mention. Besides, the muscular force of the stomach must be strained to decompose such solid viands, and I should think the diaphragm seriously injured—"

"You, Alphonso," continued Mrs. Russel, addressing the footman, and cruelly interrupting the learned harangue of the cook, "must take more care in cleaning the pictures. There is a fine large painting of one of the old English artists, over the door, in the best drawing room, the colours of which are quite faded; I am afraid you have used something improper to clean it."

"Indeed, Madam," returned Alphonso, "I think the fault is in the picture itself. It did not dry well originally; I don't think the oil that was used in its composition had the carbon and hydrogen mingled in proper proportions. You know, Madam, that oil in general has an amazing affinity for oxygen,[85] and absorbs it rapidly; now, though the oil of this picture has been exposed for years to the action of the common atmospheric air, yet it has never thickened properly into a concrete state."

"Mrs. Russel!" cried Abelard, venturing to sigh a little louder.

"Oh, Mr. Abelard!" exclaimed the fair Eloisa,[86] with a pretty affectation of confusion, "how you startled me! I declare you made me raise the adnatae of my visual organs,[87] like one of the anas genus[88] when the clouds are charged with electric fluid, whilst my heart leaped from its transverse position on my diaphragm, and seemed to stick like a great bone right across my œsophagus."

"How wretched I am to have occasioned fears in that lovely bosom. Hem, hem! might I hope to be indulged with a short interview."

"In a moment, dear Mr. Abelard! I will attend to you; I will but just finish my directions. The duke, you know, gives a grand dinner to-day, and my heart palpitates in my bosom with fear lest I should commit some error. These town-bred people are so particular."

"*You* need not fear any scrutiny."

"La, Mr. Abelard! Eustace!" addressing the butler, "mind you must take care not to bring any variety of wines to the table: nothing is drunk now but port and sherry, and even they are going out of fashion. Have plenty of strong ale, however, and porter, for they are now reckoned the most elegant liquors for the ladies."

"I shall do my utmost endeavour to obey your injunctions, Madam." said Eustace, bowing respectfully, "but I cannot imagine that any species of corn, even if it have undergone the vinous fermentation, can produce a liquid so agreeable to the palate, as well as conducive to the sanity of the body, as the juice of the grape."

"Cannot you spare a single moment to listen to me?" sighed Abelard.

"I have nearly done: I have only to beg that you, Evelina and Cecilia," addressing the housemaids, "will carefully superintend the arrangement of the dormitories: let the air out of the beds[89] and re-inflate them—examine the elastic spring mattresses—mend the gossammer curtains—sweep the velvet carpets, and take care the tubes for withdrawing the decomposed air, and admitting fresh, are in proper order; also, clean out the baths attached to each chamber, and take care there is an abundant supply of water."

"I am told that ablution in the common aqueous fluid is becoming more fashionable than any medicated baths," said Evelina, "and that some people of rank actually use a composition of alkali and oil[90] to remove the pulverous particles that may have lodged upon their epidermis in the course of the day."

"I fear from the commands you have issued, Madam," rejoined Cecilia, "that you were oblivious of the alteration that has been effected in the superior dormitory. The air there is no longer changed by means of tubes—but there is a fan-feather ventilator fixed in the ceiling, which by its gentle undulations occasions a free circulation of the aeriform[91] fluid. I do not think, however, that it is quite adequate to supply the place of the tubes, as upon entering the room this morning, I perceived a strong sensation of azote,[92] and found that the proportion of nitrogen more than trebled that of oxygen throughout the whole apartment."

"I am sorry for it, but as it cannot be avoided we must submit. Now, Mr. Abelard, I am ready to attend to you."

"I have taken the liberty of—of—wishing," said the butler, in his turn affecting confusion, "to show you a little poetry. These are some verses of my own,[93] in the acromonogrammatic style, only every line begins with the same word with which the last ended, instead of the same letter. Will you permit me to read them to you?"

Mrs. Russel graciously simpered assent, and Abelard, unfolding the paper, read as follows:—

> ON LOVE.
> OF all the powers in Heaven above,
> Above all others, triumphs Love;
> Love rules the soul-the heart invades,
> Invades the cities and the shades.
> Shades form no shelter from its power,
> Power trembles in his courtly bower.
> Bower of beauty-art thou free?
> Free thou art not-nor canst thou be!
> Be every other class released,
> Released from love, thy woe's increased;
> Increased by all the weight of care,
> Care flowing from complete despair.

"Charming!" exclaimed Mrs. Russel, "only I own I don't understand why despair comes in the last line."

"Despair—despair: oh! to rhyme with care, my Eloisa. I hope I shall have no other reason to talk of despair."

"Oh dear; Mr. Abelard, do not endeavour to take undue advantage of my tenderness."

"Forbid, Heaven!" exclaimed he, taking her hand, when their love scene was cruelly interrupted by the unexpected sight of Edric, who happened at this moment to pass in Lord Gustavus de Montfort's balloon. The recognition was mutual, and Edric was so exceedingly agitated by this encounter, which convinced him that his father was in town, that he determined to delay his journey no longer, as his dread of meeting him was excessive. He therefore resolved to seek his tutor, and, if he found him inclined to procrastinate, to set off without him. On reaching the doctor's chamber, however, he found half his uneasiness converted into laughter at the ludicrous situation of the poor philosopher, who, surrounded as he was on every side by a crowd of tradesmen clamorous for orders, looked something like Mercury encircled by a tribe of discontented ghosts upon the banks of the Styx.

"Yes, yes, Mr. Jones," said he; "I see you understand me. The coats are to be those woven in machines, where the wool is stripped off the sheep's back by one end, and the coat comes out completely made, in the newest fashion, at the other."

"Very well, Sir," said Mr. Jones, wagging his ears in token of assent;[94] for in those days of universal education, even the muscles of the head were trained to perform functions which in former days it was only supposed possible they *might* attain: "You are quite right, Sir,—no person of fashion ever wears any thing else now."

"Oh, Edric!" cried the doctor, "I shall be ready to attend to you directly:— and so, Mrs. Celestina, you must make the soup, if you please, water-proof; and you, Mr. Crispin, must have the boots ready to dissolve, at a moment's notice. Oh, dear! oh, dear, what a perplexity I am in, my head is going just like a steam-boat, at the rate of sixty miles an hour?"[95]

"Upon my word, doctor," said Edric, looking round in dismay, "if we are to take half the things assembled here, I do not know where we shall find a balloon large enough and strong enough even to raise us from the ground."

"I will show you one," replied the doctor, mysteriously; and solemnly drawing forth from his bosom a key, which appeared to have boon suspended by a ribbon from his neck, he slowly opened, with great difficulty, a secret drawer in his escritoire, and produced from its inmost recesses a small bottle of Indian rubber[96]. The gravity of the doctor's manner, and the length of time that he had employed in this operation, had excited Edric's curiosity, and he burst into a violent and uncontrollable fit of laughter when he saw the result.

"What is the matter, Edric?" asked the doctor, with the utmost solemnity; "what can be the occasion of this unceremonious and ill-timed levity?"

"Parturient mountains,[97] my dear doctor," replied Edric, still laughing,— "you know the rest."

"Ridicule, Edric," said the doctor gravely, "is by no means the test of truth. Fools often,— nay, generally, laugh at what they cannot understand, and when I shall have explained the motives of my conduct, I trust you will feel ashamed of your present weak and unseasonable mirth. Caoutchouc, Edric, is a substance capable of astonishing dilation and contraction; whilst the peculiar elasticity and tenacity of its fibres give it a strength and solidity, very rare in bodies when in a state of extreme tension. But before I inform you of the novel use to which I intend to apply it; there are several very extraordinary phenomena relating to elastic bodies, which I am happy to have an apposite opportunity of explaining to you." (Edric yawned.) "You know, elastic substances have the power of wonderfully resisting a force which would annihilate solids, apparently infinitely stronger than themselves, as a feather-bed will repulse a cannon-ball that would penetrate with ease through a thick table. Now the reason for this is evident: the elastic body has the power of summoning all its forces to its assistance, for the effect of a blow may be traced even to its remotest extremity; whereas the solid substance can only oppose its enemy by the mere resistance of the identical part struck."

"Certainly," said Edric, striving to suppress a yawn; "nothing can be more clear."

"Nothing," resumed the doctor. "I was sure you would admire the force of my reasoning; indeed, I see the excess of your admiration in the involuntary yawns in which you have been indulging. On some occasions, Edric, man shakes off the artificial restraints of society, and breaks forth into the full freedom of honest and unsophisticated nature:—thus it was with you, Edric. In ancient times, the extension of the jaws was held synonymous[98] with the extension of the understanding, and the opening of the mouth and eyes was considered as the greatest possible sign of pleasure that could be given. In the works of an ancient author, whose poetry was doubtless once esteemed very fine, since it is now quite unintelligible, we find the following passage: —

'And Hodge stood lost in wide-mouth'd speculation.'[99]

Again,

'His eyes and mouth the hero open'd wide.'

—And divers others, which—"

"We will leave till a more convenient opportunity, if you please," said Edric, interrupting him. "At present, do favour me for five minutes with your attention. We cannot take all these things."

"Why not?" asked the doctor, gazing at his pupil with surprise; "for my part, I do not think we can dispense with a single article."

"These cloaks," said Edric, "and those hampers, for instance, cannot be of the slightest use."

"I beg your pardon," returned the doctor. "The cloaks are of asbestos, and will be necessary to protect us from ignition, if we should encounter any electric matter in the clouds; and the hampers are filled with elastic plugs for our ears and noses, and tubes and barrels of common air, for us to breathe when we get beyond the atmosphere of the earth.'

"But what occasion shall we have to go beyond it?"

"How can we do otherwise? Surely you don't mean to travel the whole distance in the balloon? I thought; of course, you would adopt the present fashionable mode of travelling,[100] and after mounting the seventeen miles or thereabouts, which is necessary to get clear of the mundane attraction, to wait there till the turning of the globe should bring Egypt directly under our feet."

"But it is not in the same latitude."

"True; I did not think of that! Well, then," sighing deeply, "I suppose we must do without the hamper?"

"Certainly; and without those boxes and bottles too, I hope."

"Oh no! we can't do without those. Those bottles contain my magic elixir, that cures all diseases merely by the smell:—a new idea that. You know it has been long discovered, that the whole materia medica[101] might be carried in a ring, and that all the instruments of surgery might be compressed into a walking-stick. But the idea of sniffing health in a pinch of snuff is, I flatter myself, exclusively my own."

"Very likely; but we cannot be encumbered with your panacea in our aerial tour."

"Then that box contains my portable galvanic battery; that, my apparatus for making and collecting the inflammable air; and that, my machine for producing and concentrating the quicksilver vapour,[102] which is to serve as the propelling power to urge us onwards, in the place of steam; and these bladders are filled with laughing gas,[103] for the sole purpose of keeping up our spirits."

"The three first will be useful," said Edric; "but I will positively have no more."

"Adieu! adieu! then, my precious treasures!" exclaimed the doctor, looking sorrowfully around: "Dear offspring of my cares! children of my mind! and must I leave you to some rude hand, which, heedless of your inestimable worth, may scatter your beauties to the winds? Alas! alas!"

"Breakfast is ready, and my lord is waiting!" interrupted the shrill voice of one of Lord Gustavus's servants.

"Then we must go!" said the doctor; and the rest of his pathetic lamentation remained for ever buried in his own bosom.

Lord Gustavus was already seated when they entered the room, with two gentlemen, whom he introduced to our travellers as Lord Noodle and Lord Doodle. These noble lords were both counsellors of state as well as their illustrious host, and had attained that high honour in exactly the same way, viz. they had both succeeded their respective fathers. It is not easy to be very diffuse in their description, as they were members of that honourable and numerous fraternity, who never take the trouble of judging for themselves, but contentedly swim with the stream, whichever way it may flow, and have nothing about them to distinguish them in the slightest degree from the crowd. Lord Gustavus was at present their leading star, and they might very appropriately he termed his satellites. Thus, when any new idea was started, they cautiously refrained from giving an opinion till they found what he thought of it —they would then look wise, shake their heads, and say, "Exactly so!" "Certainly!" "Nobody can doubt it!" or some of those other convenient *ripieno*[104] phrases, which fill up so agreeably the pauses in the conversation, without requiring any troublesome exertion of the mental powers of either the hearer or the speaker. These gentlemen had now visited Lord Gustavus, for the purpose of accompanying him and Edric to the Queen's levee, and as soon as they had taken breakfast, the whole party, with the exception of Dr. Entwerfen, proceeded to court.

When arrived there, however, they found the Queen had not yet risen. "Her Majesty is late this morning," observed Lord Maysworth, a gentleman loaded with orders and decorations, addressing Lord Gustavus:—"I am not surprised," said his lordship, "for her most gracious Majesty told me the other day, that she has slept badly for some time."

"Which, of course, caused you great grief?" asked Dr. Hardman, a little, satirical-looking gentleman in a bob-wig.[105]

"Thinking as I think," said Lord Gustavus gravely, "and as I am sure every one here must think, or at least ought to think, her Majesty's want of sleep is a circumstance of very serious importance."

"Oh! very!" exclaimed Lord Noodle, shaking his head. "Most assuredly!" cried Lord Doodle, shaking his.

"Why?" demanded the doctor; "of what possible consequence can it be to her subjects, whether her Majesty sleeps soundly or has the night-mare?"

"Of the greatest consequence," replied Lord Gustavus solemnly.

"Nothing can be greater!" echoed his satellites.

"Well!" observed Lord Maysworth, "for my part, I am such a traitor as to think we might exist, even if the Queen did not sleep at all."

"Or if she slept for ever," rejoined the doctor significantly.

"Oh, fie!" cried Lord Gustavus; "what would become of us, if the great sun of the political hemisphere were to set!"

"We must watch the rising of another, I suppose," said Lord Maysworth.

"Yes," continued Dr. Hardman: "and then the energies of the people would be roused. They want awakening from their present slumber—they have slept too long under the paralysing effects of tyranny. The government wants reform; corruption has eaten into its root, and it must be eradicated ere England can be free, or its people happy. Would to Heaven I might live to aid in the glorious struggle; that I might see the people assert their right, and the fiend, Despotism, sink beneath their blows!"

"I have ever admired," said Lord Maysworth, "the high integrity and fine principles of the worthy doctor, which have not only obtained for him the applause of England, but the admiration of Europe. The courage, wisdom, and purity of his mind cannot be too highly extolled; and all who know him concur in calling him the firm and devoted friend of mankind. I also have been an humble supporter of plans of economy and retrenchment; and it was I who had the honour of suggesting to the council, the other day, that an humble petition should be presented; to her Majesty, requesting her respectfully to order a diminution of the lights in her saloon, proving incontestably, that there were, at least, six more than were absolutely necessary."

"Thinking as I think, and as I am sure every one here must think," began Lord Gustavus, —but, ere he had time to finish his exordium, the folding doors at the back of the audience chamber were thrown open, and the Queen appeared, sitting upon a gorgeous throne, and surrounded by the officers of her household all splendidly attired.

The usual ceremonies then took place: — Claudia smiled graciously on Edric as he kissed her hand, and inquired when he intended to depart. Edric informed her, on the morrow; when, condescending to express regret, and desiring to see him on his return, she wished him an agreeable voyage, and dismissed him.

It is one of the most glorious attributes of greatness, to have the power of giving great pleasure by saying very few words; yet, as during their ride home, Lord Gustavus could talk of nothing but the graciousness of the Queen, upon which he was still expatiating, when the balloon stopped; Edric, though he felt grateful for her kindness, was annoyed by hearing so much said of it, and hastened to leave him as soon as he possibly could with propriety. On his road to his own apartment, he heard a strange and fearful noise, like the voice of some one screaming in an agony of rage and pain, which seemed to proceed from the chamber appropriated to his learned tutor; and he was going thither to ascertain the cause, when the agitated form of the unfortunate philosopher burst upon him.

Sad, indeed, was the condition in which this splendid ornament of the twenty-second century now presented himself before the eyes of his astonished pupil. His face glowed like fire; his hat was off, and water streamed from every part of his body ill he looked like the effigy of a water deity in a fountain.

"Here is management!" cried he, as soon as his rage permitted him to speak; "here is treatment for one devoted to the service of mankind! But I will be revenged, and centuries yet to come shall tremble at my wrath."

In this manner be continued; and being too much occupied in these awful denunciations, to be able to give any information as to what calamity had brought him into this unseemly plight, it will be necessary to go back a little to explain it for him.

When Dr. Entwerfen left the breakfast-room of Lord Gustavus, which he did not do till a considerable time after the rest of the party had quitted it, he was so absorbed in meditation that he did not know exactly which way he was going: and, happening unfortunately to turn to the right when he should have gone to the left, to his infinite surprise he found himself in the kitchen, instead of his own study.

Absent as the doctor was, however, his attention was soon roused by the scene before him. Being, like many of his learned brotherhood, somewhat of a gourmand, his indignation was violently excited by finding the cook comfortably asleep on a sofa on one side of the room; whilst the meat intended for dinner, a meal it was then the fashion to take about noon, was as comfortably resting itself from its toils on the other. The chemical substitute for fire, which ought to have cooked it, having gone out, and the cook's nap precluding all reasonable expectation of its re-illumination, the doctor's wrath. was kindled, though the fire was not, and in a violent rage he seized the gentle Celestina's shoulder, and shook her till she woke.

"Where am I?" exclaimed she, opening her eyes.

"Any where but where you ought to be," cried the doctor, in a fury. Look, hussy! look at that fine joint of meat, lying quite cold and sodden in its own steam."

"Dear me!" returned Celestina, yawning, "I am really quite unfortunate to-day! An unlucky accident has already occurred to a leg of mutton which was to have formed part of today's aliments; and now this piece of beef is also destroyed. I am afraid there will be nothing for dinner but some mucilaginous[106] saccharine vegetables, and they, most probably, will be boiled to a viscous consistency.'"

"And what excuse can you offer for all this?" exclaimed the doctor, his voice trembling with passion.

"It was unavoidable," replied Celestina coolly. "Whilst I was copying a cast from the Apollo Belvidere[107] this morning, having unguardedly applied too much caloric to the vessel containing the leg of mutton, the aqueous fluid in which it was immersed, evaporated, and the viand became completely calcined; whilst the other affair—"

"Hush, hush!" interrupted the doctor; "I cannot bear to hear you mention it. Oh, surely Job himself never suffered such a trial of his patience! In fact, *his* troubles were scarcely worth mentioning, for he was never cursed with learned servants!"

Saying this the doctor retired, lamenting his hard fate in not having been born in those halcyon days when cooks drew nothing but their poultry; whilst the gentle Celestina's breast panted with indignation at his complaint. An opportunity soon offered for revenge; and seeing the doctor's steam valet[108] ready to be carried to its master's chamber, she treacherously applied a double portion of caloric: in consequence of which, the machine burst whilst in the act of brushing the doctor's coat-collar, and by discharging the whole of the scalding water contained in its cauldron upon him, reduced him to the melancholy state we have already mentioned.

The fear of the ridicule attached to this incident, in a great measure reconciled the doctor to Edric's project of a speedy departure, and the following morning they bade adieu to Lord Gustavus, and, stepping into their balloon, sailed for Egypt.

Volume 1: Chapter 9

No event of any importance occurred to our travellers in the course of their aerial voyage. They were too well provided with all kinds of necessaries to have any occasion to rest by the way, and in an incredibly short space of time they were hovering over Egypt. Different, however, oh! how different from the Egypt of the nineteenth century, was the fertile country which now lay like a map beneath their feet. Improvement had turned her gigantic steps towards its once desert plains; Commerce had waved her magic wand; and towns and cities, manufactories and canals, spread in all directions.[109] No more did the Nile overflow its banks: a thousand channels were cut to receive its waters. No longer did the moving sands of the Desert rise in mighty waves, threatening to overwhelm the way-worn traveller: macadamized turnpike roads supplied their place, over which post-chaises, with anti-attritioned wheels, howled at the rate of fifteen miles an hour.[110] Steam-boats glided down the canals, and furnaces raised their smoky heads amidst groves of palm-trees; whilst iron railways intersected orange groves, and plantations of dates and pomegranates might be seen bordering excavations intended for coal pits. Colonies of English and Americans peopled the country,[111] and produced a population that swarmed like bees over the land, and surpassed in numbers even the wondrous throngs of the ancient Mizraim[112] race; whilst industry and science changed desolation into plenty, and had converted barren plains into fertile kingdoms.

Amidst all these revolutions, however, the Pyramids still raised their gigantic forms, towering to the sky; unchanged, unchangeable, grand, simple, and immoveable, fit symbols of that majestic nature they were intended to represent, and seeming to look down with contempt upon the ephemeral structures with which they were surrounded; as though they would have said, had utterance been permitted to them—"Avaunt, ye nothings of the day. Respect our dignity and sink into your original obscurity; for know, that we alone are monarchs of the plains." Indestructible, however, as they had proved themselves, even their granite sides had not been able entirely to resist the corroding influence of the smoke with which they were now surrounded, and a slight crumbling announced the first outward symptom of decay. Still, however, though blackened and disfigured, they shone stupendous monuments of former greatness; and Edric and his tutor gazed upon them with an awe that for some moments deprived them of utterance.

The doctor, however, who was too fond of reasoning ever long to remain willingly silent, after surveying them a few minutes, broke forth as follows:—"What noble piles! What majesty and grandeur they display in their formation, and yet what dignified simplicity! Can the imagination of man conceive any thing more sublime than the thought that they have stood thus frowning in awful magnificence, perhaps since the very creation of the world, without equals, without even competitors,—mocking the feeble efforts of man to divine their origin, and seeing generation after generation pass away, whilst they still remain immutable, and involved in the same deep and unfathomable mystery as at first."

"It is very strange," observed Edric, "that, in this age of speculation and discovery, nothing certain should be known concerning them."

"It is," returned the doctor; "but the thick mysterious veil that has rested upon them for so many ages, seems not intended to be removed by mortal hands. They remind one of the sublime inscription upon the temple of the goddess Isis, at Sais:[113]—'I am whatever was, whatever is, and whatever shall be; but no mortal has, as yet, presumed to raise the veil that covers me.'"

"Your quotation is apt, doctor," resumed Edric, "for both relate to Nature. Indeed, Nature appears to be the deity which the ancient Egyptians worshipped, under all the various forms in which she presents herself; and their strange and animal deities were but reverenced as her symbols. It was Nature whom they worshipped as Isis; it was Nature that was typified in the Pyramids; and the good taste of the Egyptians made them prefer the simple, the majestic, and the sublime, in those works which they destined to last for ages. Formerly, from the immensity of their population, and high state of their civilization, labour was so divided, and consequently so lightened, that multitudes were enabled to exist exempt from toil. These persons, devoting themselves to study, became *initiati*; and either enrolled themselves amongst the priesthood, or passed their lives in making themselves masters of the most abstract sciences. The consequences were natural: they followed up the ramifications of creation to their original source; they penetrated into the inmost profound secrets of Nature, and traced all her wonders in her works: aware, however, of the taste of the vulgar for any thing above their comprehension, and of the natural craving of the human mind for mystery, they wrapped the discoveries they had made in a deep and impenetrable veil, and concealed awful and sublime significations under the meanest and most disgusting images."

"You are right," said the doctor, "in your observations upon the religion of the ancient Egyptians; but it does not appear to me that the Pyramids were erected by them."

"What! I suppose you draw your conclusions from the want of hieroglyphics in their principal chambers; and, from what Herodotus says of their having been erected by a shepherd[114], you think they were the work of the Pallic race."[115]

"No; though I allow much may be said in favour of that hypothesis, particularly as Herodotus says the kings under whom they were erected, ordered all the Egyptian temples to be closed, which we know the shepherd nor Pallic sovereign did; but I cannot imagine that an ignorant, Goth-like race of shepherds, men accustomed to live in tents or in the open air, and possessing no talents but for war, were capable of constructing such immense piles. No, no, the Pyramids required gigantic conceptions, highly cultivated minds, and unwearied perseverance; all qualities quite incompatible with a warlike wandering race. No, I do not think the Palli were capable of imagining such structures, much less of constructing them. I think they were the work of evil spirits."

"Evil spirits!"' exclaimed Edric.

"Yes," returned the doctor. "We are told that the evil spirits, after their expulsion from Paradise, were under the command of the Sultan, or Soliman Giam ben Giam,[116] as he is called by Arabic writers, but who is supposed to have been the same as Cheops; and that he employed them in this vast work."

"I do not know by what analysis etymologists can draw the name of Cheops from that of Giam ben Giam: but, supposing the fact to be correct, that they designated the same person, I think it only proves more strongly my hypothesis; for the Palli came from Mount Caucasus, where the evil spirits i were said to have been enchained, and if Cheops was a Pallic king, it is possible the Egyptians might poetically call their conquerors evil spirits."

"That is a good idea, Edric; though I do not think it by any means certain that Cheops was a Pallic king. However, we shall soon be able to see his tomb, and judge for ourselves; for we have now approached near enough to the Pyramids to descend. Foh! what a smoke and what a noise! It is enough to rouse the mummies from their slumbers before their appointed time, and without the aid of galvanism. Have you opened the valves, Edric? Oh yes! I perceive we are getting lower; we will not lose a moment before we visit the Pyramid. But what a crowd of brutes are assembled to witness our arrival! they stare as though they had never seen a balloon before. Egypt is certainly a fine, country, but the inhabitants are a century behind us in civilization."

An immense crowd had gathered together to witness the descent of our travellers, and they did indeed stand staring, lost in stupid astonishment at the strange sight that presented itself; for though the Egyptian people had occasionally seen balloons, they had never before beheld one made of Indian rubber. The odd figure of the doctor, too, amused them exceedingly, as he sat wrapt up. in the most dignified manner in an asbestos cloak, his bob-wig pushed a little on one side from the heat of the weather and the warmth of his argument; his round, red, oily face attempting to look solemn, and his little, fat, punchy[117] figure trying to assume an air of majesty. The Egyptians were amazingly struck with this apparition, and being, like most colonists, somewhat conceited and not very ceremonious in their manners, they looked at him a few minutes in silence, and then burst into immoderate fits of laughter.

The doctor was exceedingly indignant at this rude reception, and rising, shook his fist at them in anger; a manoeuvre, however, that only redoubled the mirth of the unpolished Egyptians, whose peals of laughter now became so tremendous, that they actually shook the skies, and occasioned a most unpleasant vibration in the balloon. Edric, who was almost as much annoyed as the doctor, had yet sufficient self-command to continue calmly making preparations for his descent; and without taking the least notice of the crowd below, he screwed the top upon the propelling vapour-bottle; he let the inflammable air escape from the balloon, which rapidly collapsed as they approached the earth, and throwing out their patent spring grappling-irons, they caught one of the lower stones of the Great Pyramid, and in a few moments the car in which our travellers were sitting, was safely moored at a convenient distance from the earth for them to alight. Edric now unloosed the descending ladder, and reverentially assisted the doctor, who was encumbered with his long cloak, to reach terra firma in safety,— amidst the bustle and exclamations of the crowd, who thronged round them expressing their wonder and astonishment audibly, in broad English.

"Where the deuce did this spring from?" cried one; "the car would load a waggon!"[118]

"And what is gone with the balloon?" said another; "it is clean vanished!"

"Well, I never saw such a thing in all my life before!" exclaimed a third; "I think they must be come from the moon."

"Hush! hush," cried an old gentleman bustling amongst them, who seemed as one having authority. "What's the matter? what's the matter?"

"We are strangers, Sir," said Edric, advancing and addressing him: "we come here to see the wonders of your country, and we wish to explore the Pyramids—but the reception we have met with—"

"Say no more—Say no more!" interrupted the worthy justice, for such he was. "Get about your business, you rapscallions, or I'll read the riot act![119] Here, Gregory, call out the posse comitatus,[120] and set a guard of constables to keep watch over these gentlemen's balloon, whilst they go to explore the Pyramids. Eh! but where is the balloon? I don't see it. I hope neither of the gentlemen has put it in his pocket!" laughing at his own wit.

"No, Sir," returned Edric, smiling, "though it is a feat which might easily be accomplished, for that is our balloon," pointing to the caoutchouc bottle, now shrunk to its original dimensions.

"Very strange, that!" said the Justice; "Very curious, very curious indeed! Well, gentlemen, if you wish to proceed immediately, you'll want a guide of course. These cottages at the foot of the Pyramids are all inhabited by guides, who get their living by showing the sights. They are sad rogues, most of them, but I can recommend you to one who is a very honest man. Here, Samuel," continued he, knocking against a small door, "Samuel! I say!"

Samuel made his appearance, in the guise of a tall, raw-boned, stupid-looking fellow, with a pair of immensely broad stooping shoulders, which looked as though he could have relieved Atlas occasionally of his burthen, without much trouble to himself. Coming forth from his hut in an awkward shambling pace, he scratched his head, and demanded what his honour pleased to want.

"You must show these gentlemen the Pyramids," said the Justice.

"Ay, that I will with pleasure!" returned Samuel; "I've got my living by showing them these fifty years, man and boy; and I know every crink and cranny of them, though I'm old now and somewhat lame. So walk this way, gentlemen."

"We are very much obliged to you, Sir," said the doctor, bowing to the Justice; who was in fact one of those good-natured, busy, bustling men, who are always better pleased to transact any other person's business than their own; and are never so happy as when a new arrival gives them an opportunity of showing off their consequence. Indeed, there is a pleasure in showing wonders to a stranger, that only those who have little else to occupy their minds can properly estimate: a man of this kind feels his self-love gratified by the superiority his local knowledge gives him over a stranger; and, as it is, perhaps, the only chance he ever can have of showing superiority, they must be unreasonable who blame him for making the most of it. Justice Freemantle was accordingly exceedingly delighted with travellers who seemed disposed to submit implicitly to his dictation; and he returned a most gracious reply to the doctor's thanks.

"Don't mention it! don't mention it, my dear Sir!" said he; "I am never so happy as when I can make myself useful. Is there any thing else I can do for you? You may command me, I assure you; and you may depend upon it, no injury shall be done to your luggage, whilst you are away."

"What a very civil, obliging, good-natured old gentleman," said the doctor, as they walked towards the entrance of the Pyramids; "I declare he almost reconciles me to the country, though, I own, I thought at first the people were the greatest brutes I had ever met with."

"Which Pyramid does your honour wish to see?" asked the guide.

"That which contains the tomb of Cheops, man!" cried the doctor solemnly; who, encumbered with his long cloak, and loaded with his walking-stick and galvanic battery, had some difficulty in getting on. "Won't your honour let me carry that pole and that bag?" said the man; "you'd get on a surprising deal better, if you would."

"Avaunt, wretch!" exclaimed the doctor, "nor offer to touch with thy profane fingers the immortal instruments of science."

The man stared, but fell back, and the whole party walked on in perfect silence.

In the mean time, Edric had walked on before his companions, completely lost in meditation. A crowd of conflicting thoughts rushed through his mind; and now, when he found himself at the very goal of his wishes, the daring nature of the purpose he had so long entertained, seemed to strike him for the first time, and he trembled at the consequences that might attend the completion of his desires. With his arms folded on his breast, he stood gazing on the Pyramids, whilst his ideas wandered uncontrolled through the boundless regions of space: "And what am I," thought he, "weak, feeble worm that I am! who dare seek to penetrate into the awful secrets of my Creator? Why should I wish to restore animation to a body now resting in the quiet of the tomb? What right have I to renew the struggles, the pains, the cares, and the anxieties of mortal life? How can I tell the fearful effects that may be produced by the gratification of my unearthly longing? May I not revive a creature whose wickedness may involve mankind in misery? And what if my experiment should fail, and if the moment when I expect my rash wishes to be accomplished, the hand of Almighty vengeance should strike me to the earth, and heap molten fire on my brain to punish my presumption!"

The sound of human voices, as the doctor and the guide approached, grated harshly on the nerves of Edric, already overstrained by the awful nature of the thoughts in which he had been indulging, and he turned away involuntarily, to escape the interruption he dreaded, quite forgetting for the moment from whom the sounds most probably proceeded.

"Lord have mercy on us!" said the guide; "I declare that gentleman looks as if he were beside himself! and see there! if he hasn't walked right by the entrance to the Pyramid without seeing it! Sir! Sir!" halloed he.

Excessively annoyed, but recalled to his recollection by these shouts, Edric returned.

"These Pyramids are wonderful piles." said the doctor, as he stumbled forward to meet him. "I really had no adequate conception of the enormity of their size. They did not even look half so large at a distance as they do now."

"Immense masses seldom do," replied Edric; compelling himself with difficulty to speak.

"True," returned the doctor; "the simplicity and uniformity of their figures deceive the eyes, and it is only when we approach them that we feel their stupendous magnitude and our own insignificance!"

"They give an amazing idea of the grandeur of the ancient kings of Egypt," said Edric, without exactly knowing what he was saying. "Their palaces must have been superb, if they had such mausoleums."

"How absurdly you reason, Edric!" replied the doctor peevishly; for, being annoyed with his burthens and his cloak, he was not in a humour to bear contradiction. "I thought we had settled that question before. In the first place, I think it very doubtful whether the Egyptians had any thing to do with the building of these monuments; and if they had, I think they were meant for temples, not mausoleums; and in the next place, even if they were intended for tombs, their greatness affords no argument for the splendour of the surrounding palaces; as the Egyptians were celebrated for the superiority of their burying-places, and for the immense sums they expended upon them. Indeed, you know, ancient writers say they went so far as to call the houses of the living only inns, whilst they considered tombs as everlasting habitations;— circumstance, by the way, that strongly corroborates my hypothesis, at least as far as their opinions go; as it seems to imply that both soul and body were designed to remain there."

They had now entered the Pyramid,[121] and were proceeding with infinite difficulty along a low, dark, narrow passage: "Observe, Edric," said the doctor, "how the difficulty and obscurity of these winding passages confirm my opinion: you know, the religion of the ancient Egyptians, like that of the ancient Hindoos, was one of penances and personal privations; and, granting that to be the case, what can be more simple, than that the passages the *initiati* had to traverse before they reached the adytum, should be painful and difficult of access. Besides this, as you know, the bones of a bull, no doubt those of the god Apis,[122] were found in a sarcophagus in the second Pyramid, it seems probable that it was sacred to his worship: and its vicinity to the Nile, which was indispensable to the temples of Apis, as, when it was time for him to die, he was drowned in its waters, confirms the fact. Indeed, I am only surprised that any human being, possessing a grain of common sense, can entertain a single doubt upon the subject."

"How do you account for the tomb we are about to visit being placed in the Pyramid, if you think they were only designed for a temple?" asked Edric.

"The question is futile," said the doctor. "A strange fancy prevailed in former times, that burying the dead in consecrated places, particularly in temples intended for divine worship, would scare away the evil spirits, and the practice actually prevailed in England even as lately as the nineteenth or twentieth century. Indeed, it was not till after the country had been almost depopulated by the dreadfully infectious disease that prevailed about two hundred years ago, that a law was passed to prevent the interment of the dead in London, and that those previously buried in and near the churches there, were exhumed and placed in cemeteries beyond the walls."

Edric did not reply, for in fact his ideas were so absorbed by the solemn object before him, that it was painful for him to speak, and the doctor's ill-timed reasoning created such an irritation of his nerves, that he found it required the utmost exertion of his self-command to endure it patiently. The passage they were traversing, now became higher and wider, shelving off occasionally into chambers or recesses on each side, till they approached a kind of vestibule, in the centre of which, yawned a deep, dark, gloomy-looking cavity, like a well.

"We must descend that shaft," said the guide, "and that will lead us to the tomb of King Cheops; but as the road is dark, and rather dangerous, we had better, each of us, take a torch." As he spoke, he drew some torches from a niche where they were deposited, and began to illuminate them from his own. The red glare of the torches flashed fearfully on the massive walls of the Pyramid, throwing part of their enormous masses into deep shadow, as they rose in solemn and sublime dignity around, and seemed frowning upon the presumptuous mortals that had dared to invade their recesses, whilst the deep pit beneath their feet seemed to yawn wide to engulf them in its abyss. Edric's heart beat thick: it throbbed till he even fancied its pulsations audible; and a strange, mysterious thrilling of anxiety, mingled with a wild, undefinable delight, ran through his frame. A few short hours, and his wishes would be gratified, or set at rest for ever. The doctor and the guide had already begun to descend, and their figures seemed changed and unearthly as the gleams of the torches fell upon them. Edric gazed for a moment, and then followed with feelings worked up almost to frenzy by the over-excitement of his nerves; whilst the hollow sound that re-echoed from the walls, as they struck against them in their descent, thrilled through his whole frame.

No one spoke; and after proceeding for some time along the narrow path, or rather ledge, formed on the sides of the cavity, which gradually shelved downwards, the guide suddenly stopped, and touching a secret spring, a solid block of granite slowly detached itself from the wall, and, rising majestically like the portcullis of an ancient fortress, showed the entrance to a dark and dreary cave. The guide advanced, followed by our travellers, into a gloomy vaulted apartment, where long vistas of ponderous arches stretched on every side, till their termination was lost in darkness, and gave a feeling of immensity and obscurity to the scene.

"I will wait here," said the guide; "and here, if you please, you had better leave your torches. That avenue will lead you to the tomb."

The travellers obeyed; and the guide, placing himself in a recess in the wall, extinguished all the torches except one, which he shrouded so as to leave the travellers in total darkness. Nothing could be now more terrific than their situation: immured in the recesses of the tomb, involved in darkness, and their bosoms throbbing with hopes that they scarcely dared avow even to themselves, with faltering steps they proceeded slowly along the path the guide had pointed out, shuddering even at the hollow echo of their own footsteps, which alone broke the solemn silence that reigned throughout these fearful regions of terror and the tomb.

Suddenly, a vivid light flashed upon them, and, as they advanced, they found it proceeded from torches placed in the hands of two colossal figures, who, placed in a sitting posture, seemed guarding an enormous portal, surmounted by the image of a fox, the constant guardian of an Egyptian tomb. The immense dimensions and air of grandeur and repose about these colossi had something in it very imposing; and our travellers felt a sensation of awe creep over them as they gazed upon their calm unmoved features, so strikingly emblematic of that immutable nature which they were doubtless placed there to typify.

It was with feelings of indescribable solemnity, that the doctor and Edric passed through this majestic portal, and found themselves in an apartment gloomily illumined by the light shed faintly from an inner chamber, through ponderous brazen gates beautifully wrought. The light thus feebly emitted, showed that the room in which they stood, was dedicated to Typhon,[123] the evil spirit, as his fierce and savage types covered the walls; and images of his symbols, the crocodile and the dragon, placed beneath the shadow of the brazen gates, and dimly seen by the imperfect light, seemed starting into life, and grimly to forbid the farther advance of the intruders. Our travellers shuddered, and opening with trembling hand the ponderous gates, they entered *the tomb of Cheops*.[124]

In the centre of the chamber, stood a superb, highly ornamented sarcophagus of alabaster, beautifully wrought; over this hung a lamp of wondrous workmanship, supplied by a potent mixture, so as to burn for ages unconsumed; thus awfully lighting up with perpetual flame the solemn mansions of the dead, and typifying life eternal even in the silent tomb. Around the room, on marble benches, were arranged mummies simply dried, apparently those of slaves; and close to the sarcophagus was placed one contained in a case, which the doctor approached to examine. This was supposed to be that of Sores, the confidant and prime-minister of Cheops. The chest that enclosed the body was splendidly ornamented with embossed gilt leather, whilst the parts not otherwise covered were stained with red and green curiously blended, and of a vivid brightness.

The mighty Phtah,[125] the Jupiter of the Egyptians, spread its widely extended wings over the head, grasping in his monstrous claws a ring, the emblem of eternity; whilst below, the vulture form of Rhea proclaimed the deceased a votary of that powerful deity; and on the sides were innumerable hieroglyphics. The doctor removed the lid, and shuddered as the crimson tinge of the everlasting lamp fell upon the hideous and distorted features thus suddenly exhibited to view. This sepulchral light, indeed, added unspeakable horror to the scene, and. its peculiar glare threw such a wild and demoniac expression on the dark lines and ghastly lineaments of the mummies, that even the doctor felt his spirits depressed, and a supernatural dread creep over his mind as he gazed upon them.

In the mean time, Edric had stood gazing upon the sarcophagus of Cheops, the sides of which were beautifully sculptured with groups of figures, which, from the peculiar light thrown upon them, seemed to possess all the force and reality of life. On one side was represented an armed and youthful warrior bearing of in his arms a beautiful female, on whom he gazed with the most passionate fondness. He was pursued by a crowd of people and soldiers, who seemed rending the air with vehement exclamations against his violence, and endeavouring in vain to arrest his progress; whilst in the background appeared an old man, who was tearing his hair and wringing his hands in ineffectual rage against the ravisher.

The other side, presented the same old man wrestling with the youthful warrior, who had just overpowered and stabbed him; the helpless victim raising his withered hands and failing eyes to Heaven as he fell, as though to implore vengeance upon his murderer, whilst the crimson current was fast ebbing from his bosom. The dying look and agony of the old man were forcibly depicted, whilst upon the features of the youthful warrior glowed the fury of a demon. The sarcophagus was supported by the lion, emblem of royalty, the symbol of the solar god Horus; and above it sat the majestic hawk of Osiris, gazing upwards, and unmindful of the subtle crocodile of Typhon, that, crouching under its feet, was just about to seize its breast in its enormous jaws. Neither of the travellers had as yet spoken, for it seemed like sacrilege to disturb the awful stillness that prevailed even by a whisper. Indeed, the solemn aspect of the chamber thrilled through every nerve, and they moved slowly, gliding along with noiseless steps as though they feared prematurely to break the slumbers of the mighty dead it contained. They gazed, however, with deep but undefinable interest upon the sculptured mysteries of the tomb of Cheops, vainly endeavouring to decipher their meaning; whilst, as they found their efforts useless, a secret voice seemed to whisper in their bosoms—"And shall finite creatures like these, who cannot even explain the signification of objects, presented before their eyes, presume to dive into the mysteries of their Creator's will? Learn wisdom by this omen nor seek again to explore secrets above your comprehension! Retire whilst it is yet time; soon it will be too late!"

Edric started at his own thoughts, as the fearful warning, "soon it will be too late," rang in his ears; and a fearful presentiment of evil weighed heavily upon his soul. He turned to look upon the doctor, but he had already seized the lid of the sarcophagus, and, with a daring hand, removed it from its place, displaying in the fearful light the royal form that lay beneath. For a moment, both Edric and the doctor paused, not daring to survey it; and when they did, they both uttered an involuntary cry of astonishment, as the stern, but handsome, features of the mummy met their eyes, for both instantly recognized the sculptured warrior in his traits. Yes, it was indeed the same, but the fierce expression of fiery and ungoverned passions depicted upon the countenance of the marble figure, had settled down to a calm, vindictive, and concentrated hatred upon that of its mummy prototype in the tomb.

Awful, indeed, was the gloom that sat upon that brow, and bitter the sardonic smile that curled those haughty lips. All was perfect as though life still animated the form before them, and it had only reclined there to seek a short repose. The dark eyebrows, the thick raven hair which hung upon the forehead, and the snow-white teeth seen through the half open lips, forbade the idea of death; whilst the fiend-like expression of the features made Edric shudder, as he recollected the purpose that brought him to the tomb, and he trembled at the thought of awakening such a fearful being from the torpor of the grave to all the renewed energies of life.

"Let us go," whispered the doctor to his pupil, in a low, deep, and unearthly tone, fearfully different from his usually cheerful voice. Edric started at the sound, for it seemed the last sad warning of his better genius, before he abandoned her for ever. The die, however, was cast, and it was too late to recede. Indeed, Edric felt worked up to frenzy by the over-wrought feelings of the moment. He seized the machine, and resolutely advanced towards the sarcophagus, whilst the doctor gazed upon him with a horror that deprived him of either speech or motion.

Innumerable folds of red and white linen, disposed alternately, swathed the gigantic but well-proportioned limbs of the royal mummy; and upon his breast lay a piece of metal, shining like silver, and stamped with the figure of a winged globe. Edric attempted to remove this, but recoiled with horror, when he found it bend beneath his fingers with an unnatural softness; whilst, as the flickering light of the lamp fell upon the face of the mummy, he fancied its stern features relaxed into a ghastly laugh of scornful mockery. Worked up to desperation, he applied the wires of the battery and put the apparatus in motion, whilst a demoniac laugh of derision appeared to ring in his ears, and the surrounding mummies seemed starting from their places and dancing in unearthly merriment. Thunder now roared in tremendous peals through the Pyramids, shaking their enormous masses to the foundation, and vivid flashes of light darted round in quick succession. Edric stood aghast amidst this fearful convulsion of nature. A horrid creeping seemed to run through every vein, every nerve feeling as though drawn from its extremity, and wrapped in icy chillness round his heart. Still, he stood immoveable, and gazing intently on the mummy, whose eyes had opened with, the shock, and were now fixed on those of Edric, shining with supernatural lustre. In vain Edric attempted to rouse himself;—in vain to turn away from that withering glance. The mummy's eyes still pursued him with their ghastly brightness; they seemed to possess the fabled fascination of those of the rattle-snake, and though he shrunk from their gaze, they still glared horribly upon him. Edric's senses swam, yet he could not move from the spot; he remained fixed, chained, and immoveable, this eyes still riveted upon the mummy, and every thought absorbed in horror. Another fearful peal of thunder now rolled in lengthened vibrations above his head, and the mummy rose slowly, his eyes still fixed upon those of Edric, from his marble tomb. The thunder pealed louder and louder. Yells and groans seemed mingled with its roar;—the sepulchral lamp flared with redoubled fierceness, flashing its rays around in quick succession, and with vivid brightness; whilst by its horrid and uncertain glare, Edric saw the mummy stretch out its withered hand as though to seize him. He saw it rise gradually—he heard the dry, bony fingers rattle as it drew them forth—he felt its tremendous gripe—human nature could bear no more—his senses were rapidly deserting him; he felt, however, the fixed stedfast[126] eyes of Cheops still glowing upon his failing orbs, as the lamp gave a sudden flash, and then all was darkness! The brazen gates now shut with a fearful clang, and Edric, uttering a shriek of horror, fell senseless upon the ground; whilst his shrill cry of anguish rang wildly through the marble vaults, till its re-echoes seemed like the yell of demons joining in fearful mockery.

How long he lay in this state he knew not; but when he reopened his eyes, for the moment, he fancied all that had passed a dream. As his senses returned, however, he recollected where he was, and shuddered to find himself yet in that place of horrors. All now was dark, except a faint gleam that shone feebly through the half-open gates; these ponderous portals slowly un-closed, and the form of a man, wrapped in a large cloak, and bearing a torch, entered, peering around as it advanced, as though half afraid to proceed. Edric's feelings were too highly wrought to bear any fresh horrors, and he shrieked in agony as the figure approached. The sound of his voice subdued the terrors of the intruder, and the doctor, for it was he, shouted with joy, as he rushed forward to embrace him.

"Edric! Edric! thank God he is alive!" exclaimed he. "Edric! my beloved Edric! for God's sake, let us leave this den of horrors! come, come!"

Reassured by his tutor's voice, Edric arose, and taking one hasty, shuddering glance around as the light gleamed on the sarcophagus, he hurried out of the tomb. Neither he nor the doctor spoke as they passed through the vestibule, where the colossal figures still sat in awful majesty; indeed, as their torches were extinguished, their gigantic forms looked still more terrific than before, from the wavering and indistinct light thrown upon them. Edric shuddered as he looked, and hurried on with hasty strides to the place where they had left the guide, whom they found kneeling in a corner, hiding his face in his hands, and roaring out, "O Lord, defend us! Heaven have mercy upon us! "Lord have mercy upon us! Heaven have mercy upon us!"

"He has been in that state for more than an hour," said the doctor mournfully; "for, after I came to myself again, I tried to rouse him, but all to no purpose."

"Then you also fainted?" said Edric, with difficulty compelling himself to speak.

"Why," resumed the doctor with some hesitation, "I don't know that you can exactly call it fainting; but the fact was, that when I saw you touch the plate upon the mummy's breast, and start back, looking so horribly frightened, I—I thought I had better call for assistance; so as I ran for that purpose, somehow or other, I fell down, and lay insensible I don't know how long. When I came to myself, however, I tried to rouse the guide, and when I found I could not, I came to seek you; but now that we are both recovered, I really don't know what is to become of us; for this fellow will never be able to show us the way out, and I'm sure I don't know the road."

"Let us try to find it, at any rate," said Edric faintly.

"Oh, for God's sake, take me too!" screamed the guide. "If you have any mercy, don't leave me in this fearful place."

"Take the light then, and lead the way," said Edric. The guide obeyed, shaking every limb, and every now and then casting a terrified look behind, whilst the quivering flame of the torch betrayed the unsteadiness of the trembling hands that bore it. In this manner they proceeded, starting at every sound, and frightened even at their own shadows, without daring to stop till they reached the plain.

"Thank God!" cried the doctor, the moment they stepped out of the Pyramid; looking round him, gasping for breath, and inhaling the fresh air with rapture.

"Thank God!" reiterated Edric and the guide, as they walked rapidly towards the place where they had left their balloon. When arrived there, however, they looked for it in vain; and fancying themselves under the influence of a delusion, they rubbed their eyes, and again looked, but without success.

"Dear me, it is very strange!" said the doctor; "this is certainly the place, and yet, where can it be?"

"Where, indeed!" repeated Edric; "horrors and unaccountable incidents environ us at every step; I am not naturally timid, yet—"

"Ah!" screamed the doctor, as he tumbled over a man lying with his face upon the ground; "Oh!" groaned he, as Edric and the guide with difficulty raised him; "would to Heaven I were safe at home again in my own comfortable little study, indulging on pleasing anticipations of that which I find is any thing in the world but pleasing in reality."

Volume 1: Chapter 10

We left Dr. Entwerfen in the last chapter uttering a very moral, if not a very new, exclamation on the vanity of human expectations; which had scarcely escaped from his lips, ere cruel Fate, resolving not to be accused in vain, supplied him with yet more abundant cause for lamentation. We have before mentioned, that the doctor had stumbled as he quitted the Pyramids, and that his friends raised him from the ground; but what was his consternation and dismay, when, on looking round to thank them, he found he was surrounded by armed men, who commanded him in the royal name to surrender! Sadly did the doctor turn his woful[127] eyes upon Edric, but, alas! he was in the same predicament as himself; and, in spite of their entreaties, they were marched off to prison, without being at all informed of what crime they had committed.

Sadly passed the night, and gloomy dawned the day upon the unfortunate travellers, whose minds were harassed and bewildered by the extraordinary success of their awful experiment, and whose misery was infinitely increased by the suspense they had to suffer, both on account of their ignorance of the crime of which they were accused, and its probable punishment if they should be found guilty. Soon after daybreak, however, a summons for them arrived, and they were conducted as criminals before the same magistrate who, the day before, had treated them with such officious kindness.

Very different, however, was the solemn judge who, clothed in all the insignia of magisterial dignity, now sate upon the bench, from the easy, good-tempered gentleman of the Pyramids; and the unlucky travellers saw, in an instant, that they were not likely to experience any favour from their previous acquaintance with him. The court was thronged with people: and the prisoners saw that they were regarded with curiosity, mingled with horror and supernatural fear. It is not agreeable to feel oneself an object of disgust to any one; and though Edric magnanimously and frequently repeated to himself that it was quite indifferent to him what such ignorant wretches as Egyptians thought of him; yet, if he would have avowed the truth, he would have been quite as well contented to have found himself the object of their admiration instead of their hatred; and he would have been very glad to have been safely at home again; whilst the doctor openly and loudly lamented the much regretted comforts of his own dear delightful study at Sir Ambrose's. Little time, however, was allowed for reflection;

for as soon as the prisoners were placed at the bar their examination commenced.

"So, gentlemen!" said the learned judge, "you stand convicted—no, I mean accused, of a most horrible, heinous, and sacrilegious offence—an offence that makes our hair start with horror from our heads, and every separate lock rise up in vengeance against you." The justice paused, that the prisoners might admire his eloquence; but, alas! such was the absorbing nature of self-love, that they were only thinking of what was going to be done with them, and to what this terrible exordium was likely to lead, After a short pause, Edric, supposing they were expected to speak, addressed the judge, and begged to know of what crime they were accused.

"We are strangers," said he, "and gentlemen. We were attracted to your country by an account of the wonders it contained; we declared our purposes openly; we have affected no concealment; and we have done nothing we need blush to avow—"

A confused murmur ran through the court as he spoke, expressive of the utmost disgust and abhorrence; Edric felt indignant, and he looked round proudly as he added:—

"Yes, I repeat we have done nothing we need blush to avow, and nothing derogatory to our characters as Englishmen and gentlemen."

"Sorcerers! wizards! demons in disguise!" cried the crowd. "Down with them! burn them! guillotine them! destroy them!"

"Is this fair? is this generous?" asked Edric. "If we have done wrong, let our crime be proved, and we are ready to submit to any punishment you may think proper to inflict; but do not condemn us unheard. In England, every man is deemed innocent until he be proved guilty. You boast of having imported and improved upon all the useful regulations of the mother country, and cannot surely have omitted her most glorious law. Let us then have a fair trial, and God forbid that the course of justice should be impeded."

"You talk well, Sir," said the judge; "but it's of no use here. My chair, Sir, is made of witch-elm, and the whole court is lined with consecrated wood; so you may take your familiars to another market, for here they will avail you nothing."

"Good God!" exclaimed Edric, wringing his hands, "what ignorance! what gross superstition! And yet, in this man's power are our lives!"

"Oh! oh!" said the judge, who saw his despair, though he did not exactly know the cause; "I have brought you to, have I? Yes, yes; I tell you, no incantations will be of any avail here; and so, clerk, call the witnesses—"

The first person examined was the man who had been left in charge of the balloon, and he deposed as follows:—"Why, Sir," said he, scratching his head, as though he supposed wisdom dwelt in his fingers, and that their touch might give a little to his brain, "your honour told me to call out the *posse comitutus*, and set a guard of constables over the gentlemen's whirligig; but I thought as how, seeing it was but a queer-looking thing, and not likely to tempt anybody to steal it, I might as well save the gentlemen from throwing their money away upon a parcel of idle fellows, and keep watch over it myself."

"And so get the reward instead of them," observed the judge.

"Why, your honour," said the fellow, grinning, "I thought they might give something that might do me some good, but that it would be nothing amongst so many."

"Very true!" remarked the judge; "Go on Gregory."

"Well," continued Gregory, "as I was sitting there, thinking of nothing at all, and somehow, I believe, I had fallen into a bit of a dose, I heard a queer sort of a buzzing, and I opened my eyes, and there I saw the gentlemen's whirligig buzzing and puffing like a steam-engine on fire, and i' th' midst o' the smoke I'll take my oath I saw the mummy of King Cheops as plain as I see his worship there sitting in his throne."

"Oh!" groaned the horror-struck crowd; "Oh!" groaned the judge and jury.

"Yes," continued the man; "I'll take my oath, if it was the last word I had to speak, that I saw him there vomiting fire, and his big eyes flaring like a fiery furnace."

"Oh!" groaned the judge, crowd, and jury, a degree louder than before.

"And then," resumed Gregory, something went whiz, and off it all fled together like a flash of lightning—"

"Oh!" shrieked the whole court, in a convulsion of horror. Some of the fair sex in particular, screamed and covered their faces, as though they feared the next exploit of the redoubtable magicians would be to blow up the court, and send them all flying after the resuscitated mummy.

"With your permission, Sir," said Edric, as soon as the tumult had somewhat abated, "this proves nothing against either my friend or myself. We are, in fact, injured by it, and we have a claim against you instead of your being able to substantiate a charge against us. We left our balloon, containing valuable articles, and money to a considerable amount, in your charge, or, at least, in the custody of a man whom you recommended. When we quitted the Pyramid, We, of course, inquired for our balloon—it had vanished; and instead of making us amends for our loss, you throw us into prison and tell us a wild, extravagant story of the disappearance of our property, which no man in his senses can possibly believe."

Another confused murmur, though very different in its character from the former, ran through the court on the conclusion of this speech; and the judge, if such an expression be not profane when speaking of a representative of justice, looked most excessively foolish.

"Had not your worship better call the other witnesses?" whispered the clerk, pitying the dilemma of his principal.

"True, true!" said the Lycurgus[128] of Anglo-Egypt; "our observation is premature, young man; when the case has been proved against you, it will be time enough for you to think of your defence."

Edric bowed assent, and the examination continued. The guide was the next witness.

"Well, Samuel," said the judge; "what do you know about this matter?"

"Why, Sir," replied Samuel, "ye see, my dame and I were sitting by the fire, and we'd got a black pudding, as we was a going to have for our dinners. And so says dame, 'I likes it cut in slices and fried,' and so says I—"

"Hold, fellow!" cried the judge, with great dignity. "Don't abuse the patience of the Court. We have nothing to do with your dame or the black pudding; it is quite irrelevant to the matter now before us. Go on."

But Samuel could not go on; and, like his predecessor in the witness-box, he only stood still and scratched his head.

"Why don't you speak, fellow?" asked the clerk.

"Because I doesn't know what to say," replied Samuel.

"You must tell all you know about this affair, pursued the clerk.

"But I doesn't know where to begin!" rejoined the perplexed witness; "his worship says it is not reverent,"

"Begin with the Pyramid," said the judge; "and, if you can, give a clear account of all that happened after you left the old passage by the moveable block in the wall that was last discovered."

"Why I can't say there was any thing very particular happened, as I know of, Sir," said Samuel, "after that, till we got to the shaft, and then we went down, Sir, you know, as we always does, till we came to the tomb of King Cheops; and then I turned the gentlemen in by themselves, as we always does, for the 'fect, as Parson Snorum calls it.[129] And then I sits me down i' the vault, to wait for 'em, and I'd just rolled myself up, and was dozed asleep, when I hears such a noise as if the Pyramids were all coming tumbling about my ears. So up I jumped and rubbed my eyes, for I did not know very well where I was; and then I saw something that seemed to strike the torches out of the hands of the two great sitting figures, and put them out; and then I saw a great tall figure come gliding by me; and when he came up to the light, I saw his great flaming eyes; and then I fell upon my knees, and he laid hold of my shoulder and griped it. Look, your honour!" laying bare his shoulder as he spoke, and showing the deeply indented marks of the bony fingers of the Mummy. Again a groan of horror and indignation ran through the Court; and when another witness proved that the sarcophagus of Cheops had been examined, and was found empty, the judge seemed to think it was a clear case, and called triumphantly upon Edric for his defence.

"I do not see that what has been proved," said Edric, shuddering in spite of himself, "can affect either my tutor or myself. These people say that a mummy has revived, and, quitting the Pyramid in which he had been so long immured, has flown away with our balloon: but, supposing the tale to be true, what proof have you that we were at all implicated in the business? We were in the Pyramid, it is true; but so was also this man, whom you have brought forward as a witness against us. Supposing it was the intervention of some human aid that roused the Mummy from its tomb —a fact, by the way, by no means proved, why may not he be the agent instead of us? What is there to fix the charge against us? Have we gained any thing by the adventure? Have we not, on the contrary, been serious losers by it? Where is our balloon, and the valuable articles it contained? If we are wizards, it must be confessed that we are very foolish ones; for we have lost our property, and thrown ourselves into prison, without reaping the smallest possible advantage? And if we have the power you seem to attribute to us, why do we stay here to be questioned, when we might so easily fly away in a flame of fire, or turn you all to statues, and walk quietly off without your being able to follow us?"

Every one shuddered, and many turned pale at this speech; seeming to fear that Edric was about to put his suggestions into execution; whilst the judge seemed posed, and in vast perplexity as to what he had better determine;—and the people were dreadfully afraid, lest they might, after all, lose the edifying spectacle of an *auto-da-fé*,[130] for which they had been so impatiently longing.

Edric marked the hesitation of the judge, and endeavoured to improve it to his own advantage.—"For my part," continued he, "I am a British subject, and as such, under the protection of my own Court; my Sovereign has a consul here, and to him I make my appeal. I am neither ignoble, nor unknown in my own country,—my name is Montagu, and I am brother to the celebrated general of that family,—whose victories, no doubt, have reached even this remote province!"

"My dear Mr. Montagu!" said the judge, "I really beg your pardon: why did you not acquaint me sooner with your dignity? I dare say there is no truth at all in the charge:—only assure me upon your honour that you did not touch the mummy, and that you know nothing of what is become of it at present, and I will instantly order you to be set at liberty."

"I certainly do not know what is become of it," replied Edric. "But—"

"No!" interrupted Dr. Entwerfen, coming forward with the air of a determined martyr, "I will not suffer such equivocation.—I would rather perish at the stake, than disavow, for a moment, my opinions, or betray the sacred interests of science with which I feel I am intrusted. No, Sir! my pupil cannot make the public declaration you require. I know he would not—and he cannot if he would;—on the contrary, I avow the fact. We came here for the express purpose of endeavouring to resuscitate the mummy of

Cheops, and I glory in the proud thought that we have succeeded." (a groan of horror.) "Yes, Sir, I do not hesitate to avow openly, that the grand object of my life, for several successive years, has been to detect in what consisted the strange, inexplicable secret of life. We live, Sir, we die: we are born, and we are buried: we know that time, sickness, or violence, may kill us; but who can say in what the mysterious principle of life consists? Various theories have been broached, with which, no doubt, a gentleman of your intelligence and extensive information is well acquainted;—and life has been successively stated to depend upon the heart, the brain, the circulation of the blood, and the respiration of the lungs. All, however, are fallacious; the heart has been wounded, and the brain has been removed, and yet the patient has lived, whilst the operations of respiration and circulation have been kept up for hours, in a body from which the vital spirit had departed. Weighing all these and divers other arguments in my mind, it has struck me, and indeed I may say, that after mature deliberation, I have confidently arrived at the conclusion, that both the faculties which we call life and soul depend entirely upon the nervous system. Do not all philosophers agree that we receive ideas merely through the medium of the senses?[131] And can our senses be operated upon otherwise than through the influence of the nerves? Ergo, the nerves alone convey ideas and sensations to the mind—or rather, the nerves alone are the mind. Not a single instance, I believe, is known in which life remained after the sensorium had been destroyed, or even seriously injured. What then can be more simple than to suppose life resides there? Pursuing this idea, I have long been convinced that where the nervous system remained uninjured, and the appearance of death was only occasioned by a suspension of the operation of the animal functions, that life might be restored, if, by the intervention of any powerful agency, the nervous system could be excited to re-action; and as this, of course, could not be effected where any kind of decomposition had taken place, it appeared to me that a mummy was the only body upon which the experiment could be tried with the least prospect of success. From various circumstances, however, it has never till now been in my power to realize my wishes on this head; but for a few weeks past, my pupil has entertained similar longings to myself; and yesterday saw our hopes accomplished. Yes; I flatter myself there cannot now remain a shadow of doubt to the world, that, in ordinary cases, before decomposition has taken place, that resuscitation is not only possible, but probable, and that dead bodies may be easily restored to life."

The horror and consternation produced by this extraordinary speech, amongst the Anglo-Egyptians who heard it, far exceeded any human powers of description. Their terror at what they considered as the doctor's daring impiety, being considerably augmented by their not understanding above one-tenth part of what he said,—and when he had finished, there was a dead pause which no one dared to interrupt, till a sudden gust of wind happening to blow open the door of the justice's retiring-room, the terrified crowd fell back aghast one upon another, pale and trembling, as though they absolutely expected his Infernal Majesty to appear before them in *propria persona*.[132]

When tranquillity was in some degree restored, the judge ordered the prisoners to be reconducted to prison.

"After the dangerous and impious speech we have just heard," said he, "it would be madness to trust such suspected persons at large; and yet, I would willingly take time to consider the case, and to ascertain whether this young man be indeed the person he represents himself; as, I own, I should be sorry to inflict the full penalty of the law upon the brother of her Britannic Majesty's Commander-in-chief."

Remonstrance was useless, and the prisoners were again conducted to their dungeon where they were heavily chained, and left to ruminate upon the calamities that had befallen them. Far from agreeable were these meditations; for Edric was too angry with the doctor's ill-timed candour to be inclined to speak; and the doctor was too much ashamed of the effect already produced by his eloquence, to wish to make any farther display of it. At length, as his eyes became accustomed to the faint glimmering light admitted into the dungeon, he perceived the wall to which he was chained was covered with hieroglyphics, and endeavoured to divert his chagrin by examining them.

"I congratulate you, Sir," said Edric, when he perceived this, feeling rather indignant at his tutor's coolness—"I congratulate you most sincerely upon your philosophy, and most earnestly do I wish that I could imitate it."

"Ah, Edric!" returned the doctor, "all men are not equally gifted."

"With either the art of making blunders, or forgetting them," said Edric pointedly.

"These hieroglyphics are very curious," observed the doctor, who had his own reasons for not wishing to pursue the subject; "see how beautifully the ancient Egyptians worked in granite. The fine polish they contrived to give this hard substance would be perfectly astonishing, if we did not recollect that they always edged their tools with emerald dust."

"Humph!" said Edric, in a tone which seemed to imply "and what does it matter to me if they did? "The doctor, however, was unabashed, and continued: "You see, as usual, the figure of the bull is frequently repeated here. This wall is evidently built of stones gathered from some ancient ruin. By the way, Edric, I don't think I ever explained to you why the ancient Egyptians chose a bull as one of their deities, or, rather, as their principal one. You know, that anciently the year began in Taurus, though, by the precession of the equinox, it has now advanced past Aries. Well, as the ancient Egyptians found that the sun began its career in Taurus, what could be more natural than that they should identify a bull with the vivifying principle? The same theory may account for that legend of the Chaldeans, which supposes the world to have been produced by a bull's striking chaos with his horn—which horn, by the way, was probably the origin of the fable of Amalthea,[133] or the Horn of Plenty."

Edric made no reply, and the doctor dreading a pause, which might give his pupil an opportunity of upbraiding him, went on:—"Though the Egyptians had a number of divinities, they clearly worshipped only two, viz. the principles of good and evil. Osiris, Isis, Cneph, Phath, Horus, and all their host of inferior deities, were clearly types of the first, and light and life were their essence; whilst Typhon, Campsa, and the malignant deities, exemplified the second, and their attributes were invariably darkness and death."

"For Heaven's sake!" cried Edric, "say no more upon the subject, for it is not in the power of language to describe the horror I have at the mere thought of any thing Egyptian. Let us escape from this fearful country, and I most sincerely hope nothing may ever happen to recall even its recollection to my imagination."

"Such and so changeable are the desires of human life!" said the doctor. "But a few short weeks since, Egypt was the goal of your wishes, and the prospect of re-animating a corpse—"

"Oh! do not mention it!" cried Edric, shuddering. "Oh God! how just am I punished, by the very fulfilment of my unhallowed hopes!—even now the fearful eyes of that hideous Mummy seem to glare upon me; and even now I feel the gripe of its horrid bony fingers on my arm!"

"Oh yes, no doubt," exclaimed the doctor, "he pinched hard. He was a king, and kings should have strong arms, you know."

"For God's sake! do not jest upon such a subject," returned Edric; "a subject so wild and fearful, that I can still scarcely believe but that all which has passed was a dream."

"If it be," said the doctor, "it is one from which I freely avow I should be very happy to awake, for I must confess this prison is not at all to my taste."

"And yet, is it not your fault—?" began Edric.

"Recrimination, Edric, is always folly," interrupted the doctor, who did not now feel very proud of the part he had acted before the magistrate, nor very anxious to have it alluded to;—"and instead of losing time in regretting past errors, it is the part of a wise man to endeavour to find means of remedying them, and avoiding them in future."

"Agreed!" returned Edric; "and as I presume you are now convinced your learned dissertation on the probable seat of human life was, to say the least, ill-timed, we will drop the subject. But, even if we get out of prison, what is to become of us? Our money and valuables were all in the balloon; and here we are, in a foreign country, entirely destitute."

"Not entirely, Edric—not entirely!" cried the doctor, a glow of satisfaction spreading itself again over his face; "no, no; I have guarded against that; ah, what a thing it is to have foresight! Well! some persons are certainly singularly gifted in that line, and it is a happy thing for you that you have somebody to think for you. See here!" displaying the things as he spoke; "here is a bed, bolster, and pillows, ready for inflation; a portable bedstead, linen, soap, pens, ink, paper, candles, fire, knives, forks, spoons, and money; all snugly packed up in my walking-stick!"[134]

"Your supporter," returned Edric, smiling, "as you used to call it; and as it now seems likely to prove, in more senses than one."

"Yes, yes!" cried the doctor, "only let us get out of prison, and all the rest will be easy."

"But that *only*, doctor."

"Of that, we must take time to consider."

"Well, it is some comfort that we are likely to be allowed time enough, as my hint respecting the British consul did not seem thrown away upon the judge. Oh, doctor, if you had not spoken!"

"Why, surely you would not have given him the declaration he required?"

"There was no occasion. He neither wished nor expected more than I had already said. After what I had mentioned of my family, he only wished a decent pretext for setting us at liberty."

"At any rate," said the doctor, by way of changing the subject, "you see my doctrine is proved completely by the resuscitation of the mummy, for it must have been perfectly restored to life and consciousness, or it could not have flown away with the balloon."

"For my part," returned Edric, "I can scarcely believe what has occurred to be real: there must be some deception. And yet, by whom can a deception have been practised, and for what purpose? In short, I am quite bewildered."

The doctor being much in the same condition, could only sympathize with his pupil; and in this state ewe must leave them, whilst we inquire respecting the mysterious object of their speculations.

The mummy thus strangely recalled to life, was indeed Cheops! and horrible were the sensations that throbbed through every nerve as returning consciousness brought with it all the pangs of his former existence, and renewed circulation thrilled through every vein. His first impulse was to quit the tomb in which he had been so long immured, and seek again the regions of light and day. Instinct seemed to guide him to this; for, as yet, a mist hung over his faculties, and ideas thronged in painful confusion through his mind, which he was incapable of either arranging or analyzing.

When however he reached the plain, light and air seemed to revive him and restore his scattered senses; and gazing wildly around he exclaimed, "Where am I? what place is this? Methinks all seems wondrous, new, and strange![135] "Where is my father? And where! oh, where, is my Arsinöe?[136] Alas, alas!" continued he wildly; "I had forgotten—I hoped it was a dream, a fearful dream, for methinks I have been long asleep. Was it, indeed, reality? Are all, all gone? And was that hideous scene true? —those horrors that still haunt my memory like a ghastly vision? Speak! speak!" continued he, his voice rising in thrilling energy as he spoke—"speak! let me hear the sound of another's voice, before my brain is lost in madness. Have I entered Hades, or am I still on earth?—yes, yes, it is still the earth, for there the mighty Pyramid, I caused to be erected towers behind me. Yet where is Memphis? where my forts and palaces? What a dark, smoky mass of buildings now surrounds me!—Can this be the once proud Queen of Cities? Oh, no! I see no palaces, no temples—Memphis is fallen. The mighty barrier that protected her splendour from the waste of waters, must have been swept away by the encroaching inroads of the swelling Nile. But is this the Nile?" continued he, looking wildly upon the river; "sure I must be deceived. It is the fatal river of the dead. No papyrine[137] boats glide smoothly on its surface; but strange, infernal vessels, vomiting forth volumes of fire and smoke.[138] Holy Osiris, defend me! where am I? Where have I been? A misty veil seems thrown upon the face of nature. Awake, awake!" cried he, with a scream of agony; "set me free; I did not mean to slay him!"[139] Then throwing himself violently upon the ground, he lay for some moments, apparently insensible. Then slowly rising, he looked at himself, and a deep, unnatural shuddering convulsed his whole frame. His sensations of identity became confused, and he recoiled with horror from himself: "These are the trappings of a mummy!" murmured he in a hollow whisper. "Am I then dead The next instant, however, he broke into a wild laugh of derision:—"Poor, feeble wretch!" cried he; "what do I fear?—Need *I* tremble, in whose bosom dwells everlasting fire? No—no! let me rather rejoice. I cannot be more wretched; why then should I dread a change? I should rather welcome it with transport, and bravely dare my fate."

At this moment the car of the balloon caught his eye: "Ah! what is that?" cried he; "I am summoned! 'Tis the boat of Hecate, ready to ferry me across the Mærian Lake,[140] to learn my final doom. I come! I come! I fear no judgment! *My hell*[141] is here!" and, striking his bosom, leaped into the car, and stamped violently against its sides.

At this instant Gregory awoke; his terror was not surprising. The dried, distorted features of the Mummy looked yet more hideous than before, when animated by human passions; and his deep hollow voice, speaking in a language he did not understand, fell heavily upon his ear, like the groans of fiends. Gregory tried to scream, but he could not utter a sound. He attempted to fly, but his feet seemed nailed to the spot on which he stood, and he remained with his eyes fixed upon the Mummy, gasping for breath, while a cold sweat distilled from every pore. In the mean time, Cheops had stumbled over the box containing the apparatus for making inflammable air, and striking it violently, had unintentionally set the machinery in motion.

The pipes, tubes, and bellows, instantly began to work; and the Indian-rubber bottle became gradually inflated, till it swelled to an enormous magnitude, and fluttered in the air like an imprisoned bird, beating itself against the massive walls to which it was still attached.

"Still it goes not," cried Cheops, again stamping impatiently." The quicksilver vapour bottle had fallen beneath his feet, and it broke as he trod upon it. The vapour burst from it with inconceivable violence, and tearing the balloon from its fastenings, sent it off through the air, like an arrow darting from a bow.

Volume 1: Chapter 11

In the mean time, Sir Ambrose Montagu had attended the Duke to the Queen's drawing room. The splendour of the English Court at this period defies description. The walls of the room in which the Queen received her guests, were literally one blaze of precious stones, and these being disposed in the form of bouquets, wreaths, and. trophies, were so contrived as to quiver with every movement. These magnificent walls were relieved by a colonnade of pillars of solid gold, around which were twined wreaths of jewels fixed also upon elastic gold wires, so as to tremble every instant. The throne of the Queen was formed of gold filagree[142] beautifully wrought, richly chased and superbly ornamented, whilst behind it was an immense plate of looking-glass, stretching the whole length and height of the apartment, and giving the whole the effect of a fairy palace. The carpet spread upon the floor of this sumptuous saloon was so exact an imitation of green moss, with exquisitely beautiful groups of flowers thrown carelessly upon it, that a heedless spectator might have been completely deceived by the delicacy of their shape and richness of their colouring, and have stooped to pick them up, supposing them to be real. The suit[143] of rooms appropriated to dancing was equally splendid, and fitted up in the same manner save that the floors were painted to imitate the effect of the carpet, and rows of trees were placed on each side, hung with. lamps. This imitative grove was so exquisitely managed, that the spectator could scarcely believe it artificial; and the music for dancing proceeded from its leaves, or from automaton birds[144] placed carelessly amongst its branches.

The dresses of the Queen and her attendants were worthy of the apartment they occupied. Brocaded silks, cloth of gold, embroidered velvets, gold and silver tissues, and gossamer nets made of the spider's web, were mingled with precious stones and superb plumes of feathers in a profusion quite beyond description. The most beautiful of the female habiliments, were robes made of woven asbestos, which glittered in the brilliant light like molten silver. The ladies were all arrayed in loose trowsers,[145] over which hung drapery in graceful folds; and most of them carried on their heads, streams of lighted gas forced by capillary tubes, into plumes, fleurs-de-lis, or in short any form the wearer pleased; which *jets de feu*[146] had an uncommonly chaste and elegant effect. The gentlemen were all clothed in the Spanish style, with slashed sleeves, short cloaks, and large hats, ornamented with immense plumes of ostrich feathers, it being considered in those days extremely vulgar to appear with the head uncovered. It would be difficult, perhaps, to imagine more perfect models of male and female beauty than those which now adorned the Court of Queen Claudia, for the *beau ideal*[147] of the painter's fancy seemed realized, nay surpassed by the noble living figures there collected. The women were particularly lovely, and as they stood gathered round their Queen, or lightly threaded the mazes of the graceful dance, dressed as above described, their brows bound with circlets of precious stones, and their glossy hair hanging in rich luxuriant ringlets upon their ivory shoulders, they looked like a group of Houris,[148] or the nymphs of Circe, ready with sparkling eyes and witching voices to lure men to destruction.

Claudia was very handsome, and though her countenance wanted expression, her noble figure and majestic bearing well qualified her to play her part as Queen amongst this bevy of beauties, with becoming dignity. There is something in the habit of command when it has been long enjoyed, that gives an imposing majesty to the manner, which the parvenu great strive in vain to imitate; and Claudia had this in perfection. The consciousness of beauty, power, and high birth swelled. in her bosom; and even when she wished to be affable, she was only condescending.

She now, however, received. Sir Ambrose most graciously; she gave him her snowy hand to kiss, and addressed. a few words of compliment to him, which sank deep into his heart. It is one of the privileges of greatness easily to excite emotion; one word of commendation from those above us, far outweighs all the laboured flattery of our inferiors. Thus the words of Claudia, and the warm praise she bestowed on Edmund, gave the purest transport to his father's heart; and affected him so violently, that he would have fallen at her feet, had he not been supported by Father Morris, who stood near him.

"I leave you in excellent hands, Sir Ambrose," said Claudia, smiling; "I have known Father Morris from my cradle, and estimate him as one of my dearest and best friends."

So saying, the Queen passed on, whilst Father Morris, with pallid lips and quivering limbs, conducted the Baronet to a sofa, under the shade of the harmonious trees before mentioned. The agitation of the priest was so marked and so unusual, that notwithstanding Sir Ambrose's indisposition, he could not avoid noticing it.

"Good Heavens! what is the matter with you, Father Morris?" exclaimed the Baronet. "I—I—I believe that I am ill," stammered the priest, hastening to fetch a glass of water. By the time he returned, all traces of agitation had vanished from his countenance; and the mind of Sir Ambrose was too much occupied with the thought of Edmund, to suffer him to dwell long upon the circumstance.

The following day was appointed for the triumphal entry of Lord Edmund, and the greatest part of the night preceding it, was passed by Sir Ambrose in the greatest agitation. He could not sleep; and he rose several times from his bed, in excessive anxiety, to listen for the repetition of noises which he fancied he heard: once he opened his window all was still. His room looked into the garden of the palace, which, as we have already mentioned, shelved down to the Thames, and the calm moonlight slept peacefully upon the tall, thick trees, and verdant lawn that spread before him. The evening breeze felt cool and refreshing; but Sir Ambrose sighed, and a strange fear of something he could not wholly define hung over him.

He again retired to bed, and at length sank into a feverish and uneasy dose. At daybreak, a thundering of cannon announced the arrival of the important day. Sir Ambrose started from his pillow at the first discharge, and the solemn sound thrilled through every nerve as it pealed along the sky. Scarcely had its echoes died upon the ear, when another, and another peal succeeded; and the heart of Sir Ambrose throbbed in his bosom almost to suffocation, as he sate,[149] resting his head upon his hands, and striving, though ineffectually, to stop his ears from the solemn sound, which seemed to absorb his every faculty, and strike almost with the force of a blow upon his nerves.

Whilst he was still in this position, Father Morris entered the room. "Come, come, Sir Ambrose!" cried he; "are you not ready? The Queen has sent for us, and the procession is just ready to set off."—Sir Ambrose started: he attempted to dress himself, but his trembling hands refused to perform their office, and Father Morris and Abelard were obliged to attire him, and lead him down to join his friend, the duke, who was waiting for him impatiently.

It has often been said that the anticipation of pleasure is always greater than the reality: this, however, was not the case in the present instance, as the brilliancy of Lord Edmund's triumph was far greater than even the imaginations of the spectators had before dared to conceive. The duke and Sir Ambrose, attended by Father Morris, found the individuals who were to compose the procession of the Queen assembled in the extensive gardens belonging to the superb palace of Somerset House. These fine gardens, spreading their verdant groves along the banks of the river, adorned by all the charms of nature and art, and enriched by some of the finest specimens of sculpture in the world, were now crowded with all the beauty and rank of England, who, waiting for the arrival of their Sovereign, formed an *ensemble* no other nation in the world could hope to imitate.

In the centre walk, appeared the superb Arabian charger of the Queen, led by his grooms, and magnificently caparisoned. His bridle was studded with precious stones, and his hoofs cased in gold; whilst his blue satin saddle and housings were richly embroidered and fringed with the same metal. The noble animal, whose flowing mane and tail swept the ground, paced proudly along, tossing his head on high, and spurning the ground on which he trod, as though conscious he should perform a conspicuous part in the grand pageant about to take place. All now was ready, but yet Queen Claudia did not appear.

"It is very strange, but lately it is always so," said Lord Maysworth to Lord Gustavus de Montfort, who had been for some time engaged in earnest conversation with Father Morris. Lord Gustavus started at the sound of his friend's voice in some apparent confusion, whilst Father Morris replied in his usual soft, insinuating tones, "Perhaps her Majesty may be indisposed, and may have slept rather longer than usual."

"Most likely," returned Lord Maysworth; "yet it is strange the same thing should happen so often—if you remember," continued he, again addressing Lord Gustavus, "I made the same observation the morning of her last levee. Indeed I have frequently made it lately, and I have observed that she looks pale and languid."

"Here she comes, at any rate! and for my part, I think I never saw her look better," said Dr. Hardman, who had now joined them, and who, notwithstanding his violent politics, was one of the physicians of the Court. The indolence of Claudia, which, indeed, seemed daily increasing, having induced her to overlook what another Sovereign would have resented.

Claudia did indeed look well, and her dress suited well with her style of beauty. Her trowsers and vest were of pale blue satin; whilst over her shoulders was thrown a long flowing drapery of asbestos silk, which hanging in graceful folds, swept the ground as she walked along, shining in the sun like a robe of woven silver. On her head, she wore a splendid tiara of diamonds; and in her hand, she bore the regal sceptre, surmounted by a dove, and richly ornamented with precious stones. Thus gorgeously attired, surrounded by the ladies of her household, she issued from her palace; and whilst her kneeling subjects bent in humble homage around her, she mounted her noble charger. Cannon were now fired in rapid succession; the bells of every church rang in merry peals, and martial music mingled in the clamour. The palace gates were thrown open, and the procession poured from them along the streets, where crowds of people bustled to and fro, eager to catch a glimpse of the sumptuous spectacle.

First advanced a long double line of monks, arrayed in sacerdotal pomp, and bearing immensely thick lighted tapers in their hands chanting thanksgiving for the victory They were followed by chorister-boys, flinging incense from silver vases, that hung suspended by chains in their hands, and chanting also; their shrill trebles mingling with the deep bass voices of the priests in rich and mellow harmony. The Queen next appeared, her prancing charger led by grooms, whilst beautiful girls, elegantly attired, walked on each side of their Sovereign, scattering flowers in her path from fancy baskets made of wrought gold. Behind the Queen, rode the ladies of her household and the principal nobles of her Court, the superb plumes of ostrich feathers in the large Spanish hats of the latter, with their immense mustachios, and open shirt collars, giving them the air of some of Vandyck's[150] best pictures. As they rode slowly along, their noble Arabians paced proudly, and champed the bit, impatient of restraint.

The ladies of the Court, superbly dressed in open litters, next appeared, borne upon the shoulders of men splendidly clad in rich liveries. Amongst these, were Elvira and Rosabella.

These were followed by monks and boys as before, but singing a somewhat different strain. It was now a chant of glory and triumph that swelled upon the ear, for these preceded the duke and Sir Ambrose; who, the one as uncle to the Queen, and the other as father of the expected hero, occupied the post of honour. The two venerable old men sate hand-in-hand in a sumptuous car drawn by two Arabian horses, and were followed by a large body of the Queen's guards.

The costliness and variety of the dresses worn this day were quite beyond description. Many of the ladies had turbans of woven glass; whilst others carried on their hats very pretty fountains made of glass dust, which, being thrown up in little jets by a small perpetual motion wheel,[151] sparkled in the sun like real water, and had a very singular effect.

In this manner the procession advanced towards Blackheath Square, said to be the largest and finest in the world, where the meeting between the Queen and her general was appointed to take place. Amongst the numerous balloons that floated in the air, enjoying this magnificent spectacle, was one containing Father Murphy, Clara, Mrs. Russel and Abelard—Clara's youth preventing her joining in the procession—and nothing could be more enthusiastic than their delight, as they looked down upon the splendid scene below them. Few things, indeed, could be imagined finer than. the sight of. this gorgeous *cortege*,[152] winding slowly along a magnificent street, supposed to be five miles long, leading from Blackfriar's Bridge, through Greenwich, to Blackheath.

Sumptuous rows of houses, or rather palaces, lined the sides of this superb street; the terraces and balconies before which were crowded with persons of all ages, beautifully attired, waving flags of different colours, richly embroidered and fringed with gold, whilst festoons of the choicest flowers hung from house to house. We have already said the air was thronged with balloons,[153] and the crowd increased every moment. These aërial machines, loaded with spectators till they were in danger of breaking down, glittered in the sun and presented every possible variety of shape and colour. In fact, every balloon in London or the vicinity had been put in requisition, and enormous sums paid, in some cases, merely for the privilege of hanging to the cords which attached the cars, whilst the innumerable multitudes that thus loaded the air, amused themselves by scattering flowers upon the heads of those who rode beneath.

Besides balloons, a variety of other modes of conveyance fluttered in the sky. Some dandies bestrode aërial horses, inflated with inflammable air;[154] whilst others floated upon wings, or glided gently along, reclining gracefully upon aërial sledges, the last being contrived so as to cover a sufficient column of air for their support. As the procession approached the river, the scene became still more animated; innumerable barges of every kind and description shot swiftly along, or glided smoothly over the sparkling water. Some floated with the tide in large boat-like shoes; while others, reclining on couch-shaped cars, formed of mother of pearl, were drawn forward by inflated figures representing the deities or monsters of the deep.

When the Queen reached a spot near Greenwich, where, through a spacious opening, the river, in all its glorious majesty, burst upon her, she paused, and commanded her trumpeters to advance and sound a flourish. They obeyed, and after a short pause were answered by those of Lord Edmund; the sound, mellowed by the distance, pealing along the water in dulcet harmony. Delighted with. this response, which announced the arrival of Lord Edmund and his troops at the appointed place, the procession of the Queen was again set in motion, and in a short time arrived at Blackheath.

The noble square in which the meeting was to take place, was already thronged with soldiers; whilst every house that surrounded it was covered with spectators. No trees or fantastical ornaments spoiled the simple grandeur of this immense space; the houses that surrounded it, built in exact uniformity, each having a peristyle supported by Corinthian pillars. and a highly decorated façade, looked like so many Athenian temples. As the *cortege* of the Queen entered the square, the soldiers formed an opening to receive it, and reverentially knelt on each side, with reversed arms, and bending banners as she passed. In the centre was Lord Edmund, surrounded by his staff, all in polished armour for since an invention bad been discovered of rendering steel perfectly flexible, it had. been generally used in war. Lord Edmund's helmet was thrown off, and his fine countenance was displayed to the greatest advantage, as he and his officers threw themselves from their war-steeds to kneel before the Queen. Claudia, also, descended from her charger, and as she stood in her glittering robes, surrounded on all sides by her kneeling subjects, she looked, indeed, their Sovereign. With becoming dignity, she addressed a few words of thanks and commendation to Lord Edmund; whose graceful figure was shown to the utmost advantage, as he knelt before her, his thick, dark, brown hair falling in clustering curls over his noble forehead: and his elegant form attired in a suit of closely fitting armour, over which, upon the present occasion, was thrown a short cloak of fine scarlet cloth, richly embroidered with gold, and fastened in front. By a cord and superb tassals;[155] made entirely of the same metal. In short, he looked a living personification of the God of War.

The Queen raised him from the ground in the most gracious manner; and then turning to the still kneeling soldiers, she made a short speech to them, of the same nature as that which she had addressed to Lord Edmund: after which, again mounting her palfrey, she made Lord Edmund ride by her side, and prepared to return to town. Edmund's quick eye had discovered, and exchanged looks of affection with his father and friends, though the etiquette of his present situation did not permit him to do more; and he now rode proudly by the side of the Queen, gracefully bowing to the assembled crowd as he passed, his heart beating with pleasure at the thought that his triumph was witnessed by those most dear to him; whilst his noble Arabian tossed his head and champed his bit as he pranced forward, as though he also knew the part he was performing in the splendid ceremony.

Acclamations rent the sky as the procession advanced, and showers of roses were rained down upon the Queen and her general from the balloons above; from which, also, flags waved, in graceful folds, and flapped in the wind, as the balloons floated along the sky. Every one seemed delighted with the grandeur of this splendid pageant; but no one experienced more pleasure than Clara Montagu and her companions; the raptures of Mrs Russel being so excessive, that, like the spectators of the stag-hunt on the lake of Killarney,[156] she was in imminent danger of throwing herself overboard in her ecstasy: whilst Clara clasped her hands together, in all the transports of childish delight, her sparkling eyes and animated looks bearing ample witness to her gratification.

"What shouting! what a noise!" exclaimed Mr. Abelard; "I declare it puts me in mind of the acclamations in the time of Nero, when the Romans shouted in concert, and birds fell from the skies with the noise!"

"How well the Queen looks!" observed Mrs. Russel. "It was said a short time since, that she had lost her appetite and could get no rest; but I think she doesn't seem to have much the matter with her now."

"Evelina says she's being poisoned," cried Clara, "and that the people say that it would be no great matter if she was, for then they would have to choose a Queen for themselves, and they might make what terms they pleased with her."

An awkward pause followed this speech which no one seemed inclined to break, till Clara exclaimed, "Dear me! what a pretty horse my cousin Edmund rides!"

"I think that's a purtier comes afther him," said Father Murphy.

"What, that one with his head hanging down and his mane sweeping the ground?" asked Mrs. Russel.

"Yes.—And sure, it's a very purty young man that walks by the side of him; so he is," replied Father Murphy.

"His hands are chained, so you see he is a prisoner;" observed Abelard.

"Sure, and it's a barbarous custom that of putthing chains about the hands of the prisoners," said Father Murphy, "as if it was not bad enough to be a prisoner without looking like one."

"Poor fellow!" cried Clara, "I should like to go and let him loose. He looks very melancholy!"

"How great Lord Edmund looks!" exclaimed Mrs. Russel: "I declare if he were a real king he couldn't have a grander appearance. And then to see the poor old gentleman his father, sitting there hand-in-hand with my master. I declare it does my heart good to look at them!"

Whilst the occupiers of the balloons were thus enjoying the splendid scene below them, the pleasure of the exalted personages they admired, had not been inferior to their own. The Duke in particular, seemed almost out of his senses with joy. His impatience during the whole procession from London had been excessive; and the moment he saw Edmund, he rubbed his hands in ecstasy, and jumping up in his seat almost overturned Sir Ambrose, who was also bending forward eagerly gazing upon his son.

"There! there he is!" cried the Duke. "See how handsome he looks! Oh the young rogue! There'll be many a heart lost to-day, I warrant me! Look at him, how the colour comes into his cheeks when the Queen speaks to him! Now he helps her on her horse—and now see, he's looking round for us! There I caught his eye—Look, Sir Ambrose! Don't you see him?—Surely you arn't[157] crying. my old friend? Why you'll make me as great a fool as yourself—God bless him! I am sure I don't know any thing we have to cry at; but we are two old simpletons."

Father Morris, who had joined the procession of monks, was almost as much affected as his patron. Indeed his affection for Edmund seemed the only human passion remaining in his ascetic breast. Cold even to frigidity in bis exterior, Father Morris seemed to regard the scenes passing around him but a the moving figures of a magic lantern, which glittered for a moment in glowing colours, and then vanished into darkness, leaving no trace behind:—whilst he, unmoved as the wall over which the gaudy but shadowy pageant had passed, saw them alternately vanish and re-appear without the slightest motion being excited in his mind. Under this statue-like appearance, however, Father Morris concealed passions as terrific as those which might be supposed to throb in the breast of a demon: though never did his selfcommand seem relaxed for a moment, but when the interests of Edmund were in question. On the present occasion, joy swelled in his bosom almost to suffocation, as he railed his eyes to Heaven, and, wringing his hands together, exclaimed, "Oh! it is too—too much!"

There is something indescribably affecting in seeing strong emotion expressed by those. who are generally calm and unimpassioned; thus Sir Ambrose, by whom this burst of feeling was quite unexpected, gazed at the confessor with the utmost surprise, and strange to tell, though he had known him nearly twenty years, it was the first time he had seen his head completely uncovered. Father Morris's cowl had now fallen off entirely, and displayed the bead of a man between forty and fifty, whose fine features bore the traces of what he had endured. His noble expressive brow seemed wrinkled more by care than age. and his sable locks had evidently become "grizzled here and there,"[158] prematurely. Sir Ambrose gazed upon him intently, for the peculiar expression of his features seemed to recall some half-forgotten circumstance to his mind, dimly obscured, however, by the mist of time. The earnestness with which he regarded the monk, seemed at length to remind the latter of his imprudence. He started, and, whilst a deep crimson flushed his usually sallow countenance, he hastily resumed his cowl, and appeared again to the eyes of the spectators, the same cold, unimpassioned, abstracted being as before.

The ovation had now nearly reached Blackfriars' bridge, at the entrance to which, a triumphal arch had been erected. The moment the Queen and her heroic general passed under it, a small figure of Fame was contrived to descend from the entablature, and, hovering over the hero, to drop a laurel crown upon his head. Shouts of applause followed this well-executed device; and the passengers in the balloons wondering at the noise, all pressed forward at the same moment to ascertain the cause of such continued acclamations. The throng of balloons became thus every instant more dense, whilst some young city apprentices having hired each a pair of wings for the day, and not exactly knowing how to manage them, a dreadful tumult ensued; and the balloons became entangled with the winged heroes and each other in inextricable confusion.[159]

The noise now became tremendous; the conductors of the balloons swearing at each other the most refined oaths, and the ladies screaming in concert. Several balloons were rent in the scuffle and fell with tremendous force upon the earth; whilst some cars were torn from their supporting ropes, and others roughly overset. Luckily, however, the whole of England was at this time so completely excavated, that falling upon the surface of the earth was like tumbling upon the parchment of an immense drum, and consequently only a deep hollow sound was returned as cargo after cargo of the demolished balloons struck upon it; though some of them rebounded several yards with the violence of the shock.

Amongst those who fell from the greatest height, and of course rebounded most violently, were the unfortunate individuals who accompanied Clara, an unlucky apprentice having poked his right wing through the silk of their balloon, in endeavouring to avoid the charge of an aërial horseman, who found his Æolian[160] steed too difficult to manage in the confusion. The car containing our friends was in consequence precipitated to earth so rapidly, as for the moment to deprive them of breath.

"Sure, and I'm killed entirely!" cried Father Murphy.

"Oh, my bonnet! my beautiful bonnet!" sobbed Mrs. Russel; whilst Clara, dreadfully frightened, began to cry; and Abelard, whose ideas were generally a long time travelling to his brain, particularly upon occasions of sudden alarm, stood completely silent, stupidly gazing about him, as though he had not the least notion what could possibly have happened. Indeed, it was till a full hour afterwards, that he found himself sufficiently recovered to exclaim, "Dear me! I do think we were very near being killed!"

The confusion in the air still continued; piercing screams that demons were amongst them, mingled horribly with- the crashing of balloons, the cries of the sufferers, and the successive falling of heavy weights. The situation of the crowd low, however, was infinitely worse than that of those above. The momentum of the falling bodies being fearfully increased by the distance they had to descend, those beneath had no chance of escape, and were inevitably crushed to death by the weight, whilst the agonizing shrieks of the unfortunate wretches who saw their danger coming from a distance, yet were so jammed together in the crowd that they could not fly, rang shrilly upon the ear, and pierced through every heart.

At this moment a dreadful scream rang through the crowd, and the horse of Queen Claudia, his bridle broken, his housings torn, his nostrils distended, and his sides streaming with gore, rushed past— "Oh God! the Queen! the Queen!" burst from every voice, and one general rush took place towards the spot from whence the cry had proceeded.

Beneath the triumphal arch, and partially sheltered by its shade, lay the bleeding body of Claudia, supported by Edmund. By her side, knelt Rosabella, who, assisted by Father Morris, was applying restoratives; whilst Henry Seymour was endeavouring to restore Elvira, who had fainted in his arms, and Sir Ambrose, his face streaming with blood, stood at a little distance amongst a group of courtiers, several of whom had also experienced severe injuries. The tumult in the air still continued; groans and shrieks and exclamations, that the atmosphere was supernaturally haunted, were heard in many places; and some persons declared the accident to be the work of demons. A current of wind had blown those balloons that had become unmanageable across the city while the others, their occupiers, terrified almost to madness appeared still contending with some fearful monster in the sky.

The courtiers, however, heeded not this disturbance; for all their attention was occupied by the apparently expiring Queen, whose long-drawn sighs, and convulsed bosom, seemed to threaten her instant dissolution.

"She's gone!" cried Lord Gustavus de Montfort, as her bosom heaved with a deep, heavy sigh, and then all was still.

"Yes, she's dead!" repeated Lord Noodle.

"She is certainly dead!" reiterated Lord Doodle.[161]

And then these sapient counsellors of the apparently departed Queen shook their wise heads in sympathy.

"Hush! she breathes!" cried Lord Edmund.

For some moments, the courtiers stood in breathless anxiety watching the body, and fearing to move lest they should break the awful silence that prevailed, though their hearts throbbed till the pulsations were almost audible.

Fearful was the pause that now ensued! All were suffering from the torments of hope or fear; for all knew that the interests of the whole community hung upon her breath. Most of the courtiers either hoped to gain places, or feared to lose them, whilst all trembled at the uncertainty that seemed to rest upon their future destiny, and the prospect of the anarchy which the purposed mode of electing their future Sovereign might create. The interest which the fate of the Queen excited was thus intense, and the courtiers hung over her body with streaming eyes and motionless limbs to watch the result.

At this instant, a fearful and tremendous yell ran through the air; and the car containing the Mummy, which had been for some time entangled with the other balloons, fell to the ground with tremendous force, close to the expiring Queen. The gigantic figure of Cheops started from it as it fell—his ghastly eyes glaring with unnatural lustre upon the terrified courtiers, who ran screaming with agony in all directions, forgetting every thing but the horrid vision before them.

Volume 1: Chapter 12

The tumult had now nearly subsided. The late busy crowd fled, uttering shrieks of horror and dismay; and of all the countless mass of human beings that had so lately thronged around, none remained save Edmund and Father Morris, who supported Claudia; and the Duke and Henry Seymour, who still remained near the insensible form of Elvira; whilst they, pale and immoveable as the sculptured marble of the tomb, their eyes chained as though by magic, upon the horrid vision before them, waiting in fearful expectation of what was next to happen, scarcely daring to move or breathe, the solemn silence that prevailed being only broken by the convulsive gasps of the expiring Queen, presented an awful change from the busy hum of thousands which had so lately filled the air.

"Where am I?" exclaimed Cheops, gazing wildly around—his deep sepulchral voice thrilling through every nerve:—"Where is Arsinöe? They seize her! They tear her from me! Curses on the wretches!—May Typhon's everlasting vengeance pursue them with its fury, and may their hearts wither, gnawed by the never-dying snake!"

The Mummy gnashed his teeth as he spoke, and the gloom which gathered on his dark brow grew black as night. All shuddered as that horrid glance of eternal hatred seemed to freeze their blood. They turned away involuntarily; and when they looked again, the spectre had disappeared. The shattered remains of the balloon alone lay before them rent to atoms; for happening to cross London just at the moment of the greatest confusion, it had become entangled in the crowd, and, notwithstanding the strong material of which it was composed, it had been rent asunder in the scuffle, and had fallen with its fearful occupier to the ground.

"Good God!" cried Father Morris, after a short pause; "what a horrid vision! what can it mean!"

"It seemed an Egyptian Mummy," said Edmund, shuddering; "and it spoke that language. But what can have resuscitated it? What human power can have recalled to life, a being so long immured[162] in the silent tomb!"

"Perhaps the vehicle he came in may contain something to explain the mystery," said Henry Seymour.

At this moment several persons ran past screaming with terror, and exclaiming that they had seen a demon. When the confusion excited by these trembling fugitives had a little subsided, a few of the courtiers began also to make their appearance, and return to their posts near the Queen. But all were pale, and they started at every sound, seeming ready, at the least alarm, to take flight again as expeditiously as before.

Claudia still lay insensible; her heaving chest and deep convulsive sobs for breath, alone betraying signs of life. But her fate no longer excited the deep, overwhelming interest it had done before. Whispers of wonder and superstitious horror mingled with the hopes and fears inspired by her danger; and her removal to the palace was almost regarded with indifference, so completely were the minds of men occupied by the strange spectacle they had so lately witnessed.

Every one, indeed, neither thought nor spoke of any thing but the Mummy; and a thousand rumours, each more extravagant than the last, spread from mouth to mouth respecting it. Men stood in groups whispering to each other, and scarcely daring to stir without a companion: nay, even then, creeping from place to place, looking cautiously around, and starting at every noise, as though they feared the awful visitor was returned: whilst the sages of the country gravely shook their heads, and declared that what had taken place was evidently a visitation from Heaven, in punishment of the sins of mankind. An indefinable presentiment of evil hung over the spirits of all.

Gloom, indeed, spread through every class of society: all dreaded they knew not what—and all shrunk with horror from the thought of supernatural agency. There is an invincible feeling implanted by Nature in the mind of man, which makes him shudder with disgust at any thing that invades her laws.

The body of the Queen being removed, attended by her physicians and the ladies of her household, the rest of the assembled courtiers gathered round the balloon; and exclamations of terror and surprise broke from their lips when they discovered it to be the same in which Edric and Dr. Entwerfen had so short a time before taken their departure for Egypt. The whole truth now seemed to flash upon them.

"I thought how it would be," said Lord Maysworth; "you know I told you, Lord Gustavus, that in my opinion it was an expedition that could never possibly do any good—but you were of a different belief."

"My Lord," returned Lord Gustavus, solemnly, "thinking as I think, and as I am convinced every one who hears me must think, or at least ought to think, it is my deliberate opinion, that the expedition of my youthful friend and his learned tutor was both admirably planned and well concocted, and that if it have failed in its ulterior object, it has been solely owing to some of those unforeseen events which sometimes do occur even in the best regulated arrangements, and which it was utterly impossible for any human ability entirely to ward off and avert."

"Edric's balloon! Impossible!" cried Sir Ambrose, rushing forward to ascertain the fact, and forgetting all his anger against his son in his anxiety for his fate. "Yes! yes!" continued he, looking at some of the things, as they were drawn forth and exhibited by different persons in the crowd; "those were Edric's books—that was his desk. Oh! my son! my son! what is become of him?"

Many sympathized with the unfortunate father, and more eagerly questioned each other as to the probable meaning of what they saw. No one, however, could give any explanation; and all was confusion and dismay. The bosom of Edmund, after the first moment of excitation had passed, was racked with anguish too bitter to allow him to feel curious even to know his brother's fate. But a few hours before, love and fortune seemed to unite in showering their choicest blessings upon his head, and now he was the most wretched of mankind; for if Claudia died, Rosabella or Elvira must be queen; and if Elvira should be chosen, all hopes of becoming her husband must be lost.

"Oh, God!" cried he, striking his forehead in agony, "why was I reserved for this? Why did I not perish fighting the battles of my country? And why was I saved only to be mocked with the hope of happiness, which, just as it seemed within my grasp, flies from me for ever? Wretch that I am! would that I had been never born, or at least had died in my nurse's arms, and thus escaped the tormenting pangs that now drive me to distraction!"

Whilst Edmund thus raved, the eye of Rosabella followed his every movement, and seemed with a fiend-like pleasure to exult in his agonies. "I am avenged," thought she; "he now feels what I have so often suffered. But this is not all; he must be probed to the quick ere he can know the bitter vengeance of a woman scorned."

Whilst these violent emotions were convulsing the bosoms of all around, the old duke knelt by the side of Elvira, gazing upon her with the most intense anxiety. Her gentle and feminine nature had been overpowered at seeing the blood of Claudia, and she still lay insensible, looking more exquisitely lovely than fancy can conceive. The beauty of Elvira was of the most soft and feminine description; long silken eyelashes shaded her dark hazel eyes, and gave them an expression more voluptuous than brilliant, whilst nothing could exceed the delicacy of her complexion, or the beauty of her full rosy lips. The figure of Elvira might not have served as the model of a courageous heroine, but it would have suited admirably for an Houri; and lovely as she always was, she had perhaps never looked more so than at this moment, as the returning blood softly retinted her cheeks, and her eyes gradually unclosed. Lord Edmund gazed upon her, till, maddened by the thought that he must lose her for ever, he could no longer endure his own sensations, and, darting amongst the crowd, he endeavoured to fly from the world and from himself.

The duke, on the contrary, saw the recovery of his daughter with unalloyed transport, for though he loved Edmund, and wished to have him for a son-in-law, he was by no means insensible to the prospect of seeing his daughter a Queen, and his breast throbbed with violent emotions, to which had long been a stranger.

In the mean time the Mummy had stalked solemnly through the city, urged more by instinct than design; the mist that still clung over him, making him seem like one wandering in a dream. Yet still he advanced; his path, like that of a destroying angel, spreading consternation as he went, and all he met flying horror-stricken from his sight: many, however, when the monster had passed, crept softly back to gaze after him, and amongst this number was Mrs. Russel, in whose breast curiosity, that vice of low minds, reigned predominant.

The moment their balloon fell, Mrs. Russel, attended by her faithful Abelard, had hurried home, leaving Clara in the care of Father Murphy; lest, as she said, in the confusion that might ensue, the servants might be induced to leave the Duke's house, and some evil disposed personages might strip it of its contents. Urged by this prudent motive, Mrs. Russel hastened home, and finding all safe, was just about to retire to re-arrange her disordered dress; when one of the servants rushed into the room with the account of a fearful spirit having been seen in the Strand, whose mysterious appearance, coupled with the accident that had happened to the Queen, seemed to portend some dreadful calamity which was about to fall upon the country.

"What is it like?" asked Mrs. Russel; "have you seen it, Evelina?"

"Oh yes, ma'am!" cried the panting girl; "its eyes flare like fire, and it stares so wildly round it! and as it went along, it saw a dead cat lying in the street; and it knelt down and took the creature up, and kissed it, and lamented over it[163] in such a strange way, and in such a strange language! I never heard any thing like it in my life."

"Oh, dear! I should like to see it!" cried Mrs. Russel, flying to the door, and holding it half open to secure a retreat in case of necessity. Just as she reached the street, however, fate, as though willing to gratify her curiosity, occasioned the Mummy to turn back; and with that kind of half pleasure and half pain, with which the good people of England sometimes delight to. gaze upon any thing horrible, Mrs. Russel continued to look as it rapidly approached her, till, as it reached the door, to her infinite horror it stalked towards it. Awestruck and trembling, Mrs. Russel retreated. The Mummy followed her. He stretched his hand out to her. She shrunk back aghast from his touch. "Lead on!" cried he with a voice of thunder. Mrs. Russel could bear no more, and she fled screaming to her own apartment, where her lover was awaiting her return, impatient to delight her attentive ears with a few more of his poetical effusions.

Absorbed as Abelard was, however, he was roused by this unexpected intrusion, and the blood ran chilly through bis veins, as he saw the tall majestic figure of Cheops stride across the apartment. His athletic stature, bis dark swarthy complexion, and his strongly marked features, aided by the fearful lustre of his piercing eyes, gave to his figure, swathed as it yet was in the vestments of the grave, a supernatural grandeur that thrilled through every nerve of Abelard's frame, and he shrank back with horror as his fearful visitant stalked past him.

Cheops saw his terror and smiled in proud disdain as he threw himself upon a couch, placed near a window looking upon the garden, which, as we have before stated, shelved down to the river. There he lay, his eyes fixed upon the majestic Thames, whilst Abelard and Mrs. Russel gazed with trembling limbs and pallid lips at the strange intruder, without daring either to approach or disturb him.

"Thus have I watched the Nile," said Cheops, his awful voice sounding as from the tomb, "whilst the gently rising waters have gradually swelled into the flood which was to pour joy and plenty over the land:—and thus, too, have I lain, gazing upon its streams, when, the purpose of all-bounteous Nature having been fulfilled, it has sunk back, slowly retiring to its natural bed. But, oh! how different were the feelings that then throbbed in my breast, to the corroding fire that now consumes me!—Oh! Osiris! what horrid thoughts flash through my brain!—they come like overwhelming floods pouring from heaven to the great deep, sweeping all before them in one mighty ruin.—Oh! Arsinöe! by the fell rites of Typhon, there's madness in the thought!"

Then springing from the couch, his eyes glared with yet fiercer brilliancy as he flashed them round, whilst Abelard and Mrs. Russel, terrified beyond the power of expression, flew towards the door, eyeing the motions of their dangerous guest with feelings of unspeakable horror. The storm of passions in the breast of Cheops, however, though tremendous, seemed soon allayed; for ere many moments had elapsed, he sank again upon the couch in a kind of lethargy, which, if it were not slumber, seemed at least to imply a temporary cessation from pain.

"Thank God!" whispered Abelard, as he motioned to Mrs Russel to creep out of the apartment. She tremblingly obeyed; and the moment she thought herself in safety, she threw herself upon her knees, and thanked God with more fervour than she had ever done before in her whole life; whilst the servants, who were all assembled in the ante-room, crowded round her, trembling and with pallid cheeks and white lips, clustering together like bees swarming round their queen.

"Oh, madam! madam!" exclaimed Angelina, in a whisper, "what will become of us? A serous moisture[164] transudes from every pore in my body with the chilliness of death, and my very hair erects itself with horror upon my head."

"And my heart throbs with such violence," said Cecilia, "that the whole arterial system seems deranged."

"It is evidently an Egyptian Mummy," observed Abelard and, as he seldom spoke, every word he uttered was listened to as an oracle. "Its language and its dress bespeak its origin, but by what strange event it has been resuscitated—"

At this moment a sharp knock at the door made the terrified servants all spring closer together, clinging to each other in an agony of nervous horror, and not one daring to approach the door. The knocking and ringing, however, at length became so violent, as to rouse Abelard to give the clamorous intruders entrance. It was Father Morris and Sir Ambrose.

"Oh, Abelard!" cried the latter, panting for breath; "have you heard the news? The Queen is certainly dying. And every one says the demon that appeared this morning has killed her."

"What, the Mummy?" asked Abelard. "Have you heard of it then?" cried Sir Ambrose eagerly.

"It is now in this house," said Mrs. Russel.

"In this house!" repeated Sir Ambrose with a faint scream; whilst Father Morris, who had looked pale and exhausted when he entered the hall, became still paler, and seemed scarcely able to support himself.

"To arms!" cried Cheops from the inner room; "the Palli are upon us! Cowards that we are, the enemy are at our gates!"

Screaming, and scarcely knowing where they went, the terrified servants tumbled over each other in the hastiness of their retreat, huddling themselves together in a heap, yet keeping their eyes fixed upon the door from which they expected the spectre to appear, as though charmed by the fascination of a rattlesnake.

A loud crash now produced a fresh scream; then all was still. After a long pause, which seemed. of endless duration, Father Morris, evidently with a dreadful effort, roused himself and advanced—

"Death itself is not so horrid as this suspense," said he, as he resolutely threw open the door of the room, which had contained the Mummy, and entered it. It was empty—but the broken frame-work of the window seemed to point out in what manner the awful visitor had made his exit.

It was with infinite difficulty that Mrs. Russel could be persuaded to return to this room; and when she did, the remainder of the day was passed by her, and every domestic of the mansion, in fear and trembling. When they spoke, it was in whispers, and when they moved, they crept along with stealthy noiseless steps, as though they feared the echo of their own footsteps; the eyes of all fixed timidly upon the broken window, through which the fearful stranger had disappeared.

Slowly and heavily the hours rolled on with Mrs. Russel and her constant Abelard, till , till the time appointed for dinner arrived: the servants, as they served the meal, looking timidly around, instead of regarding the dishes they carried in their hands, and the family scarcely daring to eat, and only speaking in whispers, whilst they started every moment, fancying the wild eyes of Cheops again glared upon them, and his deep hollow voice again rang in their ears; and their own tones sounded strangely hoarse and unnatural. Yet as the bottle circulated their terrors dissipated, and Abelard had just begun again to breathe some of his tenderest effusions, when the crashing of branches in the garden announced the return of the spectre, and the laugh of Cheops, strange, wild, and unearthly, again rang in their ears, like the yell of a demon; the servants, terrified at the appalling sound, listened for a moment, their limbs shaking in every joint; their teeth chattering in their heads; and terror blanching their lips and cheeks to a ghastly paleness, till, as the hideous noise increased, they could hear no more, and springing from their seats they fled shrieking from the room.

In the mean time, the sensations these extraordinary events had created amongst the people were indescribable. Strange rumours and contradictory reports were circulated, and the most incredible stories invented of all that had passed. The minds of men became bewildered; they knew not what to credit nor what to think; a gloomy presentiment hung over them; they seemed to feel some fearful change was at hand, but scarcely knew what to hope or what to fear. Business was at a stand: people indeed gathered together in the shops, but it was only to whisper secretly to each other, strange mysterious stories of the late marvellous events, which they dared not breathe in public. The extremes of ignorance and civilization tend alike to produce credulity, and. the wildest and most improbable stories were as greedily swallowed by the most enlightened people in the world, as they could have. been even by a horde or uncultivated barbarians.

The family of the Duke of Cornwall retired early to rest at the close of the eventful day we have been speaking of, hoping to lose in sleep the remembrance of the harassing events they had so lately witnessed. Lord Edmund had returned soon after the disappearance of the Mummy; but he locked himself in the chamber prepared for him, and refused to see any one, his mind being too much agitated for him to endure the common forms of society. All was soon quiet throughout the mansion.

It was midnight when, a tall figure, wrapped in a large cloak, appeared slowly gliding with catlike steps through the garden. It cautiously avoided the light, and. crept along the shadiest walks and thickest allies, carefully shrouding itself from observation, and endeavouring, by availing itself of the shelter of the trees, the better to conceal its movements. At the extremity of the garden was a terrace very little used; the door, indeed, leading to it had been so long closed up, as to be nearly forgotten, and yet it was towards this unfrequented spot that the mysterious figure directed its course. The long neglected door slowly opened, and the stream of light it admitted was obscured for a moment by a passing shade; and then all seemed dark, silent, and mysterious as before.

"It certainly went that way," said a voice, the preciseness of which marked it. as belonging to Abelard; "and it was a real, tangible, material form, as I saw its shadow intercept the light when the door was opened and it passed through."

"It is quite impossible," cried Mrs. Russel, who having been induced by the romantic butler to take a ramble with him by moonlight, had also witnessed this strange apparition; "you must be mistaken Mr. Abelard, for that door does not appear to have been opened this age. It is even nailed up, as you may see yourself if you examine it."

"It is very strange," said Abelard, after he had tried the door and found it immoveable; "I certainly saw it open."

"It must have been an optical delusion," resumed Mrs. Russel; "the retina of the eye is sometimes strangely affected, and represents objects quite different to what they really are."

"I must consult Father Morris about it tomorrow, for in my opinion it was certainly the Mummy spectre."

"La! do you think so, Mr. Abelard? why then didn't you speak to it?"

"I will if it comes again," returned Abelard.

"Oh! there it is!" cried Mrs. Russel; and the worthy pair flew back to the house, screaming in concert, and without once daring to look behind them. Scarcely, however, had the last echo of their footsteps died away upon the ear, when the figure emerged from the recess in which it had lain concealed, and again crept slowly towards the door leading to the terrace.

"Hist! Marianne!" exclaimed the stranger, pausing for a reply; but all was still. "Marianne!" repeated he still louder—"Fools! dolts! idiots!" continued he, stamping violently, as he still found his call of no avail; "they have kept me so long with their cursed folly, that she is gone. Eternal misery haunt them for their officious babbling! By heaven! if they had had the sense to climb the wall, I had been lost: but hark, she comes!"

The door now slowly opened, and a female figure holding a light appeared.

"How is she?" cried the stranger.

"Better," returned the female.

"Then it is past the power of man to kill her," resumed the first; and rushing wildly past his companion, he buried himself in the deepest recesses of the grove.

VOLUME 2

Volume 2: Chapter 1

Father Morris, when Abelard and Mrs. Russel confessed to him the following morning the strange spectre they had witnessed, treated the whole as the mere vision of their heated imaginations, and refusing to listen to any of their surmises respecting it, prepared to attend the Queen, who, finding herself sufficiently recovered to be able to attend to the duties of religion, had, from the general reputation of his superior sanctity, sent for him to confess her. Her Majesty, indeed, seemed rapidly improving, and the hopes of Edmund reviving with her health, he passed every hour he could abstract from the duties of his station at the feet of his adored Elvira, his love for whom seemed increased by the imminence of the danger he bad just escaped, of losing her for ever.

In this manner several days had passed, and the strange visit of the Mummy, and the accident of the Queen, had already taken their place on the shelf with the other *évenemens passés*[165] of the day; when one morning Sir Ambrose was startled by an earnest message from the Duke of Cornwall, entreating him to come to him without delay. Sir Ambrose immediately obeyed the summons, and found the duke walking up and down his study in a state of the greatest agitation, which Father Morris was vainly endeavouring to tranquillize.

"Oh, my beloved friend!" exclaimed the duke, springing forward, and grasping the baronet's hand the moment he saw him approach: "my dear Sir Ambrose, Claudia is no more!"

"Dead!" cried Sir Ambrose, involuntarily looking at Father Morris, whose aspect, however, still preserved only its usual cold and statue-like appearance. "Are you sure that she is dead?—I thought she was better."

"So we all did," said the duke: "but alas! we deceived ourselves, for Father Morris has just seen her expire. Oh! where is Edmund?—why is he not with you?—what will become of him? It will destroy him to lose Elvira: and I, too, that have felt so proud in the expectation of his becoming my son-in-law, oh, it will break my heart!"

"Oh!" cried Father Murphy, who was also present; "and if that's the case, why don't you let Rosabella take the crown at once, and make no more fuss about it."

"And yet," continued the duke, "I cannot hear that Elvira should he deprived of her right, she would so become a crown; and with her inflexible sense of justice, and desire for improvement, she would do so much good that I should not feel justified in depriving the country of such a sovereign."

"Thus," said Father Morris, smiling, "do we deceive ourselves; you are ambitious whilst you think that you are only just. Believe me, if you consult Elvira's real happiness, you will not impose upon the troublesome duties of a crown: she will make a better wife than a queen; for her gentle nature is less fitted to command than to obey. Rosabella has more firmness."

"I do not agree with you, Father," said Sir Ambrose; "in my opinion Elvira is infinitely better fitted to be a queen than Rosabella, for her passions are more under the control of reason."

"That is to say," resumed the monk, sneeringly, "they have not yet been called into play."

"What do you mean, Father?" began the duke.

"Nothing that could give you offence, my Lord," returned the priest. "Disgusted myself with the world, I naturally thought the princess most likely to find happiness where I seek it myself—viz. in a life of quiet and retirement."

"Enough," said the duke: "but where is Edmund? Let us seek him; no doubt he is with Elvira—poor things! we must spoil their billing and cooing."[166]

Edmund was with Elvira, and was passionately urging his suit, whilst she, engaged with her embroidery frame, listened with a half abstracted mind, and Emma duteously waited behind her chair.

"You do not love me," said he, "or you could not answer with such provoking coldness."

"Indeed I do, Edmund, but you are so unreasonable. I have already told you I have no idea of that passionate overwhelming love you appear to feel, it absolutely terrifies me, and I am sure it is not natural to my character.— (This silk is too dark, Emma)—and so, Edmund, if you feel you cannot be happy with such love as it is in my power to bestow, we had better determine at once to separate."

Good God!" exclaimed Edmund, striking his forehead violently. with his clenched hand; "how coldly you talk of our separation!"

"What can I do? I try every thing in my power to please you. (Emma, give me my scissors.) But since you will not hear reason—"

"Reason!" cried Edmund fiercely, seizing her arm, and then letting it go again; "If you talk of reason you will drive me distracted!"

"You quite terrify me with your violence, Edmund," said Elvira, rising, and preparing to quit the room.

"Oh stay! stay, my adored Elvira!" exclaimed Lord Edmund, throwing himself upon his knees and catching her hand; "for Heaven's sake, stay! pardon my impetuosity—frown upon me, treat me with coldness, disdain, or contempt, but do not, do not leave me."

"I do not know what you wish; I have repeatedly told you I am ready to become your wife whenever our parents think fit; and that I will do every thing in my power to make you happy. Do you call that coldness?"

"I do—I do indeed: freezing, insulting coldness. Oh, Elvira! I would rather see you spurn me—hear you declare you hated me, or know that you doomed me to destruction, than hear you speak of our marriage in that calm, unvaried tone."

"How unreasonable you are!" said Elvira, "as Henry Seymour says—you do not understand my character in the least."

"Henry Seymour!" cried Edmund fiercely: "how dare he pass an opinion upon my conduct? He shall account for his insolent interference."

"Oh no! no!" exclaimed Elvira, turning pale with terror; "I'm sure he meant no harm. For Heaven's sake, Edmund! my dear Edmund," continued she, earnestly laying her hand upon his arm—she paused—Edmund gazed upon her intently—she became confused, and added in a faltering voice, "do not hurt him, Edmund!"

Edmund sighed deeply: "You shall be obeyed," said he.

At this moment a slight tap at the door announced the arrival of the duke and his friends.

"So, so!" said the duke, "we have found you, have we? But you must take your leave of tender scenes for the future."

"What do you mean?" asked Edmund. "The Queen is dead," said Sir Ambrose.

The glowing countenance of Edmund turned of a ghastly paleness; and his livid lips quivered, as he leaned against the window for support.

"Assist him!" cried the duke. "He will faint! Don't distress yourself, Edmund; the death of Claudia shall make no alteration in your prospects."

"I am better," said Edmund faintly, attempting to smile, and waving of all assistance; "'Twas but for a moment: the suddenness of the shock overcame me: I thought the Queen was better."

"She was supposed so," returned the duke; "but it seems she had some internal malady her physicians were not aware of. An inward bruise, I believe. But don't make yourself unhappy about it, Edmund; I cannot hear to see you wretched. Let Rosabella take the crown, and think no more about it."

"Your Grace wrongs me," said Edmund, his fine countenance glowing with the exalted feelings of his soul. "However I may suffer from the violence of my feelings, I can never permit them to interfere with my sense of duty. Elvira has a right to ascend the throne, and if my exertions can ensure her success, she shall be Queen."

"Thou art a brave lad!" cried the duke. "And will you really try to secure the election of Elvira, when you know, by so doing, you will deprive yourself of her for ever?"

"I shall do my duty," said Lord Edmund, pressing his lips firmly together, as though to suppress his feelings. Father Morris looked at him from under his over-shadowing cowl with a kind of sardonic smile, which seemed to say "You speak well, but let us see how you will act."

"My noble Edmund!" murmured Sir Ambrose, tears rolling down his cheeks.

Elvira's eyes thanked her lover for his disinterestedness; and the glow of anticipated triumph which flushed her cheeks, betrayed, that neither her love for Edmund, nor the grief for the loss of her cousin, could suppress her joy at the flattering prospect opened before her. "Elvira!" said Lord Edmund, gazing upon her earnestly, as though he would penetrate the inmost recesses of her bosom. "What are your wishes? Do not hesitate to declare them, for alas! much hangs upon your words?"

Elvira blushed, and cast her eyes upon the ground; however, Lord Edmund comprehended but too well the meaning of her silence, and he sighed deeply. "It is enough," said he, in a mournful tone; "then the die is cast." He paused a few moments, whilst his friends, though they all looked at him with the deepest commiseration, respected his emotion too much to venture to interrupt it: then rousing himself, he hastily brushed a tear from his eye, and exclaimed, "How weak is human nature! I know my duty, and I will perform it; but yet—Oh Elvira!"

"Compose yourself, my beloved Edmund," said his father; "to-morrow you will be more calm."

"Oh, talk not of to-morrow!" replied Edmund; "to-day is the season for action; Keep the death of Claudia concealed a few hours, if possible. I will in the mean time assemble my friends: I know the army is devoted to me. A council of state will be chosen to direct the kingdom during the interregnum. I must be one of its members: some weeks must elapse before the election can take place, I think?"

"Three months is the time fixed," said the duke: "but you know the votes of all the people are to be collected, and that, with such a population as ours, will be no trifle: to be sure, it is the deputies that are to do the business, but then it will take some time to elect them."

"When the founder of the present dynasty ordained her successor should be chosen by the votes of the whole people," said Sir Ambrose; "she wisely recollected the difficulty that must arise from collecting their votes impartially, and directed they should elect deputies; but when she ordered that every ten thousand men throughout the kingdom should choose a deputy of their own rank and station to come to London to represent them,[167] she did not calculate upon the immensity of our present population, nor think of the evils the presence of such a disorderly body of men must bring upon the capital."

"Yet any attempt to reduce their number, would inevitably overturn the government," observed Father Morris; "for as it is the only act of freedom the people have long been permitted to enjoy, they will be proportionably tenacious of it."

"And the majority of these deputies are to decide the election," said Edmund, musing; "then our business must be to secure that majority. Think you that any good can be done by endeavouring to procure the return of those who are disposed to be favourable to us?"

"Very little," returned Father Morris, to whom this observation was addressed; "for the lower classes, from their conceit and pedantry, are extremely difficult to manage. Their deputies, however, notwithstanding the ordinance of the Queen, will probably be more polished, and less learned, as the lower classes will be ill able to spare the time necessary to become deputies, whilst the country gentlemen will be delighted to obtain something to do."

"We must be prompt," said the duke, "at all events. I don't like delay."

"True!" replied Edmund, starting from a reverie into which he had fallen; "I must get myself nominated a member of the council, and we must arrange our other plans afterwards."

The party now separated, and Elvira, left alone with her companion, indulged in dreams of future grandeur. "I am sorry for the death of Claudia," said she, "but I never loved her; she was so cold and uninteresting—such a mere matter-of-fact being—she had no soul, Emma, and how can one love a being so totally passionless and insipid? I wonder," continued she, after a short pause, "what Henry Seymour will think of this?"

Emma smiled. "Poor Lord Edmund!" said she.

"I know what you would say," returned Elvira; "I am sorry for him, and I admire his conduct extremely. There is really something very noble about him."

Emma again smiled, for she saw, in spite of this admiration, that in a week poor Lord Edmund would he forgotten.

In the mean time, poor Rosabella's mind was a prey to the most violent passions. A billet from Father Morris had informed her of the death of her cousin, and of the designs brooding against her interests. "I will be revenged," said she; "I will show them mine is not a soul to dwell upon impotent grief. I will assemble my friends; my father's party was strong in the state; it cannot be quite extinct. Let me see, to whom shall I apply?"

"The Lords Noodle and Doodle (both of ancient families) were both devoted to your father, and were under great obligations to him when they were young," observed Marianne.

"But they are such fools!" said Rosabella. "They are well connected," returned her confidant; "and power does not always attend upon talent."

"True, and, as they are so weak, I may guide them as I will."

"Do not rely upon that: folly is generally obstinate; and though there may be hopes of convincing a man of sense, fools will always have their own way."

"How then are they to be dealt with?"

"By letting them fancy they direct, when, in fact, they are directed. Apply to Lords Noodle and Doodle, as though for advice, more than assistance. Consult them how you ought to act, and suggest the advantages that will arise from your possessing the throne so artfully, that they may fancy what you say the dictates of their own minds, and then, if they advise any course, they in some measure pledge themselves to support you, if you pursue it."

"I do not doubt obtaining their sanction, and that of Lord Gustavus de Montfort; but I wish I could also obtain the countenance of Dr. Hardman, for he has many friends, and some talents," said Rosabella; "and I own I do not feel satisfied to trust myself entirely in the hands of any of the others."

"Talk of liberty and public spirit," replied Marianne; "promise a redress of grievances, and a radical reform of all evils, and you may secure Dr. Hardman. Yet he is not a fool; nay, he is even shrewd, penetrating, and persevering; but as lunatics are generally mad only upon one subject, so even men of sense have generally some prevailing folly, and his is, that of being thought of importance in the state. Indeed, in my opinion, there are very few human beings that we may not make subservient to our views, if we have but penetration enough to discover their weak sides, and art enough to avail ourselves of the discovery."

"The world is very much obliged to you for the high opinion you have of it," returned Rosabella; "however, I like your advice, and will pursue it. But do you think Father Morris will approve?"

"Oh, I will answer for him," interrupted Marianne.

"I will then write to each of the three lords," continued Rosabella; and appoint a time and place for an interview with each. I must attend to the doctor afterwards."

"Beware," said Marianne; "you have a difficult game to play. The old proverb says, it is well to have two strings to one's bow; but four, I fear, will be too much for you to manage."

"Fear me not," cried her mistress; "impetuous as I generally am, I can be cautious when I see occasion."

In pursuance of her resolution, Rosabella wrote to the noblemen, whose assistance she wished to secure; and receiving favourable answers, the hour of twelve that night was fixed upon for a secret meeting between Lord Gustavus and herself upon the subject. The utmost secrecy was requisite, as Rosabella knew the fiery temper of her uncle, and felt confident, that if he discovered her plans before they were ripe for execution, his vengeance would have no bounds. She wished, therefore, to ascertain her strength privately; and, as she was aware a fruitless struggle would only involve her in ruin, she resolved not to betray her intentions till there appeared at least a fair prospect of success.

For this reason, when the duke informed her of the death of the Queen, she affected only the surprise she might naturally be supposed to feel at the suddenness of the event; and appeared absorbed in grief for the loss of her cousin, without seeming even to think of the consequences likely to ensue to herself; in short, she acted her part so well, that the duke was completely deceived; and when he returned to Sir Ambrose, after his conference with her, he exclaimed, "I've had no occasion to alarm ourselves, or give ourselves so much trouble: I don't believe Rosabella even thinks about the throne; and I am sure she doesn't care a straw whether she has it or not. I am even confident, from what I have seen to-night, that I have only to express my wishes in favour of Elvira, to have her resign all pretensions immediately."

Sir Ambrose smiled and shook his head incredulously, and the duke was provoked; for, like all weak, obstinate men, he was extremely tenacious of the infallibility of his judgment.

"Why do you shake your head?" said he; "Do you disbelieve my assertion?"

"I do not disbelieve your assertion; I only doubt your penetration!"

"And why do you doubt that?"

"Because I know Rosabella."

"Then you think her indifference affected?"

"I think it too great to be real. Moderation is not by any means a characteristic of Rosabella. She is ever in extremes; and when she appears otherwise, depend upon it she is only acting a part, and she has some end in view that she hopes to gain by it."

"Well, let her be as sly as she will, she cannot deceive me! I'll watch her! I'll defy her to think, walk, look, or speak, without my knowing of it; and if I find she nourishes even the thought of rivalling Elvira she shall quit my house immediately. I will encourage no vipers."

Sir Ambrose smiled inwardly at the mistaken confidence of his friend in his own judgment. Thinking it useless, however, to irritate him by farther opposition, he endeavoured to turn the conversation upon another subject. "It is strange," said he, "how frequently I have been thinking of that Mummy. If there be no deception in the business, it is a perfect miracle!"

"And what deception can there be?" returned the duke, peevishly: "you think yourself so very wise, and that you know so much better than other people, only because you are always suspecting something wrong. Now, for my part, I think, as poor Dr. Entwerfen used to say, 'Incredulity is often as much the offspring of folly as credulity'!"

"I wonder what has become of the doctor and Edric? for, ill as Edric behaved, he is still my son; and I own I should like to know where he is."

"Oh! I don't think you have the least occasion in the world to trouble yourself about him. Depend upon it, he and his mad friend, Doctor Entwerfen are rambling about Egypt, and are happier now than ever they were before in their lives."

"If you are right," said Sir Ambrose, "and they are now in Egypt; as they have lost their balloon, they may be even in want of necessaries."

"And it is very right they should be so," replied the duke; "what business had they to go away?"

The hours of this eventful day rolled on heavily with Rosabella; the important consequences of the struggle she was about to engage in forcibly impressed her mind. Ruin must inevitably ensue if she failed, and even if she succeeded, her path seemed strewed with thorns. The anxiety natural to the intrigues she was about to be involved in, also hung about her. Though haughty and vindictive, Rosabella was not naturally deceitful. Indeed the very violence and impetuosity of her passions rendered it difficult for her to appear otherwise than she really was. The secret intercourse, however, which, through the intervention of Marianne, she had long maintained with Father Morris, had somewhat practised her in concealment, but it was still repugnant to her nature. She was now anxiously expecting a visit from the reverend father, and as he was generally remarkably punctual to his appointments, his non-appearance filled her with a sensation of dread; and a presentiment of evil crept over her, that she tried in vain to overcome.

"It is long past the hour the father mentioned," said Marianne, after a long pause, during which she had been listening with the utmost attention to every sound. "I cannot imagine the cause of his absence. Surely our plans have not been discovered." And as she spoke, her blanched cheeks and livid lips betrayed the deep interest she took in his fate.

"How gloomily that heavy bell clangs in my ear!" said Rosabella; "it seems to ring the death-knell of my hopes. A gloomy foreboding hangs upon my mind, and undefinable horrors rise in dim perspective before me."[168]

"Hark!" cried Marianne, her sense of hearing sharpened by anxiety; "he comes! yes, yes, he comes," added she, after a short pause; and in a few seconds Rosabella heard the Father's well-known step. "You are very late," said she, as he entered the room.

"Good God! what is the matter!" asked Marianne, as the haggard, agitated features of the priest met her eye. "You look like one who has held communion with infernal spirits."

"You say right, Marianne," replied the Father, in a deep hollow tone; "I have, indeed, conversed with spirits—for never could those fearful eyes that so long have glared upon me, belong to mortal."

"What do you mean?" asked Rosabella.

"I have again seen the Mummy! that fearful spectre from the tomb. I have even conversed with him, and he lives and breathes; nay even reasons, thinks, and speaks like a human being; but the cerecloths[169] of the grave are still wrapped round him, his fearful eyes glare with unearthly lustre, and his deep sepulchral voice thrills through every nerve."

"What, that horrid creature whom we saw descend from above at the very moment of Claudia's accident? Heaven grant no horrible consequences may ensue from so awful an invasion of the general laws of nature!" said Rosabella.

"Are you certain it is no deception?" asked Marianne.

"Deception!" returned the priest, "even I trembled, Marianne, when I gazed upon the countenance of that tremendous being, and read there the traces of fierce and ungoverned passions, wild and destructive in their course as the raging whirlwind. Even I, dreaded the influence he might exert upon our destinies, and shuddered at the thought of such a creature's being released from the fetters of the tomb, and sent back as a destroying spirit upon earth. The eternal gloom that hangs upon his brow, seems to bespeak a fallen angel, for such is the deadly hate that must have animated the rebellious spirits when expelled from heaven. His look is terrific; and my blood froze in my veins at his horrid laugh, which seemed to ring in my ears like the mockery of fiends when they have involved a human being inextricably in their toils."

"It may be a fiend," murmured Marianne, in a low whisper. At this moment, the clock struck twelve.

Rosabella started at the sound. "Lord Gustavus will expect me," cried she.

"Go, then," replied the priest, "with Marianne. I will follow presently."

With trembling limbs, beating heart, and all the trepidation which the consciousness of guilt cannot fail to give even to the firmest mind, Rosabella and Marianne proceeded to the terrace, where they found Lord Gustavus waiting to receive them.

"You may think it strange, my Lord," said the agitated princess, as she advanced, leaving her confidant at the gate which led from the garden, "that I should desire this meeting."

"By no means—by no means," said Lord Gustavus, condescendingly. "Indeed, I have already had some conversation with an emissary of your's, that has let me into your views; and I find from him your ideas upon several important subjects are so clear, so just, so sensible, and so accordant with my own, that I feel disposed to become your partisan, even before you utter a syllable."

"And who is this emissary?" asked Rosabella, unable to account for a reception so unexpectedly gracious, and alarmed at what she feared a premature exposure of her plans.

"Father Morris," replied Lord Gustavus, alarmed in his turn, lest he should have unguardedly committed himself: "he told me, he was an accredited agent of yours, and even induced me to—to—"

"Your Lordship need not hesitate," returned Rosabella; "I was not aware, that Father Morris had seen you, or I should not have expressed surprise."

"I have been induced then," said Lord Gustavus, "to bring with me two friends of mine, Lord Maysworth and Dr. Hardman. They are fully convinced of the justness of your ideas respecting retrenchment and reform; and they think your plans of curtailing the expenditure, by throwing all the power of the state into the hands of a few trustworthy individuals, upon whom you may thoroughly rely, (such as them or myself, for instance,) most excellent."

Poor Rosabella was here completely puzzled, as she had not the slightest idea of what plan Lord Gustavus could possibly allude to; nor indeed was it probable she should, it being entirely the offspring of the creative brain of Father Morris, invented by him solely for the purpose of the winning of the noble lords, to whom he had confided it, over to her party. Rosabella was naturally quick, and, possessing abundantly that very unexplainable, but well-known faculty, designated "tact," she instantly divined the motive that had induced Father Morris to attribute this scheme to her, and determined to avoid, if possible, betraying her ignorance.

Lord Maysworth and Dr. Hardman, who had remained at a little distance, and whom the agitation of Rosabella had prevented her before seeing, now advanced; and after having been presented to the princess, the former assured her of his devotion to her cause.

"I admire your ideas exceedingly," said he; "and particularly your intention of removing Lord Edmund from the command of the army, and placing an older and more experienced person in his stead."

"Lord Edmund!" cried Rosabella, thrown off her guard by the sudden mention of that name.

"Father Morris told me so," resumed Lord Maysworth, in surprise.

"And he told you truly," interrupted Rosabella. "Father Morris is worthy of all the confidence I can repose in him; and, in fact, he knows my inmost thoughts; but I was not aware that he had seen you."

A conversation now ensued, in the course of which Lord Maysworth detailed, with admirable minuteness, a variety of subjects calling for reform. Rosabella did not understand half he said, for his calculations bewildered her; and her mind, accustomed to soar with the eagle flight of genius, and take in oceans with a glance, could scarcely condescend to listen to the petty articles of economy in expenditure, to which it seemed principally his object to draw her attention. She assented, however, to all he said; and having let him speak as long as he liked, without showing symptoms of weariness, and having luckily said 'yes' and 'no' in the right places, he departed quite enchanted, and completely gained over to her party, declaring her to be, without exception, one of the most sensible young women he had ever conversed with in his life. To this, Lord Gustavus and Dr. Hardman assented, as she had appeared also to acquiesce in all they had said; and the noble lords and learned doctor departed perfectly satisfied.

Scarcely were they gone, when Father Morris appeared. "My dear father!" exclaimed Rosabella, enraptured at the result of the interview, "congratulate me! Lord Maysworth, Dr. Hardman, and Lord Gustavus, are our own."

"I rejoice sincerely, my child," returned the priest; "for Heaven knows I feel as great an interest in your welfare as in my own. But what did they say? Let us hear if your hopes are well founded."

"At first their expressions were rather of a negative nature—for they told me rather that a party existed against my rival, than for myself. They say the duke has many enemies, from his obstinate and conceited disposition; they said also that my father *had* had many friends."

"And do they exist no longer then, that you lay such emphasis on the word *had?*" asked Father Morris bitterly.

"They exist, but it seems my father has been so unfortunate as to lose their friendship," returned Rosabella; "Lord Gustavus even alluded to some crime, which he said he had committed."

"Crime! Did he dare to call it crime?"

"He did indeed, and it is not possible to describe the torture that rent my bosom as he spoke. I always knew my father had been unfortunate, but I never before even suspected him of having been guilty."

"Nor was he guilty, girl! none but fools or idiots dare breathe such an accusation against his name."

"Ten thousand blessings on you for relieving my mind from the agony of believing him unworthy of my love. I am perfectly satisfied with your assurance; and yet, methinks, I would fain know his history."

"Rosabella, you never knew your father; you were but three years old when circumstances occurred that urged him to commit a deed of desperation. Seek not to inquire farther; and endeavour, since misfortune has thrown a shade over your father's name, to redeem it by the lustre of your own."

"As an obscure individual, whatever might be my will, power would be wanting."

"But it shall not be wanting. You shall be Queen. I swear it, though all the powers of heaven and earth should unite to oppose my designs, and though even blood should be necessary to seal the compact—"

He was going on when a fiendish laugh rang in his ears;[170] and, looking up, he beheld the gigantic form of Cheops standing over him. The bright moonbeams showed, with horrible distinctness, the strange attire, savage features, and unearthly gaze of the Mummy, as his horrid laugh echoed from the wall behind them and pealed across the water. Rosabella had not before seen him, except when she knelt before the dying Queen; and, shrieking with horror, she fled for refuge to her uncle's garden, whilst Cheops thus tauntingly addressed the priest.

"You were conspiring mischief. Though the language your lips employed was unknown to me, that of your looks was clear. Men do not cast their eyes upon the earth, and murmur forth their accents as though they trembled at the sound of their own voices, when their purposes are such as will bear avowal. Make me your confidant, and by the aid of my serpent deity, my guardian Cneph,[171] I may assist you: but force me to become your enemy, and Typhon himself never pursued Isis and the infant Horus with more unrelenting vengeance[172] than I will follow you and destroy your plan."

Dreading alike to trust, or enrage this mysterious being, and cursing the evil chance that had led him to that spot, Father Morris, who, like all the English in those days, was an universal linguist, found himself obliged partially to obey this injunction, and inform the Mummy of his design. Cheops burst into one of his terrific laughs of derision. "And so," he said, "you would make yonder feeble girl who fled screaming at my approach, a Queen. A fit monarch for a warlike people. Can a woman's arm resist an invasion of the Palli, or a woman's hands direct the reins of Mizraim's government? Alas! alas! where am I wandering? I forgot the change wrought in my destiny, and that your people seem powerless as the sovereign you would give them. Be satisfied, I will not betray thee. Indeed, so do I hate thy countrymen, that I shall rejoice to see thee triumph in deceiving them. Beware, however, how thou attemptest to deceive me, lest my vengeance, quick, sure, and unforeseen as the secret agency of the Epoptae,[173] should fall upon and crush thee at the very moment of the fruition of thy wishes."

Fearing, whilst he hated the mysterious being thus strangely thrust into his most inmost secrets, Father Morris promised obedience, and the Mummy retreated within the walls of Mrs. Montagu's garden; ere he left the priest, however, he held out his hand to him. "Give me your hand," said he, "and let us seal our compact."[174] Father Morris shuddered as he obeyed; for the words of the Mummy recalled those he had just employed, when this fearful apparition broke in upon him, and brought with them a train of thoughts he would now willingly have shaken off. He did not dare, however, to refuse, and reluctantly held out his hand: the Mummy seized it with an iron grasp, and an icy chill seemed to creep from his hand to Father Morris's heart, as he burst into one of his demon-like laughs and left him.

Father Morris, unable to shake off the horror that oppressed him, for he felt as though he had entered into a compact with a fiend, stood gazing at the supernatural appearance of Cheops as he stalked across the terrace. His giant figure (rendered more awful by the grave-clothes that bound it) was magnified in the moonbeams, which seemed to increase, rather than to mitigate the unearthly ugliness of the apparition they shone upon. The priest was fixed in a fearful trance: in imagination, he still felt the cold and iron grasp of the Mummy, whose eyes seemed as though they were still looking into his very soul, and whose solemn accents were even now scaring his faculties. At length, however, Father Morris recovered something of his self-possession, and fled from the spot (he scarcely knew in what direction) under the fear, at every turning, of again encountering the dreaded Mummy!

Volume 2: Chapter 2

When the reverend father took refuge in his chamber after this fearful and memorable interview, he felt that strange mysterious sensation of something dreadful hanging over him, though he scarcely knew what, which so often weighs upon the mind when any great and unexpected change has taken place in our destiny. He threw himself upon a sofa, and endeavoured in vain to analyze his feelings. He was not superstitious; but there was something about the Mummy that inspired him with awe in spite of himself, and he felt that he was no longer his own master, for a supernatural power seemed to mingle with his designs, and control his actions: he endeavoured in vain to recur to the plans he had that morning arranged for gaining over partizans to the side of Rosabella; he could not govern his ideas; he could no longer direct them as be wished; one sole thought occupied his mind, one sole image floated before his senses. He held his head with his hands, he pressed them firmly against his ears, and closed his eyes, as though by shutting out external objects his mind could recover its tone. It was all in vain! the gaunt figure of the Mummy still seemed to stalk before his eyes, and his fiendish laugh still to ring in his ears. Father Morris rose from his couch and threw open his window; the cool evening breeze revived him, and restored his faculties. He now began to reason with himself.

"It is very strange," said he; "but, unaccountable though it may seem, the destinies of this fearful being are evidently interwoven with mine. His appearance here at this eventful moment, and his forcing himself upon my confidence, which a secret power superior to my own prevented the possibility of my refusing him, cannot surely be accidental. No, no—he is permitted to revisit this earth for some positive and definite purpose; perchance to counteract my plans, perchance to aid them. There is no vanity in the thought; for upon my destiny, at this moment, hangs that of a mighty empire, and I feel that I am but a blind instrument in the hands of Fate, condemned to work, mole-like, in the dark, uncertain whether I be not drawing destruction upon my head at the very moment when I fancy I am attaining the pinnacle of happiness and glory. However, I will not be wanting to myself; this strange agent may be sent to aid me, and it shall not be my fault if I do not avail myself of his assistance.

The night was now far advanced, sleep had waved his leaden pinions over the inhabitants of the late noisy city, and no sound broke upon the stillness that spread around, save the great bell of the ancient cathedral of St. Paul's, which tolled solemnly at lengthened intervals, to announce the death of the departed Queen. The contemplation of nature always soothes the mind, and Father Morris, as he gazed upon the quiet garden sleeping in the calm moonbeams, felt half his cares pass away, and refreshed by the cool breeze, which now blew keenly from the water, he closed his window and prepared to retire for the night; but what was his horror, on turning round, to find, stretched upon the couch he had so lately occupied, the dreaded Mummy!—his eyes fixed upon the brilliant constellation of Orion, and his lips murmuring an address to the deity he fancied it to represent.

"Yes, blessed Horus!" cried Cheops, as Father Morris entered the room; "thou wilt hear my prayer, for thou hast also been a stranger in a foreign land; forced even in thy mother's arms to fly, pursued by all the fury of fell Typhon's rage; thou knowest how to pity the unhappy! And thou too, bright Isis!" continued he, addressing the moon, "thou also hast known sorrow; when thy streaming tears occasioned the first overflowing of the Nile, and grief for the loss of Osiris rent thy bosom with despair—then becamest thou well fitted to be patroness of the wretched. O Arsinöe! could I but recall the fatal moment when I saw thee last!"

"Despair is sinful," said Father Morris, who now stood beside him; "repentance may obtain forgiveness even of the most heinous crimes."

Cheops started upon his feet at the sound of the father's voice, and burst into one of his fearful laughs: "And who art thou," cried he, "who presumest to preach repentance to me? Oh! I know thee now, thou art the priest whose confidant I am become. But though I will aid thee, think not I will be thy slave—no, rather art thou mine, for thou art in my power!"

Father Morris felt his blood curdle in his veins at this address, and, though he strove to speak, his tongue clove to the roof of his mouth, and he could not articulate a word.

At this moment the solemn clang of a deep-toned bell fell heavily upon their ears. Cheops started at the sound, and, springing from the couch on which he had reclined, bent forward eagerly to listen as it slowly pealed through the deep silence of the night.

"What is it?" cried Cheops; "whence comes that fearful knell, awful as the sound which is doomed to sink into the souls of the initiate of the Isian mysteries?[175] Again it tolls; speak! whence comes it? what does it foretell? Is it the signal of another change of existence, strange, awful, and mysterious, as that I have already experienced? Let it come, I am prepared. The gods cannot inflict tortures more horrid than those I already suffer. Cannot! have I said? dread Osiris, forgive the impious thought! Methinks e'en now I see thy dark blue countenance frowning in awful majesty at my unguarded rashness. Forgive me, mighty Spirit! No longer will I repine at thy decrees, but teach my proud rebellious heart submission. Alas! alas! had I before done so. But it is now too late, and happiness is lost to me for ever."

Sighing, he hid his face in his hands as he spoke; and all again was silent, save the deep-toned bell, which still fell heavily at intervals upon the ear. Slowly the hours rolled on, yet still Father Morris sate gazing on the

Mummy, till the first bright tints of morning broke through the dark grey sky, and a half-subdued hustle in the streets, as of people hurrying to and fro, announced that preparations were making to hang them with black.

The confused murmur—the busy voices hushed to whispers, and the still-continued tolling of the muffled bell, harmonized with the fearful form of the Mummy-visitant, which, now seen dimly by the uncertain shades of the breaking twilight, seemed to acquire fresh horrors from the obscure and wavering gleams thrown upon it. It was at this moment, when objects were gradually becoming more distinct every instant, that Lord Edmund rushed into the room—"Father Morris," cried he, "you must aid me, or all is lost!"

And as he spoke, he started back aghast; for the terrific form of the Mummy struck upon his sight. He had seen him, it was true, on his first descent; but the events that had since occurred, involving as they did the dearest interests of his soul, had almost driven the circumstance from his memory. Now, however, aided by the illusive light, the spectre appeared before him in all its frightful reality, and even the firm mind of Edmund shrunk back aghast from the appalling sight.

"Why do you shrink?" said Cheops, his deep hollow voice thrilling through the souls of his auditors; "why does my form appear to create such terror? Is it because a tomb has been my dwelling? Oh, degenerate race! know that the sons of Mizraim, bold, wise, and learned as they were, held that communion with the dead was needful to the living. They loved to gaze upon the empty casket, deprived of all that gave it value, for it taught the meanness of the body; and who could dwell upon the withering worthless clay, and not acknowledge to his soul how poor were its highest pleasures, when compared to the sublime aspirations of the spirit? Why then tremble? Virtue need fear no spectres, and vice might shudder at itself. If thine own conscience do not upbraid thee, what hast thou to fear?"

"Nothing!" said Lord Edmund firmly; "spectre or demon, whatever you may be, I fear you not! 'Twas but the infirmity of human nature; it is past, and I am again myself, and strong in the consciousness of the integrity of my own mind. It is not in the power of Hell itself to fright me from my purpose!"

"The integrity of thine own mind!" cried Cheops, with one of his horrid laughs; "Poor weak offspring of clay! ay, confide in thy boasted strength; rely upon thy vaunted firmness; but when the hour of trial and temptation shall arrive, tremble?"

Lord Edmund shuddered in spite of himself, and his blood ran colder in his veins! "Who art thou?" cried he, indignantly; "strange, terrible being that thou art?—and why art thou permitted to revisit earth to taunt me into madness?"

I was once as thou art," returned Cheops. "Young, ardent, and impetuous, I thought the world was made for happiness, and that men were born to be my slaves. Glory was my idol, and Fame the only meed I coveted. Deeply did I drink of her intoxicating cup; my renown spread to the remotest corners of the earth, and my power became as boundless as my ambition! To immortalize my name, I caused the erection of an enormous pyramid! and my grandeur seemed beyond the reach of destiny to destroy. But I trusted in my own strength, and I fell! Tremble then, weak man! nor dare to boast how thou wilt act until the moment of temptation shall arrive!"

The deep thrilling voice of the Mummy fell upon Lord Edmund's ear as a warning from the tomb. He too was relying on his own strength, and should he too fall? Forbid it Heaven! "No!" thought he, "in some cases I might fear; but now, when the welfare of her I love is at stake, I cannot fail!"

The Mummy smiled as he read the thoughts that passed over Lord Edmund's expressive countenance. "Thus I too thought," muttered he; "and as I was, so will he be deceived! Human nature is still the same even in this remote corner of the globe. Fool that I was, then, to attempt to reverse her decrees! Forgive me, mighty Isis!" The rest was lost in inarticulate murmurs as the Mummy's head sank upon his breast.

"Oh, God!" cried Edmund to Father Morris; "whence comes this fearful spectre? what does it import?"

"I know not," said Father Morris, in a hoarse unnatural whisper, his eyes still strained upon the Mummy. Edmund started, for the unusual abstraction of Father Morris added fresh horror to the scene: his senses seemed bewildered; he scarcely knew where he was, or what was passing around him; he rubbed his eyes, and tried to wake from what appeared a frightful dream; but in vain; the vision was still there in all its horrible distinctness, and Edmund felt a terrific creeping steal along his nerves as the hollow sepulchral voice of the Mummy again fell upon his ears.

"Alas! where am I?" continued he; "can that river[176] be a ramification of my beloved Nile? or am I indeed torn from all I prize and love, to be cast upon this secluded spot, where all seems strange and insignificant? O deity of the foaming waters! holy Sirius, hear me! Calm my troubled spirit, and grant some gracious manifestation of thy divinity to chase my growing doubts. But I deceive myself; this is not the Nile! No papyrine boats glide o'er its polished surface. No acanthus groves nor forests of lofty palm border its banks. No, no! the immortal palm, fit emblem of the soul, grows only in those favoured realms; where, spurning at oppression, it resists the feeble efforts of man to bend it to the earth, and springs upward with only added vigour from the feeble attempts made to subdue it!"

The Mummy ceased, and a solemn silence prevailed; whilst passions fierce as the whirlwind's fury flitted across his face, chilling the beholder's heart with horror at the fearful being whose bosom could conceive them.

Father Morris was not naturally timid; he even possessed uncommon strength both of nerves and mind; yet an unwonted shuddering ran through his frame as he gazed upon Cheops, and traced the workings of that demoniac mind as they were successively imprinted on his features. Involuntarily he turned away in disgust. "For God's sake, let us go!" cried he, gasping for breath; for a strange feeling that he could not define, seemed to impede his respiration.

"Yes, yes—let us go!" stammered forth Edmund; still, however, keeping his eyes fixed upon the awful object of his fear, as he slowly moved towards the door.

"Stay!" cried Cheops in a voice of thunder. Involuntarily they obeyed. "How feeble is this race of men!" resumed the Mummy; "how different from the sons of ancient Mizraim, from the Macrobian Ethiopians,[177] or even our Pallic foes; degenerate in form as well as spirit, their souls no longer seem emanations from the divinity, though perhaps the immortal spark becomes degraded and abased from its long continuance in clay, and is sunk for ever from its pristine greatness! Stay, then!" continued he; "why should you fly me? I mean you no harm, and I swear by the sacred tomb of Osiris in Philoe, that I will not hurt you. Drive me not then from amongst you, and I may aid your projects: at least, it is your duty to receive me as the destined instrument of Fate, since Osiris decrees that my soul shall quit its transmigrations in the form of animals to reanimate this worthless body. Take me then into your counsels, confide in my power and I swear by the holy dust of Isis that you shall not repent."

"Avaunt, demon!" cried Lord Edmund, and, bursting from the room, he rushed out of the house.

What farther passed between the priest and his awful visitor, was known only to themselves; for when the family descended to breakfast, the Mummy was gone, and Father Morris appeared absorbed in his usual studies, without taking the slightest notice of the terrific occurrences of the night.

The death of the Queen being now generally known, her remains, laid in state, were exposed to the lamentations of her subjects, and innumerable visitors (with that strange fondness for seeing sights, which can make even death considered as a show,) crowded to the mournful spectacle.

In an immense hall, hung with black, was placed a kind of bier, covered with black cloth, supporting the body of the deceased Queen, over which was thrown a velvet pall, so disposed, however, as to display the beautiful features of the deceased, which, though now fixed in death, still retained their native expression of majestic dignity.

Immense tapers of an enormous thickness lighted the sombre walls, hung with black cloth; whilst chorister boys walked up and down chanting hymns in honour of the deceased, and flinging incense in the air from silver vessels suspended by silver chains, which they carried in their hands; thus shedding fragrance around, and chasing the fearful odour of mortality even from the very chamber of death. Priests wrapped in funeral garments also slowly paraded the room, muttering prayers, and joining occasionally their full, deep-toned, voices with the shriller chant of the boys.

The space where the public were admitted, was railed off from the lower end of the hall; but near the body knelt a beautiful female arrayed in black velvet, and her fair face and arms shaded by a veil of black crape.

"O Osiris!" cried a figure wrapped in a long dark cloak, grasping the arm of Father Morris, "who is that lovely creature? There, bending over the last awful relics of mortality, methinks she looks beauteous as the phoenix rising from the funeral pile, and triumphing in glory over the impotent malice of the grave."

"Hush! hush! for Heaven's sake!" whispered the deep, full voice of Father Morris; "it is Elvira, the rival of Rosabella, whom you have sworn to support."

"Typhon himself could not injure her," said Cheops, for it was he; and he stood with his eyes fixed upon her, apparently lost in meditation.

"For mercy's sake, let us go on!" whispered the priest, "you will excite attention—we shall be discovered. Besides," continued he in a lower tone, "did you find a crown so delightful that you think you would injure her by depriving her of one?"

"No! by the holy limbs of Osiris!" said Cheops; and, obeying the influence of the friar's arm, he moved onwards.

"Why was not Rosabella with Elvira in the hall?" asked Sir Ambrose. "I thought it was commanded by the law that all the princesses of the Blood Royal should exhibit themselves publicly as mourners by the corpse of the deceased Queen."

"Rosabella is ill," replied the duke. "Grief for the loss of her cousin has produced an access of fever, and she is unable to quit her bed."

"Indeed!" returned Sir Ambrose, incredulously; "it is very strange! I own I did not give Rosabella credit for so much sensibility."

Notwithstanding the incredulity of Sir Ambrose, however, Rosabella was really dangerously ill; though her illness did not proceed exactly from the cause she chose to assign for it. The terror she had felt at the sudden appearance of the Mummy, whom she thought a supernatural being, at the very moment she believed the death of her cousin was darkly hinted at by the monk, operating upon an over-excited imagination, had produced fever; and for some days Rosabella was in considerable danger.

The secret exertions of Father Morris, however, in her behalf, prevented Rosabella's cause from being injured by her illness; and, by the time she was able to leave her bed, Lord Gustavus de Montfort, Lord Maysworth, and Dr. Hardman, with the Lords Noodle and Doodle, had declared themselves her adherents, bringing with them all the numerous host who, finding it too much trouble to judge for themselves, are always ready to follow in the train of a great man. The day when this important declaration was made, was that on which all the nobility of the realm assembled in that splendid monument of antiquity, Westminster Hall, to choose the council of state to govern the kingdom during the interregnum. This venerable pile, which had seen so many generations successively rise and pass away, now cleared of the incumbrances[178] with which the bad taste of the middle ages[179] had loaded it, shone in all its original magnificence, and opened wide its ponderous portals to receive the whole nobility of England upon this important occasion.

It was a glorious, and almost an awful sight, to see so many great and illustrious characters, some of whose names were celebrated even to the remotest corners of the globe, collected together in that magnificent hall. Few however, thought of the grandeur of the spectacle; the deep interest excited by the occasion that assembled them absorbing all minor feelings. The business of the day was soon entered upon; and twelve noble individuals chosen to direct the affairs of state, till another Queen should be elected.

The Duke of Cornwall, Lord Edmund Montagu, Lord Gustavus de Montfort, Lord Maysworth, and the Lords Noodle and Doodle, were amongst the number chosen; and as soon as the election was completed, the council retired together to an apartment appropriated to their use, to consult upon the measures to be taken to secure the due election of their future Queen. Then it was, that the anxious father of Elvira was paralyzed, to hear the noble lords above-mentioned declare themselves partisans of her rival; and to see others who had till then remained neuter, seem inclined to range themselves upon the same side. In vain did Edmund exert his powerful eloquence; the weight and influence of the adverse lords far outweighed all his arguments in the breasts of the auditors; and the poor old duke returned home depressed and almost broken-hearted, from the conviction he received, that the feeling of the majority of the council was decidedly against his child.

The moment the duke reached his own palace, he repaired to the apartment of Rosabella, and found her apparently in a state of convalescence, reclining upon a sofa, supported by her confidant Marianne, with Father Morris sitting at her feet. The holy father was evidently confused at the unexpected arrival of the duke; and he rose hastily in great disorder, to endeavour to account for his appearance there though, in fact, as there was nothing extraordinary in a priest visiting a sick penitent, his eagerness to exculpate himself from suspicion would have excited it, had not the duke been too angry even to be aware of his presence.

"Wretch!" he exclaimed; "vile, ungrateful wretch that thou art! Thou hast destroyed me. Thou wilt bring the grey hairs of thy benefactor with sorrow to the grave! And so treacherously too! Oh, Rosabella! how could you plot against me whilst you were enjoying the shelter of my roof. Against me, did I say? Alas! would it were only against me! But no! with fiend-like barbarity, you have conspired to destroy my child!"

The duke had here unwittingly struck a chord that thrilled through the inmost souls of his auditors—though he did not heed their confusion.

"Oh, Rosabella!", continued he, "if I could have guessed, when thou wert brought to me a little smiling infant, and I took thee under my protection to foster thee as my own child, that thou wouldst prove a serpent to sting my heart to the core! But I was told it would be so—Sir Ambrose warned me to beware. 'Your brother,' said he, 'has proved a villain; the violence of his passions has led him to commit unheard-of crimes; and may not the same furies glow in the bosom of this smiling infant? Do not desert her, but do not educate the offspring of guilt in the bosom of your own family'"

"And did Sir Ambrose say this?" exclaimed Father Morris, grinding his teeth together, and scarcely able to articulate from the strength of the emotion that convulsed his frame. The duke, however, did not hear his question, and passionately continued—"He advised well, but I was deaf to his counsel; Fate hurried me on to my own destruction, and I nourished with the tenderest care a wretch whom I have this day discovered plotting with traitors to deprive my child of her birthright."

"What do you mean, my Lord?" said Rosabella: "I do not understand you."

"Yes, yes!" replied the duke, "ask what I mean; you may well assume that face of smiling innocence—too—often has it served your purpose! Fool, idiot, that I have been to have been so easily deceived! But your arts will now be vain. Lord Gustavus de Montfort would not have openly declared himself your friend, as he did to-day, if the most insidious arts had not been practised to win him."

"And has he done so?" asked Rosabella, her eyes sparkling with joy.

"Has he done so?" repeated the duke bitterly; "no doubt you know it but too well. Also that the prosing Lord Maysworth, the enlightened Lord Noodle, and the intelligent Lord Doodle, have enlisted their empty heads and long purses upon your side."

"Have they?" cried Rosabella, transport brightening every feature.

"Oh, Rosabella!" exclaimed the duke, passion giving way to agony, and torrents of tears streaming down his aged face; "that look of affected astonishment is intolerable! You must have known all this! I am a poor, weak, old man! there needed not such plotting to deceive me. It breaks my heart to find you guilty of hypocrisy."

Rosabella was affected by her uncle's tears: all his former kindness rushed upon her mind, and Nature resuming her powerful influence, she forgot all her ambitious projects, her hopes, her fears, and her intrigues; she thought only of the feeble, miserable, old man before her; and, attempting to throw her arms round his neck, she sought to mingle her tears with his, and, clinging to his feet, implored his forgiveness. The duke, however, could not read her heart, and, blinded by his passion, saw in this action only an aggravated insult: violently he spurned her from him, commanding her to leave his house immediately, and, by so doing, extinguished for ever every gentler feeling in his niece's breast.

Rosabella's haughty spirit did not wait a second repulse. Her tears were instantly dried, and, with eyes flashing fire and cheeks glowing with indignation, she rushed out of the room, without deigning to reply.

The duke's rage, if possible, exceeded her own; and these near relations, united as they were by the tenderest ties, parted in mutual hatred, sincerely hoping, on both sides, that they might never meet again.

Father Morris and Marianne followed Rosabella; and they found, as they expected, that the violent over-excitement of the moment had given way to hysterics. These tremendous convulsive agonies soon exhausted her enfeebled frame, and she lay upon a sofa in a state of torpid languor nearly approaching to insensibility, whilst her friends consulted upon what course they should pursue. During this pause of uncertainty and painful deliberation—for as Rosabella was entirely dependent upon her uncle, the case seemed hopeless—a letter arrived from Lord Gustavus de Montfort, offering the loan of his palace and his purse to the princess. That prudent and calculating nobleman was fully aware of the situation in which Rosabella would be thrown by his declaration in her favour, and of the advantage that would accrue to himself in after-times, if she should obtain the crown, from his having at such a moment conferred an important service upon his future sovereign.

Father Morris did not hesitate to open this letter and read it. Rosabella was not in a state to be consulted. Indeed, the case was one that did not admit of hesitation; and a conveyance having been procured, the princess was removed to the house of Lord Gustavus before she had recovered the full use of her faculties.

Volume 2: Chapter 3

THE morning appointed for the election of the council of state was passed by Elvira in the most intense anxiety. For herself, she had no wish to be a Queen—nay, perhaps she trembled at the thought; but when she saw how earnestly it was desired by her father, and thought of the bitterness of his disappointment should she be rejected, her eyes filled with tears, and she felt ready to make any sacrifice to promote his happiness.

Thus, trembling with agitation, yet fearing alike every change, the fair

Elvira sate, leaning her head upon her hand, whilst Sir Ambrose, whose rank did not entitle him to a vote, Dr. Coleman, and Henry Seymour, endeavoured to console her.

"My dear young lady," said the good doctor, "indeed, indeed, I think you distress yourself quite unnecessarily. With such supporters as your father and Lord Edmund, I do not think you can fail of success."

"You quite mistake me, doctor, I assure you," returned the princess; "I think not of the crown, yet it is not possible to express what I have suffered during the last few hours. Ere my father went to the council this morning, his agitation was so excessive that I feared it would destroy him, and my impatience for his return is become almost agony."

"Let me entreat your Highness to be composed," said Henry Seymour. "You torment yourself with vain terrors. I cannot suffer myself to imagine for a moment that the duke can be otherwise than successful."

"My dear child," observed Sir Ambrose, "exert your own good sense; nothing can be more foolish than to let imaginary horrors usurp any influence over your senses; you thus suffer doubly, and often the pains of anticipation exceed those of reality. But, see, here comes Father Murphy, and my little lively niece, Clara. Well, father, what news? Will the princess be Queen?"

"Och, and there can be no manner of doubt of it!" returned Father Murphy.

Elvira turned pale. "God in his mercy grant you may be mistaken!" said she.

"Oh, dear!" cried Clara, involuntarily.

"Why do you exclaim, fair lady?" asked the doctor, smiling.

"I am so surprised—so astonished!" said the blushing girl.

"At what?" resumed the doctor inquisitively.

"That—that," said Clara timidly, "that the princess should not like to be a Queen."

"Alas! alas!" said Elvira, smiling languidly, "you are too young, Clara, to know the awful responsibility such a situation would impose. The Queen of England must devote herself to her people; once elected, she is cut off for ever from all the happiness of domestic life. She must form no ties—she must indulge in no attachments—she can never feel the happiness of devoting herself entirely to promote the welfare of one adored object. She can never know the transports of a mother!" and, sighing deeply, Elvira cast her eyes upon the ground, whilst those of Henry Seymour were fixed earnestly upon her.

"Yet all this," said Sir Ambrose, "is rather imaginary than real. The subjects of a good Queen ought to be her children; and the glory of contributing to the happiness of thousands, and ruling nations by a nod, may well compensate for the humbler comforts of a domestic fireside."

"I do not agree with you," rejoined Dr. Coleman; "I think the situation of a Queen is one both of trouble and responsibility. We all know how difficult it is to give satisfaction even in the most ordinary occurrences of life; and how much more must that difficulty be increased in such an exalted station. Besides, it seems cruel to condemn a young and beautiful woman to the miseries of celibacy. Woman naturally seems to want support; she is to man, what the clinging ivy is to the majestic oak,—its loveliest ornament; but take away the standard tree, and she falls forlorn and unsupported to the dust. Do you not think so, Mr. Seymour?"

The youth started at this appeal, for his thoughts had indeed wandered far from the scene before him. "Yes," said he, after a short pause.

Sir Ambrose laughed heartily. "Upon my word," said he, "I congratulate you, Dr. Coleman, upon your happiness in having such attentive auditors. The princess looks as if she had not heard a single word that you have said; whilst Mr. Seymour, when you appeal to him for his opinion, only starts, and says 'Yes.'"

"You are quite right, Sir Ambrose, returned Dr. Coleman, smiling good-humouredly; "and I begin to discover that reasons are quite useless when the feelings are interested."

"Och!" said Father Murphy; "and my opinion is that we have all rason to be interested; for I should not be surprised at all at all,[180] if the King of Ireland was to take advantage of our troubles, to make a descent upon us. There is no time so fitting for throwing every thing into confusion, as when nobody knows what he is doing."

"There may be much justice in your remark, holy father," said Henry Seymour, smiling; but, for my own part, I own I do not apprehend the King of Ireland has any such bloody-minded intentions."

"Report speaks highly of his son," observed Elvira.

"Not more highly than he deserves," cried Doctor Coleman enthusiastically. "The youthful Roderick is brave, noble, and generous; possessing every quality to fit him for a hero; and is quite incapable of any thing bordering upon meanness."

"Is he handsome?" asked Clara, with infinite *naiveté*, looking up earnestly at the doctor as she spoke.

"As the Achilles of the ancients," replied the doctor.

"Dear me, how I should like to see him!" said the little beauty, with the utmost simplicity:—"Should not you, Mr. Seymour?"

"I cannot say I have any curiosity," returned Henry Seymour, having infinite difficulty to help laughing.

"Dear me, how very odd!" said Clara, looking at him earnestly; "I do believe the doctor was only quizzing us, and that he's very ugly and disagreeable. Is he, Mr. Seymour?"

The air and manner with which she put this question, quite destroyed the small remains of gravity Henry Seymour had till now with so much difficulty preserved; and, bursting into a violent fit of laughter, he rushed out of the room. Every body looked astonished, and Dr. Coleman embarrassed. After a short pause, however, he seemed to recover himself. "It is very strange the duke does not come," said he, pulling out his watch. "The council must be chosen before this; and they seldom stay to deliberate long at a first sitting."

"I am miserable," cried Elvira. "If he should be ill!"

"Shall I seek him?" asked Dr. Coleman; and, reading her assent in her countenance, he quitted the room.

"The doctor is very obliging," said Sir Ambrose; "but he never did like Rosabella. He hated her father, and when. Duke Edgar—but, I forget! his history is a secret which must rest for ever in my own breast."

"Do tell me, uncle!" cried Clara coaxingly; "I should so like to hear it, and every body says you know all about him."

"And what can his history have to do with such a little chit as you?"

"I don't know," said Clara with the utmost innocence; "hut I am sure I should like to hear it."

"Why?" again asked Sir Ambrose.

"Because every body says it is a secret," replied Clara, clinging round him, and fondly stroking his face;—"so do tell me, my dear uncle, pray do?"

"You are a little coaxing witch," said Sir Ambrose, patting her long silky hair; "I would tell you any thing in reason, but the history of the father of Rosabella—"

"Rosabella!" cried the duke, bursting into the apartment with the fury of a maniac—"Rosabella! who speaks of Rosabella? She is a wretch, a vile, insidious wretch! She has destroyed me—she has conspired to destroy my child!"

And as he spake, the agonized old man sank into a chair, fainting with exhaustion, whilst a sanguine stream gushed from his mouth and nostrils, a blood-vessel having been ruptured by the violence of his emotions. Elvira shrieked in anguish, and, dreadfully terrified, threw herself upon her knees beside him, imploring him to speak to her, whilst Sir Ambrose, even more alarmed than herself, ran screaming for assistance. Dr. Coleman and Henry Seymour were at hand. The duke, and his daughter, who had fainted, were conveyed to their separate apartments, attended by Clara, Sir Ambrose, and the doctor, whilst Henry Seymour and Father Murphy were left together.

"O Beauty!" thought Henry Seymour, as he watched the lovely form of Elvira, looking like some fair flower drooping on its stem, carried past him, "how omnipotent is thy power! Even the savage monarch of the forest, tamed by thee, has crouched beside a maiden's feet! How heavenly does she look! pure as the immortal spirit, when, ere his breast was sullied by the grosser passions, man first conversed with God!"

"And sure if it's the princess ye're thinking of," said Father Murphy, tired of being so long silent, "ye've rason to look so sadly after her, for it's all over, and she'll never be Queen."

Henry Seymour started: the voice of the holy father sounded harsh and discordant in his ears; it had dispelled all his fairy dreams; and with a movement of impatience he threw open some folding doors, and walked into the garden. Father Murphy followed him.

"And where is it that ye're going?" asked he.

"I would be alone," said Henry in a commanding tone.

"And so ye shall be," returned Father Murphy, "when I'm after laving ye; and that I will do in a whiffey. But—"

"Begone!" cried a peculiarly low, hollow voice which sounded close to the friar's ear. He started, and as he looked up, the withering glance of Cheops fell full upon him; he screamed wildly and fled, uttering shrieks of terror.

Cheops looked after him with a scornful smile, and then fixing his superhuman eyes on Henry Seymour, he waited for him to speak. Few were the human beings who could have met that scowl unmoved. Those wild eyes, shaded as they were by the thick dark brows above them, always seemed to sink direct to the beholder's soul: Henry Seymour, however, shrank not from their gaze. A long pause ensued.

"You wish for help," said Cheops, "and it is in my power to assist you. I know you well, you are not what you seem; but fear not, and all your hopes shall be fulfilled."

"Alas! how can they?" said the youth, "when I know them not myself."

"Hear me!" returned Cheops; "you love Elvira, you would fain become her husband, and would yet not deprive her of the crown.

Even now, you were revolving in your mind a scheme to reconcile these two apparently incompatible objects; but, besides innumerable minor obstacles, one great one destroys your plans—you have a father."

"In the name of Heaven!" cried Henry Seymour wildly, "who and what art thou?"

But, ere he had finished speaking, the Mummy was gone. "Fiend! demon!" cried the youth, "what means this unreal mockery? But thou shalt not escape me thus."

In the mean time, the duke had somewhat recovered, and, by permission of Dr. Coleman, Lord Edmund and Sir Ambrose were admitted to his chamber. The reverend Fathers Morris and Murphy were there already.

"I believe it is quite against the rules," said the doctor, "to allow visitors to a patient in the duke's state;—but he is so irritable, I fear keeping him in suspense might occasion a relapse."

"I am sorry to see you thus, my dearest friend," said Edmund, pressing the duke's hand warmly; "you have always been a second father to me, and, God knows! I love you as myself."

The Duke fervently returned his pressure, but he could not speak. "My dear, dear friend!" said Sir Ambrose, the tears trembling in his eyes."

"Come! come!" said Dr. Colman; good-humouredly, "I must not let you agitate my patient. Lord Edmund is only come, my Lord Duke, to take leave. He is going to join the army to try to exert his influence amongst the soldiers."

The duke shook his head.

"I must not have you despair," said Sir Ambrose; "we shall beat them yet: not but that we must fight hard, for Rosabella is as crafty as a fox, and you see what a party she has made:—besides, she's as selfish as her father."

"No," said the duke feebly, and speaking with great difficulty; "Edgar was not selfish."

"The influence of natural affection is astonishing!" said Sir Ambrose; "since it makes you speak thus of one who has so grossly injured you."

Edgar's faults," replied the duke, scarcely able to articulate, "were rather those of circumstance than of feeling. I am convinced of it, and forgive him. Nay, if he were alive, and I could see him, I would clasp him to my heart."

"Och!" said Father Murphy, "and that's said just like yourself; for there's nothing so like a Christian spirit as forgiving our enemies;—and so may Heaven prosper and bless all that love ye, and send all that hate ye to the Devil."

"But how does that accord with the Christian spirit you were talking of?" asked Dr. Coleman, smiling.

"Och!" replied Father Murphy, "and it's clane another thing. For none but the Devil's own brats could hate the duke, and he's a right to his own, surely."

Dr. Coleman, though not quite convinced by the sophistry of the holy father, did not attempt to controvert it; and the party, fearing to fatigue the duke, soon after separated.

A few hours after this conversation, Father Morris was walking in one of the shadiest parts of the garden of the Duke of Cornwall's mansion,[181] where the thick trees spread over his head, and by their umbrageous foliage, almost shut out the light of the sun. In the very centre of this gloomy grove, a funereal urn had been erected by one of the former possessors of the mansion, over which hung a weeping willow. The monument had once been gaudily adorned with bright colours and gilding, to mark the armorial bearings and dignity of the dust that mouldered below. Now, however, damp and neglect had hastened the work of Time in that secluded spot. The once white marble was stained with a dirty green, and moss had grown round the crumbling monument of former greatness: the plaister effigies of the arms had cracked, and peeled off in places; whilst wild-flowers had taken root in the fissures, and reared their blooming heads, and twined their fantastic wreaths around the mouldering stone, hanging in wild luxuriant festoons over this emblem of decay, as though to mock the feeble efforts of man to perpetuate his name, and assert triumphantly the supremacy of Nature.

Father Morris was struck by the effect produced by this apparently simple circumstance, and he stood with his arms folded on his breast, attentively gazing upon the urn: "And for this," thought he, "yes, even for such perishable baubles as these, does man risk his immortal soul. For this, for honours that decay even whilst we gaze upon them; for fame, which the slightest breath may blow away, light as the thistle's down; for wealth and power, which, past a certain point, pall on the senses; and for ambition, we sacrifice all the mind holds dear to it. And what is ambition? What real happiness can fame, wealth, or power bestow? I will repent; it is not yet too late:—for worlds I would not harm that poor old man. Yes, he has still a heart. I am not wholly lost. Oh! how his look, his voice thrilled to my inmost soul, and awakened feelings I thought for ever dead.

Oh, Julia! Julia![182] surely thy blest spirit would rejoice if angels can still feel for mortals, at my repentance. Oh, if one fatal act could but be recalled, and one fiend be satisfied, I might still be saved!"

And overpowered by his emotions, even his firm heart was softened; he leant his head against the mouldering urn, and, hiding his face in his cowl, he wept. Blest were those bitter tears, and sweet were the sensations that stole over the mind of the monk as they flowed; for they were the first fruits of human feeling that had long touched that savage breast. Soothed by their healing balm, and half forgetting the cares that hung about him, Father Morris still reclined against the tomb; whilst mild and pleasing images floated before his fancy, and the fairy form of Happiness rose again upon his sight, and, though dim and indistinct by distance, seemed once more to beckon him forward through the mist of time. Lost in these meditations, the most delightful he had long indulged in, the father remained unheedful of the lapse of time, till he was startled by a tap upon his shoulder, and, turning, he beheld the giant form of Cheops.

"Fiend, demon, devil!" cried he, passionately; "avaunt! and tempt me not!"

The Mummy burst into one of his frightful laughs of derision. "What!" said he, "have you forgot your friend? your confidant? your confederate? And is it thus you treat him? Have you forgot our compact and your oath? which, if it were necessary, was to be sealed with blood?" (The friar shuddered, whilst Cheops continued:) "Pshaw! pshaw! talk not of temptation! The passions in that breast defy its power; for demons scarce could credit them. Fear not temptation then, most pure and most immaculate priest! for know, I can read thy heart: and I—yes, even I—shudder at the wickedness it conceals!"

"My feelings are changed—I repent!"

"Impossible! your repentance is but as a passing shade before a glowing fire, which, even if not removed, would be soon devoured by the flames!"

"I tell you, my purpose is changed:—I will no longer plot against the duke; and Elvira, if she will, may be Queen."

"And do you think a crown so enviable then," said the Mummy, repeating the friar's own words, once addressed to him, "'that you think you would injure her by depriving her of its cares?'"

"Devil!" cried the father, unable to resist the feelings these words had conjured up.

"And these are mortals," said Cheops; "they sin, and they repent![183] Thus adding hypocrisy to guilt, and doubling their crimes by the knowledge they have of their enormity!"

"Demon!" returned Father Morris; "the words of that old man wrung my heart; and I would sacrifice all the world can give, to throw myself upon his breast, and obtain his forgiveness."

"I believe you think so *now*," said Cheops maliciously; "but when Rosabella shall be Queen, and wealth and dignities shall be dispensed by Father Morris; when nobles shall bend humbly before him, and, hanging upon his smile, beg favours from his hand, then—"

"Curses on thee, fiend!" cried Father Morris, rushing from the grove, and pressing his cowl round his head with both his hands, as though he feared the horrid laugh of Cheops should echo in his ears, and sting him into madness.

"Weak, feeble worm!" exclaimed Cheops, with a scornful laugh, looking after the friar as he darted from his sight; "and yet this man boasts of his intellect; ay, and rules his fellow-men almost to his will! Degenerate wretches! O powerful Osiris! if from thy dread abode thou deignest to look down upon thy votary, pity him now! condemned to waste his days amongst this hated race! And thou, fell Typhon! dread avenging deity! say, will thy awful wrath accept of victims such as these? Alas! I fear vengeance like thine will not be thus appeased! and that thy never-dying fire will still gnaw my vitals. Oh! these mortals *think* they suffer: but what are their torments when compared to mine?"

As he spoke, he gnashed his teeth in fury, whilst again the expression of passions, too tremendous to be conceived by mortals, darkened on his brow.

Volume 2: Chapter 4

"I am really glad we have left the house of my uncle," said Rosabella to Marianne, the morning after her removal to the palace of Lord Gustavus; "for though there is something revolting to my feelings in being dependant upon a stranger, yet as it may soon be in my power to repay any obligations I may receive from him, it is better than the treachery I was obliged to practise towards the duke. There is something so mean in treachery!"

"We are always apt to feel most disgusted with those vices most repugnant to our nature, said Marian smiling, "whilst we are merciful to those we practise. However, I can't say I think there is much difference."

"What!" cried Rosabella indignantly; "do you class those vices that spring from at noble though mistaken spirit, with those that are the natural offspring of base, grovelling minds?"

"No," returned Marianne, "for I think the latter preferable, as the mind that produces them is incapable of making nobler efforts; whilst the others, by degrading their possessors, show forcibly the monstrous depravity of the human heart."

"I do not understand you," said Rosabella.

"Nor is it necessary you should." rejoined her confidant.

Rosabella was not quite satisfied with this summary manner of dismissing the argument, and was proceeding to question her confidant's maxim, when a tap at the door announced a page from Lord Gustavus, who came to know if the princess would honour his master with an audience.

"Certainly," said Rosabella; and in a few minutes Lord Gustavus entered her boudoir.

"I hope your Serene Highness has rested well," said the noble lord with his usual pomposity; "I feel better this morning."

"I am perfectly well, I thank your lordship!" returned Rosabella; "and the relief I have experienced, by having the weight that has so long hung upon my mind relieved by my removal to your hospitable mansion, has proved an excellent soporific."

"That being the case," said Lord Gustavus, "perhaps your Highness will have no objection to indulge the noble lords who already have declared themselves on your behalf, as also some others of their friends who are anxious to enlist under your banners, with an interview: for thinking as think, and as I am convinced every reasonable person in the kingdom must think, no time ought to be lost in a matter of so much and of such infinite importance."

Rosabella, thinking *par merveille*[184] exactly the same as the noble lord, instantly gave him her hand to lead her to his library, where the illustrious personages he had spoken of were waiting to receive her. It has been already said that Rosabella was beautiful and now that her recent illness, and the agitation natural to the novelty of her present situation had softened the usual pride and haughtiness of her demeanour, she looked perfectly lovely. It has often been allowed, that a beautiful woman never looks so well, as when in affliction; there being something in the. appearance of a timid helpless female, looking up to man for protection and support, that rouses every generous and manly bosom in her behalf; whilst that wretch must indeed be lost to every sense of feeling and humanity, who could be deaf to the prayer of beauty in distress. Thus the appearance of Rosabella caused a general sensation in her behalf, whilst her usual pride and haughtiness, which were well known, only made her present diffidence and agitation, her downcast eyes and trembling voice, appear still more interesting from the strong effect of contrast they produced.

The persons collected in the library of Lord Gustavus were all affected by her manners; and though perhaps it would have been difficult to find a group of individuals more various in their usual habits and modes of thinking, yet upon this one point they were agreed. The personages who composed this worthy assemblage, were Lord Maysworth, the Lords Noodle and Doodle, Dr. Hardman, and the young Prince Ferdinand of Germany, who had been taken prisoner by Lord Edmund, and was now upon his parole of honour, till the conditions for his ransom could be arranged. He was at present the guest of Lord Maysworth, who having in his youth received great obligations from the German Emperor, was now glad of an opportunity to show his gratitude to his son; and who had now brought him to Lord Gustavus, to introduce him to the Princess Rosabella.

Prince Ferdinand was ardent and romantic, and he was just at that happy age when all appears bright and blooming, before reality has destroyed the flattering dreams of hope; when we are ready to believe all we wish, and imagine human nature without a blot. Alas! why are the delightful moments of life so transient; and why can we never partake of pleasure without having our relish for it destroyed!

Confiding, however, and unsuspicious as Prince Ferdinand was, he was certainly excessively astonished to hear Lord Maysworth, the advocate of freedom and equality, eloquently plead in Rosabella's behalf that her father was the elder brother of the present duke, and that consequently her claim was strengthened by all the magic powers of primogeniture, and he was still more surprised by his assertion that the present duke had rendered himself unpopular by advising the late Queen to rebuild the late palace at Richmond,[185] by which several hundreds of workmen were kept in employ during the whole of the preceding winter, and saved from perishing.

"Good heavens!" cried Prince Ferdinand, "Can you blame that? Was it not better than suffering them to perish with cold in the streets?"

"No danger of that, your Highness—no danger of that" returned Lord Maysworth—"nobody can perish of cold in our streets, because, you know, we have always pipes of hot air in them to make them quite warm.[186] And as to the palace, it is really quite melancholy to think how many thousands of the public money were expended upon it. Oh! I assure you, it is quite impossible to find a man more deservedly unpopular than the Duke of Cornwall."

"Oh, quite impossible!" said the Lords Noodle and Doodle, shaking their heads.

"Thinking as I think, however, and as I am confident every one here must think," said Lord Gustavus, "it will be imprudent to depend entirely upon the duke's unpopularity: Lord Edmund is beloved by the army; and, as he is decidedly upon the side of Elvira, we cannot be too cautious."

"Oh, no, certainly!—we cannot be too cautious," echoed the two repeaters.

"It is a glorious circumstance, however," said Dr. Hardman, "that the choice of the Queen rests entirely with the people; their voice alone will decide the glorious struggle, and their free unbiassed[187] opinions alone give the Monarchy its future Queen."

"Yes," said Lord Maysworth, "it is true, it rests with them alone to decide the question; and for this reason do you not think it will be as well, my lords, for each of us to repair to his country seat, and endeavour, by his influence in the neighbourhood, to procure the election of such deputies as may be disposed to vote favourably to our wishes."

"The plan is excellent!" cried Dr. Hardman.

"Excellent!" exclaimed Lord Gustavus.

"Excellent!" echoed his attendant satellites.

"Then it only remains for us to put it in execution," said Lord Maysworth.

"If the princess will excuse my absence—" began Lord Gustavus.

"Oh, my Lord!" interrupted Rosabella hastily, for she dreaded his long speeches beyond the power of description, "think not of me: I must be, indeed, unreasonable, if I could complain of your absence, when it is for my service you will be employed."

"The princess speaks like an oracle," said Dr. Hardman; "and I think we cannot do better than put her wishes in execution."

"Farewell then, my friends," said Rosabella, her voice trembling with emotion as they parted, "and may success attend you; for the present, my poverty, in all but gratitude, prevents my wishes; but the time may come, when you shall find the powerful Queen will not forget the favours conferred upon the dependant princess."

"Oh!" cried the noble lords and Dr. Hardman, "do not mention reward; patriotism and the disinterested love of our country alone dictate our actions—we think of nothing else!"

"'Twould be treason, and worse than blasphemy," said Prince Ferdinand, "to mingle the thought of self-interest with such purposes. Who indeed can see the Princess Rosabella, and suffer the paltry thought of self to interfere with his devotion to her interests?"

Rosabella smiled graciously upon the youthful speaker, though she did not speak.

"If, however," said Lord Maysworth, "the interests of the state should require a general more experienced than Lord Edmund, I have served, and I would willingly forego the transports of domestic peace to devote myself to the welfare of my country."

"Or, if the state should need a minister," observed Lord Gustavus, "thinking as I think, and as I am sure every one else must think, she has a right to command the services even of one so devoted to retirement as myself."

"For my part," said Dr. Hardman, "I wish neither place nor pension; but if my humble services in a medical capacity—"

"Fear not," returned Rosabella, "but that all your wishes shall be gratified; for, if I should be Queen, I shall only regard myself as an agent to dispose my power to the hands of those most worthy of it."

As she said this she withdrew, having the rare happiness to leave all her auditors perfectly satisfied with her conduct. In fact, such was their delight, that each stood for some moments after her departure lost in contemplation, indulging in day-dreams of the delightful anticipations her words and manner had excited, till, like Farmer Ashfield and his dame in "Speed the Plough,"[188] they were in imminent danger of running foul of each other in their abstraction: the entrance of a servant, however, roused them from their reveries; and, feeling somewhat alarmed of having so far forgotten the dignified sentiments they had been professing, they retired to their respective homes to take measures to put the scheme that had been suggested into execution.

"How I hate that Lord Gustavus," exclaimed Rosabella when she reached her boudoir. "Even if he makes a sensible observation, he adds so many explanations to it, that the spirit evaporates."

"Yes," returned Marianne, "he has yet to learn, that to tack explanations to wit, is like adding water to wine; you diminish its strength and spoil its flavour; but even he is preferable to Lord Maysworth."

"Oh! I don't think so," cried Rosabella, "for a ridiculous fool is always better than a prosing one. I can laugh at Lord Maysworth, but Lord Gustavus sends me to sleep."

"When an important enterprise is undertaken," said Marianne, "it will not do to be very scrupulous about the tools one employs to accomplish it. It is the part of a man of talent to discover the weaknesses of the human beings around him, and make them each subservient to his purpose."

"At any rate, that is not difficult in my case, "rejoined Rosabella; "for my good friends are so eager to show themselves off, that, I must do them the justice to say, they neither give me the trouble to find out their weaknesses, nor the way to win them. Prince Ferdinand is the only one who possesses a single spark of noble feeling."

"And he, I think you say, seemed struck with your appearance?"

"He appeared to be so."

"We must improve that prepossession. The alliance of Germany may be invaluable to us. You must encourage the hopes of the prince, and do all you can to fan his infant passion into a flame."

But I love Edmund."

"Pshaw! how can you be so childish? I do not wish you to love Prince Ferdinand. If you can contrive to make him love you, it will be all that is necessary."

"But do you consider the cruelty of trifling with his feelings?"

Marianne laughed. "I did not imagine you so romantic," said she tauntingly. "Do not alarm yourself; the rage for dying of love is gone by: therefore, notwithstanding the power of your charms, you must excuse me, if I presume to doubt their murderous properties."

Rosabella was too much mortified by the manner in which her confidant treated her scruples, to wish to continue the conversation; though the reasoning of Marianne produced its full effect upon her mind, and even, in spite of herself, influenced her conduct.

In the mean time, the family of the duke experienced considerable uneasiness on account of Clara, whose health gradually declined.

"I cannot imagine what is the matter with Clara?" said Sir Ambrose one day to Dr. Coleman; "I wish you would talk to her a little.—Here, Clara, my dear, do just step this way.—You will be quite shocked, doctor, at the change in her appearance. Poor girl! I don't think she has ever properly overcome the fright she experienced at the first sight of the Mummy, for she has never seemed herself since-but here she comes.—Clara, I sent for you to speak to Dr. Coleman."

Dr. Coleman was excessively struck by the alteration in Clara's appearance. The beautiful, lively, blooming girl was changed to a pale shadow-like being, whose existence seemed to hang upon a thread, and whose fragile form the first ungentle breeze would annihilate.

"What is the matter with you, my dear child?" asked the doctor.

"Nothing," said Clara, sighing.

"And I don't know any thing that can be worse," said Father Murphy, who happened to be present; "for that's the speech a young lady always makes when she's in love, and I don't know any disease that's harder to cure."

"In love!" cried Sir Ambrose, roused by that ill-omened word, which generally grates so harshly upon the ears of parents and guardians.

"In love!" repeated he, looking earnestly at his niece; "who can she possibly be in love with?"

"Ay, that's the question," said the duke; "for I'm sure since she has been here I have never trusted her from under my own eye; and I'll defy her to fall in love without my knowing it. No, no, she cannot be in love."

"Och! and that's no reason at all," cried Father Murphy, "for I never knew of watching doing any good at all in such matters."

"Well, Clara," said Dr. Coleman, "you hear Father Murphy's opinion; do you plead guilty to the charge?"

Clara's blushes became deeper, and her agitation so excessive, as Dr. Coleman fixed his eyes upon her, that, finding she could not bear his looks, she burst into tears, and hurried out of the room. Poor Clara! the fangs of the most cruel of passions had indeed pierced thy heart, though thou wast unconscious of it thyself!

It may be remembered, that, on the day of Edmund's triumph, Clara had been forcibly struck by the fine figure and noble appearance of a youth, who had walked as prisoner in the procession. It was Prince Ferdinand; who, having formed a strong intimacy with Lord Edmund, had been an almost constant visitor at the house of Mrs. Montagu ever since. Clara was just at the age when the human mind first begins to feel the want of something to love. In her own family, her affections had been thrown back upon herself; and, being driven to the regions of fancy to find an object to occupy her heart, she would often wander for hours together in the garden, picturing to herself adventures, which she would paint in all the vivid colours of imagination; till, lost in creations of her own, she would almost forget the tame, cold realities of life.

Of course, all these imaginary adventures could not exist without a hero; but Clara could never fix upon any definite form to bestow upon him, till she had seen Prince Ferdinand. Then, all her dreams seemed realized; and the secret God of her idolatry appeared to stand before her, in *propria persona*. Clara was now perfectly happy; and as, from the prince's frequent visits to her cousin, she now often passed whole days in his society, though he perhaps scarcely saw her, or at most regarded her but as a pretty child, yet she was satisfied: she saw him, and she heard him speak; what more was wanting to complete her dream of bliss?

Lord Edmund's departure for the country, however, broke this magic charm. Prince Ferdinand came no more to Mrs. Montagu's; and Clara heard of him only as the devoted admirer of Rosabella. Jealousy till that moment had been scarcely known to her, even by name; but it now shot its fiercest pangs into her heart. She had never been accustomed to conceal her feelings, and they now destroyed her. The climax, however, was still to come. One day, as she was mournfully pacing the terrace in her father's garden, she was startled by the appearance of Prince Ferdinand himself: her agitation was excessive; her lips trembled, and she panted for breath; but he passed on without noticing her—yes, it was he, the cherished idol of her thoughts, the hero of her dreams;—and he had passed without seeing, or at least without seeming to behold her. Was it possible he could have seen her and passed so coldly?—was it possible she could be so totally indifferent to one who was all the world to her? Oh! there was madness in the thought! she could not hear her own reflections. What would become of her, she knew not—she cared not; and, in an agony of despair, she plunged into the thickest grove of the garden.

Though it was summer, the day was cold and chilly; a drizzling mist fell fast, and a thick fog from the river wrapped the grove in gloom. Heedless however of the weather, Clara hastened on to the spot where stood the marble urn; but as she approached it, she started back, for close beside it stood the hideous figure of Cheops, dimly seen through the gathering gloom.

"Fear not!" said he in a softened, though still hollow voice; "tell me your woes, and, if I can, I will assist you."

"Alas! it is in vain," cried Clara in an agony of despair too profound even to admit of her feeling the fear generally experienced by all who saw the Mummy; "no one can relieve me,—I have no hope!"

Cheops smiled. "Poor child!" said he, "it is always thus when Eros first creeps into the soul, covering his arrows with roses, so that they are not seen till their barbed points rankle in the heart! I cannot tell how much I pity thee! So young and lovely too, it is hard that even thou shouldst not be exempt from the common lot of mortals! Yet do not despair."

"I do despair!" cried Clara, darting away from him; "I am truly wretched!"

From this moment Clara saw the Mummy almost daily, and her mind acquired new force and energy from his society, though her health visibly declined.[189] It was not, indeed, possible for human beings to hold daily intercourse with Cheops without feeling their souls withered. The glowing tints of youth and health faded rapidly from the cheeks of Clara; she became pale and spiritless, whilst she appeared to have lost all interest in the common affairs of life. Her fits of abstraction, however, her dejection, and her solitary wanderings, at length became so evident as to excite the attention of her mother, and the scene we have just described was the result.

Nothing could be more painful to poor Clara than the questioning she had undergone. She rushed from the presence of her parents to her favourite garden, to think over what had passed, and implore the assistance of the mysterious being with whom she had associated herself. He was not there, however; and though she repeatedly called upon his name, he came not. The weather was now delicious; the autumnal tints, that had just begun to change the lovely verdure of summer into a glowing brown, gave richness to the landscape. Since the abolition of coal and wood fires, the air of London had become pure and bright, though it still remained soft from its vicinity to the river, and it was thus highly favourable to vegetation: whilst, as no house was permitted to approach within a certain distance of the Thames,[190] the sumptuous gardens that bordered its banks were beautiful in the extreme. That of Mr. Montagu, which has been so often alluded to, was in particular laid out in the greatest taste; and its grateful shade and delicious fragrance calmed poor Clara's troubled spirits, and soothed them to repose. Nothing, indeed, could have a more lulling effect upon the harassed senses than the scene before her. The air was perfectly still; not a leaf was agitated, not a flower stirred; all nature seemed to repose, but Clara alone felt restless. The questions of Dr. Coleman, and surmises of Father Murphy, had created a variety of new feelings in her mind; and she wandered up and down, oppressed by a sensation of melancholy which she had never felt before. She could not define her own sensations; she could not analyze her thoughts; and, as she sauntered to and fro without any determinate object, she listlessly pulled the leaves from a rose that she carried in her hands.

The scattering of the rose-leaves, however, recalled her to herself, and she smiled as she saw the mischief she had done. "Alas! poor rose!" sighed she, apostrophizing the flower; "I know not why I have destroyed thee!" Then walking hastily away, she plunged into the thickest part of the grove. "Why am I thus agitated?" said she to herself. "Why do I feel thus miserable and discontented? Can it be love? Love!" she repeated, whilst deep blushes glowed upon her cheeks, and she started at the echo of her own voice. She threw herself upon a turfy bank under a shady tree, and, resting her head upon her hand, watched through the leaves the light fleecy clouds that drifted along the sky, till, oppressed by the painful nature of her own sensations, she sighed heavily, and tears swam in her eyes.

At this moment, footsteps rapidly approached; and Clara, springing upon her feet, hastily drew her hand across her eyes, and hid herself amongst the trees.

Dr. Hardman and Father Morris, who approached, seemed absorbed in conversation; and Clara, who dreaded Father Morris excessively, kept herself concealed, to avoid meeting him. We have already mentioned, that she was simple and innocent to a degree; but hers was the simplicity of ignorance, not folly. Her natural abilities were excellent, and her mind uncommonly strong. She therefore neither screamed nor fainted, though, from her present position, she became auditor to a scene of the deepest villany.[191] Notwithstanding the influence which Rosabella's party had at present in state, Father Morris was not satisfied. He wished to make her election certain, and this could he only done by removing Elvira. Dr. Hardman was her physician—the rest may be easily imagined.

Clara trembled, and her flesh seemed to creep upon her bones, as she listened to this horrid conference. But her terror was even increased when they changed the subject, and spoke no longer of an intended murder, but of one which had been already committed. Clara shook in every limb, and her lips and cheeks became blanched with fear; yet she uttered no cry, nor betrayed her presence by the slightest motion. At length they went, and

Clara stood like one awakened from a fearful dream, almost doubting the reality of what she had heard.

An hour elapsed, yet Clara still stood motionless. What should she do? Would her unassisted testimony be believed in matters of such awful import against the weight and influence of two persons of so much consequence in the state? No, she felt it would not. Yet, if she remained silent, she would be accessary to the murder of Elvira. What could she do? what course ought she to pursue?—she knew not. A chaos of thoughts seemed whirling through her brain, and threatened almost to drive her to madness. The longer she thought, the more she became confused; and she began to fear her senses were actually leaving her, when a solemn voice sounded in her ear. Well did she know those deep and awful tones—they were those of Cheops; and, confiding the awful secret to him, she promised to comply implicitly with his injunctions.

It was the day following this adventure, that, as Father Murphy and Abelard were conversing tranquilly together, lamenting over the degeneracy of the age, their conference was interrupted by the sudden appearance of the duke.

"Where is Sir Ambrose?" cried he in a state of violent agitation—"where is Sir Ambrose? I must see Sir Ambrose immediately."

"Calm yourself, for Heaven's sake!" said Father Morris, who had followed him unobserved. "This violent agitation will destroy you: remember your recent illness, your age, your weakness—"

"Where is Sir Ambrose?" cried the duke.

"This vehemence is unbefitting of your station," continued Father Morris: "moderate it, I entreat you—it can do no good."

"Will no one call Sir Ambrose?" reiterated the duke: and as the baronet, who had been summoned by Abelard, appeared, he threw himself into his arms, sobbing like a child.

"Oh, my dear, dear friend!" exclaimed he, "they are determined to ruin Elvira. Lord Gustavus and his adherents are gone to their country-seats to try to influence the election of the deputies; and my child can have no chance against such treachery."

"If that be all," said Henry Seymour, who had accompanied the baronet, "why not follow their example? your influence must, at least, be equal to theirs."

"He is right," rejoined Sir Ambrose. "I know not why we did not do so sooner; but, even now, it is not too late."

"And what end can possibly be produced by such a measure?" asked Father Morris, scowling darkly at the youth: "the freedom of the election should be inviolable."

"But!" hastily interrupted the duke, "if they attempt to control it, we may surely—"

"I was not before aware," said Father Morris, in his cold, ironical manner, "that the circumstance of others doing evil was any reason for our committing sin."

"Nonsense!" cried the duke; "here can be no sin in securing the election of my daughter; and so, Sir Ambrose, we will set off to-night, if you please."

"With all my heart!" said Sir Ambrose: and the two old men and Henry Seymour hurried away, leaving the monk alone. He did not, however, long remain so, for in a few seconds Cheops was at his side.

"So, Sir," said Father Morris, scowling upon Cheops with a look of deadly hatred, "you have proved yourself my friend, in suffering this babbling boy to counteract my views. Did you not boast he was your slave?"

The Mummy met his glance without shrinking; and, bursting into one of his fearful laughs, exclaimed tauntingly, "And so he is: but I thought you had determined not to oppose the duke any longer. It seems, then, I did not understand your reasoning in the garden."

"Fiend! cursed mocking fiend!" cried the friar, gnashing his teeth.

"Nay!" returned Cheops, "why blame me? Was I wrong in believing what you said? Was it, then, only a part you were acting to deceive me?"

"Demon! thou canst read my heart; but it is thy wish to drive me to distraction."

"No, no, my good Father Morris, my worthy friend, I honour you too much! If I can read your heart, I must be charmed to see such devotion to your friends, such candour, openness, and integrity."

"Taunting devil! be my sins what they may, thy presence is a penance that might redeem them. By Heaven! hell itself were easier to endure than those bitter scoffs."

"And darest thou talk of Heaven?" said the Mummy in an awful voice, that thrilled through the father's soul; whilst his eyes glared with such supernatural lustre that the priest could not bear their beams, and sank upon one knee before him, bending his head to the ground. "'Tis as it should be!" continued Cheops, with one of his fiendish laughs. "Yes, he is mine—he bends before my will! Now will I tell thee what thy feeble reason was too powerless to discover: I am still thy friend. The duke and Sir Ambrose will only injure their cause by the ill-judged measures they will take to promote it. They had the advantage of justice, honour, and open dealing upon their side; was it nothing to deprive them of these fair sounding words? Will they in future be able to complain of corruption, when they have attempted to corrupt? Had it not been so, even if success had crowned your efforts, would not the minds of men have been inclined to the side of injured integrity? for so they might have termed the party of the duke. Might they not also have said the election was secured by bribery and deceit; and upon the first discontent that arose against Rosabella's government, would they not have recurred fondly to the recollection of the honest, open dealing plain speaking duke! Men naturally love and respect virtue, though they may be seduced for a time by the allurements of vice. Thus, though they might not have had strength of mind to resist the arts of your party, their best feelings would have still remained upon the side of Elvira. This can now no longer be the case. The duke and Sir Ambrose voluntarily throw away their strongest hold—they rush blindfold to destruction. They degrade themselves to your level;[192] whilst, as they are unused to deceit, they will not succeed in their endeavours, and disgrace will be their only reward. Now, do you blame me?"

"Blame you!" exclaimed Father Morris; "you are my friend, my best, my only friend my preserver."

"With regard to Edmund," said Cheops, "we must excite his jealousy. If he were detached from Elvira, her cause would perish."

"It would, it would!" cried Father Morris.

"Try then thy efforts," said Cheops; "and if thou canst excite suspicions, fan them gently to a flame, yet without seeming to do so. Do not attack Elvira openly, or assert broadly that she loves another; but hint it darkly that your victim cannot misunderstand, and that the damning certainty may flash upon his mind with greater force than mere words can give. Well knowest thou what I mean, and well hath Nature modelled thee for such a part. That downcast look, that insinuating voice, and half ironical manner; the infernal deity himself could not well have wished a more fitting agent to execute his designs on earth than thou. Work then upon Edmund, and success cannot fail to follow your attempts."

"Thou Machiavel!"[193] cried Father Morris; "my friend, my dearest friend, my benefactor: oh! how I could fall down and worship thee!"

A sardonic smile curled the haughty lips of Cheops. "Learn then to obey in silence," said he, "nor dare again to blame designs far beyond your comprehension!"

Volume 2: Chapter 5

The day following was appointed for the departure of the two families of the duke and Sir Ambrose for the country; and the whole preceding evening was passed by the two old men in arranging their plans, and forming new schemes to ensure success. Elvira took no part in this conversation, though certainly the person most interested: she was thoughtful and *distraite*;[194] she was too restless to remain in one place. She walked to the window; she returned, and she again sat down. She attempted to work, to read, to draw—all was in vain; all seemed tasteless and insipid. Again she went to the window, and, opening its folding doors, stepped out upon the balcony. It was a delightful night, and the air felt soft and warm. Vines, laden with their luscious fruit, twined from pillar to pillar of the balcony, forming a kind of verdant network, whilst the moon shone bright upon the lovely scene beyond. Below, a smooth green lawn stretched forth like a velvet carpet, bounded on each aide by Chinese rose-trees, the delicate tints of which looked still more transparently beautiful in the lovely light. Behind these, rose trees of a loftier height and deeper shade, whilst. at the extremity of the lawn wound the river. The clear moon-beams trembled on the gently rippling stream, and gave a transparent brightness to the graceful foliage of a weeping willow, which hung over the water, and quivered in every passing breeze.

Elvira gazed upon the fair scene before her, and sighed heavily as she gazed. A gentle sigh softly echoed hers, and she started to find that Henry Seymour was standing before her.

"How beautiful is Nature," said he, "when undefiled by the follies and sins of man. How one might forget the world, and all its busy turmoil of deceit. When one gazes thus upon the sublime and lovely face of Nature, how poor do all the arts, the ambition, and the pitiful contrivances of man appear. The soul seems elevated to its proper sphere, and to long to throw off the frail covering of clay, which yet chains it down to the grovelling passions of earth, and to soar triumphant to its native skies."

His fine eyes were turned to heaven as he spoke; and Elvira gazed upon them and his noble countenance beaming with enthusiasm, till she quite forgot to reply.

"Do you not agree with, me, Elvira!" said he, in a tone of the softest melody, fixing his eyes upon hers with a look that sank deep into her heart. Again she sighed deeply, but she could not speak. "Oh, Elvira," continued he. taking her hand; "will you forget me? will not the remembrance of this night form a tie between us, when we shall be far, far apart?"

"Apart!" cried Elvira almost with a shriek of surprise.

The youth sighed; and, gazing earnestly upon her blushing face, whispered tenderly, as he pressed her hand to his heart, "O that I could flatter myself sorrow mingled with that sigh."

"Why, what is this?" said the old duke, bustling to the window; "the doctor tells me you are going to leave us. Surely you might contrive to stay till after the election."

"I am very sorry, Sir," said the youth; "but the circumstance that calls me away—"

"Ay, ay, the doctor told me; a near relation dangerously ill, that can't die in peace till he's seen you. "Well, well, my boy, such things must be; and if he's doomed to die, I only wish him an easy death, and you a good legacy."

"I cannot tell you how sorry I am to part with you," said Sir Ambrose, who now advanced, "nor how sincerely I wish you good fortune."

"Thank you, thank you, Sir," said the youth: "alas! I now feel how poor words are to express my gratitude for all your kindness. But—"

"I am sorry to hasten you, Mr. Seymour," said Dr. Coleman, who now approached; "but time wears apace."

"True, true," said Henry, "I had forgotten. Once more farewell. God bless you all!" and he hurried away, as though fearful of his own resolution if he ventured to stay another second. For the rest of the evening, Elvira was silent and abstracted; the suddenness of the blow seemed to have stunned her, and she felt like one wandering in a dream. Was he really gone? Should she never see him more? were questions she scarcely dared even to ask herself. "He was nothing to me, a mere common acquaintance," she repeated incessantly; and yet she felt a wearisome void, a sickening disgust and impatience at every thing around her, which she had never experienced before. "What can be the matter with me," said she peevishly; "I shall never see him again; and it is the excess of weakness to feel an interest in the fate of one, who is evidently so indifferent about me; and yet he seemed affected when he said we were about to part. Was he really so? But of what consequence to me is it whether he were so or not. I shall never see him more." And Elvira sighed involuntarily at the thought. "I am devoted to other prospects. I—in short, I will think of him no more." And, in pursuance of this magnanimous resolution, she thought of nothing else all night.

The following day, Elvira and her friends went into the country; but, as Cheops had predicted, the duke and Sir Ambrose proved quite unequal to the task they had undertaken, and they only lost their popularity by the attempt. Men were disgusted to see personages hitherto considered so respectable descend to meanness, and the shallowness of the artifices by which it was intended to impose upon them excited their contempt. In the mean time, Lord Edmund was not more successful in London than his friends in the country: he had marched a chosen body of troops within a convenient distance of the metropolis; in consequence of which ill-judged measure, the members of the council, to show that they were not influenced by the fear of military authority, and to vindicate their independence, invariably opposed every measure that he suggested.

As the law, however, forbade any decisive promises till the actual day of election, there was still hope, though the friends of Elvira struggled on, rather from a wish not too hastily to abandon her cause, than from any rational, well-founded prospect of success.

In the midst of these anxieties, Elvira's health indeed seemed rapidly declining. A weight that nothing could alleviate, hung upon her spirits; she made no effort to secure voters; but pale, silent, and melancholy, she glided about—the ghost of her former self. Still, however, she was lovely; the increased delicacy of her complexion, and shadowy lightness of her form, harmonized well with the general style of her beauty; whilst her fine eyes, shaded by their long silken lashes, only shone more brilliantly from the glowing hectic of the cheek below.

The time fixed for the important ceremony now rapidly approached; the election of the deputies was concluded, and the families of the duke and Sir Ambrose prepared to return to town. The night, however, before they departed, the duke gave a grand *fête champêtre*[195] to the neighbouring gentry; and as a considerable number of the deputies were expected, he particularly enjoined Elvira to exert herself to the utmost to win their suffrages. Never perhaps had Elvira looked more beautiful than she did that night, as, pale, trembling and timid, she received her numerous guests; and never, perhaps, was effect more magical than that which her appearance produced. Her very diffidence and modesty attracted; and the reserve, with which she shunned, rather than sought the attention of the crowd, completed the enchantment.

"It is her fear of seeming to wish to interest us," whispered one deputy to another, "that makes her treat us so coldly."

"Yes," replied the other; "and I like her the better for it. If she were to attempt to make herself agreeable, I should hate her; the duke and Sir Ambrose have sickened us of that!"

The fete was given in the gardens of the duke, which were beautiful and extensive, and now brilliantly illuminated by lamps suspended from the trees. There was something, however, not quite congenial to Elvira's taste in thus marrying the gorgeous splendour of art to the simplicity of nature, and she sighed heavily as she watched the flaring lamps scorching the calm pale verdure of the trees.

"Now this is as it should be," said the old duke, as he led his daughter to the pavilion appointed for her to receive her guests; "Elvira now looks like herself. Does she not, Dr. Coleman?"

The doctor shook his head: "I fear," began he—

"Oh! we will have no fears to-night!" cried the duke gaily; "remember, Elvira! every thing now depends upon you. Play the part of the smiling, condescending hostess; win the hearts of the deputies, and you will make that of your old father leap for joy. We shall have a gay party, sha'n't we, doctor?" continued he, eyeing the groups as they advanced. "I wish your friend, Henry Seymour, were here amongst us."

Elvira started, and deep blushes suffused her cheeks at the mention of this name. The doctor eyed her attentively, though he replied as though he had not noticed her agitation. "It was urgent business, you know, that obliged him to leave England."

"He was a charming youth," said the duke; "so gay and yet so fearless. I think, however, I observed that his spirits seemed much depressed the last time I saw him."

"You know he said it was the death—I mean the illness of a relation, that compelled him to go."

"Young men don't generally feel so much for the illness, or even death of old ones," returned the duke: "now, if I were to judge, doctor, I should think it far more likely it was some love affair. But we can't stay talking about it now. I must go, and attend to my guests: and do you mind, Elvira, and make yourself agreeable."

Poor Elvira, however, was, perhaps, never less fitted to obey her father's injunctions than at this moment; for the conversation she had just heard, had quite deranged her nerves. Her father's supposition inflicted a deep pang on her heart; and though she went through the duties of her station mechanically, her mind wandered to Henry Seymour.

It was a lovely night, and the general effect of the scene, as groups of elegantly-dressed people flitted to and fro through the lighted groves, was striking in the extreme. Beautiful flowering exotics decorated the pavilion of Elvira, and the balmy air that fanned their blossoms, seemed loaded with sweets; whilst the richly illuminated castle, rearing its lofty towers in awful grandeur in the distance, had the appearance of a fairy palace.

Elvira listlessly gazed upon the magic scene, till she felt almost fainting with the fatigue her situation as hostess imposed upon her; and she looked with a languid and almost despairing eye upon the crowds that came still pouring into the gardens. The throng, however, now opened, and a tall and dignified figure found its way through the mass. It was Lord Edmund: he approached rapidly, and threw himself at Elvira's feet: "My adored Elvira!" exclaimed he.

"You here, my Lord?" cried the princess; whose eyes, enfeebled by exhaustion, had not permitted her to recognise him till he was immediately before her: "I did not expect to see you here to-night!"

"Does my presence pain you then?" said Lord Edmund, looking at her attentively. "They told me you were ill, and I do indeed find you changed."

"I am better now," returned Elvira faintly.

"Do not deceive yourself," cried he, with the most intense anxiety. "You are ill—you are not equal to this fatigue. Retire from this scene, it will destroy you."

I dare not," replied Elvira, still more feebly, "without permission from my father; though, I own, I do feel exhausted!"

Lord Edmund waited for no more; but darted to find the duke, and obtain his wished for sanction. The next instant, his place was supplied by Prince Ferdinand, who had been invited into the country a few days before by the duke; and who, with the inconstancy natural to his disposition, had now become as deeply smitten with Elvira, as he had before been with Rosabella.

Elvira, however, saw him not; and, looking gratefully after Lord Edmund, sighed profoundly as she lost sight of him among the crowd.

"Happy Edmund!" said the prince; "what would I not give to create a feeling in that lovely bosom, like that caused by thy absence!"

Elvira blushed at the earnest gaze of the youthful German, as she replied, without exactly knowing what she said, "Do you suppose, then, that the absence of Lord Edmund gave me pain?"

"What other cause can I divine for your melancholy?" said Ferdinand. "Adored by every heart, admired by every eye, and blest at once with rank, beauty, and affection, what can Elvira wish?—and what can cloud her brow with sorrow, or heave her lovely bosom with a sigh, unless it be the loss of the favoured lover whom ambition bids her sacrifice?"

"And think you so poorly of me," returned Elvira indignantly, "as to suppose, if I really loved Lord Edmund, that ambition would tempt me to sacrifice him?"

"Can a heart like yours then be really dead to love?" said the prince, gazing upon her earnestly. "Can Nature have formed such exquisite beauty, and forgotten to give a soul to pity the wretches it must make?"

Elvira blushed deeply as he spoke, for his ardent look embarrassed her; and her eyes having been modestly withdrawn, again met those of Lord Edmund, who had returned without her perceiving him. 'Twas but for a moment, however, that she gazed upon him, for she shrank aghast from his withering glance. Jealousy and hatred curled his lips, and darkened upon his brow; whilst his features seemed so changed, that Elvira could scarcely believe he was indeed the same she had so lately spoken with.

"I beg your Highness's pardon," said he haughtily; "I would not have presumed to intrude, if I had known you were engaged. fancied that you wished to retire, and had obtained the duke's permission for your doing so; but—"

"Oh, thank you! thank you, Edmund!" cried Elvira; "most gladly will I seek my chamber." Then marking a slight smile upon Prince Ferdinand's face, she hesitated, for she recollected the interpretation he had put upon her melancholy and indifference. Lord Edmund's agony was beyond description: he saw her hesitation; he saw her look at Ferdinand, and fancying she sought his approval before she would retire, his jealous rage was unbounded, and, darting at her a look of ungovernable passion, he sprang from the pavilion, and was out of sight in an instant. Elvira could not hear his look, nor his unreasonable jealousy; and, exhausted by her previous fatigue, she fainted. A crowd soon gathered round her, and she was carried to her chamber in a state of insensibility.

"Mark me!" said a figure muffled in a thick cloak, speaking in a deep, low whisper, as he laid his hand; upon the arm of Father Morris, who stood gazing after Elvira, with a look of intense anxiety; "she must not die; for if she does, I swear by the holy tomb of Osiris at Philaa,[196] Rosabella never shall be Queen!"

From that hour, Elvira recovered; and the consumptive symptoms, that had so strongly excited the alarm of her friends, entirely disappeared.

Lord Edmund was conversing earnestly with one of the deputies, and, notwithstanding his jealousy, advocating the cause of Elvira with vehemence, when he was informed that she had fainted: his first impulse was to fly to her assistance; and when he found she had been removed to her chamber, his heart smote him for the cruel manner in which he had left her.

"She was really ill," thought he; "and, in her feeble state, my harshness overpowered her. But never again shall my foolish jealousy disturb her peace. No! let her scorn me—hate me, if she will. I will hear all the tortures she can inflict, rather than again hazard wounding that gentle bosom. Let her smile on whom she lists, even upon that hated German, I will not repine: if she be happy, I will ask no more."

Thus thought Edmund, and he knew not that be deceived himself, till he saw Prince Ferdinand, who, with the happy elasticity of youth, was chatting gaily with one of the beauties of the court. "Love him!" thought he, as a scornful smile passed over his features—"love him, did I say? Oh, no! it is impossible; I could not endure to see her love that coxcomb:" and, shuddering with the torments of jealousy, he turned away.

Cheops was near him, muffled in a thick cloak that shrouded him from observation; the Mummy marked the changes in Lord Edmund's countenance, and read well the feelings they betrayed.

"Yes, even he," said he, with one of his fearful laughs, "will soon be mine; for never yet did man trust in his own strength, that did not fall."

Volume 2: Chapter 6

The day of election now rapidly approached. The duke, Sir Ambrose, the rival candidates, and the opposition lords, were all in London. The deputies were also assembled; and though it was forbidden to declare publicly for whom they intended to vote, till the decisive moment arrived; yet the popular feeling seemed so strongly in favour of Rosabella, that there appeared scarcely a chance for her rival.

Exulting in her expected triumph, and confident of success, Rosabella sate in the splendid *boudoir* allotted to her use in Lord Gustavus's house, musing on her hoped-for grandeur. A large mirror was opposite to her; and as Rosabella saw her own fine figure reflected in it, joy sparkled in her eyes. and her mind wandered enraptured through scenes of future glory. Thus, completely absorbed in pleasing meditations, Rosabella was not aware that

Cheops stood before her, till she heard his full, deep-toned voice repeating her name.

"Rosabella!" said he—"Rosabella! Queen of England! hail!"

"Cheops!" exclaimed she.

"Hail to the Queen of England!" resumed he: "no longer need you stoop to solicit suffrages: your fate is sealed!"

"Think you that I am quite safe?" asked the princess; her eyes sparkling, and her cheeks glowing.

"Certainly—there cannot be a doubt."

"Then I may bid defiance to these wretches, and need no longer submit to their caprices, or be subservient to their humours."

"Not unless you like it."

"Like it!" exclaimed Rosabella, her eyes flashing fire; "can you suppose I like to practise meanness?"

"Policy, indeed, recommends a contrary course," continued the Mummy; "as, if you do not assert your own independence, they will encroach upon your condescension, and treat you as a slave."

Rosabella bit her lips, and her bosom swelled with indignation.

The Mummy took no notice of her agitation, but went on. "Let them not bind you by any promises. Prove yourself a free and independent sovereign. Trample upon, them, and they will crouch at your feet: but crouch to them, and they will trample upon you!"

"You say right," said Rosabella proudly; "and my would-be masters shall soon find their error. They think weakness has made me submit to their arrogance; but they shall see their folly."

The influence the Mummy exercised over the minds of all those he came in contact with was astonishing; and, in pursuance of his advice, Rosabella, from this moment, resumed her usual imperious manner; and received the compliments paid to her with the air rather of an empress long seated upon the throne, than that of an aspiring candidate for regal honours, dependant only upon the favour of the people. This excessive confidence, however, displeased the deputies.

"She hardly leaves us a choice," said they; "for she seems to command us to choose her. Notwithstanding the strength of her party, and the weakness of her rival, we don't think she should take the thing quite in her own hands: the old Queen ordered that the people should choose her successor; but this princess seems to have chosen herself. It is very kind of her to wish to save us the trouble; but, with her good leave, we think we might have managed to go through it without her help."

These murmurs, however, though deep, were not loud; the party of Rosabella being too firmly established for any one to dare openly to oppose it. The opposition lords had all returned to town, and, though they had not completely succeeded in the object of their journey to the country, they had at least satisfied themselves; and by the activity they had displayed, given themselves, as they imagined, a just title to the gratitude of their future Queen.

In the mean time, the friends of Elvira almost despaired; few persons of note declared themselves her advocates; and though the favourable impression she had made upon the deputies still faintly operated, the feeling was fast fading away. An invincible repugnance to appear as the leader of a party, oppressed her; and she shrank from the public gaze with a sensation little short of horror. Lord Edmund, however, still remained her firm and almost her only friend. Yet, though he exerted every nerve on her behalf, even he despaired of obtaining her election. Sometimes, indeed, as he gazed upon her beauty, a selfish feeling crept over his soul, and he could scarcely repress an emotion of joy, as he thought of the possibility that she might still be his; for the very qualities that impeded her success, only endeared her yet more fondly to his heart. The next instant, however, his nobler feelings would reproach this selfish joy, and with a kind of penitential sorrow, he would strive by fresh efforts to destroy the hopes, for the gratification of which his very soul panted.

"I presume," said Lord Gustavus de Montfort to Rosabella, the day before that appointed for the election, "your Highness does not intend to make Lord Maysworth a minister as well as a general; for, thinking as I think, and as I am confident every one else must think, I feel assured he has no talents for the cabinet."

"As Queen of England, my Lord," returned Rosabella proudly, "I will not be dictated to though I will do my best to choose such ministers as may, in my judgment, be most likely to promote the welfare of my country."

Lord Gustavus was thunderstruck, and he gazed after her, as she retired, with mingled feelings of astonishment and indignation. "You are not Queen of England yet, however," said he to himself, "and it is possible you never may be. What pride! what haughtiness! If I had been a slave, she could not have shown more contempt. 'When I am Queen of England,' said she, I 'will not be dictated to.' 'Queen of England,' said she? Humph! thinking as I think, and as I am sure every one else must think, it is possible, that that is a contingency that may never arrive. Humph! 'I will not be dictated to'—Humph! Well, certainly I must confess I never heard a more dignified '*will not*' in my life."

It was the hour when Lord Gustavus was accustomed to hold a kind of levee where the partizans of the princess had been in the habit of assembling, under the guise of casual visitors; and as he thus cogitated, Lord Maysworth and Dr. Hardman were announced.

"My dear Lord Gustavus," cried the former, "you cannot imagine how impatient I feel to have to-morrow over. The uniform of the household-troops is horrible: I have determined to change it the very instant I am appointed commander-in-chief."

"If you should obtain that situation," replied Lord Gustavus doubtingly.

"What do you mean?" asked his friend, in astonishment. "I thought the means we had taken must infallibly ensure success."

"They must ensure the election of Rosabella," replied Lord Gustavus.

"And is not that all we wish?"

"Not quite," returned Lord Gustavus drily.

"I do not understand you," said Lord Maysworth.

"What can you mean?" demanded Dr. Hardman.

"I mean," replied Lord Gustavus, in his usual cold, precise manner, "that, thinking as I think, and as I am sure every one else must think, from the conversation that has just taken place between the princess and myself, I am convinced that our possession of the places she has promised to us, is by no means the necessary consequence of her accession to the throne."

"Oh!" cried his auditors, looking perfectly aghast: a farther explanation confirmed their fears. "I could not have believed it!" exclaimed both; and as the partizans of Rosabella continued to arrive, they were successively apprized of and paralyzed by the appalling news. Divers were the sensations thus excited: but amongst all, notwithstanding their professed disinterestedness, there was not one whose sentiments remained unchanged by the intelligence.

In the mean time, Rosabella, in the solitude of her own chamber, became aware of the imprudence she had committed, though she brooded in secret over her uneasiness, and felt too proud to avow it even to Marianne; whilst that faithful confidant, quite unsuspicious of the error of her mistress, exulted in her expected triumph with as much transport as though it had been her own.

"To-morrow," said she, "I shall have to do homage to my Queen, and I shall have the rapture of seeing crowds kneel humbly at her feet. Oh, would the happy day were come! how tedious will seem this long, long night! how wearisome will be the hours! Does not your heart also throb, my princess? To-morrow I shall see my Queen. To-morrow! oh, would it were to-day!"

The important day at last arrived, and the delegates, assembled in Blackheath Square, awaited with impatience the arrival of the princesses. Each was to deliver a speech; after which, a nobleman was to be permitted to address the mob on her behalf, and then the majority of their votes was to decide.

The rival princesses appeared, and were hailed with enthusiasm. They were dressed with the utmost simplicity, in the purest white; whilst from their heads hung long veils of gossamer web, the ample folds of which effectually shielded their persons from observation. They were followed by their respective suites; Lord Gustavus and the opposition lords being most conspicuous in that of Rosabella; and Lord Edmund in that of Elvira. The Duke and Sir Ambrose, attended by the reverend fathers Morris and Murphy, were amongst the number of spectators: the two former feeling too much agitated to allow of their appearing as actors in the scene; and the others being, from different reasons, equally disqualified from taking a part in it.

All now was silent—the tumultuous, wave-like heaving of the multitude ceased; and every one listened in breathless expectation—for the princesses were about to speak. It was an awful moment: the poor old duke's heart beat almost audibly; he sate, his eyes fixed upon the ground, not daring to look up, and holding the hand of his friend, Sir Ambrose, firmly in his own. It was Rosabella who was to speak first: she advanced with a firm, decided step; and when the attendants, drew back the veil that covered her, the assembled multitude uttered a shout of admiration at her beauty. Her dark eyes flashed fire, as she proudly surveyed the crowd; and anticipated triumph gave an animated glow to her fine features. She looked, indeed, already a Queen, and seemed born only to command, and be obeyed. The multitude were awed by her presence; and listened with uplifted eyes, and the most profound silence, whilst she thus addressed them:

My Lords and Gentlemen,
"I feel the presumption I am guilty of, in thus venturing to address so august an assembly; but I trust the magnitude of the occasion that calls me forward may afford an excuse for my temerity I come, gentlemen, to offer myself to you as your Sovereign, and the exalted nature of the trust I wish you to repose in me inspires me with courage to deserve it. Yes gentlemen, I say to deserve it; for I should consider myself unworthy to be appointed your Queen, if I were to shrink from performing any of the duties attendant upon the station; and one of the most arduous of these do I consider that of thus addressing you. I am aware, that, upon occasions like the present, it is usual for the aspiring candidate to promise miracles of reformation, that are to be effected upon the obtaining of power; I promise nothing of the kind, for I will tie myself to no promises. Elect me for your Queen, and I will fulfil the duties of my rank, according to the best of my own judgment. I will not submit to dictation; neither will I be censured by my subjects. I will be a free, independent Sovereign, or I will remain a subject. I scorn to attempt to practise any deception upon you. I wish you to see me as I really am; and then, if you think me worthy of the high office I aspire to, then, at least, I may assure you, you shall never have reason to blush for your choice; nor shall the proud character which England has so long maintained, ever suffer a stain upon its glory at my hands. No, my countrymen, haughty as I may be deemed, I assure you, with sincerity, that I have ever held the name of Englishwoman as my noblest boast; and that

I would not relinquish my title to it, were kingdoms offered in exchange. I can say no more. If you approve me as your Sovereign, your voices will obtain the fulfilment of your wishes; if you do not, worlds would not tempt me to accept the throne."

Rosabella now sate down amidst thunders of applause, whilst acclamations of "Long live Rosabella!" rent the air. These symptoms of approbation were, however, only produced by her beauty and her commanding manner; for when men came to analyze her speech, they found much in it to disapprove. The haughty manner in which she had disavowed control, indeed was neither calculated to win new friends, nor secure those she already had: as the counsellors who had so warmly supported her cause, had certainly not imagined, that by so doing, they should shut the door of preferment against themselves; and what hope of promotion or power could remain during the reign of a Queen who had thus openly announced her intention of acting entirely for herself?

The prejudices of the people, too, were wounded; they had been so accustomed to promises of reformation and relief from taxation, upon the accession of a new Sovereign, that they were disappointed at not receiving them, although they knew from experience, that they meant nothing: just as persons fond of flattery cannot live without it, though they are well acquainted with its fallacy. Besides, even experience cannot make some people wise; and though the hopes of the English had been so often disappointed, it was pleasant still to have something held out to them to hope for. These thoughts soon arose in the breasts of the multitude; and a rising murmur was beginning to swell upon the ear, when the assembly was hushed to silence by perceiving Lord Noodle had risen, and was about to address them.

"My lords and gentlemen," said he, "it is with feelings of considerable embarrassment that I rise to address you. Every thing that can be said, has been said; and every thing that has been said, ought to have been said; and every thing that ought to have been said, has been said. 'What, then, can there possibly be left for me to say?

"Let it not be supposed, however, by my saying this, that I have nothing to say for myself; on the contrary, I think every body must allow I have said a great deal upon the said subject;" (here the noble lord tittered at his own wit, and well it was that he did so; as, if he had not, perhaps nobody might have found it out;) "say what I will, however, one thing must be clear, and that is, (if I was to speak for an hour I could say no more;)—that is, that you must have a Queen; and that you cannot choose a better one than the noble lady who has just sat down!—and so, gentlemen, she having finished, I think I cannot do better than follow her example!"

Shouts and roars of laughter followed this speech, to the infinite delight of the enlightened orator; and he bowed and bowed on all sides, till his little head and bobbing periwig seemed to have acquired the gift of perpetual motion.

No sooner was the tumult a little subsided, than Elvira came forward to address the people. When her veil was removed, her agitation was extreme. Elvira was delicately fair, and the "eloquent blood spoke in her cheeks"[197] in a thousand varying tints; for a few seconds she stood, her eyes fixed upon the ground, apparently endeavouring to collect herself: then raising her eyes, she seemed on the point of speaking, but her courage failing as she surveyed the immense multitude, every eye fixed upon her, and every ear listening for her words, the sounds died upon her lips, and after a few ineffectual attempts to speak, she buried her face in her veil, and sobbed aloud.

Who can describe the agitation of her aged father at this moment! When she appeared, he had risen, and, leaning forward, listened with a fearful eagerness, as though his ear would drink in every syllable, and as though his own death-warrant hung upon her words. He became pale as he saw her agitation, and his countenance varied with every variation of her's; till, when he saw her total inability to speak, his lips became of livid whiteness, he uttered a piercing shriek, and fell senseless to the ground!

A bustle immediately took place; the duke was carried off; and Elvira remained pale, trembling, and almost fainting, leaning against one of the pillars that supported the canopy over the platform upon which she stood. An artful pause ensued, which was at last broken by Lord Edmund rushing forward, and eagerly addressing the crowd in the following words:

"My friends and countrymen,

"If one spark of kindness and compassion dwell in your breasts; if your hearts are open to noble feelings; if you can pity defenceless age and helpless womanhood, listen to me now! Hear me whilst I plead the cause of the timid female now before you; who, agitated by the solemn occasion for which you are convened, and awed by the august majesty of this assembly, finds it impossible to give vent to her feelings in words; for difficult, indeed, is it to express by words the strong emotions of the heart. Oh! would to Heaven, my friends, that I could lay her heart open before you, that you might there read the love of her country—the devotion to your dearest interests—and the generous wish to sacrifice her domestic happiness to secure yours, that prompt her this day to appear before you. Do you fear tyranny? Is this trembling woman likely to impose it? Do you wish remission from oppression? Is not she who evidently possesses such extreme sensibility likely to relieve your cares? Can her breast, which now throbs with emotion, ever be deaf to the cry of misery? No, no; that gentle spirit which shrinks from exposure in the garish light of day, will devote itself to soothing your woes, and lightening your burdens. Do you wish for victory? Has not my arm been hitherto successful, and am I not devoted to Elvira?

"My countrymen, I plead not from interested motives, God knows I do not! Nay, there may be some among you who know I now plead for the destruction of my dearest hopes: but the welfare of my country is more to me than my own. I give my country the treasure that might have been mine: contented, if by the sacrifice of my own happiness, I can secure that of thousands.

My countrymen, I cannot more strongly prove my devotion to your interests, for if you choose Elvira for your Queen,[198] my widowed heart will have no bride but glory. Take, however, the treasure I resign to you. Prize her as she deserves, and Heaven in its mercy grant that prudent counsellors and sagacious statesmen may so direct her steps, that victory may shine on her banners, wisdom in her counsels, and happiness in her kingdom!"

Lord Edmund stopped, overpowered by his own emotions; and his agitation found an echo in the bosom of every auditor. The effect of his speech was instantaneous: cries of "Elvira shall be our Queen!" "Elvira for ever!" rose in deafening tumult from the crowd, nor did there appear a single dissentient voice. In fact, after all that can be said upon the subject, feeling is the only true eloquence. The passions of the crowd were strongly excited: the fainting of the duke; the agitation of Elvira; and the speech of Lord Edmund, who was the hero of the day, absolutely had driven them distracted. They shouted again and again that Elvira, and Elvira alone, should be Queen, and, forming a triumphal car, placed her in it, and dragged her along to Westminster Abbey, where the ceremony of the coronation was appointed to take place. This venerable pile, which had stood for centuries, and resisted alike the war of nature, and the destroying hand of innovation, with which the barbarous taste of the middle ages had endeavoured to destroy its grandeur, shone forth in all its original splendour, and afforded another magnificent proof of the length of time the labours of man survive the term of his fragile existence.

It had been a brilliant sight, when Westminster Hall was crowded with the nobles of the land, to choose the council of state; but far more splendid was it now, when, after the religious part of the ceremony of the coronation had been performed in the Abbey, the trembling and beautiful Queen entered its sumptuous walls, surrounded by her counsellors, and welcomed with transport by her kneeling subjects. All had been previously prepared for the ceremony, as the ordinance of the old Queen had directed the coronation to take place immediately after the election; and the venerable Hall was now crowded with the nobles and ladies of Claudia's court, splendidly attired, waiting for the Queen, whom the choice of the deputies might give them, with the most eager impatience. Elvira was received with transports; and though, perhaps, under different circumstances, her rival might have been honoured with equal rapture, yet, as Elvira knew it not, the thought did not damp her pleasure.

In the mean time Father Morris had remained aghast, a prey to the combined tortures of grief, rage, and disappointment. The crowd had disappeared, yet still he stood gazing upon the platform, the speechless image of despair.

"For Heaven's sake, do not remain here," cried a voice he knew only too well; and, obeying the impulse of Marianne's arm, he suffered himself to be led from the scaffold, where all his hopes had perished. There was a small house, at no great distance from the spot, where the partizans of Rosabella had held frequent conferences respecting their plans for securing her election; and to this place Marianne led the disappointed friar.

"Curses on the fiend that has betrayed me to my ruin!" said he, as he threw himself upon a sofa in this abode: "may demons haunt him here, and eternal misery be his portion hereafter!"

The fiendish laugh of Cheops rang in the father's ears as she pronounced these words; and ere he finished, the hated form of the Mummy stood before him.

"What, Father Morris!" cried the Egyptian, "is this your treatment of your friends? Fie! fie! is this your strength of mind? I am ashamed of you. Is it the part of a man of courage to shrink from such a slight reverse? However, I am still your friend, and if you will follow my advice—"

"Avaunt! demon!" cried Father Morris; "tempt me no more! Ruin hangs upon thy words, and it is thy advice that has destroyed me."

"Say rather, your own evil passions," returned the Mummy.

"Fiend!" exclaimed the monk; "was it not by thy advice Rosabella rejected the address I had prepared for her, and determined to deliver her own sentiments extempore."

"Such an expression of her genuine feelings was likely to produce ten times the effect of a studied address. The oration of Lord Edmund was from the feeling of the moment, and you saw its power was magical."

"And it was not by your desire that the fool Lord Noodle seconded her, instead of Lord Gustavus, as I had intended?"

"A ridiculous fool was more likely to put the people in good-humour than a prosing one."

"Yes, yes, I know; it was thus you made your plans seem feasible, but how have they succeeded?"

"Success is not always the test of merit. How could I foresee the fainting of the duke, and the agitation of Elvira? That timid silence said far more for her than words: if she had spoken, she would have had no chance."

"Would she were dead!" said Father Morris, grinding his teeth.

"So would you seal your ruin. Rosabella would be suspected, and her chance of reigning destroyed—destroyed for ever."

"What shall I do?"

"Let Elvira reign!—Nay, start not! for it is but for a time: she will naturally make Edmund her first counsellor from gratitude for the service he has rendered her; and, as he has sense and talent, he will as naturally either reject employing the noble lords who were your friends entirely; or, at best, give them but subordinate situations. Their hopes having been previously raised, they will feel this disappointment bitterly, and look back with longing eyes to Rosabella, by whom they were promised place and power. That princess must moderate her natural haughtiness: if she wish to reign, she must submit to bend before she rise; for, though ambition be the most lofty of all passions, perhaps no one makes its votaries occasionally condescend to greater meanness. At present patience alone is required. Novelty is always delightful; but the pleasure it produces can never be lasting: and the expectations of men having been raised too high by the brilliancy with which a new government is certain to commence, they will soon be disposed to quarrel with every thing that may chance to fall short of the standard they will then propose to themselves: though this same standard, if they give themselves time to consider, they would find far too exalted for mortals to have ever any hopes of reaching. Their extravagant expectations not being realized, they will then plunge into the opposite extreme; they will see every thing with a jaundiced eye; and, not liking to own they find themselves deceived, they will overturn the government of Elvira to conceal for ever the folly they have been guilty of."

"But will not the government of Rosabella afterwards share the same fate?"

"No: for they will have learnt wisdom by experience; and having just suffered from the inconveniences inseparable from a revolution, they will idolize every word and action of Rosabella, to spare themselves the necessity of again undergoing the same horrors, and yet avoid the charge of inconsistency. They will thus fear even to censure; and will gloss over any thing that may not quite please them, rather than run the risk of again interrupting that tranquility which the late disturbance has made them taste the sweets of."

The sophistry of Cheops was well suited to the feelings of his hearers; and well did he know how to work upon the passions of those he conversed with. The indignation of Father Morris and Marianne subsided, and they again became the Egyptians devoted slaves. Cheops watched them as they retired; a smile of derision curling his haughty lip.

"Fools that they are!" said he, as again a fearful expression flashed across his saturnine countenance: "by Typhon! they are scarcely worth deceiving, for they rush blindfold into the net."

In the mean time, nothing could exceed the grandeur of the scene exhibiting in Westminster Hall. The ceremony was finished; for the Queen had taken oaths of fidelity to the interests of her new subjects, and had received their humblest homage in return. A sumptuous banquet was now served, where all that could please the eye mingled in luxuriant profusion with all that could tempt the appetite. Music completed the charm; and as the harmonious notes swelled through the lofty dome, it seemed a choir of angels rejoicing from on high. Thus, whilst all that could gratify the senses was combined, the fairy loveliness of Elvira seemed to fit her well to be the goddess of the scene; and the figure of the poor old duke, her father, gazing at her with indescribable rapture—the tears trickling down his furrowed cheeks, and his long white hair hanging loose upon his shoulders, completed the interest of the picture.

Great and glorious was the triumph of Elvira: but, whilst the nation rang with acclamations of joy, and bonfires and illuminations proclaimed the transport of the people, who shall paint the despair, the desolation, of the unfortunate Rosabella? Forlorn and deserted by her friends; despised and injured by him she loved; disappointed in the fairy dreams of her ambition; and disgusted with a world that had rejected her—what could she do? where find a refuge from her woes?

Rosabella sought no refuge: wretched as she was, her proud spirit still supported her: she neither retired from society, nor gave herself up to the paroxysms of despair. Hers was not a mind to brood over useless grief. She felt her wrongs, it is true, and most keenly did she feel them, but she wasted not her time in lamentation, and burnt only to avenge them. Marianne had communicated to her the advice of Cheops, and her whole soul was now devoted to revenge. For this, she determined to obey his injunctions; to bend her haughty spirit to his wishes; to conciliate the friends that had deserted her; and to submit to any meanness to keep up a party in the state. This done, she resolved to watch for the errors unavoidable in a new government; to take advantage of every weakness, and foment every discontent; in short, to open a chasm under her rival's feet, and then, like the lion pismire[199] on the brink of his sandy trap, to rest concealed until the entanglement of the expected prey enabled her to rush upon and destroy it.

Elvira's disposition was naturally noble; and, satisfied with the possession of the throne, she sought no farther triumph. Her generous soul was touched by the apparent resignation of her rival, and she endeavoured, by every means in her power, to console her for her disappointment. The duke had quitted the country, and now resided entirely with his, daughter; whilst upon Rosabella, Elvira, with the utmost delicacy, conferred a palace and a separate establishment.

Notwithstanding, however, the delicacy with which Elvira's favours were conferred, Rosabella could not forget that they *were* favours, and hers was not a mind to brook dependence. Her hatred for her cousin thus increased with the weight of her obligations, whilst that of Elvira had vanished with the occasion that gave it birth. It is, indeed, scarcely possible for a proud, haughty temper, like that of Rosabella, to love the person to whom it owes every thing. Such dispositions find infinitely more pleasure in obliging, than in being obliged—pride being gratified in one ease and humbled in the other. People are thus often devotedly attached to their protegées, as they seem, in some measure, creations of their own, and lavish favours upon them with a profuse hand; but they often expect such devotion in return, that love withers into slavery, or changes into hatred, and what was once gratitude, soon becomes mortification.

Elvira had an arduous part to sustain. It was difficult to find the medium between giving too much or too little; and more difficult still, to discover a means of giving at all, without hurting the feelings of Rosabella. The sense she had of this, rendered the manner of Elvira towards her cousin, occasionally, cold and restrained, and Rosabella felt acutely the slightest change. She, indeed, saw every thing with a jaundiced eye: she imagined insults, where none were intended; she shrank from the slightest observation, that could be supposed to allude to her present situation; and she appeared to feel so much pain whenever she was in the society of Elvira, that the intercourse between the cousins gradually dwindled to a mere formal interchange of visits, and the customary ceremonials of court etiquette.

The cousins thus completely estranged from each other, Rosabella's palace became the resort of the discontented. The King of Ireland had died soon after the departure of the Duke of Cornwall for the country, and those malcontents, formerly in his pay, being repulsed by his son, now, crowded round Rosabella. Men of talents, but of dissolute habits; daring spirits that preyed upon themselves for want of employment; and desperate characters, to whom every change was agreeable, as they had nothing to lose, and every thing to hope for by a revolution, vied with each other in devoting themselves to her service. It was often grating to Rosabella's feelings to associate with wretches such as these; but to what cannot proud spirits sometimes submit, to gain the determined purpose of their souls! Every thing is swallowed up in one vast overwhelming passion, and minor difficulties are neither seen, thought of, nor felt.

Thus, Rosabella scrupled not to waste her time in the society of such beings as Lord Noodle and his friend Lord Doodle; she even stooped to flatter them, and occasionally to ask, and appear to follow their advice: she endured patiently the dictatorial prosing of Lord Gustavus, and listened with an appearance of interest to the wearisome pettinesses of Lord Maysworth. All she thought of, was whether any particular line of conduct were likely to conduce to placing her on the throne; and if it were, be it what it might, the haughty Rosabella instantly condescended to practise it. Taught by the late events not to rely too confidently upon her own strength, she rushed into the opposite extreme, and descended even unto servility.

In the mean time, the attention of Elvira was completely devoted to the establishment of her government. She had many qualities worthy of her rank; and some of the most conspicuous were her nobleness in forgetting injuries, and her inflexible sense of justice: thus, though she had made no promises herself to her people on the day of her election, she justly considered those made by Edmund on her part as equally binding, and endeavoured by every means in her power to redeem the pledges he had given. Cheops had judged rightly in supposing she would make Edmund her prime minister—her gratitude to him, indeed, was bounded; and though her noble and generous disposition prevented her depriving the lords who had voted against her of their dignities, yet that the strong mind, and commanding genius of Edmund would make them dwindle into nonentities, he had also been equally correct in predicting. The noble lords, quite unconscious of their own inefficiency, were indignant at finding themselves subalterns where they had hoped to be commanders, and rallied round the standard of Rosabella, who, on her part, received them so graciously, that her former haughtiness was forgotten.

Elvira was not aware of their defection, or if she were, she thought them too insignificant to merit notice, her attention being entirely occupied in affairs which she considered of infinitely more importance. Though the laws of the old Queen had been excellent, many abuses had crept into the manner of putting them into execution; and these Elvira now, with the aid of Edmund, set herself diligently to work to discover and correct. She could not, indeed, have chosen an assistant more competent to the task. The penetrating mind and commanding genius of Edmund were unequalled. With a single glance, he saw where errors had been committed, and how they ought to be amended. Whilst under his auspices, vice was punished and virtue rewarded, goodness, though in rags, was raised to affluence, and villainy compelled to disgorge its ill-gotten wealth. Justice was impartially dispensed to all, and the first Monday in every month, the Queen proceeded in solemn state to the grand square at Blackheath, to receive there, in person, the petitions of her subjects.

The crowd assembled upon these occasions was immense. However well a constitution may be organized, it is impossible to give satisfaction to every one; and even under the best-regulated governments there will be always some who fancy themselves aggrieved. Besides, as free access was allowed on these occasions to every one, numbers went merely to see the Queen; and nothing could be better contrived for letting her Majesty know the real feelings of her subjects, than this arrangement; as, from the people being placed in lines, along each of which the Queen walked, she became alternately in personal contact with every separate individual. Like every thing else, however, that sounds perfect in theory, difficulties arose when this plan came to be put in practice: it was originally intended that the Queen should receive, with her own hands, and read herself, all the petitions that might be presented; but when it was found their numbers frequently amounted to some thousands, this scheme was abandoned as impracticable, and the Lords Noodle and Doodle were appointed to the important office of walking behind the Queen, carrying large bags, in which the petitions were deposited, and from which they would probably never again have emerged, if they had not been dragged to light by the persevering and indefatigable exertions of Lord Edmund.

The people, however, were not aware of this, and there was something in the show that delighted them. It was indeed a fine sight, to behold so many hundreds of human beings anxiously watching the movements of their beautiful Queen, as she glided along their ranks, smiling graciously upon all, and looking like an angel sent upon earth to dispense blessings to mankind: ladies of honour walking behind her, with pages bearing their train, and the two aged counsellors of state, bending. beneath the weight of their ponderous bags, bringing up the rear.

Thus gloriously commenced Elvira's reign. The people, delighted with the attention paid to their wishes, and struck by some instances of the Queen's love of justice and hatred of oppression, lauded her to the skies; the nobility, hoping riches and power from her liberality, almost worshipped her; and the ambassadors of foreign powers, dreading the valour of Lord Edmund and his soldiers, offered the humblest homage at her feet. In short, all seemed to smile upon her, and the kingdom to bid fair shortly to rival even the imagined happiness of Utopia itself.[200]

Volume 2: Chapter 7

In the mean time, what had become of Edric and Dr. Entwerfen? Gloomy indeed were the reflections of our travellers when they found themselves immured in a dungeon, so far from all they loved or reverenced, without friends, and accused of a horrible crime, from the guilt of which they felt it would he vain for them to attempt to free themselves. Days and weeks rolled on, yet no change took place in their destiny. Every night the grating of a rusty key in the lock announced the arrival of the gaoler, bringing their daily pittance of bread and water, but he never spoke, nor could the most earnest entreaties of the doctor and Edric bring one word from his lips.

Despair at length began to invade the bosoms of the travellers; till one day, as they were examining, for the thousandth time, the hieroglyphics on the stones in the wall, Edric perceived that one of them was loose. With infinite difficulty they removed the stone, and found a long vaulted passage, dimly lighted by an opening at the farther extremity. The transport of the prisoners, on making this discovery, was unbounded, and can only be imagined by those who have felt the loss of liberty, and rejoiced at its recovery.

When their first raptures had a little abated, they began to consult upon the best means of availing themselves of their good fortune, and preventing pursuit. The doctor had luckily several chemical preparations in his walking-stick; with one of these he dissolved the iron of their chains, so as to free Edric and himself from their weight, and then, smearing them over with the remainder of the composition, he laid them in a heap, exclaiming with a laugh, "The jailors will be dreadfully frightened when they find these fetters; for though they look perfect to the eye, they will crumble to pieces at the slightest touch."

Edric was too anxious to effect his escape, to listen to his tutor's exultation; and his arrangements being made, the travellers, with trembling steps and throbbing hearts, explored the vaulted passage, and found, to their infinite delight, that it had led them to the borders of the Nile. A small boat was anchored to the shore, and its crew, an old man and his son, who gained their living by conveying goods up the Nile, were peaceably taking their supper on the bank.

Edric and the doctor had taken the precaution to replace the stone that had concealed the vaulted passage, and having smeared the opposite wall with phosphorus, they had no doubt that when the jailor entered the prison, which he generally did in darkness, he would be too much alarmed to take any effectual means for pursuing them till it should be too late. Having luckily also plenty of money, that certain road to the human heart, they easily persuaded the old man to take them on board, and in a short time they embarked in his fragile vessel and set sail.

Slowly and silently they floated along the majestic river, which rolled in solemn waves like an inland sea, and swept proudly on to the ocean, seeming to scorn the degenerate land it left behind; and without one pang did our travellers quit for ever the fertile plains and gorgeous cities of Egypt. One only thought swelled in their bosoms, and that was joy at their escape. Offering up silent prayers of thanksgiving, our travellers continued their progress down the river, and, when morning dawned, and the enormous forms of the Pyramids were seen grimly frowning through the mist, they shuddered involuntarily, and, devoutly crossing themselves, muttered new prayers for protection and deliverance.

After a long and tedious voyage, our travellers at length reached the sea in safety. The mouths of the Delta were at that time the seat of extensive, and almost universal commerce; and our travellers trembled lest they should here encounter some emissary of their enemies, who might reconvey them to the prison from which they had so miraculously escaped. They found, however, the belief of their supernatural disappearance too strongly impressed upon the minds of the multitude for even a suspicion of their existence to remain; and they stood upon that sumptuous quay, surrounded by Greeks, Russians, Egyptians, Arabs, and Turks, without exciting a single remark, or obtaining the slightest attention. They wished to proceed to Constantinople, then the capital of the powerful empire of Greece,[201] and entered into conversation with the master of a felucca,[202] for that purpose.

"I will attend to you directly, gentlemen," said the sailor, leaving some persons with whom he had been previously talking: "but I have been listening to such a horrid tale!"

"What was it?" asked Edric, suspecting the subject, but aware that to seem incurious upon such an occasion, might betray that they were already only too well informed.

"Two sorcerers," returned the man, "have been taken into custody, for blowing up the Pyramids and bewitching the mummies!"

"And how were they punished?" asked Edric.

"Oh, you haven't heard half they did yet!" said the man. "When they were put in prison for their pranks, the Old One[203] came to their help, and carried them off in a flame of fire, leaving a long train of light after them in the sky, like the tail of a blazing comet. Dick Jones[204], who was telling me, swears he saw them all going off together. The old one hanging by the Devil's horn, and the young one keeping fast hold of his tail!"

"Shocking!" said Edric; scarcely able, however, to repress a smile at this proof of the vividness of Dick Jones's imagination.

"I haven't told you half," resumed the man. "All Grand Cairo[205] rings with it; several have gone mad, and others died with fear; and the man who was with Dick Jones, and who was one of the soldiers of the guard set over them, assured me as a positive fact, that the chains they had had on, and left behind them, crumbled between his fingers like a bit of rotten wood."

"It is very awful!" said Edric.

"Ay, is it not?" rejoined the man; "thank God I was not there to see! I am sure the very look of one of those conjurors would have driven me mad! I never could abide such things."

Edric now, with some difficulty, persuaded the man to return to the subject of their transit.

"I am very sorry, Sir," said he; "but I don't think there'll be a vessel going out to Constantinople for this week at least; for they've got the plague there,[206] and our magistrates won't let a ship that has been there, return to our harbour again without performing quarantine; and that is such a hindrance to trade that our folks don't like it. But perhaps you're in no hurry, and can wait?"

"Oh yes, We can wait quite well!" said the doctor, trembling with anxiety to be off.

The sailor, however, had no occasion to say more; for the bare mention of the plague was quite sufficient to deter our travellers from visiting Constantinople; and finding he was bound for Malta; and that no other vessel would quit the harbour that day, they hastily embarked, notwithstanding his vessel was old and inconvenient, and not forwarded by steam, and though the superior certainty of the steam-packets was now so generally felt and acknowledged by all, that perhaps this was the only common sailing-boat in the harbour. The joy of our travellers at their deliverance was, however, too great to permit them to dwell upon trifles; and as the cabin was scarcely habitable, they resolved to remain on deck the whole of the voyage, being determined to submit to any thing sooner than delay their departure. Accordingly they stretched themselves upon their cloaks, and, reclining against some ropes, watched attentively the lovely scene around them. The evening was beautiful, and, as the shores of Egypt swiftly receded from their view, they felt their minds soothed by the contemplation of the grand scene that presented itself. There is, indeed, something in the awful majesty of the world of waters, which, like the gigantic monuments of Egypt, powerfully affects the mind by its very simplicity, and, by raising the soul far above the common trifling occurrences of life, soothes it to tranquillity.

The voyage was long, for contrary winds impeded their progress; and one evening, after Dr. Entwerfen had remained for some time gazing steadfastly on the water, with a look of deep abstraction, he exclaimed suddenly, "There will be a storm!"

"Impossible!" returned Edric. "The sun set in unwonted splendour, spreading its rays of purple and gold through the waters like a jewelled diadem; and the wind is even now dying away to a gentle breeze, which scarcely curls the surface of the ocean as our bark dances gaily over it."

"That is a bad sign," said the doctor. "Have you not often heard that a storm is generally preceded by a calm? You will find it no metaphor now."

The moon soon shone brightly; and as the ship ploughed her way slowly through the almost motionless waves, its beams sparkled through the spray, which fell in silvery showers over the prow. All now was still, except the heaving of the vessel, and the monotonous splashing of the waters as she slowly worked her way through them. The wind gradually sunk, and the sails only feebly flapped in the breeze that could no longer inflate them, till at last even that failed, and the vessel, completely becalmed, lay like a log upon the water, which spread like a vast and tranquil mirror around her.

Bitterly now did our travellers regret the precipitate haste that had made them embark in such a frail, unmanageable boat; and they regarded with longing eyes the compact steam-packets that glided past them; their black smoke curling in the air as they were wafted swiftly along. It was too late, however, to repent; and the doctor consoled himself by taking advantage of the effect produced by the thick black smoke, as they saw it rising in the distance, to illustrate the lecture he had formerly given his pupil, on the theory of combustion and decomposition of amphlites,[207] till he fairly lulled him to sleep.

Morning came, hut brought not with it the wished-for breeze. Edric rose, and walking upon deck, encountered the doctor. "How still all seems!" said he; "Nature seems to sleep: but 'tis an awful stillness, such as falls upon a dying patient, prophetic of his end. Nature seems exhausted, and I could fancy is seeking a short repose to rally her energies. for some decisive blow,"

"You are fanciful, Edric," said the doctor; "you alarm yourself unnecessarily. The violent shock your nerves have sustained, unfits you for exertion, and renders you disposed to see every thing in a gloomy light."

"I beg your pardon, Sir," said a ragged English sailor, who happened to be on board; "in my opinion the gentleman is right, for every thing portends a storm. Cirro-strati streak the sky, and as they join with the fleecy cumuli below them in cumulus-strati,[208] nothing can more clearly indicate wind and rain, and probably thunder. And see, too, how the dark, frowning nimbus spreads its black shade along the edge of the horizon, and how the birds fly cowering, almost touching the waters with their wings as they flit along. Now it begins, hark!"

Whilst the sailor had been speaking, the clouds had thickened gradually, and the sky had grown dark as night. A hollow murmuring was heard, which seemed to gather fury as it came, till it burst over the devoted vessel with terrific violence, and rent the sails to atoms, whistling round in fearful gusts, as though mocking the mischief it had done. The sea now heaved mountains high. The forked lightning played like writhing serpents along the deep black sky; now streaming like floating ribands in the air, and then darting downwards like fiery arrows. Thunder rolled heavily in the distance, approaching however nearer and nearer, every peel reverberating through the sky, as though echoed back by unseen rocks, till at last a tremendous crash announced the fall of the electric fluid. Our travellers were preparing to retire below, when, just as they reached the cabin stairs, the heavens seemed to open, and a ball of light-blue fire, of a most vivid brightness, shot downwards from the chasm, and struck the mast of the labouring ship. Immediately after, a loud crackling noise rattled over their heads, and then all again was still, save the howling winds, and the groans of some prostrate seamen, wounded by the scattered fragments of the splintered mast.

The rain now descended in torrents, and the feeble vessel, at one moment raised to a fearful height, then dashed down, and apparently engulphed by the heavy seas that washed over her, seemed every instant doomed to destruction, and to escape only by a miracle. The shouts of the seamen, and creaking of the strained timbers of the ship, mingled horribly with the howling of the wind, and roar of the billows. Every instant it was expected she must go to pieces; for she had sprung a leak, and the water rose so fast as to baffle every attempt made to check its progress. The seamen were now in despair: they broke open their trunks, and dressing themselves in their best clothes, they filled their pockets with all the valuables they could find: then, whilst some went to prayers, others broke open the captain's spirit-chest, and many rolled overboard in a state of intoxication, whilst the ship, now become a perfect wreck, drifted before the wind, and was rapidly sinking. The storm, however, seeming to abate, the master ordered out the boat, and all the seamen who retained their senses, eagerly sprang on board. Our travellers attempted to follow, but the seamen pushed them back, and exclaiming the boat was full, rowed off, leaving them to their fate.

The English sailor had been in the act of stepping on board the boat, the very moment she pushed off, and the sudden shock precipitated him into the sea. A piercing scream burst from his lips, as his body, with a dying effort, sprang from the waves, which seemed to rise after him and suck him back into their gulph. Our friends heard the cry, and rushed to the side of the vessel, but alas! they were powerless to save him: the ship drifted rapidly by, they saw his hands gleam for a moment through the waves, as he raised them in agony, and then the roaring billows rolled on, deep, black, and gloomy as before.

The horror of Edric and the doctor was excessive; but the impending terrors of their own fate prevented the possibility of their minds dwelling long upon his. The storm, however, visibly abated, and the dismantled hulk they were upon, lightened by the desertion of the sailors, still swam: light, fleecy clouds now scudded rapidly along the skies, and the moon, struggling to break forth from behind them, shed a faint and watery gleam upon the scene.

Our travellers now, by the feeble light afforded by the moonbeams, perceived the boat labouring heavily through the dark-grey sea, and struggling to reach a long black line of rocks, distinctly marked in the distance, against which the still boiling waters broke with tremendous roar, curling in whitened foam as they laved their craggy sides; whilst the wreck our travellers were upon, seemed rapidly drifting upon the same point. Death now appeared inevitable, as it was impossible their shattered bark could resist the shock, if it should be tossed against these jagged crags; and every moment she seemed rising upon a wave that must dash her upon them, and floating back to escape only by a miracle. The doctor and Edric became giddy with these repeated shocks, and in despair fancied themselves resigned; or rather, stunned by the misfortunes which had followed each other with such overwhelming rapidity upon their devoted heads, they awaited their fate with an apathy which they mistook for resignation.

The seamen in the boat still continued labouring on, straining every nerve to reach the shore, though ineffectually; for the foaming surge beat them back with repeated, with resistless violence. With anxious eyes and beating hearts, our friends marked the progress of the boat; till, giddy with watching, and feeling their spirits exhausted as they surveyed the fruitless struggle of the toiling boat-men, they hid their faces with their hands, and shut it from their sight.

At this instant a wild and piercing cry rang in their ears:—'twas from the boat. She had swamped; the human beings she contained were all swallowed up in the boiling waves, and that shriek of agony was their funeral knell. A horrid silence followed this appalling scream, unbroken save by the lashing of the billows against the rocks, and the low, half-suppressed moaning of the winds,—till the senses of the travellers became bewildered, and they shrieked in agony. Their peril indeed grew every moment more intense, for every wave carried them nearer and nearer to those frowning crags, whilst their dark sides, rearing themselves in awful majesty, seemed mustering their strength to repel the insolent intruders that sought to invade their territory. The doctor and Edric in the mean time, suffering a thousand deaths in the protracted horrors they were compelled to endure, and which they could neither mitigate nor evade, shrank back with the shivering of affrighted nature trembling at dissolution, every time the wave on which their vessel floated seemed to dash against the shore.

At length, however, the fate they had so long dreaded arrived. Their shattered hulk was raised on a tremendous billow, and thrown with fearful violence upon the rocks, with a force that shivered it to atoms, and engulphed the doctor and Edric in the boiling surge. The next wave, however, returning, swept them along in its bosom, and threw them, perfectly insensible, though locked in each other's arms, upon the shore.

Volume 2: Chapter 8

It was morning, and the glowing sunbeams danced gaily on the sparkling waters of the dark blue deep, as, gently rippling, it laved the rocky shore on which Edric and his tutor had been thrown; and seemed to smile, as if in mockery of the mischiefs it had wrought. There, sheltered by a rock, whose jutting crag had saved them from being carried back into the devouring ocean, lay our travellers, apparently buried in sleep; returning consciousness not having yet dispelled the torpor produced by the fearful terrors of the night. The sun now shone brightly, and its glowing heat revived Edric from his trance. Slowly and heavily he unclosed his languid eyes, and, forgetting where he was, attempted to rise. He succeeded; but weak and dizzy, he only staggered a few paces ere he again fell: the roaring of the ocean still sounded in his ears, his senses swam, and, giddy and enfeebled by his previous exhaustion, he fancied himself still tossed upon the foaming billows. For some time, he lay in a state of torture, the thrill of returning circulation tingling through his veins, till the recollection of what had passed flashing across his mind, he again endeavoured to rouse himself, and seek his tutor. The unfortunate doctor, however, appeared to be no more, and as Edric gazed upon his inanimate form, he might have exclaimed with Prince Henry, "I could have better spared a better man."[209]

At this moment, Edric recollected the strong chemical preparations the doctor generally carried about him, and, searching his pockets, found a potent elixir. With some difficulty, he forced a few drops down his throat, taking a dose also himself. The effects of the medicine were soon visible: the doctor heaved a deep sigh, and, opening his eyes, gazed vacantly around, whilst Edric himself felt perfectly restored.

"Where am?" cried Doctor Entwerfen, as soon as he was sufficiently recovered to speak, and then, as some of the horrors he had so lately witnessed recurred to his mind, he exclaimed "I will never disclose it—no torture shall compel me; where is the justice? He fled away in a flame of fire hanging to the Devil's horn. Ah, Edric! where are we? Ah! I have had such a horrid dream."

"Alas!" returned Edric, "it is but too real!"

"What! what!" cried the doctor, getting up and staring wildly around him; "I remember now, we were drowned—but where—where are we?"

"I know not," replied his pupil mournfully. "You forget I have been exposed to the same perils as yourself, and that I am equally ignorant where fate has thrown us. I should think, however, from the position we were in when the storm began, that we are somewhere on the shores of the Mediterranean; but whether in Europe or Africa, I have as yet had no means of ascertaining."

"We must explore," said the doctor solemnly; "we ought not to remain in doubt another instant upon so important a subject. Follow me!"

They now quitted the rocky beach on which they had so long lain, and advanced towards some cliffs which shut them out from the view of the surrounding country. When they had surmounted this natural barrier, they found the prospect that presented itself superb; and their eyes wandered with delight over orange groves and forests of cork-trees; whilst the green shining leaves, and rich scarlet blossoms of the pomegranates, and light tender waving foliage of the olive, afforded variety to the scene. The burning heat of the sun's rays felt softened by the breezes from the sea; a balmy fragrance seemed to pervade the air; birds flew twittering around them, or, perched upon the branches of the trees, made the groves resound with melodious harmony; whilst butterflies of the most brilliant colours fluttered from flower to flower, and innumerable buzzing insects seemed to fill the air with motion.

"What a lovely country!" said the doctor, as he and Edric penetrated into the deep recesses of a shady grove; "and how delightful is this sensation of refreshing coolness, after having been exposed to the burning rays of the sun! It is yet early, for the sun has not yet reached far above the horizon, and the dew-drops still glisten in his rays like diamonds hanging from every leaf. Where can we be? Surely we are not dead, and now in Paradise!"

Edric smiled: "I rather think," said he, "that we are in Andalusia. I have often read of the exquisite beauty of some of the southern provinces of Spain, and this seems well to accord with the ideas I have always entertained of that country."

They now approached what appeared to be a cemetery, and which was tastefully adorned with weeping willows hanging over the graves; whilst roses, and a thousand beautiful flowering shrubs, flourishing in wild luxuriance from the genial nature of the climate, spread around, and gave this receptacle of the mouldering remains of mortality the aspect of a blooming garden.

"How different from the Pyramids!" exclaimed the doctor and Edric at the same moment.

"The tomb-stones seem to have inscriptions upon them," continued the former, after a short pause; "let us approach and examine them: they will at least declare the country we are in, by the language in which they may be written."

The idea struck Edric as feasible, and they entered the cemetery. "You are right, Edric," said the doctor; "we are in Spain, for here lie the mortal remains of Don Alfonso, that mighty hero of the Bourbon race,[210] who, you doubtless remember, was the first that conquered the northern part of Africa, and by transferring the seat of the Spanish empire to Fez, contributed so powerfully to the civilization and conversion to Christianity of all that vast territory."

"And who destroyed Spain as a monarchy, by so doing," added Edric.

"It is true," replied the doctor, "that Spain, finding itself too mighty for a province, shook off in consequence the yoke of his descendants, and erected its present republic, which it most probably would never have done if the seat of government had remained at Madrid. But that is trifling compared with the inestimable benefits produced to the world at large, by the civilization and reduction to a Christian state, of such a mighty empire as that of Morocco. Had it not been for that, we might still have remained in the degrading ignorance in which mankind were immersed for so many centuries respecting the interior of Africa:—Timbuctoo would never have risen to its present eminence in science and commerce;[211] the real course of the Niger[212] would never have been discovered: and the sources of the Nile[213] still remained wrapped in oblivion. Yes, mighty shade! thou wert indeed a hero! Calumny may assail thy fame, and unenlightened minds cavil at the wonders of thy glory; but one firm and attached votary still remains to thee, and thus he humbly bends to do thee homage."

So saying, the doctor prostrated himself upon the tomb, and reverentially kissed the cold marble inscribed with the hero's name.—"Hold! hold!" cried a man, rushing from behind a small temple, and seizing him, whilst in an instant Edric and his tutor found themselves surrounded by soldiers, whose grim visages spoke them inured to blood and warfare.

"Wretch!" exclaimed the leader, apostrophizing the terrified doctor; "but thy life shall soon pay the forfeit of thy crimes. Away with him!" continued he, addressing his soldiers; "hear him before the next alcaide,[214] and let him there suffer the punishment the law enacts against all those who dare to praise the actions or worship the memory of the tyrannic Alfonso[215]—Away with him, I say."

"Mercy! mercy!" implored the doctor,

"Impossible!" said the leader sternly; "do you not know that this is a land of liberty, and that we abhor the very name of tyranny and oppression? How then can the admirer of a tyrant hope for mercy at our hands? Away with him, I say, and with his companion too; for as they appear to be associates, no doubt their principles are the same."

"And do you call this a land of liberty?" asked Edric reproachfully.

"Hear him! he blasphemes!" cried the soldiers; "gag him if he dare again to breathe such impiety!" and amidst their shouts and execrations, Edric and his tutor were dragged away. Taught by this lesson that the liberty of the republican Spaniards did not extend to the tolerance of any opinions except their own, Edric and the doctor did not again venture to speak; and they soon, to their infinite dismay, found themselves in the presence of the alcaide; who, however, luckily for our travellers, happened to be a man of some sense and liberality. He smiled when he heard the substance of the facts gravely stated against the prisoners. "This case requires a private hearing," said he: "Velasquez, conduct the prisoners to my own apartment."

We will have no private hearing," clamoured the people and the soldiers. "The crime was public, and the punishment should be so too; we will not be gulled."

"But, gentlemen," said the magistrate, "supposing these prisoners to be part of a gang of conspirators who have been plotting against the state, it might defeat the ends of justice to have them examined publicly; as it is possible—mind, gentlemen, I only say, as it is possible—some traitors may lurk even among the crowd before me, who might give intelligence to other parties interested, who might be thus enabled to make their escape."

"Ay, now you speak reason," said the mob; "we are always willing to listen to reason;" and without farther remonstrance they permitted the alcaide and the prisoners to retire.

"You see, gentlemen," said the alcaide, shutting the door of the room carefully, and placing chairs, in which he invited his prisoners to sit down, "that all is not liberty which is called so, and that a mob can occasionally be as tyrannical as an emperor. I know that in reality there is not a shadow of complaint against you; yet I dare not release you, as my own life would be the forfeit if I did. You must thus submit to a temporary restraint, which you may rest assured I shall not only endeavour to shorten, but shall render as light as possible whilst I am compelled to inflict it."

"My dear sir," said the doctor, we are exceedingly obliged by your kindness. If we had not met with you, I do not know what would have become of us. I could not have believed people were in existence so illiberal as these Spaniards, or that any human beings could be so weak as to fancy themselves in a land of liberty whilst they are practising the most refined tyranny."

"And yet my countrymen are neither fools nor hypocrites," returned the alcaide; "but, like many other people, they deceive themselves, and talk about freedom till they fancy they possess it. Their great fault, however, has been, that they did not know where to stop; and as even virtue becomes vice when carried to the extreme, so have the most sublime principles of liberty and patriotism become degraded in their hands, by being attempted to be carried to an exaggerated degree of perfection!"

"Oh, England! England!" sighed the doctor; "would to Heaven I had never left thy happy shores! Alas! alas! what a crowd of horrible events have occupied the last few months!"

"Why did you leave your country, since you so bitterly regret it?" demanded the alcaide.

"Because we could not be contented," replied Edric. "Devoted from my earliest youth to the pursuits of science, I craved ardently for knowledge denied to mortals; I aspired to penetrate into the profoundest secrets of Nature, and burnt to accomplish wishes destined never to be realized. The desire of seeing foreign countries also filled my soul: I longed to travel, to acquire new ideas and meet with strange and wonderful adventures; I sickened of the quiet and tranquillity of home. 'Give me change,' cried I in my madness, 'give me variety, and I ask no more; for even wretchedness itself were better to bear than this tiresome unvarying uniformity.' The unreasonableness of my wishes deserved punishment, and I have been curst with the very fulfilment of my wishes."

"Is this gentleman also a votary of science?" asked the alcaide, who had appeared musing whilst Edric spoke.

"What a question!" exclaimed the doctor, in a transport of indignation. "What! has my whole life been devoted to scientific pursuits! have I deprived myself of rest and almost of food! and wasted the midnight lamp in bringing to perfection some of the most sublime discoveries ever vouchsafed to man, to be insulted with such a doubt as that? Know, sir, that you see before you Doctor Entwerfen, the fortunate inventor of the immortalizing snuff,[216] one single pinch of which cures all diseases by the smell; the discoverer of the capability of caoutchouc being applied to aerial purposes; and the maker of the most compendious and powerful galvanic battery ever yet beheld by mortal!"

"Then you are the very man I want," said the alcaide; "go to prison contentedly, and rest satisfied that your confinement will be of very short duration. In a day or two I will see you, and explain the project I have conceived for your deliverance."

So saying, he summoned his guards, and, ordering them to convey the travellers to prison, the doctor and Edric were dragged away, and, being immured in separate dungeons, were left there to ruminate upon the varied and busy scenes in which they had been so lately engaged. Sadly and heavily passed the time; yet days and weeks rolled on ere they again saw the alcaide. At length, when they had begun almost to despair, they were reconducted to his presence.

"Do you understand the management of an electrical machine?" asked he abruptly.

"Certainly!" cried the doctor, transported with joy at the question, before Edric, who was half blinded by the sudden change from his gloomy prison to the broad light of day, had sufficiently recovered himself to reply.

"Then it is in your own power to set yourselves free," continued the alcaide. "The principal general of the army stationed here is ill; a powerful party exists against him who wish his death, at the head of whom stands the leader who was the cause of your being taken into custody. The general himself is a mere nonentity; but the opposite party, to which I belong, wish to save his life, as his name affords a sanction under which they can act. He is now ill of a palsy, and has been recommended to try the effects of an electrical shock. A machine has been with difficulty procured in this remote district; but the philosopher of the army being lately dead, and another not having been yet appointed, no one here knows how to apply it. Now, if you—"

"Say no more!" cried the doctor, interrupting him, in a transport of delight; "say no more—I see, I comprehend the whole! I shall restore him, and receive my liberty as the reward. Nay more, I shall obtain immortality amongst the Spaniards by the deed; their poets will sing my fame, and their historians will pause upon the fact!"

"You will undertake it then!" said the alcaide, and, reading an indignant affirmative in the doctor's looks, he led the way to a camp, at a short distance from the village, where the paralytic general was sitting in a kind of throne, placed without his tent, and surrounded by the principal officers of his staff; the electrical machine, a large, clumsy, heavy-looking thing, standing before him. The doctor looked with dismay at this unwieldy apparatus, so different from his own neat, powerful compendium of science, as he was wont to call it; and saw with infinite horror that even its construction was totally different from those he had been accustomed to. His natural vanity and presumption, however, revolted from making this mortifying acknowledgment, particularly after the boasts he had been indulging in to the alcaide; and, relying upon his general knowledge of the principles of science, he walked boldly up to the machine, with as much composure and self confidence as though he had been accustomed to the management of it all his life.

A considerable trepidation, however, crept over him as he examined it and found its movements intricate and complicated in the extreme; and his hands trembled, and a thick film came over his eyes, as he attempted to charge and adjust the cylinder. No time, however, was allowed for deliberation; he was ordered to apply it instantly; and, terrified by the recollection of the prompt manner in which the Spaniards were accustomed to make themselves obeyed, and the already long and severe imprisonment he had undergone, he set it in motion: an unlucky wire, however, which he did not quite understand, pointed upwards, and he tried in vain to arrange it; he tried again, but was instantly felled to the ground by a tremendous shock, whilst a loud crash of thunder burst with violence over his head, and a vivid flash of lightning proclaimed that the ill-managed machine had drawn down the electric fluid from a heavy cloud, that happened unfortunately to be just above them, upon the head of the unfortunate general, whom it scorched to a cinder, levelling some of his officers to the earth, and scattering the rest in all directions. For the moment, the doctor himself was blinded by the sudden light, and, when he recovered his sight, the first thing that met his eyes was his friend the alcaide sticking fast by the skirts of his coat in a hedge.

Terrified at the mischief, he had done, the first impulse of the learned doctor was to run away; but, notwithstanding the general confusion and dismay, the first intimation he showed of his design, drew around him a crowd of soldiers, like peasants round a mad dog, who seemed to think him as little entitled to mercy as though he had really been one of those unfortunate animals. "Cut him down!" cried one—"blow his brains out!" shouted another—"chop his head off!" screamed a third; and summary punishment would instantly have been inflicted, if the alcaide, who in the mean time had contrived to extricate himself from his uncomfortable situation, had not interfered. "Villain!" cried he, as soon as he had recovered his breath—for being rather fat, he found flying exercise rather too violent to suit his taste; "is this the manner in which you treat me? Was it for this I brought you to the camp, and would have made your fortune? Wretch that you are! hanging is too good for you, and impaling alive mercy to what you deserve.—Away to prison with him! he merits not a death so easy as you would give him; carry him back to his dungeon, and let him there await what punishment the council of state may judge fit for killing a general and frightening an alcaide out of his senses."

"Mercy! mercy!" screamed the doctor; but his cries were disregarded, and he and Edric were dragged back to prison, deprived of every hope of obtaining forgiveness. Sadly and silently passed the hours in this gloomy abode; for, though the doctor and his pupil were now permitted to be together, little communication took place between them, as, though Edric was too good-natured to upbraid his unfortunate companion, yet it was past the power of human nature not to feel enraged at the folly that had drawn them into so disagreeable a situation.

The poor doctor, however, needed not to be upbraided; for the reproaches of his own conscience were more bitter than any Edric could have lavished on him. "I am lost!" cried he; "ruined, and utterly undone! Not only my body will perish miserably, but my fame, my immortal fame is destroyed—oh! I shall go distracted!"

In this manner he lamented; wringing his hands and tearing his hair, whilst Edric felt too angry to attempt to console him.

"Speak to me, Edric, dear," cried the poor doctor at last, quite in despair at his silence; "for Heaven's sake, speak to me! Do let me hear the sound of some voice, besides my own and that of those cursed Spaniards. Oh, Edric! Edric! solitary confinement is quite enough to drive a man distracted; but to have a companion in such a place as this, and he to refuse to speak—Oh, Edric! Edric! your heart must be turned to stone, if you can resolve to use me so cruelly."

Edric was moved by the doctor's sorrow.

"What do you wish me to say?" asked he, smiling.

"Oh, now that's like yourself," cried the poor doctor; bursting into tears, and throwing his arms round Edric's neck, whilst he sobbed upon his shoulder like a child. "Now I shall die happy! I don't care what they do to me; I am quite ready for any thing that may happen."

Edric was affected by the doctor's manner, and returning his embrace warmly, he could not restrain his own tears.

"Oh! my dear, dear Edric!" cried the doctor; "how I love you! would to Heaven I could save you! I would not care for myself."

"And I would not accept of liberty without you, my dear tutor, I assure you!" returned Edric "No, no! the perils we have undergone together have added new force to the ties that formerly united us; and our fate now, be it good or ill, shall be the same. It is possible, however, that there may be some means of escape."

"Alas! no!" said the doctor mournfully; seeing Edric look round at the walls and windows: "this is the same dungeon I have been so long confined in, and not even a mouse could get out of it without the keeper's permission."

"What is to be done, then?" cried Edric.

"Ay," returned the doctor; "what, indeed! However, it is certainly a great comfort to have a companion in one's misery; and though my prospects are certainly not much improved since you joined me, my cares are lessened at least one-half."

"Oh! my poor father!" exclaimed Edric, "The hardest part of my fate seems to die without obtaining his forgiveness! Alas! If he could see me now, he would surely repent his ill-timed severity. Fain would I also know what has passed in England since we left it: if Edmund be married, and if Claudia still reigns. It was spring when we left England, it is now winter: alas! alas! how many changes this brief space of time may have produced. If, however, my father's life has been spared, I care not for the rest."

"How little did we anticipate," said the doctor, "when we first proposed to travel, the misfortunes that were to attend us! Alas! they seem a just punishment for our crime, in presuming to wish to pry into secrets never intended to be revealed to man."

"Can you believe it!" returned Edric, "in spite of all the misfortunes I have suffered, a restless curiosity to know the fate of the Mummy we so strangely resuscitated, haunts me incessantly, and gives an added bitterness to my other sufferings. I can scarcely believe but that the scene in the Pyramid was a delusion, and that we are still labouring under the effects of a frightful dream."

"If it be a dream," said the doctor, "it is one from which I should be very glad to be awakened."

Volume 2: Chapter 9

A few days after this, the prisoners were honoured by another visit from the alcaide.

"Thank God!" cried Edric involuntarily, as soon as he saw him; for, as he felt confident that the anger he had expressed against them, had been assumed, he hoped he was now come to save them.

"Alas!" returned the worthy magistrate, "I fear you have little reason to be thankful. All my endeavours to save you have only succeeded in obtaining a few hours respite, and tomorrow morning you are condemned to be burnt alive."

Oh!" shrieked the doctor; whilst even Edric's courage could not prevent his turning deathly pale.

"It is dreadful," said he, "to die thus so young in a foreign country, and by such fearful means."

"Oh! Don't talk of it," sobbed the doctor. "My poor dear, dear Edric! Save him, sir! in mercy, save him! Though I may be doomed to pay the penalty of my folly, it is very hard he should suffer."

"It is, indeed," returned the alcaide; "and my wish to save him, joined to the hatred I bear the present general, has made me a traitor to my country. I see you look astonished, but to explain what I mean, it will be necessary to give you a short sketch of the present state of this country, which I will endeavour to do in as few words as possible. You know, no doubt, that Spain was once a powerful empire, till the ill-judged policy of one of her monarchs, in removing the seat of government to Africa, occasioned her fall: for the tree of majesty becoming too widely extended, it was but natural that some of its branches should strike root for themselves, and detach themselves entirely from the parent stem.

"This was the case with Spain; and her first directors as a republic happening to be intelligent men, the infant state grew and flourished, exciting the admiration of its neighbours, and the envy of its mother country. Unfortunately, however, the wheel of fortune is always turning, and Spaniards, as I before said, not knowing where to stop, have gone on, getting worse and worse by degrees, till they have become the bigoted and intolerant wretches you have found them. In fact, the army now rules the state, and the people, finding the tyranny of the soldiers insupportable, have been for some time attempting to throw off the yoke. They were long unsuccessful, as they found the discipline of the soldiers far outweighed all their bravery and self-devotion. In their distress, however, they called in the aid of Roderick the Second, the young and warlike King of Ireland. This powerful monarch, who realizes in himself all the romantic qualities of the ancient knights of chivalry, hastened instantly to their assistance, and they are now combating under his auspices with every prospect of success. His progress has been magical; success has followed ever he has gone, and his army now lies at a little distance, though he landed in the north of Spain. It is to him, therefore, that I have sent secretly, giving him (in the hope of saving you) instructions, by which, if he follows them, he cannot fail of surprising the camp."

The doctor and Edric, though they were fully aware that they were principally indebted to the hatred the alcaide bore the present general for the steps he had taken in their behalf, yet felt and expressed themselves properly grateful; and the alciade quitted the prison, leaving the flatterer Hope behind to console them for his absence, mingled, however with the natural anxiety, which they could not help feeling, lest the well-arranged plan laid for their escape should fail. Morning had just dawned, after a tedious and miserable night, and the doctor and Edric were yet shivering from the damp cold which often precedes the break of day, and which now seemed to have struck a chill to their inmost souls, when the door of the prison opened, and a file of soldiers appeared, ready to conduct them to the place of execution. The doctor's heart beat thick, so as almost to impede respiration, and a heavy film spread before his eyes; whilst the agitation of Edric, who had, however, now quite forgiven him, was scarcely inferior to his own. Fervently they embraced, and then submitting to be pinioned, they were forced to march to the spot appointed for their sacrifice, where an immense crowd awaited their approach.

The doctor's heart sunk within him as he looked down from the kind of terrace upon which the ceremony was to take place, upon the mass of human heads jammed together below, every face regarding him with a gaze of anxious expectation; and as he turned from these eager looks with a thrill of horror, his feelings were yet more forcibly harrowed up by the sight behind him. This was composed of two iron stakes fixed firmly in the ground, and provided with ponderous chains so as to prevent the remotest possibility of escape, whilst the enormous heaps of green wood piled round each, gave a frightful idea of the intensity of the lingering torments the unfortunate prisoners were condemned to suffer. The mind of Edric, in the mean time, was not much more composed than that of his friend. He also had looked round, and whilst nature shuddered at the thought of the horrid death awaiting them, the immensity and compactness of the crowd seemed to destroy all probability of a rescue, and the hope which had till then supported him, fled from his breast; whilst, as his eyes again met those of the poor doctor, mournful, indeed, was the glance that they exchanged.

It is an awful thing to die! and though there are occasions when death may be braved, or at least met with unabated courage; yet when it comes on thus slowly and deliberately, seen from afar of, and yet impossible to be avoided, the firmest mind will find it difficult to bear its approach unmoved. That of Edric, however, notwithstanding it had been weakened by his long confinement, and by the delusive flattery of hope, did not shrink from the trial: and calmly he even saw the crowd divide, to make way for the executioner, who slowly advanced, preceded by a band of martial music, playing a mournful air, the drums being covered with black crape, and followed by a long train of soldiers, in mourning cloaks, with their arms reversed. Nothing could be more appalling than this lugubrious procession: the executioner, musicians, and soldiers, being all shrouded in their gloomy cloaks, (the very hoods of which were drawn over their heads,) had the air of demons coming to bear away the miserable victims to everlasting perdition; and the mind of the unhappy doctor not being able to endure such accumulated horrors, he sunk upon his knees, uttering shrieks of anguish whilst the cold sweat ran in large drops from his forehead, and every nerve quivered with agony.

The procession had now nearly reached the prisoners, and even Edric's firmness gave way, as he saw the executioner spring upon the terrace, and advance towards him. A convulsive throb of anguish seemed to rend his heart, and his lips and cheeks turned of a livid paleness. But how was he surprised, and what a sudden revulsion of feeling did he not experience, when the supposed executioner, after having unbound his arms, put a sword into his hands, and whispering,—"Now is the time, defend yourself!—our soldiers are in green," left him completely free.

Completely overcome, Edric stood for a moment lost in amazement, unable to credit the evidence of his senses, and gazing after his deliverer, who, the moment he had also unbound the doctor, threw off his disguise, and shouting "Roderick forever!" disclosed to the multitude below the dreaded form of the Irish hero himself. Shouts of "Roderick for ever!" now rent the skies; the soldiers who had followed their monarch, and several others who had lurked concealed amongst the crowd, threw off their disguises at the same moment, and formed round the leader; whilst the main body of his troops, left behind in the care of experienced generals, tutored for the purpose, charged the affrighted Spaniards in the rear.

The confusion and dismay that now prevailed were quite beyond description. The terrified Spaniards, who, naturally superstitious, had long fancied the wonderful acts of heroic valour attributed to Roderick could only be performed by magic, were now firmly convinced that his sudden appearance amongst them was an act of especial favour from his Infernal Majesty himself! and finding themselves attacked on all sides, imagined their enemies multiplied by the powers of darkness, and fled without striking a blow. Roderick and his soldiers returned laughing, after they had pursued them a little way, to ransack and burn their camp; which when they had done, they retired to their former station; having previously promised the alcaide to spare the town, and not to push the consequences of their victory farther.

Roderick the Second, surnamed the Great, was then in the flower of his age.[217] He had not long ascended his throne; and his father, who had been a prudent prince, having left behind him a well-established government, able statesmen, and a considerable sum in the treasury, Roderick had little to employ his mind at home. Brave, ardent, and enterprising, burning for conquest, and spurning the quiet of domestic peace, the overtures of the Spaniards had met his most ardent wishes; and he had embraced their cause with an eagerness and impetuosity that had hitherto carried every thing before it. The greatest part of Spain lay at his feet. Even Madrid was his! but it was to attack Seville, that queen of cities, that he was now in Andalusia. This city was still in the power of his enemies, and Roderick, having made

Cadiz his head-quarters, was about removing thither, when the message of the Alcaide, had induced to undertake the romantic enterprise he had just so successfully accomplished. Romance was, indeed, a leading feature in Roderick's character, he delighted in surprises and disguises, and loved to give a kind of theatrical effect to every thing he did.

He had not been upon good terms with the late King, his father; in fact, no two characters could be more diametrically opposite: it had been the policy of the late King, to foment secretly the discontents nourished amongst the English; but the spirit of Roderick revolted at conduct he considered so base and mean. The Spanish war, on the contrary, exactly suited his disposition: to aid an oppressed people to throw off the yoke of their oppressors, seemed noble and generous; and he engaged in the enterprise with all the energy of his bold and daring temper. His soldiers adored him, and his people warmly seconded his efforts; for, as the seat of war was far removed from them, and as the treasury of the late King defrayed the expenses, they felt none of the inconveniences of war, and gloried in the triumphs of their Sovereign. Thus, Roderick's praise was the theme of every tongue: even the Spaniards worshipped him almost as a god, and their active imaginations magnified his exploits, till both friends and foes alike regarded him as a being who had only to will to conquer, and whose prowess it was perfect madness even to struggle to resist.

Such was the monarch our travellers now anxiously awaited, till suspense became almost agony. At last the joyful sounds of "He comes! he comes! Long live the mighty Roderick!" burst upon their ears, and the travellers bent forwards, eagerly expecting, yet dreading to see, a countenance stern and fearful as that of Cheops in his tomb: but how were they astonished to behold, in the redoubtable Roderick, only a tall handsome young man, riding carelessly upon a beautiful Barbary charger, and laughing and talking gaily with his officers as he came along.

"What!" cried the doctor indignantly, "would you attempt to make me believe that slight blooming boy a conqueror? the thing is impossible! It is quite ridiculous to mention it. Those laughing eyes, smooth down-like cheeks, and white teeth, may he well adapted to win a lady's heart, but I am sure they never can belong to a hero!"

The King, in the mean time, was equally struck with the doctor; and seeing something peculiarly honest and simple in his fat, round, oily face, he felt a lively interest for him, and an excessive curiosity to know what could possibly have brought a man, apparently so harmless and inoffensive, into so perilous a situation. The fine person of Edric, disfigured as it was by the troubles he had undergone, also attracted his attention; and as he rode up to his guests to question them as to their adventures, (the noble barb that carried him, pacing proudly along, as though conscious of the illustrious burthen he bore,) even the doctor was compelled to admit, the face and figure of his rider bespoke firmness, intellect, and dignity.

"What crime had you committed amongst the Spaniards?" asked he, as he approached, addressing himself to the doctor in a full, mellow, yet commanding tone. "It must have been of the blackest die, if we are to judge by the enormity of the punishment."

"I am innocent!" cried the doctor, "an' it may please your Majesty! I am quite innocent."

"It will please me very much to find you so," said Roderick, smiling; "but assertion is nothing—what proof have you?"

"My friend here will bear witness in my behalf," said the doctor solemnly, not feeling at all pleased with what he thought the King's unseasonable disposition for merriment; whilst as he stood looking very cross, his red face and bald head streaming with perspiration from anger and vexation, his clothes having been torn to rags, and his hat and wig lost in his late troubles, he struck Roderick as presenting so very whimsical and ridiculous a figure, that after looking at um a few minutes, the Merry Monarch burst out into a violent and almost convulsive fit of laughter.

"Well!" said the doctor, still more gravely, "I am glad your Majesty seems so well amused; but for my part, I don't see any thing at all agreeable or entertaining in being about to be burned alive?"

The doctor's solemn look and lengthened face, as he made this naive remonstrance, only increased Roderick's peals of laughter. "I beg your pardon, Sir," said he, addressing Edric, as soon as he was able to speak; "I really beg your pardon; but your friend here is so exceedingly amusing, that I am really under infinite obligations to him, and know not how I shall ever be able to repay him."

"It is we who are under obligations to your Majesty, for which we can never be sufficiently grateful," said Edric gravely; for he also was not very well pleased at seeing his friend so openly ridiculed; as, though he did sometimes take the liberty of smiling at the learned doctor's innocent follies himself, he did not like to see him made the laughing stock of another. Roderick, however, saw and instantly understood the ill-humour of Edric; and as he applauded its motive, he endeavoured to divert it by every means in his power, and soon completely succeeded. Few people, indeed, knew so well how to make themselves agreeable as Roderick; and though Edric, at first, felt indignant that the King should treat him so much like a child, as to suppose his displeasure could be easily joked away, yet this feeling insensibly wore off, and he soon thought Roderick the most fascinating of human beings. Indeed, that heart must have been hard that could have withstood unmoved the fascinations of Roderick when he wished to please. His bright laughing eyes that looked the very colour of gladness, and his arch smile, might have subdued the melancholy of a stoic; whilst his character had something bewitching in its very failings. He had been all his life the spoiled child of fortune, and though his rashness and impetuosity, his pettishness and his caressing manners, his bravery, haughtiness, and obstinacy; his fondness for any thing that promised a frolic, and his chivalrous devotion to noble and grand enterprises, formed a singular melange, he was, perhaps, more beloved than he would have been if his character had been more perfect; and it was this very inconsistency that made him so completely the idol of his soldiers.

"Believe me," said he, addressing Edric, "that it is impossible for me to describe the pleasure I feel in having had it in my power to be of service to you; and though I should have been happy to relieve any of my fellow-creatures in distress, yet I must own I am glad you are Englishmen. It was the policy of my late father to act as the enemy of England; but I have always been her friend. I am sure that Nature intended the English and Irish for brethren; and I am too sincere a votary of the goddess to wish, even in the slightest degree, counteract her designs."

"Your sentiments perfectly coincide with mine," said Edric; "and as it has been my fate to live in habits of intimacy for several years with a very worthy countryman of yours, Father Morris, confessor of the Duke of Cornwall, who was the most intimate friend of my father—"

"Father Morris!" interrupted Roderick.

"Yes," returned Edric, surprised at the wonder expressed by the King. ls it possible you can know him?"

"The name appeared familiar to me, that was all," replied Roderick, evidently finding it difficult to repress a strong inclination to laugh. Edric looked at him with Still increasing astonishment, not being able to discover any thing in the slightest degree ridiculous in what he had said; and Roderick's disposition to mirth seemed to increase in exact proportion to Edric's gravity. At length, perceiving he remained silent, Roderick with infinite difficulty contrived to say,—

"Go on, my dear Mr. Montagu, I entreat you to go on; never mind me; it is a strange thought that has just entered my head."

"Mr. Montagu!" exclaimed Edric. "I was not aware that your Majesty was acquainted with my name; I do not recollect having mentioned it."

"Perhaps, however, the doctor did," returned the King; "or the alcaide might have told me, or my servants may have seen it marked upon your trunks or your linen, or—"

"Your Majesty need not give yourself so much trouble to explain a circumstance in itself perfectly immaterial," replied Edric. "I have no wish to conceal my name; I was only astonished to find your Majesty so well acquainted with it."

"Well, well," cried Roderick, somewhat impatiently, "the circumstance is, as you say, quite immaterial, so pray go on with what you were saying of Father Morris."

"I was simply observing that though an intelligent and highly cultivated man, he has strong prejudices, and that his dislike to the Irish is carried to an extravagant excess. My own feelings have always been the reverse of his, and I am happy to say I have always entertained a favourable opinion of your Majesty's countrymen."

"Which I hope the thoughtlessness of their King will not induce you to change. I trust you have too much good sense, Mr. Montagu, to feel offended with what you may call the frivolity of my manner. My heart, I hope, is good, though I own even I cannot say much in favour of my head. I am a laughing philosopher however, a sort of Democritus the second; and finding it more agreeable to laugh than cry, I generally try to extract amusement from every thing that happens to fall in my way. We shall soon know each other better, and so now, as doubtless you may wish for repose after the fatigues you have undergone, you will perhaps like to retire to the tent prepared for you."

The doctor and Edric willingly assented and repaired to their new abode, completely puzzled by what seemed to them the extraordinary and inconsistent character of the King.

Under this gay, laughing exterior, however, Roderic hid a sound penetrating mind, and a firm determined spirit; whilst, though no one enjoyed more to ridicule occasionally the foibles of his subjects, no one knew better how to check them, and bring them back instantly to their proper stations, if they ventured a hair's breadth beyond the limits he prescribed to them. He had thus the art to make himself feared as well as loved, and to rule his subjects despotically, though he never spoke to them without a smile.

Such as I have described him, it may be easily imagined Roderick was not long in winning the affections of his new friends, and he, in his turn, was equally delighted with them. The noble, generous, and inquiring spirit of Edric exactly accorded with his own; and the follies of the learned doctor afforded him never-ceasing amusement, whilst Edric, delighted to meet with a companion who could understand and sympathize with his feelings, felt happier than he had been for years; and the learned doctor, proud of being admitted to the intimacy of such a man as Roderick, declared all his troubles were repaid, and that he now considered himself as the most fortunate of mortals.

Volume 2: Chapter 10

The Spanish nobility were daily collecting round the Irish King. To one of the most distinguished of these, the Duke of Medina Celina, Roderick was particularly anxious to introduce Edric. For this purpose, therefore, as soon as the army of Roderick returned to his head quarters at Cadiz, where the duke had remained, the friends went together to pay him a visit.

Edric was exceedingly interested by this call. The duke's family consisted only of himself and his granddaughter, the Princess Zoe, but the appearance of both was excessively striking. The duke was a blind old man with white flowing hair and a long silvery beard, clad with almost patriarchal simplicity; whilst Zoe, who sate closely by his side, and seemed devoted to his comfort, was beauty itself. Exquisitely lovely, however, as her features were, they excited rather pain than pleasure in the mind of the beholder, from their excessive paleness. Her dress was simple: a robe of black silk fitted tight to her slender shape, and her jet black hair was simply braided on her forehead, and confined in a net behind.

When she saw the strangers, a slight blush stained the usual alabaster fairness of her complexion, and a trifling agitation was visible in her manner. It was but for an instant, however, that this glowing tint suffused her pallid cheeks, or that her fine features betrayed agitation. Her usual calm dignity of expression was immediately re-assumed, and her countenance regained its marble whiteness. There was, indeed, something very singular in the whole countenance of this young beauty, for, notwithstanding the exquisite loveliness of her features, her charms were rather those of a statue than of a human being. Her fine features were strictly Grecian and perfectly regular, but they were always fixed in one unvarying expression; whilst her large black eyes fringed with long silken eyelashes, and her glossy raven hair, contrasted strangely with the spotless fairness of her complexion; the whole gave her the air of some unearthly visitant from the tomb.[218]

Zoe had been unfortunate from her birth. Her mother having accompanied the old duke upon an embassy to Constantinople, had happened to please the fancy of the reigning Emperor so forcibly, that, contrary to the advice of his counsellors, he had married her. Disproportioned marriages, however, are seldom happy ones: and that of the parents of Zoe formed no exception to the general rule. The Emperor soon repented his rashness, and, becoming tired of his wife, treated her with coldness and neglect; whilst she, far removed from all her former friends, and finding herself despised by the man for whose sake she had sacrificed every thing, lingered a few years and then died unheeded and forlorn, leaving only the hapless Zoe to lament her fate.

The Emperor married again; and Zoe had dragged on a miserable existence, till in an insurrection of the Greeks, her father had been murdered, and she herself compelled to fly from Constantinople. She had repaired first to Africa; but finding her grandfather was in Spain, she had followed him thither, and still remained with him, under the protection of Roderick.

It was, indeed, the aristocracy of Spain for which the Irish hero was now principally fighting; for they had suffered most severely from the licentious conduct of the soldiers, and were most earnest in imploring his assistance. When the seat of the Spanish monarchy had been removed to Africa, most of the nobles had followed in its train, whilst those that remained had become objects of hate and suspicion to the republican governments that ensued. Still, however, the *amor patriae*[219] glowed strongly in their breasts, and chained them to their country; they submitted patiently to innumerable grievances, till, a few months before they applied to Roderick, finding the insolence of the soldiers become insupportable, they determined to throw off the yoke, and re-establish a monarchy in Spain.

For this purpose, they had invited Don Pedro, a younger branch of their former Royal family to come over from Africa to accept their throne. He complied, and had brought in his train many of the old nobility; and amongst the rest the venerable Duke of Medina Celina, whose most passionate wish it was, that he might die and be entombed in Spain. Don Pedro had been unsuccessful, and had fled; but many of those who had accompanied him remained, and with the resident Spanish nobility now formed the splendid Court of Roderick at Cadiz.

The duke received Edric kindly, and treated Roderick with that enthusiastic devotion, which is, beyond all other praise, flattering to the mind of man. Zoe never spoke, nor did her features betray that she took the slightest interest in the scene before her. It has been before observed, that education was carried to such a pitch in England, that all, even the common people, were universal linguists. Instruction indeed, in that respect, was imparted in many brief and ingenious modes; and knowledge being thus rendered so cheap and easy, as to be *á la portée de tout le monde*,[220] it of course was going partially out of fashion with the higher classes; but as Sir Ambrose piqued himself on his devotion to all the old customs, he would not swerve from them in the education of his sons; and in consequence, Edric was almost as learned in this respect as a servant or a labourer.

This had often been a source of chagrin to him at home, as it prevented his feeling upon equal terms with those in the same situation of life as himself, and had contributed greatly to give him those shy and reserved manners we have noticed. On the present occasion, however, Edric found his learning advantageous, as it enabled him to enjoy thoroughly the animated and entertaining conversation of the old duke. After a lively and spirited discussion of the manners of the age generally, and the state of Spain in particular, the friends retired, having first obtained a promise from the duke and Zoe to be present at a grand tournament Roderick intended giving on the following day.

"Well, Edric!" said Roderick, "what think you of the Princess Zoe?"

"That she would be charming if she had a little more soul."

"I am surprised at *your* making such an observation, Edric, I thought you were fond of still life, or you would not feel so anxious about your Mummy."

"Oh, for God's sake!" said Edric, "do not joke me upon that subject; it is too solemn, too awful!"

"At least, your doubts are now satisfied," said the King.

"Not at all," returned Edric; "for I cannot help imagining it was only permitted to appear resuscitated to punish my presumptuous daring; and its mysterious disappearance, added to the strange and fearful adventures that have since attended us, only confirm my opinion."

"It must have been a horrible feeling when you first saw it stir," observed Roderick.

"Words cannot express the agony of that moment," replied Edric, "when I saw my strange unearthly wishes gratified, and felt the impiety I had been guilty of in having formed them; and I would have given worlds to restore the Mummy to the deep sleep I had disturbed. It was, however, then too late."

"Can you form any idea of what has become of it?"

"None. If the Egyptian's story be correct, it contrived to re-inflate the balloon, and that carried it away, though it is quite impossible to say how far it might go, as the Mummy could not possibly understand the management of the machine, though he might accidentally fill it."

"Would it relieve you to think the Mummy safe in England?"

"Oh no! I shudder at the thought."

"Well, well, then it is useless to make yourself unhappy about the subject. Depend upon it, all is for the best. I am sure, for my part, I am very much obliged to the resuscitated gentleman; as, if it had not been for his freak of flying away with your balloon, you would not have been here at the present moment, and I might never have even known that such a person was in existence. However, now you are here, you must not leave me; and when we have finished our campaign, we will return to Ireland together, and pass the remainder of our lives in peace and tranquillity."

Edric smiled, for the very idea of peace and Roderick seemed incongruous.

The tournament was held on a fine plain on the mainland, a few miles from Cadiz, and nothing could exceed the brilliancy of the show. "The sun shone o'er fair women and brave men,"[221] for even in winter, the bright beams of an Andalusian sun give a glowing animation to the scene. The busy murmurs of the crowd, the prancing of the horses, and the gay laugh of the light-hearted Irishmen, as they paid their highflown compliments to the Spanish beauties, were, however, soon interrupted by the firing of cannon, and a pause ensued, which was at length broken by loud shouts of "Roderick! Roderick, forever! Long live the Conqueror of Spain!" And immediately, the pressure and hustle of the people, and the sound of warlike music which gradually swelled upon the ear, announced the arrival of that illustrious Sovereign upon the field.

Roderick was, as usual, riding upon Champion, his noble barb,[222] and surrounded by the officers of his staff; but he was not talking to them with his accustomed familiarity; his countenance even wore an air of sadness and reflection, very unusual to it. However, as he rode along, his fine horse tossing his head and spurning the ground as he advanced, he looked completely the powerful Sovereign that he really was.

His dress was exceedingly becoming. Roderick knew mankind too well not to appear to adopt, in some measure, even the prejudices of those he associated with; and knowing the partiality of the Spaniards for dress and appearance, his own was magnificent. A tight vest and pantaloons of black satin displayed the elegance of his figure to the best advantage, whilst a short cloak of the same material, hung from his shoulders in graceful negligence, and his head was covered with a large Spanish hat of black velvet, having a. magnificent plume of ostrich feathers, secured by a diamond aigrette[223] in front. A superb collar of diamonds also adorned his breast, and a deep frill of vandyk lace[224] was fastened round his neck.

Splendid, however, as was the attire of Roderick, it was far exceeded by his personal advantages; and no one could look upon that fair, open brow, those bright blue eyes, that manly, though youthful form, that glossy chesnut hair and curling mustachios, or, what was more than all, upon the fascinating smile of the mouth they decorated, without feeling deeply interested for their possessor.

The fascinating manners of Roderick have been already mentioned; but, upon the present occasion, his usual *gàité de coeur*[225] was tempered by an air of dignity and command which became him equally well, and which powerfully told, that though he might sometimes condescend to seem amused with trifles, he could, when he pleased, be indeed a king.

The affairs of Spain were now beginning to assume a favourable appearance, and, consequently, the people were better disposed to be amused; whilst, as a truce had been granted for some weeks, during a negotiation for peace which was carrying on, the combined Spanish and Irish soldiers shut up in the Isle of Leon, and thrown entirely upon their own resources for amusement, like most persons in similar situations, grasped eagerly at every trifle that seemed to promise variety and amusement.

Roderick was perfectly aware of this; and it was partly to afford employment for his officers, and partly to gratify his own taste for the pursuits of chivalry, that he had proposed the present tournament. The lists were marked out, and a flourish of trumpets summoned the combatants to the field. Two of the Irish officers were the first who engaged, and whilst every eye was occupied in watching their movements with the most intense anxiety, Roderick took an opportunity of whispering to Edric that he had just received news from England.

"Well!" cried Edric, his eyes sparkling with impatience.

"Elvira is elected; but I am afraid there is a strong party in the state against her."

"And my father?"

"He is well, and Edmund is prime minister!"

"What says Rosabella?"

"She is silent; and therefore I fear—"

"You are right. In such a case, Rosabella's silence can only portend a storm."

"The duke has left the country, and now resides entirely in town."

"What a change," said Edric, "a few short months has produced! all is altered. I was excessively shocked when you informed me of the death of Claudia; but this news, though it surprises, does not displease me; and, thank God! my father is well."

The defeat of one of the combatants, and the shouts and triumph attending the success of the other, now interrupted the conference; and the rush of all parties towards the King separated him from Edric, who walked quietly away from the crowd to meditate upon the news he had received. The train of thought thus conjured up was so pleasing, that he was soon completely lost in it. His father, his brother, and all the scenes of his childhood, those early recollections so dear to every heart, seemed to rise before him, and he had forgotten Spain and all that it contained, when he was roused from his reverie by a piercing scream; and, looking round, he saw the Princess Zoe, near whose palanquin[226] he had accidentally placed himself, attempting to break from her carriage in a state of the most violent agitation.

Astonished beyond the power of expression at her emotion, Edric hastily assisted her to unfasten the door of her palanquin, and offered her his arm: Zoe took it without speaking, and with trembling steps hurried across the plain. In a few minutes, however, the cause of the princess's agitation was explained; for, as they approached the spot she evidently wished to reach, Edric saw the body of Roderick extended upon the ground, apparently without life or motion. Uttering an exclamation of horror, he attempted to rush towards him, but the princess held his arm firmly, and prevented him. Quite astonished, he looked up in her face; she was still dreadfully agitated, but she did not speak, and only pressed her finger against her lips.

In a few minutes, Roderick opened his eyes, and the princess again pressing Edric's arm, said in a hurried, though low tone, "Let us go!" Edric obeyed; and they walked hastily back to the palanquin in perfect silence.

When Edric had assisted the princess into her carriage however, and was about to retire, she pressed his hand, and said again in her peculiarly low soft voice, "Do not speak of this!"

"I will not," said Edric; and bowing respectfully as he pressed her hand, to his lips, he walked away excessively surprised at the scene he had witnessed. Upon reaching the King, he found he had been thrown from his horse, and so slightly hurt as not to think it necessary to interrupt the amusements of the day; which concluded after a brilliant display of Irish and Spanish valour, without any other incident worthy of notice.

A few days after this adventure, as Edric was sitting, lost in thought, in his own apartment, musing, as was his custom whenever he was alone, upon the strange adventure of the Mummy, and endeavouring in vain to imagine what might be its probable fate, he was startled by the door of his room flying suddenly open, and Roderick's rushing in pale and in violent agitation.

"Oh, Edric!" cried he, "I am ruined! my fame is lost for ever! whilst I have been loitering away my time here, the enemy has obtained the assistance of the French: they have taken Madrid, and almost all the towns between that and the frontier! An immense army is marching upon Seville, and they intended to have blocked me up here, amusing me with their pretended treaties, till they had caught me in their snare."

"And how has their plot been discovered?"

"The Princess Zoe—yes! I know what you would say—she loves me, and though I love her not, nay, though I am devoted to another, if I reconquer Spain, myself and crown shall be thrown at her feet;—but, if I fail, I will never live to be the herald of my disgrace."

"It is unworthy of Roderick to despair: it will be by treachery, if you are vanquished."

"Hold!" cried Roderick, driven almost to frenzy at the thought. "For mercy's sake, talk not so calmly of my being vanquished. I will conquer—I will redeem my name, or perish in the attempt; and if they do vanquish me, it shall be my corpse alone that they shall conquer, for the immortal spirit shall escape their fury."

"Alas! alas!" said Edric; "your words have again conjured up the fiend that so long has haunted me:—*does* the immortal spirit escape?"

"Edric," returned the King, "this is not a moment for metaphysical subtleties; we must act, and that immediately and decisively. We must advance upon Seville, and, if possible, get possession of that city before the army of the enemy shall reach it: this blow will strike the Spaniards with awe, and before they have recovered themselves, I shall have made myself master of half Spain. I know the character of the people I have to combat; I must carry every thing by a *coup de main*,[227] or I shall fail."

It was impossible to deny the justice of this observation, and Edric warmly seconded the preparations of Roderick to march immediately upon Seville. These preparations were soon made; for Roderick was so completely idolized by his soldiers, that they regarded his will as law, and were ready to march at an hour's notice, though they knew not where they were going. Dr. Entwerfen was excessively agitated when he found he was going now really to engage in war; not that the base emotion of fear took possession of his soul, but a slight trepidation, such as that which scandal says even heroes feel at their first battle, crept over his nerves, and gave him an odd kind of sensation, which, he said, was only anxiety to engage.

No one knew where they were going; it was only rumoured, indeed, that hostilities were about to recommence, and, as the doctor said, it was very disagreeable to be unacquainted with the theatre of their future glory. Roderick was amused, notwithstanding even the agitation of the moment, with the efforts of the doctor to discover the secret, and told him, as though in confidence, that they were going to attack Lisbon. Delighted with this news, which he firmly believed, the doctor strutted about with indescribable dignity, walking upon the tips of his toes, pressing his lips together, and swelling out his cheeks like a cherub in a country churchyard, whilst he seemed absolutely bursting with the importance of the secret he carried. All was now ready; but before Roderick quitted Cadiz, he took leave of the Princess Zoe.

"It would be unjust to your merit, and my gratitude," said he, "to insult you with words; but if I survive, the devotion of my whole life—"

"Stay!" interrupted Zoe, "nor overrate so strangely the value of the service I have been so fortunate as to render you. Besides, even if your estimate were just, know that the services of Zoe are not to be purchased. No, prince; judge me not so meanly. Had I not determined that we should never meet again, the intelligence you so highly value would never have reached your ears. My greatest enemy is dead; and to-morrow I return to my native land, where the rebels have no longer the power to injure me. Demetrius, the ancient minister of my father, arrived yesterday, with the permission for my return, and I do not hesitate an instant—yet, before I go—"

"Speak," cried Roderick hastily; "command my life! my throne! my fortune!"

Zoe smiled. "The favour I have to request is trifling. I have a favourite page, who dreads to return to Greece, and I would willingly place him under your care."[228]

"He shall be my brother!" exclaimed Roderick enthusiastically; "my friend! my companion in arms! He shall live with me, fight with me, and—"

Again a faint smile played on Zoe's marble features, like the ghost of departed joys; it was but for an instant, however, and it added fresh darkness to the succeeding gloom. "I wish no privileges for my page," said she gravely, "beyond those usually bestowed upon his class. Treat him kindly, but promise me you will not over-indulge him, or will not leave him with you."

"You have only to command," said Roderick, "and you may rely upon obedience."

"Adieu! then," exclaimed the princess, extending her hand, whilst a slight blush stained her alabaster complexion. "God bless you!—we may meet again."

Roderick kissed her hand as he would have done that of an empress. "Heaven grant we may!" exclaimed he, "for, rest assured, no earthly pleasure could afford me half the joy."

"None?" asked Zoe incredulously.

"None!" repeated he firmly; unless, perhaps," added he with, a smile, "the re-conquering of Spain."

"Then you will accept my page?"

"As a gift from Heaven!"

"He shall join you ere you cross the bridge: once more, adieu!"

"Adieu!" cried Roderick, and Zoe vanished. In half an hour the troops were under arms, and had quitted Cadiz; but Roderick, in the bustle and confusion attendant upon the removal of so large a body of men so suddenly, had quite forgotten the Greek page. As he was crossing the bridge, however, his noble barb started, and Roderick, looking for the cause, saw a slight, graceful boy, who, kneeling, presented him with a letter; it was from Zoe.

"I forgot to tell you," wrote she, "that my page is dumb. As his loss of speech, however, was accidental, he is, notwithstanding, perfectly intelligent, and will obey your slightest gesture."

Ordering some of his attendants to provide a horse, Roderick desired the page to mount it, and ride by his side: the boy crossed his arms upon his breast, and bowed his head in token of obedience, and then lightly vaulted into the saddle.

Volume 2: Chapter 11

The army of Roderick advanced rapidly through a lovely country richly tinted by the rays of a southern sun. Nothing, indeed, could be more beautiful than the scene. Though spring was only just bursting from the icy chains of winter, vine-covered cottages peeped through orange groves loaded with their fragrant flowers; whilst behind, the dark foliage of the lofty palm-trees gave depth and richness to the landscape. Innumerable flowers perfumed the air, and the sky glowed with azure and gold.

Under these circumstances, the advance of Roderick's army, though rapid, resembled rather the journey of a party of pleasure than a fatiguing and toilsome march; and when, just as the sun was setting, they approached a small village, Edric paused on the summit of a hill, to survey with delighted admiration the lovely scene below. A white church peeped from between a thick cluster of trees, and romantic cottages covered with wild festoons of luxuriant plants, were scattered about at intervals; whilst sitting before the doors, were placed groups of peasant girls, singing patriotic airs to their mandolines or lutes, and others were dancing gaily beneath the shade of some widely spreading trees. Neat dresses of black serge fitted tightly to the shape of these girls, and displayed the graceful elegance of their figures to the utmost advantage. Their long dark hair was bound in a simple net; and their sparkling eyes beamed with animation and love, whilst the clear dark complexion, well proportioned forms, jet black hair, and aquiline noses of their male partners, still, notwithstanding the lapse of so many centuries, strongly marked their Moorish origin. Songs of joy and lively music swelled upon the gale; but these sounds of peace and happiness were soon changed to shrieks of terror, as the unfortunate peasants saw the army of Roderick wind slowly through the trees, and they fled screaming for mercy, whilst all their little store of wealth fell an easy prey to the foe they left behind.

Edric shuddered at the pillage that ensued, and warmly remonstrated with his friend.

"My dear Edric," said Roderick, "these things are inevitable; though what you see here can give you but a very faint idea of the dreadful havoc and devastation of war. My soldiers destroy nothing, and generally even pay for what they take: but commonly in an enemy's country, men burn what they cannot make use of, and treat the unfortunate inhabitants with the most appalling cruelty. However these are things we cannot reason about."

"I think not," returned Edric; and finding his remonstrances unavailing, he had the discretion not again to allude to the subject, till the army approached Seville. The first view of this splendid city, illumined by the glowing rays of the setting sun, struck our young philosopher most forcibly. "Oh, Roderick!" cried he, "look at that long line of sumptuous palaces, adorned with marble pillars, and the finest statues; those lovely gardens—those bowers of roses; and those crystal fountains, whose sparkling spray looks dazzling in the sunbeams."

"Well," said Roderick, "I see them all, and more, the lofty spires of the town rising beyond, their gilded vanes glittering in the sun."

"And can you look upon this fair scene?" asked Edric, "and not feel compunction? Alas! alas! that the cruel hand of man should dare to destroy so lovely a picture!"

"My dear Edric," returned Roderick, smiling, "you would never do for a conqueror. If you make war a profession, Glory must be your mistress, and to obtain her, you must sacrifice all your better feelings. But, ah! what is that? look yonder, Edric!"

"I see nothing but a volume of fleecy smoke curling up between the trees," said Edric; "which harmonizes well with the lovely scene around—that scene which the grim hand of War is destined so soon to desolate. Oh, Roderick, can it be possible, that you, whose kind and charitable nature would not crush a worm to death unnecessarily, should—"

"They have fired the suburbs!" cried Roderick, interrupting him; and clapping spurs to his horse, he darted forward like an arrow discharged from a. bow. His suspicions were correct. Light clouds of white vapour hung high in the clear blue heavens; whilst below, a thick yellow smoke, mingled with flames, spread wide ruin and devastation. Crackling pieces of wood, sparkling like a *feu d'artifice*,[229] were thrown up with violence at intervals, and the scorching heat felt intolerable, as showers of sparks, and pieces of ignited matter, rained thick and fast upon the plain.

Edric and Roderick were on a gentle eminence when they first saw the city; and, deceived by the remarkable optical delusion often observable in similar situations, they had fancied it very near them. When they plunged into the valley, however, they soon discovered that this was of very considerable extent; and their horses, weary with their toilsome march, with difficulty made their way through the thick underwood and tangled grass that every moment threatened to impede their progress. At length, they entered into the mazes of a wood, that quite obscured the city from their sight; and when fair Seville again broke upon them through an opening in the trees, she appeared one vast mass of flame.

"Good Heavens!" cried Edric, "surely they will not burn the city! What a multitude of human beings will he sacrificed if they do!"

"I hope they will not he so foolish," said Roderick, "yet I own I fear; no—no—" cried he, after a moment's pause; "see, see! the smoke divides, and as the wind bears the rolling volumes asunder, the city's walls still stand: no fire as yet has touched the glory and the bulwark of proud yet fair Seville."

The glowing embers still crackled as they approached, and still threw up occasional showers of sparks fearfully glaring amidst the darkness of the night, which now closed in upon them with a thick gloom very unusual to that climate. The flames had caught the bridge ere the army of Roderick reached the banks of the river; and the fiery bow, glowing through the surrounding darkness, looked like the fabled arch[230] over which the Mahometans believe the souls of the dead are destined to skait[231] into Paradise.

At length the army of Roderick found their progress stopped by the deep and rapid waters of the Guadalquiver; the black smoking remains of the bridge which had once stretched across the river, seeming to forbid their farther progress. Magnificent palaces lay around them, crumbling into ruins, whilst their half-burnt roofs fell occasionally with a tremendous crash. Fearful indeed was the spectacle that presented itself, and the once superb suburb seemed the very temple of Desolation. Vases and statues lay overturned, and blackened by the smoke. Majestic trees, scorched by the flames, and their shrivelled leaves stripped from their withered branches, stretched forth their bare arms forlorn and desolate, like bereaved mothers mourning over their murdered children. A chill drizzling mist began to fall, and all looked dreary and uncomfortable around.

Roderick stood upon the banks of the river and marked its dark rolling waters, in which the fire that still crept amongst the ruins on the other side reflected its red lurid glare. "We must pass the river," said he; "these Andalusians are too crafty to have destroyed this fine suburb, in itself a town, had not some imperious reason urged them to it. They want to gain time; but we must show them that we dare brave the combined terrors of flames and water, when Glory gives the word."

"And what is this Glory you pursue so madly?" asked Edric. "May not Prudence be admitted to its councils? And will it not be more certain if we wait till morning to seize it? The night is dark and gloomy; 1 think it forbodes a tempest; and at any rate it will be difficult to ford this black rolling stream in the obscurity. To-morrow with the dawn we will effect a passage; our troops will be then refreshed with rest, and we shall be ready to encounter with vigour the dangers that may oppose us."

Roderick smiled sadly. "Tomorrow, Edric," said he, "it may be too late. To-morrow, the army our enemies expect may advance upon us, and either obtain possession of the town, or cut off our retreat. We have traitors amongst us; for even now, secret as our movements have been, you see the enemy has had notice of our approach."

"Why should we pause?" cried Lord Arthur O'Neil, one of the Irish lords who had followed his Sovereign to the field. "Your Majesty may confide in your soldiers.—Tired! An Irishman knows not the meaning of the word. Shall the heroes of Burgos, Valladolid, and Salamanca,[232] complain of fatigue? Have you forgotten how they fought and conquered? Have you forgotten the proud day before Madrid, when a handful of Irish fought and defeated a whole legion of Spaniards? Can we think of these things, and yet talk of fear? Oh no, surely not! Surely if we did, every warm drop of blood in our veins, every spark of enthusiasm in our hearts, would give the lie to the assertion. Lead us on, brave Roderick! Damp not the spirit of your troops by unnecessary delays, but lead us forward to victory."

"Lead us to victory!" shouted the officers and troops; and Roderick, animated by their cries, gave orders for the instant fording of the river. The evening had now quite closed in; not a star broke the thick dull grey of the heavens, and the sky began to look dark and threatening. The lowering clouds grew gradually darker and darker; whilst a dusky veil seemed to fall over the distant turrets of the town, and to envelope them in gloom.

The fire that still raged in the suburbs, had now seized an ancient castle, and a thick yellow smoke burst from its embrasures: it seemed like a huge giant vomiting forth flames. In the mean time, heavy clouds that had gathered over their heads, seemed big with destruction, and a low moaning sound was heard at a distance as though the winds were sighing over the fate of the unhappy wretches, who were soon to fall victims to their fury! The hollow murmuring continued; it grew gradually louder and louder; and at length, burst with tremendous violence in fearful blasts over the heads of the army. It was now as dark as night, and the thunder rolled with awful grandeur; the rain descended in torrents, and the flashes of lightning showed by glimpses the pouring vengeance of the clouds, and the still smoking fragments of the ruined bridge.

It seemed madness to attempt the passage of the river at such a moment; but the determined spirit of Roderick, when once resolved, was not easily to be shaken, and crying out, "Glory and Roderick for ever!" he attempted to plunge into the boiling flood. At this instant the heavens seemed to open, and a vivid ball of bright blue fire to dart from them. The lightning had struck a tree, beneath which a group of soldiers had taken shelter, splitting it asunder and scattering the branches in all directions; whilst the groans of the unhappy wretches, crushed by its fall, mingled horribly with the howling wind and crashing thunder. Nothing, however, could intimidate the daring spirit of Roderick, and calling upon his soldiers to follow him, he struck his spurs into Champion, his faithful barb, and the noble animal plunged with him into the stream. The river, swollen by the torrents of rain, now rushed along in roaring waves like the sea. Champion, and the horses of those who had followed the example of their Sovereign, were soon obliged to try to swim, and struggled in vain to reach the opposite shore. The impetuous current, however, swept them down the river, and soon the cries of the drowning men, and the plunging of the horses, added fresh horror to the roar of the raging waters.

Fearful was the struggle, till, after a few horrible moments of almost supernatural exertions, the storm partly ceased; and though the wind still continued to howl at intervals, and the thunder to roll, its growl became fainter and fainter; and soon nothing was heard but the splashing of the waves, and the struggles of the swimming animals who tried in vain to stem the boiling current.

Champion had made most violent efforts to save his master, but he strove in vain! he only floated upon the waves. No longer could he toss his head and proudly champ his bit; his strength was fast leaving him: his long thick mane and heavy armour weighed him down. His feeble eyes, however, caught a glimpse of the opposite shore; they had almost reached it, and the noble animal, collecting all his strength for one attempt, sprang forward: but, alas! his heart broke in the effort; his strength failed; the slippery clay slided[233] from beneath his feet, and the lifeless body of poor Champion fell back into the river, dragging his illustrious master with him. Roderick was too much exhausted to swim; and, encumbered by the dead body of the horse, he was fast sinking to rise no more, when a powerful arm caught hold of him.

"Take this knife!" cried a voice that he knew to be Edric's: "disentangle yourself from the horse, and I can save you!"

His words recalled the fleeting spirit of Roderick; he grasped the knife and hastily cut asunder the cord that confined his cloak round his neck. It was this cloak which had become entangled in the saddle, and the moment it was released from the neck of Roderick, it floated down the stream with the body of poor Champion, whilst the fainting Monarch was dragged on shore by his friend Edric. The storm had now entirely ceased; the water began to get more tranquil, and the moon, breaking from the clouds that drifted rapidly across the skies, showed the opposite bank so plainly that the rest of the army passed with little difficulty. In the mean time, restoratives had been applied to Roderick, and he opened his eyes. A slight shudder, however, ran through his frame, as he looked around, and, heaving a deep sigh, he hastily reclosed them, as though he wished to shut out for ever the recollection of what had just passed. 'Twas but for an instant, however, that the manly mind of the Irish hero indulged in this overwhelming sorrow; the next, smiling though mournfully he took the hand of Edric, and looking at him with affection, he said, "I owe my life to you. God only knows whether the boon be worth the meed of thanks, or whether you have not been cruel to my people in saving me. They have small reason to wish my life, if I am often to be seized with such freaks as these. Good God! I shudder when I consider that the lives of several of my fellow-creatures have been sacrificed to my misguided folly. Poor Champion too," drawing his hand across his eyes to wipe away his tears, and then again trying to smile. "You will laugh at me, Edric, but you don't know how much I feel the loss of that horse. Poor fellow! how nobly he breasted the tide, and struggled on. But he is gone, and it's of no use thinking of him."

And as he spoke, he resolutely started from the bed upon which he had been laid, and again dashed the tears from his eyes. "I have other things to think of that are of far more importance than poor Champion; and yet, poor fellow, I can't forget it was his obedience to me that destroyed him! Poor fellow! You would have been sorry for him, Edric, if you had heard how deeply he sighed when we were in the middle of the water, and I forced him to go on. But I will think no more of him. Summon my officers, and let us hold a council as to our future proceedings."

The council was called, and it was soon ascertained that the army had sustained no other loss than poor Champion, a few other horses, and about eight or ten of the King's bodyguard, who had thrown themselves into the river the moment they had seen their master do so. Roderick felt keenly the folly that had occasioned the loss of these brave men and useful animals; but as he was aware that he was now surrounded by his soldiers and the allied Spaniards, and that it is always necessary for a Monarch to seem great, whether he be so or not, if he wish to be obeyed, he had too much self-command to show any signs of weakness, and gave orders for the commencement of the siege of the town with as much coolness as though he had merely quietly marched up to its walls.

In the mean time, Dr. Entwerfen had safely floated over the stream, riding astride upon one of the ammunition waggons, which were contrived of cork, and supported by bladders, or rather balloons, filled with gas upon each side; whilst the middle part, upon which the doctor rode, being nearly in the form of a barrel, the worthy gentleman had formed no bad representation of Bacchus as he swam merrily across; for the learned doctor, having wisely considered how much the interests of science would suffer if any accident befel[234] his precious person, had waited till the river was as smooth as glass, before he would venture to traverse it.

It was perhaps also well for Roderick, that he now found himself upon the theatre of war: that he had orders to give—decisions to make; in short, that he had sufficient to occupy his mind, and prevent its dwelling upon the unpleasant circumstances that had just passed. Occupation, indeed, is the only sure remedy for grief. The consolations of friends and hopes of religion may do much; but constant employment is the most effectual medicine for woe that the skill of man has yet been able to discover.

Roderick now enjoyed the benefit of this invaluable panacea in its fullest extent; for he had much to do. Notwithstanding all their affection for him, his army could not conceal from themselves, that he had sacrificed several valuable lives unnecessarily by his rashness, and their confidence in his prudence was proportionably diminished. Roderick saw, and was mortified by this; the more so, as he felt it was occasioned by his own folly; and he struggled to do something to retrieve the confidence he had lost. There is, perhaps, no situation more painful to a noble, high-spirited mind, than the consciousness of error; and the feelings of Roderick upon this occasion were an ample penance for his faults.

During the whole of the passage of the river, and the encampment of the army upon the opposite side, under the very walls of the city, not a single soldier of the enemy had been seen: but when that was completed, and the harassed host of Irish had stretched their weary limbs upon the earth, to seek a few minutes' repose before the attack that was ordered at daybreak, lights could he plainly seen moving to and fro in the city, and the heavy tramp of the soldiers heard as they paraded the walls. All now was still; a calm seemed to have succeeded a mighty tempest.

A tent had been erected for Roderick and his chief officers; and there the Monarch now sate gloomily musing, whilst his officers were scattered, in various attitudes of repose and thought, around him. Alexis, the Greek page, who had with difficulty passed the river, lay at his feet. At length, all slept but Edric and Roderick. After a long pause, the Irish hero looked at his friend, and seeing him gazing at him with a look of the tenderest concern—"Edric," said he; "I suffocate here; will you walk forth?" Edric willingly consented, and they sallied from the tent.

The moon now shone brightly, and the night was calm and still. They walked together towards the banks of the river. Those waters, which so lately had raged like a roaring lion seeking to devour, now rippled gently along, dancing in the sunbeams, and seeming almost to smile at the mischief they had done.

Roderick could not bear the sight; remorse for his impatience struck like a barbed arrow through his heart, and he turned hastily away. He now looked at the scene that lay before him towards the town. The moon shone brightly upon the tents of his soldiers, which contrasted strongly with the black and disfigured ruins of the suburbs, amongst which they had been hastily pitched; whilst the lights in the city, seen only from the summit of the walls, made it look almost like an eagle's nest suspended between heaven and earth. Roderick grasped Edric's hand. "How calm," cried he, "how peaceful seems the scene before us! Alas! how different from that which so lately—but ah! what's that?" exclaimed he, suddenly interrupting himself; "surely I heard a groan."

Edric listened, and distinctly heard the feeble moaning of a human voice. Neither Roderick nor himself uttered a syllable; but both darted to the spot from whence the sounds proceeded. Just at a bend in the river, surrounded by lofty trees, now scorched and half destroyed by the fire, had stood the *maison de plaisance*[235] of one of the Spanish nobles. It had been built in the Italian style; hedges of myrtle and pomegranates had bloomed in the garden, and a raised terrace had surrounded the house, ornamented by statues. Now, however, this terrace was covered with fallen pillars and broken vases—ruin and desolation spread around. The trellis-work, against which, different creeping shrubs had been trained, hung in wild disorder, torn from the walls, and crushing with its weight the shrubs to which it had once served as a support.

Edric and Roderick entered the dwelling, for the cry seemed to proceed from its ruins. With hasty steps they traversed the deserted chambers, in which magnificent tapestry hung in tatters from the walls, whilst shattered remnants of valuable pictures and shivered mirrors showed the grandeur that had once been there. All now, however, was desolation! the gilded walls and ceilings looked black with the smoke, and the splendid furniture lay half-burnt and half-destroyed upon the ground. Roderick and Edric, however, did not stop long to survey the misery around them, for they hurried hastily forward to the place from which the cries had proceeded. As they approached, they found they were the accents of a female voice that had attracted them; and advancing a few steps farther, they beheld a sight that filled them with pity.

Beneath a fallen column, in the ruins of which she was so entangled that she could not move, lay, or rather stooped, a beautiful female, bending over the apparently lifeless body of an old man, whose fine features and venerable appearance were sufficient of themselves to create a deep interest in his behalf, but which interest was trebly increased by the evident anxiety painted upon the beautiful face of the female.

"Oh, Heavens!" cried she, as soon as they approached; "if you have any mercy or Christian charity in your disposition, succour this poor old man. Those cruel wretches have left him to perish miserably: though we are strangers, we are human beings, and have committed no crime."

By this time, Edric and Roderick had arrived near enough to draw her from the column, when they perceived, to their infinite horror, that her arm was broken, and that she was otherwise seriously hurt. "Oh, think not of me," cried she, finding they wished to succour her before they attended to the old man, who appeared to be dead; "save my father, I am quite well—can I help you?" and heedless of her own pain, the heroic girl assisted in dragging her father from his dangerous situation.

"I fear he is dead," whispered Roderick.

"Oh! say not so," shrieked Pauline, for that was her name; "he must, he shall recover. Give him air," continued she, endeavouring with the one trembling hand, the use of which remained to her, to unfasten his collar. Edric gazed at her with admiration, and, struck with her filial piety and generous self-forgetfulness, he felt an interest for her that he had never before experienced for woman. He assisted her pious cares, and finding the old man still insensible, he bore him in his arms to the banks of the river, and sprinkled him with its waters.

Whilst he was thus engaged, the little fat Dr. Entwerfen, quite out of breath with his exertions, came puffing up, in something between a run and a trot. "Oh! Edric dear!" cried he, gasping for breath, "I've found you, have I; but, heyday! What's the matter? You haven't been killing any body, have you?"

"Doctor!" exclaimed Edric, "I am rejoiced to see you; this gentleman has been hurt by some falling ruins—will you bleed him?"

The doctor had studied surgery in his youth, and had since practised frequently for charity; and, being in all things in which his particular foibles were not concerned, a man of sense and feeling, he instantly comprehended the importance of the case, and drawing forth his lancet, after having first bared and bound up the arm of his patient, he bled him. At first the blood dropped slowly, drop by drop; but it soon began to flow more freely, and then the patient, heaving a deep sigh, opened his eyes.

Pauline had been bending over her father with an intenseness of anxiety that repressed every personal feeling; but the moment she heard him sigh, the unnatural strength that had supported her gave way; nature could bear no more, and she fell senseless to the ground.

Every one flew to her assistance, and Dr. Entwerfen, in particular, was quite in agony. "Dear, pretty creature!" cried he, pushing his wig on one side, in his hurry to raise her up—"Pretty dear! I do declare her arm is broken, and her shoulder dreadful lacerated! Poor thing! I wonder how she could contrive to hold up so long."

"It is wonderful!" repeated Edric. "It is the triumph of mental energy over bodily suffering."

"See! she opens her eyes! she survives!" exclaimed Roderick. "Had I not better return to my tent for assistance?"

"There are some soldiers just there," replied the doctor, pointing to a group of men a few paces distant; "they came with me to protect me, but I outran them when I saw Edric."

The soldiers soon formed a litter, upon which M. de Mallet, for that was the name of the old man, and his daughter were conveyed to the tent of Roderick, where proper surgical aid was afforded them. And whilst they are recovering from the injuries they had received, we will take the opportunity of informing our readers of the circumstances that had placed them in so unpleasant a situation.

M. de Mallet was a Swiss noble; and upon the usurpation of the then despot of Switzerland,[236] he had vehemently defended the liberty of his country. The tyrant had imprisoned him, and he had with difficulty made his escape, followed by his only daughter, who was devotedly attached to him, and who, in all his dangers, had never quitted his side. She had lost her mother in her earliest youth, and since that period, all her thoughts and cares had been devoted to her father.

To comfort him, had formed the sole occupation of her life; and self was quite forgotten in her anxiety for his welfare. After escaping from Switzerland, they had taken refuge in Spain, flattering themselves, that, as it was a free country, they should there be safe and happy. But, alas! they soon found the charms of freedom were more ideal than real; and M. de Mallet, though he had been an enthusiast for liberty under the despotic government of Switzerland, found the sweets of freedom not quite so great as he had imagined amongst the Republicans of Spain; the pride of the nobles, and the conceited ignorance and insubordination of the people, being, as he found by sad experience, things much more agreeable to talk about than endure. In Switzerland, he had called the one, proud independence, and the other manly daring; but he now discovered nobles and democratic chiefs can be tyrants as well as kings; and that the mob is a many-headed monster most exceedingly difficult to manage.

At first, M. de Mallet and his daughter were rapturously received in Spain. No human beings could be more interesting: applauses filled the air whenever they appeared; addresses were presented to them from all quarters, the people crowded to see them, and the Spanish nobles vied with each other in offering them an asylum. All this was very fine; but, unfortunately it was too charming to be lasting. As M. Mallet and his lovely daughter had been often seen congratulated, and condoled with, there was nothing now to be done, and the enthusiasm of the Spaniards began rapidly to abate. In the first moment of triumph, M. de Mallet had blindly believed every thing the people had advanced, and had fancied himself, really as they called him, a hero and a martyr. He thus felt sensibly the change of feeling they so soon evinced; he became disgusted with a people so fickle; and, being too candid to conceal his sentiments, he suffered the Spaniards to perceive his disgust. The total alienation of the remaining interest they felt for him, was the natural consequence.

In the heat of enthusiasm, M. de Mallet had accepted freely the offer of a Spanish nobleman to make his house his home; but, with the usual tenacity of a generous mind in a state of dependence, as soon as he fancied he saw a coldness on the part of his host, he left him instantly, and hastened to the house of another, who had been still more warm in his offers of friendship. He, too, soon became cold; and M. de Mallet, like the hare with many friends,[237] though overloaded with professions, found himself completely desolate when he really wanted protection.

M. dc Mallet had provided no funds when he left his native country, and his estates having been confiscated, he was thus thrown entirely upon the bounty of strangers. Too high-minded to endure dependence, and too proud to humble himself to labour, M. de Mallet had solicited and obtained the promise of a post in the Spanish army; and the directors of the government having promised him a place in the garrison of Seville, he had proceeded a few weeks before to the house of the Duke of Sidonia, the governor of that city, for, the purpose of taking possession. The duke, however, received him coldly, amusing him with procrastinating promises, till M. de Mallet found too late he had been duped by the directors; who, to rid themselves of his importunities, had sent him to Seville, merely on account of its distance from Madrid, and the difficulty he would have in returning to torment them, instead of having any real intention of complying with his wishes.

Indignant at the treatment he had met with, M. de Mallet expostulated warmly with the duke; and the violence of his feelings produced an apoplectic seizure. The duke, though indifferent to the suit of M. de Mallet, was not destitute of the common feelings of humanity; he had him, therefore, carried to a chamber, where proper surgical assistance was afforded him. This scene took place at the duke's country-seat, upon the banks of the river; and M. de Mallet had remained there till, aided by a strong constitution and the vigilant attention of his daughter, he was fast recovering. When, however, intelligence being received of the rapid approach of the army of Roderick, the duke ordered the suburbs to be burnt, including his country-house; his unfortunate guests had entirely escaped his recollection; and the Spaniards appointed to destroy the suburbs, having performed their task with the utmost barbarity, tearing to pieces and destroying what they could not burn; the servants had flown at their approach, entirely forgetting M. de Mallet and his daughter; who, being in a distant quarter of the mansion, knew nothing of what was passing, till they were roused to a sense of their situation by the flames attacking their apartment. With piercing screams Pauline succeeded in rousing her father, and forcing him from the chamber; but they knew not where to fly. The crackling flames seemed to pursue them wherever they went, and the falling timbers threatened every instant to destroy them. At last they reached the hall, and Pauline's beautiful features beamed with joy at their approaching deliverance, when the tottering roof gave way, rocking a few moments with a fearful cracking noise, and then falling with a tremendous crash. Pauline saw it coming; but there was not time to escape; and uttering a faint cry, she threw herself before her father, striving to shield him with her delicate body from the coming danger.

Feeble, however, would have proved this slight and fragile barrier to ward off the impending peril, had not fortunately one of the descending rafters struck against a projecting pillar, and thus formed a kind of arch, which served to protect them from farther injury; the falling of the roof having also nearly extinguished the fire. Pauline's arm had been broken with the blow, and her shoulder dreadfully lacerated; yet still the heroic girl supported herself; and, sustaining with her remaining arm the apparently lifeless body of her father, who, stunned with so many misfortunes, lay insensible at her feet, she endeavoured by her cries to draw the attention of some one to the spot; as she found her father and herself were so entangled in the ruins, that it was impossible they could be extricated without powerful assistance.

The keenest interest was excited by Pauline and her father in the breasts of Edric and Roderick; but, powerful as it was, it was destined soon to give way to yet more painful sensations; for scarcely had they been removed to the tent, when Roderick, perceiving the first feeble tints of day streak the horizon, gave orders for the assault. The city was strongly fortified, and even where the ancient bulwarks had decayed, the governor had hastily supplied their place with wood so skilfully painted to resemble stone, as quite to deceive the eyes of his opponents. Thirty towers were ranged at intervals along this formidable-looking wall; and on one side appeared a citadel strongly garrisoned, which commanded that space between the river and the city where the army of Roderick was now encamped, and which was aided by a kind of ditch which served occasionally as a covered way.

The sun now rose, in all its splendour, spreading its rich tints of purple and gold over the scene, and sweeping away before it the mists of morning. Soon, however, was its brilliancy to be obscured, and the savage rage of man to deface the beauty of nature; soon did roaring cannon and flashing weapons imitate a contention of the elements; and soon did the gashed and bleeding forms of the assailants strew the ground, rendered slippery by their blood. The besieged defended themselves vigorously; three times did Roderick and his followers attempt to scale the walls, and three times were they repulsed; but at length a breach was made, and Roderick, transported with joy, threw himself into it, shouting to his soldiers to follow him. They obeyed; and the siege would have been at once terminated, had not a cloud of dust, rising in long black columns in the distance, through which the reflection of arms shone dazzling in the sun, given new spirits to the besieged, and discouraged the besiegers.

Deep masses, half hidden by this heavy cloud and appearing only more vast from the obscurity thrown over them, advanced rapidly, seeming to come on with the mighty force of the raging sea when it rushes along with irresistible violence and sweeps before it every thing that dare oppose its fury.

The garrison of the town, animated at the sight, rallied their half-exhausted forces, and drove back the assailants with such carnage that the line of their retreat was marked by a long stream of blood and expiring bodies. Roderick, for the first time in his life, refrained from renewing the attack, for, as he feared being surrounded, he determined to draw off his forces, and give battle to the combined French and Spanish army that was now fast approaching.

Volume 2: Chapter 12

Notwithstanding the danger of his situation, Roderick was delighted at the sight of the allied army. "Now we shall fight," cried he, "and not be thrown down like dogs from the walls to perish. I could not bear to see my brave soldiers so sacrificed. But now that we shall meet fairly upon the open field, and struggle hand to hand, and man to man, we cannot fail to conquer!"

"Heaven grant us victory!" said Edric, sighing.

"Why, and so it will, man!" repeated Roderick gaily. "Come, come! rouse, and cheer thy spirits, for the moment of glory ought not surely to be that of gloom!"

The force of the enemy had, in the mean time, rapidly advanced, and the two armies were now opposite to each other; the river curving round that of Roderick like a silver band. The situation of the Irish hero was, indeed, now become hazardous in the extreme; and, if defeated, he could neither retreat nor advance without being exposed to imminent peril, as the river lay before him, and his rear was open to attacks from the town. But neither Roderick nor his soldiers ever contemplated the possibility of defeat; they breathed nothing but victory; and, as the confidence, of success often ensures it, they had hitherto found themselves invincible, principally from the firm belief they entertained that they really were so. Roderick divided his army into three parts, and, determining to lead the van himself, he gave the command of one of the other divisions to Lord Arthur O'Neil, son of the Earl of Tyrone; and confided the other, which consisted entirely of Spaniards, to the conduct of the Spanish general, Don Alvarez Rippeardo, upon whose prudence he knew he might confidently rely: whilst he retained Edric, the doctor, and Alexis, the Greek page of Zoe, immediately about his own person.

The battle soon raged with terrific grandeur; the shouts and cries of the combatants, mingling horribly with the roar of the cannon, which echoed from the walls of the town, seemed to leap from hill to hill, and reverberate in the distance like peals of rolling thunder. Roderick, in the mean time, performed prodigies of valour. Not satisfied with directing the movements of his troops, he fought bravely, sword in hand, like a common soldier, with all that prodigious energy and unexampled good fortune, which had previously induced the belief amongst the lower classes of Spaniards, of his being assisted by supernatural agency. A square was attacked and seemed upon the point of giving way; but when Roderick saw its danger and threw himself into the centre, the soldiers were inspired with unwonted courage, and, fighting like lions about to be despoiled of their prey, repulsed the enemy with tremendous slaughter. In fact, nothing could resist the valour of Roderick's arm; like Homer's Achilles, he seemed ready to triumph even over Fate herself.

An unexpected occurrence, however, notwithstanding his prowess, was very near turning the tide of the battle against him. Lord Arthur O'Neil, whom he had placed at the head of one of the divisions, though brave as an individual, was nothing as a chief; and, unequal to the responsibility of the task he had undertaken, stood hesitating and uncertain what to do, whilst the moment for action passed away. His division had been sent round to attack the enemy in the rear; and Roderick having advanced farther than he would have done, had he not depended upon their assistance, their inaction seemed likely to produce the most fatal consequences. Edric saw Lord Arthur's uncertainty; and, comprehending in an instant both the cause and its effects, he put himself at the head of a few men and galloped to his relief. Arthur, bewildered and overwhelmed, willingly resigned his command; and Edric, leading his division to the charge, changed instantly the fortune of the day. The victory that followed was decisive. Those combating in front against Roderick, astonished at hearing the din of battle in their rear, wavered and became irresolute; whilst disorder being once thrown amongst such a mass of men, horses, and ammunition-waggons, its consequences were irreparable. The rout soon became general. The French and Spaniards fell over each other in dismay; whilst, in some instances, their confusion was so excessive, that they turned their arms upon their own troops, mistaking them for those of their opponents.

The pursuit of the flying foe being confided to the Spanish division of Roderick's army, that victorious monarch returned himself in triumph to his camp before the city. Gloom hung over the walls of Seville, as that proud city expected to become instantly the prey of the conqueror. Roderick, however, finding the garrison were still determined to resist, and that his own soldiers were exhausted by the fatigue they had undergone, resolved to defer the attack till the next day. Then retiring to his tent, he ordered his officers and nobles to be summoned to hold a council of war as to their future proceedings. A crowd had, in consequence of this summons, already collected round the Monarch when Edric appeared amongst them. Roderick saw him, and hastily rushing forward, clasped him in his arms. "My dearest friend!" cried he; "yesterday you saved my life, but to-day you have preserved my honour. I do not attempt to thank you, for I feel the utter incompetency of words to express my feelings. Do not, however, look miserable, Arthur," continued he, addressing the unfortunate general "for I do not blame you. It was my fault for putting you in a situation you were not competent to fill. For the future, you and Edric shall change places; and then I trust, whilst I have still the pleasure of employing my friends, the interests of the state will not suffer."

A page now appeared, bearing a ribband,[238] attached to which, were fastened some glittering crosses. "It is well," said Roderick, taking the ribband in his hand. "Edric," continued he, "I hope you will oblige your friend by accepting these splendid baubles from his hand. They can confer no additional honour upon you in his sight, but they may aid in establishing your authority amongst the soldiers you in future will command, who regard these trinkets with respect.

Edric gracefully bowed assent, and kneeling before the Monarch, received his new honours with as much grace as Roderick bestowed them; the assembled officers and nobles pressing round, and offering their congratulations. Whatever they might say, however, no one present really felt a tenth part of the delight experienced by Dr. Entwerfen upon the occasion. His transport, indeed, quite defies description; for he danced, sang, jumped, nay, absolutely screamed with rapture; till at last, quite unable otherwise to give vent to the violence of his emotions, he sprang to the pillar of the tent, and clinging round it, embraced it with all his strength. All these antics had been slily[239] watched and enjoyed by Roderick, even through the circle that surrounded him: he lost sight of the doctor, however, when he darted away; and it was not till the officers and nobles dispersed, that the King discovered his learned friend, to his infinite amusement, still hugging the post.

It has been already observed, that an unconquerable love of mischief mingled with the thousand good qualities that formed the composition of Roderick, and that he was continually getting into scrapes, and playing tricks upon all the unhappy personages who happened to fall in his way; though his invincible good-humour, and a certain indescribable degree of the *bon enfant* peculiar to his character, rendered it quite impossible for any one seriously to resent his pranks.

It was not, indeed, in nature, for any human creature to be long angry with Roderick; and thus being certain of not giving lasting offence, whenever he was not positively engaged in war, the restless activity of his disposition made him frolic about, like a spoiled and petted child, who, even at the very moment of his sins being forgiven, is entirely occupied in plotting some new exploit.

Under these circumstances, it may be easily imagined what an infinite fund of amusement the confiding simplicity of Dr. Entwerfen had proved to Roderick, and innumerable had been the tricks he had played off upon him during their long and tedious sojourn in the Isle of Leon. The important events that had since occurred had, however, entirely occupied the Monarch's attention, and the poor doctor had been suffered to enjoy a long respite, till this sudden view of his unabated enthusiasm presented an opportunity too tempting for the laughter-loving Monarch to resist.

Accordingly that evening, one of Roderick's pages, affecting an air of profound secrecy, presented the doctor with a mysterious bag, containing several small balls of dough, and a billet from the King, in which he informed the doctor, that these balls when boiled would be converted into a gunpowder of such amazing strength and efficacy, that ten grains of it would be sufficient to blow up a whole city; and that having become possessed by accident of the invaluable secret of their composition, he wished to use them for the destruction of Seville; and not having in his whole camp so skilful an experimental philosopher as the doctor, he had determined to confide their preparation exclusively to his care.

It is impossible for words to do justice to the importance that swelled in the breast of the doctor as he perused this epistle. He strutted, puffed himself out, and did his very utmost to look big—a feat he doubtless might have contrived to accomplish, had not Nature perversely determined to counteract his endeavours, and confined his stature to about four feet eleven. As it was, however, he certainly did make the most of himself, and being firmly resolved not to lose a single instant in putting the designs of the King into execution, he hastened to a vacant place between the camp and the city, where some cauldrons had been hastily erected for cooking the soldiers' food, and there commenced his operations.

In the mean time, Roderick, who had no idea the doctor would be so expeditious in his movements, was busily engaged in superintending the removal of the wounded, and in giving orders of the assault which was to take place upon the following day. He had indeed much to do; for awfully heavy is the responsibility of a general who is not entirely divested of feeling for his men; and the heart of Roderick, though a mistaken thirst for glory had made him a conqueror, was kind and generous, nay even tender in the extreme.

Urged by his compassion, he thus could not rest satisfied, after the more arduous labours of the day were over, without visiting himself the hospitals of the sick. He saw their wounds dressed, and tried to soften their pains, whilst he spoke kindly to them, and praised their valour. Thus employed, as he passed from tent to tent, the eyes of his soldiers beamed with rapture at his approach; and even in the agonies of death, they raised their feeble voices to call down blessings upon his head. Alexis followed his master in this excursion, and his fine eyes sparkled with pleasure as they followed the godlike form of Roderick through the crowd. The Monarch, indeed, himself, started with amazement as, turning suddenly, he accidentally met their gaze. "This page," said he to Edric, who happened to be near, "possesses a glance of fire—I really never saw more expressive features."

"It is often the case," returned Edric calmly, as he assisted one of the surgeons to bind the arm of a wounded soldier. "The dumb frequently employ gestures to make themselves understood, and their features insensibly become more expressive from the muscles being more frequently brought into play."

"You fought like a hero, my brave fellow!" said Roderick to the poor man Edric had been assisting. "I hope your hurt is not serious!"

"And if it were through my heart," said the man, "it's no more than I'd be proud to bear for your Majesty, any day of my life."

"Oh, these Irish!" sighed an old Andalusian soldier, who lay near, and happened to understand them. "They are brave as lions in the field, but gentle as doves when they are in a chamber."

"Have your wants also been attended to?" asked Roderick.

"Yes, God bless your Majesty!" returned the soldier. "If the devil does help you when you are fighting, I am sure it is God's own spirit makes you so good to your soldiers afterwards."

"If the devil helped me to-day," said Roderick, laughing, "I am sure I am very much obliged to his Satanic Majesty, for I never was in greater, peril. Do not look so grave, Edric, you know I am only joking; and that whatever my tongue may say, my heart only feels gratitude where it is really due:" and as he spoke, he devoutly crossed himself.

"I know," said Edric gravely, "that your heart is infinitely better than your head."

"The fault of my countrymen," cried Roderick, again smiling, "or rather the fault of nature, for they, poor souls, can't help it. Our imaginations are so vivid that, like a restive horse, they are apt to take the bit in their teeth and gallop away at full speed, in spite of all that the sage Dame Reason, who still keeps uselessly pulling the rein, can do to prevent them."

As soon as the more important duties of his station were fulfilled, Roderick intended paying a visit to Doctor Entwerfen, to discover what effect had been produced upon the doctor's mind by his treacherous letter; but Edric proposing that they should see the fair Swiss, as common politeness required they should inquire after her arm, the poor doctor was driven entirely from his thoughts.

A separate tent had been pitched for the reception of M. de Mallet and his daughter; and when our friends entered it, they found that worthy gentleman quite recovered, and his lovely daughter reclining upon a kind of couch, and looking more beautiful than ever. Her angelic features had, it is true, lost the animation they before expressed, but their present languor made them infinitely more interesting than their former energy. Softness was indeed the characteristic of Pauline's beauty. Her figure, though slight and sylphic, was yet round and full enough to please a voluptuary. Her complexion was exquisitely fair, but a beautiful rosy tint glowed on her cheeks, whilst her clear blue eyes and golden hair gave her the look of a seraph; and when she raised those bright blue eyes in gratitude to Edric, her look sank deep into his soul, and he thought he had never before seen beauty.

Such was Pauline; and when she spoke, Edric, as he listened in rapture to the soft melting tones of her melodious voice, felt he could no longer resist, but yielded up his heart a willing captive to her charms. Yes; the calm, the reasoning, the philosophic Edric was actually in love. He, who had so despised and ridiculed the passion, and who had affected to doubt its very existence, was now become one of its most devoted victims.

Roderick was almost as much charmed as Edric with the beauty of Pauline, and as the circumstance that had at first introduced her to their notice formed so striking a contrast to the softness and delicacy of her present appearance, that it was scarcely possible to suppose her the same person, a feeling of curiosity mingled with the interest she excited. When our friends entered the room, M. de Mallet rose to receive them: "I know not how to thank you," said he; his voice almost stifled with emotion: "my own life was of little value; but for that of this dear child—" he could not proceed.

Roderick took his offered hand. "My dear Sir," cried, he, "talk not of thanks; Edric and myself are but too well repaid in seeing you thus recovered; and I am sure we shall ever esteem the day when we were so fortunate as to be of service to you, as the happiest of our lives!"

"You are too good," exclaimed M. de Mallet—"too good!" and he could no longer restrain his tears.

Roderick was deeply affected; he could not bear to see an old man weep; and he again took M. de Mallet's hand, pressing it respectfully to his lips: "My dear Sir," exclaimed he, "what I have as yet been able to do for you is nothing; but if you will return with me to Ireland, I may be able—"

"Hush! my good friend," replied M. de Mallet; "I do not doubt your kindness nor your power; but I have had too much of professions!"

"My father," said Pauline, interposing her soft sweet voice, "has suffered much; forgive him if he seem ungrateful for your kindness; but repeated disappointments sour the spirit. We have seen much trouble!" and her voice trembled as she spoke.

"Alas! —if *you* have, not been exempt from trouble, who shall dare complain?" exclaimed Edric, in a voice as soft and tremulous as her own.

Pauline turned her beautiful eyes upon him:

"Pardon me, Sir," said she, "that I have not before thanked you! be assured it has not been for want of feeling your kindness; but sometimes the heart is too full for utterance."

"Thanks from your lips, madam," returned Roderick, "would be a reward for any service."

Pauline blushed: "You too, Sir, were kindness itself," rejoined she: "think not I am insensible to your favours; but I am a bankrupt even in thanks. Alas! fate destines us to incur continually obligations which we can never repay."

A grateful heart is more than words," said her father; "and in that, my child, I know you will never be deficient; but to whom are we indebted for such kindness?"

"I am the King of Ireland," said Roderick, smiling; "surnamed the devil's favourite here in Spain."

"Is it possible?" cried M. de Mallet; "do I, indeed, see the illustrious Roderick?"

"And this," continued Roderick, without noticing his exclamation, "is my friend, Mr. Montagu, an Englishman; who, like many of his countrymen, not contented with enjoying every luxury at home, rambles into foreign climes, to grumble and find fault with every thing he may chance to meet."

"Do not believe him, madam," cried Edric; "my countrymen are fond of travelling, it is true; and may find fault occasionally with what they think deficient in a strange land; but I assure you, we travel from a desire of improving ourselves and acquiring knowledge, whilst we only find fault in the charitable hope that our censures may produce amendment."

"That is, supposing your censures are just," replied Roderic; "but that we sometimes take the liberty to doubt."

"I think nothing more unreasonable than to censure customs merely because we are not used to them," said M. de Mallet; "for my part, when I travel, I make up my mind to be satisfied with every thing, as I think I have no right to quarrel with inconveniences I have sought myself."

It would be well," rejoined Roderick, "if all were of your opinion, and if those who cannot be contented abroad would try to rest contented at home. But you speak as though you had travelled, and I think your daughter mentioned yesterday that you were strangers in Spain."

"We are Swiss," replied M. de Mallet; "my name is de Mallet, a name which you may have heard as belonging to a champion of liberty. Powerless as my efforts have been, I was that champion, and the reward of my labours is poverty and disgrace in a foreign land."

"But surely," said Roderick, "the Spaniards as a nation of freemen would receive a martyr for liberty with open arms, and would treat him as a brother."

"Yes, yes," replied M. de Mallet bitterly; "I have had a tolerable specimen of their fraternal affection: they received me with protestations, fed me with delusive promises, and then left me to perish miserably."

"Not designedly, my dear father," said Pauline; "I cannot suppose they left us to perish designedly."

"Oh, no!" cried Roderick; "that must have been impossible: tigers must have been moved to pity by that voice. They never could have intended to leave you to perish."

"Sire," replied M. de Mallet gravely, "you forget my daughter and I are but plain simple Swiss; we are unused to flattery and to the language of Courts; do not then address expressions to us above our comprehension, which may lead us to forget the distance fortune has placed between us."

"Speak not of the difference of rank," interrupted Roderick impatiently; "beauty and merit, like that of your daughter, place her upon a level with a throne."

"Pardon me, Sire," replied Pauline, blushing, and casting her eyes upon the ground; "I am perfectly aware of the humility of my station. I am aware that I was not born to be a companion of kings and princes, nor have I any wish to exalt myself above the situation in which nature has placed me. My duty to my father led me to follow him to the Spanish Court. It was the first that I had seen; and, forgive me, Sire, if I say I sincerely hope it may be the last."

"But you must not judge of us by the Spaniards."

"I know it well, report has always spoken of the Irish hero as noble, generous, and kind: even his enemies have done justice to his merits, and the fame of Roderick has spread to every corner of the globe. I know that he is incapable of treating my father as he has been treated by the directors of Spain; but I know also, that he is so far superior to myself as to make his notice a condescension which I dare not flatter myself will continue, and of which I know myself perfectly undeserving."

Edric's eyes expressed his admiration, and Pauline's glowing cheeks proved she saw and understood their meaning. Roderick, however, was not quite so well pleased; he felt himself rebuked, and Roderick did not like to feel himself in the wrong.

"You are too modest," said he; then turning to Edric, "Edric," continued he, "have you any idea what is become of Dr. Entwerfen?"—then again addressing himself to Pauline, he added, "Apropos—you will be very much amused with the learned doctor, Mademoiselle de Mallet; but I give you fair notice before you see him, that you must not laugh at him before his face, for Edric is as tenacious of the feelings of his tutor as of his own."

Pauline's eyes expressed her approbation of Edric's delicacy upon this point; and, as they met his, they conveyed more pleasure to his heart than language could express. From this moment, Pauline and Edric seemed to understand each other, for they felt there was a community of feeling between them. The mute intelligence of the eyes sometimes says more than whole years of commonplace intercourse; and thus Pauline and Edric felt like old friends, though they had scarcely exchanged half a dozen sentences.

"Was not that the gentleman that relieved me from my swoon?" asked M. de Mallet.

Before Roderick had time to answer, an officer rushed into the room, looking the very image of despair, and, approaching Roderick, bent his knee before him.

"What is the matter?" cried the Monarch sternly. "Speak! If you have committed a fault, you have less to fear from my justice than my mercy, for misplaced lenity only encourages crime."

"Pardon, Sire!" exclaimed the officer, still kneeling; "but—but—"

"Speak!—no evasion."

"Your Majesty commanded that we should watch that no harm happened to Dr. Entwerfen, and—and he has been taken by the enemy."

"Fool! dolt, blockhead!" cried Roderick; and, taking leave of M. de Mallet and his daughter, he and Edric hastily quitted the tent.

The balls the Irish King had given the doctor were simply formed of dough, the same as that used in the making of bread, with only the addition of a little bit of quicksilver rolled up in the centre of each. This, the merry Monarch knew, as soon as it was exposed to the action of heat, would make the dumplings dance about, as though they were bewitched; and he anticipated great amusement from seeing the doctor's exertions to keep them in the pot, and his despair at not being able to do so. To prevent the possibility of mischief, however, he had desired a select guard to keep watch over the unfortunate philosopher, and never to lose sight of him, taking care to prevent, if possible, his being exposed to any danger. These fellows, however, did not perform their duty, and it was to their negligence that the unhappy fate of the doctor was owing.

The moment the doctor had received the fatal balls, he hastened to the cauldron, and, hastily kindling a fire, began to try the experiment. The balls more than answered Roderick's expectations, for, as soon as they were affected by the heat, they began to jump out of the pot, one after the other, with the most determined perseverance. The doctor was in a violent heat from being exposed to the steam of the cauldron; and he threw off his coat to cool himself; his wig also slipped off, in his exertions to recover the provoking balls, he being obliged to skip after them with the utmost agility as they rolled bounding along; and no sooner had he caught one and put it back into the pot, than another would jump out and begin a new set of vagaries. The doctor, though tired and provoked, did not however relax his labours even for an instant, and he was running, panting and out of breath, after one of these mercurial harlequins, when he was stopped by a rough arm, whilst a man in a gruff voice demanded what he was doing there?

The doctor looked up, and finding with horror that he was surrounded by eight or ten armed Spaniards, answered, in trembling accents, "that he was making gunpowder."

"Gunpowder!" exclaimed one of the men. "But what were you doing with those balls?"

"I was boiling them," replied the doctor, with great awe.

"You seemed to be playing with them, I think," resumed the man. "Were you running after them to make gunpowder?"

"Yes, they wouldn't stay in the pot; and I was obliged to run after them, to catch them."

The soldiers burst into a horse laugh at this *naïve* reply, and their merriment offered a ridiculous contrast to the doctor's woful[240] visage. They now prepared to retire, dragging the doctor with them, totally heedless of his supplications for pardon and declarations of innocence. They declared him to be a spy, and swore that they would hang him as such as soon as they should get within the town. The soldiers who were appointed to guard the doctor, and who, by indulging in a comfortable game at piquet, had neglected their charge, now came up, and, dismayed at seeing the doctor in custody of a force too considerable for them to engage with, fled to inform their Sovereign, trembling, however, all the time at the consequences of their disobedience.

When Roderick and Edric reached the plain, the group of soldiers, with the poor doctor in the midst of them, were just entering one of the gates of the town through which they had made their sally. The rays of the setting sun fell full upon the poor doctor's bald head and shining face; and these, and his white shirt sleeves, as he raised his hands in a supplicating manner towards Heaven, made him a conspicuous object even at a distance, till he was hidden from the sight of his friends by the heavy gates closing upon him. Roderick and Edric were in despair at the loss of their favourite; and to see him, dragged away so barbarously, without having the power to assist him, was enough to try the philosophy of a stoic. It was no wonder, therefore, that it was too much for the patience of the Irish hero, who had rarely known disappointment or control: he raved, stamped, and, unable to contain his rage, ordered an instant attack of the place.

The enemy, imagining the Irish too much fatigued with the battle they had just fought, to assault the town that night, were far from expecting an attack; but, encouraged by the successful opposition they had before made, they received the assault with firmness, and repulsed it with vigour. The cannon roared with tremendous fury on both sides, and whole columns of men were swept away as grass falls before the scythe. The impatience of Roderick increased every moment, and the discharge from a petard having set fire to the wooden bulwarks of the town, he threw himself upon the blazing breach, sword in hand, heedless of the crackling timbers and fast spreading flames, whilst Edric and some of his most devoted soldiers followed him, and they were all soon warmly engaged with the Spaniards who opposed their entrance upon the walls. A loud shout from below, however, soon engaged their attention; the besieged had made a sortie by means of the covered way; and Edric and his royal friend, finding their retreat would he cut off if they stayed, were reluctantly compelled to retire with their followers. Roderick, indeed, was struck down by a Spanish soldier, whilst in the act of leaping from the walls. The soldier, seeing the effect he had produced, was about to repeat his blow, and the Irish hero must have perished before he could have recovered himself, if Edric had not interposed, and received the gash instead of his friend; then instantly turning round, he cut down the soldier. In the mean time, Roderick had revived, and he and Edric fought their way back to the rest of the army. It was now getting quite dark, and the besieged falling back within the town, the army of the Irish Monarch returned once more to their camp.

"How provoking!" cried Roderick, the moment they entered his tent, taking off his helmet, and giving it to Alexis the Greek page: "I shall never be happy again, if they hurt the doctor. Take my sword also, Alexis: but what is the matter with the boy? methinks he looks wondrous pale. Does he not, Edric!" Then turning to Edric, he was excessively shocked at the change in *his* appearance. It has been before stated, that Edric received the blow the Spanish soldier intended for Roderick. The wound had bled profusely, but the blood having congealed, the flow had stopped, and Edric, aided by his own courage, presence of mind, and firmness, bad been enabled to sustain himself till he had reached the tent. Now, however, that the necessity for exertion had ceased, his pallid looks and ghastly countenance bespoke what he had suffered. He had received one horrid gash upon the temple, and the coagulated blood upon his face and hair contrasted frightfully with the whiteness of the rest of his face. In fact, he looked like the ghost of some poor murdered wretch appearing to implore vengeance upon his destroyer.

He had seated himself at a table, resting his arms upon it, and supporting his head with his hands. He attempted to smile in answer to Roderick's inquiries; but the effort was too much for his already exhausted strength, and his head fell heavily upon the table. Roderick flew to support him, and dispatched Alexis for a surgeon. "My dear! dear Edric!" cried he, "speak to me! for God's sake, speak to me! Do not let me think that I have destroyed my friend. Oh, Edric! 'tis Roderick calls. Speak! speak, for God's sake, speak!"

Edric was, however, incapable of speaking; and the torture of the Irish King, when he found his friend could not answer him, was beyond description.

"My beloved Edric!" exclaimed he, wringing his hands in an agony of grief, "I implore you to answer me. Alas! he cannot: he is no more. Curses on my folly! I might have been blest and happy: but, in pursuit of the phantom Glory, I have sacrificed all I ever loved on earth. Oh! would to God that I had never visited Spain!"

A heavy groan behind him startled Roderick as he finished speaking and turning round he beheld Alexis, who had now returned with the surgeon. The boy's appearance was singular; his complexion was usually a clear dark brown, with a rich glow of colour, and remarkably full rosy lips; now the deep colour on his cheeks remained unfaded; but his lips had assumed a ghastly livid hue, his limbs trembled with agitation, and a dark mysterious expression seemed to sit upon his features. Roderick looked at him with amazement and almost horror, as strange suspicions arose in his mind respecting him.

Before the Irish army had left Cadiz, it had been whispered that the Duke of Medina Cellina's claim to the throne was at least equal to that of the Prince whom Roderick was fighting to establish. The duke, indeed, had many partisans, but his age and blindness enfeebled their efforts. An express from Cadiz had just brought intelligence that the duke was dead; and as Zoe was his sole heiress, this extraordinary agitation in her page looked at least suspicious.

"I must beware of him," thought Roderick, regarding him attentively; "for as Zoe knows that, notwithstanding my obligations to her, I shall never permit any monarch to reign in Spain but Don Pedro whilst I live, my life will be the first sacrifice required in her cause."

Thus mused Roderick, though it was but for an instant, that even the dread of personal danger could divert his thoughts from his friend.

The surgeon, when he probed Edric's wounds, however, declared to the great joy of the King that they were not dangerous, and that he had only fainted from loss of blood. He was now placed upon a conch in the same tent with that of the King; and Roderick, soon after stretching his fur mantle under him, threw himself upon his bed; if not to sleep, at least to muse upon the eventful occurrences of the day.

"Here is the lump of a spy," said one,

"And here that of a rogue," rejoined another.

"Yes, the organs of observation and self-appropriation," resumed the first, "are strongly developed. That head is enough to hang an angel!"

"Alas! alas!" cried the poor doctor; "would to Heaven that I had not lost my wig!"

"It would have been of no avail, if you had retained it," said one of the judges gravely, "as it would have been forcibly removed; and even if you had worn your own hair, you must have had your head shaved; for, knowing the general corruption and inaccuracy of witnesses, the judges of this enlightened court reject verbal testimony altogether, and form their correct and infallible judgments upon the sure and undeviating basis of that most profound and useful of all sciences—craniology."[241]

"And happy are the prisoners judged by so wise a rule," said another.

"Yes," rejoined a third; "for, though the minds of men are weak, and their judgments liable to err, the broad and general principles of science must ever remain unchangeably the same."

In this manner they went on, whilst the poor doctor, looking ruefully from one to another, as they severally pronounced their opinions, stood the very image of despair.

"Let us question him," resumed the first magistrate: "what were you doing when you were taken?"

"I was making gunpowder," sighed Dr. Entwerfen.

"The wretch!" exclaimed all his judges together; "he acknowledges he was manufacturing weapons for our destruction."

"And how were you making this gunpowder," resumed the judge.

"I was boiling it," moaned the doctor.

"Boiling it!" exclaimed the judges; "what a villain!" and they all shook their wise heads in concert. The poor doctor could not bear this; and throwing himself upon his knees begged stoutly for mercy.

"In my opinion," said one, "we should be guilty of a crime in letting him escape."

"I think so too." cried another.

"I would not have such a sin upon my conscience for the world," exclaimed a third.

Whilst the unfortunate doctor, reading his condemnation in their countenances, groaned aloud in the agony of his spirit.

At this moment, the deep awful roar of a cannon was heard, and Dr. Entwerfen leaped from his knees. "Thank God! thank God!" cried he, strutting up and down, and wiping his forehead with his pocket handkerchief, as the continued roar of the cannon rolled awfully along, rebounding from house to house, and shaking the very court in which they stood.

The magistrates looked aghast, whilst their pallid lips and trembling limbs told that, however great they might be in the council, their courage was not particularly conspicuous in the field.

The doctor, in the mean time, kept ejaculating, "I'm safe! I'm safe! See what a thing it is to have a friend for a sovereign: no, no! what did I say? a sovereign for a friend, I mean. Ay, ay! that's it! that's it!"

Thus did the doctor exult, whilst the citizens crowded round their chiefs, begging for directions, and not knowing whither to fly for safety. In this dilemma, the exclamations of the doctor attracted their attention; and, enraged to see him rejoice at their misery, the magistrates ordered him to prison, whilst they consulted as to what steps it was most advisable to take.

The poor doctor's joy was thus quickly changed to grief; and he lamented loudly his foolish transports of delight, without which, he might perhaps have passed unnoticed in the crowd. It was too late, however, for repentance; the command had gone forth, and the unfortunate doctor was dragged away to a loathsome dungeon. The assault was, as we have seen, repulsed, and it being too late, when it was over, to think of hanging Dr. Entwerfen that night, the magistrates retired to their beds, determined to have him executed the first thing in the morning.

All was now still; the plain between the camp and the city, which had so lately echoed with the heavy tramp of horses and human beings, now slept tranquilly in the moonlight; undisturbed, save by the groans of some expiring wretch, or by the busy labours of those employed to remove the dead and relieve the wounded. Roderick had thrown himself upon his couch, and dozed, but in a disturbed slumber; whilst Alexis, placed at a table, was writing dispatches from the dictation of Don Alvarez de Ripparda, who had returned from the pursuit, and sate opposite to him; whilst Lord Arthur O'Neil nodded at his side, and Edric lay reclined on another couch, at a little distance, near the opening of the tent.

All was silent, save the whispered voice of the Spanish general, the heavy breathing of Lord Arthur, and the measured steps of the sentinel, as he paced his weary round. Edric listened till he grew tired of the same sounds falling uninterruptedly upon his ear, and turning on his couch, tried to divert his attention by gazing upon the objects before him. The strong light from the lamp placed upon the table, fell upon the fine features of Alexis, as he looked up to the Spaniard; and Edric thought, as he gazed upon them, that he had certainly seen those features before, though where he could not remember; and fatigued with the effort of trying to recollect, he turned to survey the noble Roderick, as he lay gracefully stretched upon his couch. One arm was raised above his pillow, and the other fell carelessly by his side, whilst the fine contour of his head and neck was fully displayed, the rich, thick, glossy curls that generally hid his forehead being thrown back. His coral lips were half open, and his long black eyelashes fringed his closed eyelids; whilst his dark whiskers and mustachios, with the rich brown tint that glowed upon his cheek, contrasted finely with the whiteness of his throat. "God bless him!" thought Edric, "and send him all the happiness he deserves!" And then seeming fearful to disturb him, he looked again towards the town. The curtain of the tent was partly looped up, and Edric watched, with interest, the lights of those still employed in their several duties of burying the dead, and relieving the wounded. The figures of the persons engaged in these painful duties were frequently imperceptible; and the lights gliding to and fro, apparently without any human means, looked like ignes fatui, or an assemblage of ghosts at their infernal revels.

Edric sighed as he surveyed them, and his thoughts flew back, he knew not by what connection of ideas, to his native land. He thought of his father, his brother—of the good old Duke of Cornwall—of Rosabella and Elvira, till, one by one, the lights appeared to die away; the images that floated before his fancy became gradually fainter and fainter; his thoughts more confused: the scene before him faded rapidly from his sight, and, in short, he was fast sinking into repose, when he was roused by a piercing scream, and raising himself in his bed, he beheld a spectacle which froze his blood with horror.

Thick, black, pointed columns of smoke arose from the town through which, first a red glow, and afterwards sparks, appeared at intervals. At first, Edric could not imagine what it was; he rubbed his eyes, and almost fancied it was a display of fireworks; but, presently, long spiral columns of flame burst through the smoke, and, uniting in one immense body of fire, rose up to heaven, and seemed to swallow up the devoted city.

The moment the flames broke forth, one fearful scream seemed to burst from every lip, the soldiers flew, *en masse*, to the tent of their monarch; and Roderick sprang from his couch, when he heard their hurried footsteps. "What is the matter?" cried he, rubbing his eyes, and half blinded by the sudden glare of light.

"The city is on fire!" exclaimed a thousand voices at once, and Roderick rushed forth upon the plain. The air felt hot and scorching: "Save them! save the inhabitants!" cried Roderick; "promise them quarter—peace! any thing to save them! Let all the soldiers fetch water from the river! I will have no plunder. He dies who touches an article belonging to the town, or injures a single creature escaping from it. Let us fight like men! It is beneath us to take advantage of misfortune!"

The orders of Roderick were as promptly obeyed as given; the monarch himself leading the way to the town, and assisting in endeavouring to quench the flames. The gates were thrown open, and men, women, and children rushed forth half naked, and were received and supplied with food and shelter by the army of the Irish hero. The Irish adored their sovereign; his valour, his rashness, and his romantic generosity, won their hearts; and even his most discontented soldiers loved whilst they blamed him: thus his will was law—nay,' there was something so noble in his orders, that his soldiers were proud of implicitly obeying them, and not the meanest slave of the camp would have presumed to violate them in the slightest instance. The flames had now caught some cotton-mills on the river, which had been spared in the previous conflagration, and they burst forth in fresh volumes of fire, as the light materials they contained added fuel to the flames. The buildings in the town were mostly old, many of them wood, and some were large warehouses filled with the most combustible substances, which burnt with added fury as the long pointed flames lapped them into their devouring vortex; curling round them, and wrapping them in columns of fire as they, one by one, fell victims to their rage. The town was now half destroyed, and the flames were fast approaching the citadel; the governors of the city had been roused from their beds, and had taken refuge, half naked, in the camp of Roderick; but the prisoners yet remained in the citadel, shut up, however, in dungeons below the surface of the earth. Roderick had anxiously inquired of every one for Dr. Entwerfen, and at last, to his infinite horror, he learnt he was in this fated citadel; he rushed forward in agony to save him, for he knew that the powder was kept there. He was aware too, that the flames had already seized the fortress: long ere he could reach it, indeed, a tremendous explosion took place—a vast burst of fire rushed forth, scattering red flaming furniture, bricks, pillars, and every kind of rubbish in all directions, and then all sank to comparative darkness. The fire seemed to have spent its fury in that last effort, and, though it still feebly crept along in a half-smothered flame, its violence was passed. Dreadful, however, was the scene that now presented itself, for Seville was levelled with the dust. Black disfigured smoky ruins supplied the place of what had once been lofty towers and sumptuous palaces; the splendid cathedral, that had withstood the rage of centuries, was now no more; and human bodies lay in the streets, thrown in fearful heaps, some half burnt, and others blackened and dried by the scorching fury of the flames.

Roderick, however, stayed not to examine the effects of the fire; he rushed over heaps of yet hot ashes, and threw himself amongst the still smoking ruins of the citadel. A Spanish soldier, whom he had saved from destruction a few minutes before, was his guide, and, under his directions, Roderick hastened to the dungeons: he hurried from one to the other, releasing the unhappy wretches confined there, searching everywhere for the doctor, but in vain: at last he heard his well-known voice—the dungeon door was thick, but it could not resist the impatience of Roderick—he could not wait for the soldier to assist him to open it—he burst the fastenings asunder, and in an instant the poor doctor, sobbing with joy, was locked in the monarch's arms. Some of the soldiers of Roderick had followed him to the citadel, and he left it to them and the Spaniard to release the other prisoners, whilst he returned with his dear doctor in triumph back to the camp.

VOLUME 3

Volume 3: Chapter 1

WHEN Roderick and Dr. Entwerfen returned to the camp, they found Edric most impatiently awaiting their arrival. He was too much agitated to speak; and the worthy doctor found all his troubles amply repaid by the interest his friends took in his welfare.

Whilst Dr. Entwerfen was employed in relating his adventures to Edric, Roderick was occupied by a task far more difficult and important than any he had yet undertaken, viz. that of organizing and of providing for the disorderly multitude that had thronged into his camp from the city: their number was immense; men, Women, and children, crowded round their deliverer, falling upon their knees, blessing him and kissing the edge of his, garments. Roderick was affected even to tears: "For Heaven's sake, my good friends," said he, "spare me; I have done but my duty; I have been but an humble instrument in the hands of Providence; address your thanks to him: there they are due."

Roderick, however, was quite aware it was not enough to have saved these people: he knew he must do something to provide them with food and lodging; and that if he did not, when the first moment of enthusiasm should be passed, unpleasant scenes must inevitably take place. He accordingly made dispositions to this effect, with a prudence and sagacity that would have done credit to far more advanced years. Temporary huts were erected, till the streets of Seville could be cleared of the ruins that encumbered them, and the houses in some measure repaired. Shelter for the inhabitants being thus provided, Roderick harangued the magistrates, directing them to take the people under their direction. These sapient ministers of justice gladly gave him possession of the town, which Roderick was too generous to assume without their permission, and acknowledged themselves and the garrison prisoners of war. The peasants, when they found the kindness with which the citizens had been treated, flocked in with provisions, and the camp of the Irish monarch soon resembled an immense fair.

Alexis had followed his master during the whole of these arrangements, and had frequently sighed deeply as they proceeded.

"What is the matter with the boy?" said Roderick in one of these moments: "I cannot imagine why he looks so melancholy!"

The boy enthusiastically clasped his hands together, looking up to Heaven, as though murmuring an inward prayer.

"What can this mean?" exclaimed Roderick with astonishment.

The boy took his master's hand, pressing it first to his lips, and then vehemently to his heart, and knelt before him, reverentially bending his forehead to the earth. The next moment, however, officers entering for directions, the attention of Roderick was diverted and Alexis forgotten.

In the mean time, M. de Mallet and his daughter, who had been exceedingly agitated by the events of the day, thought not of repose, but sat in the tent prepared for them, conversing upon the merits of their deliverers.

"I never saw a finer countenance," said M. de Mallet, "so noble, so animated, and yet so good."

"Good indeed," ejaculated his daughter; "surely if we could believe a superior spirit would ever descend upon earth, such would be the form he would assume!"

"How kindly he spoke, and how considerately!" exclaimed the father.

"How attentive he seemed, and how delicate!" rejoined the daughter.

"Such a majestic figure!"

"Such a graceful manner!"

"It is so rare to find such condescension in so great a monarch."

"Monarch!" cried Pauline: "were you speaking of Roderick, father?"

"And of whom were you speaking, child?" returned her father, turning quickly round, and fixing his eyes upon her.

"Of—of—Mr. Montagu, father," replied Pauline, casting down her eyes and deeply blushing.

"Pauline!" said M. de Mallet. She started at the sound of her father's voice, and looked timidly up in his face. "Pauline," repeated he, "my dear child, beware!"

At this moment a roar of cannon shook the tent; the sound echoed by the walls of the town, and leaping from hill to hill in lengthened peals, Pauline sunk upon her knees, hiding her face in her father's lap. "My child! my beloved child!" cried M. de Mallet, bending over her as though to shield her from danger, "Heaven defend thee!"

In this painful situation, the father and daughter continued till the cannonading ceased.

All was now still; and awful was the calm that succeeded such a tumult. Pauline raised her head, and looked fearfully around. "Come, my child," said her father, "let us endeavour to ascertain who are victors."

Pauline rose from her knees, and, leaning upon her father's arm, accompanied him to the opening of the tent; but she shrunk back, shuddering at the horrid scene that presented itself. Their tent was situated at the extreme edge of the camp, and commanded a view of the whole field of battle where the combat of the morning had taken place. The plain that stretched to their left, lay covered with the bodies of the dying and the dead, whilst a multitude of horses broken loose, galloped over the field, plunging, snorting, and crushing beneath their hoofs, the bodies of their fallen riders.

In some places, the branches of half broken trees strewed the ground, whilst their mutilated trunks, perforated with shot, remained as melancholy relics of their former beauty. Swords and helmets, mingled with overturned waggons and military utensils of all kinds, were scattered in wild disorder around. The earth, ploughed up by the cannon balls in deep furrows, save where the ridges had been beaten flat by the feet of the combatants, looked wild and uneven as the waves of the mighty ocean arrested in the moment of tempest. Blood lay in pools upon the ground; and clotted gore, mingled horribly with remnants of human bones and brains, hung to the still standing bushes, disfiguring the fair face of nature.

Pauline shuddered, and turned eagerly to the other side of the landscape, which commanded a view of the town. Here still, however, she found nothing but death and war. It was the moment when the explosion of the petard set fire to the wooden bulwark; and Roderick and Edric leaped through the flames upon the beach. The bright glare of the blazing bulwarks relieved strongly their dark figures, and Pauline distinctly saw and recognized them for a moment, though the next they were lost in a cloud of smoke. She screamed, and grasped her father's arm in convulsive agony. M. de Mallet was scarcely less agitated than herself; and, as the smoke cleared away, they saw distinctly through its flaming volumes, Roderick and Edric upon the breach, opposed by a crowd of Spaniards, and fighting with inveterate fury. "Roderick is on his knees," cried M. de Mallet. "But see! he rises suddenly, and plunges the Spaniard, who had raised his sword to cut him down, into the flames." Pauline did not speak; but she gasped for breath, and held her father's arm yet more tightly than before. Edric was now seen grappling hand to hand with a Spaniard, when the fire and smoke closed upon him and hid him from their view. The next instant, a tremendous crash was heard, and loud shouts, followed by a rush of men; it was the sortie of the besieged.

"Oh, heavens!" cried Pauline, turning pale, and resting her head upon her fathe"s shoulder, "war is a dreadful thing."

"You are faint, my child," "replied M. de Mallet; "this is no fitting scene for you. Shall we go in?"

"Oh, no, no!" cried Pauline feebly; "I cannot leave the spot." Here shouts of "Roderick! Roderick for ever! Roderick and glory!" rung in their ears. Pauline shuddered; a faint sickness crept over her; the scene seemed to swim before her eyes; and she would have fallen, but for the supporting arm of her father. At this moment, some soldiers, carrying a bier, passed at a little distance from the tent. Upon it lay the body of an officer; his head hung back, his long thick hair was matted with gore, and a ghastly wound gaped on his uncovered breast. Pauline could bear no more—she thought it was Edric, and she fell fainting into her father's arms.

M. de Mallet bore her back into the tent, and as soon as she was sufficiently recovered to enable him to think of any thing but herself, he dispatched one of the soldiers, appointed to attend them, to ascertain if the

Irish monarch had escaped. The soldier did not return; and M. de Mallet, too impatient to remain in his tent, sallied forth to learn the news himself. Scarcely was he gone, however, when the soldier's wife, whom he had called to the assistance of Pauline, perceived the town was on fire. Pauline's agitation now became excessive; she trembled in every limb, and listened till the sense of hearing seemed agony. She could not comprehend the cause of the noise and bustle made by the citizens, as they came crowding into the camp; she looked forth, but the throng of half naked men, women, and children, that came hurrying along, seemed inexplicable; she stopped a woman, who, half dressed, had her clothes tucked up in one hand, whilst with the other she led two half naked children—"What is the matter? asked she. "Roderick," cried the woman bewildered in her grief, "God bless the noble Roderick!"

"Where are you going?" demanded Pauline of two young men, bearing between them a bed containing their sick father.

"Roderick!" shouted the pious Spaniards. "Heaven, in its mercy, bless Roderick!"

Pauline was proceeding in her inquiries, though without the smallest hope of receiving a direct reply, the hearts and minds of Spaniards being so full of Roderick, that no other name could find utterance from their lips, when she perceived her father.

"My dearest father!" cried she, running to him; "now I shall know all! What is the matter?"

"Roderick, the noble Roderick is safe!" repeated M. de Mallet. Pauline was chagrined—she longed to hear of Edric, and she envied, for his sake, the renown of the Irish hero.

"Can you, too, speak of nothing but Roderick?" said she, somewhat reproachfully.

"And of whom else should I speak?" replied her father. "Who else deserves to be spoken of?" for surely he is the bravest! the noblest of men!"

"I do not doubt it," observed Pauline coldly. "Every tongue utters his praise—every breast swells with gratitude at his goodness—and every hand is raised to Heaven in prayers on his behalf.

"Have there been many persons killed?" asked Pauline.

"How can you ask so foolish a question?" replied her father. "Do you not see the ground heaped with slain?"

But persons of note,[242] I mean?"

"Let me see; I think they said there were the Generals H— and M—, and Counts L—, P— and T—."

"Oh!" groaned Pauline, impatiently.

"And besides, I think they say M. Montagu is seriously wounded."

"I feared so!" sighed Pauline, "he is so brave."

"Yes—every one says he is brave, and implores blessings upon his name—for he saved the life of Roderick!"

Pauline's countenance had beamed with triumph at the commencement of this sentence but it rather fell at the conclusion. She did not quite like her hero to owe his glory to any one but himself.

M. de Mallet continued: "His bravery and nobleness of spirit were unequalled. Every one praises him. There is certainly something very extraordinary in the character of the English. Their daring tempers and love of adventure lead them to quit peace and riches in their native country, to seek glory and distinction elsewhere. This Mr. Montagu[243] is really an exalted young man."

Pauline's eyes flashed joy—she felt she loved her father better than ever—she could have embraced him as he spoke, for the praise of Edric sounded as the sweetest music in her ears. Strange that so slight an acquaintance should have produced so strong a passion! but such and so inexplicable is love.

Pauline had now patience to hear the explanation of her father respecting Roderick. She even felt pleasure in the repetition of his exploits, for he was the friend of Edric; and she retired to rest—happy in herself, and contented with all the world; having been first assured by her father that the surgeon confidently expected Edric would soon recover. Pauline, however, would have been very much puzzled to explain the cause of the excessive contentment that she felt. The situation of herself and father was as hopeless as ever. They were still prisoners in a strange land, without fortune, without friends; but so little does happiness depend upon external circumstances, that the breast of Pauline seemed to have been a stranger to it till now.

After arranging every thing for the comfort of the refugees and his own soldiers, Roderick took a few hours of hurried repose. When he rose in the morning, he sent his compliments to M. de Mallet and his daughter to demand permission to wait upon them. This was instantly and gladly accorded, and in a few minutes the Irish hero was in their tent.

"I condole with your Majesty upon the situation of your friend," said M. de Mallet, the moment he saw him: "I hope he is better."

The monarch smiled; he forgave the abruptness of the question, in favour of the excellence of the motive, and he replied that Mr. Montagu was fast recovering. He regrets exceedingly," added he, "that it is not in his power to pay his devoirs[244] here"—bowing to Pauline, "and well can I sympathize with him, as I know what he loses."

Pauline inquired modestly the particulars of the combat. "Upon my word, Madam," replied Roderick, "I know very little about it."

"I thought your Majesty had been engaged."

"That is the very reason. If I had not, the case might have been different; but as it was, I only just saw a great many people that tried to kill me, and a great many that I tried to kill, and the smoke hid all the rest."[245]

"A very satisfactory account of a battle, upon my word," cried de Mallet, smiling; "but other people saw more of your Majesty's acts than you did yourself; and they say, you performed prodigies of valour."

"It is very kind of them to say so," said Roderick, "for I am sure it is more than they know."

"Your Majesty's modesty wishes to throw a veil over your valour," observed Pauline, "but luckily it cannot be concealed."

"Your praises, Madam, would make any man a coxcomb," returned the Monarch: "I own I have not the courage to refuse commendations from your lips."

Pauline blushed—she fancied she had said too much, and now remained silent.

"I cannot describe how much I admire your Majesty's leniency to the inhabitants of the city," said M. de Mallet: "it proves your benevolence is equal to your valour, though indeed it was sound policy to act as you have done; for by this you have conciliated the hearts of the Spaniards; whereas, if you had exercised any cruelty, they would have risen against you *en masse*; but this, I dare say, your Majesty considered."

"Indeed," replied Roderick smiling, "my Majesty considered no such thing; I only thought as a man: I did not like to see my fellow-creatures burnt to death, or poniarded if they attempted to escape; I should not have liked it at all, if I had been in a similar situation, and so I did all in my power to save them —that is all I know about the matter. But to change the subject, I have a great favour to beg of you, Mademoiselle de Mallet."

"What is it?" asked Pauline: "your Majesty has only to speak to be obeyed."

"Oh! for Heaven's sake, do not talk of obedience—it is I who should obey—I only ask a favour, and that is, that you will permit me to bring Dr. Entwerfen to kneel at your feet and kiss your fair hand, in token of his homage."

"I would not advise Pauline to let him kneel," said M. de Mallet laughing, "as I fear, if she does, there will be some difficulty in getting him up again."

"Your Majesty's commands,—" said Pauline.

"Do not talk of commands," interrupted Roderick; "I hate the word."

"Your Majesty's wishes, then," continued Pauline smiling, "shall be complied with."

"This evening, then," cried the gay monarch, "the doctor shall make his appearance. Till then, adieu!"

"Will your Majesty have the kindness to present my best wishes to Mr. Montagu for his recovery," requested M. de Mallet.

"Certainly," replied Roderick; "but am I to tell Edric that Mademoiselle de Mallet has no wishes for his welfare?"

"I wish—I hope—that is, I think—" stammered Pauline.

"My daughter means her sentiments are exactly similar to my own upon the subject," said M. de Mallet gravely; for he was not at all pleased with the interpretation he thought the King might put upon the embarrassment of his daughter.

"Very well!" repeated Roderick provokingly: "I shall tell Edric, that M. de Mallet and his daughter think exactly alike of him.—That is it, is it not?"

M. de Mallet was about to reply, when the King, nodding and Waving his hand, bade them adieu, and hurried away. "I don't know what to make of the Irish hero," said M. de Mallet, the moment he had left them. "With all his good qualities, there is something very strange about him: I don't know what to make of him!"

Pauline sighed assent; though she did know what to make of him very well, for she fancied he saw, and ridiculed her partiality for Edric. This idea roused every spark of pride in her nature; she could not bear the thought of being supposed to give her love unsought, and she determined when she next saw Roderick to show by her coldness and indifference, when Edric was mentioned, how completely he had been deceived.

When Roderick left the tent of M. de Mallet, he returned to Edric, whom he found pale and feeble.

"You are the happiest fellow in existence, Edric!" said he: "I would willingly give all my glory, and even my demoniacal renown, that the Spaniards talk so much about, to be able to call up such blushes to the cheek of beauty as your name can raise. Oh! if you had seen Pauline. By Heaven! she is the loveliest creature I ever beheld in my life!"

As he spoke, Alexis, the Greek page, who had been crouching rather than sitting at the foot of Edric's couch, resting his head upon his hands, and looking absorbed in grief, uttered a faint cry, and rushed out of the tent.

"There is something very extraordinary about that boy," said Roderick, looking after him.[246]

"There is, indeed," replied Edric, "and I have something that I wish to communicate to you respecting him:" and in a few words he related what had passed the preceding night in the tent.

"Impossible!" cried Roderick, "you must have been dreaming, Edric! What communication would the boy hold with Alvarez? You know he is dumb. Besides, even if Alvarez were inclined to plot against me, he is too prudent and reserved to make a confidant of a beardless boy!"

"I simply relate the facts as they occurred," said Edric; "I do not pretend to explain them. But I can assure you, I was neither dreaming nor delirious."

"It is very strange!" repeated Roderick musing, and it corresponds remarkably with what I have observed myself." For some moments he remained lost in thought; but it was not in his gay and joyous nature to suffer any thing to depress him long; and the next instant, Alexis was forgotten.

The fall of Seville, and the destruction of the army sent to defend it, produced a powerful effect upon the destinies of Spain. The Cortes again sent ambassadors to negociate[247] with the Irish hero; but, taught by experience, he now received them haughtily, refusing to treat with them but as a conqueror; and to put his threats in execution he determined to advance immediately upon Madrid.

"We must follow up our victory," said he to Edric, after he had somewhat contemptuously dismissed the deputies from the shattered remnant of their allied army, who came to sue humbly at his feet for peace. "These people are treacherous beyond description. They do not understand leniency, and they must be treated with sword in hand. I am thoroughly tired of them; their fickleness and uncertainty have quite disgusted me; I will therefore march to Madrid, establish Don Pedro as their sovereign, and take my leave of them for ever."

"I am rejoiced to hear it!" exclaimed Edric. "You will then return to Ireland, and devote your time to your own subjects."

"I will try to satisfy them as well as I can; but as perfection cannot be expected all at once, you must not be surprised if some day I should fly off in a tangent, and take it into my head to colonize the moon."[248]

Edric laughed: "If you promise to wait till then," said he, "I shall be satisfied."

"You may not find my project so wild as it appears," rejoined Roderick. "The moon is a very pretty, mild, modest-looking planet, and I must own I should like amazingly to see what kind of inhabitants she contains; and if I should determine to go there, here is a gentleman who I am sure will be quite ready to accompany me."

Dr. Entwerfen entered the tent as he spoke. "Of what was your Majesty speaking?" asked he.

"Of a voyage to the moon," said Roderick.

"Will you go with me?"

"With all my heart," cried the little doctor, rubbing his hands and looking all glee at the thought.

"There, I told you so," said, Roderick, laughing.

"I should have thought the many adventures you have met with had cured your passion for travelling," rejoined Edric.

"Cured him! Given him a zest for it, you mean," replied Roderick. "The appetite for travelling always grows with what it feeds upon; and though the doctor may boast

> 'That he *has* fair Seville seen,
> So *is* a traveller, I ween,'[249]

yet I do not doubt but that he is just as eager to explore new places as ever."

"Yes," returned the doctor, "I certainly did see Seville."

"Every part of it, my dear fellow, from its palaces to its dungeons," resumed Roderick; "nay, I believe you were very near being indulged with a view of its ropes."

The doctor did not quite relish this raillery. "I can assure your Majesty—"

"*Apropos de bottes*," cried Roderick, interrupting him, "I had entirely forgotten I promised to introduce you to Mademoiselle de Mallet. We will go now. Will you accompany us, Edric? I am sorry to ask you to do any thing so disagreeable; but I think it will be but decent to kiss hands, take leave, and all that sort of thing, before we set out for Madrid: besides, it maybe as well to make some kind of provision as to what is to become of them in our absence."

"Then you will not take them with you?" said Edric, despondingly.

"Who ever heard of such a thing?" cried Roderick; "How could I possibly ask the lovely Pauline to endure the inconveniences of travelling with a camp? I really have not the assurance to attempt it."

Edric sighed deeply; and his countenance assumed an expression of so much melancholy that Roderick laughed immoderately: "I could not have believed it possible," cried he, "that you could ever become such a sighing Strephon;[250] the thing's incredible!"

"The pain of my wounds," said Edric, blushing; for even philosophers don't like to be laughed at.

"The pain in your heart!" repeated Roderick, mimicking him. "'But, come! come! I can pity you. I have been in love at least fifty times myself—so I know what it is."

"But I am not in love," remonstrated Edric.

"Denial is one of the most dangerous symptoms," resumed Roderick, gravely. "Experienced physicians rarely think their patients really ill, till they are not conscious of it themselves. Let me feel your pulse."

"Psha," said Edric, impatiently.

"Will you go then!" asked Roderick, laughing; and to avoid being farther tormented by his raillery, Edric hastily rose from his couch, and declared himself ready to attend him. The injuries he had received, having been only flesh wounds inflicted with a sabre, had now nearly healed; and the only change they had produced in his appearance, had been to make him look more pale and interesting, one arm being supported by a sling, and a bandeau bound round his forehead. Pauline's eyes sparkled when she saw him, in spite of her intended indifference; and she could not command her voice so entirely, but that its tremulous tone betrayed her inward agitation.

Edric's eyes also involuntarily expressed his pleasure; whilst the gay laugh and arch look of Roderick told that he was perfectly aware of what was passing in the mind of each. Doctor Entwerfen, however, saw nothing of the kind, his mind being quite absorbed in the delightful contemplation of his own glory. He had been presented to M. de Mallet by Roderick, as "his friend and counsellor, the learned and justly celebrated Dr. Entwerfen;" and that moment seemed a sufficient reward for a whole life of misery, the doctor's ecstasy upon the occasion being so unbounded, that he neither knew what he did nor what he said. Whilst Roderick had been speaking, indeed, he had been in perfect agony; stretching himself out on tiptoe, opening his hands and closing them again with every sentence, as though bursting with impatience to speak, that he might by his eloquence confirm the monarch's eulogium, yet trembling every instant lest he should interrupt it.

M. de Mallet had been a dabbler in scientific experiments in his youth, and, pleased to find a person. who could talk to him, and understand his ideas upon the subject, he soon drew the doctor on one side, leaving his younger friends to be entertained by his daughter.

The conversation which ensued may be easily imagined. Lovers are not famed for any eloquence but that of the eyes, and those of Edric and Pauline were sufficiently expressive, whilst the languor of indisposition, under which they were both suffering, shed a pleasing softness over their ideas very favourable to the developement[251] of the tender passion. Whilst Roderick, who notwithstanding his love for mischief was really good-natured, no longer tormented them with his raillery; and Edric so well improved his time, that when M. de Mallet had finished his conference with the, doctor, and Roderick informed him of his intention of leaving Seville upon the following day, after appointing him governor of the city, Pauline turned deathly pale, and every hope of happiness seemed to fly from her breast for ever.

M. de Mallet, however, was not at all aware of his daughter's anguish; and, thanking the king gratefully for the high honour conferred upon him, his fancy began to revel by anticipation in the delights of governorship; and in ten minutes he had arranged in his mind as many improvements and alterations as it would take fifty years to accomplish.

"Farewell," continued Roderick, "I trust we shall meet again, if not here, at least in another and a better world. Permit me, lady!" continued he, slightly touching with his lips the pallid cheek of Pauline. To-morrow with the dawn we advance, and we have so much to do ere then, that we must deny ourselves the pleasure of again enjoying your society. Farewell, Governor, you will find the necessary papers to install you here," (giving him a packet) "and the soldiers have orders to obey you as myself. Come, Edric."

Edric advanced, and bowing, took the hand of Pauline and pressed it respectfully to his lips;—his heart was too full to speak. Pauline could scarcely restrain her tears, and shaking hands with the doctor, she hastily retired to a part of the tent enclosed for her use.

"My daughter is not well," said M. de Mallet, "these scenes of blood and war are too much for her nerves; but she will soon recover when you have left us."

"I doubt that," murmured Roderick in a half whisper; and soon after the friends retired. Edric was not insensible to Pauline's emotion; and as he more than suspected the cause, a pleasure, unknown before, throbbed in his bosom. His eyes sparkled, and his whole appearance presented so complete a contrast to his usual depression, that Roderick could not resist the temptation of again rallying him most unmercifully upon it. "Talk of medicine," cried he, "there is no elixir like the magic of a pair of bright eyes. All the physicians in my camp can effect nothing like it. Nay, you need not blush so, Edric! I did not imagine you were so far gone as that."

"I do not blush, that I am aware of," returned Edric, somewhat peevishly; for he did not relish being teazed;[252] "at least, I am sure I have no occasion for blushing."

"Well, then, don't look so like a bashful maiden, disavowing her first attachment, with a 'La, Pa! how can you think so!'—I did not suppose you were capable of such affectation."

"I am not aware that I have been guilty of any."

"Come, then, own the truth candidly—you love Mademoiselle de Mallet?"

"How can you think so?" replied Edric, blushing deeply in spite of his efforts to look composed.

"You are indifferent to her, then? Dear me, I had no idea of it, I never was more completely deceived in my life! Well, if that's the case, I will resume my first design of trying my own fortune."

"How can you be so provoking?"

"Why it is very hard, if you are not in love with her yourself, that you should wish to prevent every one else from being so."

"Your Majesty's rank, I should think, would prevent your even thinking of Mademoiselle de Mallet."

"Why should my rank prevent the possibility of my being happy?"

"Your Majesty's rank prevents the possibility of your marrying Pauline; and I should hope you would not dare to entertain dishonourable views respecting her."

"Dare! dishonour! Do you remember whom you are speaking to, Edric?"

"Perfectly; for I have not forgotten Roderick, though he appears to have forgotten himself."

"Edric! But I won't be angry with you. When people are in love, they never mean what they say; in fact, they very seldom know what they are talking. about. I remember once when I was in love myself—"

Alexis, who had waited at the entrance of the tent during the visit his master had paid to M. de Mallet, and was now following them, sighed heavily at this remark. Roderick heard him;—"What is the matter with the boy?" said he:

"Were you ever in love, Alexis?"

The page sighed yet more deeply than before, and, crossing his arms upon his breast, bent his head in token of assent.

It is to be much lamented you cannot tell us all about it," continued Roderick; for you could never choose a more fitting moment for such a tale; as you may depend upon the sympathy of Mr. Montagu, even if I should be so barbarous as to refuse you mine:—

'We pity faults to which we feel inclined,
And to our proper failings can be kind;'[253]

as one of your own poets says. Eh, Edric! Don't you think he's right?"

"I think you are very provoking."

"That is because I am touching upon a string that happens to be not quite in tune; so no wonder it jars a little. Do you not remember the old proverb—

'Touch a man whose skin is sound,[254]
He will stand, and fear no wound:
Touch a man when he is sore,
He will start, and bear no more.'"

"How can you condescend to repeat such nonsense?" cried Edric, indignantly. "It is unworthy the poorest beggar in your dominions!"

"And how can you condescend to be moved at such nonsense, Edric?" replied Roderick, laughing. "Come, come! own the truth, for it is useless to attempt any longer to deny it. Say, candidly, that you are in love with Mademoiselle de Mallet, and I will teaze you no longer."

"In love is too strong a term. I admire, esteem, and respect Mademoiselle dc Mallet. I even think her possessed of a thousand charms and a thousand virtues; but as to being in love—"

"Well, well! we will not quarrel about words. I do not think you will ever make a romantic lover. You Englishmen are too reasoning and prudent ever to fall violently in love. Your blood is as cold as your climate. Now we take the thing quite differently; with us love is a devouring flame! a fire that absorbs our whole being—a stream that sweeps every thing before it—a madness—a delirium! In short, I don't know what it is!"

"I think not," said Edric, drily.

"Psha, psha!" continued Roderick; "if it could be described, it would not be worth feeling. It is all spirit! all soul! if you tie it down to rules, it evaporates. Don't you think so in Greece, Alexis?"

The page bowed, and shaking his head, pressed his finger upon his lips.

"True," returned his master; "I had forgotten: but if you cannot speak, you can write. Take these tablets, I should like to know your opinion."

The page took the tablets, and wrote with astonishing rapidity—"Since your Majesty condescends to ask my opinion, I think that the love which can stay to reason, or hesitates to sacrifice every thing to the beloved object, does not deserve the name."

"Bravo, my little hero!" cried Roderick, tapping him upon the shoulder; "spoken like a true Greek. An Irishman, however, would have said nearly the same."

The boy's slender figure trembled in every nerve at his master's touch, and his cheeks were flushed with unwonted passion, though his eyes remained fixed upon the ground, from which indeed he rarely raised them. Roderick gazed upon him a few minutes in silence, as though he wished to read his inmost soul. Then turning abruptly to Dr. Entwerfen, who had taken no part in the last conversation, he demanded gaily what he was thinking of.

"I was thinking, your Majesty," said the doctor, gravely, "that it is a long way from hence to Madrid, and that it will be very fatiguing for your men to march so far."

"Upon my word, doctor," said Roderick, laughing, "you have really made a most sublime discovery, and I perfectly agree with you in the justice of your conclusions."

"That being granted," continued the doctor, "if any means could be devised by which your army could be transported to the gates of the city without the trouble of walking there, it would be a good thing."

"Certainly," said the King; "the fact does not admit of a dispute."

"The only difficulty is to contrive how it is to be done," resumed the doctor, musing.

"Ay, there's the rub," cried Roderick, laughing immoderately; "however, if any one can do it, I'm sure you can, my dear doctor. So rally your energies and consider the best means of commencing operations: I am sure, if you exert yourself, you cannot fail of success."

"Your Majesty does me honour, and I will endeavour to prove I am not undeserving of the confidence you repose in me," said the little doctor, drawing up himself to his full height, and puffing out his cheeks as he walked on absorbed in meditation. "I have it," cried he, suddenly stopping short; "what does your Majesty think of an immense raft?"

"Excellent, my dear doctor! I see but three objections to making one large enough to convey the whole army:—First, that we have no timber to make it of;—secondly, We have no horses to draw it;—and thirdly, the roads are not wide enough to admit it."

"Balloons would do, but we have them not," resumed the doctor, still profoundly cogitating, with his eyes fixed upon the ground, and his hands in his breeches-pockets.

"What think you of packing the soldiers up in bombs, and shooting them out of mortars?" asked Roderick.

"Your Majesty is pleased to jest," observed the doctor, gravely; "but ridicule is not argument."

"Certainly not," replied the King; "and you mistake me greatly if you thought I meant to ridicule your plan. I only wished to remark that I feared it would be rather difficult to put it in execution."

"That which can be accomplished without difficulty," said the doctor, solemnly, "is scarcely worth the trouble of undertaking, and quite below the consideration of a man of genius. Difficulties to a man of science are but incentives to action."

"Most sensibly observed, my dear doctor," cried Roderick; "however, as we have now reached our tent, I must leave you to contrive some plan to bring us back from Madrid, as I am afraid we cannot wait now to put your designs in practice to enable us to get there: we must march with the dawn. Of course you will accompany us."

"Certainly!" returned the doctor, still musing; then muttering to himself—"I don't much like the plan of shooting off the soldiers, it would take such large mortars and so much gunpowder:—however, there is no knowing what might be done: I will think of it:"—he retired to his tent, though no sleep visited his eyes that night, so completely had the idea of packing up the soldiers in bombs taken possession of his imagination.

Roderick's arrangements were soon made, for Nature had certainly intended him for a general. His intelligent mind foresaw every thing, and provided against every contingency. Brave in the field, and prudent in council, the only fault of Roderick as a soldier was that he sometimes suffered himself to be carried away by his ardour when it would have been wiser to delay. But this very impetuosity had its charms in the eyes of his soldiers, as he never hesitated to expose himself to the same dangers or to undergo the same privations as themselves, and they would all have followed him willingly into the very jaws of destruction.

After arranging every thing for the morning's march, the Irish hero snatched a few hours of repose. With the dawn, however, the drums beat the reveille,[255] and the Irish army left Andalusia to advance by rapid marches upon Madrid.

Volume 3: Chapter 2

Whilst these scenes were taking place in Spain, Elvira was beginning to discover, in England, that it was not quite so delightful to be a Queen as she had previously imagined. The contending parties in the state had been roused into action by the late struggle, and party spirit is of all others the most difficult to conquer. Besides this, the choice of Elvira having been rather a matter of feeling than of judgment, men felt dissatisfied at having suffered themselves to be hurried away by their passions, and, as is usual in such cases, they were disposed to vent the ill-humour they felt at their own conduct upon every thing which chanced to fall in their way. Thus, even the best measures of Elvira's government were warmly criticised; and as she unfortunately altered some of her laws in consequence of these objections, the critics were encouraged to proceed; and fancying her plans to be the result of weakness, when they were in fact only produced by her natural candour and love of justice, the people became more outrageous and troublesome with every concession that was made to them.

Elvira's intentions were excellent, but by unfortunately wishing to please every one, she destroyed their effect. This made her councils vacillating, and her measures uncertain: nothing indeed but the strength of mind and commanding genius of Edmund, joined to his complete devotion to her cause, could have prevented the ruin of her government almost in the moment of its formation. From a mistaken motive of generosity, she had retained in her council those lords who had most vehemently opposed her, though, in compliance with the wishes of Edmund, they were shorn of their beams. This was a fatal error; half measures are always dangerous: the lords in question should have been discarded altogether, or retained in their former seats; as it was, Elvira had made them enemies, and yet left them the power to sting her.

The emissaries of Rosabella were also very active, and the ferment of the public mind excessive. The taste the people had just enjoyed of power, had only been enough to make them long for more. They had only just began[256] to relish its sweets, when the dish was snatched away from them, with which, if it had been left them to devour, they would have soon been cloyed. Discontents became general, disturbances arose, which were no sooner quelled in one quarter than they broke out in another, and these petty insurrections, though almost too trivial to mention, were excessively annoying. For trifling inconveniences, like a host of flies buzzing round a nervous man on a sultry day, are often more irritating to the temper, than serious grievances; and the noble mind of Edmund was wearied by subduing such paltry enemies;

"They want employment," said he one day to the Queen, after reading a dispatch containing an account of one of the most vexatious of these tumults; "you must build bridges and cut canals to amuse them."

The active mind of Elvira caught eagerly at the idea, and she vainly fancied her name would be handed down to posterity as one of the greatest of Queens, who, though in the bloom of youth and pride of beauty, did not hesitate to sacrifice herself for the good of her people, and to devote that time to their welfare and the improvement of her kingdom, which others of her age and rank wasted in mere amusements.

Delighted with the thought, Elvira did not delay a moment before she prepared to put it in practice; and she was found for several days together constantly surrounded by her counsellors, and seated at a table absolutely loaded with papers, which she was busily employed in inspecting and arranging.

Plans for the erection of public buildings, for hospitals, bridges, museums, and churches, schemes for new manufactories, hints for new establishments conducive to the public good, and sketches of new discoveries, lay in heaps before her; mixed with addresses of compliments, votes of thanks, complaints of grievances, petitions, secret informations; and in short all that multifarious collection of paper, with which a monarch is sure to be surrounded who is said to be anxious to ameliorate the condition of his people, or who is unhappily reported to possess a genius for improvement.

Unfortunate is the man possessed of power, of whom such reports are current. He is directly surrounded by projectors, each presenting a scheme more futile than that of his predecessor; and discontented dependants, each bringing a long list of grievances, half of which are imaginary, but which have been conjured up by the complainants that they may not lose the precious right they enjoy of complaining.

Elvira had not yet found the evils of power; but she now tasted of its sweets, and was enchanted. It seemed to her the most delightful thing in the world to hold in her hands the destinies of thousands of her fellow-creatures; and she thought not of the heavy responsibility it entailed, nor how often her path would be followed by curses instead of blessings. Some one has said that every time a sovereign confers a favour, he makes one ungrateful subject and nine discontented ones; but Elvira and Edmund as yet had not discovered the truth of this maxim. Since their present plan had been suggested, every thing with them had been the *couleur de rose*.[257] I say, them, for Edmund was associated with Elvira in all these gigantic schemes of improvement; and as he had conceived the first idea of them, so it was he only who could carry them into execution. His active mind required something to employ it; and the same strong feelings which had formerly been devoted to love and glory, were now turned into another channel.

The energies of Elvira's mind had also been awakened by the struggle for the crown, and the passion awakened in her breast by the youthful stranger; and she now felt that she could not quietly return again to the commonplace stillness of every-day life. The passions when once roused from their dormant state, must have something to occupy them, or they will prey upon themselves. Thus we generally see great warriors, or statesmen, or in fact any class of men who have passed their lives in activity, wither away when forced to the dullness of an obscure retirement: their minds and bodies decay alike from want of stimulants to call them into action.

The improvement of her people supplied this stimulus to the mind of Elvira,—but alas! she entered upon it rather with passion than judgment, and had not patience to wait to see her plans gradually carried into effect:— No—no—she could not endure any thing slow: with her every thing must be done by a *coup de main*; and as the people and the buildings were so stupid as not to be made perfect by the first attempt, she was continually disappointed and discouraged. In fact, by attempting to do too much, she did nothing.

When Elvira ascended the throne, she determined no public act should take place without the approbation of her council; and these noble lords were one day debating upon the propriety of a new road, that was proposed to intersect the entire kingdom at right angles, when Lord Gustavus de Montfort rose to oppose it, upon the ground of the injury it would do to private property if carried into effect.

Elvira could not endure Lord Gustavus: his cold, prudent, calculating manner, without a single spark of imagination, disgusted her beyond description; and the only good quality he possessed, that of being indefatigable in following up his point, completed her abhorrence. Wit and eloquence were quite thrown away upon him, for he understood neither the one nor the other; and when any new or brilliant scheme crossed Elvira's imagination, and she described it to her council with all the fire of genius and animation, there he sate with his calm, cold unvarying countenance, ready to damp it with a doubt. Lord Maysworth also was her aversion; his narrow mind, which could only take in such trifles as escape the observation of men of genius; his mean and paltry spirit, and his grovelling ambition, were all her detestation; whilst Lord Noodle and Lord Doodle, who, though ciphers in themselves, yet, like their prototypes, prodigiously increased the weight of the figures placed before them, completed the group.

Much, however, as Elvira disliked these members of her council, she felt unequal to resist their combined influence; and she was just upon the point of being teased into their opinions contrary to her own judgment, when Lord Edmund entered the room. Indescribable was the effect produced by his presence; for indeed his commanding talents swayed all before them; and Elvira could not help smiling when she saw her counsellors of state shake their wise heads, and imagine they were assisting the debate with their wisdom, whilst, in fact, they were mere tools in his powerful hands. It is true they were the agents that produced the intended effect; but his was the master spirit that set them in motion, and taught them where to go. His powerful intellect caught in an instant the comparative merits and disadvantages of the plan now in discussion, and his nod decided its fate; whilst the council, though they implicitly obeyed his will, had not the least idea that they were doing so; as he had the address so to form his opinions, as to let each person imagine them the suggestions of his own breast.

The council, however, though they implicitly obeyed his will, had not the least idea that they were doing so; as he had the address so to form his opinions as to let each person imagine them the suggestions of his own breast.

Whilst the principal personages in the cabinet, fancying they were leading, were thus blindly led, the nonentities of course followed in their train, and our old friends the lords of ancient family were perfectly astonished when they heard the magnificent plans and sagacious councils attributed to them, and sate quite lost in admiration of their own wisdom, whilst their little heads and enormous perriwigs kept bobbing with at least threefold their accustomed rapidity.

Elvira's ascension to the throne had induced both her father and Sir Ambrose to leave the country; the duke inhabiting his former palace, and Sir Ambrose taking possession of a moveable house in its immediate neighbourhood, where the worthy Baronet found himself perfectly happy in the society of his old friend, and his pretty niece.

"I begin to repent that my daughter is a Queen," said the duke to Sir Ambrose, one night after supper, when the whole party were sitting cosily round the fire in Sir Ambrose's library. "I have not half the enjoyments I used to have when I could have more of her society. Now when I see her, it is but for an instant, and she can scarcely stay to ask me how I do, before she flies off to some of her new plans of improvement."

"The face of the country will be quite changed in a few years, if all the plans of the Queen prosper," said Father Morris in his usual smooth hypocritical manner.

"I hope not!" cried Sir Ambrose; I hope it's no treason, duke—but I must confess I wish your daughter had never been Queen, if she can't leave things as they are."

"They are such wildgoose schemes[258] too that she takes into her head," said the duke piteously. "Only imagine, Sir Ambrose, she showed me this morning a plan for making aerial bridges to convey heavy weights from one steeple to another; a machine for stamping shoes and boots at one blow out of a solid piece of leather; a steam-engine for milking cows; and an elastic summer-house that might be folded up so as to be put into a man's pocket!"

"It is really provoking; and Edward is quite as scheming and visionary. I absolutely think, if we were both to die, they would not feel more than a temporary uneasiness at our loss, their minds are so completely occupied in these gigantic projects."

"I fear so indeed; all things were otherwise formerly, I remember the time," &c.

But why detail their reminiscences; it may be easily imagined how comfortably two old men would amuse themselves over a good fire, commenting on the glorious days when they were young; when all went right, or, what was nearly the same thing, when all appeared to them to do so; quite forgetting that age has other eyes than youth, and that the change was in themselves, not the times: we have other things to attend to. Clara was at a splendid party given by Elvira, and Father Morris soon left the duke's library to join her.

It was a ball; and the splendid court of Claudia seemed yet more brilliant under the reign of her successor. It was the first time Clara had ever been at court, and the effect the gorgeous magnificence of the scene had upon her was powerful in the extreme. She forgot her cares, her sadness, and her love—all seemed enchantment; and the old lady, who acted as her chaperone, was quite horrorized at her *gaucherie*.[259]

Brilliant as all was, however, the lovely goddess of the temple far exceeded even the splendour of the shrine; and the beholders gazed upon her with indescribable rapture. Beautiful as the fairy image of a dream; kind, affable, and condescending to all, Elvira glided through the crowd, followed by her suite to the concert-room. Here, all that the imagination of man could devise of harmony, enchanted the ears. But harsh was every other sound to that which stole upon the senses when Elvira was induced to forget her rank and mingle her voice with the music.

Elvira's singing was perfection: "clear as a trumpet with a silver sound;"[260] the round full notes now swelled upon the ear in liquid melody, and then died away, soft and sweet, yet distinct even in their faintest strains. Prince Ferdinand was at her side, and his ardent gaze bespoke the intenseness of his admiration. Elvira had not before seen him since the night when her conversation with him had so powerfully excited the jealousy of Edmund; and as she now observed his manner had again attracted Edmund's attention, she blushed yet more deeply than before.

Edmund saw her blushes; and, stung almost to madness by the sight, rushed violently out of the room.

The night was cold and damp, a drizzling mist fell fast, and that peculiar chill that marks the first approaches of winter, hung in the air; but Lord Edmund thought not of the weather, and he strode bareheaded through the palace-gardens with hurried steps and the actions of a maniac; whilst the thick gloom that pervaded the sky, contrasted fearfully with the brilliantly illuminated apartment he had just quitted. The gloominess of the scene, however, harmonized well with Edmund's feelings; he felt soothed insensibly; and though he still stalked moodily backwards and forwards, he became gradually more calm.

"Ungrateful woman," thought he, "to treat me thus! Does she not owe every thing to me? I could bear her coldness; I could resign her to a throne;

but the idea of her loving another drives me to distraction!—Curses on that fiend! It must be by his infernal arts that Ferdinand has triumphed. The cold, the chaste Elvira could never give her love thus—thus almost unsolicited, and at first sight if it were not the work of magic. By Heaven, I would risk my soul for vengeance on that demon!"

As he spoke, his eyes fell upon a thicket near him, and he fancied he saw the figure of a man, half obscured however by the mist, emerge from its gloomy recesses. He gazed intently, and the figure glided slowly on with cat-like, creeping steps. The mind of Edmund was worked up to frenzy he almost fancied a demon had appeared obedient to his wish, to receive his pledge, and work his bidding. "Speak!" cried he, in a voice that sounded fearfully amidst the surrounding stillness—"Speak! art thou a demon, or a mortal?"

All was silent: the figure glided on; and Lord Edmund, oppressed by supernatural terrors, and shuddering at the sound of his own voice, could bear no more; he darted upon the figure, and grasping it roughly, he exclaimed, "Man or devil, I fear thee not, and thus will I grapple with thee."

"Gently, my son," replied the well-known voice of Father Morris; "in what have I offended you?"

"Pardon, holy father," returned Edmund "I knew you not—I knew not what I did—my passion blinded me."

"And what has caused this passion? The mind of Edmund is too noble to be lightly moved."

"Oh! talk not of the nobleness of my mind, father; I feel I am but a poor weak worm. Nobleness belongs to God alone; 'tis blasphemy to apply the term to man."

"Tell me your grievances. They must, I am sure, be great, or they would not thus affect you. It is my holy office to console affliction. Speak then, my son; for, remember, that though joy is doubled by being partaken, grief is lessened by being shared—and woe robbed of half its bitterness."

"I have little to confess, father. I was weak and foolish; but Elvira—"

"And are you astonished at a woman's fickleness? Light as the eider down, and unstable as the changing wind, inconstancy is natural to the sex—they crave incessantly for novelty;—and as vanity is their only real passion, if that be gratified they ask no more."

"And has not Elvira's vanity been gratified even to satiety? Have I not idolized, worshipped her? Was it not my power that made her what she is? And is this my reward? To be scorned, deserted, laughed at, and for what? A stranger!—a boy!—my prisoner!"

"Whom do you mean?" asked the friar.

"Prince Ferdinand," returned Edmund.

"Impossible!" cried Father Morris, starting with well-feigned astonishment. "Elvira cannot, surely, love Prince Ferdinand! And yet, now

I recollect, I saw her talking to him, even now, with an appearance of deep interest, when I passed through her splendid chambers."

"Damnation!" exclaimed Lord Edmund vehemently, driven to distraction by this speech; for, strange to tell, though we may be certain of the reality of our own sufferings, they always seem to come with double poignancy when we hear them related by another.

"Calm yourself, my son," said Father Morris in his silky tones, eyeing him with about as much compassion as an angler feels for the writhing of a worm upon his hook. "These bursts of passion are unworthy of you."

"Oh, father!" cried Edmund, softened almost into tears, "you know not how I loved that woman. Your grave, serious feelings, disciplined by the restraint of a cloister, mortified by your renunciation of all earthly pleasures, can form no idea of the depth and fierceness of mine. Your passions, father, are dead within you; subdued by holy penitence to calmness; but mine rage with the fury of a volcano, and destroy me! O that my fond attachment, my long devoted services, my adoration, should be thus rewarded. Yes—my adoration, for I have adored her, father! I worshipped her like a goddess; and though I doted on her charms, and would have endured unheard-of torments to have been blest with their possession, yet, did I not sacrifice my hopes?—did I not relinquish the treasure when just within my grasp, because her happiness was dearer to me than my own? And now to see her lavish her favours on that boy! She smiled upon him, father, and he dared to take her hand and press it to his lips. I saw him kiss it, not with the calm respect of a kneeling subject, but with the fervour, the impassioned ardour of a lover; and then he looked at her—curses on the thought!—and she did not reprove; but, casting down her eyes, softly blushed consent. Damnation! I cannot endure it."

"Passion, my son, entails its own punishment. You see every thing with a jaundiced eye. Elvira's nature is gentle and yielding; she feared to hurt his feelings by her harshness. 'Tis but the natural consequence of that very softness you so often have admired. Why should you quarrel with it now? 'tis still the same that charmed you, save that now it is extended to another, and will be soon, no doubt, to all the world. Elvira has been educated in retirement, and, seeing only yourself and Edric, you thought her conduct was the effect of partiality for you, when it was in fact but her natural manner. She is now upon a larger theatre; and you must expect to see myriads of kneeling victims worship her beauty, and pay homage at her feet! And do you suppose she will be displeased at their attention? No; she is far too gentle; she has no firmness; and the same submission she now pays to you, she will, if you offend her, easily transfer to another. She is not formed to govern; she would obey and be happy; hut the weight of government would overwhelm her if she were left alone to sustain it. Shake off, then, these selfish feelings, and be again yourself. You have often said, you only wished her happiness; and if that he the case, even if she should really love Prince Ferdinand, you ought to rejoice to see her in his arms."

"Sooner would. I perish, sooner would I involve all in one universal ruin! But it is impossible; she scarcely knows him."

"And if it were so, still you would be wrong to blame Elvira for what, in fact, she cannot help. Her yielding softness is the defect of her character."

"Fool that I was, that very softness caught me, and my fond heart fell captive to its chains. But it was folly, infatuation! I see my error; Rosabella has more character. She *can* love."

Lord Edmund crossed his arms upon his breast and was soon lost in a *reverie*, which Father Morris was careful not to interrupt, but which was broken by the approach of Trevors, his lordship's aide-de-camp and secretary.

"What do you want?" asked Lord Edmund sternly.

"I came to seek your Lordship. I feared you were unwell, as I missed your Lordship from the party."

"*You* missed me!" repeated Lord Edmund bitterly. "You missed me! and did no one else discover my absence? Was it so marked that my servant could observe it, and yet no one else?"

"Did not the Queen inquire for Lord Edmund?" asked Father Morris.

"I did not hear her Majesty," replied Trevors.

"How was she engaged? what was she doing?" demanded Lord Edmund.

"She was sitting, talking to Prince Ferdinand, my Lord."

Lord Edmund gnashed his teeth together, grinding them with fury, and rushed back to the house without speaking, whilst Trevors followed at an humble distance.

"He has it," cried Father Morris triumphantly—"he has it, and he is mine for ever."

Several days elapsed from this period before Elvira again saw Lord Edmund. She was surprised at his absence; as indeed he was so interwoven in her schemes and plans, that nothing went on well without him.

"Will your Majesty have the goodness to affix the royal seal to this ordinance?" asked Lord Gustavus one morning.

"I don't know," replied Elvira. "I can't tell what to do. I wish Lord Edmund were here."

"He may soon be sent for," said Lord Gustavus pompously. "Though, with all due deference to your Majesty's better judgment, it does not appear to me that his presence is exactly requisite."

Lord Edmund, however, was summoned, and he came; But oh! how changed since Elvira had seen him last! His face looked pale and thin, his cheeks were sunken, and his eyes hollow and heavy, whilst his deep voice sounded hoarse and unnatural. Passion had passed through his soul, and withered as it went. Elvira's heart smote her as she gazed upon him.

"You have been ill, Edmund!" said she, in tones of melting softness. "Why was I not informed? Surely you could not think I would willingly neglect you? Could you judge so harshly of me?"

The firm breast of Edmund softened as she spoke, and tears swam in his eyes as he struggled to reply with calmness—yes, tears; the brave, the warlike Edmund, whose strength of mind and firmness had resisted unequalled dangers, now trembled before a woman.

"You must have some advice," continued Elvira. "Dr. Coleman, Dr. Hardman, can you not prescribe for your patient?"

"His Lordship appears feverish," said Dr Coleman. "No doubt he has rested ill."

"Yes—yes," rejoined Dr. Hardman, with a malignant smile. "His Lordship's eyes betray his want of rest."

"I have been slightly indisposed," said Lord Edmund, rallying his spirits to speak: "but I am better. Is there any thing in which my services can be useful to your Majesty?"

"Her Majesty wishes you to inspect this bill," replied Lord Gustavus solemnly, "before she gives it her royal assent."

Lord Edmund's eyes sparkled. "Then she still thinks my opinion of importance," thought he.

"Lord Edmund's illness, I hope, is passed," said Dr. Hardman maliciously; "for he certainly looks better even since he came into the room."

Lord Edmund was better; a sudden revulsion of feeling had taken place within him, and hope was again illumined in his bosom. Passion again rushed through his soul. "She must, she shall, be mine," thought he, whilst fire flashed from his eyes. "The hated law shall be repealed. Difficulties only increase the value of the prize, and they vanish before a determined spirit. What! shall I, before whose arm whole nations have fallen vanquished, shrink like a coward from the first trouble that assails me! Oh, no! I will not be so weak; opposition shall only animate my courage. Treasures would be scarcely worth acceptance if they lay beneath one's feet—a brave man spurns an easy victory! I will exert my powers, and Elvira shall be mine."

Father Morris was at the levee, and he watched with anxious eyes the fluctuations in Edmund's expressive countenance. "Perdition seize her beauty!" muttered he; "with one look she undoes whole months of labour. But he shall yet be mine—Cheops has sworn he shall,—and Rosabella shall be Queen. Be the Mummy mortal or fiend, he is resistless; he has unbounded power over the human heart, and what he wills must be accomplished."

Some weeks elapsed, during which Lord Edmund, restored to his former influence in the government, laboured assiduously to prepare the minds of the people for abolishing the law that prevented the marriage of the Queen. With the greatest care he endeavoured to make Elvira popular. For this purpose he persuaded her to remit those burthens that weighed most heavily upon the people, replacing them by taxes levied in a more indirect way; for the mass of a population seldom grumbles at taxation, unless it see the trifles for which it pays: men do not regard the giving double the real value of a commodity, a tenth part so much, as paying even a small direct sum for the use of any of the common necessaries of life.

By judiciously acting upon this principle, Edmund made himself adored; and whispers even were buzzed about, lamenting that he was not King. This was the point to which Edmund had wished to bring the people; and he pursued his plan by supporting the poor against the rich, and rigorously punishing the magistrates or officers of justice who attempted to oppress the people. The multitude generally hate those entrusted with the execution of the laws, perhaps upon the same principle as the bleeding culprit abhors the sight of the whip that has flogged him; and their natural conceit and presumption were flattered by the attention paid to their complaints; till, by his judicious management, Lord Edmund found that he had obtained the entire devotion of the mob, and could wield them at his pleasure.

Time rolled on, and winter had already wrapped its frozen mantle round the world, when one day Father Morris abruptly entered the apartment of Rosabella. "It is all over," cried he, as he threw himself in despair upon a couch. "Edmund has obtained the consent of the people for the Queen to marry, and no doubt in a few weeks he will be the husband of Elvira!"

"The husband of Elvira!" cried Rosabella, her eyes flashing fire, and her cheeks glowing, whilst every fibre quivered with agitation, and her fine features bespoke the tremendous passions of a demon. "Then may everlasting misery attend the fiend that has deceived us; that has led us on step by step to our destruction, and is perhaps even now mocking our despair! Yes, yes," continued she, as the fiendish laugh of Cheops rang in her ears, and his detested form stood again before her,—"I expected this; you come to enjoy your triumph and mock our credulity; but know, this arm is yet powerful enough to revenge my wrongs; it shall annihilate my rival; and thou, wretch! detested hideous wretch! thou too shalt feel its vengeance!"

"This to your friend!" said Cheops with a bitter smile: "fie! fie! How blind is human reason when the passions intervene!—all is for the best—have patience; wait a little, and my promises will yet be accomplished."

"If Elvira had died," murmured Father Morris, a dark frown gathering upon his brow.

"You would not be now alive," said the Mummy. "But fear not, all is as you can wish."

"As we can wish?" cried Rosabella indignantly.

"Yes, as you can wish," returned Cheops firmly. "Edmund has obtained permission for Elvira to marry any natural born subject of the realm; but she will not wed him, for she loves another, and that other is a foreigner. He will be enraged at her refusal, and jealousy will alienate him from her cause.

He will then naturally espouse that of her rival from ambition and revenge. Rosabella will be Queen, and the law which prevented the marriage of the Sovereign being abolished, Edmund will become her husband—if not from love, at least from ambition."

"O Cheops! 'tis useless to resist—we are thy slaves,—do with us as thou wilt."

"Say rather you are slaves of your own passions," murmured the Mummy; and they parted.

It was a clear frosty day in November, when Elvira, scarcely knowing why, wandered into the garden belonging to her splendid palace of Somerset House; and, entering a pavilion, reclined upon a couch placed opposite to a window that commanded a view of the river. The pavilion was decorated with the utmost taste. Its windows, opening to the ground, were shaded with curtains of gossamer net, lined with pink; the walls were beautifully painted, and divided into panels by highly ornamented columns; books, drawings, and musical instruments, were scattered around; whilst tripods, supporting vases filled with the rarest exotic flowers, shed sweet fragrance through the air; and the carpet was so soft and thick, that it felt like moss beneath the feet.

Even in this temple of luxury, however, its fair possessor was not happy. She sighed as she surveyed the gorgeous refinement around her, and felt forcibly the insufficiency of greatness. Listlessly she turned her eyes upon the figures painted upon the walls: they represented the loves of Mars and Venus: they were exquisitely painted: the artist had given to the life the tender modesty of the goddess, and the ardent passion of her lover. Elvira gazed upon his glowing countenance and sparkling eyes; and then, looking down, sighed yet more heavily than before.

She dismissed her attendants, retaining only Emma; and long her eyes were fixed on vacancy, and her mind absorbed in mournful contemplations; when suddenly she was startled by the entrance of a page, and the appearance of Lord Edmund Montagu, who followed almost at the moment of the page's repeating his name: his countenance beaming joy, and hope dancing in his eyes.

"Oh, Elvira!" he cried, "you are now mine —mine for ever! The people permit you to marry. The lords in council have signed the law; the people have proclaimed it with acclamations. You are free! you are no longer debarred from the inestimable pleasures of domestic life—you are independent—you may marry any natural born subject of the realm, and will you now be mine?"

"And so relinquish my independence the moment obtain it," said Elvira, smiling.

"Oh, my loved! my adored Elvira! consent to make me happy! Believe me you shall be free, and still as much a Queen as at this moment." "Edmund!"

said Elvira seriously, "you deserve more than I can give you; for I will not insult you by supposing you would be satisfied with the possession of my crown without my heart;—and that it is not in my power to bestow."

"My dearest Elvira, you but fancy this. I know your feelings are warm, your sensibility acute, and your generosity unbounded—can you then want a heart?"

"Alas, no! but I have discovered I possess one, only in time to know also that I have given it to another."

"And is that other a youth and a stranger?" asked her lover, gasping for breath.

"He is," replied Elvira, blushing, and looking down.

"Then, indeed, I am wretched!" cried Lord Edmund; and, striking his clenched hand vehemently against his forehead, he darted out of the room.

Elvira gazed after him with a feeling almost amounting to horror. Terrified at the strength of the passions she had awakened, she appeared stupified,[261] and stood looking like a child who had accidentally cut the string which confined the wheels of some powerful machinery, on hearing its fearful clatter above its head.

"Oh, madam, madam!" cried Emma, wringing her hands, "what will become of us? Your Majesty has offended Lord Edmund for ever, and for that wretch, who, I am certain, is a fiend incarnate!"

"Peace, Emma!" said Elvira, "you forget my rank—I will not be dictated to."

"Pardon me, dear madam, you know I love you, and—"

"I know, also, that you presume upon my love. Begone!"

Emma obeyed, and Elvira was left alone.

Dreadfully agitated, and quite unable to compose herself or arrange the chaos of her thoughts, she walked to the windows of the pavilion, and, opening one of them, looked out upon the gardens. It is already said that these delightful grounds were thrown open to the public; but, in consequence of the ease with which they might be enjoyed, a few half-pay officers, attorneys without clients, physicians without patients, clergymen looking out for livings, hissed players, disappointed authors and discarded servants, alone strolled through their romantic walks, and paused occasionally to gaze upon the beautiful works of art with which they were decorated. The English were now decidedly the first sculptors in the world. Chemical preparations alone being used to supply light and heat, smoke was unknown, and the atmosphere being no longer thick and cloudy, marble bore exposure to it without material injury. Besides this, perhaps no nation in the world produced more beautiful models of male and female beauty than England; and now that the women had long thrown off those deformers of the human shape ycleped stays, their forms developed themselves into perfect symmetry. Elvira, however, thought not of the gardens, nor of the works of art they contained; yet as she stood at the window, though absorbed in her own reflections, her eyes rested upon the exquisite statues before her. The inanimate marble seemed endowed with soul and spirit; whilst the graceful forms it represented seemed to pause only for a moment, and to be ready to start again into life and action after a short repose—in short, they appeared to breathe; and the spectator felt almost surprised, when his eye had turned from them, to find them still in the same attitude when he looked again.

The river was frozen, and persons glided along it in glittering *traineaux*,[262] or skated gracefully with infinite variety of movement; whilst, every now and then, a steam-percussion-moveable bridge shot across the stream, loaded with goods and passengers, collapsing again the instant its burthen was safely landed on the other side.

Pleased with the busy scene around her, Elvira stood and gazed, till half her troubles seemed to vanish, and a pleasing train of thought crept over her mind. "What have I done?" thought she,—"and yet I do not repent—No, no! I could not act otherwise. The noble and devoted love of Edmund deserved my warmest gratitude, and I have done right to own the truth to him, painful as it has been to me to do so, rather than torture his generous bosom by exciting hopes I never meant to realize. Yes, I have done right," repeated she aloud; "and I am perfectly satisfied with my conduct."

"Then you have reason to be contented," said the deep voice of Cheops, immediately behind her; "for few indeed are the mortals that can say so with justice!"

The solemn tones of the Mummy sank like a foreboding of evil upon the heart of Elvira, and she shuddered involuntarily.

"You think I have done wrong then?" said she.

"I did not say that," returned he calmly.—"But had I not known the sex, I might perchance have felt surprised that you should avow, unasked for, a secret to Lord Edmund which you have sedulously endeavoured to keep concealed even from me."

"Alas," cried Elvira, "my motives—"

"Were those of a woman," interrupted Cheops; "a being fated to work mischief. I do not blame you; for you have only acted according to your natural instinct."

"What do you mean?" asked Elvira, turning pale and trembling, for the words of the Mummy created an undefinable dread upon her mind.

"Listen!" said Cheops, "and I will tell you.—If you had confided your secret to me, it would have produced good, for I should have aided your passions, and I cannot give assistance unless it be required;—but by telling it to Lord Edmund you have produced evil, for he mistakes your lover for another, and the consequences may be fatal. Thus, it is clear that you could not have done otherwise than as you have; for when was a woman known to hesitate between good and evil, and not choose the latter?"

"Mistakes my lover for another!" exclaimed Elvira. "For God's sake, explain yourself!"

"He thinks you meant Prince Ferdinand," said the Mummy coldly, "and he is now seeking him in order to destroy him."

"Oh, God!—Oh, God!" cried Elvira in the bitterest agony: "what will become of me? where is Edmund! Let me fly to implore him? to spare the prince!"

"It does not appear to me," said Cheops still more calmly, "that your endeavours to preserve him are at all likely to produce the effect you wish; for, as Lord Edmund already believes you love the prince, and as that belief is the reason of his hatred, your showing a violent anxiety for his welfare does not appear to me exactly the mode most calculated to destroy his suspicions."

"True! true!" cried Elvira, wringing her hands. "Alas! alas! what will become of me?" Whilst, as she spoke, a piercing cry rang in her ears, and a sudden rush of all the persons in the gardens took place towards one particular spot. Scarcely knowing what she did, Elvira followed the crowd, and shrieked with indescribable terror as she heard the clashing of swords.[263] Pale and trembling, she hurried forward, and arrived just as Prince Ferdinand, uttering a deep groan, fell beneath the sword of Lord Edmund. Elvira screamed, and throwing herself upon the body, endeavoured in vain to revive it, quite forgetting in the excess of her agitation the crowd that surrounded her, and the interpretation that might be put upon her behaviour. One sole idea occupied her mind, and chilled it with horror: it was, that her imprudence had most probably deprived a fellow-creature of existence.

Lord Edmund in the mean time stood in statue-like insensibility, gazing upon her with feelings of unutterable anguish. Her grief, her violent emotion, seemed to confirm the passion she had avowed; and if she loved, his exertions had only paved the way for the success of his rival. The thought was madness. Lord Edmund gnashed his teeth, his countenance changed, blood gushed in torrents from his side, for he too was wounded, and he leant fainting against a tree.

The confusion that now prevailed was indescribable. It was high treason to draw a sword in the precincts of the royal palace; and the guards, who were instantly assembled, took the offenders into custody. They were both incapable of offering any resistance, and they were hurried away to prison amidst the exclamations of the mob. Elvira had fainted, and she was carried back to the palace; whilst the whispered speculations of the crowd, upon the strangeness of the scene, arose in half-stifled murmurs like the distant roar of ocean. The attention of the spectators, however, was soon fixed upon the poor old Duke of Cornwall. He had stood bending forwards—his hands clasped, and his eyes riveted upon his daughter during the whole of her ineffectual attempts to revive the prince. The old man seemed turned to stone: he neither moved, nor spoke; his glassy eyes were set, and his livid lips slightly quivered; at last he uttered a faint groan, and fell senseless into the arms of his attendants in a fit of apoplexy. The spectators thought him dead, and fancied his heart had broken, on discovering this unexpected weakness on the part of his adored daughter.

Every one was powerfully affected, and every one seemed bursting to speak; though no one knew exactly what he might venture to say. Lord Gustavus looked stern, Lord Maysworth important, and Dr. Hardman sly; whilst the Lords Noodle and Doodle shook their little heads, till they seemed in imminent danger of becoming separated from their bodies. Rosabella's heart alone swelled with rapture, and her eyes beamed with ill-concealed triumph.

"The Mummy was right," thought she;— "Elvira must fall, and Edmund will be mine."

Volume 3: Chapter 3

The evening of the day on which Prince Ferdinand and Lord Edmund were committed to prison, Sir Ambrose, as he was writing in his study, was startled by a loud scream; and flying to the spot from whence it proceeded, he found Clara lying upon the ground insensible, whilst Abelard was stooping over her, and endeavouring to render her some assistance.

"Good God!" cried Sir Ambrose, "What is the matter?"

"It is all owing to the carelessness of the domestic assistants at the next door," replied Abelard. "No. 7, is just come back from Brighton,[264] and one of the assistants being occupied in making observations on the sky, instead of minding what he was doing, pushed the house a little on one side as it was slipping into the sockets; and poking their horizontal spout through our library window, they have knocked down this shelf of books, and frightened poor Miss Clara out of her wits."

"Stupid idiots," said the baronet; "they might have killed her if the books had fallen upon her."

"I beg your pardon, Sir Ambrose," said the culprit, putting his head through the window; "I do not conceive Miss Montagu would have been injured even if the books had fallen upon her. The weight of her body, I should apprehend, must be nearly equivalent to that of the books; consequently, the resistance she was capable of opposing, being fully equal to the blow she would have received, the effect must have been neutralized."

"Confound your explanations!" said Sir Ambrose, whose anger was increased tenfold by this speech; you've killed my niece, and now you want to drive me distracted. I am always willing to hear reason, but I hate explanations."

"Your honour must excuse me," remarked Abelard, pausing in his attempt to raise Clara: "but your honour's syllogism is not well maintained. Your Honour has been pleased to state that you love reason, and yet your Honour professes to hate explanations. Now to explain, and to give reasons, are synonymous."

"The Devil take your logic," cried Sir Ambrose; "Clara! my dear Clara! open your eyes, my love! are you hurt?"

"I would not say any thing disrespectful to Sir Ambrose for the world," resumed the man whose carelessness had occasioned Clara's accident, "but I cannot refrain from observing to you, Mr. Abelard, that even now, his Honour's last proposition was by no means selfevident. The copula, and the predicate[265] did not agree, for how could the Devil, personified in his Honour's speech as an active agent, *take*, that is seize, or lay hold of your logic, Mr. Abelard, a thing which is not tangible?"

"Perhaps his Honour spoke metaphorically," observed Abelard; "and then you know one is allowed a license."

"Oh, if his Honour spoke metaphorically it alters the case completely," returned the man.

"And you would let my niece lie and die whilst you are settling the point?" cried Sir Ambrose, as he raised Clara himself, and placed her upon a chair. "How are you, my dear child?" continued he in a softer tone; "What is the matter? Where have they injured you?"

"Oh, my dear uncle!" sighed Clara, "Edmund is in prison, and he certainly will be beheaded."

"In prison, child! you must be dreaming."

"Indeed I am not, uncle: I heard the men who are placing the adjoining house say so. He has fought with Prince Ferdinand in the palace garden."

"My boy, my darling boy!" cried Sir Ambrose, and rushed out of the room in despair.

"Follow him, for Heaven's sake, follow him, Abelard," said Clara. The worthy butler obeyed, wringing his hands, and lifting his eyes up to heaven; whilst Clara remained perfectly motionless, and apparently absorbed in thought.

"I will save him," said she after a short pause, "or perish in the attempt."

In the bitterest anguish of mind, Sir Ambrose hastened to the palace; but he was refused admittance, as he was informed the Queen was in a high fever. He inquired for his friend the duke: he too was invisible, his late attack having placed his life in imminent danger. Dr. Coleman was in attendance on the Queen; and the lords of the council, though they affected to sympathize with the unfortunate father, evidently, though covertly, rejoiced at the disgrace of their most powerful rival. Repulsed on every side, Sir Ambrose now proceeded to the prison; but here also he was refused admittance, and sadly and slowly he returned home in despair, resting his sole remaining hopes upon the advice and assistance of Father Morris, upon whose gigantic strength of mind he was accustomed implicitly to rely in all the impotency of age and misery.

The prison to which Ferdinand and Lord Edmund had been conveyed was situated in a close disagreeable part of the city of London, called Kensington.[266] It had been formerly a palace, and had been surrounded by a noble park miscalled a garden. The devastating hand of improvement had however, as usual, waged war against all the sublimer charms of nature, and the majestic beauties of Kensington fell victims to its fury. Narrow, unwholesome streets now rose where spreading oaks had once stretched forth their venerable arms, and verdant lawns had become dirty causeways; whilst ponds were turned to water pipes, and Jacob's well kept clean a common sewer. As Ferdinand and Edmund, however, had never seen Kensington in its pristine glories, they could not now regret the change: and it was to them neither more nor less than a place of confinement, a spot very few people show any manifest relish for.

Immediately upon their arrival, Prince Ferdinand and Lord Edmund had their wounds dressed by the automaton steam surgeon[267] belonging to the prison, which, being properly arranged and wound up, staunched the blood, spread the plaisters, and affixed the bandages with as much skill as though it had done nothing but walk a hospital all its life. As soon as these operations were performed, the prisoners were locked up in separate cells, and left to meditate upon their situations.

"Good Heavens!" cried Ferdinand, looking round with astonishment at the elegant apartment he was shown into, adorned with a painted velvet carpet, silk curtains, and chairs and tables inlaid with brass and ivory; whilst a sumptuous canopy hung over a bed of down on one side, and divers little Cupids supported lights, held back curtains, and performed numerous other useful offices in different corners. "Can this be a prison?[268] Neither Paris nor Vienna possess palaces half so splendid!"

The surprise of Ferdinand was natural, as he was still almost a stranger in England, and did not know that our happy island had been long blest with a race of people who thought prisons should be made agreeable residences, and had gone on improving them till they had ended in making them temples of luxury. In spite of all the conveniences of his prison, however, Ferdinand was perfectly wretched. He could not imagine what reason Lord Edmund had had for fastening a quarrel upon him; for, as his passion for Elvira, though violent, had been quite as evanescent as that he had formerly entertained for Rosabella, he had not the least idea of having excited Lord Edmund's jealousy. Fatigued at length with forming fruitless conjectures, he threw himself upon his bed of down, and soon lost the remembrance of his cares in a refreshing slumber.

In the mean time, Clara was revolving in her mind the best method of putting in practice a wild scheme that she had formed, of visiting Prince Ferdinand in prison. She did not dare confide her plan to any one, for she found that anybody she might consult would either laugh at her folly or betray her secret. Besides, to obtain any assistance, she must give some motive for her conduct; and as Clara did not exactly know her own reasons for thus acting, it was quite impossible she could make out a case to satisfy another. To go, however, she was determined when the family of her uncle were all retired, she wrapped herself in a large mantle, and with some difficulty contrived to reach the street. The night was cold and dark; a thick mist fell, and Clara seemed chilled to the heart; yet a feeling she could not account for, urged her on. Clara was young and romantic; she loved Prince Ferdinand, and she fancied him in danger. How she was to save him she knew not, and yet it was solely the hope of saving him that urged her forward.

She had discovered he was confined at Kensington, and thither she bent her steps:—but as she passed the palace, she found a crowd of balloons floating around it, laden with persons whose anxiety respecting the Queen had kept them waiting, and induced them to besiege her door personally with their inquiries; whilst the lighted flambeaux, belonging to these aerial vehicles, flashed brightly in the air, and looked like a multitude of dancing stars, as they rapidly crossed and recrossed each other above her head.

This little incident completed poor Clara's bewilderment; and, terrified lest she should be seen and recognized, she hurried on without exactly knowing where she was going, till, perplexed by the different appearance the streets seemed to assume in the darkness, and her own fears, she found to her unspeakable dismay that she had lost her road. In the greatest agitation and distress, she now wandered to and fro, whilst her embarrassment was increased every moment by the ill-timed raillery of the passers by. At last, she became quite surrounded by a group of people, who assailed her with so many questions and jokes, that the poor girl, quite overpowered, stopped short, and burst into tears.

"Och! and what are ye about to be after disturbing a poor young cratur like that," cried the well-known voice of Father Murphy, as the friar's portly figure was seen bustling through the mob. "What are ye afther there? Don't you see the poor thing has lost her way in the darkthness; and if ye bother her so, how d' ye think she'll ever be able to find it?"

Never did any music sound so harmoniously in Clara's ears, as the father's rich deep brogue; and darting forwards she threw herself at his feet, and, clasping her arms round his knees, she exclaimed—"Oh! save me! I am Clara! Clara Montagu!"

"Clara!" cried Father Murphy, in the utmost astonishment. "Clara! why, what in the name of Heaven brings you out, child, at this hour of the night?"

"Oh! Don't ask me, father," returned Clara, gasping for breath; "that is, I will tell you presently. But take me away; for the love of the blessed Virgin, save me from these men!"

"Come here, my child," said the Father, drawing her arm within his own, and walking away with her; "let us lave these people. And now," continued he, when they were already at some distance from the crowd, "you must tell me, child, what brings ye here?"

This question, though it was a very natural one for the friar to ask, was beyond Clara's power to answer. In fact, she trembled so dreadfully that she could scarcely stand; and when she attempted to speak, her teeth chattered in her head so violently, that she could not articulate a syllable, "Poor thing," muttered the compassionate priest, after waiting a few minutes in vain for an answer, "she'll be bether presently."

All now was dark, and they walked slowly on some paces without speaking, when four bright flashes from a neighbouring clock announced the completion of some hour, and the next instant the solemn deep-toned bell distinctly pronounced the word "one," and then all again was silent.

"I had no fancy it was so late," said the father, whose disposition was naturally too cheerful to let him ever remain long silent.

"Did you think it was one o'clock, Clara? I little thought I should ever be wandering with you, dear, in the streets at such a time of night. I can't help fancying it's all a dream, any how: so speak, darling, it you can, and tell me all about it."

Clara felt still more faint, and only replied by clinging yet more firmly to the friar's arm. Father Murphy was frightened and thought the was going to die.—"Oh murther!" cried he, "what will I do? she brathing her last, sweet cratur, and nobody by to help her, and I not knowing how to comfort her."

The delicate form of Clara seemed every instant to become more heavy, as she still clung almost unconsciously to the friar's arm, and gasped feebly for breath.

"Oh! what will I do? what will I do?" repeated the poor father, looking eagerly around for aid: all however was dark, and gloomy and silent as the grave. Suddenly, however, a bright meteor-like substance appeared at the edge of the horizon, and the friar, to his unspeakable transport, discovered it to be a patent night fire-stage balloon.[269] He hailed it, and in a few moments it was hovering over their heads; the accommodation ladder was let down, and Clara and her companion having ascended to the car, the balloon again rapidly sailed along.

"Where are we going?" asked Clara faintly.

"Och!" returned the friar, "and that's what I never thought of asking, darling; but Heaven be praised that ye are so much better as to be able to bother yourself about it."

"We are going to Kensington, miss," said the balloon conductor.

"Kensington!" repeated Clara, clapping her hands together in transport—"thank God!"

"It's a very good thing to be thankful any how," said the father; "but I own I don't see why you should cry out in such rapture, when you find we are going the wrong road."

"Oh! no, no, father," returned Clara, "not the wrong road; for Kensington is the goal of all my wishes."

"Poor thing! she is certainly disthracted," thought Father Murphy. "The loss of her cousin has deprived her of her senses; but I will let her take her own way; perhaps she'll be better presently."

"Where will you like to be set down?" asked the man.

"Near the prison," cried Clara eagerly.

"Near the prison!" repeated Father Murphy, shrugging his shoulders. "Ay, ay, I was right."

Not another word was spoken till the balloon stopped and the passengers were set down: all still was dark, save a land-light that gleamed from the battlements of the prison, and showed a tall, clumsy-looking figure that marched with heavy, measured steps to and fro before the gates, whilst at a little distance lay a party of soldiers bivouacking. Clara shuddered as she looked at them, and hastily turning away, timidly approached the figure, and begged it to let her into the prison. It continued its march, but as it did not speak, she attempted to pass by it.

"No admittance," said the figure, as she touched it, in trying to reach the door. "I implore you," cried Clara, wringing her hands in agony.

The figure did not reply, but continued its solemn tramp unmoved; its hollow steps falling heavily upon the ear at regular intervals. Driven to despair, Clara again endeavoured to rush past it; but she was again repulsed as the figure reiterated its monotonous "No admittance!" Clara threw herself upon her knees before it in agony.

"Clara! Clara dear! "cried Father Murphy, attempting to raise, her, "you are certainly quite beside yourself; don't you see it is an automaton? nothing can stop it but the proper check-string, and that is in that little guard house, round which you see the soldiers lying."

"Then *they* can admit me," cried Clara wildly, "they are *men*, and will surely listen to me:" then before the father could stop her, she flew towards them, and throwing herself at the feet of the commanding officer, implored his pity. The officer was a man of feeling, and, touched with compassion at her evident anguish, had promised to grant her petition ere Father Murphy, who was too fat to move with much agility, could reach them. "Thank you!

thank you!" cried Clara, kissing the officer's hand. "God bless you!"

The officer smiled at her warmth. "Wait here a little," said he: "I will soon return and admit you, if I obtain permission; but State Prisoners are ordered to be guarded so closely, that I dare not take any step respecting them, without consulting the governor."

"So then you'll get in after all," said Father Murphy, who had approached near enough to hear this last speech. "Well, well, what a world this is we live in! Here have been dukes and princes begging for admission unsuccessfully, and yet a little saucy girl, only because she happens to be half distracted, is let in at the very first word."

Clara did not reply; but wrapping herself in her cloak, sate down on a large stone near the gates to wait the officer's return. The solemn automaton had been stopped for a moment to allow him to pass, but it had now resumed its slow measured step, and Clara's heart sickened at the sound. The mist cleared away, and the night became fine, though cold, whilst the moon having struggled through the clouds that rapidly scudded across the sky, shed her pale feeble light upon the scene. Clara shuddered as she looked at the dark heavy building behind her, and, wrapping her cloak tighter round her, fixed her eyes anxiously upon the sky, watching the varied shapes assumed by the clouds as they drifted along, and sighing heavily as they passed.

"Now tell me dear," said Father Murphy, seating himself beside her, "what ye mane to Say to yere cousin when ye get in to see him. Spake freely, for the devil a word the spalpeens[270] yonder shall hear of what ye're going to say, by rason of their being all fast asleep."

"My cousin!" exclaimed Clara. "Who? what?"

"Your cousin Edmund, that ye're come so far to see," resumed the father.

"My cousin!" replied Clara; "Oh! ay, true. It was my cousin that fought with him, you know. But I don't want to see my cousin."

"Not want to see your cousin!" reiterated Father Murphy, his eyes almost starting from his head in the excess of his astonishment. "Why did you come here then?"

"To—to see Prince Ferdinand," said Clara in a faltering voice, looking down, and blushing.

Father Murphy's astonishment was now far too great for words, and he could only look at her in speechless horror as he revolved some plan in his mind for getting her quietly back to her friends.

"How wild she looks!" thought he: "she must be put in confinement; there is no saying to what lengths, so strange a delusion may carry her."

Whilst the poor father was thus cogitating and repeating to himself divers coaxing forms of words, by the help of which he hoped to persuade her to return, the automaton again stopped, and, the prison door flying open, the officer beckoned Clara to advance. She flew towards him. Clara!

Clara dear!" said Father Murphy, "had you not better go home?" But Clara heard him not; she was already in the prison; the doors had closed, and the automaton sentinel had again resumed his measured, beaten track.

"Oh dear! oh dear!" cried the unhappy Father Murphy, "what will I do? How will I get her out? Poor Sir Ambrose—he will break his heart. I dare say he knows nothing about it. These kind of fits always come on suddenly."

Thus lamenting, the worthy father walked up and down before the prison in a state of pitiable distress, till a bright thought flashed across his mind, and he set off as fast as his trembling limbs could carry him to put it in execution.

In the mean time Clara had followed the officer into the prison, and her heart beat faster as she advanced, for her undertaking now appeared to her in a new light, and she trembled as she thought of the interpretation the Prince might put upon her boldness. It was, however, too late to repent; she had not even time for hesitation. The officer is already at the door, the bolts are withdrawn, and Clara finds herself in the presence of Ferdinand. Confused and horror-struck at what she had done, she, however, scarcely knew where she was, every thing seemed to swim before her eyes, and, gasping for breath, she caught firm hold of the door-way for support.

For some moments, Ferdinand was not aware of her presence, as he sat gloomily resting his head upon his hand, his elbow supported by a table, upon which lay a variety of papers, whilst Hans, a favourite servant, who had followed him from Germany, stood beside him.

Awed by his abstraction, and abashed by the presumption she had been guilty of, in intruding, unsolicited, upon his presence, Clara still stood irresolute, fearing alike to advance or to recede, till the officer, impatient at her delay, cried, in a loud voice—

"Walk in, if you please, Ma'am, that I may re-lock the door. I shall return to let you out in an hour."

The sound of the officer's voice caught the attention of Ferdinand, and he looked towards the door-way, from the shade of which the trembling Clara was now forced to advance.

"Miss Montagu," cried Prince Ferdinand, who had seen her at one of Elvira's parties, and had thought her so pretty as to inquire her name,—"this is an unhoped-for pleasure; I did not expect this."

"I came—I came—" stammered Clara: and here she stopped short, for upon recollection she really could not tell why she did come.

"I am delighted to see you," said the prince, smiling, and taking her hand, "whatever may be the cause that has procured me this honour."

"I—I—I—had—rather—sit—down," stammered Clara, without having the least idea what she was talking about.

"Well then, we will sit down," said Ferdinand: and, gently placing her upon a chair, he drew one to her side, and again took her hand.

His touch thrilled through Clara's whole frame. She felt his ardent gaze upon her face, and dreadfully agitated, fearing she knew not what, she turned away from him, and tried to withdraw her hand.

"I—I—I—believe—I must go," said she.

"So soon," cried Ferdinand, again smiling, for it was impossible to mistake the cause of her confusion. "I thought the gaoler said he should not come again for you in less than an hour."

"Did he!" repeated Clara, quite unconscious of what she said, and without daring to look at him.

"My dear Miss Montagu, will you not bestow one look upon me!" cried Ferdinand, in his most insinuating tone, sinking upon one knee before her, and gently encircling her slender waist with his arm, as he turned her towards him. Clara could not resist his imploring eyes; her heart beat, she blushed, she trembled, she looked upon the ground; when suddenly Ferdinand uttered a faint cry, and started upon his feet. Clara gazed at him with wonder, for that countenance, so lately beaming with love and tenderness, now seemed aghast with horror. She followed the direction of his eyes, and beheld in the door-way the giant form of Cheops; whilst the Mummy's appalling laugh resounded in his ears. Involuntarily Clara shuddered, and hid her face in her hands.

"By the silver bow of Isis!" cried Cheops tauntingly, "I admire your charity, Miss Montagu. Why do you hide your face? But so it is, true merit is always bashful, and the beneficent spirit that prompted Clara Montagu to visit the distressed, and even prefer a stranger to her own cousin, makes her blush to avow her goodness."

"Mercy! mercy!" cried Clara, falling at his feet. "You know my heart, and I implore your assistance."

"And you shall have it," returned Cheops. "As for you," continued he, addressing the prince; "what is your wish?"

"Deliver me from this prison, and make Clara mine, and I will be your slave."

"It is well," said the Mummy. "Clara, you must retire with me; this is no place for you. As for you, prince, Lord Maysworth and Father Murphy will be admitted to your presence in the course of a few hours, to consult with you respecting your defence. Follow their advice, and fear nothing. Rely upon me, and you shall be safe. Come, Clara! you must return to the house of your uncle. Father Murphy wisely informed me of your folly, and invoked my aid. I come accordingly to relieve you from the dilemma in which your rashness had involved you. Let us retire, and your imprudence will be overlooked in consideration of your youth. Adieu, Prince! we shall meet again!"

The Mummy and Clara now withdrew, leaving the prince's mind much relieved, as his confidence in his new friend was unbounded; whilst the discovery he had made of the devoted love of Clara soothed his troubled spirit, and robbed his confinement of half its bitterness.

Volume 3: Chapter 4

In the mean time, Lord Edmund's mind had been tortured by the bitterest anguish, and his agitation, added to the pain of his wounds, had produced a considerable degree of fever. The conduct of Elvira, and the anxiety she had evinced respecting the prince, seemed to confirm his worst suspicions. "O God! O God!" cried he, as he paced his prison in agony; "I could have borne any thing but this—it is too, too much. By Heaven! I could sell myself to everlasting perdition to be revenged."

As he spoke, he heard the key of his dungeon door grate in the lock, and he shuddered, for he almost fancied some hideous spectre would appear in answer to his call, and he felt indescribably relieved when he heard the gentle, insinuating tones of Father Morris. Sweet is the voice of friendship to the disappointed spirit, and soft falls the balm of consolation from those we love, upon the wounded heart. Edmund's bosom thus throbbed with transport when he saw the reverend father, and, throwing his arms round his neck, he sobbed like a child.

"My dear Edmund," said the priest, also excessively affected, for he really loved Edmund, "it breaks my heart to see you thus—cruel Elvira!"

"Oh, blame her not, father!" exclaimed Edmund; "I cannot bear that even you should blame her. She is deceived—she is under the influence of infatuation. We cannot control our hearts, you know, father."

"But that she should be capable of loving another, when your services, your devoted affection—"

"Alas! alas! father, love is not to be bought by services. All she could give she has given; I possess her friendship and esteem."

"And are you satisfied with those?"

"Satisfied! Oh heavens!"

"At any rate, I suppose you could bear to see her married to Prince Ferdinand, if you thought it would contribute to her happiness."

"Married to him!" cried Edmund, gnashing his teeth in agony—"married to him! Oh any thing but that: but I will never live to see it."

"You are not likely," calmly returned the priest; "for, as the state requires a victim, and Elvira will certainly not resign her Endymion,[271] you will doubtless be sacrificed to save him."

"Hold, hold!" cried Edmund, driven to madness by the thought; "do not dare to repeat those cursed words; I could die to serve her, but I will not be sacrificed. What! am I to be made a tool, a child, an idiot?—destined to labour for my rival, and denied even the poor satisfaction of showing the extent of my devotion? But I will not die so calmly; Elvira shall not forget me—I will see her—she shall at least know my sentiments; and if she treats me with scorn, I will die, it is true, but it shall be by my own hand, and at her feet. I will not he sacrificed— will not steal out of life like a common criminal.—No; the world shall know my wrongs—I will be heard, I will not fall unnoticed and unknown. Take this chain, Father Morris; give it to her, and tell her I implore, by the recollection of the moment when she bestowed it upon me, that she will grant me an interview. If she refuse me—but no, no, she cannot."

Father Morris took the chain, and, promising to see the Queen, withdrew, leaving Lord Edmund in a state of indescribable agitation. He was not left long, however, to his solitary reflections, for, as he paced with hasty strides his prison, and turned as he reached the wall, the Mummy, Cheops, stood before him.

"Ah, wretch!" cried Edmund, "what brings you here? Came you to torment your victims?"

"I came to help and comfort the unfortunate," said the Mummy.

"Begone!" cried Lord Edmund, "I do not want your pity, and your proffered help I scorn."

"Spare your scorn, proud Lord," returned Cheops, "*it* will not aid you, though I might."

I want no aid!" exclaimed Lord Edmund: "and, least of all, such help as you can give me. I despise alike your pity and your vengeance. Come what will, I rely upon myself. Conscious of my own integrity, I do not fear to fall, though demons should assail me. Avaunt then, fiend, for over me thou hast no power!"

Cheops burst into one of his fiendish laughs, and exclaiming, "That time will show," disappeared.

Edmund felt relieved by his absence, though, in spite of his boasted firmness, and the sovereign contempt he expressed for the Mummy, he could not prevent his mind from dwelling upon the circumstance. The appearance of Cheops, indeed, never failed to excite a deep and powerful interest in the minds of all who conversed with him, whilst his appalling laugh struck terror to the firmest breast, and even those who affected to despise his menaces could not prevent their minds from dwelling upon his words. This irresistible power had its full effect upon the mind of Edmund, and, though he endeavoured in vain to shake it off and rouse his mind to think of other things, still the gigantic Mummy seemed to stalk before him. In vain did he strive to picture to himself his interview with the Queen; the hideous features of the Mummy rose in his imagination instead of the lovely form of Elvira, till at length, fatigued and exhausted, he threw himself upon his couch: yet even in his dreams the same image haunted him, and the same words rang in his ears.

Whilst these scenes were taking place in the prison, Elvira was suffering all the torments of a burning fever; she was, indeed, seriously ill: the excessive agitation of her mind, and the horror she felt at the idea of being the murderer of Ferdinand, had overpowered her reason; and by the time Dr. Coleman arrived, (he having been sent for on the first alarm,) she was quite delirious. The thought that she alone had caused the danger of Ferdinand, occupied her mind; and, not being able to bear the idea that her folly might occasion the destruction of a human being, she raved of him incessantly, and repeatedly offered to sacrifice her life to preserve his.

Her ravings were heard by her domestics, and being neither exactly understood, nor correctly repeated, their reports, aided by the artful insinuations of Father Morris, soon produced rumours throughout the city, that the Queen was violently in love with Prince Ferdinand, and had gone mad because the law did not permit her to marry him. The effect this idea produced was prodigious; it was implicitly believed, for the lower classes are naturally fond of the marvellous, and, when there are two sides to a question, are very seldom disposed to err by judging too favourably; whilst the indignation it excited was unbounded. In some cases, men are more tenacious of their prejudices than of their rights. Thus, then, though the English, by consenting to the marriage of their Queen, had deprived themselves of the important right of electing their own Sovereign; they considered what they had done as trifling, when compared with the horror they felt at the thought of submitting to a foreign King: whilst the emissaries of Rosabella, taking advantage of this feeling, by alternately playing upon their fears, and magnifying their terrors, worked them up almost to a state of desperation.

The party of Elvira, in the mean time, was quite unable to stem the torrent opposed to it. The Queen and her father were both too ill to leave their beds, and Lord Edmund was in prison.

"What will become of us?" whispered Emma to Dr. Coleman, one day in the chamber of Elvira, when she fancied the Queen to be asleep. "To-morrow Prince Ferdinand and Lord Edmund are to be tried, and, they say, not even the Queen has power to pardon them if they are convicted."

"It is but too true," returned Dr. Coleman; "they must die, and the punishment is horrid. The criminal is doomed to be burned by a slow fire."

"Horrible!" cried Emma; "and this only for drawing a sword in the vicinity of a royal palace."

"Alas! that is not all! Ferdinand is accused of wishing to marry the Queen; and the laws that devote to a horrid death the man who shall presume to address her in the language of love, yet hold good against foreigners."

"I cannot believe Prince Ferdinand ever dared even think of the Queen," said Emma.

"God only can judge the heart," observed Dr. Coleman; "but, I am sorry to say, the proofs are very strong against him: I have heard, from undoubted authority, that persons will swear they heard him absolutely make love to the Queen; and that she promised to marry him if she could obtain the consent of her people."

"It is false!" cried Elvira, starting from her bed, and standing suddenly between them—"false as hell! Prince Ferdinand never addressed a single syllable breathing of love to me in his existence. He is the victim of a mistake, or rather of my folly; but he shall not die—I will save him, or perish in the attempt!"

The calm, decided tone in which Elvira spoke, and her spectral appearance, produced an almost magical effect upon her auditors, and they stood awestruck and aghast, whilst Elvira continued:—

"Dress me, Emma; I will see my people; I will appeal to them myself. It is the day for receiving petitions in Blackheath Square: there will be a multitude assembled. I will go there in person, and address them."

"It is the raving of delirium," whispered Emma to Dr. Coleman; "what shall I do?"

"Do you dare to hesitate?" said Elvira, whose sense of hearing, sharpened by her recent illness, enabled her to catch distinctly the words of her favourite.

"Humour her," returned Dr. Coleman; "in her present state, opposition would be fatal."

"It would indeed be fatal," said Elvira, seating herself in a large arm-chair, whilst the temporary colour her previous exertion had given her, faded from her cheeks, and she looked the image of death.

"She will faint!" cried Emma, flying for aid.

"It is impossible for her to go in this state!" said the doctor.

"Impossible!" cried Elvira, starting up wildly, and her cheeks again glowing with the deepest crimson, whilst her eyes sparkled with superhuman fire; "what is impossible to a determined spirit? Haste! haste! Emma, and let me go, whilst I have yet strength; for go I will, though death await me there. My rashness has endangered the life of Prince Ferdinand, and I will die to save him!"

Farther opposition was useless, and the doctor retiring, Emma hastily attired her mistress. The people were expected to assemble as usual in the Square, though, from the illness of the Queen, a deputation of nobles had been appointed to receive the petitions. The feelings of Elvira were wrought up to an unnatural energy: every limb trembled with agitation, and every nerve thrilled with impatience, whilst she was dressing; and when she was ready, she descended the staircase, leaning upon the arm of Emma, her cheeks flushed with a hectic glow, her lips quivering, and her eyes shining with unusual brightness.

At the foot of the staircase they met Cheops. He stedfastly[272] regarded the Queen, and smiled at her agitated appearance with his usual calm scorn

"Oh!" cried Elvira, the moment she beheld him, "my pride is humbled. I own I love Seymour. Aid me to save Ferdinand and I am thy slave,"

"Appeal to your people," said Cheops, his eyes flashing with proud triumph; "your feelings will give you eloquence. But do not confine yourself to obtaining the power to pardon Ferdinand. Demand to be free; the people will refuse you nothing. Tell them, first, that they have insulted you by giving you permission to marry, and then dictating whom you shall choose. Require perfect freedom. They will comply, and bow their necks beneath your footstool. But rest not satisfied with any thing short of actual submission. Endure no conditions. This is the moment to decide your future destiny. Act with energy, and you will be happy. But if you falter, destruction is your portion."

"I will obey you to the letter," said Elvira, as she walked with a firm step past him, and sprang into her balloon, followed by Emma.

"Oh, my dear, dear mistress!" said that faithful confidant, "do not listen to that wretch; he is a serpent sent to wile you to destruction. Do be advised; do return and relinquish this mad enterprize."

Elvira did not reply. Her feelings were too highly wrought to permit her to speak, and bending eagerly forward, she watched, with an impatient eye, the streets and houses they flitted over, scarcely able to bear the agony of suspense during the time necessarily lost in the transit, and seeming every instant to long to precipitate herself forward to the goal of her wishes.

The balloon now rose unusually high, whilst masses of fleecy clouds hid the town from their view, and looked like flocks of sheep beneath their feet.

"We are going wrong!" cried Elvira, in agony; "we shall be too late."

"No, no," said Emma, "I feel we descend again—we are arrived."

And as she spoke, the balloon sank rapidly, whilst the clouds opening, discovered the immense Square below them, apparently paved with human heads.

"Thank God! we are not too late!" cried Elvira, clasping her hands together, and sinking back upon her seat; whilst the balloon-conductor directed the machine to the palace usually appointed for the reception of the Queen. Elvira did not wait to arrange her dress; she did not wait to take refreshment, or even to rest a single moment from her, fatigue, but she rushed upon the terrace the instant she quitted the balloon, and presented herself before her astonished people, every limb quivering from the violence of her agitation.

The crowd was immense. The extensive space looked one compact mass of human heads; but Elvira's courage did not fail her. Though she had now no Lord Edmund to support her, and no father or applauding friends to listen as she spoke, yet the enthusiasm of the moment gave her strength.

She forgot every thing but the cause that brought her there; and her mind, thrown back upon its own resources, rallied its energies, and seemed to gather courage from the thought; whilst her sylphic figure appeared to dilate in size, and assume an almost awful dignity from the grandeur of the spirit that animated it, as she thus stood before her subjects, her life or death hanging upon their will.

Her arrival had been hailed by the loudest shouts of wonder and of joy; but when the multitude saw she wished to address them, the tumult was hushed, and they waited in breathless silence for her speech. The deep stillness that prevailed amongst this so lately bustling crowd of human beings, and the thought that every ear and every eye were turned towards her, slightly affected the nerves of Elvira, and her lips trembled as she began to speak; but as she became warmed with her subject, her voice gradually assumed its natural depth, melody, and sweetness; whilst its full tones sank deep into the hearts of her auditors, and carried conviction as she went on.

She first appealed to their gratitude; and, after alluding to all she had done to secure peace and plenty to their domestic firesides, she reverted to the misery of her own situation, before the laws had been revoked that had condemned her to celibacy. She powerfully painted the harshness of the destiny that debarred her from the blessings she had so lavishly bestowed upon others. She alone, of all her subjects, had been destined to the wretchedness of a solitary life, unsoothed by the tender cares of a husband, uncheered by the affection of children. She alone had been doomed to wither away her youth in cheerless widowhood. Their fiat had changed her destiny; but was it the part of a noble and generous people, whilst they conferred a benefit to encumber it with restrictions? No; she was confident the liberal spirit of the English would spurn the sordid thought, and shrink from such a manner of obliging. "Make me free!" said she, "really, absolutely free, and I promise solemnly you shall never have occasion to blush for your Queen."

As she spoke, her cheeks glowed, and her eyes sparkled with unwonted fire; whilst the people, struck by the suddenness of her appearance, and her enthusiasm, and carried away by the force of the sentiment that could metamorphose the tender, gentle Elvira into the exalted being before them, shouted applause; whilst cries rang loudly through the air of "Long live Elvira!" "Marry whom you list, we shall still be your slaves! Still be our Queen, and let your children and children's children reign over us, when you shall be no more."

Delight danced in the bright eyes of Elvira, and a blush of pleasure mantled on her cheek, as she gracefully thanked them. "And yet my friends," continued she, in a fainter voice, "there is another privilege I would demand at your hands. I am called free and absolute, yet I am chained by the laws.

Unloose these bands; give me at least the power to pardon. I know, that if I wished it, I might reverse these laws at my will, as the power of the Queen that made them was not greater than that which you have bestowed upon me. But I wish not to do so: I would rather accept that from your hands as a favour which I might exact as aright. Give me then, my people, the most blessed attribute of royalty. Let me pardon. Can you refuse me this?"

"No, no!" shouted the people with enthusiasm; "we are your slaves! Do with us as you list. The laws are yours; and though you change them at your pleasure, we will obey! Long live Elvira! Elvira for ever! From henceforth we own no law but her will!"

Elvira's rapture was unbounded; she forgot the unstable nature of the vox populi, and triumphed in the devotion of her people; whilst they, in return, shouted forth her praise, as she warmly expressed her gratitude, in tumultuous transports The air rang with acclamations; and Elvira, looking proudly round upon her obsequious subjects, felt herself indeed a Queen. There is perhaps no sensation in the world more delightful than thus to feel oneself the idol of the multitude, to see every eye beaming with admiration, to hear every voice resounding praise, and to know every heart is devoted to one object. The human mind cannot enjoy a higher gratification than in the consciousness of power; whilst the man thus exalted, seems raised to the level of a divinity, and triumphs in the worship of his fellow-creatures: but, alas! such glory is too much for mortals, and nothing can be more evanescent, or rather, nothings, more certain prelude to disgrace.

Elvira, however, knew not that her popularity was too great to be lasting. She implicitly believed her people would continue to feel what they now expressed, and, catching the spirit of the moment, she persuaded them to sign an abolition of the laws, and a confirmation of her absolute power. The people obeyed with rapture; the enthusiasm that animated them had not yet abated; and even if Elvira had desired their lives, they would have obeyed. They considered her inspired, and it seemed sacrilege even to hesitate to comply with her commands.

So powerful was the energy of a woman's will, and so sure it is that a determined spirit may overcome any difficulties when once roused resolutely to exert itself. Such also is the influence of beauty and eloquence upon the human mind, and so weak is judgment when attacked through the medium of the senses.

In the mean time, the council of Elvira had met in their usual apartment, and were holding a solemn consultation, previous to going to receive the petitions, on the propriety of addressing the people whom they might find assembled in the Square, respecting the illness and consequent incapacity for reigning of the Queen.

"Thinking as I think, and as I am confident every one here must think," said Lord Gustavus de Montfort, "there is no middle course to be pursued:

a regency must be appointed[273] or the government will be over-turned."

"Oh! there is no doubt, we cannot exist without a regency," said Lord Noodle.

"Yes, yes! we must have a regency!" cried Lord Doodle.

"It appears to me, to say the least of it, premature," observed the Duke of Essex, a highly respectable nobleman, who had hitherto observed a cautious neutrality; "I think, before deciding upon so important a question, we should at least examine her Majesty's physicians, and be guided by their report."

"His Grace is quite right," said Lord Noodle.

"We ought to examine the physicians," said Lord Doodle.

"One of them has just entered the council-chamber," observed Lord Gustavus; "I presume he brings the usual daily bulletin of her Majesty's health: is it your pleasure, my lords, that he be examined?"

"By all means!" cried all the noble lords simultaneously, and Dr. Hardman advanced. "How is her most gracious Majesty?" asked Lord Gustavus, with his usual solemnity.

"Alas! my lord," said Dr. Hardman, "her Majesty has slept badly, and is much worse this morning."

"Is she still delirious?" asked the Duke of Essex.

"Quite, your Grace," returned the doctor, shaking his head.

"Then I fear there is no hope?" said the duke.

"None!" said Lord Noodle, shaking his head.

"None!" echoed Lord Doodle, shaking his.

"Thinking as I think, and as I am sure every one here must think," said Lord Gustavus, "we must not suffer the interests of the people to be invaded with impunity. The constitution requires watching over, and I consider this a matter that ought to he inquired into."

"Then you think the senses of the Queen irrecoverable?" asked the Duke of Essex, addressing Dr. Hardman.

"Not irrecoverable, I hope, my lord duke, "replied the doctor; "though I own her delirium is alarming."

"What does she rave about," asked Lord Doodle; curiosity being the only mark he ever gave of his being a rational animal.

"It is a delicate subject," returned the doctor; "and if your lordships will excuse me—"

"Oh, no! you must tell us," said Lord Doodle.

"Thinking as I think, and as I am sure every one else ought to think," said Lord Gustavus; "concealment in this case would be a crime."

"Since your lordships command me," replied the doctor, "however reluctant I may be to betray her Majesty's secrets, it is my duty to obey. The Queen raves incessantly of Prince Ferdinand."

"I feared as much," said the Duke of Essex.

"And do you think if she recovers she'll want to marry him?" asked Lord Doodle.

"I fear it cannot be doubted, my Lord." returned the doctor.

"Then, thinking as I think, and as every free-born Englishman ought to think," said Lord Gustavus, "she will forfeit her crown."

A deep silence followed this daring speech, yet, though no one assented to it, no one attempted to contradict it. In fact, every man seemed afraid of committing himself; for, though every one thought Lord Gustavus would not have ventured so far, had he not felt assured the party against the Queen was strong, yet no one liked to be the first to declare himself her opponent. This awkward pause was broken by the entrance of Sir Ambrose and Father Morris, who came with a message from the Duke of Cornwall, imploring them not to decide upon any measure hastily, and informing them that on the following day his physicians assured him he would be able to assist their deliberations in person.

"We all esteem and respect the duke," said Lord Gustavus. "But, thinking as I think, and as I am confident every one who hears me must think, not even our respect for him ought to induce us to consent that the Queen should marry a foreigner! No, no, we must not let private feelings make us risk the interests of the people."

"I dare say they will not be in any danger," murmured the soft, insinuating voice of Father Morris— "I dare say they will run no risk. Foreigners have sometimes been known to respect the interests of a people, and reign as gloriously as native-born monarchs."[274]

"Not often, I believe, father," said Sir Ambrose. "At any rate, I am sure it would break the duke's heart to see his daughter married to Prince Ferdinand, and I am sure it would break mine to see him King of England. Weak, silly Elvira! I cannot account for her infatuation; and I have no patience with her, for causing all this misery solely by her folly."

"You use strong language, Sir Ambrose," said the Duke of Essex.

"Not stronger than the occasion requires, my lord duke," returned the worthy baronet. "I have known the Queen from her childhood, and loved her as a daughter; but now—"

"The matter must certainly be inquired into," said Lord Gustavus. "It is the duty of every well-disposed patriotic Englishman not to suffer the slightest invasion of the constitution. Our laws are our bulwarks; we ought to die to defend our laws; and if the Queen be no longer in a fit state to administer them, or if she even contemplate the design of putting the administration of them into hands in which their purity will be contaminated, then, thinking as I think, and as I feel confident every individual who hears me must think, or, at least, ought to think, there can remain only one course for us to pursue."

"Perhaps," said Father Morris, "we may be deceived, and the delirium of the Queen may be transient, or, at least, her mentioning the name of Prince Ferdinand in her ravings quite accidental. It is not well to be too rash—"

"Oh, no, reverend father," replied Lord Gustavus; "you deceive yourself. Your abstraction from the world, and the goodness of your heart, lead you to judge too favourably of others. But we, who know the world, see deeper. You, holy father, can form no idea of the folly of human passions; you are above their weaknesses, and cannot suspect that in another which you are incapable of feeling yourself: but, as I said before, we, that know the world, see deeper. Elvira is in love with Prince Ferdinand, and is quite capable of sacrificing her throne and people to the caprices of a romantic passion."

"Impossible!" cried Father Morris, with well-acted astonishment,"

"It is very true, notwithstanding," said Lord Gustavus, shaking his head sagaciously; Whilst his attendant satellites, the Lords Noodle and Doodle, shook theirs for sympathy.

"Impossible!" cried Sir Ambrose; "she cannot surely carry her infatuation to such a height: she is too noble: but even if she be so mad, will no one step forward and save her from destruction?"

"I do not see how any one can save her, if such be her intentions," said the Duke of Essex. "Women are proverbially self-willed; and, now that the people have put the laws into her own hands—"

"The people were cajoled into consent," exclaimed Lord Gustavus; "but if the Queen be so mad as to intend to marry the prince, she must lose her throne and suffer death, for the laws against foreigners remain inexorable."

"Yes, the laws are inexorable!" echoed the Lords Noodle and Doodle.

"Good Heaven!" cried Sir Ambrose, it possible I am in England, and yet hear such barbarous sentiments openly avowed? No one has more right to feel anger at the folly of Elvira than myself; but even I cannot bear such cruelty. What! is a young and beautiful woman, in the very flower of her age, to be doomed to destruction, merely for having shown a susceptible heart? Forbid it, Heaven! And what are we that we should dare to judge so harshly and refuse mercy to a fellow-creature? Are we not all feeble? Do we not all err? And if we show such cruelty in judging such a trifling offence, how shall we expect mercy for our own more weighty ones? Have mercy, then. Let us show ourselves men! Let us dare to exert our reason and throw off the shackles of prejudice. We boast that the law in this case makes us free, and arms us with power against our Sovereign. Let us use that power, then, and show that we are really free by daring to act justly. If we do not, we are slaves!"

"It cannot be," said Lord Gustavus; "you talk well, Sir Ambrose, but words are nothing against facts. If the Queen intend to marry Prince Ferdinand, she must either be insane or intend to subvert the constitution; and, in either case, thinking as I think, and as I am sure every reasonable person in the kingdom must think, she is no longer competent to reign, and is no longer worthy to live. Eloquence is a fine thing, and I do not deny that the worthy baronet speaks fluently; yet, notwithstanding all he can say, or indeed all that can be said, upon the subject, law is law."

"Yes, law is law!" echoed the repeating lords.

"Sir Ambrose, I thank you from my soul!" cried the old Duke of Cornwall, starting from the midst of the crowd. "You have, indeed, proved yourself my friend; but I should blush to think that my daughter was slandered in my presence, and that I left it to another to undertake her defence. Yes, gentlemen, Elvira is slandered—I will venture my life upon her innocence. Her heart is English, my lords, thoroughly English; she will marry no German; no—no, my poor, dear Elvira never dreamed of such a thing; she is innocent." And here the poor old man, overpowered by his emotions, could not proceed, but, leaning upon the shoulder of his friend Sir Ambrose, wept bitterly. It is hard to see the tears of aged men; and every one was affected: they had started at the sudden appearance of the duke amongst them; for his gaunt looks and wasted form, aided by the belief of his serious illness, gave him more the aspect of a spectre than a man: and now his trembling voice, and grey hairs, as he attempted to vindicate his child, came home to the hearts of his auditors.

"Alas! why is not Edmund here!" sighed Sir Ambrose; "he would not have left the cause of Elvira to such feeble hands. But he is gone, and, wretched father that I am! I may soon no longer possess my darling boy. Six months ago, two brave sons were the pride of my heart, and the admiration of every eye. Where are they now? the one wandering in foreign climes, exposed to every misery of want, and the other confined in a prison and doomed to suffer an ignominious death. Alas! alas! Why has my life been spared to endure such misery?"

Whilst the old man thus lamented, a bustle was heard amongst the crowd, and the noble lords of whom it was composed, dividing, made way for Elvira! With glowing cheeks and sparkling eyes, the Queen walked proudly along the lane made for her, having a roll of parchment in her hand, and with dignity took her seat upon the vacant throne. A solemn silence prevailed: the conspirators were awed by the sudden appearance of their Sovereign; and those who had hitherto remained neutral, surprised, stood hesitating, unknowing how to act. Elvira paused a few seconds, sternly surveying the crowd, and finding that no one attempted to speak, she exclaimed, "How now, my Lords? what means this silence? I came to assist your councils, not to interrupt them. Go on, I pray you; for surely such enlightened senators can have no sentiments they fear to breathe before their Queen."

"We were surprised at the sudden appearance of your Majesty," said the Duke of Essex, "as, from the report of your Majesty's physicians, we had feared your Majesty's illness—"

"My illness was of the mind, my Lord Duke!" said Elvira, "and this is the medicine that has cured it. Look, my lords," continued she, unrolling the parchment she carried, and suddenly flashing it before their eyes— "behold my panacea! Now I am, indeed, a Queen; for my people have made me absolute, and, abolishing all laws, have placed their lives and fortunes at my feet."

Lord Gustavus and his adherents stood aghast, gazing upon the Queen and the parchment she held so triumphantly, without the power of uttering a word.

"Ere this," continued the Queen, "the purport of this parchment has received some thousand signatures; yet I do not wish to abuse my power. Go, my lords; I have no longer occasion for your counsels; when I have, I will summon you."

The dignified manner in which Elvira waved her hand as she said this, prevented reply; and the lords of the council dispersed, without daring to utter a single syllable. The duke and Sir Ambrose alone remained. "My dear father, cried Elvira, throwing her arms round his neck, whilst the overstrained feelings that had so long supported her gave way, and she sobbed in agony upon his shoulder.

"Remove her to her chamber," said Dr, Coleman, who now appeared; "this agitation will destroy her—her exhausted frame is not able to endure it."

In fact, the Queen was now completely overpowered, and was carried off by Emma and her attendants in violent hysterics.

Lord Maysworth had not been present at this scene, for his time had been otherwise engaged; and, to explain what occupied him, it will be necessary to go back to the prison of Prince Ferdinand. It may be recollected, when Cheops removed Clara, he had informed the prince that Lord Maysworth and Father Murphy would be with him in a few hours. The Mummy's information was correct, for at the appointed time they came.

Och!" said Father Murphy, "and where's Clara? So they 've let me in after all, ye see; for, knowing Lord Maysworth was your friend, I went to consult him, and he talked to them and tould them how barbarous it was to deny a poor fellow that was just going to be burnt alive, the consolations of religion;—they hadn't the heart to refuse me."

"Oh!" groaned Prince Ferdinand; "is there no hope of escape?"

"I fear not," said Lord Maysworth; "for, notwithstanding the enormous expense attending public executions, the people are so fond of them, that it is necessary to indulge them now and then; and they are so devoted to Lord Edmund that his adversary has no chance. Besides, they say there are plenty of witnesses to prove that you have addressed the most impassioned language to the Queen; your enthusiasm one night at her singing—"

"I remember," cried Prince Ferdinand; "idiot that I was—oh! curses on my folly."

"Ah, that's right," exclaimed Father Murphy; "indulge yerself a little, my honey, and it will do ye good. I don't know a prettier amusement than cursing and swearing, and finding fault when one's in trouble; and I'd be far from denying ye a little harmless indulgence; for, as ye're to die so soon, it would be cruel, ye know, not to let ye have all the consolation ye can get hold of."

"Oh!" exclaimed Prince Ferdinand, "I am the most wretched of human beings."

"And ye may say that, for I don't see any great hope ye have, in respect that the people must have a victim, and they'd like you better than Lord Edmund. But never mind that, for the worst that can happen at all, is that ye'll be roasted alive!"

"Wehe mir!"[275] exclaimed Hans; "and can nothing be done?—for though roasting alive may be the worst that can happen, I don't think my master such an amateur in cookery as to wish to try the experiment."

"Och!" cried Father Murphy, "and I'm quite of your opinion; and so, if the prince would just try, and get ready a word or two of defence—or if some clever person that knows the world like yere lordship, for instance, would just give him a word or two of advice—the thing would be entirely done, and all right."

"Oh!" cried the prince, clasping his hands together, "save me! I implore you to save me!"

"I will do all I can," said Lord Maysworth, smiling most graciously; "rely upon me, prince; the suggestion of the holy father shall be attended to. The gratitude I owe your father, demands my greatest exertions—and I am most happy to have an opportunity of serving his son. This worthy father's plan is excellent: I wonder it did not strike me before. Confide securely in me, prince; a proper defence shall be prepared, and I think by it you may escape."

So saying he retired, leaving Prince Ferdinand somewhat consoled by his assurances, but by no means reconciled even to the possibility of being roasted alive. The intermediate time between this conversation and the day fixed for the trial of the prince, was spent by Lord Maysworth in preparing, with the assistance of those "learned in the law,"[276] this defence: and when it was finished, his rapture was beyond description. Three times did he read it over with still increasing satisfaction, for, as he considered it as his own production, he regarded it with all the true, yet indescribable rapture of a doting parent. We are all so fond of our own children, whether of the mind or of the body, regarding them as emanations from ourselves, upon which we may indulge our self-love without the grossness of undisguised vanity, that the transport of Lord Maysworth is not surprising; though he actually carried it so far, that, notwithstanding his professed attachment and gratitude to the German Emperor, I believe if the means of procuring the prince's escape had been offered to him, he would rather have let him stay at the risk of being burned alive, than have lost the pleasure he anticipated on hearing the delivery of his speech.

The important day arrived, and the prince, accompanied by his faithful Hans and Lord Maysworth, proceeded to the court; the latter carrying his beloved brief in his own pocket, rightly considering it far too estimable to be entrusted into any other hands than his.

The court was crowded to an excess—for strange tales of the passion and illness of the Queen had gone forth into the world, each edition more wonderful than that which went before it, and the people now thronged to see the prince with that extraordinary feeling, so common amongst the English, which makes them stare at a great man in much the same way as they would at a wild beast.

An automaton judge[277] sat with great dignity upon a magnificent throne, looking, though a little heavy, quite as wise and sagacious as judges are wont to look. A real jury (that is, a jury of flesh and blood,) was ranged upon one side of him, and some automaton counsel sate in front, their briefs lying upon the table before them, and having behind each a clerk ready to wind him up when he should be wanted to speak; it being found that the profession of the law gives such an amazing volubility of words, that it was dangerous to wind up the counsel too soon, lest they should go off in the wrong place, and so disturb the silence of the court. In different parts of these counsel were holes,[278] into which briefs being put they were gradually ground to pieces as the counsel were being wound up, till they came forth in words at the mouth: whilst the language in which the counsel pleaded, depended entirely upon the hole into which the brief was put, there being a different one for every possible tongue.

All now was ready; the prisoner with his friends placed themselves at the bar, and the judge and jury prepared to hear and decide with all due decorum. The signal to begin was given, and the brief for the crown being put into the English department of the counsel appointed to conduct the prosecution, the clerk began to wind away, and in a few minutes the counsel burst forth in the following impassioned strain of eloquence:—

"My Lord, and Gentlemen of the Jury,

"It is with feelings of the most unfeigned regret that I now rise to address you. Sensible—oh! how deeply sensible, of my insufficiency! and of the much greater competence of any one of my learned brethren at the bar; how willingly would I resign the task to any one of those eloquent gentlemen, feeling so indisputably convinced as I do, of their eminent talents and of their merit; and of their great, oh! how much greater fitness for an undertaking of this magnitude than myself!"

"Ach! Es ist aus mit ims! wir sind verlohren!"[279] cried Hans; "if thou art so unfit for the task, I wonder why the deuce they employed thee!"

"Peace, fool!" said the prince; "do you not see that this is only the exordium? these are words of course."

The orator had paused for an instant from some error of his machinery; but his clerk setting him in motion again, he went on as follows:

"But having being deputed to act, I will not shrink from the arduous duty imposed upon me; I will, therefore, state the principal points of the case; prove my facts by witnesses; and then leave the decision to the well-known judgment and penetration of the enlightened and intelligent tribunal before me!"

It was here intended the counsel should bow to the court, but, owing to his defective machinery, he only gave a kind of jerk, and then continued:—

"My Lord, and Gentlemen,

"It sometimes falls to the lot of members of my profession to relate astounding circumstances and soul-harrowing facts!—facts that pierce into the inmost souls of their auditors, and rend their tortured spirits by their iron fangs! as the teeth of the tangible arrow pierce into and rend asunder the clods of inanimate earth over which it is dragged! But what I shall have to tell you, gentlemen, will make even facts like these hide their diminished heads, and run skulking into corners like owls trembling, and flying hooting away on being exposed to the scorching glare of the noon-day sun.

"Do you not tremble, gentlemen?—do not your hearts pant in breathless expectation of what is coming? Indulge your anticipations—bid fancy take her wildest flight, and let imagination conjure up all the horrors of the infernal regions. Paint the angel of death hovering upon leathern wings over a devoted city—and shrieking mothers imploring mercy in vain for their murdered children! Paint all the multiplied horrors of famine, fire, and carnage! paint miserable starving wretches screaming wildly for food, and, in the agonies of despair gnawing the flesh from their own withering bones!—Paint flames surrounding with their pointed arms an helpless family crying in bitter anguish for the aid that cannot be afforded them!—paint witches celebrating their detested sabaoth![280] Imagine demons indulging in their infernal revels! Yes, paint and picture to yourself all these, and ten thousand other horrors, each more frightful than the last;—dwell upon them—let them haunt your imaginations; but whatever you may fancy, picture, or paint, nothing can ever equal the horror you will feel when you learn the crime of which the prisoner at the bar stands accused. Know then—my tongue falters as I speak, and my quivering lips almost refuse to give utterance to the appalling sounds—know that he has dared, impiously and presumptuously dared, to fall in love with the Queen!!!

"I see your indignation at such baseness—I feel the virtuous shame that burns upon every cheek—yes, yes, my friends, I too am an Englishman, and I, like you, spurn with disdain the thought of submitting to a stranger. What do we want with a King? Has not the country been happy, prosperous, flourishing—respected at home, and honoured abroad, under the dominion of a Queen?—Yes, yes, my friends, it has, and, under her gentle sway, the murderous weapon of war has been converted into a plough-share; the nodding helmet and ponderous corslet into the peaceful wig and graceful gown; and the grim aspect of frowning ruin and grinning desolation into the gentle smiles of benignant peace and overwhelming plenty. Long, long may gentle peace continue to shed her benignant smiles upon us.—Long, long may we sit beneath the grateful shade of her olive branches; and long, long may their feathery foliage hang in graceful festoons above our heads, and their pale green wreaths encircle our brows; for in the arms of peace lie joy, ease, and happiness—her smile gives health and contentment, and her blessing wealth.

"And what threatens to affright this bewitching deity from our shores? 'Tis this audacious stranger, who deserves the bitterest punishment for his unparalleled atrocity. But this is not all;—not satisfied with endeavouring to destroy the happiness of the Queendom, and overturn the laws enacted by the wisdom of our ancestors, he has done more: yes, intolerable as his crimes have been, there is still one more deadly behind. Shudder, my friends, and turn away your eyes as the fear-inspiring words drop from my tongue.—He has dared to draw arms within the precincts of the reginal palace.

"Insufferable audacity! Hear this, ye shades of former royalty, and tremble in your Elysian groves, at the profane hand that has dared thus to invade your august privileges. Can it be believed? Will after-ages credit the report? Oh no, no! the fact will appear too monstrous for even credulity itself to swallow!

"When the crime, the fatal crime was committed, earth trembled beneath his feet: the winds hushed their murmurs, and all nature stood aghast. The frightened ocean receded from its rocky bed. Pluto rushed shivering from his nether throne, and Neptune waved in vain his tranquillizing trident. The elements were convulsed; lightning streamed from the swords of the combatants, and thunder rolled above their heads as they stood like two heroes of Arabian fiction wielding the elements in their wrath!

"But I have done, my lord and gentlemen. I say no more; for I scorn to prejudice your minds against the prisoner, or make the slightest appeal to your feelings to condemn him. However, this I must say, that if ever a case could rouse every nerve of a true-born Englishman against it, it is this. Does any man dread to be torn from the calm delights of his comfortable fireside, where he was surrounded by his adoring wife and attentive children, and doomed to incur all the wretchedness of misery and want?—let him condemn the prisoner. Does any man dread being dragged across burning sands, or forced to wade up to the knees in water through marshy deserts?—let him condemn the prisoner. Would any man shudder to be obliged to sleep upon the hard cold ground, his limbs racked with rheumatism, and his body exposed to all the vicissitudes of hunger, thirst, and inclement seasons, whilst his life is endangered every instant?—let him condemn the prisoner;—but if he prefer these horrors to the comforts of a warm down bed, or if he enjoy the prospect of having his substance devoured by tax gatherers, to support the expenses of a foreign war, then let the prisoner be acquitted. But unless he can make up—his—mind to—under-go—privations—like—these—let—him—aid—by—his—vote—to—condemn—the—wretch—who—

And here the orator stopt[281] abruptly, being quite gone down. He had indeed uttered the last words gradually slower and slower, and at lengthened intervals, because the attendant clerk had unfortunately given him a turn too little, and had not screwed him up quite tight enough. The witnesses were now called. Several spoke to the circumstance of the extravagant admiration expressed by the prince of Elvira's singing; others deposed to the fact of the combat, and others mentioned the Queen's sighing and abstraction; but the principal one distinctly stated, that he had heard the prince make the Queen an offer of his hand in the gardens of the Somerset House, and that she had consented to marry him if she could obtain the consent of her people. A general thrill of indignation ran through the Court at this evidence, and it was with difficulty that silence was obtained for the pleading of the defendant. At last all was still, and the attendant clerk began to wind up the counsel for the prince. Lord Maysworth watched the moment; but being afraid to trust his beloved brief into any hands but his own, unfortunately in his agitation, he popt[282] it into the wrong hole, and when the counsel began to speak, he burst forth in French! Words are wanting to express Lord Maysworth's unutterable consternation at this unfortunate accident.

"Stop! stop!" cried he, "Hush! hush! Can nobody stop him?" but the inexorable counsel would not stop:—for once wound up, and properly set in motion, not all the powers of Heaven and earth combined could stop him till he had fairly run down.

"What shall I do?" cried Lord Maysworth, in an agony of despair; "for, if the judge and jury don't understand French, my fine oration will be utterly lost."

"Oh, if that be all," said the clerk, "your lordship need not distress yourself, for as soon as I found what was going on, I ran up to the judge and pulled out his lordship's French stop!"

"And the gentlemen of the jury?"

"Oh, they all understand French."

"It is well," said Lord Maysworth, "though I am still sorry the hole happened to be French, as I am afraid the verbosity of the language may deteriorate the strength of my expressions."

Thus muttered the noble lord, not sorry, however, I believe, if the whole truth were to be openly declared, that he had an excuse in the change of languages for the failure of his speech, if it should not happen to meet with that brilliant success that he felt so perfectly confident it deserved.

The counsel, in the mean time, went on. The following is a translation of his speech:—

"My lord, and gentlemen of the jury.

"It is with feelings of considerable diffidence and hesitation, that I rise to address you, after the flood of eloquence that has poured from my learned brother. I, gentlemen, am not gifted with such an enviable facility of speech; nor is my imagination endowed with that creative power he has so forcibly displayed. I cannot, gentlemen, like him

> Uprear the club of Hercules—For what?
> To crush a butterfly, or brain a gnat.[283]

"Nor have I the least intention of drawing either Neptune or Pluto from the quiet nap they have been taking for so many centuries to assist in our debate. I assure you, also, gentlemen, that I shall neither disturb the ocean from its rocky bed, nor make Nature stand aghast;[284] No, my lord and gentlemen, my intentions are perfectly pacific, and your harassed imaginations may repose tranquilly upon my speech, after the tumultuous one of my learned brother, as the way-worn traveller rests peaceably upon the soft green turf, after having been tossed about upon the heaving billows of the tempestuous ocean.

> 'Tis sweet to rest, from dread of danger free,
> And mark the billows of the foaming sea;
> 'Tis sweet, a little skiff to safely urge
> Through the tempestuous ocean's boiling surge;
> To hear the pattering rains against the root,
> And feel your hospitable mansion proof.
> But sweeter far the troubled mind's repose
> When of a speech like this, it hears the close.[285]

"When I listened to the powerful exordium of my learned friend—and I did listen to him with the most profound attention—I confess my imagination was too highly excited to be satisfied with so lame and impotent a conclusion.—'What!' cried I, 'have the laws of nature been reversed—have demons been disturbed in their infernal revels, and witches called from their dusky caverns, merely because a beautiful woman has excited a tender passion in the breast of a youthful stranger!' Is this so extraordinary an occurrence that it should create such excessive wonder? Are our hearts so dead to beauty that such a catastrophe should occasion surprise? Forbid it, Heaven! No! whilst our hearts still throb in our bosoms, may they ever beat responsive to the attractions of the fair! May we never become insensible to the charms of the loveliest objects of creation! May we ever own their witchery, and bend beneath their magic sways! Or man, degraded man! would soon sink below the level of the brutes. View man as he degenerates when secluded from the influence of female society;—is he not rough, brutal, and unpolished? Does he not want all those winning graces and those delicate attentions that form so undeniably the charm and solace of life? In proportion as our sensibility, as our goodness, and all the best feelings of our nature are awakened, we become susceptible of love. It is indeed, excessive sensibility, and a kindly feeling to our fellow-creatures, that creates it. Does there exist a generous or noble mind that has not felt this passion? No, not one! there is, indeed, something generous and ennobling in it. We cannot prefer the welfare of another to our own, nor be completely absorbed in another's being, with the devotedness of true love, without becoming purified in our ideas, and raised from that disgusting selfishness which is ever the inspirer of base and mean actions.

> Yes, love indeed is light from Heaven,
>   A spark of that immortal fire,
> With angels shared, by Alla given,
>   To lift from earth our low desire.
> Devotion wafts the mind above,
> But Heaven itself descends in love.[286]

"And from this heavenly, this inspiring feeling, shall my unfortunate client be debarred? Hear me, ye shades of heroic lovers, who, though dying for the hopeless object of your passion, have still exclaimed, with the enthusiastic devotion of a modern poet—

> Lead on, lead on, though horrors wait
> In awful fury round thy gate!
> And danger, death, and grim despair,
> Forbid my hopeless passage there!
> If love, still smiling, beckon on,
> The path is passed, the gate is won![287]

"And ye poets and philosophers, who have painted love as the oasis of the Desert, the green spot in memory's waste, where affection still lingers even when hope decays; have you no compassion for my unhappy client, whose only fault was 'that she was beautiful, and he not blind?'[288] And is this an offence for which a man deserves to be burnt alive? Forbid it, humanity! forbid it, mercy! No, no! such inhuman cruelty exists not in the breasts of Englishmen. I know, I feel that you must acquit my client on this head.

"But this is not the only charge brought against him; he is accused of having violated the sanctity of a royal palace, by drawing his sword within its precincts. To describe the enormity of this crime, my learned friend has brought forward such an overwhelming torrent of eloquence, that unhappily his meaning was swept away in the current of his words. At least I suppose so, as, with all my industry, I have been totally unable to find it. As, however, I cannot imagine my learned friend could have harangued so long without having some meaning in what he said, I suppose it has slipped undiscovered into some sly corner, where it lies, poor thing! quite concealed, and almost crushed to death by the ponderous. weight of metaphors heaped upon it. Gentlemen, my client drew his sword in the Royal Garden. This is the plain statement of the fact, when stripped of the load of ornaments with which my learned friend has encumbered it. My client, a stranger to the English laws and customs, chanced to be walking in the public garden belonging to a Royal palace. He there met a nobleman of the court; from causes irrelevant to the question before us, high words tool; place between them. My client was grossly insulted in a manner impossible to be borne by a man calling himself a gentleman, or making the least pretensions to honour. He drew his sword to defend himself. Can any thing be more simple? And yet for this, all created nature is thrown into confusion, and Neptune and Pluto called shivering from their beds. Gentlemen, my learned friend's brain was teeming with a monstrous conception, and longing to be delivered; he dragged it into the speech with which we have just been favoured. Not satisfied with piercing us through with the fangs of a mental arrow; plunging us into all the disasters of War, and distracting our imaginations by exhibiting the combined effects of plague, pestilence, and famine—he has entangled, in his snares, these unfortunate deities, whom he has forced to upper earth to bear witness on his behalf, I am afraid, very much against their wills. Nothing, indeed, can be more distressing than to see an unfortunate thought thus hunted through the meandering of a sentence; a crowd of unmeaning words, like a pack of hungry dogs pressing close at its back, till at last worn out and completely exhausted, it sinks feebly away, and gives up the ghost so quietly, that no one can reasonably imagine what can possibly have become of it.

"Thus it was with the argument of my learned friend, it has vanished amidst the bustle he created around it. One thing more, my Lord and Gentlemen, and I have done; for (shall not, like my learned friend, after disclaiming all intentions of appealing to your feelings, endeavour by an artful peroration to come home to your inmost souls. It is simply this, that my client is a stranger, the son of a powerful foreign monarch, and, of course, as he has never taken any oath of allegiance to the English government, he is not amenable to the English laws. After stating this fact, I sit down, confidently assured that your verdict will be in my favour, and that, by it, you will again vindicate that proud right you have so long and gloriously maintained of acting always as enlightened and free-born Englishmen."

As the orator sat down, a tumult of applause rang through the hall, and the delight of Lord Maysworth can be only justly appreciated by an author who recollects what he felt when he first heard of the success of a favourite work. But he had little time for exultation, as the Judge, having been wound up in his turn, now began to sum up the evidence. Slowly and heavily did he go on, the machinery that composed him wanting oil, and creaking ominously as it moved, whilst, ere he had half finished, a cry was heard through the outer court, and instantly a rush of people announced the arrival of the Queen.

After the exertions made by Elvira the previous day, her fever returned, and she lay insensible to every thing that passed till she was restored to recollection by the tolling of a deep-toned bell, which was always set in motion the moment a prisoner was put upon his defence. She heard the solemn sound distinctly; the court where state criminals were tried, adjoined the palace, in order that the Queen might have an opportunity of hearing appeals, or deciding on any difficult case that might arise; though as offences against the state had been very rare in the female dynasty, (whether from the goodness of the people or the severity of the punishment, I leave it for my readers to determine,) the privilege had been seldom called in action, and the bell now grated harshly as it tolled. Elvira, however, had heard of the custom, and its cause flashed instantly upon her mind, as she started from her bed, and listened to the solemn sound as it fell slowly and heavily upon her ear, every knell seeming to strike upon the naked nerve.

"Emma!" cried she, "let me go—quick, let me save him, or I shall be too late." Emma obeyed; but whilst she was attiring her mistress every moment seemed an age, and Elvira listened to the heavy tolling bell till the sense of hearing became agony; and, unable to endure any more, she pressed her hands firmly against her ears to shut out the dreaded sound. At length she was ready, and hurrying to the court, arrived just at the critical moment I have mentioned.

"Stop!" cried she, "I command you to stop proceedings. The prisoner is free. My people have given me a right, to pardon all offences, and I thus first exercise it. Set him free!"

The guards obeyed; and it not being possible to stop the automaton judge till he had run down, he was carried out of court, repeating, (for it happened he was summing up the evidence at that moment,) "And the

Queen said she loved him, and would sacrifice even her life for his sake."

"You are free, Sir," said Elvira to the prince. "I only blush that a stranger should have been so inhospitably treated in my court. My illness, however, must plead my excuse; and I can only now show my sorrow by releasing you from the parole of honour you have given.

You are absolutely free, prince, not only from these chains, but also to leave the kingdom whenever you shall think fit."

The prince, in a transport of gratitude, knelt and kissed her hand; and then retired with his friends to the house of Lord Maysworth; whilst Elvira, satisfied with herself, and hoping she had disarmed scandal by desiring the prince to quit the kingdom, returned to her palace more happy than she had felt since the fatal combat in the garden.

Volume 3: Chapter 5

The effect produced by the scene just described upon the minds of the multitude was magical. It seemed a confirmation "strong as proofs of holy writ"[289] of all that had been urged against the Queen, and alienated from her side even those who had remained neutral.

"I really could not have believed it possible," said the Duke of Essex, as he retired slowly from the court.

"Thinking as I think, and as I am confident every one else must think," said Lord Gustavus, "she seems to have lost all sense even of common decency."

"What do *you* say to this, Sir Ambrose?" asked Dr. Hardman triumphantly.

"Nothing," replied Sir Ambrose, sighing.

"Then the case is hopeless," said the Duke of Essex; "for I know Sir Ambrose so well, that I am certain if a single word could be said in the Queen's behalf, he would not remain silent."

"Your grace judges me too favourably," returned Sir Ambrose; "for there is, on the contrary, much to be said for the Queen, if I had been disposed to say it. You see the story of her wishing to marry Ferdinand was evidently false, for she desired him in plain terms to quit the kingdom."

"A mere blind," cried Lord Gustavus, who felt he had now gone too far to recede; "an absolute farce; and I am only astonished a man of your penetration, Sir Ambrose, could have been deceived by it."

"It has long been the proudest boast of the English law," said Sir Ambrose, "that every one is presumed innocent till he be proved guilty; and I confess I do not see why the Queen should alone be made an exception to the rule."

Lord Gustavus made no reply, and the party proceeded to their several homes. The following day was appointed for the trial of Lord Edmund, and the court was, if possible, yet more crowded than before; for the singular termination of Prince Ferdinand's trial had created the most intense anxiety upon the part of the mob to know what would be the result of that of Lord Edmund. It has been already stated that he was the idol of the people, and now thousands of human voices shouted his praises to the sky, and heaped curses and execrations upon his enemies.

The tumult, however, was hushed to breathless expectation when it was announced that the officers of justice were gone in search of the prisoner; and innumerable human beings stood craning their necks over the lane made for his approach through the crowd, all eager to catch the first glimpse of him. But what language can express their disappointment and surprise when they saw the officers return, pale and trembling, fear painted upon their countenances, and their teeth chattering in their heads!

"He is gone," they cried: "the prison door was locked, and the windows fast, but he is gone; and doubtless some evil spirit has carried him off."

Great was the consternation excited by this unexpected news; every one rushed to the prison, and each in turn was struck with horror on finding it exactly in the state the officers had described.—"It is the Mummy that has done this," said the people, whispering amongst themselves: "some horrible event certainly hangs over us; and it is in vain to attempt to resist our destiny! All is supernatural, and we are merely blind instruments in the hands of Fate."

The disappearance of Lord Edmund had, however, nothing supernatural in it; and, indeed was effected by very simple means, and mere mortal agents. The agitation of his mind after his interview with Cheops became excessive, and every hour seemed stretched to an unnatural length as he anxiously awaited Father Morris's return; but the monk came not. Lord Edmund's impatience increased every instant, till it became absolute agony; yet still he was alone. He paced his chamber with uncertain steps—his brain burning with incipient madness, till, no longer knowing what he did, he dashed his head against the walls, and tore off his hair by handfuls. In this state the gaoler found him; and reporting his condition, his trial, which was to have taken place previously to that of Ferdinand, was postponed a few days to allow time for his recovery.

Bleeding and blistering reduced Lord Edmund's fever; but his soul was still on fire. In the paroxysms of his disorder, no less than in his lucid intervals, one sole idea seemed to have taken possession of his fancy; and he inquired incessantly if Father Morris were returned? No, no, was the continual answer to his queries; till the heart of the poor prisoner sickened within him at the sound. At length, he appeared well enough to take his trial, and the day was fixed, as we have already stated. The mind of Edmund now seemed tolerably composed; but it was the stillness of apathy, rather than that of resignation; and on the night preceding the day fixed for his trial, some of his former anxious and tormenting fantasies returned.

"I will shake off this weakness," said he; "I will read;" and, drawing his chair near the fire, he took up a book: it was in vain, however; for though he read over the same page repeatedly, he could not compose his mind sufficiently to comprehend its meaning. He threw his book aside, and, fixing his eyes upon the fire, was soon lost in gloomy meditations: when a slight noise attracted his attention; and, looking round, he saw a panel in the wall slowly detach itself, and Father Morris appear in the aperture, followed by another figure, closely wrapped in a large black cloak.

"Father Morris!" cried Edmund; "is it indeed Father Morris; or some kind spirit that has assumed his shape?"

"It is indeed I, my son!" returned the priest; "and I come to rescue and console you."

"Methinks you come somewhat late, father," said Edmund, rather coldly; "for I have suffered much since I saw you!"

"Others have suffered also," resumed the monk, "and for your sake! Notwithstanding you have fancied yourself neglected and forgotten by all the world, there is one human being who has never ceased to watch over you; who thinks only of you; who makes your happiness her only care; and who would sacrifice her life to preserve yours!"

Edmund's heart beat, and his cheeks glowed as he exclaimed, "And this kind friend is—"

"Now before you!" interrupted the monk; tearing aside the cloak that shrouded his companion, and discovering Rosabella!

"Rosabella!" exclaimed Edmund; a slight shade of disappointment passing over his features.

"Oh Edmund!" cried Rosabella, throwing herself at his feet, "can you forget that I have overstepped the bounds prescribed to my sex: will you not hate me?"

"I do not blame you. I were unworthy of the name of man if I could. But father, what says Elvira? Have you delivered the chain?"

"She refuses either to see or hear from you."

"Cruel woman! But perhaps she dreads to see me?"

"I know not; but she treated your petition with contempt. 'Tell him,' said she, 'it is not possible he can have aught to say that can interest *me*. I will not hear his suit.'"

"Proud, haughty princess! But was this all?"

"No: I again entreated her to see you, when she turned from me in scorn, and bade me leave her. 'Talk not to me of Edmund,' cried she, with a look of ineffable contempt. 'Has he not wounded Ferdinand, and would you have me forgive him?—a thousand deaths are not sufficient to punish such a crime!'"

"What strange infatuation!"

"Strange, indeed—for she has interrupted his trial and set him free; besides which, they say she has actually offered her hand and he has refused it; yet still she dotes upon him to distraction. 'Go,' continued she, when I had finished all I had to say, 'and tell Edmund, that I neither hate nor despise him, for he is incapable of exciting any emotion in my breast; however, if he wishes to make amends for his past conduct, and be restored to my favour, his first step must be, humbly to beg pardon of the prince.'"

"Damnation!" cried Edmund, starting up fiercely: "she did not, surely she could not, say that?"

"Indeed she did, my lord."

"Then may ten thousand curses light upon me if I forgive her! Pardon of that wretch! my slave! my prisoner! no, sooner would I expire in horrid torments—sooner be torn asunder by wild beasts.—Pardon of that boy!—oh! she could not mean it."

Whilst Edmund thus raved, Father Morris and Rosabella watched his torments with much of the same coolness, as a French philosopher would those of an unfortunate animal upon which he was trying experiments.[290] No feeling of compassion entered their souls, and they only waited to see the effect their words would produce. It may easily be perceived that the whole scene which Father Morris related as having passed between him and Elvira, was a fabrication; but Lord Edmund saw not this, for jealousy often throws a veil over the eyes of its victims, which gives a delusive colouring to every thing they see. Thus, Lord Edmund believed every word the father uttered, and his whole frame trembled with agitation as he paced the room with hasty strides. At last, he threw himself upon a chair—"Beg his pardon!" exclaimed he: "Oh Elvira! Elvira!" and he hid his face his hands, whilst the big tears trickled through his fingers, and Lord Edmund, 'the stern, courageous soldier, the philosopher, the hero, and the statesman, wept, actually wept, like a feeble child.

"Oh Edmund!" exclaimed" Rosabella, approaching him, and taking his hand—"I cannot bear to see you in distress. Would to Heaven that by the sacrifice even of my life I could relieve you!"

"Rosabella, you will drive me to distraction."

"Not for worlds, Edmund; on the contrary, were I mistress of worlds, I would cast them at your feet."

"I know it—I know it; but spare me now."

"Spare you, Edmund! Spare what? spare my reproaches, mean you? Alas! you need not fear them. Am I not devoted to you? Is it not for your sake that I have thus passed the boundaries of my sex? Are you disgusted with my boldness? But no: you will surely forgive me, for my only motive has been to save you, and my only hope of happiness is bound up in yours."

"Rosabella!" repeated Edmund, "I believe that you love me."

"Love you! Oh heavens! can you doubt my love?"

"I do not doubt it, and this last action proves it more than words. I have long done you injustice; can you forgive me, Rosabella?"

"Oh Edmund!" exclaimed the princess, whilst her full heart heaved almost to bursting and the tears streamed down her face.

"I have been the victim of infatuation," continued Edmund; "I have loved a false, ungrateful woman, who has betrayed me. But I see my folly; and if tears of penitence shed at your feet can earn my pardon—if you will accept a broken, bleeding heart—"

"Oh Edmund!" interrupted Rosabella, throwing herself into his arms, "say no more—I am yours—yours for ever—your devoted slave—"

"Not my slave, Rosabella," said Edmund, gently disengaging her from him, and placing her upon a chair, "but my wife, my beloved wife."

"Your wife!" exclaimed Rosabella, Edmund's wife! am I indeed so blest? Oh no! surely it is a dream, a fond delusive dream! You cannot surely be serious."

"Is this a moment for jest?" asked Edmund calmly.

"It certainly is not," said Father Morris, whose agitation had been nearly equal to their own, and who had stood gazing upon them with looks of the fondest affection. "We must immediately escape, or it will be too late; it wants but two hours of daybreak, and, with the dawn, Lord Edmund's trial will commence."

"True, true!" cried Rosabella, "I had forgotten. Dearest Edmund, you must condescend to fly, or your precious life will be sacrificed."

"But how shall I escape?"

"Through this panel. A balloon waits at a little distance, and this cloak will conceal your person from observation."

"Dear Rosabella!"

"Come, come," cried Father Morris, we have no time to lose. Though Ferdinand was acquitted you must fall, for the state requires a victim."

Lord Edmund waited for no more; the name of Ferdinand was torture to him; and, hastily disencumbering himself of his chains, he followed the father and Rosabella from the prison. He sighed, however, and looked back for a moment with regret ere he quitted the outer walls, for he thought of Elvira. Rosabella's quick ear caught the sigh and her subtle spirit divined its meaning; but this was not a moment to complain, and stepping into their balloon they were soon out of sight of London. They proceeded to a palace of Rosabella's, a few miles out of town, and there, the following day, Edmund became her husband.

In the mean time, the excessive agitation Elvira experienced on the day of Prince Ferdinand's trial brought on a return of her fever, and it was several weeks ere she was sufficiently recovered to leave her bed. When she did so, however, she was really shocked at the state in which she found her kingdom. When she first began to reign, carried away by the enthusiasm of the moment, she had taken too much of the executive part of the government upon herself; and as her illness had been too sudden to allow her to appoint a regency, no one knew who ought to supply her place. All therefore was confusion and disorder, and Elvira shrunk disgusted from the chaos before her. She had now no Edmund to smooth the way for her, and the native energy of her mind was gone. Pale, heart-broken, and dispirited, she felt languid and incapable of the slightest exertion. What had formerly been a pleasure, was now become an overwhelming burthen, and the weight of life seemed insupportable.

She was now weary also of the fatigue necessary to carry on the plans she had projected for the benefit of her people. At first, when all seemed new and delightful, she had devoted herself entirely to their interests: she had denied herself even the most trifling pleasures, and scarcely allowed herself the time absolutely necessary for food and rest. This was all very well, whilst her plans had the charm of novelty, and were supported by passion. But now that novelty had worn off, and they had assumed the dull wearisome appearance of duties—when repeated disappointments had extinguished almost the hope of success, and when she found her people expected, nay, demanded as a right, that which she had originally granted them only as an especial mark of favour, she discovered, though too late, the folly of the toil she had imposed upon herself.

She now also discovered that improvement to be effectual must be slow: that people don't like to be forced out of old habits, till they have seen the effect of new ones proved by experience, and that nothing is so difficult as to improve people against their wills. Increase the resources of a country, throw money into the hands of the middling and lower classes, and they will improve themselves; but, at least, nine-tenths of a population will never suffer themselves to be improved. Those only who have attempted this thankless and painful office can fully estimate the sufferings of the unfortunate Elvira, who, disappointed in all she undertook, found life become tasteless and insipid, and was completely wretched,—though surrounded by all the gifts of beauty, power, and fortune.

Every thing seemed to conspire to increase her misery. Those whom she raised from indigence to affluence treated her with the most provoking insolence and discontent. A plan which had been opposed by the lords Gustavus de Montfort and Maysworth, and which she had persisted in having tried, had completely failed, and the noble Lords had triumphed in the most provoking manner in her disappointment. In short, every thing went wrong; and Elvira, disgusted with the world, felt mortified and disgusted with herself.

"How hard it is," thought she, frequently, as she tossed upon her sleepless couch, "that I who, since my accession to the throne, have devoted myself entirely to the interests of my subjects, should be thus wretched; whilst tyrants, who live but to oppress, sleep quietly upon their beds of down. Alas! why cannot I be as they are? Why cannot I divest myself of reflection, and enjoy the pleasures that surround me? But what pleasures can I enjoy? alas! the world presents nothing that can interest me; an insipid vacuum spreads through creation; my heart is cold and desolate; my affections are thrown back upon myself, and I am miserable."

Thus raved Elvira, and, absorbed in painful meditations, she neglected the duties of her station, and resigned herself to despair, whilst the people, attributing her evident wretchedness to her grief for the absence of Prince Ferdinand, who had left London immediately after his trial, and had not since been heard of, became every hour more and more discontented with their Queen.

In the mean time, the marriage of Lord Edmund, though not openly avowed, was generally suspected; and the party of Rosabella gained strength every day, whilst mysterious rumours were whispered from mouth to mouth, and divers hints given that many knew more than they chose to say; though from the immense number of these mystery-mongers it seemed, as in the celebrated scene in the Barber of Seville,[291] that every one was in the secret, though nobody was to divulge it. The listlessness of Elvira soon produced the most serious effects. A kingdom without a government, or rather a government without a chief, cannot long go on well. It is like a ship at sea without a pilot, and it must founder upon the first rock that impedes its course.

When the vigour of government is from any cause relaxed, there are always plenty of persons ready to take advantage of the opportunity afforded them to commit evil with impunity; and crimes of every description multiplied so fast under the negligent sway of Elvira, that the people became clamorous in their complaints. But to whom could they address themselves? The Queen was rarely visible—Lord Edmund was gone, and the lords of the council were too busy *talking* about the interests of the people to think of *really attending* to them; whilst the duke and Sir Ambrose seemed too old to be likely to trouble themselves by intermeddling with an affair of state. To them, however, the people looked as a dernier resort; and as it seemed indelicate to apply to the duke when the person they complained of was his own daughter, they entreated Sir Ambrose to present a petition to the Queen in their behalf.

The worthy baronet acceded to their request, and though almost bent to the earth by age and misery, prepared once more to appear at court. The loss of his beloved Edmund had affected the old man deeply: he considered his flight before trial as a confession of guilt, and the thought of disgrace weighed down his grey hairs with sorrow to the grave. The distress of the people, however, roused him from the apathy into which he was fast falling; and when he waited upon the Queen, it was with all the energy of his former years.

The Queen received him sullenly. "I cannot help it Sir Ambrose," said she; "I am sorry for my people, but I cannot do any thing to relieve them. I feel that I am fast sinking into the tomb; do not then disturb my last moments by fruitless solicitations."

"Last moments!" cried Sir Ambrose, indignantly; "rally your energies, and you may live half a century. You give way to a morbid sensibility that oppresses you; and, because some of your hopes have been disappointed, you shrink from the duties that you have imposed upon yourself, and talk of your last moments. Shame! shame! Elvira! rouse yourself from this lethargy, and be indeed a Queen. Remember, that though Nature has ordinarily denied your sex the power of triumphing in the field, she has yet left a far greater conquest for you to achieve—the conquest of yourself; for it is far more glorious to subdue the wayward desires of the human heart, than to lead scores of monarchs captives in your chains. Struggle then with your feelings: conquer those fatal passions that threaten to destroy you; show yourself worthy of your crown, and be again the Elvira for whom even in her childhood, I anticipated greatness."

"It is too late," interrupted the Queen impatiently—"it is now too late. Urge me no more, Sir Ambrose, or you will drive me to despair."

Sir Ambrose was provoked at her obstinacy, and a pause ensued, which was broken by a tumultuous noise and shouting. It was the people at the gates of the palace, who, impatient at the length of Sir Ambrose's stay, were now becoming clamorous for an answer.

"What shall I say to them?" asked the baronet.

"Tell them I deny their suit!" replied the Queen. "Away, away, away! I would be quiet; go without reply; I will hear no more; I will not be tormented:" and waving her hand for him to depart, she hurried to her chamber. Finding there was no alternative, Sir Ambrose was compelled to appear before the people and acquaint them with the will of their Sovereign. The tumult became more violent as he spoke. An English mob is proverbially impetuous; and now their rage rose beyond control. "The Queen! the Queen!" they shouted; "we will see the Queen!" The crowd increased every moment—the multitude heaved in tremendous waves like the rolling billows of the sea, and the hum of thousands of human voices filled the air. They threatened to storm the palace. A man in complete armour, his face entirely concealed by his vizor, headed their attempts; the outer gates were forced, and the throng rushed tumultuously into the court of the palace.

All there was confusion: soldiers might have been summoned, and the place defended; but there was no one to give orders; and the servants ran to and fro in the greatest possible distress, without knowing either where they were going, or what they intended doing. In the midst of this bustle, Elvira sate burying her face in her hands, and obstinately refusing to take the slightest interest in the scene. The door opened violently, and Sir Ambrose and some of her principal servants rushed in. "For God's sake, save yourself!" cried they. "If your Majesty were safe, we care not for ourselves."

"Fly!" cried Sir Ambrose, throwing himself upon his knees before her, his white hair streaming almost to the ground; "for God's sake, fly!" It was too late, however, then, had the Queen been disposed to obey him; for, as he spoke, the outer door burst open with tremendous violence; the palace seemed to shake to its foundation with the shock; and in an instant the chamber was filled by the infuriated populace.

"Seize the Queen, but do not injure her!" cried a voice that thrilled through every nerve of Sir Ambrose. "Spare the old man; do not hurt a hair of his head." Sir Ambrose looked up; the voice came from the man in armour; but it was the voice of Edmund. A crowd of overwhelming thoughts rushed through his mind, and, overpowered by their weight, he sank senseless upon the ground. "Take him away!" cried Edmund; (for it was indeed he;) "take him away! but see that ye hurt him not: he dies that injures him."

"Edmund!" cried Elvira, struck also by his voice—

"To prison with her!" exclaimed he.

"To prison, Edmund! do you doom your Queen to prison? Is it thus you treat your Sovereign?"

"I own no Sovereign here but Rosabella."

"But, by what right can she be called your Sovereign?"

"By that which made you Queen. The people's voice. It lies with them to crown or to dethrone!"

"Oh Edmund! mercy!"

"Away with her! I'll hear no more."

The guards seized upon the unfortunate Queen, and, in spite of her entreaties, hurried her away. Edmund did not trust himself to look at her. For a moment he hid his face in his hands; then rousing himself, he exclaimed, "Now to proclaim the Queen!" The people followed him with shouts of applause, and before evening Edmund and Rosabella were unanimously acknowledged as King and Queen of England.

Volume 3: Chapter 6

Notwithstanding the able manner in which the revolution had been effected, England was still in a state of tumult. Though the army had been seduced by the example of Edmund, and the people had been obliged to submit, they were by no means perfectly satisfied with their new government; and

Rosabella found, too late, that though the throne might be compared to a bed of roses, it was not without its thorns. The discontented nobles who had aided her cause were also extremely displeased by what they called the trifling value of the rewards bestowed upon them; though, in fact, they rated their services so high, that Rosabella found her whole kingdom did not possess the power of repaying them to their satisfaction.

It was also a considerable grievance of these haughty nobles, to see Prince Ferdinand return to the English Court immediately after the dethronement of Elvira, and be received with open arms by Rosabella, who, with the anxiety to conciliate the friendship of foreign powers, usually displayed by those whose thrones feel far from secure at home, loaded him with favours, and even gave him a post of honour in the command of her own body-guard.

Whilst the unreasonableness of her people thus embittered Rosabella's political life, her domestic happiness seemed to rest upon a yet more unstable foundation. She knew that though she possessed Edmund's hand, his heart was still devoted to Elvira; and jealousy made her view all his actions in a distorted light. If he were sad, she was sure he was thinking of her rival; and if gay, she fancied it a masque put on only to deceive her. She was thus completely miserable, and Edmund was as wretched as herself. He felt that he had sacrificed himself to revenge, and sold his peace for a bauble, which, when obtained, did not seem worth the trouble of possessing. His father too—Sir Ambrose, his doating[292] father, was now entirely estranged from him, as he repeatedly declared he would never forgive a traitor, who could forget his oath of allegiance for his own aggrandizement.

"No!" exclaimed the old man, "I loved, I doted upon Edmund; but the Edmund I loved is vanished. My darling son was brave and noble, not a deceptive scoundrel. No, no, my old heart may break:—nay, I hope it will—but never whilst I live shall a deceitful traitor be pressed against this breast."

Edmund was inconsolable; he passionately loved his father, and could not bear his anger; besides, he felt that the reproaches of the old man were seconded by those of his own heart. It is painful at any time to bear the censures of the world, but they fall with double weight when we know that they are deserved. Edmund was dissatisfied with himself, and, consequently, disposed to quarrel with the world. He fancied it looked coldly upon him, and, in return, he affected to despise it. A hundred times a day he repeated that he was perfectly indifferent to every thing that was said of him; whilst his nervous anxiety to peruse the newspapers, and make himself perfectly acquainted with every popular rumour, proved that he was only too sensible to every word that was uttered. Edmund had made the mob his idol, he could not live without its applauses, and wretched indeed are those who thus depend on others for their hopes of happiness.

Edmund's disgust at his new rank and situation was soon still farther increased by a visit from Lord Gustavus, who, with several other lords, was deputed to present to his Majesty the complaints of the Commons. They wanted to be enfranchised, they desired innumerable rights and privileges, and in fact they wanted to be all kings; for if half that they demanded had been granted, Edmund must have made them more powerful than himself. He pointed this out to Lord Gustavus, and condescended to reason with him upon the folly of their desires.

"Impossible!" cried Lord Gustavus. "Your Majesty must excuse me but I cannot listen to such arguments; I came here to defend the liberties of the people. Reform is necessary—without reform, nothing can go on well. Evils must be, torn up root and branch."

"Are not my subjects healthy, wealthy, and prosperous?" asked Edmund. "Have they not been successful at home and abroad? Do not the English peasants live as well as most foreign princes, and what more can they require?"

"Liberty, Sire," returned Lord Gustavus. "What are all these pretended advantages without liberty? mere toys; gaudy apples, but rotten at the core. Of what use, indeed, are all the blessings of life, without liberty to give them zest, and radical reform to purge them of all impurities?"

"But listen to reason."

"Reason! Thinking as I think, and as I ani sure every rational being must think, your Majesty must forgive me if I assert, that even Reason herself does not deserve to be attended to, when she is basely enlisted upon the side of Tyranny."

"Nay, then," said Edmund, "it is useless to attempt to argue with you. I thought you had made Reason your goddess; but if you worship her only as long as it suits your own purposes, I have done. You may retire. I shall take the petition into consideration, and give it an answer when I may think fit."

Edmund, who, from being degraded and debased in his own opinion, no longer possessed that confidence in himself that carried conviction with all he said, had yet sufficient dignity in his manner to awe those to silence who dared to dispute his commands; and Lord Gustavus and his colleagues, not presuming to make farther remonstrance, retired in dudgeon. This incident contributed to sicken Edmund of reigning: he became disgusted with his Queen, his court, his kingdom, and his country, and, secluding himself as much as possible from public life, left the care of managing the affairs of state to Rosabella and Father Morris, who now throwing off the disguise he so long had worn, appeared openly as the dispenser of her favours, and the arbiter of her actions.

The spirit of poor Sir Ambrose was quite broken by these misfortunes. The defection of his son, and the ingratitude of his confessor, stung him to the core. He retired again to the country, where with his friend the duke, Clara, and Father Murphy, he contrived to exist, though but the shadow of his former self. The duke was also grievously changed, and it was melancholy to see these two poor old men wandering about their splendid gardens and magnificent palaces like roaming ghosts, permitted to revisit for a time the scenes of their departed happiness. Clara now became the sole stay that bound these old men to life. Her character had developed itself wonderfully in the midst of the striking events she had witnessed. Firm, courageous, and enterprizing, though still gentle——the lively girl seemed changed into the intelligent woman,[293] whose active mind and comprehensive spirit foresaw every thing and provided against every emergency. Clara was still young; but her spirit was mature beyond her years, and her attention to the duke and Sir Ambrose was unremitting.

"Well!" would they often say, "though we have lost much, we ought still to be thankful that Clara is spared to us:" and then with tears trickling down their aged cheeks, they would join in imploring Heaven to shower down blessings upon her head. In the mean time, however, Clara herself was far from happy. She would, it is true, exert herself to appear cheerful, but it was evident it was an exertion; and often, when the duke and Sir Ambrose had seated themselves at a party at chess, she would steal out unobserved and retire to a little pavilion in the garden, near what were formerly the apartments of Father Morris, as being the most secluded spot she could find; this part of the mansion having been carefully shut up and avoided by every human being, since the departure of the priest, as infectious; the indignation the worthy and attached servants of Sir Ambrose felt towards Father Morris for his desertion of their master, being extended even to the rooms he had occupied.

In this secluded spot Clara often sate for hours, lost in meditation, her head resting upon her hand, and her eyes fixed in vacancy. Winter had now given place to spring, and all nature seemed to revive with that gay and joyous season. The heart of Clara, however, was still lonely; she fancied it could enjoy no second summer; and she felt almost disposed to quarrel with all around her for displaying a gaiety in which she could not participate. Nothing makes a broken heart feel more gloomy than to see all other objects look gay. It turns from them in disgust, and feels its own misery doubled by the sight of their happiness.

One evening as Clara was sitting absorbed in melancholy reflections, she was startled by hearing a deep-drawn sigh heaved heavily behind her. She turned, and fancied she could distinguish a figure in the midst of the twilight;—but, magnified by the obscurity, the figure seemed of gigantic proportions. Uttering a faint scream, she attempted to fly—when a hand of iron grasped her arm, and arrested her progress. An icy chill shot to her heart, whilst the well-remembered voice of Cheops sounded in her ears.

"Clara," said he, in his deep sepulchral tone, "would you save your Queen?"

"With the sacrifice of my life, if necessary," replied Clara firmly.

"Clara," continued the Mummy, "I have marked you attentively,—and as I do not know any individual possessing more strength of mind and personal courage than yourself, I have fixed upon you to be my assistant in this enterprize. The life of Elvira is in danger; and even my influence cannot much longer save her, if she remain in the power of Father Morris. Besides, the lesson she has already had, has been sufficiently severe. I will aid her to escape, and you must assist me. You shall go to Ireland; and there, if the warlike Roderick be not deaf to the cry of beauty in distress, through his aid Elvira may hope redress,—at least, she must implore his help.—Rosabella is now at a palace near this, and she has brought her rival in her train; for, with the usual jealousy and suspicion of tyrants and usurpers, she scarcely dares to trust her from her sight. Besides this, her diabolical revenge is gratified in making Elvira wait humbly near her throne, and serve in those palaces where she once commanded. Moved by this ungenerous conduct, and the patience with which the unhappy Elvira bears her sufferings, the nobles and people of the realm begin to pity her: and when they are disgusted with the haughtiness and intolerance of Rosabella, they sigh for the return of the gentle Elvira. Father Morris perceives this, and determining to rid Rosabella of her rival, the fair Elvira fades beneath his arts, like a flower withering on its stem."

"She must be saved!" said Clara, with enthusiasm; "she *shall* be saved!—Point but out the means, and I am devoted to her service."

"You must assume these weeds,[294] and follow me," said Cheops, pointing to a bundle in a corner of the pavilion, which Clara had not before noticed. "In half an hour I will return for you."

"And my sudden disappearance," rejoined Clara, "will it not excite suspicion?"

"The river is deep and rapid," returned Cheops; "some of your clothes left upon its banks—"

"I comprehend," cried Clara eagerly; "but the poor old duke, and Sir Ambrose?"—

"Their anxiety and distress may be great, but cannot be lasting: the feelings of age are blunt, and—"

"Oh, no!" exclaimed Clara, "you are deceived;—nay, I think that age feels grief more acutely than youth. The mind has lost its elasticity—hope is dead within it, and the old brood over their secret sorrow till they destroy their—"

"By Osiris! thou art a most extraordinary girl," said Cheops; "the old do brood over grief, but why say this to me? Do I not know it well—too well?" continued he, looking at her earnestly. Clara turned pale, and trembled—he saw her agitation; and, hastily averting his eyes, continued in a calmer tone,—"Whatever the sufferings of the old men may be for the moment, I suppose even you will allow the life of Elvira more than counterbalances them;—and, by inflicting this temporary pain, you will save them from the more lasting agony they would endure from her death: for Father Morris is so subtle, that it would be dangerous to give them the slightest hint of our intention, lest he should worm it from them. Be ready then, Clara; resign thyself to my instructions, and, above all, fear not."

Clara bent her head in token of assent, and Cheops disappeared. Upon examining the clothes, Clara found them to be the dress of a Greek peasant boy, numbers of whom at this period were rambling over England singing wild romances to their harps or lutes, and telling fortunes in a kind of doggrel[295] rhyme. Exposure to the air tanned most of these wandering minstrels brown, and Clara found a bottle of liquid in the parcel to stain her face and hands. She bound up her flaxen ringlets, and, covering her head with curls of a jetty blackness, she found the metamorphosis so complete that she scarcely knew herself as she saw her figure reflected in a large mirror behind her. It was now nearly dark, but Cheops had left the necessary implements for striking a light, and Clara made her toilette without the least difficulty.

Anxious were the moments, however, that passed after her task was completed, till the arrival of Cheops; and when he did come, she saw he was attired as herself. He grasped her arm, and without speaking led her to the banks of the river. Clara shuddered as she found herself alone in the power of this mysterious being, and saw the river roll deep and dark beneath her feet. Cheops felt her shudder, and cried with one of his horrid laughs, which sounded fearfully amidst the stillness of the night, "What! do even *you* fear me? Is there *no* courage in this degenerate race? None? What do you fear? If you dread to trust yourself in my power, or think yourself unequal to the task you have undertaken, retire: there is yet time, and I wish no unwilling agents. Poor child!" continued he, looking at her with feeling; "thou dost not know me, but for worlds I would not harm thee!"

"I will go with you," said Clara resolutely; "I do not shrink. Let what will await me, I will not recede: though unheard-of torments may attend me, I will endure them."

"By the Holy Gods of my forefathers," cried Cheops, "she is a brave girl! Yes, Clara, I will trust thee; and though we should encounter horrors fearful as those which menace the initiati in the dread Isian mysteries, I will not doubt thy courage. A determined spirit, Clara, may subdue even Fate."

As he spoke, he threw the clothes she had brought for the purpose carelessly upon the banks of the river; and then again seizing her arm, he dragged her forward with such rapidity, that in an incredibly short time they approached the palace of Rosabella. The mansion looked the region of enchantment. Brilliantly illuminated, light streamed from every window; and through the colonnade of the great hall, groups of elegantly dressed people were seen gaily moving to and fro, some dancing, and others listening to harmonious music.

Clara, though terrified and exhausted, felt still irresistibly impelled to proceed, and, still guided by her strange companion, entered, unobserved, the outer court of the palace.

"Prince Ferdinand of Germany commands the guard to-night," whispered Cheops, in a low, unnatural voice; "it is well, he shall go with us."

"But will he?" asked Clara tremblingly.

"Will he?" returned Cheops, with his peculiar sneer: "dost thou doubt my power, girl?"

Clara and Cheops had now reached a place from whence, unobserved, they could survey the whole of the splendid apartment before them. They had, in fact, entered the hall, and placed themselves in a kind of recess shaded by projecting pillars, from whence they could see every part of the saloon. Clara was astonished to find herself so easily in the presence of the Queen, for she knew not how they had attained their present situation; and she would have spoken to ask Cheops, but he laid his finger upon his lips: and whispering—"Hippocrates was the only son of Isis and Osiris!"—she comprehended he meant that wisdom and Knowledge produced Silence, and she did not dare to breathe a syllable.

Rosabella sate upon a splendid dais, gorgeously attired; her black eyes flashing with added brilliancy from the deep rouge upon her cheeks; whilst her raven hair was adorned with diamonds, and a splendid tiara of the same precious stones sparkled on her forehead; a robe of crimson velvet, bordered with ermine, fell in graceful folds over her fine figure; whilst her swanlike neck and snowy arms, exposed perhaps more than delicacy might strictly warrant, were also loaded with costly jewels. Around her, stood the ladies of her court, and amongst the rest, Elvira, plainly attired in a robe of dark grey silk. No ornaments shone amongst her golden tresses, and her naturally fair complexion seemed faded to a sickly and unnatural whiteness.

The indignation of Clara could scarcely be restrained at this sight; but Cheops laying his hand upon her arm, they stood suddenly before the Queen.

"Ah! who are these?" cried Rosabella, starting. Cheops took no notice of her surprise; but, tuning his lute, began to sing a few doggrel verses in praise of her Majesty.

"What means this mummery?"[296] asked Rosabella; "how came these minstrels here?"

"It is doubtless a device of the King," returned some of her ladies, "to amuse your majesty."

Rosabella smiled; attentions were now so rare upon the part of Edmund towards her, that she felt gratified that it should even be supposed he wished to please her, and, addressing the minstrel more graciously, asked what brought him to England. He sung his reply and in the same doggrel rhyme asked the Queen to let him tell her fortune.

"What say you, ladies," said Rosabella, again smiling, "shall we hear our destiny?"

The ladies, delighted at any thing that promised an interruption to the general gloom which hung over Rosabella's court, gladly assented; and, to Clara's infinite surprise, the Mummy addressed a few doggrel verses to each whilst the voice in which he repeated this nonsense, was so different from his usual deep sepulchral tones, that Clara's wonder became mixed with fear, and she shuddered with horror as the conviction, that the being with whom she had associated herself was indeed a demon, flashed across her mind.

When Elvira's turn came, Clara perceived her colour was heightened, and that she trembled excessively, yet the Mummy's verses to her were as unmeaning as to the rest. Whilst this scene was passing, the King and Father Morris approached. The former stood silent and abstracted, apparently quite unconscious of the group before him; whilst Father Morris gazed at them intently, with a satirical sneer upon his countenance, as though in thorough contempt for such folly.

"How can you endure such mummery?" said he to Rosabella, after a short pause.

"Any thing for a change," said she, sighing. The father's dark eye glanced upon the King, and then upon Rosabella, as with a gloomy frown he stalked on. The Queen coloured, and hastily waving her hand to the minstrel, as a sign that he might depart, she turned away, and the disappointed ladies were reluctantly obliged to follow in her train. In a few minutes, however, a page returned with a chain and a purse of gold, which he gave the minstrels, and retired. Clara was upon the point of refusing her share of this bounty, but a look from the Mummy made her sensible of her error, and she took it without uttering a syllable. Her hesitation, however, did not pass unnoticed, and she found, to her infinite horror, when they quitted the palace, that two of the Queen's servants had followed them. Clara trembled excessively, and clung tightly to the Mummy's arm for protection; but that mysterious being still stalked on with the same indifference as before. Clara longed to give him some intimation of the danger that awaited him, but she could not speak; the words seemed to swell in her throat and almost choke her, whilst she found herself dragged along by an irresistible influence, too powerful to admit of her even struggling against it. Inexpressible agony, however, seized her as she found herself hurried on towards the river; and when, as they reached the brink, she beheld Cheops stamp, with almost supernatural force, upon the fragile bridge which stretched across the water, and saw the slender plank sink beneath his weight, she could bear no more, and, screaming with horror, rushed forwards to save him. A strong arm, however, pulled her back; she felt herself whirled round, and for the moment her senses seemed to desert her. The next instant she found she had been dragged under some bushes, and saw their pursuers rush down to the place where the broken bridge had been.

"They are gone, by Jupiter!" said one; "I heard them fall into the water. It was a tremendous crash."

"I heard them," returned the other; "they fell as heavy as lead; and how they screamed!"

"The young one screamed," said the first; "but the old one groaned."

"What does it matter," resumed the second, "whether they screamed or groaned? They are gone to the devil a little before their time, and so we have only to go hack as we came. Between ourselves, it was nonsense to take the trouble to watch them; They were evidently only what they seemed to be; and even Father Morris, suspicious as he is, gave us no orders about them."

"Thy dull head cannot see," said the first. "The father's negligence was the very motive of my vigilance. Things are not with him as they have been—he wants to rule the Queen with a rod of iron, and Rosabella will not endure control. Now, it struck me when I saw the youth's hesitation, that all was not right, and, I thought, if I could discover what had escaped him—"

"I see," said the other; "his lifeless trunk might have had the honour of serving as a stepping-stone to enable you to rise."

"It was possible," returned the other, laughing; and they retired, their voices gradually dying away till they became inaudible in the distance. Clara now perceived that the Mummy stood beside her. He did not speak, but pressed his finger upon his lips in token of silence, and for some minutes they stood fixed to the spot:—till, as the last faint echo of the servants' footsteps died away, he again seized the arm of Clara, and hurried her away towards a gloomy cave.

They stopped at the entrance; and though the poor girl was still too much terrified to speak, yet she felt somewhat relieved by the discovery that the Mummy had evidently saved her from danger, instead of, as she feared, precipitating her into it. She still gazed with awe, however, at his strange unearthly figure, as he stood with his eyes fixed earnestly upon a star, and apparently occupied in muttering prayers addressed to it.

"Clara!" at length said he, his deep, full voice echoing solemnly through the vaulted cave; "Clara!" again he repeated, whilst the blood of his terrified companion seemed to curdle in her veins at the awful sound. She, however, slowly and tremblingly advanced—he grasped her arm—she attempted to shrink back, but seemed fixed as though by magic;—"Hear me," continued the Mummy, in a low, hollow tone, which appeared to rise from the tomb, and contrasted fearfully with the lighter accents he had employed as a minstrel. "Elvira understood my signal, and she will soon be here; but you must do the rest. Prince Ferdinand keeps guard to-night. Pass through this cave; the outlet will bring you to his station. Throw yourself at his feet, and appeal to his compassion in whatever language the feelings of the moment may inspire. He will readily listen to you, for he has not forgotten your visit to him in prison, and will swear to devote himself to your service. Tell him you accept his offers, and entreat him to convey yourself and the Queen to Ireland—where Roderick will receive and protect you. He will immediately comply; and his being the companion of your flight, will induce the belief that you are gone to Germany, and will consequently prevent the least danger of pursuit."

At this moment a slight figure, wrapped in a large mantle, appeared at the entrance of the cavern. "Elvira!" cried Cheops, and the stranger sprang forward. "Then I am right," exclaimed she, whilst her whole frame trembled with agitation.

"This is your guide," said Cheops, in his deep sepulchral tone; "follow her and you will do well. Farewell! but we shall meet again." Then bending over her, he pressed his lips to her forehead, and to that of Clara.

Both shuddered at the touch of those cold marble lips, and an icy chill ran through their veins, as the fearful conviction that their companion was no earthly being thrilled in their bosoms. Even the strongest minds dread supernatural horrors, and our fair fugitives turned involuntarily away. When they looked again, the Mummy was gone, and the darkness appeared so profound that they were obliged to grope their way cautiously along. Fearing alike to remain or to advance, they proceeded with trembling steps slowly along a narrow passage; their minds filled with that vague sense of danger that generally attends the want of light, when Imagination pictures terrors which do not really exist, and Fancy lends her aid to magnify those which do.

By degrees, however, the Queen and her companion became accustomed to the darkness; and as the pupils of their eyes dilated, they were enabled to discern the objects around them. Innumerable fantastic shapes, however, now appeared to flit before them, and grim giants to frown awfully from every corner of the gloomy vault they were traversing. The dim and indistinct light threw a misty veil round the projecting corners of the rocks that gave them a fearful and unnatural grandeur; whilst the fair friends, overpowered with terror, gazed timidly around, and stood a few moments not daring to advance into the darker abysses of the caverns, and yet dreading alike to remain where they were, or to return.

"We must go on," said Elvira at length, her voice echoing through the cave, till she started at the sound.

"Oh God!" cried Clara; "hark! a thousand mocking demons seem to repeat from every rock 'Go on!'"

"Go on!" again rang in a thousand varied tones through the cavern.

"Let us proceed," whispered Elvira, shuddering; "this is a fearful place!"

And they hurried on as fast as their trembling limbs could carry them, along a dark and gloomy passage, leading in the direction pointed out by the Mummy. In a few minutes, however, a bright though glimmering light appeared afar off, like a star, which, gleaming through the darkness, seemed a beacon of hope to guide them on to happiness. A slight current of air, too, now blew freshly in their faces, and their spirits rose, as with quickened steps they hastened onward in the direction from whence it appeared to proceed.

The light now seemed rapidly to enlarge, and the wind blew more freshly, whilst the Queen and her companion distinctly heard the heavy stamping of horses, which vibrated fearfully on the hollow ground, and grew louder and louder every moment as they advanced.

"Ah! what is that?" cried Elvira trembling, clinging closer to her companion.

"It is the bivouack[297] of Prince Ferdinand," replied Clara; "the Mummy told me we should find him here, and that he would aid us."

"Ah, that fearful Mummy," murmured Elvira softly; "if he should deceive us, and this should be only a plan to betray us to our enemies?"

"Fear not," said Clara; "come what may, we must dare the worst."

They had now reached the outlet of the cavern, and found an opening large enough to admit of a single person. Cautiously advancing towards it, they paused for a few moments ere they descended, to gaze upon the scene below. A troop of soldiers were scattered round, in various attitudes of repose, under a small grove of trees, whilst their horses grazed at a little distance. The prince alone seemed awake, and he lay apart from his companions, stretched upon a grassy bank, a thick tree spreading above him, his head resting upon his hand, and his eyes fixed upon the ground. The moon shone brightly, and played upon the Prince's polished armour, like summer lightning dancing on a lake. His helmet was thrown aside, and his countenance looked pale and sad, whilst his frequent sighs betrayed the uneasiness of his mind.

"Let us advance," said Clara, "and try to move him to compassion."

Elvira complied; and with light and timid steps, fearing almost to breathe, lest they should break the slumbers of their enemies, they approached the prince. All was still, save the hard breathing of the sleeping soldiers, and the measured champing of the horses; their stately figures strongly relieved by the dark grey sky beyond, and their long manes and tails sweeping the ground. The prince was now listlessly tracing figures in the grass with the scabbard of his sword: he started as they approached, and hastily demanded the cause of their intrusion.

"Mercy!" cried Elvira, sinking upon her knees before him; "mercy!" She could say no more, but gasping for breath, she stretched out her arms imploringly, whilst every thing around seemed to swim before her eyes, and the figures of the prince, the trees, the horses, and the sleeping soldiers, appeared all dilated to gigantic magnitude. She entirely forgot the pathetic appeal she had intended making to the prince's feelings, and every faculty seemed suspended in the intenseness of her anxiety.

"For Heaven's sake, good youth," exclaimed the prince, addressing Clara, "explain the meaning of this scene! Why does this lovely female kneel to me, and why does she implore my mercy?"

"Because she has no other hope, save in that and Heaven," said Clara solemnly; "it is the Queen."

"Elvira!" cried the prince: then raising her eagerly, he continued—"Your Majesty may command my services; only tell me how I can assist you."

A few words from Clara explained the urgency of their situation; and the prince, promising to meet them with horses in an hour, persuaded them to return to the cavern till he should join them. Heavily rolled the minutes of this tedious hour, which seemed destined never to have an end, till the nerves of Elvira and Clara were wrought up to such a pitch of agony, that death would have appeared a blessing. At length, the prince came, bringing with him only his faithful Hans.

The sight of him was sufficient to rouse the almost fainting spirits of the Queen; and, without speaking a single word, she and Clara hurried after their conductors, to the wood where the horses were waiting for them.

They mounted, still in perfect silence, and hurried through the most intricate paths they could find; for, as morning dawned, they feared inevitable destruction. Before it became quite light, however, they had reached a thick wood, near the centre of which, they found a half ruined hut; and here did the ci-devant[298] Queen of England and her suite try to obtain a few hours' repose. But, alas! sleep fled from Elvira's eyes; she could not forget she was a fugitive in her own kingdom, flying with terror from those very people who, but a few months before, had almost worshipped her as a goddess; and not even the exhaustion of her body could overcome the hurry of her spirits, whilst every time she closed her eyes, and felt a soft dose creeping over her troubled senses, she started up again in horror, fancying her pursuers had overtaken her.

Consternation reigned in the palace when the flight of Elvira, and the defection of Prince Ferdinand were made known there. "She is gone to Germany!" was the universal cry, and troops were directly dispatched to all the sea-ports, whilst a whole fleet of balloons were ordered to scour the air in all directions, and arrest every aerial vehicle they should meet with, whose passengers could not give a perfectly satisfactory account of themselves. These commissions were executed to the letter, as the guards now sought by extra diligence to excuse the negligence with which they had suffered the Queen to escape; and numerous were the wandering lovers, absconding clerks, and unfaithful wives, who were brought before the Council instead of Elvira and the German Prince, of whom, however, nothing could be heard, their measures having been taken too well to expose them to detection.

In the mean time, the hat and mantle of Clara having been found upon the banks of the river, the duke and Sir Ambrose were inconsolable; and dispatched emissaries every where in search of her. Amongst the rest, Father Murphy and Abelard were sent to the summer palace of the Queen, to inquire if she had there been heard of. Rosabella and her Court, however, had removed to London immediately upon the flight of Elvira being discovered, and the disconsolate searchers having inquired of every one they met in vain, wandered through the gardens, restless and forlorn, till at last they found the mysterious cavern. The aspect of the place was dreary in the extreme: a few stunted shrubs grew upon the banks of a dark, dull rivulet, and Father Murphy shivered and crossed himself as he looked around.

"Och, murther! and this is an awful place, Mr. Abelard," said he; "and I'm after thinking the sooner we get out of it the better."

"Ah, what is that?" cried the butler, springing forward eagerly, and snatching at something in the bushes that looked white.

"It is Clara's pocket-handkerchief, poor darling!" said the friar; "see, here is her name worked upon it by her own pretty fingers:" and as he turned to examine it, his foot slipped, and he rolled into the water, floundering about like a huge porpoise.

Oh dear! oh dear!" cried Abelard, "he will certainly be drowned. Submersion in an aqueous fluid is almost always destructive of animal life, and I see little chance that he has of escape."

"Och! and will ye let me drown while ye're talking?" asked the indignant priest. "Before it's the good-natured thing ye'd be doing in pulling me out, will ye let me be suffocated?"

"No, no, certainly not!" returned Abelard; "my agony is unspeakable at your distress. I only doubt how I shall be able to raise you without a lever or pully. The application of the mechanical powers—"

"May go to the devil," cried Father Murphy, as he crawled out without assistance: "and so you would have let me drown, whilst you were talking of the mechanical powers?"

"Excuse me, father," returned Abelard; "friendship is a powerful affection of the human mind; it invigorates, it warms." "Does it," said the priest, shaking himself like a water-spaniel; "then I should be very glad to have a little of it at present, for I am shivering with cold.

"I am surprised to hear you talk of cold, father," said Abelard. "You are, surely, too fat to feel cold; for animal oil is universally allowed to be a bad conductor of caloric."

Father Murphy did not speak, but his look was sufficient, and his teeth clattering in his head afforded an ample commentary upon the text.

"It is strange," continued the butler, "that fat people generally seem ashamed of their obesity; for they have many advantages which lean people never can enjoy. For instance, they ought never to feel any violent craving for food. Fat serving as an interdium,[299] through which the nutritive-matter extracted from food passes, before it is assimilated to repair the loss of the individual, ought to serve as a magazine to supply his wants; and a fat man should be able to abstain from food much longer than another; because, during his abstinence, the collected fat must be rapidly re-absorbed."

"Oh!" groaned Father Murphy, "would to Heaven I had a broiled rump steak at this moment, smoking hot, and swimming in gravy; and a fine frothing pot of porther!"

"A rump steak is no bad thing," resumed Abelard, his mouth watering at the bare mention of the savory viand; "and I do not wish it to be understood, by any means, that a man can live without eating. On the contrary, the indivisibility and individuality of the living body, can only be maintained by an incessant change of the particles which enter into its composition; part of the animal food being reduced into chyle, and part becoming bones; which are, in fact, only secretory organs, incrusted with phospate[300] of lime. The lymphatic vessels remove this salt, and—"

"Och! and it's Clara you are forgetting all this while," interrupted Father Murphy. "The purty creature —sure, and it's her manthle after all, so it is; and here we are talking of stuff and nonsense; and quite forgetting she's drowned, and kilt all over, pure soul!"

"Alas! alas!" returned Abelard, "I have not forgotten her; and I assure you, I feel my lachrymal gland suffused almost to overflowing, whenever a thought of what may be her fate shoots across my pia mater."

The despair of the duke and Sir Ambrose, when they saw their emissaries return with the clothes of Clara, may be easily imagined; and when they heard of the flight of Elvira, and the threats which Father Morris now openly indulged in, that the ex-Queen should be publickly[301] executed if found, for having endeavoured to raise an insurrection, the climax of their misery seemed full.

In the mean time the party of Elvira did not dare to leave the hut in which they had remained pent up the whole day; their horses being crowded within its walls, as well as themselves, to prevent the possibility of discovery. At length, the shades of evening began to fall, and they again set forward at a rapid pace: though the agony they had suffered all day from fear of detection—the narrow space in which they had been cooped up, together with want of food, had exhausted the Queen so much that the morning found her unable to proceed without refreshment, and about day—break they were obliged to approach a cottage to implore assistance.

The cottager and his son were out at work; but the woman of the house agreed to give the fugitives the shelter they requested. The prince, delighted at receiving this permission, flew back to the Queen to lift her from her horse; but, alas! Elvira was not in a state to enjoy even the most welcome tidings. Pale and livid as a corpse, her head hung upon the prince's shoulder as he bore her into the house, and her terrified friends thought she had expired. A little warm milk, however, revived her, and she opened her eyes.

"I am ready—quite ready—to go on," said she gasping for utterance, and again sinking back in a fainting fit.

"It is impossible she can proceed in this state," said the prince to Clara, in a whisper; "what will become of us?"

"We must remain here quietly, till she is better," said Clara.

"But if we should be pursued and taken?"

"We cannot die better than in such a cause," said the heroic girl.

"It is strange," said the prince, looking at her earnestly, "that the Queen has been able to inspire such enthusiastic devotion in such a mere boy."

Clara blushed, and cast her eyes upon the ground, whilst the prince gazed upon her blushing cheeks still more earnestly, till she turned away from him abashed. He took her hand; "I cannot be mistaken," said he, "it is, it is, Miss Montague!"

Clara's agitation betrayed her. "I must attend the Queen," said she, breaking from him; and the prince, respecting the awkwardness of her situation, forbore to urge her farther: he felt, however, completely happy. Clara was too artless to conceal the interest he had excited in her breast, and it was not in the nature of man to be indifferent to the devotion of so young and lovely a creature. His eyes, however, alone expressed his happiness; and Clara, who felt his delicacy in refraining from making any farther observations on her disguise, found her love for him increased tenfold by his forbearance.

A few hours' repose restored Elvira so much, that she wished to pursue her journey immediately, and it was with the greatest difficulty that the prince persuaded her to wait till nightfall. "You must recruit your strength," said he, "or you will never be able to plead your cause with Roderick. He is too stern a hero to be won as I was."

"Oh, it is impossible to describe how I dread to meet him," cried Elvira; "I tremble at his name. A being so fierce and stern as he is, will perhaps not even condescend to listen to a woman's prayer, and he will spurn me from him."

"Impossible!" cried the prince; "though, I own, I wish we could do without him."

Whilst the principals were thus employed, the cottager's wife was endeavouring to learn from Hans who and what they were. "That poor lady seemed dreadfully tired," said she. "When she came, she looked just like a drooping daffadowndilly;[302] when the gentleman lifted her from her horse—oh! it was quite moving to see her!"

"Ja!" said Hans.

"However, though her illness should occasion a little delay," continued the cottager; "I opine that you must be unreasonable to grumble, when you consider the delightful occasion it affords you of refreshing your olfactory nerves by partaking of a little of this odoriferous atmosphere."

"My what nerves?" asked Hans.[303]

"Your olfactory nerves," replied the learned cottager, with a look of the greatest possible contempt: "that is, the nerves that line the membrane of the nasal organ. Every child knows that the nasal fossae are formed to receive sensations, as by their depth and extent a larger surface is given to the pituitary membrane, and these soft sinuses, or cavities, are enabled to retain a greater mass of air loaded with odoriferous matter."

Poor Hans stood aghast at this explanation, which he found something like that said to be given by Dr. Johnson, when he called net-work a complicated concatenation of rectangular angles;[304] and afraid to speak, lest he should draw upon himself a new volley of words as astounding as the last, he remained silent, staring at his companions with much the same, kind of feeling as that with which a wild man of the woods just caught, might be supposed to gaze upon enlightened Europeans.

"Can you give me some more warm milk?" asked Clara, who now descended in search of refreshments for the Queen.

"Do you think so much of the tepid lacteous fluid good for the lady?" asked the cottager, as she put some milk into a saucepan.

"She can take nothing else," returned Clara.

"How delightfully that girl sings!" continued she, listening with rapture to a milk-maid, who was chanting an Italian bravura as she was milking her cow.

"Yes," replied the cottager; "Angelica sings well. The parieties[305] of her larynx are in a very tense condition, and her trachea is quite cartilaginous. But here comes my good man," continued she; "he has been hard at work all day in the roads, and I am sure he must want some refreshment."

"I do indeed feel excessive lassitude, missis," said the cottager, as he came in; "and I want something to eat. What have ye got? Do see, will you, for it's dreadful hard work breaking stones; most we had to-day were primitive limestone, but I found a few fine specimens of quartz. The crystals were quite rhomboidal,[306] and I stopped at least half an hour admiring them."

"Rock crystals are often found amongst quartz," said his wife; "so I don't think you had any occasion to lose your time in admiring them, when, you know, you break stones by measure, and your wife and children are starving for want of bread."

"Do not distress yourself upon that head, my good woman," said Clara; "we have money, and our gratitude will not permit you to want any thing that we can give you."

"Thank you, thank you, "cried the woman; "it's a pleasure to serve a generous gentleman like your honour."

"What a charming voice you have!" said Clara, turning away to avoid the woman's praises, and addressing herself to the milk-maid; who, having finished her task, now stepped over the stile that divided the field from the garden of the cottage, with a pail of milk upon her head, and advanced gracefully in measured steps towards them.

"I am very happy to have pleased you, Sir," replied the girl, dropping her foot into the fourth position,[307] as she made an elegant curtsy, and then glided gracefully on.

"Stay, stay!" cried Clara; "won't you give us another song before you go?"

"You must excuse me, Sir," said the girl, again gracefully curtsying; "I am exceedingly sorry to be obliged to refuse a gentleman of your appearance; but singing requires an alternate enlargement and contraction of the glottis, an elevation and depression of the larynx, and an elongation and shortening of the neck, very difficult to be performed with a pail of milk upon one's head."

"Set down the pail, then," said Clara.

"Indeed I can't, Sir; for I have not a moment to spare. I just met some gentlemen of my acquaintance on the hill, and as I expect them here every moment, I must snatch an instant or two to arrange my toilette."

"Gentlemen of your acquaintance!" cried the mother; "what gentlemen can you have met with here, child, that know you?"

"My cousin John that went for a soldier some time since, and a party of his companions."

"And what brings them in these parts? No good, I fear; for John was always a wild good-for-nothing lad."

"It is no evil, I assure you, mother," said Angelica pertly; "but you are always fancying the worst. John is become a man of consequence now, and he is at the head of a party of soldiers, searching for some state prisoners. He'll be made a captain if he finds them: and I hope he will, with all my heart."

"Where are they now?" asked the mother.

"In the wood," replied the girl; "and my brother is gone to help them to search, as he'll get a share of the reward if they find the fugitives whilst he is with them."

"And you'd go too, if you'd any wit," said the wife to her husband, who had now seated himself comfortably before the fire, and seemed very unwilling to be disturbed. Inspired, however, by his wife's remonstrances, he roused himself, and, stretching his heavy limbs, rolled rather than walked away. Angelica had also retired, and Clara was left alone with the woman. It has already been mentioned, that presence of mind was one of Clara's distinguishing characteristics; and, perceiving the danger of the Queen, she was aware not a moment was to be lost. The observations of the woman to her husband, and, in fact, her whole manner, showed that avarice was her master passion, and upon this hint Clara spoke. She offered her abundance of gold; she enlarged upon the greediness of the soldiers, who, if she waited for their approach, would perhaps cheat her of her share in the promised reward, or, at least, give her such a trifle as would not to be worth having; and at last drew forth the glittering metal and spread it before her eyes. Gold softens the hardest heart, and the cottager's wife could resist no longer, but promised to connive at their escape.

Clara instantly ordered Hans to prepare the horses; and, informing the prince and Elvira of what had passed, the whole party again set forward on their eventful journey.

Volume 3: Chapter 7

In the mean time, Roderick had been completely victorious in Spain. He had reached Madrid and established Don Pedro as King; and was now on his return to Seville, where he had left M. de Mallet and his charming daughter. Edric, of course, accompanied him; but the rest of the army had marched to Cadiz to embark, the Greek page only attending upon his master.

"Well, Edric!" said the King, laughing, as they approached Seville, "does not your heart beat with pleasure at the thought of quitting Spain?"

"How can you torment me so, Roderick?"

"Torment you! why I thought you would be in raptures; though I must own, if you are, they are the most melancholy raptures I ever beheld in my life."

"This raillery is not generous. It is unworthy of you. I own I love Mademoiselle de Mallet—but I despair."

"And why?"

"Alas! how can I ask her to share the fortunes of a banished man?"

"Am not I your friend?"

"I know it; but I cannot brook dependence even upon you."

"I do not wish you to be dependent; but what can I do to serve you? Shall I make war upon this cross old father of yours?"

"Oh, do not speak of him so lightly! Say what you please of me, but spare my father!"

"I respect your feelings; and as I can say no good of him, I will have the discretion to be silent."

Edric felt no inclination to reply to this remark, and they travelled on in perfect silence till they reached Seville. Here they found every thing changed: the town had been partially re-built, and the lovely groves of orange and myrtle trees in the vicinity, glowing with all the rich luxuriance of a southern spring, gave no idea of the scene of ruin and desolation; it had before presented. They inquired for the house of M. de Mallet, and upon entering the inner square, or court-yard, they found him seated under the piazza that stretched round it, enjoying the evening breeze, whilst his fair daughter was occupied in reading to him.

A fountain played in the centre of the court, its sparkling spray descending in silvery showers; whilst innumerable orange trees and flowering shrubs, which were placed around, perfumed the air with their delicious fragrance; and a light awning, spread over the roof of the court, mellowed the light to a soft though glowing tinge, which gave an air of voluptuous languor to the whole scene.

The delight felt by M. de Mallet and his daughter at again seeing their deliverers was enthusiastic; and though it was most openly expressed by the father, the burning cheeks and sparkling eyes of Pauline spoke quite as intelligibly her silent transport.

"We have long expected you," said M. de Mallet; "for I cannot describe how anxious we are to leave this country. Pauline has wearied Heaven with prayers for your safety, and as I have felt my strength decay daily, I too have prayed for your return, for I have a secret to confide to you that weighs heavily upon my spirits."

"To confide to us?" cried Edric.

"Yes, to you," said M. de Mallet. "It is true I have not known you long; but some circumstances make men better acquainted in a month than the ordinary routine of life does in years. Thus, the kindness with which you have treated me, and the important events in which I have seen you engaged, have made me consider you as old and tried friends, and have induced me to confide to you a secret which I have hitherto guarded with the utmost scrupulous fidelity."

"What can you mean?" asked Edric in astonishment; whilst Pauline gazed upon her father with a look of the most intense anxiety.

"Pauline is not my child!"[308] said the old man impressively. Pauline uttered a cry of agony that thrilled through the souls of her auditors, and threw herself at his feet, looking up in his face with an expression of the bitterest anguish, as though she implored him not to desert her. M. de Mallet's agitation was equal to her own, and, as he fondly regarded her, he continued: "Yes, miserable being that I am! I am not her father. Alas! often when I have beheld her enduring hunger and thirst for my sake; when

I have seen her delicate frame exhausted with fatigue or shivering with cold, whilst still with angelic sweetness she has seemed to forget her own sufferings, and to think only of alleviating mine—oh, then, how I have burned to tell her that I did not deserve her kindness, and that I was an alien from her blood!"

"Oh father! my dearest father!" cried Pauline, her eyes streaming with tears; "what do you not deserve from me? What is there that I could do, that could half express my love and gratitude? Alas! though I am not your child, the tender care you took of my infancy—your kindness, your affection—" Pauline could not continue, her sobs impeded her utterance.

"My dear child!" said M. de Mallet: and folding her in his arms, he mingled his tears with hers; whilst Roderick and Edric were both too powerfully affected to interrupt their sorrows, and stood gazing upon them in silence, though both ardently desired an explanation of this seeming mystery. After a short pause, M. de Mallet resumed: "I see the astonishment I have caused you, and my heart bleeds for the pain I have been compelled to inflict upon Pauline, but I could not die in peace without disclosing the truth."

"Oh, do not talk of dying!" cried Pauline, still clinging to him with the fondest affection.

"And who are the parents of Mademoiselle de Mallet?" demanded Roderick.

"Alas! I know not," returned the Swiss. "About twenty years ago, I was travelling in England with my wife, who, afflicted with an incurable disease, had been advised to try the skill of English physicians, they being considered the most able in the world. One night, my poor wife being exhausted with fatigue, we stopped at a small inn in a village near the sea coast. The night was tempestuous, and a blazing light in the kitchen tempted us to wait there whilst the parlour was prepared for us. A woman sate near the fire, with a lovely little girl, about two years old, playing at her feet. My poor wife was always passionately fond of children, though Heaven had never blest us with any; and attracted by the exquisite beauty of the little cherub, she took it in her arms and began to caress it.

"Is your honour fond of children?' asked the woman with an evident affectation of vulgarity.

"'I dote upon them,' replied my wife. 'Oh Louis,' continued she, addressing me in French, 'if I could have such an angel as this to supply my place to you, I think I could be resigned to die.'

"'If your honours like the child, you may have her,' said the woman.[309]

"I started: but recollecting that, from the over education of the lower classes in England, they were all linguists; the circumstance of the woman's understanding what We said, did not appear extraordinary. 'She is my child,' continued the woman; 'I live hard by—and have only taken shelter here from the storm. The landlady knows me very well. My husband has been dead some months; and, as I find it hard work to maintain myself and the child too, I own I shall be glad to place her in hands where she is sure to be taken care of.'

"The woman's tale seemed plausible; and my wife and I were easily induced to conclude the bargain that gave us possession of Pauline! We visited the cottage of this woman the next morning, and found her story true, excepting that she had only lived there a few weeks. This, however, appeared immaterial; as indeed she had not fixed any definite time for the period of her residence, and gave some reason which I have forgotten for having left her former abode when her husband died. Soon after this, we left England, taking Pauline with us: her beauty increased with her years; and when my poor wife died, which she did a few months after our return to Switzerland, Pauline formed the sole consolation of my life. Two or three years afterwards, a friend of mine visiting England called by my desire upon the reputed mother of Pauline. He found the cottage deserted, and the landlady of the inn told him, that the woman had left the place a few hours after we had done so ourselves.

"This circumstance, combined with the evidently affected vulgarity of the woman, and the elegance and delicacy of Pauline, has always induced me to suspect I was the dupe of a deception, and that the child had been stolen from parents in a superior rank of life to that in which I found her. Whether my conjectures are correct, I know not; but when I have surveyed the beauty and graces of my child, my breast has smote me for confining her to my own humble station, and I have determined, whenever circumstances would permit, to take her to England, and endeavour, if possible, to elucidate the mystery that hangs over her destiny."

"Accompany me then to Ireland," said Roderick, "and when you have stayed there till you are tired, if you still wish to prosecute your researches, I will give you letters of introduction to the English Court, and I sincerely hope we may find our fair friend to be a princess of the blood at least."

In the mean time, M. de Mallet's narrative had caused the greatest agitation in the breasts of Edric and Pauline, "Not his daughter!" thought the former; "whose can she be, then?" and his imagination ran wild amongst a variety of dreams and fancies, each more extravagant than the last: for, to suppose the elegant and accomplished Pauline the daughter of a mere peasant was impossible; and the transporting hope that she might yet be his, with the consent of his father and the approbation of all his friends, danced before him; whilst Pauline, uncertain what to think, and unable to analyze her own sensations, felt, even amidst the desolation in which the avowal of M. de Mallet had involved her, a faint emotion of pleasure still throb at her heart, when she reflected that now her country was that of her lover's, and that it was possible—she dared go no farther, for her senses seemed unable to support the intoxicating thoughts of what might follow.

It had been agreed that our friends should remain a few days at Seville, to give the army at Cadiz time to recover from the fatigue of their march previous to their embarkation; but the morning after their arrival, a courier arrived with despatches from England, which made Roderick impatient to leave Spain immediately. He was at breakfast when these letters, which had been forwarded to him from Cadiz, were put into his hands. He changed colour, and, starting from his seat, begged Edric to follow him into the garden.

"Good God, what is the matter?" asked M. de Mallet.

"Nothing, nothing!" replied Roderick; "but that I must return to Ireland immediately."

And waving his hand as though to repel farther inquiry, he left the room; Edric followed in silence. "Edric," said the Irish Monarch, throwing himself into a garden-seat and burying his face in his hands; "Elvira is dethroned, and perhaps murdered, all owing to my cursed folly in remaining so long in Spain."

"Elvira!" exclaimed Edric, looking at his friend in the most profound amazement; for he could not imagine why he took so deep an interest in her fate.

"I see your astonishment, Edric," resumed the King; "but I have not now time to explain whys and wherefores. Suffice it to say, that I adore Elvira, and if she perish, I will not survive her."

A piercing shriek burst from the thicket as he uttered these words, and both Edric and Roderick sprang involuntarily to the spot—it was vacant; they searched the wood, but no creature was to be seen.

"It was fancy," said Edric.

"It was the Mummy," murmured the King, "come to chide me for doubting his promises for an instant."

"The Mummy!" cried Edric; "good God! what do you mean?" and he gazed with horror upon the wild and haggard countenance of his friend, who he seriously believed had become distracted. His look recalled the fleeting senses of Roderick, and with a ghastly smile he replied, "I am not mad, though I have enough to make me so. We must return to Ireland without a moment's delay, and there reinforce my army. Elvira must be restored immediately, for her life is in danger from every moment's delay."

"I hope not," said Edric; "for, though I detest Rosabella, I do not think her capable of assassination."

"If she be not, Father Morris is," returned Roderick, in a. low voice, with a look of intense feeling.

Edric turned pale.—"In the name of God, tell me who and what you are?" said he earnestly; "and how you have obtained this close knowledge of the English Court."

"I am called the Devil's favourite, you know," returned Roderick, smiling, in spite of his distress, at his friend's embarrassment, "and it would be very hard if my patron did not give me a hint now and then upon subjects of importance."

"How *can* you jest upon such a topic?" asked Edric reproachfully,

"True," returned Roderick; "as you say, the subject is not one to joke upon: for we must quit Seville in a few hours, and leave M. de Mallet and the pretty Pauline to follow us under the escort of my Greek page; or rather, what perhaps you would prefer, you shall stay behind to take care of them, and Alexis and I will proceed alone."

"Oh Roderick!" exclaimed Edric, "how can you imagine I could leave you?"

"Not even for Pauline?" asked the King, smiling.

"Not even for Pauline," repeated Edric firmly; "my love for you surpasses even the devoted love of woman; and whilst I breathe neither peril nor pleasure shall tear me from your side."

"My dear Edric!" said Roderick; the tears glistening in his eyes: the next instant, however, he dashed them away, and added gaily, "But come, we must go and make our bows and take our leave like pretty behaved cavaliers; and you may trust my discretion, Edric, that I will not tell Pauline of your want of gallantry."

The Greek page looked the image of despair, when he heard his master's commands that he should remain behind; and passions, dark as the lowering heavens before a. storm, hung upon his brow. He offered no opposition, however, to his master's will; and crossing his arms upon his breast, bent his head in token of obedience.

The voyage of Edric and Roderick to Ireland was rapid and favourable in the extreme; and on their arrival, their reception was enthusiastic. The Irish are proverbially warm-hearted, and the rapture with which they now greeted their victorious Monarch defies description. Triumphal arches were erected, the walls were hung with tapestry, and the streets strewed with flowers, to greet his entry into his capital. Roderick did not refuse these honours; but it was evident to all who knew him well, that his mind was occupied with other things; and, in fact, he took his measures so promptly and so decidedly, that, by the time his army, with M. de Mallet and his daughter, Dr. Entwerfen, and the Greek page, arrived from Spain, he had assembled a force quite sufficient for the restoration of the Queen.

The very day that Elvira fled in terror from the power of her rival, the combined army of Roderick began its march to hasten to her assistance; and it had nearly advanced through the whole of the tunnel under the sea, which separates the two kingdoms, without opposition. Orders were now given for the soldiers to rest for the night, and tents were rapidly pitched for that purpose. Roderick, however, could not sleep; and he stood with his arms folded, gazing at the singular scene before him, the innumerable torches fixed against the dark sides of the tunnel shedding their lucid light around, and showing distinctly the long line of white tents that stretched as far as the eye could reach; whilst the distant roaring of the sea above their heads, sounded like the hoarse murmur of gathering thunder.

Whilst Roderick was thus engaged, Edric perceived a group of people enter the cavern from the English side, and eagerly inquire for the King. They were brought before him; they were four in number: but one stayed behind, holding their horses, which looked dreadfully jaded and distressed; whilst the other three, a man and two women, approached and threw themselves at Roderick's feet: "Good God! it is Elvira!" exclaimed he.

"Henry Seymour!" screamed the Queen, and fell senseless upon the ground.

In the mean time all was anarchy in England. Disgusted with the world and with himself, the King secluded himself from society, and passed his time entirely upon a small estate adjoining the chateau of his father. Sir Ambrose and he often met; but they never spoke, though their hearts yearned towards each other. With all his good qualities, Sir Ambrose was prejudiced and obstinate; he loved his son passionately, but he could not endure a rebel, and the poor old man was fast sinking into the grave, for want of the very consolation he would not condescend to receive.

Edmund also was wretched: the habits of respect in which he had been always brought up towards his father, prevented his daring to intrude upon him against his will, though he would willingly have relinquished his empty title of King, and have exposed himself to all the miseries of absolute want, to have obtained the privilege of throwing himself upon his father's neck, and receiving his forgiveness. The title of Edmund was, indeed, now only an empty one. Rosabella alone exercised the power of a Sovereign, and her haughty temper and capricious tyranny made her universally detested. Monarchs to be respected must be firm; and whilst they continue to inspire respect, they may sometimes venture to be tyrants. But Rosabella was no longer respected; he was despised; and the Commons finding themselves oppressed, and their complaints completely unattended to, began to regret the gentle sway of Elvira. "She, at least," said they, "treated us with kindness; and if she did refuse our petitions, it was with gentleness. But now we are treated with scorn, and trampled beneath the feet, not only of the Queen, but of her confessor. We will not, we cannot bear it."

Sad and mournful also was the life of the Duke of Cornwall: for days and hours he would wander in the gardens of his chateau with his friend Sir Ambrose, and lament sorrowfully over the complete destruction of his hopes. In these walks they often saw Edmund, gliding at a distance like a solitary ghost, and plunging amongst the trees when he thought himself observed. "How changed Edmund is become!" said the duke. "Alas! how guilt corrodes the heart! He has destroyed my daughter, and he is now suffering the penalty of his crime."

"Say not so," rejoined Sir Ambrose, who could not bear to hear his son blamed by any one but himself; "if Elvira had not eloped with Prince Ferdinand—"

"Eloped with Prince Ferdinand!" cried the duke,—"I did not expect this. What! can you, Sir Ambrose, join in the general voice? Will you slander poor Elvira? Elvira, whom you have known from her cradle—whom you have loved and fondled as your own child?"

"Patience! patience! my good friend."

"I have no patience, I can have no patience, when I hear my daughter scandalized—my poor motherless girl. Remember, if she should err, she lost her mother in her childhood—she has been always brought up with me, and as she has been the playfellow of your sons, from her earliest infancy, perhaps she may not act according to those rigid restraints imposed upon her sex, by those who have been always secluded from the society of men. But she means well, Sir Ambrose, she means well always, and I'd answer for her virtue with my life. Besides, you know, she has always been used to have an intimate friend of the other sex;—You know Edmund—"

"No one ever blamed her whilst Edmund was her friend."

"And who dares blame her now? No one, I trust, whilst I have an arm and a sword ready to defend her."

"My good friend, you reason like a fond father; who, though he sees, is willing to excuse the faults of his offspring: your judgment condemns Elvira, even more than mine."

"No, no,—if I thought her wrong, I should not blame her as you do. Your partiality to Edmund blinds you, and you fancy my poor child has a thousand faults, because she was not sensible to the merit of your son."

"You mistake me quite; my opinion of Elvira would be just the same if Edmund were not in existence: though I acknowledge frankly, that every time I see his fine noble countenance, worn with care—his pale cheeks and sunken eyes—I feel a pang through my inmost soul. It is a strange infatuation that she should repulse my noble boy; and yet elope so readily with a youth she scarcely knew."

"Take care what you say, Sir Ambrose—take care what you say,—I will not have my child insulted."

"I do not wish to insult her—I speak but the truth—I do not even think her guilty, though the whole Court rings with her shame."

"Guilt! shame! And this to me? Oh God! Oh God! I have lived too long! To hear my child thus basely slandered, and be unable to resent it!"

"Base! and is this the conclusion of our long friendship—Base! and have I lived to be called base, for merely blaming a coquettish wanton?"

"Wanton!" cried the duke, and transported by his passion he struck Sir

Ambrose violently. The aged baronet could not endure this insult; his sword flew from his scabbard, and in a few seconds these ancient friends were engaged in mortal combat.

It was a shocking thing to see these two old men, their white hair streaming in the wind—their venerable features wrinkled with age, and their feeble frames tottering for support—fighting with all the vindictive fury of youth. How fearful is the storm of passion! How vile the human heart when left to its own workings! Every gentler feeling was extinguished in the breasts of the two veterans. and only brutal rage remained. For some time victory was doubtful: but at last Sir Ambrose fell, and in another moment the sword of his antagonist would have passed through his bosom, had not a powerful arm arrested the stroke. It was Edmund! he had heard the clashing of swords at a distance, and, rushing to the spot, arrived just in time to prevent the fatal blow.

"Oh my father!" cried Edmund with a thrill of horror, "for God's sake, do not die till you have forgiven me! He hears me not!" cried he, wringing his hands in unutterable anguish. "Oh, for mercy's sake, speak! Do not destroy me."

Sir Ambrose feebly opened his languid eyes: "Farewell," said he, faintly: "God bless you!"

"Oh, do you forgive me!" shrieked Edmund, falling upon his knees.

"I do," said Sir Ambrose: "and—the—duke;" the words feebly ebbed from his lips; and, as he spoke, the fearful rattle of death gurgled in his throat, and with a convulsive sob he expired.

Sadly did the duke now gaze upon his fallen foe, but when he found him dead he was distracted. Madly he tore his hair, and threw himself upon the corpse; but his agonies were in vain, the vital spark was extinct. Edmund stood also for some seconds gazing upon the body, without any distinct idea existing in his mind; but when the whole sad reality rushed upon him, he could not endure his own thoughts, and darted away with the velocity of lightning. The duke heeded not his departure; he had thrown himself upon the body of his departed friend, and the whole universe seemed to contain for him only that bloody corpse. "I have killed him! I have killed him!" cried he, "I have killed him!"

His fearful shrieks soon drew many persons to the spot. "I have killed him!" screamed the duke, in answer to all interrogations; "I have killed him!" Abelard was one of the first collected round this mournful spectacle. "What can we do?" said he to Father Murphy,— the case seems desperate."

"I've killed him!" again screamed the duke in agony.

"He's entirely mad," said Father Murphy, "and there's no doubt of it."

"I've killed him!" repeated the duke, with a still more piercing shriek; "I've killed him!"

"Oh he is mad," cried all the spectators, whilst they attempted to remove him from the spot. With infinite difficulty they succeeded, he still clinging to the corpse, and screaming "I've killed him!" till his voice was lost in the distance.

Whilst these scenes were transacting at the English Court, the army of Roderick marched through the kingdom without opposition, for the people every where, tired of the tyranny of her rival, received Elvira with open arms, and the chief nobility vied with each other in opening their houses to entertain her and her suite as she passed along.

It was a fine evening in March, and the night was clear, though cold, when Elvira, with hurried steps, paced the fine terrace belonging to the castle of one of these noblemen. The Queen was evidently lost in reflection, and as she occasionally stopped, she threw back her long hair and looked up to the sky with an air of intense anxiety. "It is a lovely night!" murmured she: "Heaven grant that peace may still attend us! yet, I fear I know not what of danger. Oh, if the forces of Rosabella should resist—and Roderick should fall—and for me—"

She paused, for the thought seemed too dreadful for endurance. The moon shone brightly in the heavens, and the stars sparkled like diamonds on the clear blue sky; whilst Elvira, raising her eyes to heaven, and clasping her hands together, seemed lost in silent prayer. Her fair face, shaded by her long black veil, looked even more lovely than usual, in the soft light thrown upon it; and, as she stood thus apparently quite absorbed in inward devotion, she seemed almost a celestial being descended for the moment upon earth, and about to remount to her native skies.

A figure, wrapped in a dark long cloak, now appeared at the extremity of the terrace, and advanced slowly towards the Queen. Two other figures also emerged from the shade, and followed, though at a considerable distance. Elvira was not aware of their approach till the first figure stood behind her, and seizing her arms, threw a cloak over her head to stifle her cries; and then, with the help of the others, was hurrying her of. At this moment, Roderick sprang actively upon the terrace, and with one blow from his vigorous arm, felled the first assailant to the ground. Then, drawing his sword, the enraged Monarch would have instantly dispatched him, had not the supposed assassin uttered a piercing scream, and, clinging round his knees, implored mercy. The moon shone full upon the boy's face, and disclosed to Roderick's astonished eyes the features of the dumb page. "Alexis!" cried he.

The boy sprang from the ground.

"Roderick!" screamed he; "then I am ruined!"

"Stay!" returned the King, grasping his arm, and preventing his escape; "who, and what are you? Speak, or dread my vengeance."

The boy's heart beat almost to suffocation; every nerve throbbed with the most violent emotion, and drawing a dagger from his belt, he attempted to plunge it into the heart of Roderick. "Ah!" cried the King, starting aside in time to prevent the blow; whilst ere he could prevent it, the page had buried the weapon in his own bosom.

"Good God!" exclaimed Roderick, "what can this mean?"

The whole of this scene had passed with such rapidity, that Elvira had scarcely time to recover herself, or to be aware of what had happened. The two assistants had fled the moment they perceived the King; and Elvira, with trembling steps and pallid cheeks, approached the spot where Roderick knelt beside the bleeding page.

Kneeling beside him, she attempted to staunch the blood which flowed rapidly from the wound, but in vain; for the boy's life was evidently fast ebbing.

Brian, a servant of the King, who had followed his master to the terrace, aided her endeavours; but Roderick remained fixed and immoveable, his eyes chained as by the power of fascination upon the page, who now slowly unclosed his eyelids, and heaving a deep sigh, fixed his languid eyes upon those of Roderick.

"Zoe!" cried the King.

"Yes," returned the page, gasping for breath, and speaking with difficulty; "Zoe! I am indeed that wretch. I loved you, Roderick; I would have died for you. I do die for you; but—but—Elvira—"

"What meant your outrage upon her?"

"What did it mean?" cried Zoe, her eyes flashing fire, and her whole frame supported by a supernatural energy; "did I not see that you loved her, and could I endure to resign you to another? No," continued she, starting from the ground; "I would have killed her, and, had she perished, I should have died contented."

The violence of the action made the blood gush in torrents from her wound; and, pale and feeble, her failing eyes closed. She staggered a few paces, fell, heaved one convulsive struggle, and Zoe was no more!

Sadly did Roderick gaze upon that form which had so lately thrilled with feeling—now cold and inanimate at his feet: the victim of passion lay before him. Her hopes, her fears, her rage, and her love, had passed away, and there her body remained a senseless clod of clay, till it should be resolved into its original elements. By this time, some of the servants of the castle, who had been summoned by Brian, approached; and the old Earl of Warwick, in whose castle the fatal scene had taken place, rushed upon the terrace, calling wildly upon his people to save the Queen.

"Is it the Lady Elvira that ye mane?" asked Brian; "Och an't plase yere honour, and she's safe, every inch of her."

"And what has been the matter?" asked the Earl."

"Och and your lordship may well ask that; but the divil a bit any body can tell you but one, and that's myself. Ye see, my master, his most gracious

Majesty, and me were walking in the garden; that is, he was walking and I was watching, for fear any harm should happen to him; for the life of such as he isn't to .be trusted to chance in a strange country, and I guess he was thinking of the Queen, though he never said nothing about it. And so when we came near the terrace, it was so dark, ye couldn't see yere hand before you. And then the moon peeped through the clouds, like a pretty face looking through a ground-glass window. And then she came out as bright as a silver mirror; and the Queen looked so pretty as she stood praying, that my master couldn't find it in his heart to interrupt her; and for me, I wasn't the man to be even thinking of such a thing. And then two black-looking spalpeens, bad luck to them! stole out behind her, and there wasn't two, for there were three of them—with never a livin' soul beside, to be seen in respect of being near her: but God never would suffer a rale lady like herself to want as friend to comfort her when she'd be in naad[310]—and my master wouldn't let her be after coming to harm, for he jumped upon the terrace entirely like a hound springing at the deer—and saved her, which nobody but himself could have done like it, for the very life of 'em. And when I came, there was the man lying dead that would have killed the princess, and it turned out he wasn't a man at all, but a woman."

The story of Zoe is soon told. Bred in a warm climate, and naturally enthusiastic in her disposition, she was the child of passion. The misfortunes she had experienced in Greece, by depriving her of all she loved, had thrown her affections back upon her own bosom, and they had preyed upon themselves.

To give vent to the feelings that oppressed her, she created an image of perfection in her own mind, and this she worshipped in secret.—When she saw Roderick, however, all was changed; a new world seemed to open upon her. The idol of her fancy, indeed, stood before her; for Roderick realized all her wildest dreams. He became her god. His heroism, his person, his talents, caught her imagination, and the violence of her passions completed the delirium of her soul. Notwithstanding, however, the intensity of her feelings, no thought of grosser texture contaminated her mind. Her love was as that of angels, pure and undefiled:—she regarded Roderick as a thing enshrined, almost too holy for mortal vows to worship; and she would have considered it sacrilege to dare even to think of him as a husband.

With these feelings, she had watched over him, with almost a mother's love; and when she informed him of the conspiracy against him, she resolved, with all the romantic self-devotion of a fond woman, to follow him unknown and in disguise; without any plan, however, but that of being near him, or any hope but that of contributing to his happiness. Money, and the assistance of one or two devoted servants, who contrived to follow in Roderick's train, had enabled her to accomplish this. She had felt a momentary jealousy at his anxiety for Pauline, and she had been half induced to favour the plots of the Spanish general, to take Roderick prisoner; but that feeling had worn away, when she discovered the mutual passion of Edric and the fair Swiss. Now the case was different, and, maddened by the thought of Roderick's devotion to Elvira, she had determined to destroy her. Her trusty Greeks would have assisted her plan, but they fled at her detection.

Inexpressibly shocked at what had taken place, Roderick could scarcely bear again to separate himself, even for an instant, from Elvira. "Do not bid me leave you," said he, looking at her with the fondest affection; "You shall accompany me, even to the field. Oh! would to Heaven you would give me a right to be near you for ever."

"Alas! alas!" replied Elvira; "I tremble for the result of this fatal contest. Oh that I were but a humble peasant!"

"Would to Heaven you were!" cried Roderick, with enthusiasm; "for happy as I always am in your presence, never do I feel so much so, as when we seem, as at present, secluded from the world. Then I could forget your rank, and all the artificial restraints grandeur has thrown around you; and without remembering that I am Roderick, and you Elvira, think only of a pair of simple lovers, whose weightiest care was their attendance upon their flocks, and whose only happiness consisted in loving and being beloved."

"Alas, Roderick!" replied Elvira; "do not speak of love. After the dreadful scene we have just witnessed, I tremble at the passion. No, be my friend, Roderick. Friendship is more sure than love. On that, we may confidently rely; but passion destroys itself with what it feeds upon—intense feelings cannot last."

"Oh Elvira! say not so," cried Roderick, fixing his eyes earnestly upon her blushing countenance—whilst she, trembling and agitated, betrayed by her confusion the passion she would have fain concealed.

How feeble are words to express the transports of such a moment! 'Tis the oasis in the desert of life—the bright gem that casts a radiance even upon the dross with which it is surrounded. Man is born to misery—thick clouds hang over him, and obscure his path—dangers await him at every step. One single ray alone breaks through the gloom—bright as the fairy dreams of childhood; but, alas! equally fleeting. 'Tis love—pure, passionate, unsophisticated love—the only glimpse of heaven vouchsafed on earth to man. And this was what was now felt by Roderick and Elvira, as he, throwing himself at her feet, vowed eternal constancy, and persuaded her to acknowledge that her hopes of earthly happiness centered in him alone.

But why do I profane such a scene, by attempting to describe it? Those who have loved, have only to recollect what they felt upon a similar occasion; and to those who have not,—Heaven help them!—not all the eloquence of

Cicero himself could give the least idea of any thing of the kind. Suffice it to say, that before Roderick and Elvira parted, she consented, if success should crown their efforts, to become his bride.

The state of England, at this moment, defies description. The death of Sir Ambrose and the insanity of the Duke of Cornwall were events so shocking in themselves, that it was not surprising they produced a violent effect upon the minds of the people. Edmund. had disappeared, and Rosabella, instigated by Father Morris and Marianne, became every day more rapacious and tyrannical; whilst even they quarrelled amongst themselves, and wretchedness prevailed throughout the kingdom.

This was the state of the public mind when the news of the invasion of Roderick first reached the ears of Rosabella.

"Marianne!" she exclaimed, "summon Father Morris. We are ruined," continued she, as the reverend father entered—"absolutely ruined. Roderick is invincible, and he supports Elvira! Where is Cheops?"

"Ay!" returned Father Morris, "where is Cheops? It is that accursed fiend that has led us on to destruction? His counsels have destroyed us; for, though plausible in appearance, they have been as deceitful as the oracles of old."

"Yet you trusted him!" said, Rosabella. "I hated him from the first; but you trusted him. You thought him all perfection: he flattered your vanity, and you weakly believed every thing that he asserted."

"Weakly!" cried Father Morris, his lips quivering with rage.

"Yes, weakly!" returned Rosabella; "for a child would have seen through his artifices; but you were deceived by them, and have been his dupe, his tool, his plaything."

"This to me!" cried Father Morris, gnashing his teeth together with passion.

"Yes, to you," returned Rosabella coolly; "for why should I longer conceal my sentiments? I will no longer be your slave. You have made me deserted by my husband—hated by my subjects—and detested by myself. I will, therefore, no longer follow your councils; from henceforward I will act for myself. Adieu, we meet no more as friends!"

And as she spoke, she walked out of the room, leaving the priest motionless with astonishment.—"This to me!" cried he to Marianne, as soon as he recovered himself sufficiently to speak—"to me, who have sacrificed every thing for her! Did I not place her on the throne? Have I scrupled even to imbrue my hands in blood for her sake? Have I not committed crimes for her that weigh heavily upon my soul? Did I not poison Claudia? and should I not also have destroyed Elvira, if Cheops had not saved her? Oh, Marianne, am I awake? Is it not a cruel dream? Is it possible it can be Rosabella! Rosabella! *my* Rosabella! *my child!* my own Rosabella! that uses me thus?"

"Hush! hush!" cried Marianne; "'tis but the passion of a moment. Be composed. Rosabella still loves you; but, irritated by the desertion of Edmund, and the news she has just heard—"

"Oh, Marianne!" interrupted the friar in agony, "you may easily reason, for you never had a child; but if Heaven had blessed us with one, you might have felt for my anguish."

"I do feel for you," returned Marianne; "but does she not treat me with equal scorn? Since the absence of Edmund she has become distracted, and I, who know the agonies a woman endures when she finds herself deserted by the man she adores, can feel for her."

"And who first gained her Edmund? Would he ever have become her husband, had not I induced him?"

"I believe not; neither would she have been Queen but for you."

"No—no. Oh! how I have toiled for that ungrateful girl! How I have adored her!"

"You have been a devoted father."

"Have I not, Marianne? I have at least endeavoured to expiate my sin. I have done penance—I have spent nights unnumbered in painful vigils. I have scourged my body, till the feeble flesh has shrunk beneath the torture; yet still my mind remains unappeased. Remorse still gnaws my vitals! Oh, Marianne! how poor is earthly grandeur to a mind diseased!"

In this manner did these companions in iniquity confer; till at length, hating each other and themselves, they gave vent to mutual upbraiding, and parted with undisguised hatred and contempt. Such, indeed, is the disgusting nature of sin, that though a man may shut his eyes to his own defects, or rather, see them through the magic prism of self-love; yet he almost always abhors them when he sees them reflected in another.

Thus it was with Father Morris.—Marianne had been his associate in many scenes of vice; he had, in fact, first led her from the paths of virtue, and, as usual in such cases, he now hated the creature he had made.[311]

Father Morris was indeed that brother of the Duke of Cornwall, whose crimes and punishment have been before slightly hinted at. He had married in early life a beautiful and accomplished woman;[312] but, instigated by the machinations of Marianne, whom he had previously seduced and abandoned, he had become jealous of her, and, in a paroxysm of rage, had deprived her of life. This was the crime he had since endeavoured to expiate by the penance of his whole life. Vain, however, had been his endeavour! The mortification of the body avails little, where the humiliation of the spirit is wanting; and Father Morris, notwithstanding his apparent repentance, was proud, envious, and intolerant.

In a fit of remorse, after the death of his wife, he had embraced a monastic life, and in order to subject himself to a perpetual penance, had placed himself as father confessor to Sir Ambrose. No situation, in fact, could have been more painful to a proud spirit than this; yet this daily misery Father Morris felt a pride in supporting without murmuring.

It is strange, but true, that haughty spirits sometimes feel almost pleasure in trying their powers of endurance to the utmost; for there is a self-satisfaction in thinking we have borne what seems almost too much for mortals, that often consoles a man under the acutest agonies.

This was the case with Father Morris, and the daily tortures which he endured without shrinking, almost reconciled him to himself. Ambition, however, was still his master-passion, and as his monastic vows prevented its indulgence in his own person, he devoted himself to the advancement of his child. How he succeeded, and how he was rewarded, has been already shown.

Volume 3: Chapter 8

"Have you heard the news?" asked Lord Maysworth one morning, bustling into the breakfast-room of Lord Gustavus de Montfort.

What is it?" demanded that noble lord, who was sitting at breakfast with his usual satellites.

"The King of Ireland has arrived at Oxford with an immense army, intending to re-establish Elvira."

"Impossible!" cried Lord Gustavus.

"Impossible!" echoed the satellites.

"Something must be done," said Lord Maysworth.

"Thinking as I think, and as I am confident every one who hears me must think, or at least, ought to think," said Lord Gustavus; "no government can he worse than the one we have at present."

"The Queen has not performed one of her promises," subjoined Dr. Hardman; "and her caprice and cruelty are beyond endurance."

"Her extravagance is unbounded," said Lord Maysworth.

"And her arrogance extreme," rejoined Lord Gustavus.

The satellites shook their heads in chorus.

"In my opinion," said Lord Maysworth, "we had better seek Elvira and try to propitiate her. She was used to be mild and gentle."

"But will she not be too much exasperated with our former desertion, to listen to us?" asked Dr. Hardman.

"I think not," said Lord Gustavus pompously.

The result of this conference may be easily imagined. Rosabella found herself deserted; many who would not have had courage to abandon her cause, had they not found precedents for their conduct, fled in the suite of the rebel lords. Roderick rapidly advanced, and his army was every day, augmented by the discontented English.

"I am lost, Marianne!" cried the Queen, when she found the enemy was within a day's march of her capital; "I am ruined past redemption."

"Do not desert yourself," said Marianne, "and you may yet be saved. If you despair, it is a virtual acknowledgment of the weakness of your cause."

"What will become of me?" continued Rosabella, wringing her hands; "no earthly help can save me."

"But courage may," said the deep voice of Cheops, who had entered the room unobserved.

"Ah!" screamed Rosabella; "it is the fiend!"

Cheops laughed, and the unearthly sound rang hoarsely in the ears of his auditors.

"Speak, demon! or whatever thou art," cried Marianne; "shall we perish?"

"You shall meet with your reward!" said the Mummy calmly: "Are you satisfied?"

"Oh, Rosabella!" screamed Father Morris, rushing into the room in an agony of despair; "save her! save my child!"

"Your child?" cried Rosabella; "can it be possible that *you* are *my* father?"

"I am—I am;—but fly—fly—and I forgive every thing; only let us fly!"

"Alas!" cried Marianne; "he has but too much reason for his agony. The enemy have entered the city."

"What will become of us?" ejaculated the friar. "Fiend! monster! barbarian!" cried he, addressing Cheops, and seizing him roughly by the arm; "deliver us! It was thy accursed counsels which involved us in ruin. Save us!"

"My counsels that led you to ruin!" returned Cheops, with one of his bitter laughs; "say rather, your own passions;[313] Did I urge you to murder Claudia? Nay, did I not save Elvira? Did I not warn you that the throne and misery were inseparably connected? And have not all my promises been fulfilled to the very letter?"

"Yes, yes; to the letter," returned Father Morris; "but not in spirit."

"By the sacred hawks of Osiris kept at Edfou![314] I swore Rosabella should be Queen, and you her favourite minister."

"Talk not of what is past," cried the priest impatiently; "tell me how to act. The foe is at the gates of the palace."

"Did you not say there was a secret passage, leading from this chamber?"

"There is! there is!" cried Father Morris, with rapture; "we will there lie concealed, and may surprise them."

Cheops laughed:—"Am I still your foe?" asked he, with his usual bitterness.

"Name it not, name it not!" cried Father Morris; "we have not an instant to lose. Hurry into the subterranean passage. I hear the horses of the enemy in the court of the palace!"

"Thebes was perforated with passages, yet she has fallen," muttered Cheops, as he followed the friar and Rosabella through the opening into the secret chamber; Marianne joined them, and the spring pannel[315] closed.

Nothing could be more flattering than the reception Elvira met with from her people. Roderick had placed her at the head of his army, and the people hailed her appearance with rapture. Not a blow had been struck, for the army of Rosabella had joined her banners; and Elvira advanced to London without opposition. Too mild and forgiving to indulge a single feeling of revenge, she felt rejoiced that her rival had escaped, and wished no pursuit to be instituted.

Edric, however, was not so quiescent. A thousand circumstances flashed upon his mind, to prove that the accession of Rosabella had been long planned by Father Morris, and he felt convinced he had been the dupe of the plans they had laid to induce him to quit the kingdom.

"I will find him," said he, "and expose his infamy. He shall not escape me thus."

Vain, however, was his search, and he returned to the room so lately occupied by Rosabella restless and dispirited. Elvira was now in this splendid chamber, surrounded by her friends; and, trembling with agitation, was awaiting the expected arrival of her father.

"Oh, Heavens!" exclaimed she, as the poor old man was led in; "Roderick! my beloved Roderick! can we not save him!"

"Alas!" returned Roderick, "I fear—but compose yourself, my dearest girl; all may yet go well."

"Where is Elvira? my child, my darling Elvira!" cried the old man: "I did not kill her! No," whispered he, drawing near to Roderick; "I killed *him*, it is true, but it was for her sake. He slandered my child, and I could not bear that."

"Oh God! oh God!" cried Elvira! "have mercy upon him! It breaks my heart to see him thus. Leave us, I implore you," she continued, addressing her friends; "I cannot bear that even you should see the extent of his malady. Leave him with me, and perhaps my presence may recall his lost recollection."

Finding opposition only incensed her anxiety, her friends at length consented; and Elvira was left alone with her father. Kneeling by this side as he lay stretched upon a sofa, the Queen endeavoured to console him; but he knew her not, and wrung her heart by calling vehemently upon Elvira. "If I could see my child," said he, "I should die contented. Call my child! Where is Elvira? Yes, yes, I know she is a Queen, and cannot come to me! Yet I think even a Queen might look at her poor old father: I only want her to look at me!"

Whilst this scene was passing, Rosabella and her friends lay concealed in the secret chamber; and, through the moveable pannel, watched every thing that passed. "Now is the time," cried Father Morris; when he saw that Elvira, exhausted by her grief, had hidden her face in her hands, to indulge her tears unrestrainedly.

"You ensure your own destruction if you kill her!" said Cheops.

"I care not," returned Father Morris; and removing the pannel, he approached. Elvira saw him not: and the shining dagger already was aimed at her breast, when it caught the eye of the maniac; and returning reason flashed through his mind.

"Edgar!" cried he, with a piercing scream, "spare my child!"

The cry roused the friends of Elvira, who had remained in the antechamber, and they rushed in. In an instant the room was crowded; Father Morris was secured; and his confederates (from his having left the pannel open) discovered.

"Edgar!" cried the duke; "yes, it is Edgar! my brother! my only brother! and this is Elvira. She is not fled; I knew she was not! She is safe!"

"And is it possible," cried Edric, "that you can be Duke Edgar!"

"I am that wretch!" said Father Morris.

"Then Rosabella is—"

"My child! and for her I have become the wretch I am! Yet to her I have done my duty; and if she be spared—"

"Ah!" cried M. de Mallet; "it is, it is—yes, I am not deceived, that is the woman who sold us Pauline."

"Who, which?" exclaimed Edric eagerly.

"Here," cried the Swiss, pointing to Marianne.

"Marianne!" exclaimed Edric.

"Yes," said she, "Marianne! He is right; it was I, and now is the moment of my vengeance. Seduced and deserted by this man," pointing to Father Morris, "my passions, always impetuous, panted for revenge. I instigated him to murder the wife for whom he had abandoned me—I stole his child and sold her to a stranger—and I substituted my own wretched offspring, whom I had had by a man he abhorred, in its place."

"What!" cried Father Morris, his livid lips quivering with anguish; "is not Rosabella my child?"

"No," said Marianne; "twenty years ago I sold your child to this gentleman," pointing to M. de Mallet. "He was a foreigner, and I believed, by placing her in his hands, you would never see her more."

"Then who is Rosabella?"

"My child, and by your servant Jacques."

"Curses on thee, woman! What! have I then destroyed myself here and hereafter for the offspring of that wretch? A man I detested, abhorred, despised!"

"Yes," said Marianne, with a fiendish laugh.

"You abandoned me, and I swore to be revenged: he heard my oath, and by promising to assist me obtained my consent to be his paramour. By his aid I effected all the rest. He has long been dead, but still I have pursued my plan; and when I saw you risking body and soul for Rosabella, I have gloried, for I was revenged."

"Fiend!" cried the priest; and rushing upon her before any one could prevent him, he stabbed her to the heart, and then instantly withdrawing the dagger buried it in his own bosom. "Still I am revenged!" cried Marianne, as heaving a deep sigh she expired. Father Morris never spoke again.

My tale is nearly closed, for dull must be the mind that cannot picture all the rest. The duke recovered his reason, and enjoyed all the happiness his bosom was yet capable of, in witnessing the union of his daughter and Roderick, whom he had loved as Henry Seymour, and now adored as the hero of Ireland. He gave Pauline a noble fortune, as his niece, and she married Edric; who, in the absence of his brother, took possession of his father's wealth, and fixed his residence in his former dwelling, where, after all his troubles, Dr. Entwerfen found himself comfortably re-established in his ancient chamber; whilst Clara, by becoming the bride of Prince Ferdinand, enchanted her mother, and secured her own happiness.

The coronation of Roderick and Elvira, as King and Queen of the United Kingdoms of Great Britain and Ireland,[316] was superb, and far excelled that in which Elvira had previously been an actress. Taught wisdom by experience, however, she no longer placed implicit reliance upon the shouts of applause that followed her footsteps;—yet, even with the reflection that all the promises she received might be evanescent, she could not resist the emotion of pleasure that swelled her breast, when, after the priest had pronounced the nuptial benediction, she walked with Roderick, the chosen of her heart, through a long line of kneeling subjects, and heard every mouth implore blessings on their heads, and bestow praises on her choice.

Proudly did Elvira look around as she reached the entrance of Westminster Hall; yet, ere she entered it, a rush and hustle in the crowd attracted her attention, and a man, clad like a monk, threw himself before her. Elvira screamed; when the man, throwing back his cowl, fixed his heavy eyes upon her and exclaimed, "Do you not know me, Elvira?" It was Edmund.

"Alas! alas!" cried he, "the demon was right; I trusted in my own strength, and I have fallen, miserably fallen. Though I knew it not, ambition was my god—and every thing else weighed lightly in the scale. Yet, even when my ambition was gratified, I was wretched; for I loved you, Elvira, even whilst I plotted against you;—and as my own heart reproached me, I felt every wrong you suffered far more poignantly I than you could yourself. My poor father too!—but all is over now, and I am doomed to bitter expiation of my sins,—bitter indeed, for oh, how far beyond all other sufferings are the never-dying tortures of remorse. One thought alone haunted my mind,—

one image alone floated before my senses. I could not die till I had obtained your pardon. Pardon me then, Elvira! See! thus humbly at thy feet I implore thy forgiveness; crouching in the dust, and bending my neck to be thy footstool!"

"Rise, I entreat you, rise!" said Elvira; "and he assured I forgive you—nay, that I pity you from my inmost soul."

"She pities me!" cried Edmund; "yet I can bear even this: even pity. And am indeed fallen so low as to be pitied! Yes, yes, I am indeed to be pitied."

"I did not mean to wound your feelings," returned Elvira, "believe me, Edmund. Tell me, what is there I can do for you?"

"Nothing!" cried he wildly; "the world is nothing for me now. Pity that unhappy woman that was my wife; and as for me, forget me!"

"Never!" said Elvira; "for never can I forget your disinterested love and your devoted affection. The heart, however, is capricious; and mine, though» sensible to your merits, was destined for another."

"And well does that other deserve your love;—for even jealousy itself must own that Roderick is worthy to be your husband. Yes, to him I can resign you. Farewell, Elvira! you shall never see me more! Let my brother take my inheritance! May you be happy! God bless you! God bless you!"

And starting from his knees, he disappeared, before she could reply.

The spirits of Elvira were agitated by this event, which threw a damp over the remaining festivities of the day; and, trembling and unnerved, she proceeded to the magnificent hall, where a sumptuous banquet was prepared for her reception. For some days after this event, the attention of Roderick and Elvira was occupied in arranging the different affairs of the kingdom; whilst Edric and Pauline, with the old Duke of Cornwall, M. de Mallet, and Father Murphy retired to the house of the former in the country, where Dr. Entwerfen was already comfortably established.

A thousand emotions swelled in the heart of Edric as he approached this venerable mansion, and saw again its well-known turrets peeping through the trees. Strange, indeed, are the feelings that oppress the mind, when the wanderer returns, after a long absence, to the habitation of his forefathers. A mingled crowd of contradictory sensations, of disappointed hopes, of undefined fears, float through his fancy; and, as well-remembered objects recal[317] the visions that formerly delighted him, he starts at the difference the experience of their fallacy has made in himself, and he sighs in vain for a return of the blissful ignorance he formerly despised. All too appears changed! As the human mind judges only by comparison, the eyes become dazzled by distant splendours, and that which to the eyes of youth had appeared superb, seems to the maturer judgment of manhood, tame, vapid, and insipid,—whilst the imagination which had fondly cherished the favourite dreams of childhood, and decked them in all the vivid colours of fancy, feels disappointed and disgusted, though it scarce knows why, to find the reality so different from the image it had pictured to itself.

Such were the feelings of Edric as he entered the grand hall of this residence of his ancestors, and gazed upon the well-remembered faces of the crowd of servants assembled to meet him. At the head of these was Davis; his tall thin figure waving to and fro, and his long thin white hair floating upon his shoulders; and the more spruce and gallant aspects of Abelard and his devoted Eloisa, the late Mrs. Russell, who had blest him with the possession of her fair hand a few days before, and now stood blushing and simpering, with all the affected modesty of a bride of sixty, to receive the congratulations of those around her.

"Welcome! welcome, my dear Edric!" cried Dr. Entwerfen, rushing down-stairs to meet them, his sleeves tucked up, and his wig thrown back, in a very experimental-philosophic manner; "rejoice with me too, for I have recovered my balloon! My darling caoutchouc bottle of inflammability! My immortalizing snuff, and, more than all, my adored galvanic battery! Yes, my compendium of science, my epitome of talent, and my most inestimable treasure, is safe! Not, indeed, that which was employed in galvanizing the Mummy, but its counterpart, its duplicate, its prototype. The Mummy came to England, and the balloon being recognized to be mine, it was placed in my apartment, where it has remained ever since, stowed up in safe but inglorious obscurity, till my return."

"Och! and that's a clear case!" said Father Murphy; "and there's no doubt of it."

Leaving the delighted doctor to show the treasures of his laboratory to M. de Mallet, Edric retired to his chamber, and after surveying again and again the well-known objects it contained, he hurried to his favourite grove.

It is singular how inanimate objects, which have been long unseen, recal the thoughts and train of feelings indulged in when one last beheld them: thus, the house, the groves, the walks, the gardens, and the river, recalled all its former longings to Edric's mind; and he again burnt to converse with a disembodied spirit, as he entered the grove where he had formerly so often ruminated, and indulged dreams wild and improbable as the delusions of delirium. The day was beautiful; it was one of those bright glowing mornings in April, when dew drops hang upon every thorn, when the sun shines brightly through the clear pure air, and all nature seems awaking to new life and vigour from repose.

Edric entered the grove, and threw himself upon that very bank where he had reclined only a few months before, under such different feelings. The river, the grove, the bank, were all the same; he only was changed. "And yet," said he, "is not my mind still as unsettled as before? Am I not still wandering in a labyrinth of doubts? Unknowing where to turn; and yet tormented with a restless desire to discover my way. What can have become of the Mummy, I so strangely resuscitated? It is strange, that since the restoration of Elvira it seems to have vanished, and yet all here speak of it as of a living animated being. Would that I could see it. O Cheops! Cheops—"

Suddenly a strange unearthly voice seemed to murmur harshly in his ear—"Go to the Pyramid! There and there only can thy hopes be gratified." Edric started upon his feet—no one was near him, and not a sound broke the awful stillness that reigned around, save the gentle rippling of the river that flowed at his feet. He gazed wildly on every side, hoping, yet fearing to behold the ghastly being, he fancied his words had conjured up. It was in vain; no dark figure interposed between him and the clear bright sunshine; no gloomy shadow stretched along the plain; all looked gay as youth and happiness; yet still that awful voice rang in his ears, and thrilled through every nerve.

"I will go the Pyramid," cried he energetically; "I will again enter that horrid tomb—but I will go alone."

In pursuance of this sudden, but irresistible desire, Edric hastily prepared to return to Egypt; and feigning that he was called to London by business of importance, to satisfy the anxious curiosity of Pauline, he departed. Indescribable emotions throbbed in his bosom as he took his seat in the stage balloon which was to convey him to Egypt; but when he saw the towers and temples, and, above all, the pyramids of this mysterious country, lying beneath his feet, his agitation increased almost to agony; It was with infinite difficulty that he obtained permission again to visit the objects of his journey; as, since the mysterious disappearance of the Mummy, the tomb of Cheops had been closed from mortal eyes. The interference of the British consul, however, at length obviated all objections, and Edric (whose impatience had become absolute torture from the delay) once more entered that awful receptacle of fallen greatness.

Scarcely a twelvemonth had elapsed since he had last trodden those solemn vaults, yet what a change had taken place in his destiny! When he considered the number and variety of the events that had befallen him, he could scarcely fancy it possible that they had been crowded into so short a space of time; and, instead of a year, centuries seemed to have rolled over his head. His feeling of personal identity seemed confused—his senses became bewildered, and he mechanically followed his conductor almost without knowing whither he was going.

At last the guide stopped—"This is the tomb of Cheops," said he; "I suppose, Sir, you will enter it alone."

Edric started—the words of the guide seemed to ring in his ears as the knell of death, and he shuddered as the thought crossed his mind that some horrid and appalling punishment might even now await him for his presumption. Desperately he snatched the torch from the hands of his guide and advanced ALONE.

Darkly did those gloomy vaults seem to frown at his approach, and fearfully did his footsteps resound as he slowly penetrated into their deep recesses. At length, he reached the tomb, but the brazen gates were closed, and he attempted in vain to open them. He placed the torch upon the ground, and again tried to unclose the fatal portal; he exerted his whole strength, but still it resisted his efforts. Rendered desperate, he now threw himself against the gates with almost superhuman force. Suddenly a hollow sound murmured through the cavern, and a current of wind rushed by with mighty and resistless fury. The brazen gates flew open with a fearful clang, and the torch fell and was extinguished. The next moment the sepulchral lamp shot forth a faint gleaming light, which brightened by degrees into a steady, flame, whilst heavenly music sounded faintly upon the ear, dying gradually away in murmurs, soft as those of the Æolian harp.[318]

The brilliant light of the lamp now glowed with noon-day radiance, and showed distinctly every corner of the fatal chamber. Edric looked timidly around, and shuddered as each well-remembered object met his eyes; but what was his horror and surprise when, glancing at the marble sarcophagus of Cheops, he beheld the gigantic figure of the Mummy standing erect beside it! It was again simply wrapped in the garments of the tomb, and its glassy eyes; rigid features, and statue-like form, chilled Edric to the heart. He looked at it a few moments in silence, till it raised its arm and seemed about to address him; when, shrinking back with indescribable horror, he uttered a faint shriek, and hid his face in his hands.

"Why dost thou tremble?" asked the Mummy in a deep hollow voice that thrilled through Edric's very soul. "Didst thou not come here to seek me, and dost thou shudder to behold my form? I am now before thee. Ask what thou wilt, I am permitted to reply. Why art thou silent? Why does thy heart seem to wither in my presence? Alas I alas! is no mortal to he found free from the debasing influence of fear? Thou art called bold, courageous, and noble. Thou hast dared to soar above thy fellow-men, and thou hast ardently wished to see me. Behold I am here, and now, weak, fearful, and inconsistent as thou art, thou shunnest my approach."

"I do not shun thee," said Edric, removing his hands, and endeavouring to look calmly on the fearful being before him, though the flesh seemed to quiver on his bones with the effort—"I do not shun thee; but the nerves will shrink though the mind be firm. I did wish to see thee; for ardently do I still desire to know the secrets of the tomb."

Cheops burst into one of his fearful laughs.

"Weak, silly worm! are you not satisfied then? How would this knowledge avail you? Has any thing but misery attended your former researches? And can any thing but misery attend the knowledge you now covet? Learn wisdom by experience! Seek not to pry into secrets denied to man!³¹⁹ If you wish still, however, to be resolved of your doubts, behold me ready to satisfy them; but, I warn you, wretchedness will wait upon my words."

"Then I no longer seek to hear them; for, even weak as you esteem me, I can learn wisdom from experience. Thus, then, I tear the tormenting doubts, that have so long haunted me, from my mind, and bid them farewell for ever!"

"It is well," said Cheops, his eyes beaming with joy. "Then my task is accomplished. I have at last found a reasonable man;³²⁰ I honour you for you can command yourself and now you may command me."

"I wish it not," said Edric.

"Have you no curiosity?" asked the Mummy, with a ghastly smile.

"None," returned Edric; "unless it be that I would fain know your history, and the meaning of the sculptures upon your tomb."

"What are they?" demanded Cheops.

"A youthful warrior is bearing off a beautiful woman in his arms, whilst an old man laments bitterly in the distance."

"I was the warrior," said Cheops; "and the beautiful female was Arsinoë. I loved her, and to gratify my impetuous passion I tore her from the arms of her father by force."

"The warrior is afterwards contending with the old man who falls beneath his blows—"

"He did, he did," cried Cheops; "he died by my hand; and eternal misery haunts me for the deed."

"And this old man was—"

"My father!" cried the Mummy, writhing in agony.

"And Arsinoë —"

"My sister—my own, my beloved sister!"³²¹

A solemn pause followed this speech, for Edric was too much shocked to speak again to the awful being who had avowed such crimes, and upon whose face were traced passions too horrible to be imagined. After a short silence Cheops again exclaimed—

"Yes, yes; I see your horror, and it is just; but think you that I do not suffer? know that a fiend—a wild, never-dying fiend rages here," continued he, pressing his hand upon his breast. "It gnaws my vitals it burns with unquenchable fire and never ceasing torment. Permitted for a time to revisit earth, I have made use of the powers entrusted to me to assist the good and punish the malevolent.³²² Under pretence of aiding them, I gave them counsels which only plunged them yet deeper in destruction, whilst the evil that my advice appeared to bring upon the good was only like a passing cloud before the sun: it gave lustre to the success that followed. My task is now finished;—be happy, Edric, for happiness is in your power; be wise, for wisdom may be obtained by reflection; and be merciful, for unless we give, how can we expect mercy? Rely not on your own strength seek not to pry into mysteries designed to be concealed from man; and enjoy the comforts within your reach—for know, that knowledge, above the sphere-of man's capacity, produces only wretchedness; and that to be contented with our station, and to make ourselves useful to our fellow-creatures, is the only true path to happiness."

The Mummy ceased to speak, and his features, which had appeared wild and animated during his conversation with Edric, became fixed—the unearthly lustre that had flashed from his eyes, faded away, and gave place to a glassy deadness—his limbs became rigid, and as the light of the lamp gradually sunk to less distinctness, the ghastly form of the Mummy seemed rapidly changing into stone. Edric felt that the moment when it was possible for him to hold communion with this strange being was rapidly passing away, and almost shrieked as he exclaimed, "One question! only one ere it be too late." The Mummy feebly raised his languid eyelids, but Edric felt his blood freeze at the unnatural glare.

With a violent effort, however, he rouzed[323] himself to speak. "Was it a human power that dragged you from the tomb?"

"The power; that gave me life could alone restore it," replied the Mummy in slow measured accents, as it sank gradually back into its former tomb. Edric shuddered, and involuntarily rushed forward, but the Mummy no longer lived or breathed. Cold, pale, and inanimate it lay, as though its sleep of two thousand years had never been broken.

"Oblivion laid him down upon his hearse!"[324]

and no mortal ever more could boast of holding converse with THE MUMMY.

Endnotes

1 The spirit of Samuel is called up by the Witch of Endor, on the instructions of Saul, to reveal the result of his conflict with the Philistines. In Biblical tradition, this is a problematic passage: the use of necromancy is forbidden, but Samuel's ghost also reveals that God has rejected Saul: "the Lord is departed from thee and become thine enemy ... Because thou obeyest not the voice of the Lord" (1 Sam. xxviii.16–18). The quotation foreshadows the use of Cheops, "called up" by Edric: a supernatural figure who likewise reveals the moral failings of his society.

2 *Claude Lorraine:* c. 1600–1682. French painter working mostly in Italy; a pioneer of landscape painting.

3 *Shakspeare:* spelled thus in text.

4 *by adopting Catholicism:* the process of Catholic Emancipation was under way by 1827, with the formation of the Catholic League by Daniel O'Connell (1823) and the subsequent Campaign to remove political restrictions on Roman Catholics, thrown into greater relief by the Act of Union (1800) between Great Britain and Ireland. Eventually, the Roman Catholic Relief Act, with the support of the Duke of Wellington (whose brother was Lord Lieutenant of Ireland 1822–1829), was passed in 1829 during Wellington's first period as Prime Minister; and Roman Catholics were allowed to sit in Parliament.

5   *ignes fatui:* luminous emissions of marsh gas (will-o'-the-wisps).
6   *otium cum dignitate:* leisure with dignity
7   *Cincinnatus:* Roman general c.519–c430 BC. A legendary symbol of patriotic service thanks to his relinquishment of dictatorship and retirement to private life after twice leading Rome to victory against her enemies.
8   *faineant:* ineffective, "do-nothing".
9   *like another Washington:* George Washington, following the French and Indian War of 1754–1763, resigned his commission and spent 16 years in "retirement" as a plantation owner before the 1775 Revolution in which he commanded the Revolutionary Army.
10 *"the little sea-girt isle,":* Ben Jonson's Ode "In Celebration of Her Majesty's Birthday. 1630" has "This sea-girt isle", but there are also echoes of Shakespeare's *King Richard II, Act 2 scene 1*;
    "... this sceptred isle,
    This earth of majesty, this seat of Mars,
    This other Eden, demi-paradise,
    This fortress built by Nature for herself
    Against infection and the hand of war".
11 *Entwerfen:* German "design" or "plan".
12 *having been a warrior in his youth:* (This added comment in 2nd ed. sets us up for later developments.)
13 *doating:* spelled thus in text.
14 *steam-mowing apparatus:* part of the future technology, noted with appreciation by John Claudius Loudon in his *Gardener's Monthly* review.
15 *developement:* spelled thus in text.
16 *Telegraph:* Claude Chappe's optical telegraph of 1792 used visual semaphore signals. The electric telegraph was not devised until 1816, when Francis Ronalds devised a system using static electricity, rejected by the Admiralty as "unnecessary". He published his work in *Descriptions of an Electrical Telegraph and of some other Electrical Apparatus* (1823). Sir Ambrose is using a Chappe system (he is shown interpreting codes) but some other system is clearly used for the transmission of the "peal of silver bells" that indicate a forthcoming transmission.
17 *You convinced me so clearly of the possibility of resuscitating a dead body:* an echo of Mary Shelley's *Frankenstein*.
18 *galvanic:* The experiments of Luigi Galvan (passing electrical currents through the muscle tissue of frogs' legs, and observing the reaction) seemed to indicate the presence of a kind of vital force or "animal electricity" which might reanimate dead bodies.
19 *You know a chamber has been lately discovered in the great pyramid:* According to the account given by Herodotus in Book Two of his *Histories*, Cheops on building the Great Pyramid ordered the building of "underground sepulchral chambers" (Herodotus, 151). Giovanni Caviglia, exploring on behalf of the British Consul Henry Salt, descended into the chambers of the Great Pyramid in 1817, as witnessed by the explorer and archaeologist Giovanni Belzoni in his *Narrative of the Operations and recent Discoveries in Egypt and Nubia* (136–38).
20 *develope:* spelled thus in text.
21 *disclose their origin:* despite the explorations and excavations of Belzoni, Caviglia, and others much of the history of Egypt remained a mystery until after Jean-François Champollion worked out a system of decoding hieroglyphs in 1822. Dr. Entwerfen in Vol. 1 Ch. 9 remarks that there is doubt about the very origins and purpose of the pyramids. Edric and Dr. Entwerfen's entry into the Pyramid in Vol. 1 Ch. 9 echoes Belzoni's account.
22 *soulagement:* relief.
23 *acatalepsy:* in Sceptic philosophy, the sense of not being able to come to certain knowledge of something: an example of the jargon with which the lower classes (such as Abelard) now speak.
24 *—he never speaks of himself:* the "dashes" with which the phrases are punctuated in 1st ed, are lost in the 2nd ed., but their retention makes the distinction between reported and direct speech clearer.
25 *his vermicular repast:* i.e. eating worms.
26 *graculi:* jackdaws (rather than *corvii*, or crows, though jackdaws are also members of the crow family), which are known for carrying off shiny objects such as jewellery (or, Davis claims, embers).
27 *incendriae aves:* the Latin would have the sense or "fire-raising" or "arsonist" birds.

28 *phlogisticated carbon:* embers from fires (the now-outdated theory that burning involves an element (phlogiston) which is released during combustion).
29 *pluviosity:* rain.
30 *speed with the velocity of the electric fluid:* the marvels of electricity, such as Luigi Galvani's 1780s experiments with passing electric currents through animal tissues (popularised by Humphrey Davy), and Michael Faraday's discoveries in electromagnetism in the 1820s are the background to Abelard's Puck-like claim for super-speed.
31 *somnifugous:* sleep-preventing.
32 *a saline secretion distils from every pore of my skin:* he is sweating.
33 *Stentor:* Greek herald in the Trojan War, noted for his powerful voice.
34 *get a balloon ready, and let us be off directly:* "this very hour I will engage a sailing balloon; I shall be there in forty-eight hours at furthest, perhaps in less, if the wind is fair." (Mary Shelley, *The Last Man,* Ch 5).
35 *"De gustibus non est disputandum":* "In matters of taste there can be no disputes."
36 *mob cap:* round bonnet covering the hair.
37 *in allusion to his own name:* alluding to the famous 12th century romance of Abelard and Heloise.
38 *the Paraclete:* the Biblical "Holy Spirit" (presumably a reference to asceticism rather than indulgence).
39 *eryptae:* protuberances (taste-buds).
40 *butyraceous:* having the qualities of butter.
41 *muriate of soda:* salt.
42 *Fecula:* starchy substances extracted from plants as food.
43 *Hebe:* Greek goddess of youth, cupbearer to the gods.
44 *an ingenious scheme had been devised:* a system of delivering mail by rocket was first suggested by the German writer Heinrich von Kleist in an article in the *Berlinner Arbendblätter* newspaper (October 10, 1810). Although no contemporary experiments with the technology appeared to have taken place, there were attempts later in the 19th Century in the Tonga Islands and a suggestion by the rocketry pioneer Hermann von Oberth in June 1928 which was followed by several shortlived experiments in Austria, Britain, India, and elsewhere (Ley, 1954).
45 *Apropos de bottes!:* Literally "with regard to boots" (*À propos* of nothing: ie changing the subject to something completely unrelated.)
46 *en philosophe:* Acting like a philosopher (lost in thought, absent-minded).
47 *King Cheops:* Foreshadowing the later appearance of the revived mummy of Cheops.
48 *re-animation may be produced:* See Mary Shelley's introduction to the 1831 third edition of *Frankenstein,* when she talks about experiments said to be undertaken by Erasmus Darwin, and their implications: "perhaps a corpse would be re-animated: galvanism had given token of such things" (Shelley 1992: 8).
49 *you fancy:* italics in text.
50 *sepulture:* internment.
51 *being once governed by an old woman:* Of course from 1876 it was, when Victoria was proclaimed "Empress of India", though JWL was not to know that!]]
52 *before they were converted to Christianity:* Sometime in JWL's future-history. Interestingly, despite the focus upon Egypt, at the time of the novel's composition being transformed from a region of the Ottoman Empire to a *de facto* power in its own right by the Pasha Muhammed Ali, JWL also seems to assume the eclipse of Islam.
53 *the celebrated court of Timbuctoo:* The almost legendary city of Timbuktu, at one point part of the 14th-15th Century Mali Empire was the focus of much European interest for its alleged wealth and culture, including the expeditions of Mungo Park (1771–1806), who died on his second attempt to visit the city. The first European known to have entered Timbuktu was Alexander Gordon Laing (1794–1826), who was killed shortly after he left the city.
54 *the rising states on the banks of the Niger:* The source and complete route of the Niger river was then not fully known by Europeans. Most of the "African" states mentioned in *The Mummy!* are European colonies, but it is unclear about the status of these "interior" countries, whose histories date back to powerful local Empires.
55 *America:* The USA, under President John Quincy Adams, was then in dispute with Britain over trade

in the West Indies, and had (1812) fought an inconclusive war against Britain. The "breath stopped by a bowstring" reference suggests that the fictional American "despotism" has a Native American flavour.

56 *stage-balloon:* as opposed to stage-coach.
57 *I'll warrant every one of them above three hundred years old:* the "treasures" are popular ballads recognisable for JWL's readers. The running joke is the inability of the "future" to distinguish between "high" and "low" art, with the further implication that we do not really know the status of many fragments from earlier times that we revere as "classics".
58 *Tragical end of poor Miss Bailey:* "Unfortunate Miss Bailey" first used in *Love Laughs at Locksmiths* (1803) by George Colman the Younger (1762–1836), and issued as a broadside ballad.
59 *Cherry Ripe:* A well-known song throughout the 19th Century (and occasionally revived today): words by poet Robert Herrick (1591–1674) and music by Charles Edward Horn (1786–1849).
60 *I've been roaming:* a broadside ballad; there are a number of similar titles but probably "I've Been Roaming" by Charles E. Horn, which first appeared on broadsheets around 1825.
61 *The loves of Captain Wattle and Miss Roe:* "Captain Wattle and Miss Roe", a broadside ballad published 1798, attributed to Dibdin, Charles, 1745–1814.
62 *Jessy the flower of Dumblane:* a very popular Scottish song, composed some time before 1816; still sung and recorded. Composed by Robert Tannahill of Paisley and set to music by Robert A. Smith.
63 *Dunois the brave:* a popular broadside ballad, also published 1825 in Thomas Tegg's collection of songs *The Sky-Lark.*
64 *At Wednesbury there was a cocking:* "The Wednesbury Cocking" is a well-known folk-song, also appearing as a broadside ballad and with a number of "literary" references. Samuel Butler refers to it in *Alps and Sanctuaries of Piedmont and the Canton Ticino* (1881). Wednesbury is a "Black Country" town south of Birmingham, and so the song would be "local" to JWL; possibly the reason why it is the subject of such detailed critical analysis.
65 *Stopt:* spelled thus in text.
66 *developes:* spelled thus in text.
67 *Sheridan:* Richard Brinsley Sheridan (1751–1816), playwright and theatre manager, author of *The Rivals* (1775) and *the School for Scandal* (1777).
68 *a tailor's bill of the immortal Byron:* Lord George Gordon Byron (1788–1824), the towering poetic figure of his age. The scale of his debts in his youth was by no means the only scandal attached to him. His poetry is frequently quoted or echoed throughout *The Mummy!.*
69 *"The Great Unknown!":* Sir Walter Scott, whose immensely popular "Waverley" novels were published anonymously, attracting this nickname. It was not until 1827 that he publicly acknowledged his authorship. (The exclamation "Great Scott!" has sometimes been associated with Sir Walter, although the evidence usually cited is Mark Twain's use of the exclamation in *A Connecticut Yankee in King Arthur's Court* (1889)). JWL was obviously an admirer of Scott, whose "Waverley" novels began in 1814, and by 1826 had reached its 18th title, *Woodstock.* She wrote to him on at least two occasions and Rauch (2001: 221) suggests that this might be about support for her application to the Royal Literary Fund (Feb 1929) or possibly a request to meet. The wording of her letter of 12 December 1929 is unclear about her reason for writing, merely acknowledging the "impossibility" of his granting her request and apologising for writing. She seems to mention the review in the "Literary Gazette" (18 Oct 1827) which refers to her as a "young author", or possibly the scathing condemnation of the "journeyman book-maker" in the *Monthly Review* of November 1827), although would they have been "just read" in 1829? The "new work" she refers to in the letter would be *Stories of a Bride* (Henry Colburn, 1829). Her 'impudent' request could perhaps also have been for him to review *Stories.*
70 *law the chimney through which the fiery passions of the world expend themselves in smoke:* unidentified.
71 *adytum:* innermost sanctuary (e.g. of a Greek temple)
72 *he saw a house in the suburbs gently slide out of its place:* the moving houses are an extrapolation of the then-novel railways (they move, of course, on rails and are propelled by steam).
73 *Somerset House:* begun (as Somerset Place) by the Duke of Somerset before his execution in 1552. During an extensive procedure of rebuilding over the next few centuries, it was used as a residence by royal consorts and from 1630–1635 contained a chapel where the Roman Catholic Henrietta

Maria, wife of Charles I could worship. This, and its use after the Restoration by Catherine of Braganza, the wife of Charles II, gave it an association with Catholicism. Demolished in 1775, it was rebuilt as an imposing site for public offices and learned societies by Sir William Chambers.

74 *exordium:* introduction.
75 *carte blanche:* complete freedom to act.
76 *popt:* spelled thus in text.
77 *a strong south country brogue:* reflected in the spellings in the text.
78 *but it was that myself:* the text reads "but '*I it was that myself...*'": a possible slippage of punctuation.
79 JWL was to use this surname for the pedagogic mother in *Conversations Upon Comparative Chronology* (1830).
80 *l'ami de la maison:* "friend of the house" (general favourite)
81 *bienseances:* rules of etiquette or decorum.
82 *hussey:* spelled thus in text.
83 *remember, nothing can be too plain for great people:* this is the topsy-turvey future, where the fashion is "for great people to have only one dish, and that as plainly cooked as possible", and porter and strong ale a fashionable drink "for the ladies" (a little later). In the 1st ed., this dialogue, or much of it, is between Mrs Montagu and Angelina.
84 *canaille:* rabble.
85 Oxygen: the "discovery" of oxygen as an element in the late eighteenth century has been claimed by various scientists including Joseph Priestley (1733–1804) who published his findings in 1775) and Antoine Lavoisier (1743–1974), who named the element in 1777.
86 *the fair Eloisa:* a stereotypical name for a pastoral damsel.
87 *the adnatae of my visual organs:* growths (i.e. eyebrows). In 1st ed, this dialogue is between Sir Ambrose and the butler Abelard.
88 *one of the anas genus:* "anas" is latin for "duck". Presumably the image is that of a startled duck taking flight "when the clouds are charged with electric fluid". Variants of the phrase "like a dying duck in a thunderstorm" are common from the late 18th century. The OED cites Sir Walter Scott's *Peveril* (I.x1. 269): "Closed her eyes like a dying fowl—turned them up like a duck in a thunder-storm."
89 *let the air out of the beds:* inflatable beds: more future-tech.
90 *a composition of alkali and oil:* Or, in other words, the upper classes, or some of them, actually use *soap* when they wash!
91 *Aiériform:* Light, insubstantial.
92 *Azote:* Lavoisier's term for nitrogen (from the Greek "without life").
93 *some verses of my own:* The verses shown to Sir Ambrose in 1st ed.
94 *wagging his ears in token of assent:* not quite the evolution of form, but suggesting that the future might result in different abilities.
95 *sixty miles an hour:* steamboats were relatively new technology, but this is much faster than anything possible at the time. (His head is in such a spin that he is confusing his instructions, resulting in surreal possibilities.)
96 *Indian rubber:* India(n) rubber or caoutchouc: mainly imported from South America although an Asian version was known from 1798. Its elastic properties made it increasingly useful although it was something of a curiosity in Britain until some time after Faraday analysed its properties in 1770. Entwerfen explains it as something exotic.
97 *Parturient mountains:* He is referring to a Latin tag: "Mountains will be in labour, and an absurd mouse will be born" (Horace, *Ars Poetica*). All that work [i.e. the slow and solemn dramatic production of ... *a small bottle of Indian rubber*] and nothing much to show for it.
98 *synonymous:* corrected from "synonimous" in 1st ed.
99 *And Hodge stood lost in wide-mouth'd speculation:* 'Where Hob stood lost in wide-mouth'd speculation!' from 'Sir Joseph Banks and the Emperor of Morocco' by the satirist Peter Pindar (John Wolcot, 1738–1819). Lisa Hopkins (2003: 13) draws attention to the slight misquotation to make the point that JWL's intention is to emphasise the lack of meaning in the "unintelligible" texts left to future readers, implying that "the literature which incorporates the radical vision of Mary Shelley will also perish."
100 *the present fashionable mode of travelling:* Space travel. As Rauch points out (*The Mummy.* 1994, xiv)

this explanation is awkward. JWL (or Entwerfen) seems to think that the balloon can ascend until it is beyond the Earth's gravitational attraction and wait in a stationary position until the globe turns. Edric, though, realises that England and Egypt are not in the same latitude, and so this will not work: the balloon will have to be directed (somehow) and the breathing apparatus is not necessary if they stay within the atmosphere. Given JWL's consistent comic dialogue, it is more likely that the error is Entwefen's than hers.

101 *materia medica:* technical term for the body of collected knowledge about medicines, from *De materia medica* by Pedanius Dioscorides (1st century AD).
102 *quicksilver vapour:* Mercury vapour, an advance on steam! Associated with alchemy and medicine (especially the treatment of syphilis). The vapour of mercury is highly poisonous, and this may be another underlining of Enterwerfen as "mad scientist".
103 *laughing gas:* Nitrous oxide, isolated in 1772 by Joseph Priestley (associated with the "Lunar Society") and later developed by Humphrey Davy, who coined the term "laughing gas". Davy's study of the gas, *Researches, chemical and philosophical* (1800) included accounts of its use as a recreational drug, and prints showing its use were circulated in the early 19th century.
104 *ripieno:* musical term for instrumental parts as accompaniment rather than solo. (Literally "padding" or "stuffing".)
105 *bob-wig:* Wigs were out of fashion by 1827. Bob-wigs, smaller than the full formal wigs, were introduced in legal circles in the 1780s.
106 *mucilaginous:* Sticky or gelatinous.
107 *Apollo Belvidere:* a Roman copy of a Greek statue, discovered in 1503. The joke is partly the "culture" of the lower classes, but partly that the figure was regarded as the epitome of male beauty, so Celestina is neglecting her duties for a bit of beefcake.
108 *steam valet:* an automaton or robot.
109 This is not entirely futuristic speculation. By the 1820s, Muhammed Ali, who had been Pasha of Egypt since 1806, had taken advantage of Napoleon's brief occupation of the country to introduce an industrial revolution along European lines and institute a programme of modernisation. Dams and bridges, and construction projects, and factories and cotton mills were already springing up along the banks of the Nile, and more land was opened up for cultivation. (Wilkinson, 87, 101).
110 *fifteen miles an hour:* a considerable speed for land travel.
111 *Colonies of English and Americans peopled the country:* In this future, Africa is colonised by Europe, though there are hints that some African countries are independent.
112 *Mizraim:* the Biblical name for Egypt.
113 Sais: the city of Saïs mentioned by Herodotus as a site sacred to Athene. Plutarch's *On Isis and Osiris* says "In Saïs the statue of Athena, whom they believe to be Isis, bore the inscription: 'I am all that has been, and is, and shall be, and my robe no mortal has yet uncovered.'"
114 *having been erected by a shepherd:* possibly from Herodotus Book 2: "Here then they reckon one hundred and six years, during which they say that there was nothing but evil for the Egyptians, and the temples were kept closed and not opened during all that time. These kings the Egyptians by reason of their hatred of them are not very willing to name; nay, they even call the pyramids after the name of Philitis the shepherd, who at that time pastured flocks in those regions."
115 *Pallic race:* Pelasgians: forerunners of the Greeks.
116 *Soliman Giam ben Giam:* In some Islamic traditions, the Biblical Solomon ruled the djinn. The Egyptian historian Muhammed Al-Maqrizi (1364–1442) collects stories about Cheops (Khufu) but JWL's source for this link is doubtful. (https://en.wikipedia.org/wiki/Khufu#Diodorus_of_Sicily)
117 *punchy:* paunchy.
118 *waggon:* spelled thus in text.
119 *riot act:* An act of 1714 to enable magistrates to declare gatherings of 12 or more unlawful assemblies which must disperse.
120 *posse comitatus:* Citizens whom the magistrate or equivalent can call upon to help preserve the peace.
121 *They had now entered the Pyramid:*
122 *Apis:* the god Apis was identified as a bull.
123 *Typhon:* The giant whom Zeus defeated and cast into Tartarus. Herodotus identified him with the Egyptian god Set.

124 entered *the tomb of Cheops:* Italics in text.
125 *Phtah:* Ptah, the Egyptian creator-god.
126 *stedfast:* spelled thus in text.
127 *woful:* spelled thus in text.
128 *Lycurgus:* Legendary law-giver of Sparta who according to Plutarch's *Lives* established the institutions of the Spartan state.
129 *for the 'fect, as Parson Snorum calls it:* There is a Parson Snorum mentioned in an aside in John Eyre's *Consequences* (1794) so this could be a running if obscure joke.
130 *auto-da-fĕ:* "act of faith": public penance and execution of heretics under the Spanish Inquisition.
131 *Do not all philosophers agree that we receive ideas merely through the medium of the senses?:* the argument from, e.g. John Locke's *Essay Concerning Human Understanding* (1690) that ideas are not innate but are produced in the mind by sense-impressions, that is explored in *Frankenstein* Vol. 2 Ch. 3 when the creature describes how he comes to self-awareness and awareness of the outside world.
132 *propria persona:* a legal term: acting for one's self. More loosely, "in person".
133 *Amalthea:* Foster-mother of Zeus. In one legend she is personified as a goat; when the baby Zeus broke off one of her horns, this became the Cornucopia, or Horn of Plenty, a never-ending source of nourishment.
134 *all snugly packed up in my walking-stick!:* more examples of Entwerfen's ingenuity.
135 *Methinks all seems wondrous, new, and strange!:* The future-shock Cheops experiences is reminiscent of many time-travellers, and readers may have been reminded of the reports of the "reanimated" Roger Dodsworth, a widely-circulated hoax which inspired Mary Shelley's short story "Roger Dodsworth: the Reanimated Englishman" (unpublished until 1863). Shelley's "Valerius: The Reanimated Roman", written c. 1919 but unpublished in her lifetime, has the hero disgusted by the decadence of the Italy into which he is revived.
136 *Arsinöe:* As we later learn, in the final chapter, his sister. This seems to have nothing to do with the actual Cheops, though Arsinöe II (316 BC – ?270 BC) was the sister and wife of Ptolemy II who was Pharaoh 283–246 BC.
137 *papyrine:* made of papyrus.
138 *strange, infernal vessels, vomiting forth volumes of fire and smoke:* steam-boats, developed in the late eighteenth century, came in the early nineteenth century to operate commercially in the USA and Britain. The first steam-boat on the River Thames was the *Margery* in 1815. By the 1820s, several steamship lines were running between London and Margate, and across the Channel.
139 *I did not mean to slay him!:* the mystery set up by this source of Cheops' guilt is resolved in the final pages.
140 *the boat of Hecate, ready to ferry me across the Mærian Lake:* one of the Greek goddess Hecate's realms was the underworld. The souls of pharaohs were ferried into the afterlife.
141 *My hell:* italics in text.
142 *filagree:* (filigree: spelled thus in text.)
143 *Suit:* suite.
144 *automaton birds:* like the fashion in some Oriental courts – a fashion continued with the women in "loose trowsers" and looking like "Houris".
145 *trowsers:* spelled thus in text.
146 *jets de feu:* jets of fire.
147 *beau ideal:* highest standard of excellence.
148 *Houris:* The beautiful "virgins" who will reward the faithful in the Muslim paradise.
149 *sate:* spelled thus in text.
150 *Vandyck's:* Anthony Van Dyke 1599–1641, Flemish artist who became a court painter in England in the reign of Charles I.
151 *a small perpetual motion wheel:* another of JWL's not altogether serious examples of future technology.
152 *cortege:* slowly-moving procession.
153 *the air was thronged with balloons:* very much the kind of scene on the "March of Intellect" prints circulated during the 1820, or the later illustrations of Albert Robida (1848–1926)
154 *inflammable air:* hydrogen, identified and named thus by Henry Cavendish (1766). The name

"hydrogen" was given by Antoine Lavoisier in 1783. The gas was used in balloons by Jacques Charles (1783), in an ascent witnessed by hundreds of thousands. Among the characters of William Blake's satire "An Island in the Moon" (1784, but unpublished in his lifetime) is "Inflammable Gas the Wind-Finder".

155 *tassals:* tassels (spelled thus in 1st ed.).
156 *the spectators of the stag-hunt on the lake of Killarney:* Killarney was famous for stag hunting. *A Guide to the Lakes of Kilarney* by Rev. G. N. Wright (1822) footnotes (p. 35) the "extravagent portraying" of "the author of The Hibernia Curiousa": "There is, however, one eminent danger that awaits the hunter, which is, that he may forget where he is and jump out of the boat." The Hibernia Curiosa (anon 1764) has "him" rather than "the hunter" and in the context is describing how the best way for spectators to enjoy the hunt is from the lake, so this might be JWL's direct source.
157 *arn't:* spelled thus in text.
158 *"grizzled here and there,":* The quotation marks indicate this is a quotation. The eponymous Marmion in Walter Scott's poem (1808) is described thus:

His forehead by his casque worn bare,
His thick mustache, and curly hair,
Coal-black, and grizzled here and there,
But more through toil than age; (Canto 1: 5)

159 *the balloons became entangled with the winged heroes and each other in inextricable confusion:* This and other scenes recall the profusion of balloons, winged flyers, and other futuristic technologies in the satirical prints by "Paul Pry" issued as "The March of Intellect".
160 *Æolian:* Æolius, Greek god of the Wind.
161 *"She is certainly dead!" reiterated Lord Doodle:* The "Thompson Twins" effect of repeating the obvious.
162 *recalled to life, a being so long immured…* Punctuation as in 1st and 2nd eds.
163 *it knelt down and took the creature up, and kissed it, and lamented over it:* Cats being sacred to the Ancient Egyptians.
164 *serous moisture:* The "serous fluid" is fluid within or exuding from body cavities.
165 *événemens passes:* past events.
166 *their billing and cooing:* heavily ironic, as is immediately shown.
167 *every ten thousand men throughout the kingdom should choose a deputy:* This future is undemocratic by our standards, but considerably more so than the pre-1832 Reform Act system of Parliamentary representation known to JWL.
168 *A gloomy foreboding hangs upon my mind, and undefinable horrors rise in dim perspective before me:* typical gothic rhetoric.
169 *cerecloths:* Wax-impregnated cloth used to wrap corpses.
170 *a fiendish laugh rang in his ears:* This melodramatic occurrence is the first instance of Cheops as the "moral compass" of the story, noticing the "mischief" being conspired.
171 *Cneph:* as understood by Herodotus, the creator-god who took the form of a serpent.
172 *Typhon himself never pursued Isis …:* After becoming pregnant with Horus, Isis flees from Set, who has killed and dismembered her husband Osiris. The identification of Set with Typhon, the giant who battled with Zeus and was exiled to Tartarus, is drawn by Herodotus from earlier Greek sources.
173 *Epoptae:* Initiates in the Eleusian Mysteries.
174 *and let us seal our compact:* The Mummy is the external emblem of Father Morris's own devious plotting.
175 *Isian mysteries:* to do with the goddess Isis.
176 *that river:* the Thames (presumably he is looking out of the window.)
177 Macrobian Ethiopians: The "long-lived Ethiopians" of Herodotus Book 3
178 *incumbrances:* (spelled thus in text) encumbrances
179 *bad taste of the middle ages:* the "gothic" in architecture.
180 *I should not be surprised at all at all:* The repetition of "at all" and the pronunciation of "reason" as "rason" are further examples of Fr. Murphy's "strong south country brogue".

181 *the garden of the duke of Cornwall's mansion:* "of Mr Montague" as in text, but this should probably be "the garden of the Duke of Cornwall". This appears to be an error in the revision. Sir Ambrose Montagu and his retinue are staying with the Duke of Cornwall (Vol 1 ch 4). In the first edition, they are staying with Sir Ambrose's brother and sister-in-law, Mr and Mrs Montagu, who have been written out of the second edition, although "by one of those singular coincidences in real life, which would be called improbable in a novel, ... Mr. Montagu's mansion adjoined that of the duke." (Vol 1 Ch 8). Later references to Edmund as "Mr. Montagu" possibly explain why JWL decided against two "Mr. Montagus" in the text, and the retention of "Mr. Montagu" here shows that confusion is certainly possible.

182 *Oh, Julia! Julia!:* Who is Julia? This is another set-up to be revealed at the end.

183 *they sin, and they repent!:* It is the blatant hypocrisy of those who repent only to fall further into sin when subject to further temptation that so disgusts Cheops.

184 *par merveille:* by chance, for a wonder.

185 *the late palace at Richmond:* 16th century palace built by Henry VII (formerly Earl of Richmond) on the site of Sheen Palace. Elizabeth I used it as a home, and died there in 1603. It was demolished after the Civil War. JWL is referencing various schemes in which former soldiers after the Napoleonic Wars were saved from destitution by such "public works".

186 *nobody can perish of cold in our streets...:* more of what readers of pulp sf in the 1930s would refer to as "gosh-wow technology", but it also serves to underline the complacency of the ruling class.

187 *unbiassed:* spelled thus in text.

188 *Speed the Plough:* Comedy by Thomas Morton (1764–1828), first performed in 1798, known for the (off-stage) character Mrs Grundy who became a byword for convention and interfering censoriousness.

189 *her health visibly declined:* There is a hint of vampirism here.

190 *as no house was permitted to approach within a certain distance of the Thames:* The mobile houses again.

191 *villany:* spelled thus in text.

192 *They degrade themselves to your level:* the "good" side are induced to use unsavoury methods which, as they are not used to, they will fail in.

193 *Machiavel:* The Shakespearian "Machiavell" (Machiavelli). The "Vice" of the Elizabethan drama.

194 *distraite:* distracted.

195 *fête champêtre:* garden-party or (high-class) picnic, sometimes involving fancy-dress.

196 *Philaa:* Philae: island said to be the site of a tomb of Osiris, and a major temple-complex.

197 *eloquent blood spoke in her cheeks:* John Donne "The Second Anniversary".

198 *if you choose Elvira for your Queen:* Possibly echoes of George IV's exclusion of his Queen, Caroline of Brunswick, from his coronation (19 July 1821).

199 *lion pismire:* The larvae of the Myrmeleontidae family of insects, which dig pits to entrap their prey (which includes ants).

200 *even the imagined happiness of Utopia itself:* Thomas More's *Utopia* (1516).

201 *Constantinople, then the capital of the powerful empire of Greece:* At the time of publication, Greece was in the middle of its war of independence against the Ottoman Empire. An independent Greece was agreed in 1830, and the 1832 Treaty of Constantinople established Greece as an independent state ruled by the German Otto of Bavaria.

202 *felucca:* traditional sailing-boat of the eastern Mediterranean.

203 *the Old One:* euphemism for the Devil.

204 *Dick Jones:* this may be Egypt, but the peasantry have English names.

205 All Grand Cairo: A correction [[Sumatra]] (1st ed.). Indonesia is of course Islamic and the contacts between Sumatra and the Middle east date from the 13th century, but why this reference is not clear.

206 *they've got the plague there:* plague is still a feature of this future. The plague is also central to Mary Shelley's *The Last Man:* the apocalyptic plague on the novel also begins in Constantinople (Volume 2 Chapter 12).

207 *amphlites: ampholytes* are compounds that when dissolved in water can act either as acid or as a base.

208 *Cirro-strati streak the sky, ... cumulus-strati:* more "useful knowledge" of the working-classes. The modern classification of cloud-types was designed by Luke Howard (1772–1864) in his *Essay on the Modification of Clouds* (1803).

209 *I could have better spared a better man:* Shakespeare, *Henry IV Part 1* Act V Sc 3: Prince Henry spies Falstaff (who has just shammed dead):

Poor Jack, farewell!
I could have better spared a better man

210 *Don Alfonso, that mighty hero of the Bourbon race:* His conquest of North Africa is part of JWL's future-history.
211 *Timbuctoo would never have risen:* the rise of Africa is still largely due to colonialism from Europe.
212 *real course of the Niger:* not known by Europeans until Richard Lander (1804–1834) followed the river to the Atlantic in 1830.
213 *sources of the Nile:* also at time of publication a mystery to be solved. The source of the White Nile in Lake Victoria was claimed by the explorer John Hanning Speke (1827–1864) in 1858 and later confirmed by Henry Morton Stanley (1841–1904) in his expedition of 1874–77.
214 *alcaide:* commander or local military governor.
215 *the tyrannic Alfonso:* In conquering North Africa, Alfonso "destroyed the monarchy". Spain is now a republic, though a republic more after the post-revolutionary French model than a democracy, preaching liberty but practising tyranny. Similar anti-democratic sentiments appear in *Stories of a Bride*, particularly in the story "The Mystic".
216 *Doctor Entwerfen, the fortunate inventor of the immortalizing snuff:* more mad-scientist knockabout comedy.
217 *Roderick the Second, surnamed the Great, was then in the flower of his age:* The Irish are dominant, romantic, powerful.
218 *the air of some unearthly visitant from the tomb:* a deliberate touch of the supernatural.
219 *amor patriae:* love of the fatherland.
220 *á la portée de tout le monde:* within everyone's reach.
221 *The sun shone o'er fair women and brave men:* Byron, "The Eve of Waterloo" (*Childe Harold*, Canto III. Stanza 21.): "The lamps shone o'er fair women and brave men,"
222 *barb:* Berber (North African) horse.
223 *aigrette:* head-dress so-called because it often incorporated, or was intended to suggest, a white egret's feather.
224 *vandyk lace:* the wide lace-edged collar popularised in the paintings of Anthony van Dyke (1599–1641).
225 *gàité de Coeur:* light-heartedness.
226 *palanquin:* covered litter.
227 *coup de main:* sudden attack.
228 *I have a favourite page, who dreads to return to Greece, and I would willingly place him under your care:* as will be revealed, some Shakespearean cross-dressing to add to the melodramatic mixture.
229 *feu d'artifice:* firework display.
230 *the fabled arch:* As-Sirāt, the bridge over which the souls of the Faithful enter paradise on the day of Judgement. Below it are the fires of hell. JWL may be thinking of Bifrost, the rainbow bridge which connects Valhalla with Middle-Earth in Norse mythology.
231 *skait:* spelled thus in text.
232 *the heroes of Burgos, Valladolid, and Salamanca:* Salamanca (22 July 1812) was one of the decisive battles of the Peninsular War, conducted by the Irish-born Arthur Wellseley (Duke of Wellington.) In May 1813, after being repulsed the previous year, he successfully captured the city of Burgos.
233 *slided:* as in text.
234 *befell:* spelled thus in text.
235 *maison de plaisance:* country house.
236 *upon the usurpation of the then despot of Switzerland:* more future-history.
237 *like the hare with many friends:* allusion to a fable by John Gay (1685–1732), best known for *The Beggar's Opera*. In *Fables*, (1757), the farm animals are friendly with the hare, but when the horns of the hunt are sounded the hare goes in turn through all her friends who find excuses not to help.
238 *ribband:* a ribbon, but sometimes meaning something somewhat more formal or decorative than the

modern term, or the strip of wood or fabric on which the decorations were attached.
239 *slily:* spelled thus in text.
240 *woful:* spelled thus in text.
241 *craniology:* the study of differences in the size and shape of human skulls between "races" or groups of humanity. What they are actually doing is practicing *phrenology*, developed as a "science" in 1796 by Franz Joseph Gall. Phrenology suggests that character traits are located in parts of the brain which shape the skull, thus by locating "lumps", the subject's psychological and moral character can be discovered. While the Italian criminologist Cesari Lombroso later in the 19th century popularised theories that propensities to criminal behaviour (and the "primitive" stereotypes in racial categorisation) were shown by these physical attributes, phrenology as a science was debunked by the early 20th century. JWL is clearly using the unfortunate Dr Entwerfen to mock believers in this "most profound and useful of all sciences".
242 *persons of note:* Echoing the tally of the slain after Agincourt in Shakespeare's *Henry V* Act 4 Sc 8: "None else of name." JWL pointedly does *not* name the "notables" who have been slain.
243 *Montagu:* Montague in text.
244 *devoirs:* obligations.
245 *I only just saw a great many people that tried to kill me:* untraced as a quotation, but a very vivid description of Napoleonic-era warfare.
246 *"There is something very extraordinary about that boy," said Roderick:* Shakespearean cross-dressing only works if the other characters are a bit dim.
247 *negociate:* spelled thus in text.
248 *if some day I should fly off in a tangent … to colonize the moon:* another touch of science fiction? The possibility of the moon as a world, with inhabitants, that could actually be reached (as opposed to a location for utopian or satirical romances) goes back at least to John Wilkins, Bishop of Chester's *The Discovery of a New World* (3rd ed. 1640) in which he speculates about travel to the moon. Speculative fantasies such as Godwin's *The Man in the Moone* (1638), Cyrano de Bergerac's *L'auture Monde* (1657) , David Russen's *Iter Lunare* (1703) and Daniel Defoe's *The Consolidator* (1705) all involve space travel. Nicholson (1948) and Parrett (2004) survey many of the fictions that JWL might have had access to. Did she know of Edward Francis Burney's 1815 illustrations to the unpublished "Q.Q. Esq's Voyage to the Moon"? (*Illustrated London News*, (6 June 1959), 982–3.)
249 *That he has fair Seville seen …:* "he that hath not Seville seen, is no traveller, I ween," is quoted as a "proverb" in the picaresque novel *L'Histoire de Gil Blas de Santillane* (Alain-René Lesage, 1717–1735). It was translated into English by Tobias Smollett, 1748. The emphasis in the text is Roderick's teasing of Dr. Entwerfen.
250 *such a sighing Strephon:* a lamenting shepherd from the beginning of Sydney's *Arcadia* (1598).
251 developement: spelled thus in text.
252 *teazed:* spelled thus in text.
253 *We pity faults …:* possibly an echo of William Whitehead's "Essay on Ridicule" (1743): "We pity faults by nature's hand imprest/Thersites' mind, but not his form's the jest."
254 *Touch a man whose skin is sound:* untraced, possibly a fictional "old proverb".
255 *reveille:* military signal to awaken the troops.
256 *began:* spelled thus in text.
257 *couleur de rose:* optimistic (as in "seeing through rose-coloured spectacles").
258 *wildgoose schemes:* Elvira's "projects" seem straight from a "March of Intellect" satire.
259 *gaucherie:* awkwardness.
260 *clear as a trumpet with a silver sound:* From Dryden's *Palamon and Arcite:* "Whene'er he spoke, his voice was heard around, / Loud as a trumpet, with a silver sound;" also cited in Walter Scott *Waverley* Ch 21.
261 *stupified:* spelled thus in text.
262 *traineaux:* sleighs.
263 clashing of swords: although transport and horticultural technology seems to have developed, weapons technology apparently has not.
264 *No. 7, is just come back from Brighton:* What has happened is a clumsy adjustment of one of the "moving houses" back into its usual position.

265 *The copula, and the predicate:* "copula" is a word that links the subject in a sentence to the subject complement (in this case the verb "take"). The "predicate" is the part of a sentence containing a verb and stating something about the subject (in this case "take your logic"). The nature of the quibble is explained by the clumsy domestic: the humour(?) is in the way one part of the sentence is personified as an active tangible agent ("The Devil") that can "take" things and the other (logic) is an abstract concept. Abelard points out that "The Devil take" can be construed as a metaphor rather than an *actual* devil *actually* taking.

266 *a close disagreeable part of the city of London, called Kensington:* Then, as now, a fashionable area, although the 2017 destruction by fire of the residential tower block Grenfell Tower in the north of the borough has drawn attention to features more akin to those of JWL's future.

267 *automaton steam surgeon:* another example of robots.

268 *Can this be a prison?:* more topsy-turvey. This future believes that prisons "should be made agreeable residences". The attempts of reformers such as John Howard (1726–1790) and, especially, Elizabeth Fry (1780–1845) are hinted at. Howard's 1777 report on *The State of the Prisons* influenced future reform. Fry campaigned to improve the conditions of women prisoners in Newgate during the first decades of the 19th century.

269 *fire-stage balloon:* systematic fire-fighting was until the 1833 London Fire Engine Establishment: a matter of "brigades" operated by various insurance companies.

270 *spalpeens:* rascals (Irish).

271 *Endymion:* In Greek mythology, shepherd who was loved by the moon-goddess Selene.

272 *stedfastly:* spelled thus in text.

273 *a regency must be appointed:* the Prince of Wales (the future George IV) became Prince Regent in February 1811 on the illness of his father, George III (seen, as here, as as much a derangement of the senses as a physical illness).

274 *Foreigners have sometimes been known to respect the interests of a people, and reign as gloriously as native-born monarchs:* following the Hanoverian George I in 1714, Britain was ruled by a dynasty of "foreigners".

275 *Wehe mir:* woe is me.

276 *"learned in the law,":* The quotation marks signify that this is a quotation of some kind, a tag or a cliché. We learn the truth in a few lines.

277 *automaton judge:* the legal profession is reduced to a series of automata.

278 *In different parts of these counsel were holes:* somewhat like player-pianos, though these were not patented until 1841. JWL would have known of the less sophisticated "barrel pianos" used by street musicians and in places of entertainment.

279 *Ach! Es ist aus mit ims! wir sind verlohren!:* "Oh we're done! We're lost!"

280 *Sabaoth:* technically "hosts" or "armies" but the "witches' sabbatt" of folklore is what is imagined.

281 *stopt:* spelled thus in text.

282 *popt:* spelled thus in text.

283 *Uprear the club of Hercules—For what? / To crush a butterfly, or brain a gnat:* from John Wolcott (as "Peter Pindar") "Lines on Doctor Johnson" (Monthly Magazine vol 36 part 2 Nov 1 1813), describing Johnson's style:
"Uplifts the club of Hercules—For what? / To crush a butterfly, or brain a gnat."

284 *make Nature stand aghast:* variants of this and other phrases reach the point of cliché in apocalyptic literature.

285 *'Tis sweet to rest, from dread of danger free …:* untraced. Possibly original to JWL.

286 *Yes, love indeed is light from Heaven …:* Byron, "The Giaour", (1813).

287 *Lead on, lead on, though horrors wait …:* untraced. Possibly original to JWL.

288 *that she was beautiful, and he not blind:* Byron, "The Lament of Tasso" (1817): "that thou wert beautiful and I not blind".

289 *strong as proofs of holy writ:* Shakespeare *Othello* Act 3 Sc 3: "Trifles light as air are to the jealous confirmations strong as proofs of holy writ."

290 *an unfortunate animal upon which he was trying experiments:* animal experimentation or vivisection, allegedly justified by the contention of René Descartes (1596–1650) that animal perception was that of automata or machines, was increasingly controversial. Anita Guerrini (Knellwolf &

348] *The Mummy! A Tale of the Twenty-Second Century*

Goodall, 2008: 71–85) draws attention to the French scientist François Magendie (1783–1855) who demonstrated in London in 1824 and whose work was widely cited in activity against animal cruelty.

291 *in the celebrated scene in the Barber of Seville:* 1775 play by Pierre Beaumarchais (1732–1799). Rossini's opera *The Barber of Seville* (1816: first performed in England 1818) places the "shaving scene" in Act 2, where the singing-tutor Basilio appears, to be utterly confused by what is going on.

292 *Doating:* spelled thus in text, but see next paragraph.

293 *the lively girl seemed changed into the intelligent woman:* possibly the most significant change in the novel.

294 *weeds:* clothing (as in "widow's weeds", worn during a period of mourning, and thus probably with an implication of drabness or obscurity.)

295 *doggrel:* Doggerel (spelled thus in text).

296 *What means this mummery?:* Lisa Hopkins (2003: 10) points out the play on words here.

297 *bivouack:* bivouac: temporary camp.

298 *ci-devant:* former.

299 *interdium:* intermediate layer.

300 *phospate:* spelled thus in text: phosphate.

301 *publickly:* spelled thus in text.

302 *daffadowndilly:* daffodil.

303 *"My what nerves?" asked Hans:* Hans, being German, does not have the over-education of the British lower classes.

304 *a complicated concatenation of rectangular angles:* Johnson's Dictionary (1775) defines "Net-work" as "any thing reticulated or decussated, at equal distances, with interstices between the intersections". JWL's version of this definition is also in Mrs Henry MacKarness, *The Young Lady's Book: A Manuel of Amusements, Studies and Pursuits* (1876) and S. Annie Frost's *The ladies' guide to needle work, embroidery, etc* (1877)

305 *parieties:* walls of a bodily cavity.

306 *rhomboidal:* in which adjacent sides are not equal and angles are not right angles (i.e. diamond-shaped).

307 *fourth position:* a position in classical ballet, feet turned out (toes pointing in opposite directions) one in front of the other.

308 *"Pauline is not my child!":* the wrapping-up of loose ends and revelations of identities in this chapter is either the work of a novice author desperate to complete her work, or a writer who understands exactly the comic effect such a pile-up of plot-twists can create.

309 *If your honours like the child, you may have her ...:* the "adoption" of random children by aristocratic travellers was not confined to the pages of melodrama. Percy Shelley, with the apparent approval of Mary, made at least one attempt. Their attempt to adopt Marguerite Pascal in Champlitte, in 1814 on their journey to Switzerland, was rejected by the girl's father. (Seymour, 107). The episode is not recorded in Mary Shelley's published *History of a Six Weeks' Tour* (1817).

310 *naad:* need.

311 *as usual in such cases, he now hated the creature he had made:* a common trope in melodrama, but the echo of Victor Frankenstein's relationship with his creation is clearly there.

312 *a beautiful and accomplished woman:* The "Julia" whom Fr. Morris/Edgar apostrophizes in Volume Two Chapter Three, although with all the sudden revelations of this chapter the reader might be forgiven for not remembering this.

313 *say rather, your own passions:* In this, Cheops is the "moral chorus". It is Father Morris's own nature that has led him to sin.

314 *Edfou:* temple dedicated to Horus.

315 *pannel:* spelled thus in text (and also below).

316 The United Kingdom of Great Britain and Ireland came about with the 1800 Act of Union. Previous to that, the "kingdoms" had been united through the titles of British monarchs as King/Queen of Great Britain and King/Queen of Ireland, although there were separate Parliaments for each nation. The Act was a result of the defeat of the 1798 uprising, in which Protestant Republicans and many Catholics rose to demand independence, and was in part an attempt to temper the excesses

of the "Protestant Ascendancy" and the possibility, with contemporary movement towards Catholic Emancipation, of a French-allied Irish parliament. The satirical point here, of course, is that a (Catholic) England is now subordinate to a strong Ireland ruled by the dashing and virile Roderick.
317 *recal:* spelled thus in text.
318 *Æolian harp:* played by the movement of wind (Aeolus, the Greek god of the wind) across the strings.
319 *Seek not to pry into secrets denied to man:* there is knowledge which must be denied to humanity – not quite the scientific approach!
320 *I have at last found a reasonable man:* the "reasonable man" is one who knows not to push curiosity so far. Edric is not, therefore, Victor Frankenstein.
321 *My sister—my own, my beloved sister:* this seems to have little or nothing to do with any legends attached to the historical Cheops, though the practice of Pharaonic "interbreeding" was well known and the (much later) Arsinoe II, (b.316 BC) was married to her brother Ptolemy II.
322 *Permitted for a time to revisit earth ...:* it turns out that there was a greater moral force behind all this, and Entwerfen's regenerative "science" is undermined.
323 *rouzed:* spelled thus in text.
324 *Oblivion laid him down upon his hearse:* Walter Raleigh "Oblivion laid him down on Laura's hearse:" ("A Vision Upon this Conceit of the Faery Queene" (1595), the preface to Spencer's *Faerie Queene*).

THE MUMMY!
A TALE OF THE
TWENTY-SECOND CENTURY

By Jane Webb Loudon

Edited by Nickianne Moody and Andy Sawyer

PART TWO:
Background and Changes

Sources of The Mummy!: "An encyclopedia of the future"[1]

The Mummy! was a calculated attempt at popular literary success. In her introduction, Loudon presents her account of the 22nd Century as an answer to her search for literary novelty. "[T]he deep mine of invention cannot be worked out; there must be some new ideas left, if I could but find them," she writes; to be answered by the spirit of her inspiration offering a "Chronicle of a future age." Writing the future is something unknown, untried, but the "spirit" advises her to embrace the sense of difference which will come about as new governments, strange discoveries, and stranger modes of life come into view. This – the idea that the future is very much a legitimate area of literary speculation, and that the future will be very different indeed from the present – is the heart of many forms of what we now call science fiction, but JWL is drawing upon several popular threads in what is clearly an attempt to make the story a best-seller.

One is the "discovery" of Ancient Egypt. The flood of artefacts from and information about Egypt after the Napoleonic wars resulted in much popular enthusiasm. The diplomat Henry Salt (1780–1827) acquired much material for the British Museum through the activities of agents such as the Italian-born Giovanni Belzoni (1778–1823) who brought to London the vast head of Rameses II which inspired the "Ozymandias" sonnets of 1808 by Percy Shelley and his friend Horace Smith. Smith, interestingly, explicitly draws Shelley's meditation on the hubris of lost civilizations into ironically contemporary relief as a future explorer among the ruins of London wonders, like Shelley's "traveller", what "unrecorded race" constructed these colossal fragments. Belzoni opened an exhibition in Piccadilly in May 1821 at which a mummy was unwrapped, and almost 2000 visitors attended the first day (Tyldsley, 101). Jane Webb, searching for a subject, could hardly have missed the craze for Egyptian artefacts. *The Literary Gazette* in March 1826 reported on the presentation of the mummy of an Egyptian crocodile to the French Academy of Sciences. Peregrine Wilton's poem "To an Egyptian Mummy", published in the *Literary Gazette* of August 1827, expresses the enigma of a long history of which much was known through second-hand Classical sources such as Herodotus (the main source for the history and mythology of *The Mummy!*) and the presence of actual objects, but whose voices had not yet been heard:

> What were thy race, thy deeds, thy name?
> Dark as the tomb.

Since the discovery of the Rosetta Stone in 1799, various scholars in Britain and France had tried to decode hieroglyphics by comparing the scripts on the Stone. Jean-Francois Champollion finally cracked the code in 1822, but his conclusions were not fully accepted until some years later. The life of Cheops JWL gives her readers was based (very loosely) upon accounts in Herodotus: the murder and incest that (we discover) condemns him to the fate of tempter and guide in this complex melodrama has no source other than an author's desire to provide gothic shivers and a background context to the Mummy's diabolical laughter and ghastly stare. The popular fascination with Egyptology lasted through the 19th century with numerous authors, including Theophile Gautier, Louisa M. Alcott, and H. Rider Haggard drawing upon a range of motifs (including mummies) and well into the 20th, with a well-established folklore centred around the alleged "curse" that followed the discovery of Tutankhamun's tomb by the archaeologist Howard Carter in 1922 (Daly:84–116; Luckhurst:153–207).

A second thread was a complex mix of topical references which may be overlooked by the reader today. Alan Rauch (2001: xvi) notes the background to the accession of George IV, after a long Regency, to the throne in 1820 and the controversy over his marriage to, and separation from, Caroline of Brunswick and the way attempts were made to prevent her from attending the coronation and remove her claim to a royal title on the grounds of her adultery. The 1820s also saw bitter arguments over Irish Home Rule and Roman Catholic Emancipation—a Bill to allow Catholic representation in Parliament was passed in 1829. The novel's comical Irishmen, the absolutist Catholic monarchy, and the invasion by the King of Ireland clearly come from the way that Loudon was responding to pressures and anxieties, and much-discussed topics, that would be on the minds of her readers. Paul Alkon's attack upon the "Bowdlerised" abridged version published by Michigan University Press is partly through a sense that Rauch's abridgement and introduction minimise the different ways in which Loudon is presenting a picture of *contemporary* Britain rather than an anticipation of a future one. Towards the end of the novel (Vol 3 Chapter 4), the rivalry between Elvira and Rosabella for the Queenship of England echoes the constitutional squabbles of recent history. Because of Elvira's illness and incapacity, "a regency must be appointed". There is controversy over her headstrong desire to marry the foreign Prince Ferdinand and therefore lose her right to the throne "for the laws against foreigners remain inexorable". Elvira's passion has been underwritten by the people ("marry who you list, we shall still be your slaves!" yell the mob, in an ironic revisioning of the vocal support for Caroline of Brunswick during the government attempts to legislate a dissolution of her marriage to George IV by means of the 1820 "Bill of Pains and Penalties").

Other ingredients from popular fiction were added to the mixture: the

Machiavellian priest Father Morris and his comic foil Murphy, a touch of Shakespearian cross-dressing which demands considerable suspension of disbelief, and the energetic and attractive heroine Clara, by far the most positive and interesting of the female characters. Her transformation from a lively girl into an intelligent woman, and her mature sensitivity, cause Cheops to call her "extraordinary" and see her as something rare among the "degenerate race" he is thrust among. His attempts to aid her are not the Machiavellian moral temptings he applies to others, but genuine altruism. Cheops himself lurks and laughs "fiendishly" and "diabolically" too often to make him the genuinely "new" hero the author aspires, in her introduction, to create. (Her attentions, one suspects, were in fact rather upon the glamorous Irish prince Roderick, whose glossy curls and coral lips Edric admires at one point in the novel, whose practical joking and teasing reflect the vein of humour that runs through it, and with whose pseudonym "Seymour" she lightly disguised her own voice in *Conversations Upon Comparative Chronology* and "A Walk in a Flower-Garden"). The hasty explanations and revelations in the penultimate chapter are comic in their constant unmasking. Indeed, when we return to the introduction, with its "I could think of nothing that had not been thought of before", we surely realise that part of the novel's satirical focus is upon those very "deep mines of invention" that the struggling novice author has seen as entirely barren.

A further air of "topicality" might have come from reports of the "reanimated" English traveller Roger Dodsworth, a widely-circulated hoax circulated in newspapers and magazines during the summer of 1826, which inspired Mary Shelley's short story, unpublished until 1863, "Roger Dodsworth: the Reanimated Englishman" (Robinson, 1975). Indeed, the comparison of past and present recorded in the "Letter From the Gentleman Preserved in Ice" printed in the *New Monthly Magazine* of July 1826 might have been in JWL's mind as she records the initial confusion in Cheops when he awakens in 2126 to find the world completely changed.

However, the novel's achievement does not lie in its employment of genre tropes. Central to the argument for suggesting that this weird Gothic romance is a *science fiction* novel is JWL's conscious exploration of difference. Its 22nd-century setting is innovative: at that time future-settings were rare. I. F. Clarke's *The Tale of the Future* gives 1664 as the first date in which a "future-fiction" was composed, and it was well into the second half of the 19th century before such fictions became anything like commonplace. JWL's admiration for Walter Scott (whose works she is careful to show surviving, at least in a manner, in her 22nd Century, and who is frequently referenced within the novel) is partly admiration of a pioneer of the art of attempting to create a plausible *past*. The techniques of the historical novel need to be developed before we explore the future. The future is more complicated. It could be a dream-vision of a technologically utopian world. It could be apocalypse. It could be anything in between. The future of *The Mummy!* may exist to mock the present, but it reminds us that the future will not be the same as the past.

Second, Edric's employment of Dr Entwerfen's galvanic battery to revive Cheops proves him to be, like Mary Shelley's Victor Frankenstein, a savant who rejects the received wisdom of the past to embrace understanding of the mysteries of life and death. "You convinced me" (he says to his spiritual advisor, Father Morris) "so clearly of the possibility of resuscitating a dead body, that since that moment I have been tormented by an earnest desire to communicate with one who has been an inhabitant of the tomb."[2] Like Frankenstein, Edric is afflicted by a scientific *hubris* that knows no bounds, but is only one step (if that) beyond the curiosity that was inspiring genuine scientific understanding in the world around the young Jane Webb. While she satirises science, eventually leaving Edric to draw the conservative conclusion that there are divinely-protected areas of knowledge men must not meddle in, the *way* she satirises it reveals her own knowledge and understanding. Entwerfen's gadgetry is, like the character, played for comic effect; but its comedy reflects the unsettling effect of actual technology. More generally, the topsy-turvy world of plain-living, ignorant aristocrats and jargon-spouting commoners in *The Mummy!* is part of the conversation about the education of the working classes which resulted in Henry Brougham's Society for the Diffusion of Useful Knowledge. Reaction included such commentary as the ballad "The March of Intellect" published as part of the *Noctes Ambrosianae* sequence in *Blackwood's Magazine* in which

> All ranks are so dreadfully wise,
> Common sense is set quite at defiance,
> And the child for its porridge that cries,
> Must cry in the language of Science.

and the blacksmith

> can tell you that iron is hot,
> Because it is filled with caloric![3]

The "elaborate and scientific expressions" of the "vulgar" characters like the butler Ambrose are certainly the subject of mockery:

"Take heed you do not forget your message by the way," repeated Sir Ambrose, smiling.
"Not all the waters of Lethe could wash such somnifugous tidings from my memory," replied the butler. "Your honour's words are imprinted upon

the mnemonic organ of my brain; and my sensorium must be divided from my cerebellum ere they can be effaced." (Volume 1 Chapter 3).

But the aristocracy is not spared. The Duke of Cornwall's "plainness and simplicity", in contract with his butler, is such as "sometimes almost to degenerate into rudeness". The comedy includes the introduction of characters such as Lords Noodle and Doodle who, like Hergé's Dupont and Dupond (Thompson and Thomson) in the *Tintin* albums, repeat each other's dialogue in vain attempts to create meaning out of banality. Jane Webb's use of "scientific" language is parody, but, her subsequent career seems to prove, is by no means an attack upon the concepts of "useful knowledge" and self-improvement. Her tone is certainly not that of Theodore Hook's futuristic (set in 1926) "satirical squib"[4] with the familiar "March of Intellect" title, in which the Duke and Duchess of Bedford are regarded with contempt by a footman who despises the Duke's geographical ignorance and their daughter is ridiculed by two under-servants for not being able to answer a simple question about the rules of chess. Hook simply reveals the fear of a ruling caste that their underlings should speak to them as equals. By imagining an entire world of difference, from the industrial development of Egypt and the changed dress-codes of women to the future's baroque gadgetry and the loss of so much of her present's culture, Jane Webb was able to tackle the "the novelty of the illusions" presented to her in her introduction with confidence and extrapolate from the absurdities of her present with greater effect.

And third, the "estranging" effect of science fiction is shown in the way the recent technology of *ballooning* is extrapolated into the normal mode of transport.

In both Shelley's and Webb's novels it is the speed and ease of balloon travel which is emphasised. The 1820s was the overture to the great age of steam railway. Although "It was not until the Liverpool & Manchester Railway was formally opened by the Duke of Wellington on Wednesday, 15 December 1830, that the Railway, a public carrier of passengers and freight on rail by mechanical traction under statutory authority, stood plain for all to see"[5] (Robbins, *The Railway Age* (1965): 21), the Stockton & Darlington line, using steam locomotives to carry freight, was opened in 1825. Loudon, by 1827, has already incorporated the possible impact of the railway into her imagination. Her future aristocrats are able to transport their town houses to the country by rail; a river is crossed by a "steam-percussion moveable bridge". The romantic image of flight, the fusion of possibility and impossibility in these descriptions of what stood as a symbol of humanity's dominance over the natural order, "the power of man over the elements" which Mary Shelley rhapsodises in *The Last Man* (Shelley, 1998: 71), here stands for the apogee of human use of technology to change the world, a fitting image at a time when great changes were forthcoming and the relationship of society to technology was being rewritten.

Images involving balloons were issued as part of the "March of Intellect" series of satirical prints by "Paul Pry" (William Heath, 1795–1840), and the songs and essays which poked fun at the wave of education and self-improvement among the literate working and lower-middle classes.[6] Whether from *The Last Man* or some other source, ballooning touched the imaginations of the teenage Brontes in their juvenile world-building. Charlotte Bronte wrote, in her "Tales of the Islanders" (1829). "As soon as we had read this letter, we ordered a balloon, the which when it was brought we got into & then steered our way through the air towards Strathfieldsay." (Alexander, 2010,:20).[7] Almost contemporaneously with *The Last Man* and *The Mummy!*, in 1826 the *London Magazine* published a weird dream-fiction entitled "Aerostatic Speculations Over London, in a Balloon Constructed Under the Scientific Direction of Signor Asmodeus of Madrid". Although not an "anticipation" in the sense which (at a pinch) Shelley and Loudon may be read, it establishes ballooning as part of a common-stock of images there for the author of speculative, satirical, or weird fiction, as science-fictional as the spaceships of Jules Verne or Percy Gregg[8] or those that flourished in the pulp magazines of the 20th century.

The reviewer in the *Literary Gazette* of October 1827 (possibly William Jerdan) is guarded. "Excepting for its gay sarcasm, the future is stubborn material for a writer," he or she writes, identifying the anonymous novelist as "a young author", and concluding that "the fancy of a writer in this class [i.e. that of the tale of the future] is less likely to be responded to by the fancies of others than if either present or past were the theme." (*Literary Gazette* Oct 1827: 661) Later, in his autobiography, Jerdan, talking about his interest in Webb's early career, calls *The Mummy!* "a production of great talent and imaginative power" (Vol 4 p. 321). Others may not have shared Jerdan's judgement. The brief review in *John Bull* concentrates on the revival of Cheops and concludes "This part of the story would have been very fine, had not the conception, in some degree, been forestalled by Mrs Shelley's Frankenstein; but if "The Mummy" has less originality, in its scenes of terror, it may safely be affirmed that, in its comic or burlesque passages, it possesses indications of humour, of which "Frankenstein" is entirely destitute." (October 22 1827, 330)

If the *John Bull* reviewer thought that *The Mummy!* had more laughs but fewer thrills than *Frankenstein*, what impressed John Claudius Loudon about the book was not so much its satire but its speculation. Although his "[E]xtravagant and impracticable ideas will sometimes aid in forming new and useful combinations" is perhaps a clumsier tag-line than "Extravagant fiction today … cold fact tomorrow", the motto used by Hugo Gernsback to launch, in 1926, *Amazing Stories*, the first English-language magazine specifically devoted to what he called "scientifiction"[9] (scientific fiction) and later "science fiction", the publication of *The Mummy* and JWL's manifesto-like call for a fiction that looks into the future and explores *change* is certainly as important a moment as Gernsback's, even though few English writers were to follow her example until later in the century.

The novels published in quick succession by two women in the early nineteenth century did not immediately establish an identifiable genre in the way that the late nineteenth century "scientific romance" or magazine "scientifiction/science fiction" in the USA allowed space for speculative debate in the form of fiction. Reasons for this could include the need for a more identifiable discourse of science and fiction to be established in the coming decades; the more closely observed nature of a society transformed by the consequences (foreseen and unforeseen) of mass capitalism and technological advancement; the way paradigm-shifts such as Darwinism and Marxism established spaces for speculation and bitter argument about biological or political futures; or the application of the rhetoric of utopia and dystopia to all these developments. From 1871 onwards, fictions about future-wars or powered flight (and later, travel between the planets) offered increasing scope for ways in which anxieties about the present and aspirations about the future could be turned into fiction, and the growth of a mass reading public interested in such speculations was, in Loudon's time, some way in the future. It was not until 1894 that Lewis Hind, editor of the *Pall Mall Budget*, asked a young science journalist named H. G. Wells to turn his expertise into a series of science-based stories. As for Loudon herself, once her search for novelty reached a successful conclusion, she moved to different territory for *Stories of a Bride* (1829), but her life's work expands upon the fascination with science, technology, and "improvement" which pervades *The Mummy!*

Bibliography

Aldiss, Brian, *Billion Year Spree* [1973]] (London, Corgi; 1975).
Alexander, Christine, ed. *The Brontës Tales of Glass Town, Angria and Gondal. Selected Writings* (Oxford, Oxford University Press; 2010).
Alkon, Paul K. *Origins of Futuristic Fiction* (Athens, Georgia, University of Georgia Press; 1987).
Alkon, Paul K. 'Bowdler Lives: Michigan's *Mummy*' Science Fiction Studies 23:1 (March 1996), 123–30.
Alkon, Paul K. *Science Fiction before 1900* (London, Routledge; 2002).
[Anon.] '[Review of] *The Mummy*' Literary Gazette, 360 (October 1827), 660–1.
[Anon.] '[Review of] *The Mummy*' John Bull, (October 22), 1827, 330.
[Anon.] '[Review of] *The Mummy*' Monthly Review, 6:27 (November 1827), 411–2.
[Anon.] 'Obituary Notes' *Lloyd's Weekly Newspaper* (August 1 1858) 9.
[Anon.] 'Foreseen by an Artist in the Year of Waterloo: Man's Tireless Quest for the Moon.' *Illustrated London News*, (6 June 1959), 982–3.
[Anon.] 'Letter From the Gentleman Preserved in Ice' *New Monthly Magazine* July 1826, 453–458.
Beetham, M. *A Magazine of Her Own* (London, Routledge; 1996).
Beetham, M. 'Ladies Companion 1849–1870' (eds) Laurel Brake and Marysa Demoor, *Dictionary of Nineteenth-Century Journalism* (Ghent and London, Academia Press and the British Library, 2009), 340.

Belzoni, Gionvanni, *Narrative of the Operations and recent Discoveries in Egypt and Nubia* (London: John Murray, 1820).
Boniface, Priscilla (ed.) *In Search of English Gardens: The Travels of John Claudius Loudon and His Wife Jane* (Wheathampstead, Lennard Publishing; 1987).
Clarke, I. F, *The Tale of the Future* (London, The Library Association;1961).
Daly, N. *Modernism, Romance, And The Fin De Siècle. Popular Fiction and British Culture, 1880–1914* (Cambridge, Cambridge University Press; 1999.
David, Rosalie, *Discovering Ancient Egypt* (London, 1993; Michael O'Mara).
Davidoff, Lenore and Catherine Hall, *Family Fortunes: Men and Women of the English Middle Class 1780–1850* (London, Hutchinson; 1987).
Dewis, Sara, *The Loudons and the Gardening Press: A Victorian Cultural Industry* (Farnham, Ashgate; 2014).
Finch, J., *Married to the Job: Wives Incorporation into Men's Work* (London, 1983; George, Allen and Unwin).
Fraser, Flora, *The Unruly Queen: The Life of Queen Caroline* (Berkley, University of California Press; 1997).
Gernsback, Hugo, 'A New Sort of Magazine' *Amazing Stories* 1:1 (April 1926), 3.
Goldstein, Laurence, *The Flying Machine & Modern Literature* (Basingstoke, Macmillan; 1986).
Herodotus *The Histories* (trans. Aubrey de Selincourt) (Harmondsworth; Penguin, 1955).
Holmes, Richard, *The Age of Wonder* (London, HarperPress; 2008).
Holmes, Richard, *Falling Upwards: How We Took To the Air* (London, Collins; 2013).
Hook, Theodore, "The March of Intellect" *John Bull* (27 March 1826), 101.
Hopkins, Lisa., 'Jane C. Loudon's The Mummy!: Mary Shelley Meets George Orwell, and They Go in a Balloon to Egypt', Cardiff Corvey: *Reading the Romantic Text* 10 (June 2003). Online: Internet (5. 12. 2019): <www.cf.ac.uk/encap/corvey/articles/cc10_n01.pdf>.
Howe, Bea, *Lady With Green Fingers: The Life of Jane Loudon* (London, Country Life Ltd; 1961).
Hughes, K., *The Short Life and Long Times of Mrs Beeton* (London, Fourth Estate; 2005).
Jerdan, William, *The Autobiography of William Jerdan* (4 vols.) (London, Arthur Hall, Virtue And Co.; 1853.
Knellwolf, Christa and Jane Goodall (eds.), *Frankenstein's Science: Experimentation and Discovery in Romantic Culture, 1780–1830* (Aldershot, Ashgate; 2008).
Kuttner, Henry, *A Gnome There Was* (New York, Simon & Schuster; 1950).
Lawford, Cynthia, 'Diary' *London Review of Books* 21 September 2000: 36–37.
Ley, Willy, 'For Your Information: Mail by Rocket', *Galaxy* 8:5 (August 1954) 44–51.
Loudon, Agnes, *Tales For Young People* (London, Bowdery and Kerby; 1846).
Loudon, Agnes, *Tales Of School Life* (London, Grant and Griffith; 1850).
Loudon, Jane Webb, *Prose and Verse* (Birmingham, R. Wrightson; 1824).
Loudon, Jane Webb, *The Mummy! A Tale of the Twenty-Second Century* [1st ed], (London, Henry Colburn; 1827).
Loudon, Jane Webb, *The Mummy! A Tale of the Twenty-Second Century* [2nd ed.] (London, Henry Colburn; 1828).
Loudon, Jane Webb, *Stories of a Bride* (London, Henry Colburn and Richard Bentley; 1829).
Loudon, Jane Webb, 'Letter to Sir Walter Scott, December 12, 1929) (National Library of Scotland, MS 3911:149).
Loudon, Jane Webb, *Conversations Upon Comparative Chronology and the Outlines of General History* (London, Longman Rees, Orme, Brown and Green; 1830).
Loudon, Jane Webb, 'A Walk in a Flower-Garden' in S. C. Hall, (ed.) *Juvenile Forget-Me-Not* (London, Ackermann; 1833),103–120.
Loudon, Jane Webb, *Instruction in Gardening for Ladies* (London, John Murray; 1840).
Loudon, Jane Webb, *Agnes, or, The Little Girl Who Could Keep Her Promise* (London, Harvey and Darton; 1846).
Loudon, Jane Webb, *The Ladies' Country Companion, or, How to Enjoy a Country Life Rationally* (London, Longman, 1845).
Loudon, Jane (ed.), *The Ladies' Companion, At Home and Abroad* (London, Bradbury and Evans; 1849–50).
Loudon, Jane Webb, *The Mummy! A Tale of the Twenty-Second Century* [1827] (Introduction and abridgement by Alan Rauch) (Ann Arbor, University of Michigan Press; 1994).
Loudon Jane Webb, *Gardening for Ladies* (London, Constable; 2013).

Loudon, John Claudius, 'Hints for Improvements', *The Gardener's Magazine* (March 1829), 478–9).
Loudon, John Claudius, *Self-Instruction for Young Gardeners*, 2nd ed., (London, Longman, Brown, Green and Longmans, 1847).
Luckhurst, Roger, *The Mummy's Curse: The True History of a Dark Fantasy* (Oxford, Oxford University Press; 2012).
McCouat, Philip, "Forgotten Women Artists #2: Jane Loudon: Artist, Futurist, Horticulturalist and Author" *Journal of Art in Society* (November 2017) http://www.artinsociety.com/forgotten-women-artists-2-jane-loudon.html.
Maginn, William, *Whitehall, or The Days of George IV*, (London: W. Marsh, 1827).
Martin, Leopold 'Reminiscences of John Martin, K. L. by His Son' *Newcastle Weekly Chronicle* (5. Jan 1889 – 20 April) 1889.
Matoff, Susan, *Conflicted Life: William Jerdan, 1782–1869*, (Eastbourne, Sussex, Academic Press; 2011).
Nellist, Brian, "Imagining the Future: Predictive Fiction in the Nineteenth Century" in David Seed, ed. *Anticipations: Essays on Early Science Fiction and its Precursors* (Liverpool: Liverpool University Press, 1995) 111–136.
Nicolson, Marjorie Hope, *Voyages to the Moon* (New York, Macmillan, 1948).
Parrett, Aaron, *The Translunar narrative in the Western Tradition* (London, Ashgate, 2004).
Rauch, Alan, *Useful Knowledge: The Victorians, Morality, and the March of Intellect* (Durham, North Carolina, Duke University Press; 2001).
Robbins, Michael, *The Railway Age* (Harmondsworth: Penguin, 1965).
Robinson, Charles E., "Mary Shelley and the Roger Dodsworth Hoax", *Keats-Shelley Journal*, 24 (1975) 20–28.
Schenker, Heath, 'Women, Gardens, and the English Middle Class in the Early Nineteenth Century', *in* Michel Conan, *Bourgeois and Aristocratic Cultural Encounters in Garden Art, 1550–1850* (Washington DC, Dumbarton Oaks Research Library and Collection; 2002), 337 – 360.
Schofield, Robert S., 'The Industrial Orientation of Science in the Lunar Society of Birmingham' *Isis*, Vol. 48, No. 4 (Dec., 1957), 408–415.
Schofield, Robert S., 'The Lunar Society of Birmingham; A Bicentenary Appraisal' *Notes and Records of the Royal Society of London*, Vol. 21, No. 2 (December, 1966), 144–161.
Seymour, Miranda. *Mary Shelley* (New York, Grove Press; 2001).
Shelley, Mary *Frankenstein* (London, Penguin,1992).
Shelley, Mary, *Frankenstein: The 1818 Text* (New York, Penguin; 2018).
Shelley, Mary, *The Last Man* [1826] (Oxford; Oxford University Press; [Oxford World's Classics],1998.
Shteir, Ann B. *Cultivating Women, Cultivating Science: Flora's Daughters and Botany in England 1760–1860* (Baltimore, Johns Hopkins University Press; 1996).
Shteir, Ann B., 'Green-Stocking or Blue? Science in Three Women's Magazines, 1800–50', *Culture and Science in the Nineteenth-Century Media* ed. Louise Henson *et. al.* (London, Ashgate; 2004) 3–13.
Simo, Malanier Louise, *Loudon and the Landscape: From Country seat to Metropolis 1783–1843* (New Haven, Yale University Press; 1988).
Sutherland, John and Veronica Melnyk, *Rogue Publisher: The 'Prince of Puffers'. The Life and Works of the Publisher Henry Colburn* (Brighton, Edward Everett Root; 2018.
Suvin, Darko, *Metamorphoses of Science Fiction* (New Haven, Yale University Press; 1979).
Taylor, Geoffrey, *Some Nineteenth Century Gardeners* (London, Skeffington; 1951).
Uglow, Jenny, *The Lunar Men: The Friends Who Made the Future* (London, Faber and Faber; 2003).
'V', 'Aerostatic Speculations Over London, in a Balloon Constructed Under the Scientific Direction of Signor Asmodeus of Madrid', *London Magazine* 5:19, July 1826) 351–58.
Wilkinson, Toby, *A World Beneath The Sands: Adventurers and Archaeologists in the Golden Age of Egyptology* (London: Picador, 2020).
Wilson, John, "Noctes Ambrosianae no XXIII" in *Blackwood's Magazine* 18:107 (December 1825), (Edinburgh: Blackwood & Sons, 1825. 751–765.
Wilton, Peregrine, 'To an Egyptian Mummy', *Literary Gazette* 551 (August 1827), 524.

Textual change

For reasons which are not entirely clear, JWL extensively rewrote *The Mummy!* for the second (1828) edition. While the essential plot of the novel is unchanged, some of these revisions involve major alterations in structure and the loss of important secondary characters. In the first (1827) edition, the revolt, brought about in part by Queen Claudia's indolence, which Edmund quashes in the first chapter is moved in the 2nd edition to Chapter 2, with some expanded detail and greater focus upon the character of Edmund. Volume 1 ends with the dramatic appearance of Cheops in London, at what is meant to be the triumph of Edmund before Queen Claudia. The Mummy's arrival ends the ceremony, which has already been disrupted by the aerial commotion among the unruly balloon-borne spectators which will result in the Queen's death. The apparently supernatural visitation emphasises the flaws and fissures in the State that we have begun to see open up. Cheops inspires terror:

> his ghastly eyes glaring with unnatural lustre upon the terrified courtiers, who ran screaming in agony in all directions, forgetting everything but the horrid vision before them.

But this terror is very much, as we will come to see, because their own moral corruption is reflected in this visitation. Cheops is not the monstrous visitation of subsequent "mummy-fiction", which developed later in the 19th century and, as described in Roger Luckhurst's *The Mummy's Curse* (Oxford, 2012), received further injections of obsessive dread with the legends that arose after the opening of Tutankhamun's tomb in November 1922. The irony is that he himself is undergoing a moral re-education even as he manipulates the desires of the guilty.

The revised Volume 1 (now consisting of twelve, rather than eleven chapters, ends with the first chapter of the 1827 Volume 2, moved to offer a quieter, but ominous concluding note as, following the guilt-ridden confusion which afflicts the population (and, significantly, Cheops himself), we see a masked figure stalking the Duke of Cornwall's garden, a figure which the terrified servants assume is the Mummy but is in fact a confederate of Rosabella's *confidante* Marianne. Their cryptic dialogue clearly suggests that there is conspiracy afoot:

> "How is she?" cried the stranger.
> "Better," returned the female.
> "Then it is past the power of man to kill her," resumed the first ...

And the identities of "her" and the "stranger" become obvious as the story develops.

Some chapters contain little or no revision other than slight changes of vocabulary, while others, such as Volume 1, Chapters 2, 4, 5, 6, and 7 are extensively rewritten to comply with a decision to lose characters such as Sir Ambrose's brother and sister-in-law Mr and Mrs Montagu. While they are amusing, JWL might have decided to lose them because they seem so clearly to echo another garrulous, scolding wife and kindly but detached husband, the Bennets from Jane Austen's *Pride and Prejudice* (1813). This leaves Clara, their daughter, as Sir Ambrose's orphaned niece, which perhaps strengthens her background and development as a lively and competent woman. In their being written out, the Montagu's dialogue has been reassigned to other characters, most notably Sir Ambrose's butler Abelard and his *amour* Mrs Russel.

Sometimes this substitution does not always work, because the satire directed at a detached gentleman is redirected unreworked at a pretentious underling. For example:

> "It is evidently an Egyptian Mummy," observed Abelard and, as he seldom spoke, every word he uttered was listened to as an oracle." (2nd ed. Vol 1 Chapter 12)

This does not sound like the garrulous Abelard. Elsewhere, however, when Abelard reads his poem "in the acromonogrammatic style" to Mrs Russel (Vol 1 Chapter 8) the exchange seems more natural and comic than the 1st edition version where he reads it to Sir Ambrose.

But there are also other substitutions, including Father Morris for Entwerfen as the source of the idea for Edric's experiments on reanimation, which strengthens the figure of the scheming, Machiavellian monk as well as possibly foreshadowing JWL's eventual revelation that there is some grand Divine scheme within the complex network of betrayals and punishments. Similarly the movement of, and clues to the appearance and identity of "Seymour", and his connection to Father Murphy, the comic Irish priest, seem to be structural changes to provide a firmer, more connected plot (changes in Vol 2 Ch 1 suggest more vividly's Elvira's attraction to Seymour). When Edric, in Vol 2 Ch 10 of the 1st edition mentions knowing a countryman of Roderick's with whom Roderick, it turns out, is also acquainted, it is Father Murphy. This is revised (Vol 2 Ch 9 of the 2nd edition) to be Father Morris, and the exchange is used to give us more of the character of the mysterious monk: "though an intelligent and highly cultivated man, he has strong prejudices, and that his dislike to the Irish is carried to an extravagant excess."

Perhaps the most pointed joke, the Hatton garden steam-book

manufactory, is cut from the second edition. Discussing Clara's health, Mrs Montagu quotes a couplet of doggerel verse:

"It seems to me she hoards some secret care,
That breaks her rest and drives her to despair."

Her husband asks where the verse is from:

"Oh! it is one of a lot I bought the other day at the patent steam-book manufactory, in Hatton-Garden. I had been buying some other things, and so I persuaded the man to throw me in a bargain of quotations very cheap. They were all quite new, and ready cut, dried, and made up into pills for use."

This is possibly simply a casualty of having to lose or reallocate dialogue between the Montagus, However, William Maginn's *Whitehall, or the Days of George IV* (1827) gives us JWL's publisher Henry Colburn, according to Sutherland & Melnyk, 104, as "Henry the Great" who "owns a manufactory in Burlington Street as crammed with hacks as a Lancashire cotton mill is with machine-handlers". *Whitehall*, the only novel of a prolific journalist, is an unusual exercise in future-fiction. The preface tells us that "[t]his singular work was printed in Teyolunhakawaranenopolis, capital of the great empire of Yankeedoodoolia, in the year 2227, exactly four hundred years from the present date." What Maginn has actually presented to his readers is a story set in his/their present imagined as a *historical* novel, using the formulaic techniques and language of that genre. Like *The Mummy!*, it is a reaction to the popular novels of Sir Walter Scott, but unlike Jane Webb he is not using the future as a speculative playground. The pedantic and mock-scholarly footnotes and commentary may exoticize the everyday in a similar fashion to the way Entwerfen's precious fragments of balladry are highlighted (Volume 1 Chapter 6), but Maginn's satirical joking is limited to the device of imagining a future writer looking back at the nineteenth century and re-creating it in fiction along the model of Scott's romances.

The "manufactory" is described at length, (pp 303–323) describing a personage whose physical description and speech-patterns, if based upon a real individual, would be clearly recognizable to anyone who knew him, and whose working-practices are only one step behind "mechanical" manufacturing: for a Historical Novel, for instance:

"Take Pinnock and Maunders History of England, and there find a time when there was a war or a plot. Take an ass, and bray him in a mortar until you make him a hero. Saddle your ass with panniers, full of the adventures of the time, and let him work. This is the principal ingredient. For a heroine, take a young lady of mild manners, who is expected to go mad in the course of the book, and, during her paroxysms, to quote scraps of verses." (Maginn, 312–3).

And then, promotion and publicity (for which Colburn, the "Prince of Puffers" was notorious) come into action: "Serve up, hot and hot, with puffs; them you manufacture yourself, or you hire a regular baker." (Maginn, 316).

In the 2nd edition, it has to be Sir Ambrose who worries about Clara's health, so the joke is superfluous. It might, however, have been the case that the appearance of the scene in *Whitehall* touched a sensitive nerve and JWL (or Coburn himself) removed it on those grounds.

Other changes are simply changes of vocabulary or expression, even of punctuation. Sometimes they are the kind of minor but immediately effective change which is the hallmark of a skilled writer/editor, as in the case of the brackets added to Elvira's instructions aside to Emma to make it clear that she really is talking to two people at once and perhaps paying more attention to her servant than to Edmund's injured and increasingly melodramatic protestations that "You do not love me … or you could not answer with such provoking coldness." At other times they are word-changes or slight shifts in grammar, such as "not contented" to "not satisfied" and "had become" to "became" in the opening paragraphs of the first chapter. There are also the correction of errors in punctuation or spelling that one might expect in a careful revision. What is clear, however, is that JWL carefully revised the novel for its second edition. This might indicate that the first edition was rushed, that she had not fully thought through how she wanted it to appear in the haste to see what might be a life-saving publication in print, or that initial reception had caused her to think more carefully about it. It is probably safe, however, to conclude that the second edition was her "preferred" version and it has been the edition upon which subsequent reprintings (the 1872 Warne edition, most of the various online reproductions, and the 1994 University of Michigan Press abridgement by Alan Rauch) have been based.

What follows are the changes between the first and second editions, in which we can see the development of this fascinating novel.

Volume 1: Chapter 1

Changes here are minor, simply recasting sentences and punctuation, apart from the deletion of the lines referring to the uprising fomented by Roderick of Ireland and how Claudia was saved by Edmund Montagu, which is described at greater length in Chapter 2.

The religion of the country: [[In the meantime, the religion of the country]] (1st ed).

But it is not in the nature of the human mind …: [[It is not in the nature of the human mind, however, to be contented …]] (1ˢᵗ ed.).

The English people were not satisfied: [[were not contented]] (1ˢᵗ ed.).

Education became universal: [[had become universal]] (1ˢᵗ ed.).

but both shared the same fate; for the leaders of each, in turn,: [[the leaders of each in turn]] (1ˢᵗ ed.).

The prince continued inexorable: [[The prince, however, continued inexorable]] (1ˢᵗ ed).

assimilated as naturally with infidelity as with superstition: [[assimilated as naturally with infidelity as superstition]]. (1ˢᵗ ed.).

It seemed probable to thinking minds, however, that this scheme …: [[This scheme, however, though feasible in theory, seemed likely to present some difficulties when it was to be put in practice.]] (1ˢᵗ ed.).

But as she seldom did any harm, though she did not do much good, she contrived …: [[However, though she did not do much good, she seldom did any harm: she thus contrived …]] (1ˢᵗ ed.).

that any change had taken place …: Following on in 1ˢᵗ ed. is: [[The commencement of the year 2126 was, however, marked by symptoms of turbulence. The malcontents, secretly encouraged by Roderick, King of Ireland, and suffered to gain strength under the easy sway of Claudia, rose to arms in different parts of the kingdom; and marching to London, attempted to seize the person of the Queen. For the moment, the regular forces of the kingdom seemed paralysed, and the insurgents would have succeeded in their daring attempt, but for the presence of mind and valour of Edmund Montagu, a young officer of ancient family, a captain in the Queen's body-guard, who had the good fortune to rescue his sovereign. This circumstance was decisive; the rebels, disappointed in their hopes, and imperfectly organized, gave way everywhere before the regular troops, who had now recovered from their stupor; whilst the Queen, whose gratitude for the timely succour afforded by Edmund Montagu was unbounded, made him commander of her forces in Germany, and the youthful hero quitted England to take possession of his post.]]

Volume 1: Chapter 2
Chapter 2 is extensively rewritten, from entirely new material to simply

breaking up longer paragraphs. In the second edition, it is now Father Morris (now the Confessor to the Montagu family rather than the Duke of Cornwall) rather than Dr Entwerfen who persuades Edric to embark upon his scientific experimentation and reanimate a mummy. This allows the sinister and mysterious monk greater agency in his scheming. There are clearly plots going on right from the beginning. Taking the course of action which leads to the resurrection of Cheops away from the comic "inoffensive" Entwerfen and putting it in the hands of Father Morris (triggering his own downfall) adds a new level of irony to the conservative ending of the novel. Apparently a minor alteration, it is one of the most significant changes to the book.

The indolent Claudia ... From here to "The youthful general was the son of as baronet ... his soldiers loved though they feared him" is new material. Although the novel begins in both editions, "In the year 2126, England enjoyed peace and tranguility", this new material begins "The indolent Claudia had already reigned three years in the most profound tranquility; and the year 2127 was beginning also to roll placidly away...", presumably (as noted below) to flag the three centuries between composition and setting.

1st ed. begins (following on from Ch 1): [[High and distinguished as was the favour shown to Edmund Montagu, it was by no means greater than he deserved. His face and figure were such, as the imagination delights to picture as a hero of antiquity; and his character accorded well with the majestic graces of his person. Haughty and commanding in his temper—ambition was his God, and love of glory his strongest passion; yet his very pride had a nobleness in it, and his soldiers loved though they feared him.
Very different was the character of his younger brother Edric...]]

Very different was the character of his younger brother Edric: [[Very different was the character of his younger brother Edric, whose romantic disposition and contemplative turn of mind often excited the ridicule of his friends. As usual, however, in similar cases, the persecutions he endured upon the subject, only wedded him more firmly to his own peculiar opinions; which, indeed, he seemed determined to sustain with the constancy of a martyr; whilst he put on such a countenance of resolution and magnanimity whenever they were assailed by jests or raillery, as might have been imagined suitable to an expiring Indian at the stake. Unfortunately, however, his friends did not always properly estimate this dignified silence; and their repeated bursts of laughter grated so harshly in the ears of the youthful Diogenes, that he became gradually disgusted with mankind. He secluded himself from society; despised the opinion of the world, because he found it was against him; and supposed himself capable of resisting every species of temptation, simply because, as yet, he had met with nothing adequate to tempt him. Older and more experienced persons have made the same mistake.]] (1st ed.).

Perhaps the striking difference ...: [[The education of these two young men had been entrusted to tutors of characters as essentially different as those of their pupils.— Father Morris, who had had the care of the elder, was an intelligent Catholic priest, the confessor of the family. Whilst Doctor Entwerfen, who took charge of the younger, was a worthy inoffensive man, whose passion for trying experiments was his leading foible; but whose good-nature caused him to be beloved, even by those to whom his follies made him appear ridiculous.]] (1st ed.).

The confessor was an intelligent, well informed man...: [[Sir Ambrose Montagu, the father of Edmund and Edric, was a widower, and these two sons constituted his whole family. The worthy Baronet was no bad representative of what an old English country gentleman always has been, and of what it still continued, even in that age of refinement. He was as warm in his feelings as hasty in his temper, and as violent in his prejudices, as any of his predecessors In fact, the same causes must always lead to the same results; and there is something in a country life that never fails to produce certain peculiar effects upon the mind]]. (1st ed.).

Country gentlemen have always been allowed ... roll as attendant planets: (new paragraph in 2nd ed.).

Notwithstanding all the changes ... He was nevertheless far superior: (new paragraph in 2nd ed.).

He was nevertheless far superior ... Sir Ambrose, however, was far superior (1st ed.).

In common with most persons of his class ... during the morrow: (new paragraph in 2nd ed.).

One fine evening in June, 2127 ... in the library. 1st ed. has for this paragraph: [[It was one fine evening in the summer of the year 2126, when Sir Ambrose Montagu, such as we have described him, was sitting in his library, anxiously expecting intelligence from the army. To divert his impatience, he had ordered the attendance of his steward Mr. Davis, and endeavoured to amuse himself by hearing a report of the affairs of his farm; whilst Abelard, an old butler, who had been in the Baronet's service more than forty years, stood behind his placed an elegant apparatus for smoking, and a magnificent service of malleable glass, made to fold up to a pocket size, when not in use, containing the baronet's evening refreshment.]]

(The change of date between editions from 2126 to 2127 keeps the setting of exactly 300 years from composition and publication.)

The worthy baronet was above seventy: [[Sir Ambrose was above seventy]] (1st ed.).

"That was Edmund's favourite grove, poor fellow!" and the anxious father sighed, as he puffed his hookah: (new sentence in 2nd ed.).

But Edric was otherwise engaged: [[In the meantime, Edric was, as usual, engaged in those abstract speculations with Dr. Entwerfen, which now formed the only pleasure of his existence, and which he pursued with an eagerness that made all the ordinary affairs of life appear tasteless and insipid. His imagination had become heated by long dwelling upon the same theme; and a strange, wild, undefinable craving to hold converse with a disembodied spirit haunted him incessantly. He had long buried this feverish anxiety in his own breast, and tried in vain to subdue it; but it seemed to hang upon his steps, to present itself before him wherever he went, and in short, to pursue him with the malignancy of a demon.]] (1st ed.).

Father Morris to his proselyte: [[Dr. Entwerfen to his pupil]] (1st ed.). (The conversation has been revised to be between Edric and Father Morris.)

I am, indeed, half mad ... regions of ethereal space: [["I am, indeed, half mad," returned Edric, with a melancholy smile; "and yet, perhaps, you will laugh when I tell you the reason of my uneasiness. I am tormented by an earnest desire to communicate with one who has been an inhabitant of the tomb. I would fain know the secrets of the grave, and ascertain whether the spirit be chained after death to its earthly covering of clay, condemned till the day of final resurrection to hover over the rotting mass of corruption that once contained it; or whether the last agonies of death free it from its mortal ties, and leave it floating, free as air, in the bright regions of ethereal space?"]] (1st ed.)

said the priest: said the doctor (1st ed.).

resumed Father Morris; ("resumed the Father Morris" in text): [[resumed the doctor]] (1st ed.).

"*Tell it, then,*" *said the Confessor sternly:* "Tell it to me, then," resumed the doctor. (1ˢᵗ ed.).

said the father: [[said the doctor]] (1ˢᵗ ed.).

till it is become morbid: 1ˢᵗ ed. continues: [["However though I do not see any reason why your dream should make you decline my offer, I will not urge it if it give you pain."]]

"*In my opinion,*" *said Father Morris ... machine in motion:* [["You know my sentiments upon the subject," replied the doctor, therefore I need not repeat them."]] (1ˢᵗ ed.).

"*I confess,*" *resumed Edric ... an incorporeal spirit:* [["I know," resumed Edric, "you think the organs of thought, reflection, imagination, reason, and, in short, all that mysterious faculty which we call the mind material; and that as long as the body remains uncorrupted they may be restored, provided circulation can be renewed: for that you think the only principle necessary to set the animal machine in motion."

"Can any thing be more clear?" said the doctor. "We all know that circulation and the action of the lungs are inseparably connected, and that if the latter be arrested, death must ensue; How frequently are apparently dead bodies recovered by friction, which produces circulation; and inflation of the lungs with air, which restores their action. If your idea be correct, that the soul leaves the body the instant what we call death takes place, how do you account for these instances of resuscitation? Think you that the soul can be recalled to the body, after it has once quitted it? Or that it hovers over it in air, attached to it by invisible ligatures, ready to be drawn back to its former situation, when the body shall resume its vital functions? You cannot surely suppose it remains in a dormant state, and is reawakened with the body; for this would be inconsistent with the very idea of an incorporeal spirit."

"Certainly," resumed Edric, "the spirit must be capable of existing perfectly distinct from the body; though how, I own candidly my imperfect reason cannot enable me to comprehend."]] (1ˢᵗ ed.).

If you could overcome your childish reluctance ...": [["I wish you would overcome your childish reluctance to trying an experiment upon a corpse, as that must set your doubts at rest. For if we could succeed in reanimating a dead body that has been long entombed, so that it might enjoy its reasoning faculties, or, as you call it, its soul in full perfection, my opinion would be completely established."]] (1ˢᵗ ed.).

which has been dead a sufficient time to prevent the possibility of its being only in a trance, and which yet has not begun to decompose?: ⟦which has been dead a sufficient time to prevent the possibility of its being only in a trance.⟧ (1ˢᵗ ed.).

Dr. Entwerfen had been present ... opened the door to the unwelcome intruder: replaces ⟦"You say right," cried the doctor with enthusiasm. "And who can tell but that we may be the favoured happy mortals, destined to raise the mystic veil that has so long covered them? we may be destined to explore these wonderful monuments—to revive their mummies, and force them to reveal the secrets of their prison-house. Cheops is said to have built the great pyramid, and it is Cheops whom we shall endeavour to re-animate! what then can be more palpable, than that it should be he who is destined at length to reveal the mystery."

"Every word you utter, doctor, increases my ardent desire to put our scheme into immediate execution: but how can we accomplish it? How obtain my father's consent? You know it has long been his intention to marry me to the niece of his friend the Duke of Cornwall, and you know how obstinate both he and the duke are."

"Then if you remain in England, it is your intention to marry Rosabella?"

"I would perish first."

"If that be the case, I confess I do not see the force of your objection."

True; for as long as I refuse to marry her, their anger will be the same, whether I travel or remain in England. In fact, I shall be happier at a distance than here, where I shall be annoyed by having the subject constantly recurred to. Yet it pains me to speak upon it to my father. He has so long cherished the idea of my marriage, and dwelt upon it so fondly—"

"Then you had better stay,—relinquish all thoughts of scientific discoveries, and settle contentedly on an estate in the country; employing your time in regulating your farm, settling the disputes of your neighbours, and bringing up your children, if you should happen to have any."

"How can you torment me so?—If you could imagine the struggle in my bosom between inclination and duty, you would pity me."

"Do you think your presence necessary to your father's happiness?"

"No—if Edmund be with him, he will never think of me."

"And do you not think—nay, are you not certain, that an union with Rosabella would make you miserable?"

"It is impossible, to doubt it; Her violent temper, and the mystery which hangs over the fate of her father, which she cannot bear to have even alluded to, forbid the thought of happiness as connected with her."

"It is strange, so little should be known of her father. I never heard the particulars of his story."

"No human being knows the whole, I believe, but the duke and my father.

However, I remember to have heard it rumoured when I was a child, that he had committed some fearful crime, and that he was either executed, or had destroyed himself."

"Then it is not surprising that it should pain Rosabella to hear him spoken of. But to return to our subject: your answers have removed the only doubts that can arise; and after what you have confessed yourself, I can not imagine what further hesitation you can feel—"

At this moment they were both startled; and the words were arrested on the doctor's lips by a gentle tap at the door.]]

and in a few seconds was by the side of his father: whilst Father Morris followed with nearly equal expedition: [[and in a few seconds was by the side of his father.]] (1st ed.).

Volume 1: Chapter 3
This chapter is lightly edited, in the most part recasting of sentences.

"My dear Edric" exclaimed Sir Ambrose; throwing himself into the arms of his son: preceded by [[When Edric and Dr. Entwerfen reached Sir Ambrose, they found Father Morris at his side, explaining with his usual promptness and clearness the meaning of the different signs of the telegraph.]] (1st ed.).

summoned Abelard, that he might dispatch him to inform the Duke of Cornwall of the news: [[his most intimate friend the Duke of Cornwall]] (1st ed.).

as Father Morris, on account of the storm, had passed the night at the house of Sir Ambrose: (added to 2nd ed.).

Like most persons living in complete retirement ... resolved to make the most of it: (added to 2nd ed.). Flagging earlier the Duke's fondness for "petty mysteries and needless manoeuvres" emphasises his later behaviour.

for this purpose ... better suited to the ambitious Edmund: [[Those, however, who were acquainted with the characters of the young people, thought the duke had quite reversed the natural order of things by this arrangement; and that the strong mind and haughty spirit of Rosabella would have suited better with the ambitious Edmund ...]] (1st. ed.)

That Father Morris would generally retire in silence: [[That his friends would generally retire in silence]] (1st. ed.).

to decide in such matters: (Following this is): [[Sir Ambrose, wishing the connection for his sons, and respecting even the whims of his friend, had as yet never interfered, and the young people had also appeared silently to acquiesce. Rebellious spirits, however, were hidden under this apparent calm; and the duke was soon to learn from experience, that human beings were rather more difficult to manage than a drove of turkeys, or a flock of sheep; a fact, of which before he did not seem to have the slightest suspicion.]] (1st ed.).

Abelard, finding himself alone, was fain to follow his example, marvelling as he went along: [[as he went along, however]] (1st ed.).

Elvira had yet never loved; why she had not, we leave to philosophers to explain: [[Elvira was as yet insensible to love; why she was so, we leave to philosophers to explain;]] (1st ed.).

Rosabella's character was much more easy to decipher than that of her cousin: [[was essentially different from that of her cousin]] (1st ed.).

She loved Edmund, but though she loved him with all that overwhelming violence, which only a soul like hers could feel: [[with all that overwhelming violence, that only a soul like hers could feel]] (1st ed.).

Ambition was her leading passion: [[ambition, however, was her leading passion]] (1st. ed.).

Volume 1: Chapter 4
This chapter has been extensively rewritten. Sir Ambrose's brother and his unfortunate downwardly-mobile marriage have been written out of the story, possibly because the conversations between the weary Ambrose and his nagging, "vulgar" wife are too reminiscent of the Bennets in *Pride and Prejudice* (1813). JWL keeps much of the satire, but puts it in the mouths of two more empathetically lower-class slapstick servant characters.

Well, well, it is all right … his friend's remark: [["But he shall have a reward!" cried the duke, laughing; "ay and a fitting one too! Eh, Elvira, what say you?"
    Elvira blushed, smiled, and looked down, as young ladies generally do upon such occasions; whilst Sir Ambrose, who had now reached the summit of the mount, was too eagerly looking round in every direction to hear his friend's remark.]] (1st ed.).

"Go to his triumph!" exclaimed the duke, rubbing his hands in ecstacy: [[ecstasy]] (1st ed.).

Part 2 [373

and the other merely supported the head it no longer strained: [[no longer constrained]] (1st ed.).

and show the world that the exalted blood of the Montagues has not degenerated in my veins!": [[Montagus]] (1st ed.).

The events of to-day have only proved clearly the little value my society is of to my father: he is too much occupied with my brother to even think of me, and were I absent . . . : [[The events of to-day have only proved clearly the little value my society is of to my father. Were I absent . . .]](1st ed.).

I will seek my father; and, explaining my real sentiments, set off for Egypt immediately: [[I will seek my father; and, explaining my real sentiments, break off this hated marriage and set off for Egypt immediately.]] (1st ed.).

Do not distress yourself about making arrangements for my family," replied Sir Ambrose: (From here, the chapter has been extensively recast. Sir Ambrose's brother and sister-in-law have been written out of the story, and their daughter Clara becomes an orphan. This semi-estrangement and more precarious status strengthens her role in parallel with Cheops, with whom she forms an alliance based upon her own goodness rather than, as with Father Morris and Edmund, flaws of character and naked ambition.)

1st ed. reads:

[["Do not distress yourself about making arrangements for my family," replied Sir Ambrose; "for you know I have a brother living in London, and though we have not seen each other for years, I think upon such an occasion as this I ought to forget all animosity, and visit him, if he will receive me."

"True," rejoined the duke; "I never thought of that: but you are quite right. Though he did make a foolish marriage, the ties of blood are too strong to be easily shaken off, and this is an excellent opportunity for a reconciliation."

"Another thing also weighs with me," continued Sir Ambrose: "you know that though I was so much hurt at his marriage, I was in some measure the cause of it."

"You the cause of it!" exclaimed the duke, in excessive surprise.

"You know," resumed Sir Ambrose, "my brother was always a bookworm; and the last time I visited him, I found him so uncomfortable, and his domestic affairs so dreadfully neglected, that I advised him to get an active managing woman to act as housekeeper. He did so, and in twelve months made her—Mrs. Montagu."

"I always thought your brother was too learned to know any thing useful, and too clever to be able to take care of himself; but I own I never suspected him of being such a fool as to marry."

"Perhaps I was a greater one than himself in resenting his conduct, for I believed they get on very well. Mrs. Montagu does not want sense."

"I do not doubt her abilities, or that she was extremely well fitted for her original station; but very different qualities are required in the wife of Mr. Montagu from those which were suited to his housekeeper."

"I know it; and also that there is perhaps nothing more difficult than for a person in her situation to preserve the medium between affectation and vulgarity. However, I am told that though Mrs. Montagu cannot quite divest herself of the pedantry she acquired at a charity-school in her youth,[10] and though she still talks as learnedly as if she had never ventured beyond the precincts of the kitchen; yet, that she makes my brother a good wife, and they say her daughter Clara is a charming girl."

"I can imagine nothing good springing from such a source."

"Prejudice! my dear duke, sheer prejudice!"

"Well, well, I will say no more about it; for, as you justly say, if Mrs. Montagu makes your brother a good wife, and he is happy with her, I don't see any right any body else has to trouble himself about the matter: and so, as I don't like quarrels in families, I think you are quite right in wishing to see your brother. However, if they do not make you comfortable, I hope you'll remember you have another friend, and so we'll now wish you good day: come, girls!"

And the old duke trotted off, followed by his fair companions. Edric's heart throbbed violently when he found himself alone with his father; the moment was arrived he had been so ardently wishing for, and yet he was silent. He had scarcely had patience to wait the end of his father's conference with the duke; and whilst it had lasted, he had been arranging and re-arranging a thousand times in his mind, the phrases he meant to make use of; yet now they seemed to have all vanished from his memory, and he stood gazing through the open window, his mind feeling a perfect chaos, and without being able to recollect one single word of what he had determined to say. Sir Ambrose, in the mean time, felt perfectly happy, and in the buoyancy of his spirits tapped his son upon the shoulder.

"What all amort! Sir Knight of the Woeful Countenance," said he; "Come, come! I will have no gloomy looks to-day. But, hey-day! what is the matter with you, Edric? You don't smile—are you unhappy? You look as if you had something upon your mind."[11]

"I have something upon my mind, my dear father," said Edric, solemnly; "and something that I wish to communicate to you." He stopped when he had said this, but Sir Ambrose did not reply, and, for some minutes, neither spoke. At length, Edric broke the pause, which had been one of perfect agony to him, and, speaking very fast, he exclaimed, "Yet I don't know why I should hesitate. It is that I do not love Rosabella—that I never can marry her—that I should be entirely miserable even to think of it—and, that this is my fixed and unalterable determination."

"Heyday!" cried Sir Ambrose; "what is all this? Not marry Rosabella!"

"Never; no tortures should induce me! I am convinced she would make me wretched," continued Edric, hurrying through what he meant to say. "Our tempers don't assimilate. "We should both be miserable. I should be very sorry to cause either you or the duke a moment's uneasiness—very sorry—I would die first! But to marry Rosabella would be worse than dying a thousand deaths— we should be the most wretched of human beings, and you would be unhappy at seeing me so."

"Mercy on me!" cried Sir Ambrose, heaving a deep sigh, and feeling almost out of breath at the volubility of his son. "I thought you dumb just now, but I see that you can use your tongue fast enough when the subject pleases you. Not marry Rosabella! Is the boy mad? Is she not young, beautiful, and highly accomplished? What would you have, I wonder? You certainly must be out of your senses to refuse such a woman; and one too, so superior to yourself in rank and fortune."

"In fortune I allow her to be superior; but I think the mystery attached to the name of her father, more than compensates for any difference of rank"

"Don't talk about what you can't understand. Duke Edgar is dead, and his faults should be buried with him; besides, it is hard the girl should suffer for the sins of her father."

"What were those sins, my dear Sir? I have often heard them darkly hinted at, as something almost too dreadful to mention; but I never heard the particulars."

"Edric," said Sir Ambrose, solemnly, "if you have the least regard for my feelings, or entertain any duty for me as a son, never again advert to that subject. Circumstances there are relating to it, of a deep, awful, and mysterious nature, with which I am well acquainted, but which I have taken a solemn oath never to reveal. Never speak of them again; the bare remembrance makes me shudder—oh! would to Heaven I could forget them!"

"I am very sorry, Sir, that my question was such as to give you pain: but rest assured that, my curiosity shall never again annoy you."

"I am not angry with you, Edric. You could not know the feelings your question would create in my bosom, and it was natural you should wish to know something of the father of your intended wife. However, think no more of him. Consider the present duke as your future father-in-law; and if possible forget that such a person as Duke Edgar ever existed."

"You forget, Sir," said Edric, firmly but respectfully, "that I have before declared my determination never to marry Rosabella."

"Nonsense!" rejoined his father, "you don't know what you are talking about. The world would call me as mad as yourself if I were to let you act so foolishly: besides, what would the duke say?"

"To speak candidly, Sir, that is what principally annoys me; for I trust that your good sense and affectionate disposition will soon enable you to see the affair in its proper light."

"That is to say, you think I am an old fool, and that you can coax me to any thing you please. But you shall find your error. You shall learn I will not be coaxed; I will be obeyed. You shall marry Rosabella, or you shall leave my house."

"My dear father!" said Edric, attempting to take Sir Ambrose's hand.

"Away, Sir!" cried his father, shaking him off, "obedience far outweighs words. If I am your dear father, you will act in compliance with my wishes; and if you do not, it is a mockery to call me 'dear.'"

"I cannot marry Rosabella."

"Was ever such obstinacy!—such folly! The world will think you distracted."

"I care not for the world!" cried Edric, impatiently.

"Youth like!" returned his father. "It is very strange no one will be contented to take experience at second-hand. They must buy it for themselves, and sometimes pay very dear for it before they profit by its lessons. You talk like a child, Edric: when you get a little older, you will find practice and theory very different things. You say you despise the world: but you are wrong, the world must not be despised; nay more, it ought not to be even slighted. As long as you live in it, you must conform to its opinions: it is ridiculous to think otherwise. I don't like to hear people say they don't care for the world; the world must be cared for; and when people pretend to scorn it, it is generally because they are aware they have done something to make it scorn them."

"But, my dear father! you would not wish me to sacrifice my conscience to its dictates."

"And pray, Sir, what has your conscience to do with the matter in question?"

"Should I not sacrifice it by marrying a woman I feel I could never love? In my opinion, nothing can by more sacred than the marriage vow; and with what feelings could I enter into this solemn engagement in the presence of Almighty God, calling upon him to witness it, when I knew my heart was at variance with my words? My soul would recoil with horror at such blasphemy."

"You talk about your conscience, Edric,—but should you not rather say your inclinations? The person of Rosabella does not please your fancy, I suppose; and to gratify a capricious whim, you would destroy the happiness of your father, and ruin your own prospects for ever."

"It is not of the person of Rosabella that I complain, my dear father;—I allow her to be beautiful as a Venus, and that her talents even exceed her personal charms: but when I see her large black eyes flashing fury, and her rosy lips curved into an expression of indignant scorn, I forget her beauty, and think only of the fearful. passions of her soul."

"Your objections are futile, Edric; at any rate, they are of no avail. You must marry her—I am sorry it is against your inclination, but I will not have my authority disputed:—besides, the disappointment to the duke would be dreadful. It was but this morning that he proposed, that as soon as you and Edmund should marry, I should give up my estate to you, and he his to your brother, whilst we two old folks should retire to the cottage on the hill; and pass the remainder of our lives in contemplating with rapture the happiness of our children."

"I own the duke is so obstinate—"

"So, you have discovered that, have you? Well, you are right there; for when he has taken a fancy into his head, no arguments can turn him from his point. But there is a difference between obstinacy and firmness. Now, though I am not obstinate like the duke, you shall find I can be firm, Edric. However, as I have always been an indulgent father, I do not wish to decide hastily now, and I give you a week to make up your mind: at the expiration of which time you shall marry Rosabella or quit my house for ever. No reply, young man, I will not hear a word. Begone; leave me now, and in a week's time let me know your decision."

It was in vain to attempt a reply; and Edric left his father's presence oppressed by that strange, mysterious presentiment of evil, which, like a fearful cloud, dark, gloomy, and impenetrable, sometimes hangs upon our thoughts, foreboding horrors; though so dimly and indistinctly, that, like all the gigantic phantoms we sometimes fancy through the mist of twilight, their terrors seem increased tenfold by the very uncertainty that half shrouds them from our sight. Mingled with these feelings, however, was one of wild, unearthly joy. Driven from his father's house, he would be free to travel—his doubts might be satisfied—he might, at last, penetrate into the secrets of the grave; and partake, without restraint, of the so ardently desired fruit of the tree of knowledge. Nothing would then be hidden from him. Nature would be forced to yield up her treasures to his view—her mysteries would be revealed, and he would become great, omniscient, and god-like. His mind filled with a chaos of thoughts like these, which he trove in vain to arrange, and which seemed to swell his brain almost to bursting, Edric involuntarily strolled again into the wood he had so lately quitted, and again throwing himself upon the banks of the murmuring stream, he was soon lost in a reverie.]]

Volume 1: Chapter 5

This chapter is almost entirely rewritten and is presented as such below. Lost is the Duke of Cornwall's exclamation "By St Wellington!", a topical "joke" which might have been too close to the bone in the tension over Catholic Emancipation.

1^{est} ed. reads:

[[In the mean time, different emotions were agitating violently the bosoms of the two lovely heiresses of the duke. When they reached the castle, each of them retired to her separate apartment to ruminate upon what had passed. Confidence did not exist between them, for confidence requires congeniality of mind, and those of the fair cousins were essentially different. Each princess, however, had a favourite attendant, or rather a companion, in whose bosom she was in the habit of pouring her thoughts; and, on their arrival at the castle, they parted immediately, equally eager to find their respective confidants, and inform them of all that had happened. Marianne had been the attendant of Rosabella from her childhood; and haughty as the Princess naturally was, she was, like many other haughty people, completely the slave of her servant. Marianne was perfectly aware of her power, and she occasionally used it tyrannically on the present occasion, however, she was really alarmed at the glowing cheeks, sparkling eyes, and agitated frame of Rosabella, and asked, with an appearance of deep interest, if she were ill.

"In mind, though not in body," replied Rosabella, throwing herself upon a sofa, and hiding her face in both her hands. "Oh, Marianne! what a wretch I am!"

"What is the matter?" asked the *suivante*.[12] "He loves her! he adores her!" cried Rosabella, starting from her couch and traversing the room rapidly. "Curses on her beauty! O that a look of mine could wither it! or that she could feel the burning fire that rages here!" Then stopping suddenly, she gazed upon her attendant with the wildness of a maniac, and, pressing her hand firmly against her side, threw herself again upon her couch, exclaiming, "Oh, Marianne! why am I not beloved like Elvira?"

"And are you certain that she is beloved?"

"Certain!" reiterated Rosabella, wringing her hands; "Alas! alas! would I were not so certain; but can I doubt the evidence of my senses'! This day—this very day! I saw Father Morris put a letter into her hands, which was inclosed in that addressed to Sir Ambrose. I saw a blush of conscious pleasure glow upon her cheeks as she perused it, and I could have stabbed her to the heart, —yes, and exulted in her dying agonies—triumphed in her groans. Oh, Marianne! is it not extraordinary that one so great, so noble, and so. exalted as Edmund, can love such a poor, weak, feeble being as Elvira? But she loves him not; at least not as he should be loved. She is incapable of it."

"1 wonder Father Morris gave her the letter."

"He could not help it, Marianne. It fel[l] from its inclosure when Sir Ambrose tore it open; but she saw it fall. I even saw her eye rest, upon the address; Father Morris merely picked it from the ground, and placed it in her hands."

"I thought he would not have given it to her voluntarily."

"No; I think not. I believe the father is my friend, though I own sometimes it appears strange to me, Marianne, that he should seem to prefer my interest to that of every one else, when so many ties bind him to Sir Ambrose's family, and so few to me: nay, though I am often peevish and unreasonable with him, he never is offended, and appears to remain still as warmly attached to me as before:—I cannot account for it."

"He has ties that bind him to you that you know not of," said Marianne, in a low, under voice; "he was your father's friend."

"Was he?" cried Rosabella, eagerly; "then perhaps he may enable me to clear off the shade that has so long hung upon my father's name. By heaven! neither the gratification of my love nor of my revenge would give me half the pleasure."

"You had better not ask him," said Marianne, in the same low, mysterious tone; "you can learn nothing upon that subject which it would give you pleasure to hear." Then changing her voice, she added, "But what said Edric to the news of his brother's glory?"

I know not—I care not! Ice itself cannot be colder than Edric. When we met, and he offered his hand to greet me, his touch seemed to freeze my very veins. Cold, prudent, calculating, and cautious, he has all the vices of age without its excuses:—I hate him!"

"You do not then, I suppose, long for the moment when you are to become his bride?" asked the companion, with a sarcastic smile.

"Long for it, Marianne?" cried Rosabella, starting from her couch, and clasping her hands together with energy—"long for it! No; if all other resources fail, death shall free me before the hated moment arrives." And as she spoke, Rosabella walked up and down the room, in a state of violent agitation.

"But your uncle?" resumed Marianne.

"My uncle!" repeated Rosabella, stopping short, "yes, yes; my uncle is positive—and I—a poor dependant, and in his power. But even that shall not control my will. Poor and dependant as I am—I am free; and sooner would I labour for my bread, sooner would I perish in the streets, or endure unheard of torments, than live in a palace surrounded by crowds of adoring slaves, if the price were that I must call Edric husband."

Marianne, satisfied with the ease with which she found she could play upon the feelings of her mistress, now touched a chord that thrilled to softer emotions.

"I can never believe," said she, "that a mind so noble as that of Edmund, can long remain in the thraldom of Elvira. When he comes to know her better, and to feel the feebleness of her soul, he must despise her."

"Ah! do you think so?" cried Rosabella eagerly. "But you deceive yourself, Marianne; Edmund is so blinded that he fancies her very faults perfections."

"But that blindness cannot last for ever, and when it wears off, disgust must ensue."

Oh, Marianne, if it were so!" exclaimed Rosabella; and, sitting down, she rested her elbows on her knees, and pressed her hands against her beating forehead, concealing her face and remaining apparently lost in meditation. Marianne did not disturb her. She was aware that she had given her active imagination a theme to work upon, and she left her to enjoy it; tranquilly resuming her usual avocations without seeming to notice her abstraction.

Whilst this scene was passing in the apartment of Rosabella, Elvira was informing her confidant, Emma, who had been her governess and remained her companion, of the pleasure she had experienced from hearing of the success of Edmund, and from the tenderness of his letter. "How I wish I could love him as he deserves," said she, "but, alas, I fear it is not in my nature. I can scarcely even comprehend what he thinks ought to feel, and the violence of his manner terrifies me beyond expression. Is it not extraordinary, Emma, that this passion, which seems so universally extended throughout all nature, should be alone a stranger to my breast—that I alone, should be debarred from feeling its influence? Edmund complains of my coldness; and I feel that he has reason to do so. I feel that his love is different from mine: I esteem and respect him; I have even a sincere friendship for him, and no one values his worth more than I; I should also be very sorry if any misfortune were to befall him; but this is all, and I do not think I am capable of feeling more for any one."

"Indeed you deceive yourself," replied Emma; "I am sure a heart so kind and affectionate as yours is capable of love. Do not marry Lord Edmund; I am certain you do not love him as you will love one day: and if a day should arrive, when you feel a real passion, what will be your horror at the recollection of the sacred ties which bind you to one who is indifferent to you. I shudder at the thought."

"And so should I, Emma; but that it is impossible such an event can happen. If I were married to Edmund, I never could love another, even if my nature were susceptible of the passion: a fact I much doubt."

Emma shook her head incredulously. "Oh!" sighed she; "how little do you know of love!"

"I know more of it than you imagine. In my opinion, people would never fall in love, if they had abundance of other thoughts to occupy their minds. They would marry, of course: but that, as every body knows, is quite a different thing."

"Then you disbelieve in love entirely?"

"Not entirely; but I think what is generally called love is the offspring of idleness. When people have nothing to do, particularly if they happen to have warm imaginations, they amuse themselves by picturing an idol of perfection. This they endow with all kinds of virtue probable and improbable; and they are enchanted with the fantasy, because it is their own creation. They soon find a face or figure that pleases them, and to this they attach the charms they had before given their imaginary idol—no matter whether they accord or not. When people are what is called in love, they are like persons in green spectacles, they see every thing of a colour that does not really belong to it. Marriage, however, lifts up the magic veil, and displays the real faults and imperfections of each individual. The self-deluded mortals then find out their mistake, though too late; and start back aghast at the appalling spectre that presents itself, crying out bitterly against deception; whilst, in fact, they have been only deceiving themselves."

"You reason admirably; but it is only from the head, not the heart. If you had ever felt, you would perceive the fallacy of your arguments."

"I think not; for I am convinced the experience of ninety-nine persons out of a hundred would confirm what I say, if they could but be persuaded to avow their real sentiments. This, however, they are always, in such cases, very reluctant to do, as no one likes to own himself deceived."

"And do you think all love is like that you have been speaking of?"

"Heaven forbid!—No—no, Emma, do not imagine I am such a heretic as to deny the existence of true love. I only think it is very difficult to be met with. That it does exist, I firmly believe, but very few are the bosoms that are capable of feeling it."

"Now I agree with you perfectly. I thought you could not mean all you before asserted."

"Excuse me, Emma, I did mean what I said. But I did not then speak of real love; I spoke only of the passion, or rather fancy, that usurps its name. Real, pure, undefiled love is that absorbing affection that prefers another's happiness to its own; that devotion that would sink unknown to the grave, to procure another's happiness; that seeks not its own gratification, but would sacrifice all the world can give, to promote the welfare of another; that can taste of no pleasure and partake of no delight, unless it be participated by the beloved object, and even then, joys in his satisfaction more than in its own. This is what I call love. I can imagine such a passion, though I shall never feel it. However, that it may be felt I am firmly convinced; though even you must acknowledge, it is rare to find it."

"Alas! my dear mistress!" said Emma, sighing heavily. "Every word you utter, convinces me you deceive yourself. For God's sake, do not marry Lord Edmund. You could have no idea of the romantic feelings you describe, if your heart were not open to receive them. Lord Edmund does not—"

"Hush! hush, Emma!" exclaimed Elvira, playfully interrupting her. "It is of no use. Say what we will, like most people that argue, we are sure to remain of the same opinion when we have done. I don't believe anybody ever yet was convinced by words; we must wait for facts, and, *en attendant*, suppose we consult upon what dress will be most becoming for us to wear at the approaching ceremony."

Emma gladly consented; and the princess and her companion were soon involved in a maze of ribbons, crapes, gauzes, silks and satins, from which it would be quite in vain for me to attempt to extricate them.

When Edric next saw his father, after the partial explanation that had taken place between them, he was excessively surprised to find him behave exactly as usual. The youthful philosopher was rather disconcerted at this conduct, which completely deranged all his speculations. In the course of his meditations in the grove, he had magnanimously made up his mind to endure every species of persecution rather than submit in the slightest degree to alter his opinions; and such is the strange and whimsical inconsistency of the human mind, that he was actually disappointed when he found there appeared little prospect of his heroic resolutions being called into practice.

It may seem strange to those who are feelingly convinced of the substantial comforts of an hospitable mansion and well supplied table, that any one should be found quixotic enough to lament that he had lost the chance of being deprived of them; but Edric's was the age of romance. His life had hitherto passed in one dull monotonous round, and the prospect of bustle and adventure has, in such cases, most irresistible charms. He also knew nothing of the world; and was almost as ignorant of the real evils of life, as the French princess, who, hearing that some persons had died of hunger, wondered at their folly, and said that for her part, rather than be famished, she would eat bread and cheese. Thus, as we said before, Edric was rather chagrined than delighted, when his father greeted him the morning after their conference as affectionately as before, and very amicably proposed that as soon as breakfast was ended, they should take a walk together to the castle of the duke.

Unwilling to vex his father needlessly by refusing, and yet fearful of compromising his firmness, by appearing to accede to what might be treachery on the part of his opponents, our young philosopher gave a rather ungracious assent to this proposition, and remained apparently absorbed in meditation during the whole walk. They found the duke extremely busy. Like many other people who have few real affairs to occupy them, he was quite delighted with any thing that seemed to promise a little bustle, and was firmly resolved to make the most of it. He was then giving orders for an illumination, and a public dinner to his tenants; bell-ringing, speech-making, and a variety of other things, we have really neither time nor patience to enumerate. Busy as he was, however, he was glad to see our friends, and greeted them most cordially.

"You are come in the very nick of time," said he: "I was just upon the point of sending for you. Do you know, Sir Ambrose, it has struck me that this triumph of Edmund's will be an admirable opportunity for his marriage; ay, and for yours too, Edric. What say you, Sir Ambrose?"

"Oh! of course I can have no objection."

"And of course," resumed the Duke, "I do not suppose the young men can have any. "What do you say, Edric?"

But Edric did not speak: for, to own the truth, he did not exactly know what to say.

"Edric is so delighted, that it has deprived him of the power of utterance," observed the baronet, rather maliciously, perceiving the duke grow impatient.

"I trust your grace will excuse me," said Edric, at length recovering himself; "but—but—"

"But what?" said the duke, impatiently.

"I thought," resumed Edric, with considerable hesitation, "that your grace did not intend that the princesses should marry—till—till they had passed the age that would render—that is to say, that does render them eligible candidates for the throne.—"

Edric did not express himself very clearly; as he was not altogether certain of what he was saying. The duke, however, heard enough to put him into a passion.

"So I did," exclaimed he, "I know that perfectly; but I have altered my mind, I tell you: Claudia isn't above thirty, and she's likely to live these fifty years,—so it is of no use waiting for her death. Besides, I should like to see my children married before I die. I am getting old; and anxiety in these respects encreases with declining years."

"Then my anxiety ought to be greater than yours, duke, for I am the eldest," said Sir Ambrose.

"By a couple of years, at least," returned the duke, laughing, "for I suppose that is about the difference in our ages. But you don't answer me, Edric. 'Do you think you have eloquence enough to persuade your mistress to relinquish the prospect of a throne in your behalf?"

"I would not wish her to make any sacrifice upon my account," replied Edric.

"Confound such coldness! why, when I was a young man, my heart would have beat like a pendulum in perpetual motion at such a proposition. Go to her, man! and try your fortune.—

> 'She is a woman, therefore to be wooed;
> She is a woman, therefore to be won;'

or rather what, perhaps, will be better, I will send for her here, and tell her my will. Egad! I have a mind to surprise Edmund, and let you grace his triumph as bride and bridegroom."

"Rosabella would never consent to such a proposition," exclaimed Edric, willing to postpone the dreaded explanation as long as possible.

"I think not," resumed the duke, "if you woo her with that face. However, you need not distress yourself, as you will have nothing to say till you get to the altar. I'll take all the rest upon myself, and I've a notion I shall prove the better suitor. I know women well, and how to manage them. I'll defy any woman in the world to have a will of her own whilst she is in my custody. I know how to quiet them and bring them round. You shall see how I will manage Rosabella. She won't have a word to say for herself. Here Augustus, tell the Princess Rosabella I wish to speak with her."

"Hold!" cried Edric, "I cannot allow you to send for the princess till I have first explained my real sentiments—

"Nonsense!" said the duke. "However, I see there is no occasion to send for her; for yonder she comes. I will meet her and explain my sentiments, and then it will be quite time enough to talk about yours."

So saying, he broke from Edric, who attempted to detain him; and advanced to meet Rosabella.

"Good God!" exclaimed Edric, "what will become of me? this obstinate old man will tell her, I wish our union; and for worlds, I would not mortify the proud spirit of Rosabella, by publicly declining her hand. What shall I do? I must request a private interview, and throwing myself upon her mercy, persuade her to reject me."

"Then you still persist in your determination," said Sir Ambrose. "I had hoped my kindness in appearing to forget what passed yesterday, had disposed you to comply with my wishes. However, since you seem inclined to adhere to your resolution, you cannot be surprised that I should follow your example, and I can only repeat, that if you do not marry Rosabella, you know the alternative."

"I do," said Edric, firmly; "and I am prepared to meet it."

In the mean time, the duke had met Rosabella, and had evidently begun to declare his wishes to her, for the colour had fled from her cheeks, and her eyes were cast upon the ground, whilst her strongly compressed lips, as she walked silently by his side, showed that it was with infinite difficulty that she controlled her feelings sufficiently to hear him with patience.

"In short," said the duke, as they drew near Sir Ambrose and his son, "I have fixed upon the day after to-morrow for your wedding, and, though I own the time is somewhat short to make preparations, you must be satisfied to have your wedding clothes after your marriage instead of before, which I should think need not make much difference. So now all you'll have to do, will he to tell your cousin; and the day after to-morrow your name will be Montagu."

"And do you know of whom you are disposing so unceremoniously?" asked Rosabella, raising her brilliant eyes from the ground, and fixing them upon him with a look of proud scorn. The duke shrunk involuntarily from the withering glance, which seemed to fall upon him with the fabled power of that of the basilisk.

"Of whom I am disposing?" stammered he, unconsciously repeating her words, "Of whom I am disposing? Why, of my niece, to be sure," he continued, arranging with difficulty his scattered ideas. "You are my niece, are you not?"

"Yes," returned Rosabella, "unfortunately I am your niece; and I blush for an uncle who does not scruple to abuse so barbarously the last legacy bequeathed to him by an unfortunate brother. Yes, my lord duke, I am your niece—your protégée—your dependant. I am not ashamed to own that I owe my daily bread to your bounty; but notwithstanding all this, I am not aware that I am your slave, nor do I think the pecuniary obligations I am under to you, sufficient to give you the right of disposing of me as an article of furniture, or a beast of burthen."

"You mistake the matter entirely, Rosabella," said the duke; "I do not wish to hurt your feelings."

"Do you think, then, that I am formed of stone or iron, that I am to be told to marry when and where you list, without having my inclinations consulted or my affections gained? Look at the bridegroom for whom you destine me. Certainly I must be insensibility itself to resist such overwhelming ardour."

"You are right, Rosabella," replied the duke; "he is, enough to provoke a stone. I admire your spirit; a woman should not unsought be won, and he, I own, looks as if he expected you to go down upon your knees, and beg him to accept of your hand."

"You are mistaken," returned Edric, now taunted into the necessity of avowing himself, in spite of his former resolutions; "it is not merely coldness that dictates my conduct. I should have explained myself before, had you permitted it, though I would willingly have spared the princess this public declaration. However, as I am now forced to avow my real sentiments, I openly and solemnly protest, that no torments shall ever force me to become the husband of Rosabella. I am sorry—"

"Spare your pity, Sir," said the princess, haughtily, and interrupting him—"I, at least, have no occasion for it; for know, that I too would sooner experience a thousand deaths than become your wife. Nothing but the respect I owe my uncle has prevented my declaring my sentiments sooner."

"And only my affection for my father kept me silent."

"What a considerate pair! and how highly we ought to feel obliged to them!" said the duke, ironically. "And pray, if your respect and affection permit you to answer the question, what may it be your high will and pleasure to intend doing now?"

"Whatever you please," replied both Edric and Rosabella, almost at the same instant.

"Dear me! how amazingly condescending! So, as long as you are permitted to have your own way, we may have the honour of suggesting plans for your approbation whenever we please. How astonishingly kind! I am afraid we shall never be able to show ourselves properly grateful, Sir Ambrose."

"This irony, my lord," said Edric, firmly, "is unworthy both of yourself and us. I will allow that you and my father have both reason to be displeased with our conduct, as it has disappointed hopes which you have long cherished; but permit me to say, that if you had expressed your displeasure in serious, manly, and open terms as he did, it would have been much more befitting your high rank and the importance of the subject, than the taunting irony you have thought proper to make use of."

"Schooled too! by St. Wellington!"[13] exclaimed the duke. "Upon my word, these are fine times, when a man of my age and rank is to be lectured by a beardless stripling!"

"I did not mean to offend your grace," said Edric; "and I am sorry the violence of my feelings compelled me to use language unbefitting my youth, and disrespectful to an old and valued friend of my father."

"Say no more, young man," replied the duke, "apologies only double an offence. If such are your sentiments, I would rather you declared than concealed them, as I think even insolence preferable to hypocrisy. However, after what has passed, I can never meet you amicably again, and I shall even avoid entering the house of my friend, Sir Ambrose, whilst you remain in it." This was spoken with dignity, and a majestic firmness of tone. The duke's voice, however, trembled a little as he continued—"I shall be sorry to lose the society of my old friend, and I should be equally sorry to induce him to desert you, but I cannot willingly expose myself to insult; and I must accordingly decline all farther intercourse with your family."

"Decline all farther intercourse with our family!" exclaimed Sir Ambrose. "This from you, duke! And Edmund! my darling Edmund! is he to suffer for the faults of his brother?"

"How do you know that the loss of my daughter would make him suffer?" asked the duke, sneeringly. "Perhaps when the moment came for me to give her to him, he too would make a bow, and humbly asking my pardon, beg leave to decline the honour. Oh! curse such politeness!"

"My dear duke, I would answer for Edmund with my life. He adores Elvira, and loves you as a father. You, too, have always professed to love him—"

"And so I do. Didn't I rejoice like an old fool at his triumph? Didn't I determine to give my daughter, and bestow my estate upon him? And were not these proofs of love?"

"They were, they were! my dear friend! and, as he has never done any thing to offend you, why should not your favourable intentions continue?

Why should you punish him on account of this ungrateful idiot, whom I renounce for ever."

"Oh, my father! my dear father!" exclaimed Edric; "do not say for ever!"

"Yes, for ever! I repeat," resumed Sir Ambrose. "Begone and let me never see you more. I told you yesterday my determination, and as you have chosen to incur the penalty you must take the consequence. Come, my friend," continued he, taking the arm of the duke, "let us leave him to his own reflections. Thank God! we are none of us answerable for the faults of our children; and it would indeed be sad, if you and I were to break a friendship that has lasted half a century, on account of the childish folly of an inconsiderate boy!"

"It would, indeed," returned the duke; "and it would have broken my heart to have quarreled with my darling Edmund. Yet, it is hard, at my time of life, to be disappointed in one's fondest hopes."

And as he walked away with Sir Ambrose, the tears actually streamed down his cheeks. Both Edric and Rosabella were affected, but, wisely considering that they could say nothing likely to allay the storm, they remained silent till the old men had gradually disappeared.]]

Volume 1: Chapter 6

Parts of this chapter have been extensively rewritten.

When Edric left his father ... re-animation may be produced: Replaces

[[When Sir Ambrose and the duke thus withdrew, Edric and Rosabella were left alone together, and remained for some moments in perfect silence, for both felt keenly the awkwardness of their situation. After standing for some time looking as foolish as their enemies could reasonably desire, Edric bowed, and would have made good his retreat, but Rosabella stopped him.

"Let us be friends, Edric," said she, smiling and holding out her hand, "though we are no longer lovers."

Edric took the offered hand, and involuntarily pressed it to his lips. "Upon my word, you improve!" continued Rosabella gaily; "I declare I never saw such an instance of gallantry from you before, during the whole course of our courtship!"

Edric smiled as he replied, "If you knew the burthen that has been taken from my mind by the explanation of this morning—"

"Hush! hush!" cried Rosabella laughing, "Now you have spoiled all again. I was afraid your gallantry was too great to be lasting."

"I acknowledge," replied Edric, joining in her mirth, "that it is not very polite in me to rejoice in being freed from your chains; but I am no flatterer, and—and—"

"A truce with apologies," exclaimed Rosabella; "as my uncle very justly observed just now, they only make the matter worse. The case is simply this: you and I were not suited for each other; we found it out, and we are both glad to be released from ties that we discovered were incompatible with our happiness. 'Can any thing be more clear?' as Dr. Entwerfen says. You, I presume, are going to travel, and to gratify your natural love of variety and wish to acquire information; whilst I, poor unfortunate damsel that I am, must remain at home and wear the willow, till I am fortunate enough to meet with a swain who has the penetration to discover my charms."

"And most ardently do I hope that it may soon be the case!" said Edric, astonished at her affability, and feeling more kindly disposed towards her than he had ever done before. "You are right in supposing I wish to travel; but, alas! I have not now the power. My father is too much offended to afford me the means; and without money—"

"Travelling is far from agreeable," interrupted Rosabella, smiling: "is not that what you would say? Why not apply to Father Morris, then; he can, and I am sure, will help you; For myself, I am powerless, except as far as giving advice."

"Your advice, however, is excellent," replied Edric, regarding her with still encreasing amazement; "and I assure you I will follow it to the letter. I never thought of applying to the reverend father, though I now feel it is the best thing I can do."

"Why then do you look at me so incredulously?" continued Rosabella; "I can have no motive for deceiving you; and yet you look as suspicious as though you thought I had. I own my behaviour towards you is changed; but remember the different circumstances in which I am now placed. Formerly I feared even to speak to you, lest my words should be deemed an encouragement of the pretensions I supposed you to entertain to my hand. Now that we are both free, that reason no longer exists; and besides, I feel grateful to you for declaring your sentiments so openly, and thus saving me from my uncle's displeasure. 'Can any thing be more simple?' as your friend Dr; Entwerfen would say."

Notwithstanding Rosabella's apparent openness, however, and the plausible reasons she gave for her conduct, Edric could not divest himself of the idea that she wished to get him out of the kingdom as speedily as possible, for some other motives than those she thought proper to avow. There likewise appeared some mystery in her speaking so confidently of the assistance of Father Morris; for as the duke's family had a regular confessor, Father Murphy, it seemed strange that Rosabella should have an intercourse with any other priest, beyond that required by the common forms of society; and so slight an intimacy could scarcely warrant the positive assertion she had made use of. Edric, however, was too anxious to avail himself of any opportunity that offered of proceeding to Egypt, to trouble himself with long investigation of the subject; and when he quitted Rosabella, he proceeded in search of Father Morris as a matter of course, and almost without any volition of his own.

The suite of rooms appropriated to Father Morris in the mansion of Sir Ambrose was in a wing partly detached from the main dwelling; and thither Edric bent his steps. As he approached, however, to his great surprise he heard a sound of blows followed by deep groans. Knowing that it was the hour of dinner for the domestics, and that none of the other inmates of the mansion were at home but the friar and himself, he could not at first account for this strange and fearful noise; but finding, as he advanced, the sounds proceeded from the inner chamber of the priest, where no one but himself ever ventured, he soon became satisfied that Father Morris was performing a penance of self-flagellation; and as it was deemed impious to interrupt a penitence, he seated himself quietly in the outer chamber, Waiting the priest's leisure; wondering, however, to himself, what crime so holy a man could possibly have committed, that could require so severe an expiation.

When Father Morris made his appearance, it was with his usual downcast eyes and composed look. He expressed his astonishment at seeing Edric, but made no allusion to the penance he had just been performing, and listened with a cold unmoved aspect to Edric's communication.

"Then I am to understand," said he, when it was finished, "that you are like the prince we were reading of the other day, in a book we found in your tutor's library. You cannot be happy because you have never been miserable; and you are going to plunge into all the cares and troubles of the world, merely to learn how to enjoy retirement."

"Not exactly so, father;" rejoined Edric; "I have two other motives,—the anger of my father, and the earnest tormenting wish I before confessed to you, of diving into the secrets of the grave."

"And how is that to be accomplished by your leaving England?"

"I wish to try to resuscitate a mummy."

"The scheme is wild, vague, and impracticable."

"Not if Dr. Entwerfen's hypothesis be true. For, supposing the souls of the ancient Egyptians to be chained to their bodies, and to be remaining in them in a torpid state,—it is very possible that by employing so powerful an agent as galvanism, re-animation may be produced.]] (1st ed.).

If I recollect rightly ... destined to attain immortality?: replaces: [[I have already seen some wonderful instances of the vivifying power of the machine; and as the Egyptians took care to preserve the bodies of their dead quite entire, probably from the idea I have just alluded to,—I think the mummies are the best subjects we can possibly fix upon for our experiments."

"The ancient Egyptians did not imagine the souls of their dead remained in the bodies, but that they would return to them after the expiration of a certain number of years; so that your hypothesis, as far as it rests upon their opinions, falls to the ground."

Do not call it my hypothesis," returned Edric, "it is that of Dr. Entwerfen; my own opinion is decidedly different—for I cannot imagine any idea of death that does not imply a separation between the body and soul. The subject, however, is curious; to me highly interesting; and I own, candidly, there are many mysteries connected with it, which it would give me the highest satisfaction to have explained."

"And these mysteries, which have vainly excited the speculation of the learned since the commencement of the world, you think your journey to Egypt will enable you to unravel," said Father Morris, with a sardonic sneer. Edric felt irritated at his manner, and replied warmly:—

"I am not presumptuous, father; but as even you must allow, man is often but a blind instrument in the bands of fate, it is possible that the racking desire I feel to explore these mysteries may be an impulse from a superior power, and a proof that I am destined to be the mortal agent of their revelation to man."]] (1st ed.).

Egypt is rich. . . : [[Egypt is a country rich . . .]] (1st ed.).

excepting in their religion, they surpassed us: "excepting in their religion" added in 2nd ed. Following this, 1st ed. continues: [["Even in their religion?" asked Father Morris sarcastically.

"No," returned Edric; "every scheme of religion . . .]]

the most important discovery ever made by Man: From here to "When Edric entered the study of Dr. Entwerfen" 1st ed. has:
[[Deride me if you will; I feel a superior power inspires my wishes. I feel irresistibly impelled forward. I feel called upon to act by a force far superior to my own, and I will obey its dictates. You smile, and secretly ridicule my projects; but remember that excessive incredulity sometimes savours as strongly of folly as credulity itself, and that both are alike injurious to the progress of science."

"I do not doubt it," said Father Morris, with provoking coldness; "though it must certainly be allowed not to be the prevailing foible of the present day. However, without staying to discuss that point at present, I humbly suggest, that, as I happen unfortunately to be rather pressed for time, it may be as well to condescend to bestow a. few minutes' attention upon the best human means of enabling you to fulfil the high destinies that await you in Egypt—as, notwithstanding the imperious nature of the impulse that invites you there, I presume you are aware that the vulgar agency of money will be necessary as well as the scientific one of galvanism."

The feelings of Edric, were too highly wrought to hear this irony; and, snatching up his hat, he rushed out of the room, casting a look of indignation at the priest, who vainly endeavoured to stop him. Maddened by the conflicting emotions that struggled in his bosom and disgusted alike with himself, Father Morris, and all the world, Edric hurried on, totally unaware which way he was going, till his career was stopped by his coming suddenly and violently in contact with another person, who was running equally heedlessly with himself, but in an opposite direction. Both recoiled some paces from the shock, and Edric found, to his surprise, it was Abelard whom he had greeted so unceremoniously. Curiosity to know what could have occasioned the abstraction of the worthy butler, (he being generally remarkable for his peculiar attention to matters of ceremony,) diverted the thoughts of Edric from himself, and he, for the moment, forgot his own woes, whilst he inquired into those of Abelard.

"Alas! alas!" said the old man, shaking his grey head, whilst the tears streamed in torrents down his wrinkled cheeks, "that I should ever have lived to see this day! Oh, Master Edric! how could you irritate your respectable progenitor? Alas! alas! I feel my lachrymal gland suffused almost to overflowing, whenever the recollection of what has passed shoots across my piamater."

"For Heaven's sake! tell me what is the matter!"

"Oh dear! oh dear!" sobbed the unhappy butler, "that such longevity should have been granted me only that I might see so promising a young gentleman turned out of doors."

"Tell me the worst; though, indeed, I now fear I comprehend your meaning but too well."

"Sir Ambrose commands that you depart immediately, and never enter again into the mansion of your paternal ancestors."

"What will become, of me!" exclaimed Edric, clasping his hands together, and raising his eyes to Heaven; then, after a short pause, he added more composedly, "Well, come what will, I am resigned. Fate urges me onward with irresistible violence, and I feel it would be in vain to attempt to combat against her dictates. I, at least, am prepared to execute her will."

"But where will you go?" sobbed Abelard, "You will want money and friends. Alas! alas! that I should ever see the son of my old master stand in need of pecuniary assistance!"

"He but repeats the words of Father Morris," said Edric; "and yet how differently his doubts affect me. The irony of the priest drove me to despair, but the grief of this old man soothes my wounded spirit. He surely loves me."

These words were uttered in so faint a key, that the name of Father Morris only caught the ear of Abelard, and he replied:

"I don't like Father Morris, and I never did; though it is now twenty years since he first entered the family, and though I have never seen any thing in him to censure particularly, throughout the entire of that long period, yet my aversion remains undiminished. I suppose it must be a natural antipathy, and that the pores of my body don't assimilate in shape with the atoms that emanate from his."

"He drove me almost to madness," said Edric.

"I am not surprised at that," returned Abelard; "for I know he can take a fiendlike pleasure in tormenting. He can employ the most provoking, tantalizing expressions, and yet preserve the same soft, smooth voice, and keep his palebrae[14] half closed, and his visual organs fixed upon the at ground. Indeed, I never saw the iris of his eyes dilated in my life; and then he has such a manner of raising his supercilia, curving his nose, and drawing down his depressor anguli oris[15] when he listens to any one or replies to them, as to give the expression of a perpetual sneer to his saturnine countenance."

Edric's own recent personal experience bore testimony only too forcibly to the justice of those remarks; and as the wounded man shrinks from the slightest touch, so did Edric find the words of Abelard jar upon his nerves; as turning away from him to hide his emotions, he encountered the earnest gaze of Father Morris himself.

"Why do you appear astonished?" said the priest, smiling. "You are an infant, Edric; you quarrel with your best friends, and then appear surprised that you do not find them as capricious as yourself. You fancy you are very angry with me, for instance, and yet I am not conscious of having done any thing to offend you. Was it a crime to attempt to moderate an enthusiasm that I feared might mislead you? was it a fault to warn you against the dangers of a world of which as yet you know so little? No, no; I am confident your own reason and excellent good sense will acquit me, if you will but suffer them to act. Your imagination is too vivid, Edric; it sweeps away all before it. like a torrent. If you would view things calmly, you would perceive your folly. The world will teach you wisdom. Go then, travel; experience personal privations and evils of every description, that you may learn to enjoy the pleasures that even now lie within your grasp, but which you spurn from you with contempt. So true it is that we never learn, the real value of any blessing till we have experienced the misery that attends its privation."

"If this be the case," replied Edric, soothed in spite of himself, by the insinuating manner of the monk, "why should my feelings be an exception to the general rule? And since all our pleasures acquire a new zest by the force of contrast, and mine have long since lost all relish, is it not even wisdom to try the effect of change?"

"And yet it seems a folly," said Father Morris, in his smooth, plausible, hypocritical voice, with his eyes again fixed upon the ground, "to incur a certain evil in the hope of attaining an uncertain good."

Edric started, and fixed his eyes upon him, with an expression the monk well understood; and, not wishing again, to provoke him past endurance, he continued in a different tone: "But it is useless for age to preach lessons of prudence to youth, and as your father says, every one must purchase his own experience; so we will now, if you please, change the subject to that of making preparations for your journey. You are still determined to visit Egypt, I suppose?"

"It is my most ardent wish."

"Return then to your own apartment, and by to-morrow all shall be ready for your departure."

"He must not enter the house!" said Abelard; "alas! alas! that I should live to say it! Sir Ambrose has forbidden him even to cross the threshold."

"Can you not remain concealed in the apartment of Dr. Entwerfen?" asked Father Morris, after a short pause; "no one enters there but himself; and one of the windows looks upon this terrace, so that you may reach it unobserved; Abelard, I am confident, will not betray you; and I will accompany you, as I wish to consult with the doctor respecting your intended voyage."

Edric hastily assented, and bidding Abelard an affectionate adieu, he and Father Morris easily climbed through the window that led to the adytum of Dr. Entwerfen, whilst Abelard, clasping his hands together, exclaimed as he retired, "God bless him! Well, he shall not want for pecuniary assistance at any rate, if Mr. Davis and I can help it; that is one comfort."

When Edric and Father Morris entered the study of Dr. Entwerfen, ...]]

No! I cannot leave England ... life who was not fond of it: [[There was something in this violent expression of the doctor's transports that did not quite harmonize with Edric's feelings, especially as he fancied he perceived a satirical smile lurking round the lips of Father Morris.

"When shall you be ready to set off?" asked he abruptly.

"To-morrow, if you will," replied the doctor. "I have foreseen this result some time, and I have been preparing every thing accordingly. I never knew a young Englishman in my life, Father Morris, who was not fond of travelling.]] (1st ed.).

"What is the matter?" cried Edric: [[cried Edric and Father Morris, both at the same instant]] (1st ed.).

"If we do go," said Edric ... governed by an old woman: [["Undoubtedly!" replied Father Morris; "nay, if we are to judge by that, I only tremble lest you should animate the pyramids as well as the mummies, and you

must allow it would be an awkward sight to see them come tumbling and slipping along the plain."

"Sir!" said the doctor, staring at him.

"Do you intend visiting any other country than Egypt?" asked Father Morris, fearful he had gone too far, and wishing, for reasons he did not openly avow, not to offend his companions.

"I should like to see India," said the doctor; "some black-letter pamphlets in my possession, allude to its being once governed by an old woman (1ˢᵗ ed.).

"The whole of the interior of Africa must be interesting, particularly the rising states on the banks of the Niger. ⟦"must be interesting," observed Father Morris, "particularly the rising states on the banks of the Niger."⟧ (1ˢᵗ ed.).

the one we live under: ⟦"the one we live under?" asked Father Morris.⟧ (1ˢᵗ ed.).

The case is quite different: ⟦"The case is quite different," returned the doctor.⟧ (1ˢᵗ ed.). Entwerfen is suggesting that the *threat* of the use of absolute power in the context of limited freedom is preferable to its frequent and open employment.

Amen! For, as we are happy now, we should be idiots to desire a change.": ⟦"Amen!" said Edric; "for, as we are happy now, we should be idiots to desire a change." (1ˢᵗ ed.)

Perhaps I was not … I will give you a treat: ⟦"To-morrow," said Father Morris, addressing Edric, and without noticing the indignation of the learned doctor, "you must proceed to town, where you can remain at the house of a friend of mine, till you are ready for your voyage to Egypt. I would not, however, advise you to stay long before you go there; for, as your father intends visiting London in a day or two, you might meet, and the consequences be unpleasant. I have already dispatched a carrier-pigeon to advise my friend, Lord Gustavus De Montfort, of your arrival; he, I am sure, will give you a hearty welcome, and not only afford you the shelter of his house, but afford you all the assistance in his power, to enable you to make preparations for your journey; for which purpose, also, I will take care to supply you with money. No thanks," continued he; stopping Edric, who was about to speak, "I detest them. If you really feel obliged to me, you will prove it by remaining silent. I must leave you now, as my longer absence might create suspicion, Adieu! God bless you! A balloon will wait for you tomorrow morning, at the corner of the wood. The doctor will, of course, accompany you. I think you may safely rest here concealed till then. Once more, adieu!"

"Now Father Morris is gone," said Doctor Entwerfen to his pupil, "I have a treat for you.]] (1st ed.).

Volume 1: Chapter 7

Once more, this chapter has been much edited. The letter-scene with the Montagus pastiching/parodying Jane Austen's Mr and Mrs Bennet from *Pride and Prejudice* has been dropped, losing the "patent steam coffee-machine" , although the air-beds remain in Abelard's instructions to the housemaids in Chapter 8 of the 2nd edition. Mrs Montagu's instructions to Angelina: "remember, nothing can be too plain for great people. Fricassees and ragouts are only devoured by the canaille," are placed in the mouth of the housekeeper Mrs Russel in Chapter 8 of the 1828 2nd edition. The introduction of the comic priest Father Murphy is changed from his being the Duke of Cornwall's Confessor to a connection of Dr Coleman (a new character who is instrumental in introducing the mysterious "Henry Seymour" to Sir Ambrose in a lengthy passage of recast plotting.) In the 1st edition, "Seymour" does not appear until chapter 11, when he helps Sir Ambrose recover from his near-faint at Claudia's feet on hearing the praise of his son Edmund, and introduces himself as having been "introduced to the Queen, in hopes of getting a place at Court, by one of her Majesty's physicians, Dr. Coleman".

When Father Morris had left Edric... Edric and his tutor were on their way to London: The 1st ed. has:
[[The morning after the events just recorded, as Mr. Montagu, the brother of Sir Ambrose, was sitting at the breakfast-table with his wife and daughter, they were all startled by the unexpected arrival of a letter from Sir Ambrose. "Bless me!" cried Mr. Montagu, moved for once to forget his usual habits of indifference—"I do believe it is a letter from my brother."

"Your brother!" screamed 'Mrs. Montagu, starting up to examine it, and in her agitation overturning a patent steam coffee-machine, by which coffee was roasted, ground, made, and poured, out with an ad libitum of boiling milk and sugar, all in the short space of five minutes. "Oh!" continued she— "I am scalded to death!"

"I hope not, my dear," said Mr. Montagu, calmly taking up his letter, and carefully examining it on all sides without opening it. "Yes," continued he, "it is indeed from my brother, and I hope it contains no ill news, for I do not perceive any signs of mourning about it." And so saying, he very tranquilly laid his letter again upon the table, and recommenced sipping his coffee.

"La! papa, hadn't you better open your letter and read it?", asked Clara, who was busily employed in assisting her mother.

"Ah!" resumed Mr. Montagu. "True! I never thought of that,—I think I had." Then again taking the letter in his hand, he broke the seal and gave it to Clara to read.

"And do you think my daughter is to leave me when I am in this miserable condition, Mr. Montagu, to read letters from your brother, Mr. Montagu—a man who has always treated me with such disrespect, Mr. Montagu,—and I half scalded to death!"

"I am sure I'm very sorry, my dear," began Mr. Montagu—

"Oh, spare your sorrow," exclaimed his wife—"for I'm sure you don't care one single straw about me. You're a cruel man—"

"Hadn't I better read the letter?" asked Clara, trembling at the thought of the domestic sparring she saw about to ensue.

"Yes, yes! read, my dear," said her father, glad of any pretext to avert the coming storm: for though he seldom disturbed himself about any thing, provided his study was not swept oftener than once a month, and he was not obliged to submit to the insupportable fatigue of arranging his ideas in the tense form, necessary for conversation; he had yet a most inconceivable horror of his wife's fluency of tongue, thus affording a striking proof of the ingratitude of mortals, who often ungraciously find fault with the very things for which they have most occasion to be thankful; as it must be allowed that nothing could really be more convenient for a man of a taciturn disposition, than to have a wife who could manage to talk at once for him and herself too.

Notwithstanding the encouragement of her father, Clara, however, still paused, looking with a timid eye towards her mother, for that lady's permission to begin. Curiosity struggled powerfully with anger in the breast of Mrs. Montagu for some minutes; but at last the former prevailed, and with a nod she permitted Clara to read. She immediately began as follows:—

"MY DEAR BROTHER."

"Humph," observed Mrs. Montagu, "his last letter began—Sir. He's getting wonderfully civil, I think."

"Pshaw!" exclaimed her husband.

Clara continued,—"I am happy to inform you, that my dear Edmund has gained a glorious victory."

"And what is that to us, I should like to know?" said Mrs. Montagu: "for my part, I have too much pride to trouble myself about people, who don't trouble themselves about me."

Clara went on.—"We are all coming up to London, to be present at a grand triumph the Queen is going to give him; and thinking it a pity there should be a misunderstanding—"

"Ah! What's that, child?" exclaimed Mr. Montagu, laying down a problem which he had been studying ever since she began.—Read that again, Clara."—

"And thinking it a pity there should be a misunderstanding any longer existing between you and me, we being both fast approaching to the grave, intend, with your and Mrs. Montagu's permission—"

"Mrs. Montagu's permission!" cried the delighted Mrs. Montagu; "are you quite sure he says that, Clara?" and she pressed over her daughter's shoulder to ascertain the joyful fact. "Well, well, I do declare he really does say so. Look, my dear, there it is,—'Mrs. Montagu's permission.' He never called me Mrs. Montagu before. God bless him! a nice old gentleman! I am sure I shall be very glad to see him and his brave son, too. Only think, my dear! what an honour it is to have a hero in one's family! Read on, Clara; I feel quite interested to know all the particulars of my nephew's victory. You know, he is my nephew, Mr. Montagu, as well as yours, as I am your wife, and he is your own brother's son; so, read on, Clara, and let us know all about him."

Clara obeyed the moment her mother gave her an opportunity. "I intend, with your and Mrs. Montagu's permission, to take the opportunity of visiting you. I remain, with kind remembrances to Mrs. Montagu and my niece, to whom I long to be introduced, your affectionate brother,

"Ambrose Montagu."

"Very well," said Mr. Montagu, "I shall be very glad to see him; I always loved my brother, and I was quite sorry when we were not friends."

"Here is a postscript," resumed Clara and she read:

"I quite forgot to inform you, that the Queen has conferred a title upon my son, and that I shall have to present him to you as Lord Edmund."

"I am very glad to hear it," exclaimed the gratified uncle.

"And so am I," reiterated his wife. "My nephew, Lord Edmund Montagu. I wonder when they will be here: I must set about making preparations for them immediately. Strike the kitchen automaton, Clara, to summon all the domestic assistants together, that I may give my orders. Dear me! what a bustle I am in."

In one corner of the room stood a kind of organ, by playing certain notes upon which, intimation was given in the lower regions of what was wanted in the parlour; the organ having long tubes communicating with the kitchen, through which the sound was conveyed. Clara accordingly sat down, and by striking a few chords, soon assembled all the domestics of her father.

"I expect company," said Mrs. Montagu, with an air of excessive consequence. "My brother-in-law, Sir Ambrose Montagu, and my nephew, Lord Edmund Montagu, are coming to stay with us during a triumph, with which her most gracious Majesty the Queen intends to honour Lord Edmund, my nephew. When did my brother-in-law, Sir Ambrose, say that he and my nephew, Lord Edmund, intended coming, Mr. Montagu? Clara, look at Sir Ambrose's letter. 'I intend,' says he, addressing Mr. Montagu, 'with your and Mrs. Montagu's permission, to be with you on such a day,' but I forget what day he mentions."

"He does not say which day,'" replied Clara, consulting the letter.

"Well, at any rate, it will be very soon," resumed Mrs. Montagu; "and we must prepare accordingly. You know, the connexions of my brother-in-law, Sir Ambrose, are very high, and I do not doubt but his intimate friend, the Duke of Cornwall, will call to see him—nay, perhaps, he may dine at my table with the two princesses, his daughter and niece. Indeed there's no knowing, but, perhaps, even her most gracious Majesty the Queen may condescend to enter my humble doors. Do you hear, all of you?—you must all be attentive. You Angelina, as cook, will have the most upon your hands—remember, nothing can be too plain for great people. Fricassees and ragouts are only devoured by the canaille."

"I am instructed of that, Ma'am," replied Angelina, a great, fat, bonny-looking cook,—"but I flatter myself I know how to concoct dishes.—"

"That is the very thing I want to avoid," interrupted her mistress. "It is the fashion now for great people to have only one dish, and that as plainly cooked as possible. I have been told by a friend of mine, who got a peep at the great dinner the Queen gave the other day to the foreign ambassadors, that there was nothing in the world upon the table, but a huge round of boiled beef, and a great dish of smoking potatoes, with their jackets on."

"Well, Ma'am," returned Angelina, I will rally both my physical and mental energies to afford you all the satisfaction in my power; notwithstanding which, I am free to confess, that, in my opinion, the gastronomic science is now cruelly neglected, and that I do not think the digestive powers of the stomach can be properly excited from their dormant state by such unstimulating food as that you mention. Besides, the muscular force of the stomach must be strained to decompose such solid viands, and I should think the diaphragm seriously injured—"

"You, Alphonso," continued Mrs. Montagu, addressing the footman, and cruelly interrupting the learned harangue of the cook, "must have a new suit of livery. In the meantime, arrange properly the best drawing-room, and clean the pictures. There is a fine large painting of one of the old English artists, over the door, the colours of which are quite faded; I am afraid you have used something improper to clean it."

"Indeed, Madam," returned Alphonso, "I think the fault is in the picture itself. It did not dry well originally; I don't think the oil that was used in its composition had the carbon and hydrogen mingled in proper proportions. You know, Madam, that oil in general has an amazing affinity for oxygen, and absorbs it rapidly; now, though the oil of this picture has been exposed for years to the action of the common atmospheric air, yet it has never thickened properly into a concrete state."

"Eustace! you, as butler, must take care not to bring any variety of wines to the table: nothing is drunk now but port and sherry; and even they are going out of fashion. Have plenty of strong ale, however, and porter, for they are now reckoned the most elegant liquors for the ladies."

"I shall do my utmost endeavour to obey your injunctions, Madam," said Eustace, bowing respectfully, "but I cannot imagine that any species of corn, even if it have undergone the vinous fermentation, can produce a liquid so agreeable to the palate, as well as conducive to the sanity of the body, as the juice of the grape."

"And you, Evelina and Cecilia," continued Mrs. Montagu, addressing her housemaids, "must superintend the arrangement of the dormitories: let the air out of the beds and re-inflate them—examine the elastic spring mattresses—mend the gossamer curtains — sweep the velvet carpets, and take care the tubes for withdrawing the decomposed air, and admitting fresh, are in proper order;—also, clean out the baths attached to each chamber, and take care there is an abundant supply of water."

"I am told that ablution in the common aqueous fluid is becoming more fashionable than any medicated baths," said Evelina, "and that some people of rank actually use a composition of alkali and oil to remove the pulverous particles that may have lodged upon their epidermis in the course of the day."

"I fear from the commands you have issued, Madam," rejoined Cecilia, "that you were oblivious of the alteration that has been effected in the superior dormitory. The air there is no longer changed by means of tubes—but there is a fan-feather ventilator fixed in the ceiling, which by its gentle undulations occasions a free circulation of the aiériform fluid; I do not think, however, that it is quite adequate to supply the place of the tubes; as upon entering the room the other morning, I perceived a strong sensation of azote, and I am confident that the proportion of nitrogen more than trebled that of oxygen in the air contained in the whole apartment."

"I am sorry for that," said Mrs. Montagu, "as it is the best sleeping-room: however, as it is too late to change it, we must do the best we can; and so go all of you and attend to my directions, for I should be very sorry to have my brother-in-law Sir Ambrose, and my nephew Lord Edmund, put to any inconvenience, during their sojourn in my dwelling; to say nothing of the great and noble guests who may perchance also honour the mansion with their presence."]]

Edric and his tutor were on their way to London: 1st ed takes up the story here with: [[Whilst this bustle was taking place in the house of Mr.

Montagu, Edric and his tutor were on their way to London. It was with infinite difficulty, however, the doctor could be persuaded to set off without alarming the family ...]]

Sir Ambrose being too proud... 'robs care of its bitterest sting.': Another rewritten/recast section. The 1st ed. has:

[[In the mean time, Sir Ambrose had begun to repent, though secretly, of the unwarrantable severity with which he had treated his son. It is a trite though undeniable observation, that we never know the real value of any possession till we have lost it; and thus Sir Ambrose, though he had thought nothing of the respectful and dutiful attentions of his son, whilst he was in the habit of constantly receiving them, now felt their want, and regretted bitterly the ill-timed harshness that had deprived him of them for ever. Still, however, he was too obstinate to own he had been wrong; and though he knew that by recalling his son he should restore his lost happiness, he, like many other persons in similar situations, most magnanimously determined to persist in being miserable.

The Duke of Cornwall was quite astonished, and even indignant, at what he termed the inconsistency of his friend. "How can you be so weak as still to regret the loss of that peevish boy?" said he, as, on the second morning after Edric's departure, he entered the library of Sir Ambrose, attended by his confessor, Father Murphy. "Depend upon it, it is bad policy; for patience robs care of its bitterest sting, as this holy father says. You often preach that doctrine to me, don't you, Father Murphy?"

Father Murphy was an Irishman, and gifted with a rich brogue, which, aided by his comely figure, round rosy face, and little laughing black eyes, gave a peculiar raciness to every thing he said; He had not long filled the office he then held, and though he had been recommended to it, on the death of the duke's late confessor, by Father Morris, yet no two human beings could be more different than he and that reverend personage. Father Murphy, indeed, was a general favourite, and the whole household of the duke concurred in thinking him quite a nonpareil of a priest; for as he was not very fond of doing penance himself, so he was not very rigid in imposing it upon others, and consequently he and his penitents were always upon the best terms imaginable. In short, he seemed especially designed by Nature to be good friends with all the world; and on his side he certainly did the utmost not to thwart the beneficent old lady's kind intentions.

He now smiled good-humouredly at the duke's question, and replied, "Och! and is it me ye're quoting from, yere Grace? ...]]

"By the way," said the duke ... if nothing had been said of Rosabella: replaces: [[A short pause ensued, which was broken by the duke's suddenly exclaiming, "Did you not say Dr. Entwerfen has gone off with Edric?"

"Certainly, I did."
"Then, depend upon it, the whole was a planned thing. They have taken some wild scheme into their heads, and they are gone to execute it." (1st ed.).

I don't think the matter ... What is your opinion of the subject, Father Morris?: "I don't think the matter admits of a single doubt. But what do you think on the subject, Father Morris?"]] (1st ed.).

Volume 1: Chapter 8
Some of the material cut from the previous chapter is inserted here, using new characters, in doing so emphasizing the ridiculousness of "useful knowledge" in the mouths of the lower orders and the inflated vocabulary and pretentiousness of the servant classes.

they did not meet with a single adventure: [[and they did not meet with a single adventure.]] (1st ed.).

with a single adventure worthy of being recorded ... as his dread of meeting him was excessive: This is new material or recast dialogue to take into account the deletion of characters (Abelard the Butler shows his poetry to Sir Ambrose rather than Mrs Russel, who instructs the cook Angelina in the same way). 1st ed. reads:
[[It happened by one of those singular coincidences in real life, which would be called improbable in a novel, that Mr. Montagu's mansion adjoined that of the duke, Mrs. Montagu having, like most of the parvenu genus, a most violent penchant for the neighbourhood of the great; perhaps, in the hope that gentility might be infectious, and that she might catch a title by being near it. Both houses were in the Strand, which was, as we have before stated, in those days the most fashionable part of London, and both had beautiful gardens shelving down to the Thames.
Mrs. Montagu received her brother-in-law with all that awkward overstrained civility, with which persons raised above their original grade in society, generally endeavour to show their respect to those whom they consider as their superiors; whilst Mr. Montagu welcomed him with warm affection, and presented his daughter Clara to her uncle with all the fondness of a parent.
Clara Montagu well deserved his partiality, for she was a charming girl; and her light fairy form and animated features seemed to realize all that poets feign of Hebe. Sir Ambrose was delighted with her, and half his dislike of the mother banished, as he contemplated the budding charms of the daughter. It was well he had such an antidote, for poor Mrs. Montagu, in her over-anxiety to render herself agreeable, contrived to be most excessively annoying to him. Perhaps, indeed, there are few things more

troublesome than this vulgar attempt at politeness, and the good temper of the baronet was almost exhausted ere he retired for the night.

Abelard, who had accompanied his master to town, and who often officiated as groom of the chamber, assisted him to undress, and, as usual with servants in those days, took the liberty of giving his opinion freely of their hostess. Sir Ambrose felt no interest in his remarks, but he did not check them, as he hoped, after he had exhausted this theme, he might turn the conversation upon Edric. The baronet was indeed excessively anxious to hear some news of his son, though he was by far too proud to make any inquiries respecting him.

"So you really think Mrs. Montagu disagreeable, Abelard," said Sir Ambrose.

"She is a perfect nuisance, your honour, to all civilized society. Why, I have observed her all day, and I verily believe she has never left your honour for ten minutes, nor ever ceased for more than half an hour at a time, pressing your honour to eat."

"True," said Sir Ambrose, laughing, "one would think she took me for a slave, and wanted to feed me up fat before she sent me to market to be sold."

"Then she is so curious and inquisitive," resumed Abelard. "When she saw me bow to Master Edric just now, she was quite in a fever to know who he was; but I would not satisfy her."

"Master Edric!" exclaimed the baronet. "What, then I have you seen my son?"

"Yes, your honour, and it startled me so that it made me raise the adnatae of my visual organs like one of the anas genus when the clouds are charged with electric fluid; and my heart leaped from its transverse position on my diaphragm, and seemed to stick like a great bone right across my oesophagus."

"How did he look?" asked Sir Ambrose. "Not that I feel the slightest anxiety respecting him. No—no, his own conduct has quite precluded that."

"He was in a balloon, and when he saw me, he wrote something on a piece of paper with a pencil, and threw it down, desiring me to give it to your honour."

"Where is it?" cried Sir Ambrose, endeavouring to conceal his anxiety.

Abelard searched his pockets, and opened a large pocket-book, which he carefully examined, but in vain. "I am afraid I have lost it, your honour. No; here—here it is. Yes—no. These are some verses of my own, in the acromonogrammatic style, only every line begins with the same word with which the last ended, instead of the same letter. Shall I read them to your honour?"

Sir Ambrose groaned in the spirit, and the unmerciful Abelard, taking that for a token of assent, deliberately unfolded the paper, and read as follows:—

ON LOVE.

Or all the powers in Heaven above,
Above all others, triumphs Love:
Love rules the soul—the heart invades,
Invades the cities and the shades.
Shades form no shelter from its power,
Power trembles in his courtly bower.
Bower of beauty—art thou free?
Free thou art not—nor canst thou be!
Be every other class released,
Released from love, thy woe's increased;
Increased by all the weight of care,
Care flowing from complete despair.

"Humph!" said Sir Ambrose.

"I hope your honour is pleased with this little effusion of my Muse?"

"Oh yes, it is very fine, Abelard."

"And your honour thinks it well turned, and well expressed."

"Excellently! only I own I don't understand why despair comes in the last line."

"Despair—despair: oh! to rhyme with care, your honour."

"That reason is unanswerable," returned Sir Ambrose, smiling.—"And so you are quite sure you have lost Edric's note!—Not that it is of the least consequence, as nothing he could say, can possibly alter my opinion of his conduct; but, if you had had it—I thought I might as well have read it, to avoid the imputation of obstinacy."

"It is irrevocably gone, your honour."

"Well then, good night; and, if you should see Edric again, you may as well tell him the fate of his note;—for, shamefully as he has behaved, I would not give him reason to accuse me of obstinacy."

This was the second time the baronet had made the same observation; and ill-natured people might have said—but what do the remarks of ill-natured people signify to us? We hope all our readers will he good-natured ones, and as they will assuredly put the best possible construction upon Sir Ambrose's conduct, we will not be so malicious as to suggest an evil one.

Edric was exceedingly agitated by his encounter with Abelard; and, feeling convinced his father was in town, he determined to delay his journey no longer, as his dread of meeting him was excessive.]]

It is one of the most glorious attributes of greatness ... the agitated form of the unfortunate philosopher burst upon him: replaces: "During their ride home, Lord Gustavus could talk of nothing but the graciousness of the Queen, upon which he was still expatiating, when the balloon stopped; and Edric, who, though he felt grateful for her kindness, was annoyed by hearing so much said of it, hastened to leave him as soon as he possibly could with propriety. On his road to his own apartment, however, he heard a strange and fearful, noise, like the voice of some one screaming in an agony of rage and pain, which seemed to proceed from the chamber appropriated to his learned tutor; and he was going there to ascertain the cause, when the agitated form of the unfortunate philosopher burst upon him." (1st ed.).

He therefore resolved to seek his tutor: From here, the text follows the 1st ed.

Volume 1: Chapter 9
No textual changes between editions.

Volume 1: Chapter 10
No textual changes between editions.

Volume 1: Chapter 11
Here JWL cut the introduction of the mysterious "Seymour", whose slight Irish accent rather gives him away, and moves the character earlier to chapter 7 of the 2nd ed. There are minor changes, including spelling/printing errors, but some of the changes of vocabulary are deliberate changes of affect. In revising the dialogue of Father Murphy, she also emphasizes his comic "brogue". VOLUME 1 of the first edition ends with the dramatic arrival of Cheops in London as a thundering crescendo to the disaster that kills Queen Claudia.

In the mean time, Sir Ambrose Montagu had attended the Duke to the Queen's drawing room: [[In the mean time, Sir Ambrose Montagu had been presented to the Queen, and the evening after his arrival in town he attended her drawing-room.]] (1st ed.).

he would have fallen at her feet, had he not been supported by Father Morris: [[supported by a young man]] (1st ed.). This is "Henry Seymour", who is first introduced here. The 2nd ed. has him introduced by Dr Coleman to Sir Ambrose in Ch 7.

"I leave you in excellent hands ... to dwell long upon the circumstance: The 1st ed. has:
[["You seem faint, Sir," said the youth; "will you permit me to lead you to a seat."

"Thank you, thank you," cried Sir Ambrose, gratefully accepting the proffered aid, and leaning on his youthful supporter as they left the presence. The stranger carefully placed Sir Ambrose upon a sofa, under the harmonious trees we have already mentioned; and as he stood before him, asking if he should procure him some refreshments, Sir Ambrose had full leisure to survey his face and figure: both were handsome in the extreme. The youth seemed scarcely to have passed the age of boyhood, and his well-proportioned form displayed all the lightness and activity of youth; but wit and good-humour laughed in his bright blue eyes, whilst animated features and an enchanting smile completed an ensemble which few bosoms were frozen enough to resist. Sir Ambrose was irresistibly pleased, and longed to know to whom he was indebted for so much kindness. But he felt too delicate to ask the question in direct terms, and there was nothing in the youth's exterior to mark decidedly to what rank in life he might belong.

He was handsomely dressed, and his air and manner appeared slightly foreign; though this might be fancy, arising from Sir Ambrose's ignorance of the manners and habits of the Court. There also seemed something droll about him, and the air with which he submitted to Sir Ambrose's scrutiny was excessively comic.

"Is there any thing I can do for you?" asked he at length, when he thought the baronet's curiosity had had time to satisfy itself.

"Nothing," replied Sir Ambrose; but—"

"But—you would like to know who I am?"; said the stranger.

"I own," returned Sir Ambrose, blushing, "I would fain know to whom I am so much obliged."

"My name is Henry Seymour," replied the youth. "I was born in Spain, of English parents. I am an orphan and in want; and have been introduced to the Queen, in hopes of getting a place at Court, by one of her Majesty's physicians, Dr. Coleman."

"I am quite ashamed," said Sir Ambrose, "that my indiscreet curiosity—that is, that you should have thought—I mean, that I should have asked for—"

"In short," interrupted the youth, "you think, perhaps, that I meant to call you rude by giving such a long account of myself: but I always do so in similar cases; it saves trouble."

Sir Ambrose smiled. "You are a singular youth," said he; "I should like to know you better."

"And I," returned the stranger, "should be proud to obtain the friendship of Sir Ambrose Montagu, and shall always reckon the day that introduced me to his notice, as one of the happiest of my life."

A glow of pleasure spread over the animated features of the youth as he spoke, and Sir Ambrose fancied his accent sounded slightly Irish: convinced, however, that he must be mistaken, he did not remark it, but only exclaimed, "You know me, then?"

Before the stranger had time to utter a reply, the Duke of Cornwall, and the Princesses Rosabella and Elvira approached, and prevented him from speaking.

"How do you find yourself, my dear friend?" said the duke; "they told us you were ill."

"I have been slightly so," returned Sir Ambrose; "and I believe I should have fainted, and paid my respects to my Sovereign quite orientally, if this gentleman had not saved me."

"I am sure we are very much obliged to you, Sir," said the duke, turning to the youth.

"Indeed, we feel most grateful," said Elvira.

The stranger made. a suitable reply, and after a short conversation, in which Dr. Coleman joined, that worthy gentleman having been also drawn to the spot by the report of Sir Ambrose's illness, he requested the favour of Elvira's hand for the dance.

"That is a very nice young man," said the duke, when he was gone to join the dancers: "I admire him much."

"He deserves every thing you can say in his favour," returned _Dr. Coleman: "I have known him long, and I love him as a son."

"Then Elvira retired to her chamber that night, she sighed so often, and so deeply, that Emma, who assisted at her toilet, could not avoid remarking her uneasiness. "Are you ill, my dear mistress?" asked she, in a tone of feeling; "what else can have produced this sudden change?"

"I am quite well," said Elvira, again sighing.

"Why then do you sigh and look so thoughtful?"

"I was thinking of Lord Edmund."

"Indeed! I did not think he had the power to make you sigh. He has reason to feel flattered."

"Oh, Emma! I wish he were like Henry Seymour!"

"And who is Henry Seymour?" asked Emma, smiling, and beginning to suspect that she had been rather hasty in fancying Lord Edmund had occasion to flatter himself on account of the Princess's tristesse.

"One of the most fascinating of human beings," returned Elvira; "so gay, and yet so tender. He is not, perhaps, so regularly handsome as Edmund, but he has such expressive features, and his soul gives such animation to his countenance."

"Poor Edmund!" thought Emma: but as she was too discreet to say so, Elvira was not aware of the interpretation that might be put on what she was saying; and she went on, raving of the pleasures of the ball, till she was fairly in bed.]]

Clara Montagu and her companions: in 1st ed. this is [[the occupiers of the balloon of Mr. Montagu]] the scene goes on: [[Even that oblivious gentleman himself was moved to exclaim, that he never was more enchanted in his life; whilst the raptures of his spouse were so excessive, that, like the spectators of the stag-hunt on the lake of Killarney, she was in imminent danger of throwing herself overboard in her ecstasy: and Clara clasped her hands together, in all the transports of childish delight, her sparkling eyes and animated looks bearing ample witness to her gratification.]]

"What shouting! what a noise!" exclaimed Mr. Abelard: [[exclaimed Mr. Montagu]] (1ˢᵗ ed.).

and birds fell from the skies with the noise!: Followed in 1ˢᵗ ed. by [["La! papa, is that true?" asked Clara.

"Och, and that's a strange kind of a question," said Father Murphy, "and one, I wouldn't like a child of mine to be putting."

"And why not?" asked Mr. Montagu, somewhat indignantly.

"Because a child ought always to belave what his father says, before he hears him open his mouth."]]

observed Mrs. Russel: [observed Mrs. Montagu]] (1ˢᵗ ed.).

"Evelina says she's being poisoned," cried Clara, "and that the people say that it would be no great matter if she was: [["My nurse says she's being poisoned," cried Clara, "and that it would be no great matter if she was,]] (1ˢᵗ. ed.).

what terms they pleased with her: following this in 1ˢᵗ ed. is [["And is this the kind of servant you suffer to attend on my daughter, Mrs. Montagu?" demanded the indignant father, roused from his usual lethargy by the importance of the occasion; "Clara shall go to a boarding-school tomorrow, and her nurse shall be dismissed. My child shall not be taught to utter treason."

"Dear me! Mr. Montagu," replied the wife, "what a serious matter you make of a little harmless gossip!"

"Gossip do you call it?" repeated her husband; "it is such gossip as might cost me my head, and you your fortune, if it were to reach unfriendly ears."]]

a purtier comes afther him: [[a prettier that comes after him]] (1ˢᵗ ed.)

asked Mrs. Russel: asked Mrs Mongagu (1ˢᵗ ed.).

it's a very purty young man that walks by the side of him; so he is: [[it's a very handsome young man also that walks by the side of him]] (1ˢᵗ ed.)

"His hands are chained, so you see he is a prisoner;" observed Abelard: [["His

hands are chained as if he were a prisoner; and he looks like a foreigner," observed Mr. Montagu, who had relapsed into one of his fits of abstraction: "I wonder what can bring him there!"

"La! Mr. Montagu, how you talk!" exclaimed his wife, "you know my nephew, Lord Edmund, has just gained a battle, and what can be more natural than that he should have taken prisoners?"

"True," rejoined Mr. Montagu with the utmost naiveté, "I never thought of that!"]] (1ˢᵗ ed.)

"Sure, and it's a barbarous custom that of putthing chains about the hands of the prisoners," said Father Murphy: [[Och, and it's a barbarous custom that of putting chains about the hands of the prisoners," said Father Murphy,]] (1ˢᵗ ed.).

"How great Lord Edmund looks!" ... sitting there hand-in-hand with my master: [["How great my nephew Lord Edmund looks!" continued Mrs. Montagu: "I declare it he were a real king he couldn't have a grander appearance. And then to see the poor old gentleman his father, my brother-in-law, Sir Ambrose, sitting there hand-in-hand with the Duke of Cornwall himself.]] (1ˢᵗ ed.).

Whilst the occupiers of the balloons ... out of his senses with joy: [[Whilst Mrs. Montagu was thus exulting in the reflected grandeur that shone upon her, from being sister-in-law to the person who sat hand-in-hand with the duke, the joy and delight of that exalted personage had been almost as great as her own.]] (1ˢᵗ ed.).

gazing upon his son: The next paragraph runs on from this sentence in 1ˢᵗ ed.

"There! there he is!" cried the Duke: [[duke]] (1ˢᵗ ed.).

Now he helps her on her horse: [[Look! Now he helps her on her horse]] (1ˢᵗ ed.).

recall: [[recal]] (1ˢᵗ ed.).

remind the latter of his imprudence: [[recal the latter to himself]] (1ˢᵗ ed.).

the unfortunate individuals who accompanied the party of Clara: [[The party of Mr. Montagu]] (1ˢᵗ ed.).

Sure, and I'm killed entirely: [[Och, and I'm killed entirely]] (1ˢᵗ ed.)

"Oh, my bonnet! my beautiful bonnet!" sobbed Mrs. Russel; whilst Clara, dreadfully frightened, began to cry; and Abelard, whose ideas were generally a long time travelling to his brain, particularly upon occasions of sudden alarm, stood completely silent....: [["Oh, my bonnet! my beautiful bonnet!" sobbed Mrs. Montagu; whilst Clara, dreadfully frightened, began to cry; and Mr Montagu, whose ideas were generally a long time travelling to his brain, particularly upon occasions of sudden alarm, stood completely silent...]] (1st ed.).

Volume 1: Chapter 12
This is chapter 1 of vol 2 of the 1st edition, which ended with the climactic arrival of Cheops amid the chaos caused by the collapse of Queen Elvira. Apart from the placing of dialogue given to the Montagus in the 1st edition in the mouths of other characters, the changes are mostly minor alterations of wording.

Where is Arsinöe?: [[Where is Arsinöe? Where is she? (1st ed.).

it had been torn asunder in the scuffle: [[had been rent asunder in the scuffle]] (1st ed.).

to which had long been a stranger: [[which had long been a stranger to it]] (1st ed.).

amongst this number was Mrs. Russel: [[amongst this number was Mrs Montagu]] (1st ed.).

The moment their balloon fell ... finding all safe: [["The whole family had reached home in perfect safety, the lady herself hurrying her return, the moment the accident of the Queen was made known: lest, as she said, in the confusion that might ensue, her servants might be induced to leave her house, and some evil disposed personages might strip it of its contents. Urged by this prudent motive, Mrs. Montagu had hastened home, and finding all safe"]] (1st ed.).

asked Mrs. Russel: [[asked Mrs. Montagu]] (1st ed.).

cried Mrs. Russel: cried Mrs. Montagu (1st ed.). ("Russel" substituted for "Montagu" throughout the rest of the paragraph.

Where her lover was awaiting her return, impatient to delight her attentive ears with a few more of his poetical effusions: [[where her husband was already lost in some of his beloved calculations]] (1st ed.).

as Abelard was: [[as Mr. Montagu was]] (1st ed.).

Abelard's frame: [[Mr. Montagu's frame]] (1st ed.).

he shrank back with horror as his fearful visitant stalked past him.: [[he shrank back with horror as his fearful guest stalked past him]] (1st ed.).

whilst Abelard and Mrs. Russel gazed with trembling limbs and pallid lips at the strange intruder: [[whilst Mr. and Mrs. Montagu gazed with trembling limbs and pallid lips at the strange intruder]] (1st ed.).

whilst Abelard and Mrs. Russel, terrified beyond the power of expression: [[whilst Mr. and Mrs. Montagu, terrified beyond the power of expression]] (1st ed.).

Abelard, as he motioned to Mrs. Russel: [[Mr. Montagu, as he motioned to his wife]] (1st ed.).

observed Abelard: [[observed Mr. Montagu]] (1st ed.).

to rouse Abelard: [[to rouse even Mr. Montagu]] (1st ed.).

"Oh, Abelard!" cried the latter, panting for breath; "have you heard the news? The Queen is certainly dying. [["Oh, my dear brother!" cried the latter, panting for breath; "have you heard the news? The strangest vision has appeared, and the Queen is certainly dying.]] (1st ed.).

"What, the Mummy?" asked Abelard: [["What, the Mummy?" asked Mr. Montagu]] (1st ed.).

"It is now in this house," said Mrs. Russel: [["It is now in this house," cried Mrs. Montagu]] (1st ed.).

"In this house!" repeated Sir Ambrose with a faint scream: [["In this house!" repeated her brother-in-law]] (1st ed.).

It was with infinite difficulty that Mrs. Russel: [[It was with infinite difficulty that Mrs. Montagu]] (1st ed.).

with Mrs. Russel and her constant Abelard: (added to 2nd. ed.).

Yet as the bottle circulated ... shrieking from the room: [[Nothing, however, had terrified Mrs. Montagu so much as the laugh of Cheops; strange, wild, and unearthly, it still seemed to ring in her ears, like the yell of a demon; whilst, if any thing that happened, chanced to recall the appalling sound, her limbs shook in every joint; her teeth chattered in her head; terror blanched her lips and cheeks to a ghastly paleness, and she seemed every instant upon the point of rising from her seat and flying shrieking from the room.]] (1st ed.).

The family of the Duke of Cornwall: [[The family of Mr. Montagu]] (1st ed.).

Through the garden: [[through the garden of Mr. Montagu]] (1st ed.).

At the extremity of the garden was a terrace very little used: [[It has been already stated that the garden of Mr. Montagu was only separated from that of the duke by a terrace very little used]] (1st ed.)

cried Mrs. Russel: [[cried Evelina, one of Mrs. Montagu's housemaids]] (1st ed.).

the romantic butler: [[the inconstant butler]] (1st ed.)

"It must have been an optical delusion," resumed Mrs. Russel: [["It must have been an optical delusion, Mr. Abelard," said Evelina]] (1st ed.).

"I must consult Father Morris about it tomorrow: [["I must consult Father Morris about it tomorrow" resumed the butler,]] (1st ed.).

"La! do you think so, Mr. Abelard?": [["La! do you think so, Mr. Abelard?", said Evelina, turning pale.]]

"Oh! there it is!" cried Mrs. Russel: [["Oh! there it is!" cried Evelina]] (1st ed.).

Volume 2: Chapter 1
Volume 2 Chapter 2 of the 1st edition. The two revisions are afterthoughts designed to increase the dramatic tone of the short scenes.

—(This silk is too dark, Emma)—: The brackets in these interjections are not in 1st ed. Their addition shows more clearly Elvira carrying on two conversations at once, "half-abstracted", paying as much if not more attention to her embroidery.

"How unreasonable you are!" said Elvira ... "You shall be obeyed," said he: 1st

ed. continues the playful asides to Emma, more flirtatious and romantic. [["How unreasonable you are!" said Elvira, smiling. "Hear him, Emma; is he not a singular being? And if I find it so difficult to please him now, what must I expect when I become his wife?"

"Tormenting girl!" exclaimed Edmund, "you know your power but too well."

"What ridiculous creatures these lords of the creation are!" said Elvira, playfully holding out her hand to Edmund, though she still affected to address Emma; "I really don't think any of them know what they would have; and I believe the only way to manage them is to make one's-self perfectly disagreeable."

"That you can never do," cried Edmund, rapturously kissing her hand.]]

The revision is more melodramatic, with its reference to Henry Seymour as a rival.

"Oh! I don't think you have the least occasion in the world to trouble yourself about him": "do'nt" in text. Spelled correctly in 1st ed.

he held out his hand to him: [[Fearing, whilst he hated the mysterious being thus strangely thrust into his most inmost secrets, Father Morris promised obedience, and the Mummy retreated within the walls of Mrs. Montagu's garden; ere he left the priest, however, he held out his hand to him. "Give me your hand," said he, "and let us seal our compact."]] (1st ed.).

Volume 2: Chapter 2
Volume 2 Chapter 3 of the first edition.

it shall not be my fault if I do not avail myself of his assistance: Father Morris decides to use Cheops in his plans. Each is working upon the other. Following on from this in 1st ed. is [[In his present garb he creates disgust and terror; but clothed as a human being, his superhuman eloquence, and the strange fearful interest excited by his looks and manner, might render him a powerful assistant. It shall be my present business, then, to endeavour to make him serviceable to my views; and to do this I must persuade him to adopt the dress and manners of the country.]] Presumably this suggestion of a "disguise" is deleted because everyone identifies Cheops as "The Mummy" even when disguised. His "horrid" or "fiendish" laughter is a giveaway.

The night was now far advanced ... the deity he fancied it to represent: [[Pleased with the resolution he had taken, and quite forgetting the lateness of the hour, Father Morris descended hastily to the usual sitting room of Mrs. Montagu; but what was his horror, on entering it, to find, instead of the usual cheerful party he expected, only the dreaded Mummy! Cheops again lay stretched upon the couch he had before occupied, his eyes fixed upon the brilliant constellation of Orion, and his lips murmuring an address to the deity he fancied it to represent.]] (1ˢᵗ ed.).

he could not articulate a word: Following this in 1ˢᵗ ed is: [[Father Morris felt his blood curdle in his veins at this address, and, though he strove to speak, his tongue clove to the roof of his mouth, and he could not articulate a word. Cheops saw his embarrassment, and continued in a milder tone, "Fear nothing; we may be useful to each other. I would fain quit these garments of the tomb, and since. I seem destined to remain some time amongst your fellow-men, I will endeavour to assume their manners. You seem to have influence amongst them; try, then, to pacify their fears, and teach them to regard me as a fellow-being."]]
Again this is the Mummy disguising himself, which is changed in 2ⁿᵈ ed.

The death of the Queen ... to the mournful spectacle: [[the death of the Queen being now generally known, her remains, laid in state, were exposed to the lamentations of her subjects, and the family of Mrs. Montagu were amongst the earliest visitors to the mournful spectacle." (1ˢᵗ ed.).

and he rose hastily in great disorder, to endeavour to account for his appearance there though, in fact, as there was nothing extraordinary in a priest visiting a sick penitent, his eagerness to exculpate himself from suspicion would have excited it, had not the duke been too angry even to be aware of his presence.: [[and he rose hastily in great disorder, to endeavour to account for his appearance there. The duke, however, was too much enraged to listen to him, or, indeed, to notice the suspicious circumstance of his secretly visiting the princess; his passion was solely directed against Rosabella, and not even her present feeble and emaciated appearance was sufficient to disarm his anger.]] (1ˢᵗ ed.).

The duke had here unwittingly struck a chord that thrilled through the inmost souls of his auditors—though he did not heed their confusion.: [[The duke had here unwittingly struck a chord that thrilled through the inmost souls of his auditors; he did not heed their confusion, however, but went on.]] (1ˢᵗ ed.).

Volume 2: Chapter 3
Volume 2 Chapter 4 of the first edition

He is going to join the army to try to exert his influence amongst the soldiers: [[He is going into the country to try to exert his influence amongst the electors]] (1ˢᵗ ed.).

the garden of the Duke of Cornwall's mansion: "of Mr. Montague" is printed in the text, but this should probably be "the garden of the Duke of Cornwall". This appears to be an oversight in the revision. Sir Ambrose Montagu and his retinue are staying with the Duke of Cornwall (Vol 1 ch 4). In the first edition, they are staying with Sir Ambrose's brother and sister-in-law, Mr and Mrs Montagu, who have been written out of the second edition, although "by one of those singular coincidences in real life, which would be called improbable in a novel, ... Mr. Montagu's mansion adjoined that of the duke." (Vol 1 Ch 8). Later references to Edmund as "Mr. Montagu" possibly explain why JWL decided against two "Mr. Montagus" in the text, and the retention of "Mr. Montagu" here shows that confusion is certainly possible.

Volume 2: Chapter 4

This is Volume 2 Chapter 5 of the first edition.

When an important enterprise is undertaken: [[enterprize]] (1st ed.).

the family of the duke: [[the family of Mr. Montagu]] (1st ed.).

"I cannot imagine what is the matter with Clara?" ... "Clara, I sent for you to speak to Dr. Coleman.": Replaces the following in 1st ed: [["I cannot imagine what is the matter with my daughter?" said Mrs. Montagu one day to Dr. Coleman; "I wish you would talk to her a little;—Here, Clara, my dear, do just step this way.—You will be quite shocked, doctor, at the change in her appearance. Poor girl! I don't think she has ever properly overcome the fright she experienced at the first sight of the Mummy, for she has never seemed herself since. Indeed

> 'It seems to me she hoards some secret care,
> That breaks her rest and drives her to despair.'"

"What do you quote that from, my dear?" asked Mr. Montagu, more interested in his wife's quotation than the illness of his daughter.

"Oh! it is one of a lot I bought the other day at the patent steam-book manufactory, in Hatton-Garden. I had been buying some other things, and so I persuaded the man to throw me in a bargain of quotations very cheap. They were all quite new, and ready cut, dried, and made up into pills for use. But I never saw such a man in my life;—you think nothing at all about your daughter. I really wish you would question her a little, for she will tell me nothing."

"Very well, my dear, I will," said Mr. Montagu; but the next instant he was absorbed in his studies again, and had even quite forgotten that such a being as Clara existed.

"Really," said Mrs. Montagu to the doctor, "I do not think any poor woman in the world ever was so plagued as I am. You see what a husband I have. He never troubles his head about any thing; and if I were to take it into my head to walk off, I don't think he would even miss me; and then, my daughter—but here she comes.—Clara, I sent for you to speak to Dr. Coleman."]]

The "patent steam-book manufactory" is more futuristic fun and a satire on literary production. The image was used elsewhere, specifically for the output of Henry Colburn: e.g. William Maginn's *Whitehall, or the Days of George IV* (1827) described in Sutherland & Melnyk, 104 in which Colburn is "Henry the Great" who "owns a manufactory in Burlington Street as crammed with hacks as a Lancashire cotton mill is with machine-handlers". Colburn was JWL's publisher, so this might have been a dig which she felt tactless or even that he 'suggested' she remove.

Sir Ambrose, roused: [[Mr. Montagu, "roused from his lethargy"]] (1st ed.).

his niece: his daughter (1st ed.).

at the house of the duke ever since: [[at the house of Mrs. Montagu ever since]] (1st ed.).

Prince Ferdinand came no more to the duke's: [[Prince Ferdinand came no more to Mrs. Montagu's]] (1st ed.).

Volume 2: Chapter 5
Volume 2 Chapter 6 of the first edition.

groups of elegantly-dressed people: [[groupes]] (1st ed.).

Volume 2: Chapter 6
Volume 2 chapter 7 of the first edition.

This venerable pile ... shone forth in all its original splendour: Virtually the same words as an earlier description: [[This venerable pile, which had seen so many generations successively rise and pass away, now cleared of the incumbrances with which the bad taste of the middle ages had loaded it, shone in all its original magnificence]] (Volume 2 Chapter 2)

they were *favours:* "*were*" not italicised in 1st ed.

dependence: corrected from "dependance" in 1st ed.

Volume 2: Chapter 7
Volume 2 chapter 8 of the first edition.

There are no corrections in this chapter.

Volume 2: Chapter 8
Volume 2 chapter 9 of the first edition.

Can you believe it!" returned Edric ... I should be very glad to be awakened: [["Can you believe it," returned Edric, "but in spite of all the misfortunes I have suffered, a restless curiosity to know the fate of the Mummy we so strangely resuscitated, is one of the strongest feelings in my bosom."

"I can readily credit it," said the doctor; "for the same feeling operates upon me! It is, however, vain to indulge in useless regrets: we must die; and all we have to do, is to endeavour to become resigned to our fate."]] (1st ed.).

Volume 2: Chapter 9
Volume 2 chapter 10 of the first edition.

Roderick, having made Cadiz his head-quarters, was about removing thither, when the message of the Alcaide, had induced to undertake the romantic enterprise he had just so successfully accomplished.: [[romantic enterprize]] (1st ed.).

he delighted in surprises and disguises, ... so base and mean: [[it had been the policy of his father, the late King, to foment secretly the discontents nourished amongst the English; but the spirit of Roderick revolted at conduct he considered so mean and base.]] (1st ed.).

his chivalrous devotion to noble and grand enterprises: [[noble and grand enterprizes]] (1st ed.).

a very worthy countryman of yours, Father Morris: [[Father Murphy]] (1st ed.). In the 1st ed, the references are to Murphy rather than Morris, hence the slight revisions below.

with what you were saying of Father Morris: [[with what you were saying of Father Murphy]] (1st ed.).

though an intelligent and highly cultivated man ... of your Majesty's countrymen: [[that the excellence of his disposition had given me a favourable opinion of your Majesty's countrymen]] (1st ed.).

Volume 2: Chapter 10
Volume 2 chapter 11 of the first edition. The excision of the explicit likening of Zoe to a statue seems to make Roderick's joke even less funny.

she would be charming: [[she would be a Venus de Medicis]] (1st ed.).[16]

I am surprised ... anxious about your Mummy: [["Oh come! Edric," said Roderick, laughing; "that is really too bad. I'll allow that Zoe wants animation; but she has at least as much as a statue. Besides I thought you were fond of still life, or you would not feel so anxious about your Mummy."]] (1st ed.).

Volume 2: Chapter 11
Volume 2 chapter 12 of the first edition.

dreary and uncomfortable around: [[dreary and uncomfortable.]] (1st ed.)

I do declare her arm is broken, and her shoulder dreadful lacerated: [[dreadfully lacerated]] (1st ed.).

Volume 2: Chapter 12
Volume 2 chapter 13 of the first edition.

Dispatched Alex for a surgeon: [[despatched Alex for a surgeon]] (1st ed.).

when he was roused ... which froze his blood with horror: [[when he was roused by a slight sound, and looking up, saw the Spanish general and the Greek page standing by his bed-side.

Edric roused himself immediately, though he still pretended to slumber. The recollection of all he had heard respecting the Duke of Medina, Pedro, and the Princess Zoe, mingled with the suspicions that had been breathed of the mysterious page, flashed across his mind, and effectually destroyed all inclination to sleeping: indeed, a cold shudder ran through his frame, as he remembered, with horror, that if any thing were designed against Roderick, the first step of the conspirators would he to destroy him, from his known devotion to the Irish monarch, and that, in his present enfeebled state, he was quite incapable of resistance. His blood seemed to run more feebly through his veins, and he panted for breath, whilst he listened attentively, and heard the Spanish general whisper, "He sleeps, but not soundly enough for our purpose."

An icy thrill seemed to chill Edric's heart, and involuntarily he heaved a deep sigh. The supposed conspirators started, and retired. Edric, now completely roused from his slumber, gazed after them, as, with creeping, stealthy steps, they glided across the plain. Astonished at what he had seen and heard, Edric lay lost in bewildering speculations; but soon a new object caught his attention.⟧⟧ (1ˢᵗ ed.).

The moment the flames broke forth, one fearful scream seemed to burst from every lip, the soldiers flew, en masse, to the tent of their monarch; and Roderick sprang from his couch, when he heard their hurried footsteps: ⟦⟦The moment the flames broke forth, Alexis and the Spanish general hurried back to the tent, and Roderick sprang from his couch, when he heard their hurried footsteps.⟧⟧ (1ˢᵗ ed.).

Volume 3: Chapter 1

The conversation which ensued … fifty years to accomplish: ⟦⟦"I am glad, very glad, to see you so soon recovered," said Pauline, addressing Edric in a gentle tone; "I feared, that is, my father feared, your wounds were more serious."

"You see, Edric," cried Roderick archly, "it is as I said—Mademoiselle de Mallet feels for you exactly the same interest as her father does."

"I should be flattered by exciting any interest in so gentle a bosom," sighed Edric, looking at her tenderly.

Pauline sighed too—involuntarily, but remained silent.

"Do you then. feel no interest in my behalf?" continued Edric; "not even the cold, chilling feeling sanctioned by your father?"

"Oh! call not the interest my father feels for you cold or chilling!" exclaimed Pauline with energy, "I am sure—that is, I think—" and here, fearing she had said too much, she stopped abruptly, totally unable to proceed.

"Oh, go on!" exclaimed Edric, gazing earnestly upon her blushing face— "go on, I could listen to you for ever!"

"Pauline trembled, blushed, and hesitated. "I—I—I think I had better go to my father," stammered she after a short pause.

Roderick smiled: "By all means!" said he. "Don't you think so, Edric?"

Edric did not reply; for in fact he did not hear the question; whilst poor Pauline's agitation increased, and her colour changed rapidly every moment: she dreaded Roderick's raillery, and trembled so violently that she could scarcely stand.

At this moment her father returned; he looked at his daughter with some surprise, and then, turning to his guests, he apologized for her abstraction. "My daughter is unused to camps," said he, "and the scenes she has lately gone through have been too much for her nerves."

"She will now have an opportunity of recovering herself," replied Roderick; "my army will move forward to-morrow, and if you will accept the post, I will leave you governor of this city, with a sufficient garrison to keep it on my behalf."

Pauline turned deathly pale as he spoke, and every hope of happiness seemed to fly from her breast for ever.

M. de Mallet, however, was not at all aware of his daughter's anguish; and, thanking the king gratefully for the high honour conferred upon him, his fancy began to revel by anticipation in the delights of governorship; and in ten minutes he had arranged in his mind as many improvements and alterations as it would take fifty years to accomplish.]] (1st ed.).

Volume 3: Chapter 2

and his nod decided its fate; whilst the council, ... the suggestions of his own breast: [[and his nod decided its fate. The council, however, though they implicitly obeyed his will, had not the least idea that they were doing so; as he had the address so to form his opinions as to let each person imagine them the suggestions of his own breast.]] (1st ed.).

Elvira's ascension to the throne ... and his pretty niece: [[Elvira's accession to the throne had induced both her father and Sir Ambrose to leave the country; the duke inhabiting his former palace, and Sir Ambrose taking possession of a moveable house in one of the streets upon the banks of the Thames. Here the worthy Baronet found himself perfectly happy in the society of his niece Clara, (whom her parents permitted to keep his house,) and that of his old friend the duke.]] (1st ed.). These sentences are obviously designed to set up the joke in the next chapter which gives us one of the hazards of "moveable homes".

"I fear so indeed; ... I remember the time," &c.: deleted in 2nd ed.

But why detail their reminiscences ... the change was in themselves, not the times: [[Whilst these two old men were sitting comfortably over the fire, commenting on the glorious days when they were young, and when all went right, or, what was nearly the same thing, when all appeared to them to do so (quite forgetting that age has other eyes than youth, and that the change was in themselves, not the times)]] (1st ed.).

Volume 3: Chapter 3

Additions here are designed to sharpen up the comic scenes, with the early chop-logic dispute between Sir Ambrose and the clumsy domestic from the house next door as he attempts to settle it back into its usual position on its return from Brighton, and Ambrose setting the scene before Clara sets off to save Ferdinand. We were clearly meant to learn that Sir Ambrose had moved house in the previous chapter, but the sentences telling us so were cut from the second edition. The kind-hearted Father Murphy, ever-dependable for some comic relief, has his brogue strengthened.

I am always willing to hear reason …"*The Devil take your logic*," *cried Sir Ambrose:* added to 2nd ed.

"*I would not say any thing disrespectful … Where have they injured you?*": added to 2nd ed.

afther: [[after]] (1st ed.). His brogue has been increased.

darkthness: [[darkness]] 1st ed. More increase of his accent.

betther: [[better]] (1st ed.).

the goal of all my wishes: [[gaol]] (1st ed.): which makes this either a corrected typo or a pun JWL has thought better of.

disthracted: [[distracted]] (1st ed.).

Father Murphy wisely informed me … overlooked in consideration of your youth: [[He is prepared to receive you, and will forgive your absence, as Father Murphy will, ere we reach him, have fully explained its cause: and Sir Ambrose will overlook your folly, in consideration of your youth.]] (1st ed.).

Volume 3: Chapter 4
It is very true, notwithstanding: corrected from [[Is is]] (1st ed.).

to fall in love with the Queen!!!: three exclamation marks in 2nd ed. Only one in 1st ed.

"*Oh, they all understand French.*": [["O, they all understand French."]] (1st ed.).

I know, I feel that you must acquit my client on this head: The next sentence follows on with no paragraph break in 1st ed.

Volume 3: Chapter 5
'*Tell him,' said she, 'it is not possible he can have aught to say that can interest me.:* "me" not italicised in 1st ed.

Volume 3: Chapter 6
began to sing: [[Loveliest Queen! oh deign to hear
The humblest of thy suppliants' prayer;

Blandly on a stranger smile,
Who has sought thy happy Isle,
To feast his eyes upon that face,
Where majesty combines with grace.]] (1ˢᵗ ed., deleted from 2ⁿᵈ ed.).

a few doggrel verses in praise of her Majesty: (added to 2ⁿᵈ ed.).

He sung his reply: [["Full often in my native land
I've struck my lute with bolder hand;
But with the liberties of Greece,
Her minstrel's harmony must cease.
Since Iwan with a soldier's frown
Hath seized and worn th' imperial crown,
Those hearts which spurn despotic power
Must wander from their native bower,
And in far distant lands must try
The meaner arts of palmistry.
Give then your hand, fair lady! give,
And let the wandering minstrel live:
So shall he tell the varied fate
That may that lovely form await.
To other strains his voice is mute;
Broken his heart, unstrung his lute!"]] (1ˢᵗ ed., deleted from 2ⁿᵈ ed.).

whilst the voice ... flashed across her mind: (added to 2ⁿᵈ ed.).

and contrasted fearfully with the lighter accents he had employed as a minstrel: (added to 2ⁿᵈ ed.).

I am shivering with cold: 1ˢᵗ ed continues: [[to say nothing of being so hungry that I could eat my fingers."

"I am surprised to hear you talk of being hungry, father," said Abelard; "you are surely too fat to feel any craving for food. Fat, you know, is a kind of intermedium through which the nutritive matter extracted from the food, must pass before it is assimilated to repair the loss of the individual. It thus forms a kind of magazine to supply his wants; and a fat man may abstain from food much longer than another, because, during this abstinence, the collected fat is rapidly re-absorbed."]]

I am surprised to hear you talk ... a bad conductor of caloric: (added to 2ⁿᵈ ed.).

an ample commentary upon the text: the following text following on from here 1ˢᵗ ed. is deleted in 2ⁿᵈ ed.:

[["You seem cold also," said the pedantic butler; "but that must be a mistake, for animal oil is universally allowed to be a bad conductor of caloric."

"The devil take your caloric," cried Father Murphy, again forgetting his holy office in his anger; "I suppose you'll want to persuade me that I have no feeling next."

"That is far from impossible," replied Abelard, with the most provoking gravity; "for fat, by surrounding the extremities of the nerves, always obviates inordinate sensibility. At the same time, pray do not let me be misunderstood:—I do not say that fat people can do entirely without eating, for the indivisibility and individuality of the living body can only be maintained by an incessant change of the particles which enter into its composition; though merely part—"

"Hold, hold, for Heaven's sake!" groaned Father Murphy.

"—Part of the animal food is reduced into chyle," resumed Abelard; "and, as you doubtless know, another part becomes bones; in fact, the bones are merely secretory organs incrusted with phosphate of lime. The lymphatic vessels remove this salt—"

"Oh!" groaned Father Murphy, "all this is very fine, but it does not make me one whit less hungry. O that I had a broiled rump-steak at this moment, smoking hot and swimming in gravy, with a lump of fresh butter!"

"Hark!" cried Abelard, "the vibration of the air that strikes upon the tympanum of my ears, gives intimation of the approach of some tangible object."

"Alas! alas!" cried the priest, "it is certainly the spirits returned, that carried away poor Clara. Poor dear girl! that was certainly her pocket-handkerchief."

"I despair of finding her," said the butler. "Despair is sinful, my son," replied the friar; "misfortunes are sent to try us, and we ought to bear them with resignation, and without uttering a single murmur."

"But I thought you were even now complaining of being hungry, father?" said Abelard with the utmost simplicity.

"True, true!" replied the priest, a little disconcerted by this remark; "but—but—"

"It is one thing to preach, and another to practise," resumed the butler, smiling; "is it not, father? However, I certainly heard a noise; and if any one finds us here, we shall be ruined."

"Och! never mind that," said Father Murphy; "for that we are already, ye know."

"Who have we here?" cried some soldiers, who now descended into the cave; and who as before-mentioned, were particularly alert in performing their duty in examining all strangers.

"And is it me ye are asking that?" demanded Father Murphy. "for if it is, it's of no manner of use; for if I were to set about telling you, it's a hundred to one if ever ye got to the bottom of it."

"Is it possible?" cried one of the soldiers; "surely my ears deceive me, or that is the voice of Father Murphy!"

"Sure and it is!" said the reverend father; "and whose should it be but my own? D'ye think I'd use that of another person?"

"No, no!" returned the soldier, laughing; "but my astonishment was, to find the owner of the voice so near me. Though, now I think of it, it is not at all surprising, as the Duke of Cornwall is at the palace hard by, and you of course are with him."

"And how can I be with him," asked the literal Father Murphy, "when I am here? Now if an Irishman had said such a thing, they'd have called it a bull."

"Well, well, my good friend," said the soldier, "we will not quarrel for words. I suppose you came down with the duke?"

"And if you do, you never were more mistaken in your whole life!"

"I cannot in the least comprehend you."

"I don't know how ye should, for I hav'n't begun to explain myself yet: nor should I finish if I were to work at it all day; and so, as the duke is here, we'll just go to him, if ye plase."

The duke, already miserable at, the loss of Clara, had no sooner heard of the escape of his daughter, than he had determined to visit the place where she had been, principally from that restless desire of change which generally haunts the unhappy; and he was now as much surprised as the soldier to see Father Murphy there. He felt grateful, however, to the priest for his assiduous search for Clara; but as the adventure of the handkerchief rested entirely upon the father's conviction of its identity—the handkerchief itself having been lost in the holy father's unfortunate tumble into the water—the duke considered the whole adventure as rather apocryphal. He felt, however, consoled by it, though he scarcely knew why; and returned to his friend Sir Ambrose in much better spirits than he had left him.]]

"It is strange," *continued the butler ... shoots across my pia mater:* (added to 2nd ed.). (the pia mater is the innermost layer of the brain's meningeal membranes.)

It is, it is Miss Montague: [[Montagu]] (1st ed.)

Volume 3: Chapter 7
There are no revisions in this chapter.

Volume 3: Chapter 8
There are no revisions in this chapter.

Endnotes

1. Rauch, 61.
2. In the first edition, this exchange is between Edric and Dr Entwerfen.
3. "The March of Intellect: a New Song" *Blackwoods* 1825. 51–765. This has been attributed to Theodore Hook.
4. Nellist, 1995: 118.
5. See also Alan Rauch's introduction to *The Mummy!* (xix-xx11)
6. The imagery of the "March of Intellect" prints, issued between 1825 and 1829, feeds into the highly visualised scenes in Volume 1, Chapter 11 and elsewhere.
7. While the Brontes' juvenilia often features the supernatural (themselves as the Genii, intervening in their created world), this is a rare (only?) example of extrapolation from contemporary technolology.
8. See Verne's *De la terre à la lune* (1865; translated as *From the Earth to the Moon* 1869, Percy Gregg's *Across the Zodiac* (1880), Robert Cromie's *A Plunge Into Space* (1890) or H. G. Wells's *The First Men in the Moon* (1901).
9. His earlier "special scientifiction issue" of *Electrical Experimenter* (August 1923), was an earlier attempt to test the market.
10. *the pedantry she acquired at a charity-school in her youth*: Mr Montagu has married beneath his status. Mrs Montagu is, like the other lower-class characters in the novel, *educated*. The comic implications here are never developed to their full potential, which might be another reason why JWL made this major change.
11. Sir Knight of the Woeful Countenance: The phrase ("El Caballero de la Triste Figura") famously used to describe Don Quixote in Chapter 19 of the first (1605) part of Cervantes' novel.
12. *Suivante*: lady's maid, companion or, as described above, "attendant".
13. *"by St. Wellington!":* in this future, the Duke of Wellington, for the book's readers a national hero who was very shortly (4 April 1829) to make a speech in favour of Catholic Emancipation instrumental in the passing of the Bill to that effect later that month, has been canonised. This future England is of course a Catholic country. The Duke became Prime Minister on 22 January 1828, and the deletion of the joke from the second edition might have been the author's or publisher's decision that it could now be seen with more "political" overtones.
14. *Palebrae*: the palpebrae or eyelids.
15. *depressor anguli oris*: Facial muscle of the mouth.
16. Spelling as in the original. The Venus de Medici is a 1st Century BCE marble copy of a (lost) Greek bronze original, showing the goddess Aphrodite. Itself much-copied, it has been one of the most admired representations of beauty since at least the 17th century, when it was listed as part of the collection of the Villa Medici in Rome.

APPENDIX A: John Claudius Loudon's review of The Mummy!

The Gardner's Magazine March 1828 (478–9)

(As noted above, John Claudius Loudon's interest in *The Mummy!* was focused upon the novel's technological speculations, specifically, as might be expected from a horticultural specialist, those directed to agriculture. It is the playfulness of the author's imagination, however, which attracts him. "The most extravagant and impracticable ideas will sometimes aid in forming new and useful combinations," he writes, but his review is in part an engagement with the game of "forecasting". He shares with his readers the wonders which the extrapolation of new technologies might result in, but he is careful to note that the novel is "pushing to the extreme point" rather than seriously predicting.)

Part III Miscellaneous Intelligence
Art. VIII HINTS FOR IMPROVEMENTS

New Ideas – In The Mummy, a tale of the twenty-second century, an attempt is made to predestinate the application of steam, and other modern improvements, which, whether intended in the way of ridicule or effect, it may not be altogether useless to notice. A patent steam mowing apparatus is set to work in a hay field, and the weather being foggy the hay is dried with the use of a burning-glass! A field of barley, in a very dry state, is watered by the farmer, who, seeing "a nice black heavy-looking cloud sailing by", gets out his electrical machine, and draws it down in five minutes. Communications are held with every part of the world by means of telegraphs, and a private gentleman, whose son is engaged in battle in Germany, hears the result of an engagement a few minutes after it happens. A steam digging machine is mentioned; cooking is effected by a chemical preparation, without the use of fire; it is the fashion for great people to have only one dish and fricassees and ragouts are only devoured by the canaille, beds are inflated with air instead of feathers; house servants, of every description, are poets, artists and philosophers; water is turned into ice by mechanical pressure; fog and vapour is turned into snow or rain at pleasure, by withdrawing electricity, all travelling is performed in balloons; the tour of the whole world can be made in six weeks; and great people, finding it so very easy to be transported from one place to another, have left off travelling, and seldom leave their country seats. In a grand procession and ovation celebrated in Black Heath Square, said to be the largest and finest square in the world, the air was thronged with balloons, and with a variety of aerial horses, bestrode by city dandies, whilst others floated upon wings, or glided along on aerial sledges. "The throng of the balloons was very dense. Some young city apprentices, having hired each a pair of wings for the day, and not knowing exactly how to manage them, a dreadful tumult ensued, and the balloons became entangled with the winged heroes and each other in inextricable confusion. The noise now became tremendous, the conductors of the balloons swearing at each other the most refined oaths, and the ladies screaming in concert. Several balloons were rent in the scuffle, and fell with tremendous force upon the earth; while some cars were torn from the supporting ropes, and others roughly overset. Luckily, however, the whole of England was at this time so completely excavated, that falling upon the surface of the earth was like tumbling upon the parchment of an immense drum, and, consequently, only a deep hollow sound was returned as cargo after cargo of the demolished balloons struck upon it; some of them, indeed, rebounded several yards with the violence of the shock.

The country is governed by an absolute queen, who is "full of wild-goose schemes" – "Only imagine, Sir Ambrose, she showed me this morning a plan for making aerial bridges to convey heavy weights from one steeple to another; a machine for stamping shoes and boots at one blow out of a solid piece of leather; a steam-engine for milking cows; and an elastic summer-house, that might be folded up so as to be put into a man's pocket!"

Coal and other fuel having been long in disuse, smoke is unknown in London, and the English are the first sculptors in the world. The gardens of the nobility, who have town-houses, extend from the Strand to the Thames, and all of them are open to the public. Nothing in summer can be more enchanting than these gardens, filled with statues and beautiful originals; in winter the Thames "was frozen, and persons glided along it in glittering traineaux, or skated gracefully with infinite variety of movement; whilst, every now and then, a steam percussion-moveable bridge short across the stream, loaded with goods and passengers, collapsing again the instant its burthen was safely landed on the other side."

There is a patent steam book manufactory in Hatton Garden, where also quotations are cut, dried, and made up into pills for the use of authors. Every regiment, ship, and private family has its philosopher as well as its chaplain and surgeon. The government of England is an absolute monarchy; Ireland and Scotland are separate kingdoms, the Catholic religion is everywhere established; the most enlightened part of society believe in ghosts and goblins, and the reason given is "because the extremes of ignorance and civilisation tend alike to produce credulity."

The most extravagant and impracticable ideas will sometimes aid in forming new and useful combinations; and it is good to see the subject of scientific invention, and intellectual improvement, pushed to the extreme point, in order to show the absurdities to which every thing human is liable to give rise.

www.ingramcontent.com/pod-product-compliance
Lightning Source LLC
Chambersburg PA
CBHW071139300426
44113CB00009B/1018